SALFORD
RED DEVILS
150

SALFORD RED DEVILS 150

Graham Morris

Scratching Shed Publishing Ltd

Copyright © Graham Morris 2023
All rights reserved
The moral right of the author has been asserted.
First published by Scratching Shed Publishing Ltd in 2023
Registered in England & Wales No. 6588772.
Registered office:
47 Street Lane, Leeds, West Yorkshire. LS8 1AP
www.scratchingshedpublishing.co.uk
ISBN 978-1739247645

Photographs provided by Graham Morris
unless otherwise stated
Page design: Tony Hannan
Cover design: Louise Woodward-Styles
Cover images: Mark Lee – Bob Thomas Sports Photography
Kallum Watkins – Allan McKenzie/SWpix.com
Jackson Hastings – Alex Whitehead/SWpix.com
Gareth O'Brien celebrating drop-goal – Alex Whitehead/SWpix.com

No part of this book may be reproduced or transmitted in any form or by any other means without the written permission of the publisher, except by a reviewer who wishes to quote brief passages in connection with a review written for insertion in a magazine, newspaper or broadcast.

A catalogue record for this book is available
from the British Library.

Typeset in Warnock Pro Semi Bold and Palatino
Printed and bound in the United Kingdom by

Short Run Press Ltd
Bittern Road, Sowton Industrial Estate, Exeter. EX2 7LW
Tel: 01392 211909   Fax: 01392 444134

Contents

Foreword *by Paul King, Salford Red Devils chairman* vii
Introduction ix
Acknowledgements xvii

1. Cavendish: 1873-74 – 1878-79 1
   Players 4
   Results 6

2. Salford Rugby Union: 1879-80 – 1895-96 11
   Players 13
   Results 21
   Records 39

3. Salford Rugby League: 1896-97 – 2022 41
   Players 45
   Results 115
   Records 323

4. The Great War (World War One) 1915-16 – 1918-19 327
   Players 329

5. The Salford Hospital Cup 1924-25 – 1947-48 333
   Players 334

6. France Tour 1934 (Birth of 'The Red Devils') 337
   Tourists 338

7. Festival of Sports 1951-52 – 1952-53 339
   Players 340

8. The Red Rose Cup 1954-55 – 1980-81 341
   Players 342

9. Salford Chairmen, Coaches and Captains 347

10. Statistical Notes 353

Cavendish Street Chapel in Hulme, Manchester, where it all began in 1873.

Foreword
Paul King
Salford Red Devils Chairman

When I was growing up my grandfather had two subjects of conversation, his exploits from Dunkirk to Monte Cassino in the second world war and tales of the great Salford Red Devils team of the 1930s that included the legendary Gus Risman, Barney Hudson, Jackie Feetham, Albert Gear, Bert Day and many, many more outstanding players. Built by the immortal Lance Todd, that team won three championships and twice played at Wembley in the Challenge Cup Final. My own experiences began in the early 1970s. I missed out on Salford's Wembley return in 1969 but was happy to be on the terraces when Salford won the championship in 1973-74 and 1975-76.

That team was also packed with star names, the biggest of all being that of David Watkins but there were numerous other great entertainers in their line-up such as Chris Hesketh, Mike Coulman, Colin Dixon, Ken Gill, Steve Nash, Maurice Richards and Keith Fielding. But, of course, we all have our own personal favourites. Mine was that gritty Cumbrian Paul Charlton, the greatest full-back I have ever seen. Since then I have discovered new heroes including Darren Bloor, Neil Baker, Paul Shaw, Ian Bragger and Tex Evans, who all joined the club during the 1980s, Martin Birkett, Lokeni Savelio, Mark Lee and Paul Southern from the 1990s and, in more recent times, Luke Patten and Mark 'Flash' Flanagan. Just a few of the many that have played during my time.

Now, as we celebrate 150 years since our club was first created by pupils of the Cavendish Street Chapel in Hulme way back in 1873, we can reflect on the fact that over 1,700 players have represented us. Some of the names will be unfamiliar to today's supporters, as, indeed, they are to myself. But it is only right that we should acknowledge their role in bringing us to this historic landmark. Names like Harry Eagles, who is one of the most legendary figures from our pioneering years, and Jimmy Lomas, who led the first Northern Union (Rugby League) tour in 1910. Hopefully, this publication will introduce you to many of the lesser known names as well as a few old favourites as you thumb through its pages.

A club's history is built on the achievements of its players and we have been fortunate at Salford to have recruited so many talented individuals over those 150 years. Even now we are adding to the club's legacy. Two Salford players have recently received the prestigious Steve Prescott Man of Steel award as the season's outstanding player; Jackson Hastings in 2019 and Brodie Croft in 2022. Our ambition is that with current stars such as skipper Kallum Watkins, Ryan Brierley, Marc Sneyd, Andy Ackers and many others, more heroic and memorable moments will ensue in the years to come.

Please enjoy this remarkable analysis of those who have represented this fantastic old club for 150 years, beautifully compiled as always by the inimitable Graham Morris who continues to give his heart and soul to the preservation of our history. I look forward to his next update to celebrate our 200th anniversary.

Paul King
Salford Red Devils Chairman

Introduction

Salford Red Devils celebrate 150 years of existence in 2023 having been founded at the Cavendish Street School, Hulme. Formed in 1873 by pupils at the school, they quickly rose to prominence as Cavendish Football Club and, having crossed the River Irwell into the 'Royal Borough' in 1875, were renamed Salford Football Club in 1879. The latter event was recognised via a 'Centenary Match' staged in 1979 against visitors Widnes, although the true origination of the club, as stated above, stretches back six years prior to that.

For a rugby league club to survive for a century and a half is a mighty achievement given the unpredictability of sport; the highs and lows, good times and bad, and – most significantly for a professional organisation – the fluctuating state of its finances. The latter, of course, depends on the level of support a club can draw, and this usually relies on the quality and success of its team. The players provide a key role in encouraging spectators through the turnstiles and Salford are no exception.

Happily, Salford has been blessed throughout that long history with many great performers, some of whom have acquired legendary status. The trophy cabinet may not always have been brimful with silverware, but its supporters have been entertained by some wonderfully talented individuals over the years including record breakers, record signings, intrepid pioneers, overseas stars and national tour captains.

When I first attended The Willows in the 1950s my instant heroes were Scottish loose-forward Hugh Duffy and Welsh three-quarters Graham Jones and John Cheshire. And then there was Australian winger Wally McArthur who sadly, for me at least, moved on after just one memorable year. His pace and side-step was electrifying and he made a big impression on me as the most exciting player I had witnessed in the famous red jersey until David Watkins arrived on the scene a decade later.

That is the beauty of following a particular club; we all have our own favourites, our own heroes. Just as I have been enthralled by players that I have seen in action, there were many on the terraces in my younger days who still spoke in revered terms about Gus Risman and the original Red Devils of the 1930s. And there were veterans – my own grandfather included – who could go back even further. He was at the first match at The Willows in 1901 and had seen Jimmy Lomas – an undoubted legend – in his pomp but the one he talked about the most was Welsh half-back Dai John.

I am sure that if each Salford supporter sat down for an hour to compile their own Salford 'Dream Team' there would be very few that came out identical. After all, with a history that covers 150 years, there are so many players to choose from. At the conclusion of 2022 over 1,500 individuals had taken part in 5,250 matches since its foundation as Cavendish, including competitive and friendly fixtures.

Looking through the mists of time it is possible to identify 70 of those players – five of them during the club's rugby union era – as having achieved at least 200 appearances, a milestone that has seemingly become a thing of the past for Salford. The advent of summer rugby in 1996 heralded a new and exciting chapter for rugby league but one that provided fresh challenges. The introduction of player contracts, allied with the club's financial constraints has resulted in many players now signing for just two or three seasons. To illustrate the point, of those that made their debuts since the summer era began, only three have breached that 200 barrier, all having made their first appearance in the late 1990s. They are Malcolm Alker (360 matches), Stuart Littler (329), and Paul Highton (269). Littler has the added distinction of registering 163 consecutive appearances for Salford (including 16 as substitute), surpassing David Watkins' previous record of 140.

Player longevity has not been the only changing trend since the switch to a summer schedule. From the earliest years of the Northern Union Salford, in common with many other clubs, spread their net wide in pursuit of players. South Wales was always a popular hunting ground for talent and, in October 1896, half-backs Ivor Grey and Ben Griffiths, both from the Morriston club, were the first of five Welsh players to make their debuts in Salford's inaugural Northern Union season. In total 131 players from the Principality have appeared for Salford. But it was a pathway that closed after the rugby union authorities decided to go professional in 1995, Richard Webster being the last to be signed from a Welsh rugby union club when arriving from Swansea in 1993. The only Welshmen to play for Salford since are Gareth Owen (on loan from Leigh in 2002), Rhys Williams (loaned by Warrington in 2013 and subsequently signed from London Broncos for 2019), Gil Dudson (Widnes, 2019) and Elliot Kear (London Broncos, 2020).

On the opposite side of the proverbial coin, Salford has, over the past 40 years, increasingly turned its attention towards Southern Hemisphere countries, having, up to and including 2022, fielded 94 Australians, 48 New Zealanders, five Samoans, two Fijians, one Congolese, one Papua New Guinean and one South African. Just five of those were signed prior to the 1980s. The first two were New Zealanders; Joe Lavery (a 1907 New Zealand tourist transferred from Leigh in 1910) and Harry Goldsmith (who had played rugby union in the United States, signing in 1912 after a trial). Next came three Australians; Noel Sligar (a student staying in England who agreed a 12-month contract in 1928 but played just once), J. H. Smith (reportedly born in Queensland and listed as a Salford player in 1928-29 and 1929-30, making one first team appearance), and Wally McArthur (transferred from Blackpool Borough in 1957, the first Aboriginal player to join a British club).

The regular stream of players from 'Down Under' that is now such a major part of team building began slowly for Salford with two New Zealand signings; Gavin Cherrie (in 1980 – the first Salford player signed directly from an Australasian club) and Tom Murray (1982). It was in 1984 that the Reds started recruiting heavily from overseas with the arrival of four Australians, Steve Staccy being the first of those to make his debut. To complete the picture, the other non-English players to appear for Salford since breaking away from rugby union in 1896 have originated from Scotland (eight), France (three) and Ireland (two), whilst Olsi Krasniqi was born in Albania and Tim Jonkers in the Netherlands.

Arguably Salford's first 'legend' – and a real pioneer – was Harry Eagles, a forward who made 268 appearances from 1881 until 1892. He certainly holds that status in the annals of the Rugby Football Union through his unbelievable durability in the first ever rugby tour to Australia and New Zealand in 1888. He played in every one of the 35 rugby matches (plus all additional 19 games arranged under Australian Rules) which is still a tour record for that code. He was accompanied on his journey by three Salford colleagues including Tom Kent. Both Eagles and Kent – also a forward – share the distinction of being the only Salford players selected by England under the 15-man code. Unfortunately Eagles did not get to play due to an international dispute, but still received his international cap and jersey.

During Salford's rugby union era only two players made more appearances for the club than Eagles; full-back Billy Manwaring and forward Jack Roberts. Manwaring also played in Salford's initial 1896-97 Northern Union season as team captain, whilst Roberts became the Reds' first trainer in 1899.

Another immortal was Cumbrian centre Jimmy Lomas who arrived for a Northern Union record £100 transfer fee in 1901 and departed for another record amount (£300) ten years later. Arguably Salford's first 'superstar', he was the Northern Union captain for its inaugural 1910 tour to the Antipodes and his career tally of 2,312 points was a record for the sport until surpassed by Wigan's Jim Sullivan in 1928. He also notched a record 39 points (5 tries, 12 goals) in a match during 1907. Two other notables during this period are Welsh duo Willie Thomas (centre) and Dai John (half-back) who made their debuts in 1903 and 1905, respectively. Both enjoyed a long innings with over 400 appearances in careers that lasted until the early 1920s.

The 1920s was mostly a decade of poor on-field results but there were a few shining lights. Brightest of all was centre Fergie Southward – another Cumbrian – and forwards Teddy Haines and Jack Muir, who each made in excess of 300 appearances. All three were amply rewarded for their loyalty as early members of Lance Todd's great side of the 1930s.

The next colossus to arrive at The Willows was Gus Risman in 1929. The Welsh centre was just one of many exceptional players that helped create the Red Devils brand following the clubs' historic tour of France in 1934. The first Salford player to be inducted into the Rugby League 'Hall of Fame', Risman created season and career records at Salford for both goals and points. He was appointed tour captain in 1946 and, in 1951, received the ultimate accolade as one of several sporting heroes making a cameo appearance in the annual Royal Variety Performance. At Salford he was well supported by wingmen Barney Hudson and Alan Edwards, half-backs Emlyn Jenkins and Billy Watkins, and forwards Billy Williams and Jack Feetham, each one an international star in his own right.

After the Second World War fortunes faded although Salford still paraded some outstanding performers. Pre-war signings Tommy Harrison (scrum-half), Dai Davies (prop) and Syd Williams (wing) were joined by two new Welsh favourites in Dai Moses (a loose-forward who graduated to prop and played for almost 13 seasons at The Willows) and stand-off Eifion 'Jack' Davies (a prolific scorer who registered over 1,000 points).

Recruited in 1957 was centre Les Bettinson, destined to serve the club in a variety of roles over the next 34 years. Another of my early heroes was Jackie Brennan, a fans' favourite who was signed in 1959 and could play in either half-back role. Both were still playing in 1967 when club chairman Brian Snape enterprisingly recruited Chris Hesketh and David Watkins. Hesketh, a centre, was to become another Salford tour captain whilst Watkins arrived from Newport rugby union club in a blaze of publicity. He proved a charismatic player who, whether at half-back, centre or full-back, thrilled crowds with his explosive side-step. Watkins developed into a scoring machine, creating numerous club records including most goals and points in a season and career, and most consecutive appearances. In later years he became Salford's second entry into the Hall of Fame.

He played for Salford during a period when one headline signing followed another. The Rugby League transfer record was broken four times and a whole host of new club highs were created. Star-studded personnel included wingmen Maurice Richards (most career appearances and tries) and Keith Fielding (most tries in a season), full-back Paul Charlton, scrum-half Steve Nash, and forwards Mike Coulman (most career tries by a forward) and Colin Dixon, all of whom played for Great Britain.

During the 1980s and early 1990s – before the switch to a summer schedule – form fluctuated as Salford suffered four relegations, although bouncing back each time. There were still several high profile signings, most notably that of Australian Test full-back Garry Jack in 1987, whilst stalwart's such as forward Ian Blease, hooker-cum-halfback Mark Lee, and stand-off Steve Blakeley all made over 250 appearances.

The arrival of warm weather rugby league in 1996 saw the aforementioned trio of Alker, Highton and Littler establish themselves as integral members of the team whilst, following the move to the club's new stadium at Barton in 2012, full-back Niall Evalds made his presence felt scoring 111 tries in 160 appearances. Happily, the club has continued to attract remarkable players such as the Australian half-backs Jackson Hastings and Brodie Croft who both received the prestigious Man of Steel award in 2019 and 2022, respectively.

The pages that follow provide the most comprehensive set of

statistics published for Salford, covering the records of all known players reaching back to the 1870s. Extensive new research has revealed many amendments to previous publications, including those by myself, resulting in a fully updated set of facts and figures. Every player's career record in official fixtures since joining the 'Northern Union' in 1896 to the present time is given, including the date of their first and last match, previous team, and country of birth. All matches played by the club since its formation in 1873 are listed season-by-season, including friendly games. The scorers in each match are also shown, and from 1896-97 the attendance, where known, is given.

It is a compilation that represents the culmination of a long journey, albeit a personal one. I first became drawn towards recording details of Salford's matches in 1967-68. Having followed the exploits of the team since the 1950s I was, like many others at that time, enthused by the sudden, unexpected rise of the club. Chris Hesketh and Charlie Bott had been signed during the close season and the arrival of David Watkins was imminent. How could I not feel excited?

My interest in record keeping was stimulated through the influence of others. Oldham schoolmaster Tom Webb – who I later got to know very well – was the first. He had a regular column in the weekly *Rugby Leaguer* newspaper under the name of 'Arellicus' that fascinated me with its glimpses into the past. As far as I am aware Tom was the first to attempt recording the details of every game since rugby league began life as the Northern Union in 1895. I volunteered my services and visited libraries in Brighouse, St Helens and elsewhere on Saturday mornings to assist him in filling some of the gaps.

On reflection, I think Tom set himself a tall order and, despite tremendous progress, he would have struggled to fulfil his ambition was it not for the appearance of another name that the Rugby Football League owes a huge debt to. I am referring to Irvin Saxton, a Featherstone Rovers supporter who lived at Purston, near Pontefract. His ambitious plan to complete the task that Tom had started attracted many like-minded people. Supported by funding from the Rugby Football League, he unveiled the Rugby League Record Keepers' Club (RLRKC) in 1972. If Tom's enthusiasm had fuelled my interest in Salford's past it was Irvin's initiative that gave me purpose. Like a moth to a flame it was not long before I became a RLRKC member, riding on its incredible journey until it disbanded – mission accomplished – during the mid-1990s. (The RLRKC was revived in 2020.)

When I joined the RLRKC I had already invested considerable time in visiting Salford Local History Library and Manchester Central Library regularly for an hour or so after finishing work. The *Salford City Reporter*, particularly those reports by Tom Bergin (who chronicled the clubs affairs for 50 years until the early 1980s), and predecessor Alf Beecroft (who did likewise from the 1920s) – both using the *nom de plume* of 'Ajax' – provided a wonderful platform for my research.

Unfortunately, although much earlier reports in the *Reporter* were substantial, there were periods when the teams were not listed. Fortuitously other avenues for exploration came into view. The basement of Salford's Local History Library contained, in the 1970s, hundreds of bound volumes of the *Manchester Guardian* – forerunner of today's *Guardian* newspaper – that went back to its first issue in 1821. Throughout the late 1800s it provided the line-ups for many of Salford's games, with further queries resolved at Manchester Central Library in the pages of the *Manchester Courier* and Manchester-based *Athletic News*.

After several years of study at the local libraries there were still unresolved questions. Determined not to give up, I discovered that Manchester University had an archive that included football editions of early local newspapers and they generously allowed access. Another gem was the former Thompson House newspaper offices on Corporation Street, Manchester (now the site of the Printworks), which had its own library housing row upon row of bound newspapers including the short-lived 1880s weekly, the *Cricketers Herald and Football Times* and, most prized of all, the *Sporting Chronicle*, another Manchester publication. The latter proved invaluable if only because it provided elusive Salford line-ups from the World War One years.

After those routes were exhausted I still had a few undiscovered match details and decided the only way forward was to visit the local libraries of the opposition. So I found myself travelling north to Barrow, west to Birkenhead, East to Hull, south to Stockport and all points in between! My eventual reward was that I finished the quest with just one incomplete line-up. The result is that from 4,371 official matches played by Salford since its 1896 breakaway until the conclusion of the 2022 season there are just five appearances unaccounted for. There are also just 29 appearances missing from the 501 games played under the auspices of the Rugby Football Union from 1879 (when the club's name changed from Cavendish to Salford) up to 1896.

At that time I was not planning to publish those figures and, in any case, my research for the Rugby League era would be available via the RLRKC. The idea of doing so now came to me after the Salford Supporters' Trust decided in 2018 that they wanted to create a heritage list, embracing all first team players since 1896. In their 'wisdom' – I think that is the correct word! – I was invited to assist.

One complication that arose was due to the fact that the majority of my past research – covering 1896 until the mid-1970s and including the World War One friendlies – had provided most of the statistics for a book published in the 1990s, although without acknowledgement either to myself or the RLRKC. In the years since, numerous discrepancies surfaced related to the players' records section within the book that required reconciling before the heritage list could be created. There was also three subsequent decades of matches to take into account, hence my being co-opted to the heritage project.

It took quite a while to get to the finished product but the heritage list finally saw the light of day in 2019. The credit for producing that list belongs to Graham Jones and other members of the Supporters' Trust. My role was solely to provide them with the updated information and to answer their many queries. However, having personally invested so much time, allied to the fact that the club has reached its milestone 150th birthday, it felt like the perfect opportunity to publish the updated players' records and also add the details of those that represented the club prior to 1896.

In summary, the contents of this book are the product of many years of devoting my time and energy into unravelling the statistics of the club I grew up with. Some may describe such toil as self-inflicted 'hard labour' but I prefer to think of it as a 'labour of love'. Hopefully, as you peruse the following pages, you will feel that my endeavour has been worthwhile.

Graham Morris, Worsley, May 2023

Acknowledgements

I first began to research the match details for Salford during the 1970s, visiting numerous libraries and consulting a great number of newspapers, mostly covering traditional rugby league areas in the north. After all these years it is difficult to name them all with complete certainty and, therefore, impossible to give overdue acknowledgement. However, the many sources that have assisted my more recent undertaking as I updated that original research material are much fresher in my mind and, happily, I can give credit where due.

In particular, I am grateful to Michael Latham and Robert Gate for their unstinting help and support; and also to Tony Hannan for his excellent design work for the pages that follow.

There are several other people to whom I offer my gratitude, namely Steve Andrews, Danny Barton, John Blackburn, David Clegg, Tony Collins, Steven Fox, Dave Huitson, Alan Hunte, John Ledger, Pete Lowe, Martyn Sadler (League Publications Ltd), Alex Service, Andrew Shaw, Stuart Sheard, Gary Slater, David Thorpe, Graham Williams, Louise Woodward-Styles (who also produced the cover image) and Peter Worthington. I would also like to thank Duncan McCormick for his support and patience during many hours of study at Salford Local History Library. As is always the case, a variety of newspapers were consulted and worthy of particular note are the *Athletic News, Manchester Courier, Manchester Guardian, Salford Chronicle, Salford (City) Reporter, Sporting Chronicle* and *Yorkshire Post*.

I am also thankful for information contained within the pages of the following publications: *Code 13* (1986 to 1991, editor Trevor Delaney), *League Express Rugby League Yearbook* (1996 to 2022-23), *Rothman's Rugby*

League Yearbook (1981-82 to 1999), Rugby League Record Keepers' Club publications (1972 to 1994, editor Irvin Saxton), and the 'new' Rugby League Record Keepers' Club website (rugbyleaguerecords.com – organised by Neil Ormston). Other invaluable references were the Rugby Football League Archive (Heritage Quay, Huddersfield), the Oldham Rugby League Trust website (orl-heritagetrust.org.uk) and the Saints Heritage Society website (saints.org.uk).

Books that I referred to include *Castleford Rugby League Football Club 1926-2016* (Ian Garbett and Roy Garbett, 2016), *The Forbidden Game* (Mike Rylance, 1999), *The Glory of Their Times* (editors Phil Melling and Tony Collins, 2004), *Hall of Fame* (Joe Holliday, 2016), *The Headingley Story 1890-1955* (Ken Dalby, 1955), *The Headingley Story 1955-1979* (Ken Dalby, 1979), *History of the Salford Football Club* (James Higson, 1892), *The Home of Footballers* (Michael Latham, 2020), *Keeping the Dream Alive* (Dave Huitson, Keith Nutter and Steve Andrews, 2008), *Leigh Rugby League Club – A Comprehensive Record 1895-1994* (Michael Latham, 1994), *Oldham RLFC – The Complete History 1876-1997* (Michael Turner, 1997), *The Robins* (Roger Pugh, 2016), *Rugby's Great Split* (Tony Collins, 1998), *Salford Football Club – A History 1879-1949* (Tom Bergin, 1949), *They Played for Wigan* (Michael Latham and Robert Gate, 1992), and *Trinity* (Mike Rylance, 2013).

I am particularly indebted to those two excellent photographers, Bill McLaughlin and Steve McCormick, who have both generously provided most of the images that cover the later years of the club.

As always I am grateful for the enthusiastic support and help I continue to receive from the directors and staff of the Salford club itself and the endorsement of this publication. I should, however, like to emphasise that any inferences in the text are my own and may not necessarily reflect the views of the club itself.

1

Cavendish
1873-74 – 1878-79

The story of Salford Rugby League Club begins with Cavendish. James Higson's invaluable *History of the Salford Football Club*, published in 1892, tells us that 'Cavendish Football Club was formed by the Cavendish Street Sunday School, Hulme, about the year 1873'. Based on that statement, rugby historians, including the author of this book, have accepted 1873 as the year of foundation. Although that assumption is probably correct, there is no contemporary evidence to either support or contradict it. This is because the most popular local newspapers of the day, the *Manchester Guardian*, *Manchester Courier*, and *Manchester Evening News*, in common with all newspapers at that time, gave scant mention of the two fledgling football codes; Rugby and Association. Another valuable source, the Manchester-based sporting weekly, the *Athletic News* did not begin publication until June 1875.

According to Higson's book their early 'leaders' were H. McKay, J. Powell, H. Reeves, E. Turner, T. Wood, W. Wood 'and others'. There are, however, no reports of the Cavendish club in any newspaper until the 1874-75 season when the *Manchester Guardian*, dated Wednesday, 28th October 1874, informed its readers that the previous Saturday (24th) Cavendish, using 21 players, had lost at home to the 14 men of the Moss Side Wanderers 2nd team by one goal and three touchdowns to nil. Based on Higson's book, this would have been the club's second campaign. At a time when the football season ran from October to March (cricket occupying the remaining months) this was, in all probability, the first match against another club.

What cautions against Higson's suggestion that 1873 was the foundation year is that his book was published 19 years later and he did not join the club himself until 1881, implying that his suggested start date was obtained second hand. There are, however, a couple of pointers that support 1873-74 as the inaugural season. Higson clearly states that the club played its first two seasons at a ground in nearby Moss Side. This fits with contemporary newspaper reports that show they relocated for 1875-76 from Moss Side to Throstle Nest Weir on the Salford side of the River Irwell near to Ordsall. The other factor is that Higson also states: 'In those days there were very few Rugby clubs and the members amused themselves by playing sides-games, varied by occasional encounters with such junior twenties as could be found willing to enter into friendly rivalry.' In 1873 there were, indeed, few clubs around – a situation that rapidly changed as the 1870s progressed – and newcomers often began life by organising so-called 'sides-games' contested by teams selected from its own members.

The statistics for Cavendish Football Club included in this publication cover 1874-75 to 1878-79, the period before it was renamed Salford Football Club. Unlike Salford's season-by-season results in the rest of this book, all known Cavendish fixtures have been listed including matches that were cancelled or postponed and others where no subsequent result was found. This has been done with the intention of providing the reader with as full a picture as possible of the formative years of the club and the teams they arranged matches with.

In the earliest of those seasons, several fixtures that were reportedly arranged did not subsequently have a result or match report published by the press (indicated by 'NRA' under the 'result' column). This discrepancy could be because the match had not taken place, usually through severe weather or one of the combatants being unable to raise a team. It could also be that a report had not been sent in to the local newspaper. In those very early years of organised 'football' it was the practice for club members to submit match reports and, if none arrived, then there was no mention. It was often frustrating for this author to find a report of the second team's match (because one of its members had taken the trouble) but not of the first team. Poor reporting – by today's standards – during this embryonic period also meant that many of the scorers were not recorded.

Of the 74 Cavendish matches known to have taken place from 1874-75 to 1878-79, the team line-up was reported for 35 of them, ranging from none being published in the first of those seasons to obtaining all but one in the latter, a trend that reflects the escalating coverage of football during that period. Of the remaining 39 matches, further appearances were found through mention of players names in the match reports. Sadly, for the players' records section, there will be names from those pioneering years that have not been uncovered, particularly for the first few seasons, whilst for those that have been identified it is impossible to guarantee a complete record. There are also anomalies amongst the names uncovered. For instance there is a W. Wood credited with six appearances who is almost certainly Walter or William Wood – or even a combination of both – but it has proved impossible to determine which. Therefore there are three entries for 'Wood'. Despite the discrepancies, it was thought worthwhile to list those known to have played and the seasons that they are known to have played in, together with their inevitably incomplete appearance and scoring records.

In the match results section, the final scores are listed as reported at the time. Initially all matches were decided by goals only, resulting in many drawn games. From 23rd November 1875 the Rugby Football Union decreed that if goals were equal then unconverted tries should be taken into account. It should be noted that – as reported at the time – only the unconverted tries appear in the final score because any try that was converted into a goal was recorded as a goal only.

Cavendish Players

Name	First known	Last known	App	Tries	Con	D-gls
Alderson, G*	1875-76	1878-79	14	2	0	0
Alderson, T	1876-77	1877-78	17	1	0	0
Ashton, W*	1876-77	1878-79	19	4	0	0
Baird, W	1875-76	1875-76	1	0	1	0
Black, J	1876-77	1878-79	15	0	0	0
Black, R*	1876-77	1878-79	23	4	0	0
Blytheway, -	1875-76	1875-76	1	0	0	0
Bridge, W	1878-79	1878-79	2	0	0	0
Broadbent, W	1877-78	1877-78	1	0	0	0
Burslem, F	1878-79	1878-79	6	0	0	0
Bury, J	1877-78	1877-78	1	0	0	0
Butterworth, Fred*	1878-79	1878-79	12	0	0	0
Carroll, W*	1876-77	1878-79	34	1	3	1
Cooper, F	1878-79	1878-79	5	1	0	0
Davies, J	1877-78	1877-78	1	0	0	0
Dearden, A	1878-79	1878-79	3	0	0	0
Demper, -	1878-79	1878-79	2	0	0	0
Dunod, -	1875-76	1875-76	1	0	1	0
Eardley, J*	1878-79	1878-79	3	0	0	0
Faram, A	1877-78	1877-78	1	0	0	0
Fleming, JW	1877-78	1878-79	5	0	0	0
Fletcher, E*	1878-79	1878-79	8	1	0	0
Giles, E	1876-77	1877-78	2	0	0	0
Gomersall, A	1877-78	1878-79	7	0	0	0
Hardy, Tom*	1878-79	1878-79	5	0	0	0
Hay, H	1876-77	1877-78	15	1	0	0
Heinke, E	1877-78	1878-79	20	0	4	2
Hulme, G	1877-78	1878-79	6	1	0	0
Hulme, H	1877-78	1877-78	4	0	0	0
Hulme, J	1876-77	1878-79	17	3	0	0
Hulme, S*	1876-77	1877-78	5	1	0	0
Hulme, T*	1878-79	1878-79	1	0	0	0
Inglefield, WG	1875-76	1878-79	19	2	0	0
Jackson, W	1875-76	1875-76	1	1	0	0
Jones, J*	1877-78	1878-79	7	1	0	0
Jones, T	1876-77	1876-77	7	1	0	0
Kenwright, -*	1878-79	1878-79	1	0	0	0
Kilner, E*	1878-79	1878-79	5	0	0	0
Langton, B	1876-77	1877-78	6	0	0	0
Maguire, F	1877-78	1877-78	6	0	0	0
McKay, H	1875-76	1877-78	9	2	0	1
McKay, RG*	1875-76	1878-79	34	11	6	1
Nightingale, J*	1877-78	1878-79	13	0	0	0
Owen, T	1876-77	1876-77	3	0	0	0
Plaice, J	1877-78	1877-78	2	0	0	0

Cavendish Players

Name	First known	Last known	App	Tries	Con	D-gls
Powell, J*	1876-77	1877-78	2	0	0	0
Quine, W	1877-78	1877-78	6	1	0	1
Reeves, H	1875-76	1877-78	10	0	0	0
Russell, H*	1877-78	1877-78	6	0	0	0
Sutherland, A*	1876-77	1878-79	35	5	0	0
Symington, J*	1876-77	1878-79	27	0	0	0
Symington, W	1876-77	1877-78	4	0	0	0
Thomas, J	1875-76	1877-78	8	0	0	0
Thomas, -	1877-78	1877-78	1	0	0	0
Thompson, -	1875-76	1875-76	1	0	0	0
Turner, E	1876-77	1876-77	1	0	0	0
Webster, R	1877-78	1877-78	2	0	0	0
Welch, R	1877-78	1878-79	18	5	0	0
Williams, B	1877-78	1878-79	8	0	0	0
Williams, W	1878-79	1878-79	8	0	0	0
Winnard, J*	1875-76	1878-79	34	14	2	0
Wood, T	1876-77	1877-78	4	0	0	0
Wood, W	1877-78	1878-79	6	0	0	0
Wood, Walter	1876-77	1876-77	4	1	0	0
Wood, William	1876-77	1876-77	1	0	0	0
Yates, W	1877-78	1877-78	1	0	0	0
'A Goodplayer'	1877-78	1877-78	1	0	0	0

Also played after the club was renamed Salford in 1879

Cavendish Match Results

1874-75

	Opponent	Result	Scorers
Oct 24	MOSS SIDE WANDERERS 2ND	L 0-1g	
Oct 31	TRAFFORD	D 0-0	
Nov 14	GREENHEYS 2ND (Manchester)	D 0-0	
Nov 21	BIRCH 3RD	D 0-0	
Dec 5	St Stephen's (Birch)	D 0-0	
Dec 12	CLIFFORD WASPS 2ND (Manchester)	D 2t-0	no scorers recorded
Jan 9	TRAFFORD	D 0-0	
Jan 16	Wellington College (Broughton)	D 0-0	
Jan 30	ONWARDS (Didsbury)	D 3t-0	no scorers recorded
Feb 13	STOCKPORT WELLINGTON	D 1t-0	no scorer recorded
Feb 27	St Stephen's (Birch)	D 1t-0	no scorer recorded
Mar 13	St John's (Cheetham)	D 1g,3t-1g,4t	no scorers recorded
Mar 27	Clifford Wasps 2nd (Manchester)	L 0-1g,3t	

Home matches played at Moss Side, Manchester. *Result column*: Most goals (g) win. Only unconverted tries (t) are shown but do not count.

1875-76

	Opponent	Result	Scorers
Oct 2	Stretford	D 2t-1t	no scorers recorded
Oct 9	MANCHESTER GRAMMAR SCHOOL	NRA	
Oct 16	Bridgewater (Patricroft)	NRA	
Oct 23	LEVENSHULME WANDERERS	L 1t-1g,1?	no scorer recorded
Oct 30	Stockport 2nd	D 1t-0	no scorer recorded
Nov 6	CHORLTON	NRA	
Nov 13	FREE LANCERS (Manchester)	D 0-1t	
Nov 20	ST STEPHEN'S (Birch)	W 1g,3t-1t	no scorers recorded
Nov 27	GRASSHOPPERS 2ND (Manchester)	L 0-1t	
Dec 4	STALYBRIDGE 2ND	NRA	
Dec 18	STOCKPORT 2ND	W 1g,2t-0	T: Winnard 2, Alderson, C: Dunod
Jan 8	Grasshoppers 2nd (Manchester)	L 0-2t	
Jan 15	CAMBRIAN (Manchester)	L 0-1g	
Jan 22	Levenshulme Wanderers	L 0-1t	
Jan 29	Chorlton	L 0-1t	
Feb 5	Manchester Grammar School	W 1g,1t-1g	T: W Jackson, WG Inglefield, C: W Baird
Feb 12	Stalybridge 2nd	NRA	
Feb 26	Free Lancers (Manchester)	NRA	
Mar 4	STRETFORD	L 0-3t	
Mar 18	Cambrian (Manchester)	NRA	
Mar 25	BRIDGEWATER (Patricroft)	L 0-2t	

Home matches played at Throstle Nest Weir, Salford. *Result column to Nov 20*: Most goals (g) win. Only unconverted tries (t) are shown but do not count. *Result column from Nov 27*: Most goals (g) win. If equal most tries (t) win. Only unconverted tries are shown.

Cavendish Match Results

1876-77

	Opponent	Result	Scorers
Oct 14	Urmston	W 8t-0	T: H McKay
			(other scorers not recorded)
Oct 21	STRETFORD*	L 1t-2t	T: G Alderson
Oct 28	Weaste 2nd	W 1g,5t-0	T: Winnard 2, R Black, T Jones, RG McKay, DG: Carroll
Nov 4	FREE LANCERS (Manchester)	W 1g-1t	T: Walter Wood, C: Carroll
Nov 11	Birch Hornets	NRA	
Nov 18	Birch 2nd	L 2t-1g,3t	no scorers recorded
Nov 25	Rochdale St Chad's	D 0-0	
Dec 2	Levenshulme Wanderers	NRA	
Dec 16	CASTLETON	NRA	
Dec 23	BRIDGEWATER (Patricroft)	D 0-0	
Dec 30	Free Lancers (Manchester)	NRA	
Jan 13	ROCHDALE ST CHAD'S	NRA	
Jan 27	Bridgewater (Patricroft)	L 0-2g,1t	
Feb 3	URMSTON	NRA	
Feb 10	BIRCH 2ND	D 0-0	
Feb 17	Oldham	L 0-3t	
Feb 24	GRASSHOPPERS (Manchester)	NRA	
Mar 3	BIRCH HORNETS	NRA	
Mar 10	Castleton	L 1t-2g	no scorer recorded
Mar 17	Weaste 2nd	NRA	
Mar 24	RUSHOLME WORKING MEN	L 0-1t	
Mar 31	OLDHAM	NRA	

* Cavendish withdrew 15 minutes from end following a dispute

Home matches played at Throstle Nest Weir, Salford.

Result column: Most goals (g) win. If equal most tries (t) win.
Only unconverted tries shown in result

Cavendish Match Results

1877-78

	Opponent	Result	Scorers
Sep 29	Heaton Mersey Ramblers	L 1g,1t-1g,2t	T: Quine, C: RG McKay (*one try scorer not recorded*)
Oct 6	RUSHOLME	W 2g,1t-1t	T: Ashton, J Hulme, Sutherland, C: Heinke 2
Oct 13	Manchester Athletic	L 0-1g,1t	
Oct 20	BIRCH 2ND	W 3g,3t-0	T: Ashton, J Hulme, Sutherland, Winnard, C: Heinke, DG: Heinke 2
Oct 27	St Helens	W 2g,1t-0	no scorers recorded
Nov 3	CASTLETON	L 1t-1g,1t	no scorer recorded
Nov 10	Whitworth Rangers	L 0-1g,1t	
Nov 17	Patricroft Wanderers	L 0-1g	
Nov 24	Pendleton	W 2g,2t-0	T: RG McKay 2, Hay, C: Heinke, DG: Quine
Dec 1	Bury	D 0-0	
Dec 15	FLIXTON AND URMSTON	W 1t-0	no scorer recorded
Dec 22	Rochdale St Chad's	D 0-0	
Jan 5	Birch 2nd	D 2t-2t	T: Welch, Winnard
Jan 12	MANCHESTER ATHLETIC	D 0-0	
Jan 19	Farnworth	W 3t-1t	T: J Hulme, Inglefield, Winnard
Jan 26	ST HELENS*		
Feb 2	FARNWORTH*		
Feb 9	ROCHDALE ST CHAD'S*		
Feb 16	Flixton and Urmston	W 1g,4t-0	T: Winnard 2, R Black, H McKay, Sutherland, C: Winnard
Feb 23	PATRICROFT WANDERERS	W 1t-0	T: T Alderson
Mar 9	HEATON MERSEY RAMBLERS	D 0-0	
Mar 23	SWINTON 2ND	D 0-0	
Mar 30	PENDLETON	W 2t-0	T: Welch 2
Apr 6	SHARPE, STEWART'S (Manchester)	W 3g,2t-0	T: Ashton, S Hulme, RG McKay, C: RG McKay, DG: H McKay, RG Mackay

* *Cancelled due to non-arrival of visiting team*

Home matches played at Mile Field, off Trafford Road, Salford.

Result column: Most goals (g) win. If equal most tries (t) win. Only unconverted tries shown in result

Cavendish Match Results

1878-79

	Opponent	Result	Scorers
Oct 5	MANCHESTER ATHLETIC	L 0-1t	
Oct 12	Kirkstall (Leeds)	D 0-0	
Oct 19	BRADFORD ALBION	L 0-2g	
Oct 26	Flixton and Urmston	D 0-0	
Nov 2	LITTLE LEVER	W 2t-0	T: Carroll, Cooper
Nov 9	Heaton Mersey Ramblers	W 1g,1t-0	T: Welch, R Black, C: Carroll
Nov 16	Widnes	D 0-0	
Nov 23	PENDLETON	W 2g,1t-0	T: RG McKay 2, Welch, C: RG McKay 2
Nov 30	Castleton Moor	L 0-1t	
Dec 7	Manchester Athletic	W 1g,2t-0	T: RG McKay 2, Winnard, C: Carroll
Dec 14	FAILSWORTH*		
Dec 21	Rusholme*		
Dec 28	Little Lever*		
Jan 11	Farnworth*		
Jan 18	Manchester Athletic*		
Jan 25	Manchester 2nd*		
Feb 1	Pendleton*		
Feb 8	Bradford Albion*		
Feb 22	MANCHESTER 2ND	W 1g,4t-0	T: RG McKay 2, Fletcher, Sutherland, Winnard, C: RG McKay
Mar 1	FLIXTON AND URMSTON	W 3t-0	T: J Jones, Sutherland, Winnard
Mar 8	WIDNES	W 1g,2t-0	T: Ashton, G Hulme, Winnard, C:RG McKay
Mar 15	HEATON MERSEY RAMBLERS	NRA	
Mar 22	Manchester 2nd	W 1g,2t-0	T: R Black, RG McKay, Winnard, C: Winnard
Mar 29	RUSHOLME	NRA	

* Cancelled due to severe frost

Home matches played at New Barnes, Salford, from this season
Result column: Most goals (g) win. If equal most tries (t) win.
Only unconverted tries shown in result

H. EAGLES
Salford Football Club

Harry Eagles, who joined Salford after it amalgamated with his former club, Crescent, in 1881, was destined to become one of the Reds' most outstanding players during its Rugby Union era.

2

Salford Rugby Union
1879-80 – 1895-96

Having relocated to a ground at New Barnes adjoining the Salford-based Manchester Racecourse for 1878-79, secretary and former player Archie Sutherland proposed during the summer of 1879 that the club should be renamed Salford. He argued that adopting the name of the, then, borough (Salford obtained city status in 1926) would improve the quality of fixtures. Although opposed by some committee members, the resolution was passed and a new name appeared in the 1879-80 fixture lists. In his book, *History of the Salford Football Club*, James Higson describes Sutherland as 'practically the founder of the Salford Football Club'. Another notable change occurred prior to the 1883-84 season when it was decided to replace the previous livery of scarlet, amber and black hoops with an all-red jersey, the white 'knickerbockers' and black socks being retained. The club's first and only rugby union honour was achieved in 1892-93 when the Lancashire Club Championship was won.

Of 501 matches played as a rugby union club 57 are in the Lancashire Club Championship (1892-93 to 1895-96), one against the Maori touring team (1888-89), and 443 are classed as 'ordinary' (friendly) fixtures. The practice of determining the results based on the number of goals and tries scored continued until 1890-91. From 1891-92, a point system for goals and tries was instituted. The number of points awarded for the various methods of scoring are shown under each season's match results. It should be noted that, whilst every effort has been made to trace all the scorers, there are three matches during 1879-80 where this has proved unsuccessful.

During the period 1886-87 to 1892-93 it will be seen that, in the match results section, five games were played on the 'understanding' of a drawn result, whatever the final score. This was a common practice during this period if the ground was considered to be too hard from frost to be safe. The captains would agree to an 'exhibition' game with limited tackling so as not to injure the players.

The players' records section covers all matches played during its rugby union era with just 29 appearances unaccounted for, ten of which are from one match (versus Leigh, 26 April 1894). There was also seven games where Salford were short-handed, the cumulative total being 10 players. Note that in instances where a club name is shown in brackets against a player's name it indicates he was a 'guest' from that club.

Salford RU Players

Name	Pos	Debut	Last match	App	Tries	G
Alberts, S	T	20/10/1883	20/10/1883	1	0	0
Alderson, G**	F	04/10/1879	07/02/1880	6	0	0
Alderson, R	T	23/11/1895	14/12/1895	4	0	0
Aldred, G	F	26/12/1893	26/12/1893	1	0	0
Allen, J	FB	28/02/1885	20/02/1886	8	0	0
Allmark, –	F	02/01/1882	02/01/1882	1	0	0
Anderton, Jack	T	17/09/1887	22/04/1889	52	17	25
Anderton, W	F	13/09/1890	15/11/1890	9	0	0
Armstrong, –	T	21/10/1882	21/10/1882	1	0	0
Ashton, D	T	25/02/1893	25/11/1893	4	1	0
Ashton, F	T	07/11/1885	20/03/1886	4	0	0
Ashton, W**	F	11/10/1879	10/01/1880	2	0	0
Ashworth, –	F	26/04/1890	26/04/1890	1	0	0
Astin, T	F	02/01/1892	02/01/1892	1	0	0
Atkins, –	HB	24/12/1881	24/12/1881	1	0	0
Atkinson, F	F	19/03/1881	07/01/1882	3	0	0
Austin, Ted	F	11/04/1885	26/04/1890	43	4	0
Barlow, A	T	04/02/1882	04/02/1882	1	0	0
Barlow, J	F	22/11/1884	17/09/1887	67	7	1
Barrett, Alf	T	27/10/1888	30/04/1895	230	48	10
Barrett, Edwin	T	15/03/1890	03/04/1893	25	4	0
Barrington, WH*	F	21/04/1894	18/04/1896	27	1	0
Beatty, J	F	20/03/1889	15/04/1889	5	0	0
Beswick, E 'Ted' (Swinton)	T	28/02/1880	10/04/1880	2	1	1
Bevan, –	F	02/11/1895	25/01/1896	2	0	0
Birch, J	F	05/10/1889	12/09/1891	64	15	0
Black, R**	F	18/10/1879	04/12/1880	17	0	0
Blake, B	T	05/10/1895	18/04/1896	14	2	0
Blomley, J	FB	11/01/1890	14/03/1896	15	0	1
Booth, W	F	18/10/1879	19/11/1881	31	2	0
Bowen, –	T	26/10/1895	23/11/1895	4	0	0
Bowker, C	T	25/01/1890	12/04/1893	7	0	0
Bracher, C	F	02/04/1888	02/04/1888	1	0	0
Bradbury, A	FB	16/04/1887	16/04/1887	1	0	0
Bradbury, J	F	02/04/1887	16/04/1887	2	0	0
Bradshaw, F	F	17/09/1887	28/12/1889	29	1	0
Braithwaite, Edwin*	T	01/02/1896	18/04/1896	14	2	3
Brayshay, J	F	22/09/1888	12/01/1889	15	1	0
Brierley, Jack	F	02/01/1892	30/03/1895	86	6	0
Brockbank, Herbie (Swinton)	HB	04/10/1890	26/12/1891	2	0	0
Broome, A	F	31/03/1883	12/04/1884	10	0	0
Brown, J	F	02/03/1895	18/04/1896	38	1	0
Brown, W 'Billy'*	F	28/12/1895	18/04/1896	7	0	0
Brundrett, F	F	22/09/1894	19/10/1895	3	0	0
Buckley, Jim***	F	01/10/1881	14/03/1885	56	15	0

Salford RU Players

Name	Pos	Debut	Last match	App	Tries	G
Buckley, WH 'Bill'***	F	24/09/1881	18/04/1885	87	10	0
Bullock, Bob***	HB	21/01/1882	21/09/1889	86	13	18
Bumby, Walter (Swinton)	HB	26/04/1890	26/04/1890	1	0	0
Burton, W	T	15/09/1888	15/09/1888	1	0	0
Butterworth, Fred**	T	04/10/1879	12/03/1887	48	9	1
Buxton, Charlie	T	10/02/1883	29/01/1887	33	2	1
Buxton, George	HB	22/11/1884	29/01/1887	55	1	1
Campbell, W	F	23/04/1892	20/01/1894	10	0	0
Carrington, G	FB	08/11/1879	09/04/1881	15	1	0
Carrington, Tom***	T	07/10/1882	30/12/1882	4	0	0
Carroll, W**	F	11/10/1879	08/10/1881	25	1	6
Carson, R	FB	16/04/1892	18/08/1892	2	0	0
Carter, J	F	20/11/1886	11/12/1886	3	0	0
Cartwright, G	F	10/09/1892	21/04/1894	68	5	0
Casey, H	F	02/09/1891	14/11/1892	41	3	0
Chapman, Harry	T	01/09/1894	15/09/1894	3	1	6
Chapman, –	T	09/10/1880	09/10/1880	1	0	0
Cheetham, –	F	25/01/1896	25/01/1896	1	0	0
Clayton, J***	HB	24/09/1881	07/04/1883	13	1	0
Clayton, –	F	26/04/1890	26/04/1890	1	0	0
Clegg, Harry	HB	31/10/1885	16/03/1889	104	11	0
Coleman, George*	HB	22/02/1896	18/04/1896	11	0	0
Connor, T	F	01/09/1894	01/09/1894	1	0	0
Cook, Herbert	T	24/09/1887	23/04/1892	89	22	3
Coop, Tom (Leigh)	FB	16/11/1891	16/11/1891	1	0	0
Cooper, A	T	17/12/1892	21/01/1893	6	0	0
Cooper, J	F	11/04/1885	11/04/1885	1	0	0
Cooper, JE	T	15/03/1890	03/01/1891	21	2	0
Cooper, W (Pendleton)	F	26/12/1893	28/04/1894	2	0	0
Cosgrove, Tom	FB	28/09/1895	04/01/1896	15	0	2
Coulthwaite, Tom (Swinton)	F	06/10/1888	31/12/1888	3	0	0
Craven, S	T	10/12/1890	10/12/1890	1	0	0
Craven, Tom	F	26/10/1889	29/04/1893	100	5	0
Cross, Billy (St Helens)	HB	05/02/1890	16/11/1891	2	0	0
Crossley, T	HB	03/11/1888	10/11/1888	2	0	0
Crump, G	HB	10/04/1880	09/04/1881	6	2	0
Dain, K	F	07/12/1889	07/12/1889	1	0	0
Darbyshire, Sam	F	16/02/1889	07/03/1891	14	1	0
Darwell, A	FB	12/11/1887	12/11/1887	1	0	0
Deakin, S	F	26/12/1893	30/04/1895	28	2	0
Dennett, H	HB	30/09/1882	30/09/1882	1	0	0
Diggle, C	T	01/01/1895	26/10/1895	20	9	0
Ditchfield, W	HB	20/03/1889	25/03/1893	22	1	0
Dobson, J	F	11/12/1886	19/03/1887	4	0	0
Donnelly, J	F	28/02/1885	26/09/1885	2	0	0

Salford RU Players

Name	Pos	Debut	Last match	App	Tries	G
Doran, R 'Bobby'	HB	01/01/1895	09/11/1895	5	1	0
Draper, W	T	08/02/1896	08/02/1896	1	0	0
Drury, H	HB	13/09/1890	27/09/1890	3	0	0
Eagles, Harry***	F	24/09/1881	15/10/1892	268	61	1
Eardley, J**	F	25/10/1879	25/10/1879	1	0	0
Eccles, G	F	27/03/1889	27/03/1889	1	0	0
Edge, D	T	28/09/1895	05/10/1895	2	0	0
Edge, W	HB	12/09/1891	12/09/1891	1	0	0
Ellison, CW	T	22/02/1896	22/02/1896	1	0	0
Faey, –	T	06/11/1880	06/11/1880	1	0	0
Field, –	F	03/01/1880	03/01/1880	1	0	0
Fielden, JP	T	23/11/1895	01/01/1896	7	0	1
Fife, D***	F	07/10/1882	07/03/1888	9	2	0
Fletcher, E**	F	04/10/1879	19/02/1881	4	1	0
Fletcher, M	F	21/09/1895	09/11/1895	5	0	0
Foster, A	F	27/10/1888	22/04/1889	27	1	0
Fox, T	T	10/09/1892	14/11/1892	11	2	0
France, WH	HB	19/09/1891	29/09/1894	103	10	0
Fraser, –	F	19/03/1881	19/03/1881	1	0	0
Gill, –	F	15/04/1891	15/04/1891	1	1	0
Gill, C (Manchester Athletic)	F	28/04/1894	28/04/1894	1	0	0
Gill, E	F	15/03/1890	15/03/1890	1	0	0
Gleave, F	HB	06/10/1883	06/10/1883	1	0	0
Goddard, –	HB	29/09/1888	29/09/1888	1	0	0
Gorman, T	F	07/03/1888	02/02/1889	22	2	0
Green, F	HB	04/04/1891	20/04/1891	4	1	0
Green, RA	F	26/12/1888	26/12/1888	1	0	0
Gregson, A	F	28/12/1889	28/12/1889	1	0	0
Gregson, Walter***	F	05/11/1881	12/04/1884	22	3	0
Hadwin, H	F	20/11/1893	30/12/1893	3	0	0
Hadwin, JW	T	10/01/1891	10/01/1891	1	0	0
Haigh, L	F	29/12/1888	29/12/1888	1	0	0
Haigh, –	F	26/12/1892	31/12/1892	2	0	0
Hallam, Tom (Swinton)	F	26/12/1891	28/12/1891	2	0	0
Hampson, E	F	24/04/1893	24/04/1893	1	0	0
Handforth, A	F	15/09/1888	15/09/1888	1	0	0
Hardy, Tom**	F	04/10/1879	25/03/1882	28	3	0
Hargreaves, A	HB	12/10/1895	18/01/1896	12	0	0
Harley, CW	HB	04/02/1893	15/04/1893	10	2	0
Harter, Ezekiel*	T	26/04/1894	18/04/1896	11	2	1
Haslam, Sam*	F	07/03/1888	18/04/1896	114	8	1
Hasleham, Harry (Mcr Rngrs)	F	18/10/1890	26/12/1891	3	0	0
Hassall, S (Broughton)	T	28/04/1894	28/04/1894	1	0	0
Haynes, –	F	25/02/1882	25/02/1882	1	0	0
Heald, Jack	F	30/12/1882	11/04/1887	15	1	0

Salford RU Players

Name	Pos	Debut	Last match	App	Tries	G
Heald, Tom	T	25/10/1879	12/04/1884	50	5	2
Henry, ET	HB	25/03/1893	01/04/1893	2	0	0
Heswell, –	F	08/10/1881	08/10/1881	1	0	0
Higgins, P***	F	01/10/1881	15/10/1881	2	0	0
Higson, James***	F	17/03/1883	17/11/1883	2	1	0
Hildebrand, F	F	04/11/1893	11/04/1896	70	0	0
Hill, –	F	01/01/1883	01/01/1883	1	0	0
Hindshaw, A	F	14/03/1891	26/12/1893	29	3	0
Holcroft, JS	F	03/02/1883	03/02/1883	1	0	0
Holgate, W	T	15/09/1894	28/09/1895	3	0	0
Holmes, Jim (Kendal Hornets)	T	03/04/1896	03/04/1896	1	0	0
Hopewell, CM	T	15/11/1884	29/11/1884	2	0	0
Hopkins, S	T	27/02/1892	30/04/1892	3	0	0
Hopwood, J	T	28/01/1893	28/01/1893	1	0	0
Horrox, James	F	31/10/1891	30/04/1895	49	1	0
Hosker, Richard	HB	02/09/1891	05/09/1891	2	1	1
Hotchkiss, Nat (Swinton)	F	31/12/1888	19/03/1890	2	0	0
Hoyles, R	F	11/04/1887	11/04/1887	1	0	0
Hughes, C*	F	28/04/1894	18/04/1896	45	0	0
Hughes, R	F	23/01/1886	09/04/1887	20	0	0
Hulme, George**	F	04/10/1879	29/01/1887	56	6	0
Hulme, S	F	04/10/1879	02/04/1881	10	0	0
Hulme, T**	F	11/10/1879	11/10/1879	1	0	0
Hulmes, J	F	10/12/1892	25/11/1893	12	0	0
Humphries, J	F	28/09/1895	28/12/1895	7	0	0
Hurst, James	T	22/02/1896	22/02/1896	1	0	0
Jackson, AN	F	27/03/1889	27/03/1889	1	0	0
Jackson, George	F	27/11/1886	16/02/1889	60	1	0
Jackson, James	F	14/10/1882	10/04/1886	60	8	0
Jackson, John	F	10/10/1885	10/10/1885	1	0	0
Jackson, –	F	26/12/1892	26/12/1892	1	0	0
James, E	HB	08/02/1896	08/02/1896	1	0	0
Johnson, F	T	30/10/1880	02/04/1881	6	2	0
Johnson, R	F	07/04/1883	07/04/1883	1	0	0
Johnson, T	F	08/12/1888	13/04/1889	15	0	0
Jones, J**	F	04/10/1879	22/12/1883	49	4	0
Jones, JD (Radcliffe)	FB	28/04/1894	28/04/1894	1	0	0
Jones, JJ*	F	27/01/1894	03/04/1896	46	5	0
Jones, JP	F	26/09/1885	23/10/1886	21	1	0
Jones, L	F	04/10/1879	04/10/1879	1	0	0
Jordan, J	F	10/03/1894	18/04/1896	28	1	0
Jowett, H	F	13/10/1888	20/10/1888	2	0	0
Kay, E	F	26/12/1885	26/12/1885	1	0	0
Kennedy, GF	FB	18/10/1879	08/10/1881	11	0	1
Kent, Tom	F	17/09/1887	28/04/1894	172	18	2

Salford RU Players

Name	Pos	Debut	Last match	App	Tries	G
Kenwright, -**	F	02/04/1881	02/04/1881	1	0	0
Kilner, E**	F	04/10/1879	20/03/1880	13	1	0
Kinder, A	F	26/11/1881	26/11/1881	1	0	0
King, Tom	F	16/02/1889	03/04/1896	212	17	15
Kirkman, J***	F	03/12/1881	12/04/1884	2	2	0
Kneen, T	T	02/01/1882	02/01/1882	1	0	0
Knowles, Alf	F	01/01/1891	29/04/1893	77	2	0
Knowles, Frank	F	05/02/1890	29/04/1893	98	7	0
Law, W	F	20/03/1889	06/12/1890	20	1	0
Lawton, J (Pendleton)	T	28/04/1894	28/04/1894	1	0	0
Lawton, -	F	28/12/1895	01/02/1896	7	0	0
Leslie, -	F	27/02/1886	27/02/1886	1	0	0
Lightfoot, H	T	05/11/1892	18/02/1893	3	0	1
Lindley, -	T	04/12/1880	04/12/1880	1	0	0
Lord, H	F	17/03/1883	17/03/1883	1	0	0
Lunny, J	T	17/11/1890	15/04/1891	8	0	0
McClure, -	F	27/12/1888	27/12/1888	1	0	0
McEwan, W	HB	01/09/1894	05/10/1895	6	0	0
McGregor, A	T	02/11/1895	02/11/1895	1	0	0
McKay, RG**	HB	04/10/1879	23/12/1882	37	10	7
McNally, J***	F	31/12/1881	31/12/1881	1	0	0
McNally, Mick***	F	01/10/1881	24/04/1886	91	7	0
McVittie, J	F	21/01/1888	14/03/1891	86	4	0
Maguire, Paddy	F	18/10/1879	24/02/1883	49	2	1
Makin, B	F	21/03/1891	19/03/1892	27	2	0
Mallinson, J	T	12/04/1886	01/01/1890	27	6	0
Malpass, J	F	09/10/1880	18/03/1882	35	4	5
Manwaring, W 'Billy'*	FB	18/09/1886	18/04/1896	280	3	42
Marsden, -	F	19/12/1885	19/12/1885	1	0	0
Martinscroft, J	T	06/10/1888	13/10/1888	2	0	1
Mason, J	HB	11/11/1882	24/02/1883	12	1	0
Massey, GH	FB	01/01/1894	03/02/1894	5	0	0
Mather, E	F	04/11/1893	30/12/1893	6	0	0
Margury, E	HB	24/09/1881	24/09/1881	1	0	0
Medley, R (Broughton Rngrs)	F	04/04/1892	04/04/1892	1	0	0
Miles, Frank*	T	14/09/1889	13/10/1894	161	114	5
Milner, -	F	05/11/1881	05/11/1881	1	0	0
Morley, A***	F	04/11/1882	03/03/1883	5	0	0
Morris, H	T	01/01/1895	19/10/1895	14	0	0
Morris, T	F	21/11/1891	21/11/1891	1	0	0
Moss, Bob*	F	03/02/1894	18/04/1896	62	5	0
Mothersgill, W	F	10/12/1890	10/12/1890	1	0	0
Moxon, A	F	02/01/1888	27/03/1889	2	0	0
Naylor, J	HB	26/01/1895	18/04/1896	21	0	0
Newton, Joe	HB	26/12/1885	14/02/1891	111	7	0

Salford RU Players

Name	Pos	Debut	Last match	App	Tries	G
Nicholas, TL	F	02/11/1889	02/09/1893	38	11	15
Nicholls, –	F	02/04/1881	09/04/1881	2	0	0
Nightingale, J**	F	04/10/1879	13/11/1880	16	1	0
Nunn, F	F	05/12/1885	05/12/1885	1	0	0
Nuttall, G	T	26/09/1885	26/09/1885	1	0	0
Nuttall, P	F	27/03/1889	27/03/1889	1	0	0
Ogden, AE	F	05/11/1887	03/11/1888	26	2	0
Oswald, J	HB	26/12/1888	07/12/1889	8	0	0
Oswald, WG	FB	29/10/1892	12/04/1893	9	0	0
Ottiwell, A	F	22/10/1881	02/02/1889	161	12	3
Owen, J	T	26/10/1895	22/02/1896	19	1	0
Paine, JW	FB	09/10/1886	09/10/1886	1	0	0
Parker, JW	F	02/09/1891	19/09/1891	4	0	0
Parkinson, J	T	11/02/1888	24/04/1893	6	0	0
Parlane, Willie (Mcr Rangers)	HB	17/04/1893	26/03/1894	4	0	0
Paul, Arthur	FB	04/03/1893	10/02/1894	24	0	16
Pennel, –	F	09/04/1881	09/04/1881	1	0	0
Pilling, –	HB	24/12/1881	24/12/1881	1	0	0
Pollard, G	F	25/09/1893	25/09/1893	1	0	0
Powell, J	HB	25/10/1879	12/03/1881	5	1	0
Powell, -	F	26/12/1887	26/12/1887	1	0	0
Pratt, A***	HB	15/10/1881	21/03/1885	44	9	0
Price, J	F	21/03/1885	24/10/1885	5	0	0
Priestley, George	T	07/03/1888	17/11/1888	13	0	2
Quigley, J	HB	29/04/1893	02/09/1893	2	0	0
Ramage, –	T	02/02/1895	27/04/1895	2	0	0
Rangeley, James	T	02/09/1893	12/10/1895	58	16	10
Ratcliffe, F	T	04/10/1884	17/01/1885	9	0	0
Riddle, W	F	24/02/1883	24/02/1883	1	0	0
Rixon, JS (Risley)	F	14/09/1889	14/09/1889	1	0	0
Roberts, H	F	01/09/1894	01/01/1895	8	0	0
Roberts, Jack	F	03/03/1883	16/03/1895	271	100	1
Robinson, –	T	28/12/1894	11/01/1896	4	0	0
Rowlinson, JT	T	25/02/1893	01/01/1895	6	1	0
Russell, H	F	04/10/1879	02/04/1881	6	0	0
Russell, J (Pendleton)	FB	21/04/1894	26/04/1894	2	0	0
Ryan, Thomas	HB	21/09/1895	19/10/1895	5	1	0
Sanderson, D	T	04/01/1890	04/10/1890	3	1	0
Sandforth, HH	F	04/02/1888	04/02/1888	1	0	0
Seddon, Dick	T	24/09/1887	10/03/1888	21	1	2
Sellars, T	T	01/01/1895	20/04/1895	8	0	0
Shaw, Joe	F	12/04/1884	07/11/1891	196	16	24
Shawcross, J	F	10/12/1890	03/01/1891	3	0	0
Shepherd, F	F	01/01/1894	01/01/1894	1	0	0
Sherlock, W	FB	04/02/1882	17/09/1887	58	0	36
Shoreman, C	HB	11/01/1890	11/01/1890	1	0	0

Salford RU Players

Name	Pos	Debut	Last match	App	Tries	G
Slater, T***	HB	31/12/1881	26/11/1887	2	0	0
Slater, Vic	T	22/11/1884	31/03/1888	62	14	18
Smith, Arthur	HB	03/12/1887	28/09/1889	32	4	0
Smith, Joe	T	04/03/1893	13/10/1894	56	15	3
Smith, R	T	11/01/1896	06/04/1896	15	3	0
Smith, Tommy	F	22/11/1884	17/03/1894	105	6	0
Smith, –	T	24/12/1881	24/12/1881	1	0	0
Spinks, J	T	29/02/1896	11/04/1896	2	0	0
Stephens, JF	T	16/03/1895	30/04/1895	9	1	0
Stockton, –	F	15/10/1881	11/02/1882	2	0	0
Stott, A	F	17/10/1885	26/03/1887	33	1	0
Stuart, Angus	T	29/10/1881	01/04/1882	19	10	0
Sudlow, Tom	T	05/02/1890	12/03/1892	30	12	0
Sutherland, Archie**	HB	04/10/1879	18/02/1882	30	2	0
Sutton, A	HB	12/11/1881	10/11/1883	16	3	0
Sutton, Tom	HB	02/01/1882	21/01/1882	3	1	0
Swarbrick, J	F	04/10/1879	19/03/1881	20	1	5
Symington, J**	F	11/10/1879	16/10/1880	3	1	0
Taylor, S	F	04/11/1893	23/11/1895	10	0	0
Telford, Bob	FB	01/01/1884	19/03/1887	14	0	0
Tewson, J	F	11/02/1893	09/12/1894	19	2	0
Thomas, J	F	12/04/1886	12/04/1886	1	0	0
Thornley, T***	F	24/09/1881	02/12/1882	30	4	0
Tomlinson, E	F	23/10/1880	18/03/1882	32	1	0
Tonge, G	F	29/12/1888	30/04/1895	71	3	0
Travis, T	F	12/04/1884	12/04/1884	1	0	0
Tune, Jack	F	21/09/1889	30/03/1891	44	6	0
Valentine, Jim (Swinton)	T	31/12/1888	28/12/1891	4	2	2
Varley, Cornie	T	06/12/1884	21/01/1888	59	4	19
Vickers, E	F	09/02/1884	21/04/1888	79	5	0
Vickers, G	F	25/10/1884	25/10/1884	1	0	0
Vipond, Harry*	F	01/02/1896	18/04/1896	14	1	0
Walch, Sam*	HB	12/10/1889	20/04/1895	161	13	27
Walker, E	F	24/04/1893	24/04/1893	1	0	0
Walker, –	F	27/12/1888	27/12/1888	1	0	0
Wall, –	HB	15/04/1891	15/04/1891	1	0	0
Wall, J	HB	14/12/1895	25/01/1896	8	2	0
Walmsley, Bob	T	30/09/1882	10/11/1888	69	25	1
Ward, A (Blackley Rangers)	T	21/01/1893	21/01/1893	1	1	1
Wardle, ET	F	21/03/1885	21/03/1885	1	1	0
Watkin, –	F	09/04/1881	09/04/1881	1	0	0
Watson, R	T	14/12/1895	01/02/1896	7	0	0
Welch, R**	F	08/11/1879	10/04/1880	4	1	0
Whittaker, J	F	05/01/1884	05/01/1884	1	0	0
Wickman, E	HB	06/12/1890	13/12/1890	2	0	0

Salford RU Players

Name	Pos	Debut	Last match	App	Tries	G
Wignall, –	T	09/10/1880	09/10/1880	1	0	0
Wild, F	HB	02/09/1891	18/04/1896	18	0	0
Williams, Sam	F	08/10/1881	26/04/1890	170	27	2
Williamson, Hugh	T	29/11/1879	20/02/1886	50	22	0
Williamson, J	F	10/12/1890	10/12/1890	1	0	0
Wilson, C	F	12/04/1893	12/04/1893	1	0	0
Wilson, David	FB	16/02/1889	08/02/1896	18	3	1
Wilson, J	F	10/12/1890	10/12/1890	1	0	0
Winnard, J**	HB	04/10/1879	01/10/1881	20	2	0
Winnard, S	F	22/12/1883	27/12/1884	24	2	0
Winterbottom, Bill (Swinton)	T	26/12/1891	26/12/1891	1	0	0
Woodhead, –	F	27/12/1884	07/02/1885	2	0	0
Worthington, James	T	06/10/1883	21/03/1885	37	3	3
Yeates, R	F	14/10/1882	28/01/1888	58	5	0
AN Other	F	24/12/1881	24/12/1881	1	0	0
AN Other	F	07/10/1882	07/10/1882	1	0	0
AN Other	F	16/02/1889	16/02/1889	1	0	0
AN Other	HB	03/02/1894	03/02/1894	1	0	0
'Ferguson'	T	19/03/1887	19/03/1887	1	0	0

* Played further matches for Salford after the 1896 breakaway from Rugby Union
** Previously played for Cavendish prior to being renamed Salford in 1879
*** Previously played for Crescent (Salford) prior to amalgamation with Salford in 1881

Note: Goals column includes conversions, drop-goals, penalty goals, goals from a mark

Salford RU 1879-80 to 1895-96

Salford RU Match Results

1879-80

	Opponent	Result	Scorers
Oct 4	Dewsbury	L 0-3g	
Oct 11	WIDNES	D 1t-1t	T: G Hulme
Oct 18	Sale	W 3g,5t-0	T: McKay 2, G Hulme, Kilner, Maguire, Nightingale, Symington, C: Carroll 2, McKay (1 try scorer not recorded)
Oct 25	Leeds St John's	D 1t-1t	T: J Powell
Nov 8	Manchester Athletic	D 1t-1t	(scorer not recorded)
Nov 29	PENDLETON	W 2t-0	T: McKay 2
Jan 3	Pendleton	W 1g,1t-0	T: Maguire, Williamson, C: McKay
Jan 10	SALE	W 3g,5t-0	(scorers not recorded)
Feb 7	Broughton Rangers	L 1t-2t	T: J Winnard
Feb 14	Cheetham	L 0-1g,3t	
Feb 21	DEWSBURY	W 2g,1t-0	T: Booth, Butterworth, J Jones, C: Carroll 2
Feb 28	LEEDS ST JOHN'S	W 1g,1t-1t	T: Beswick, Butterworth, C: Carroll
Mar 20	Manchester 'A'	W 2g,6t-0	T: Hardy 2, Butterworth, Carrington, T Heald, McKay, Williamson, J Winnard, C: Carroll, McKay
Apr 10	BROUGHTON RANGERS	W 2g,3t-1g	T: Carroll, Crump, Sutherland, Welch, C: McKay, DG: Beswick

Result column: Most goals (g) win. If equal most tries (t) win.
Only unconverted tries shown in result

1880-81

	Opponent	Result	Scorers
Oct 9	Leeds St John's	L 0-2g	
Oct 16	BROUGHTON RANGERS	W 1g,1t-1t	T: Swarbrick, DG: Maguire
Oct 23	WALTON (Liverpool)	W 1g,2t-0	T: Williamson 2, Sutherland, C: Swarbrick
Oct 30	BREIGHTMET	W 1g-0	T: E Fletcher, C: Swarbrick
Nov 6	Rochdale Hornets	W 1g,3t-0	T: Booth, Malpass, Tomlinson, Williamson, C: Swarbrick
Nov 13	BIRCH	D 0-0	
Nov 27	PENDLETON	W 1g,4t-0	T: McKay 2, Hardy, F Johnson, Williamson, C: Malpass
Dec 4	SWINTON	L 0-2g	
Feb 19	LEEDS ST JOHN'S	L 1g-1g,2t	T: Williamson, C: Swarbrick
Mar 5	Broughton Rangers	L 1t-3g	T: Crump
Mar 12	Cheetham	D 0-0	

Salford RU Match Results

1880-81 *continued*

	Opponent	Result	Scorers
Mar 19	OLDHAM	W 2g,5t-0	T: G Hulme, F Johnson, J Jones, Malpass, McKay, Williamson, C: Swarbrick, DG: Kennedy
Apr 2	Oldham	L 0-2g,2t	
Apr 9	Swinton	L 0-7g,7t	

Result column: Most goals (g) win. If equal most tries (t) win.
Only unconverted tries shown in result

1881-82

	Opponent	Result	Scorers
Sep 24	DEWSBURY	D 1t-1t	T: Williamson
Oct 1	CHEETHAM	L 1t-2g,1t	T: Williamson
Oct 8	Manchester Athletic	L 0-1t	
Oct 15	Birch	L 1t-1g	T: WH Buckley
Oct 22	LEEDS ST JOHN'S	W 1g,1t-2t	T: J Jones, Williamson, C: Malpass
Oct 29	Swinton	L 1t-2g,1t	T: Ottiwell
Nov 5	ECCLES	W 3g,4t-0	T: Stuart 2, Eagles, T Heald, Ottiwell, Pratt, C: Malpass 2, DG: Malpass
Nov 12	CHORLEY	W 1g,4t-0	T: Stuart 2, Thornley, Williamson, DG: T Heald
Nov 19	BREIGHTMET	W 1g,2t-0	T: Williamson 3, C: McKay
Nov 26	Broughton Rangers	L 1t-1g	T: A Sutton
Dec 3	CHEETHAM HILL	W 1g,7t-0	T: McKay 2, J Clayton, Kirkman, M McNally, Ottiwell, Stuart, Williamson, C: McKay
Dec 24	SWINTON	L 0-3t	
Dec 31	Broughton	L 0-5t	
Jan 2	Manchester	L 0-2g,2t	
Jan 7	Dewsbury	W 2t-1t	T: Malpass, T Sutton
Jan 21	Cheetham	W 1g-0	T: Thornley, C: Bullock
Feb 4	Rochdale Hornets	W 3g,1t-0	T: Eagles, Stuart, Thornley, C: Bullock 2, DG: Sherlock
Feb 11	Chorley	W 2g-0	T: Stuart, A Sutton, C: Bullock 2
Feb 18	Leeds St John's	D 0-0	
Feb 25	BIRCH	W 1t-0	T: Stuart
Mar 11	MANCHESTER ATHLETIC	L 0-2t	
Mar 18	OLDHAM	W 6t-0	T: WH Buckley, Bullock, T Heald, J Jones, Malpass, Williamson
Mar 25	BROUGHTON RANGERS	W 5t-0	T: Stuart 2, Butterworth, T Heald, Williamson
Apr 1	Oldham	D 0-0	

Result column: Most goals (g) win. If equal most tries (t) win.
Only unconverted tries shown in result

Salford RU Match Results

1882-83

	Opponent	Result	Scorers
Sep 30	SWINTON	L 1t-2g,5t	T: J Buckley
Oct 7	Chorley	W 1t-0	T: J Buckley
Oct 14	ECCLES	W 1g,5t-0	T: Bullock 2, Yeates 2, Eagles, Williamson, C: Bullock
Oct 21	MANCHESTER ATHLETIC	W 1g,1t-0	T: Yeates, DG: T Heald
Oct 28	BROUGHTON RANGERS	W 1g-0	T: Yeates, C: McKay
Nov 4	Oldham	L 0-1g	
Nov 11	Broughton	W 4g,1t-0	T: Williams 2, Ottiwell, C: Sherlock 2, DG: Maguire, Sherlock
Nov 18	BIRCH	W 2g,5t-0	T: Williams 2, J Buckley, WH Buckley, Eagles, Mason, Thornley, C: Sherlock 2
Dec 2	CHEETHAM	D 0-0	
Dec 23	CHEETHAM HILL	W 2t-0	T: Eagles, Williams
Dec 30	Manchester	W 1g,2t-0	T: J Heald, G Hulme, Ottiwell, C: Bullock.
Jan 1	Bolton	W 1g,1t-1t	T: W Gregson, A Sutton, C: Bullock
Jan 13	DEWSBURY	D 0-0	
Jan 20	BROUGHTON	W 1g-2t	T: Butterworth, C: Sherlock
Feb 3	MANCHESTER	W 1g,1t-1t	T: Butterworth, DG: Williams
Feb 10	CHORLEY	W 2g,3t-1t	T: W Gregson 2, Bullock, J Jackson, Williams, C: Bullock 2
Feb 17	Swinton	L 1g-1g,1t	T: Butterworth, C: Bullock
Feb 24	Cheetham	L 2t-1g,1t	T: J Buckley 2
Mar 3	Broughton Rangers	D 1t-1t	T: J Roberts
Mar 17	Birch	W 1g,2t-0	T: J Buckley, Butterworth, Higson, C: Bullock
Mar 31	Manchester Athletic	W 2g,7t-0	T: Fife 2, WH Buckley, Bullock, G Hulme, Ottiwell, Pratt, Williams, Williamson, C: Bullock 2
Apr 7	BOLTON	W 5g,5t-0	T: J Buckley 2, Williamson 2, WH Buckley, Eagles, M McNally, G Hulme, Williams, C: Sherlock 3, Butterworth, DG: Williams

Result column: Most goals (g) win. If equal most tries (t) win.
Only unconverted tries shown in result

1883-84

	Opponent	Result	Scorers
Oct 6	WAKEFIELD TRINITY	L 1t-6g,1t	T: Williamson
Oct 13	Dewsbury	L 0-1t	
Oct 20	Cheetham	W 1t-0	T: J Buckley

Salford RU Match Results

1883-84 *continued*

	Opponent	Result	Scorers
Oct 27	OLDHAM	L 2t-1g	T: M McNally, J Roberts
Nov 10	Broughton Rangers	L 0-2t	
Nov 17	Widnes	W 1g,1t-1g	T: J Roberts 2, C: Sherlock
Nov 24	Southport	W 4g,8t-0	T: J Roberts 4, Eagles 3, WH Buckley, M McNally, Ottiwell, Pratt, C: Sherlock 3, DG: Sherlock
Dec 1	BLACKLEY	W 6g,3t-0	T: Eagles 2, J Roberts 2, J Buckley, M McNally, Worthington, C: Sherlock 4, DG: Bullock, Worthington
Dec 22	DEWSBURY	D 0-0	
Dec 29	Swinton	L 0-1g	
Jan 1	BARROW	W 2g,1t-1g,1t	T: Butterworth, Pratt, J Roberts, C: Sherlock 2
Jan 5	BUTTERFLIES*	W 2g,3t-0	T: Walmsley 2, WH Buckley, Eagles, T Heald, C: Sherlock 2
Jan 12	Birch	W 2g,3t-0	T: Walmsley 2, J Buckley, Eagles, Pratt, C: Sherlock 2
Jan 26	BIRCH	W 2t-0	T: J Buckley, J Roberts
Feb 9	Wakefield Trinity	W 1g-0	T: WH Buckley, C: Sherlock
Feb 16	Blackley	W 2g,3t-0	T: J Buckley 2, J Roberts, Walmsley, Worthington, C: Sherlock 2
Feb 23	WIDNES	W 3g,3t-0	T: J Jackson 2, WH Buckley, Eagles, J Roberts, Vickers, C: Sherlock 3
Mar 1	BROUGHTON RANGERS	W 1g,2t-0	T: J Roberts, Walmsley, DG: Worthington
Mar 8	SWINTON	W 3t-1t	T: Walmsley 2, J Jackson
Mar 15	ASKAM	W 4g,5t-0	T: J Roberts 3, S Winnard 2, Eagles, Pratt, Walmsley, C: Sherlock 3, DG: Worthington
Mar 22	Oldham	L 0-1t	
Apr 12	CHEETHAM	W 1t-0	T: Kirkman

* Butterflies was a 'scratch' team consisting of players from the Manchester area

Result column: Most goals (g) win. If equal most tries (t) win.
Only unconverted tries shown in result

Colours changed to red jersey, white shorts, black socks
(previously scarlet, amber and black hooped jersey)

Salford RU Match Results

1884-85

	Opponent	Result	Scorers
Oct 4	BIRCH	W 1g,7t-0	T: J Roberts 3, Walmsley 2, Eagles, J Jackson, E Vickers, C: Bullock
Oct 11	WIDNES	W 1g,2t-1g	T: Ottiwell, J Roberts, Shaw, C: Bullock
Oct 18	Oldham	W 1g,2t-0	T: WH Buckley, Walmsley, DG: Sherlock
Oct 25	Birch	W 1g,1t-0	T: E Vickers, Yeates, C: Bullock
Nov 1	BROUGHTON RANGERS*	A 1t-1t	T: Walmsley
Nov 8	SWINTON	L 0-1t	
Nov 15	Bradford	L 1g-3g,4t	DG: Ottiwell
Nov 22	Widnes	L 2t-1g	T: Eagles, Slater
Nov 29	HALIFAX	L 0-2g,4t	
Dec 6	Rochdale Hornets	W 2t-0	T: J Roberts, Slater
Dec 13	Walton (Liverpool)	D 0-0	
Dec 20	Stoke-on-Trent	W 3g,3t-0	T: Eagles, Ottiwell, J Roberts, Slater, Walmsley, C: Slater 2, DG: Varley
Dec 27	Halifax	L 0-2t	
Jan 10	WALTON (Liverpool)	W 3g,2t-1t	T: Eagles, M McNally, J Roberts, Walmsley, Worthington, C: Slater 3
Jan 17	Cheetham	W 3t-0	T: Walmsley 2, J Roberts
Jan 31	BRADFORD	L 0-2t	
Feb 7	DEWSBURY	W 4g,1t-0	T: J Roberts 2, J Buckley, Bullock, Slater, C: Slater 4
Feb 14	MANCHESTER FREE WANDERERS	W 1g,4t-1t	T: Pratt 2, J Roberts, Slater, DG: Varley
Feb 21	ROCHDALE HORNETS	W 1g,4t-0	T: J Barlow, Bullock, Eagles, Ottiwell, J Roberts, C: Varley
Feb 28	CHEETHAM	W 3t-0	T: Walmsley 2, Bullock
Mar 7	ASKAM	W 1g,2t-0	T: Bullock, G Buxton, DG: Walmsley
Mar 14	Swinton**	A 0-0	
Mar 21	Wigan	D 2t-2t	T: Pratt, Wardle
Apr 4	Barrow	W 1t-0	T: Slater
Apr 6	Askam	D 0-0	
Apr 11	WIGAN	W 2t-1t	T: Ottiwell, J Roberts
Apr 18	OLDHAM	W 2g,1t-1t	T: Bullock, J Jackson, J Roberts, C: Varley 2

* Abandoned 5 mins from end (crowd invasion following disputed Broughton Rangers try)
** Abandoned 10 mins from end (crowd invasion following altercation between players)

Result column: Most goals (g) win. If equal most tries (t) win.
Only unconverted tries shown in result

Salford RU Match Results

1885-86

	Opponent	Result	Scorers
Sep 26	ECCLES	D 1t-1t	T: Bullock
Oct 3	Bradford	L 0-2g	
Oct 10	MOSSLEY	D 1g-1g	T: Eagles, C: Slater
Oct 17	Tottington	W 1t-0	T: Slater
Oct 24	OLDHAM	D 0-0	
Oct 31	HULL	W 2t-0	T: J Barlow, Williams
Nov 7	Widnes	W 2g,1t-0	T: J Jackson, Varley, Williams, C: Varley 2
Nov 14	Birch	W 2g,3t-0	T: J Jackson, Varley, Vickers, Williams, C: Varley, DG: Sherlock
Nov 21	Halifax	L 0-1g	
Dec 5	ROCHDALE HORNETS	W 2t-0	T: J Barlow, J Roberts
Dec 19	Mossley	W 1t-0	T: Varley
Dec 26	Wigan	W 2g,1t-0	T: Williamson, DG: C Buxton, Slater
Jan 2	Dewsbury	L 0-1t	
Jan 23	Eccles	D 1t-1t	T: Stott
Jan 30	Hull	W 1g-0	T: J Barlow, C: Varley
Feb 6	WIDNES	W 1t-0	T: JP Jones
Feb 13	HALIFAX	W 1g,1t-0	T: C Buxton, Williams, C: Varley
Feb 20	DEWSBURY	W 2g,2t-0	T: Bullock, C Buxton, Slater, C: Slater, DG: Slater
Feb 27	Rochdale Hornets	W 1g-0	DG: Varley
Mar 20	MANCHESTER FREE WANDERERS	D 0-0	
Mar 27	TOTTINGTON	D 1g-1g	T: Slater, C: Varley
Apr 3	Broughton Rangers	D 0-0	
Apr 10	MANCHESTER	D 1g-1g	DG: Shaw
Apr 12	Oldham	D 0-0	
Apr 17	KENDAL TOWN	W 3t-0	T: Bullock, M McNally, J Roberts
Apr 24	Kendal Town	D 1t-1t	T: J Barlow

Result column: Most goals (g) win. If equal most tries (t) win. Only unconverted tries shown in result

1886-87

	Opponent	Result	Scorers
Sep 18	WARRINGTON	W 2t-0	T: Slater, T Smith
Sep 25	BRADFORD	D 1t-1t	T: Walmsley
Oct 2	RUNCORN	W 2t-0	T: Eagles, Walmsley
Oct 9	WIDNES	W 1g,1t-0	T: J Barlow, DG: Varley
Oct 16	Manchester Free Wanderers	W 1g,1t-0	T: Williams, DG: Varley
Oct 23	WIGAN	W 1t-0	T: Walmsley

Salford RU Match Results

1886-87 *continued*

	Opponent	Result	Scorers
Oct 30	BROUGHTON RANGERS	W 1t-0	T: Eagles
Nov 6	Oldham	W 2g-0	T: Eagles, C: Slater, DG: G Buxton
Nov 20	DEWSBURY	L 0-1g	
Nov 27	Broughton	W 1g,1t-0	T: J Roberts 2, C: J Barlow
Dec 11	Hull	L 1t-3t	T: J Roberts
Jan 1	BARROW*	D 1g-0	DG: Slater
Jan 8	Warrington	L 0-1g	
Jan 15	OLDHAM	W 1g,1t-1t	T: Slater 2, C: Slater
Jan 22	ROCHDALE HORNETS	W 3t-0	T: Eagles 2, J Barlow
Jan 29	MANCHESTER FREE WANDERERS	W 1t-0	T: Varley
Feb 5	MANCHESTER	W 1g,3t-1g	T: Clegg, Eagles, Slater, DG: Varley
Feb 19	Wigan	W 1g,1t-0	T: Newton, DG: Varley
Feb 26	Swinton**	W 1t-0	T: Walmsley
Mar 5	Runcorn	L 1t-2g	T: G Jackson
Mar 12	Manchester	L 0-1t	
Mar 19	Mossley	W 2g-1t	T: Eagles, Ottiwell, C: Varley 2
Mar 26	Broughton Rangers	L 0-1g	
Apr 2	HULL	W 1g,1t-1t	T: Slater, DG: Slater
Apr 9	Barrow	W 2g,1t-1t	T: Eagles, J Roberts, C: Slater, DG: Varley
Apr 11	Kendal Town	D 0-0	
Apr 16	BROUGHTON	D 0-0	
Apr 23	MOSSLEY	W 1t-0	T: Walmsley

* *Played on the 'understanding' of a drawn result due to hard, frost-bitten ground*
** *Played at Whalley Range as compromise to dispute as to who stages only fixture this season*

Result column: Most goals (g) win. If equal most tries (t) win.
However, 3 tries equal one goal. Only unconverted tries shown in result

1887-88

	Opponent	Result	Scorers
Sep 17	ROCHDALE HORNETS	W 1g-2t	DG: Kent
Sep 24	Bradford	W 1g,1t-1t	T: Anderton, Kent, C: Anderton
Oct 1	Runcorn	W 3t-0	T: Kent 2, J Roberts
Oct 8	Swinton	W 1g-0	T: J Roberts, C: Anderton
Oct 15	Dewsbury	D 0-0	
Oct 22	MANCHESTER	W 2g,1t-1g	T: Cook, Eagles, C: Anderton, DG: Ottiwell
Oct 29	Broughton Rangers	W 4g,2t-0	T: Eagles 3, Anderton, Seddon, C: Anderton 3, DG: Seddon

Salford RU Match Results

1887-88 *continued*

	Opponent	Result	Scorers
Nov 5	Manchester Rangers	D 0-0	
Nov 12	LIVERPOOL OLD BOYS	W 1g,2t-1t	T: Anderton, Newton, Shaw, C: Anderton
Nov 19	Birkenhead Park	W 2g-0	T: Cook 2, C: Anderton 2
Nov 26	MANCHESTER FREE WANDERERS	W 1g,1t-0	T: J Roberts, Shaw, C: Anderton
Dec 3	OLDHAM	W 2g,4t-0	T: J Roberts 2, Anderton, Clegg, A Smith, Williams, C: Anderton 2
Dec 10	Liverpool	W 2g-0	T: Anderton 2, C: Anderton 2
Dec 17	MOSSLEY	D 0-0	
Dec 24	BROUGHTON	W 1g,1t-0	T: Kent, DG: Seddon
Dec 26	Barrow	W 1g,1t-2t	T: Anderton, T Smith, C: Anderton
Jan 1	Rochdale Hornets*	D 0-1t	
Jan 2	Leeds St John's	L 0-1t	
Jan 7	BIRKENHEAD PARK	W 1g,6t-1t	T: Anderton 2, J Roberts 2, Clegg, Cook, Eagles, C: Anderton
Jan 14	RUNCORN	W 1g-0	T: Kent, C: Anderton
Jan 21	BRADFORD	L 0-1g,2t	
Jan 28	Liverpool Old Boys	W 2t-0	T: Clegg, Cook
Feb 4	Manchester Free Wanderers	W 3t-0	T: Anderton, Cook, T Smith
Feb 11	DEWSBURY	W 2t-1t	T: Cook, Eagles
Feb 18	LIVERPOOL	W 3t-0	T: Anderton, Eagles, Vickers
Mar 3	Manchester	L 0-1g,1t	
Mar 7	Owens College (Manchester)	W 1t-0	T: Cook
Mar 10	SWINTON	L 0-1g	
Mar 21	OWENS COLLEGE (Manchester)	W 2g,3t-0	T: Ogden 2, Gorman, A Smith, C: Shaw, DG: Ottiwell
Mar 24	BROUGHTON RANGERS	D 0-0	
Mar 31	Cardiff	L 1g-1g,1t	DG: Priestley
Apr 2	Swansea	L 0-2g	
Apr 7	Mossley	W 1g-0	DG: Priestley
Apr 14	Oldham	D 1t-1t	T: Walmsley
Apr 21	BARROW	L 0-1g	

* Played on the 'understanding' of a drawn result due to hard, frost-bitten ground

Result column: Most goals (g) win. If equal most tries (t) win. However, 3 tries equal one goal. Only unconverted tries shown in result

1888-89

	Opponent	Result	Scorers
Sep 15	RUNCORN	L 0-1t	
Sep 22	MANCHESTER RANGERS	L 1t-1g,1t	T: Bradshaw

Salford RU Match Results

1888-89 *continued*

	Opponent	*Result*	*Scorers*
Sep 29	DEWSBURY	L 1t-3t	T: Shaw
Oct 6	Rochdale St Clement's	W 1g,1t-1t	T: Mallinson, J Roberts, C: Shaw
Oct 13	Manchester	W 2g-0	T: J Roberts, C: Shaw, DG: Martinscroft
Oct 20	SWINTON	L 1t-2g,2t	T: Clegg
Oct 27	BROUGHTON RANGERS	D 0-0	
Nov 3	Liverpool Old Boys	W 1g,1t-1t	T: Austin, DG: A Barrett
Nov 10	Broughton	L 0-1g	
Nov 17	BIRKENHEAD PARK	W 1g,2t-0	T: Clegg, Eagles, Newton, C: J Roberts
Nov 24	Oldham	L 1t-1g	T: Cook
Dec 1	Manchester Free Wanderers	W 3g,2t-0	T: Anderton, Cook, Kent, Roberts, T Smith, C: Shaw 2, Anderton
Dec 8	LIVERPOOL	W 2g,2t-1g	T: A Barrett, Clegg, Mallinson, Williams, C: Shaw 2
Dec 15	BURTON-ON-TRENT	W 1g-1t	T: Shaw, C: Shaw
Dec 22	BRADFORD	W 1g,1t-1t	T: Clegg, Eagles, C: Shaw
Dec 26	Manchester Rangers	W 1g,3t-0	T: Anderton, Austin, McVittie, Mallinson, C: Shaw
Dec 27	MIDDLESEX WANDERERS	D 0-0	
Dec 29	Rochdale Hornets	L 0-2g,2t	
Dec 31	OLD LEYSIANS (London)	W 1g,2t-1g,1t	T: Valentine 2, Gorman, C: Valentine
Jan 1	BARROW	W 1g,2t-0	T: Brayshay, Mallinson, J Roberts, C: Shaw
Jan 5	Bradford	L 1t-1g	T: Eagles
Jan 12	MILLOM	W 1g,2t-1g	T: Austin, Foster, DG: Manwaring
Jan 19	Birkenhead Park	W 1g,3t-0	T: Eagles, Mallinson, J Roberts, PG: Manwaring
Jan 26	OLDHAM	W 2g,6t-0	T: Eagles 3, Clegg 2, Anderton, J Roberts, Williams, C: Anderton, Eagles
Feb 2	MANCHESTER FREE WANDERERS	W 2g,3t-1t	T: A Barrett 2, Eagles, Newton, J Roberts, C: Shaw 2
Feb 9	DEWSBURY*	W 1t-0	T: J Roberts
Feb 16	Liverpool	W 2t-1t	T: A Barrett, Mallinson
Feb 23	MANCHESTER	D 0-0	
Mar 2	BROUGHTON	W 1g,2t-1t	T: McVittie, J Roberts, DG: Cook
Mar 9	Swinton	L 0-1g	
Mar 16	MAORIS (Tour)**	L 1t-2g,1t (1-7)	T: Clegg
Mar 20	OWENS COLLEGE (Manchester)	W 1g,4t-1g	T: King 2, A Barrett, Williams, DG: A Barrett

Salford RU Match Results

1888-89 *continued*

	Opponent	Result	Scorers
Mar 23	Broughton Rangers	W 1g,1t-1g	T: Anderton, Newton, C: Anderton
Mar 27	Owens College (Manchester)	W 2t-0	T: Austin, Shaw
Mar 30	LIVERPOOL OLD BOYS	W 4g,3t-0	T: A Smith 2, Anderton, A Barrett, Cook, Shaw, C: Anderton 3, DG: Anderton
Apr 6	Runcorn	L 0-1g	
Apr 13	ROCHDALE HORNETS	D 2t-2t	T: Anderton, Cook
Apr 15	Broughton Rangers	W 1t-0	T: Eagles
Apr 20	Millom	D 1t-1t	T: Williams
Apr 22	Barrow	W 2g-2t	T: J Roberts, C: Anderton, DG: Cook

* *Away fixture switched to Salford as Dewsbury ground was staging a county fixture*

** *Inaccurately reported as 'Maoris', their official title was the New Zealand Native Football Representatives. During tour a point system operated; a try was 1 point, conversion 2, all other goals 3, thus Salford lost 7-1*

Result column: Most goals (g) win. If equal most tries (t) win.
However, 3 tries equal one goal. Only unconverted tries shown in result

1889-90

	Opponent	Result	Scorers
Sep 14	ROCHDALE HORNETS	W 2g,2t-0	T: A Barrett, Eagles, J Roberts, Williams, C: Shaw 2
Sep 21	Runcorn	L 1t-1g,1t	T: Cook
Sep 28	BARROW	W 1g,3t-1g	T: A Barrett, Eagles, King, GM: Manwaring
Oct 5	MANCHESTER FREE WANDERERS	W 4g,4t,1t	T: Cook 2, Miles 2, A Barrett, Kent, Tune, C: Manwaring 3, DG: A Barrett
Oct 12	Burton-on-Trent	W 1t-0	T: Birch
Oct 18	Swinton	L 0-1g,2t	
Oct 26	Broughton Rangers	W 4g-0	T: King, McVittie, Miles, J Roberts, C: Shaw 4
Nov 2	LIVERPOOL OLD BOYS	W 1g,6t-0	T: Nicholas 2, Birch, Cook, Miles, J Roberts, Williams, C: Shaw
Nov 9	BROUGHTON	W 1g,2t-0	T: A Barrett, Cook, King, C: Shaw
Nov 16	Old Leysians (London)	D 2t-2t	T: A Barrett, Nicholas
Nov 18	Middlesex Wanderers (Richmond)	D 0-0	
Nov 23	Birkenhead Park	W 1g,3t-0	T: J Roberts 2, Nicholas, Shaw, C: Walch
Nov 30	HUDDERSFIELD	D 0-0	

Salford RU Match Results

1889-90 *continued*

	Opponent	Result	Scorers
Dec 7	MANCHESTER	W 3t-1t	T: Cook, Miles, Shaw
Dec 21	MANCHESTER RANGERS	W 1t-0	T: J Roberts
Dec 26	Bradford	L 1g-2g	T: Williams, C: Walch
Dec 28	Liverpool	W 4g,6t-0	T: J Roberts 3, Williams 2, A Barrett, Nicholas, Tune, C: Walch, A Barrett, DG: A Barrett, Cook
Dec 30	OLD LEYSIANS (London)	L 2t-1g,2t	T: A Barrett, Eagles
Jan 1	MILLOM	W 2g,1t-0	T: Eagles, Nicholas, C: Walch, DG: Haslam
Jan 4	BIRKENHEAD PARK	W 3t-0	T: A Barrett, Birch, Sanderson
Jan 11	Huddersfield	L 1t-3g,2t	T: T Craven
Jan 18	Rochdale Hornets	W 1g,1t-0	T: J Roberts, DG: A Barrett
Jan 25	LIVERPOOL	W 5t-0	T: A Barrett 2, Shaw 2, Miles
Feb 1	RUNCORN	W 3t-1t	T: Miles 3
Feb 5	Owens College (Manchester)	W 4g,5t-0	T: J Roberts 2, Sudlow 2, Derbyshire, King, Miles, Shaw, C: Kent, Walch, Manwaring, DG: A Barrett
Feb 8	BURTON-ON-TRENT	W 1g,4t-0	T: Miles 2, Birch, Tune, DG: A Barrett
Feb 15	Manchester Free Wanderers	W 3g,14t-0	T: J Roberts 5, Birch 3, Williams 3, Cook 2, Miles 2, Eagles, Kent, C: King 3
Feb 22	Manchester Rangers	L 1g,2t-2g	T: Miles, Tonge, Williams, C: Shaw
Mar 1	Broughton	W 3t-0	T: Miles 3
Mar 8	SWINTON	L 0-1t	
Mar 15	Liverpool Old Boys	D 3t-1g	T: F Knowles, J Roberts, Shaw
Mar 19	OWENS COLLEGE (Manchester)	W 1t-0	T: Ditchfield
Mar 22	BROUGHTON RANGERS	D 1g-1g	T: Cook, C: Manwaring
Mar 29	Manchester	L 1t-2t	T: King
Apr 5	Barrow	L 1g,2t-1g	T: Birch, Cooper, Tonge, C: Shaw
Apr 7	Millom	D 0-0	
Apr 12	BRADFORD	L 3t-2g	T: A Barrett, Miles, Walch
Apr 14	Broughton and Broughton Rangers*	D 0-0	
Apr 19	DEWSBURY	W 5g,1t-1g	T: Miles 3, Eagles, McVittie, Walch, C: Walch 5
Apr 26	WIGAN	L 0-1g,2t	

* Charity match at Broughton Rangers' ground

Result column: Most goals (g) win. If equal most tries (t) win.
However, 3 tries equal one goal. Only unconverted tries shown in result

Salford RU Match Results

1890-91

	Opponent	Result	Scorers
Sep 6	BARTON	W 1g,2t-1t	T: Birch, Cook, Law, C: Walch
Sep 13	RUNCORN	L 0-1t	
Sep 20	Manchester Rangers	W 1g,2t-1t	T: Miles 2, Walch, C: Walch
Sep 27	BRADFORD	L 1t-1g,1t	T: Shaw
Oct 4	MILLOM	D 1g-1g	T: Tune, C: Walch
Oct 11	SWINTON	L 1t-1g,1t	T: T Craven
Oct 18	BURTON-ON-TRENT	W 2g,5t-0	T: Miles 4, A Barrett, J Roberts, Tune, C: Manwaring, Walch
Oct 25	BROUGHTON RANGERS	W 2t-0	T: JE Cooper, Miles
Nov 1	Liverpool Old Boys	W 3g,1t-0	T: Miles 2, Birch, J Roberts, C: Manwaring 3
Nov 8	LIVERPOOL	W 4g,2t-0	T: Miles 3, J Roberts 2, C: Manwaring 3, PG: Manwaring
Nov 15	Old Leysians (London)	L 1g-2g	T: J Roberts, C: Manwaring
Nov 17	Cambridge University	L 3t-2g,3t	T: Birch 2, Shaw
Nov 22	Wigan	L 0-1g,1t	
Dec 6	Manchester	W 2g,1t-0	T: Miles, J Roberts, C: Manwaring, DG: Miles
Dec 10	OWENS COLLEGE (Manchester)	W 1t-0	T: Kent
Dec 13	BROUGHTON*	W 1g-0	DG: Miles
Dec 27	OLD LEYSIANS (London)	W 1g,1t-0	T: Newton 2, C: Manwaring
Jan 1	BARROW	L 2t-1g	T: Miles 2
Jan 3	BROUGHTON*	W 4t-1t	T: Miles 2, Birch, J Roberts
Jan 10	St Helens**	D 0-1t	
Jan 17	MOSELEY	W 1g,2t-1g	T: A Barrett, E Barrett, Kent, C: Manwaring
Jan 24	BIRKENHEAD PARK	W 2g,3t-0	T: Miles 2, Manwaring, Shaw, Tonge, C: Manwaring 2
Jan 31	WIGAN	L 1t-2t	T: Eagles
Feb 7	Bradford	L 0-1g,2t	
Feb 14	BROUGHTON	W 1g-0	T: Eagles, C: Manwaring
Feb 21	Burton-on-Trent	D 3t-1g	T: E Barrett, Birch, Kent
Feb 28	ROCHDALE HORNETS	W 2g,1t-2g	T: Miles 3, C: Manwaring 2
Mar 7	Swinton	L 0-2g,1t	
Mar 14	LIVERPOOL OLD BOYS	W 2t-0	T: E Barrett, F Knowles
Mar 21	Broughton Rangers	W 1g-0	PG: Manwaring
Mar 28	Millom	W 1t-0	T: Miles
Mar 30	Barrow	W 1g,5t-0	T: Miles 3, A Barrett, Kent, Tune, C: Miles
Apr 4	MANCHESTER	L 1t-1g,1t	T: Miles
Apr 11	Runcorn	L 0-1t	

Salford RU Match Results

1890-91 *continued*

	Opponent	Result	Scorers
Apr 15	BROUGHTON PARK	W 3g,6t-0	T: Haslam 2, A Barrett, E Barrett, Birch, Gill, Green, C: Manwaring 2, DG: A Barrett (one try scorer not recorded)
Apr 20	MANCHESTER RANGERS	D 0-0	

* Both matches switched to Salford due to hard, frost-bitten Broughton ground
** Played on the 'understanding' of a drawn result due to hard, frost-bitten ground

Result column: Most goals (g) win. If equal most tries (t) win. However, 3 tries equal one goal. Only unconverted tries shown in result

1891-92

	Opponent	Result	Scorers
Sep 2	BARTON	L 4-5	T: Hosker, J Roberts
Sep 5	ROCHDALE HORNETS	D 7-7	T: A Barrett, J Roberts, C: Hosker
Sep 12	Bradford	L 5-15	T: J Roberts, C: Walch
Sep 19	ST HELENS	L 7-11	T: J Roberts, Dudlow, C: Walch
Sep 26	WIDNES	L 2-6	T: J Roberts
Oct 3	Runcorn	L 2-4	T: Miles
Oct 10	Swinton	L 0-5	
Oct 17	BROUGHTON	W 8-2	T: Miles 3, A Barrett
Oct 24	Broughton Rangers	L 0-10	
Oct 31	LIVERPOOL OLD BOYS	D 11-11	T: Eagles, France, Miles, J Roberts, C: Manwaring
Nov 7	Liverpool	L 0-2	
Nov 14	Old Leysians (London)	W 28-5	T: Sudlow 2, A Barrett, Kent, F Knowles, Makin, J Roberts, Walch, C: Nicholas 4
Nov 16	Cambridge University	D 0-0	
Nov 21	Burton-on-Trent	L 2-7	T: Hindshaw
Nov 28	MANCHESTER	W 2-0	T: Nicholas
Dec 5	MANCHESTER RANGERS	W 18-10	T: Nicholas 2, Sudlow 2, Makin, Miles, C: Nicholas 2
Dec 12	BIRKENHEAD PARK	W 13-0	T: A Barrett, Eagles, France, Miles, Walch, C: Nicholas
Dec 19	NEWPORT	L 2-8	T: Sudlow
Dec 26	DUKINFIELD	W 7-0	T: France, J Roberts, C: Valentine
Dec 28	OLD LEYSIANS (London)	W 19-2	T: Eagles, Kent, King, Nicholas, Walch, C: Nicholas 3
Jan 1	MILLOM	W 5-4	T: Sudlow, C: Nicholas
Jan 2	BARROW	W 7-4	T: A Barrett, Brierley, C: Nicholas

Salford RU Match Results

1891-92 *continued*

	Opponent	Result	Scorers
Jan 23	Liverpool Old Boys	W 4-2	T: Miles, J Roberts
Jan 30	Widnes	W 8-0	T: A Barrett, Miles, Nicholas, Sudlow
Feb 6	BURTON-ON-TRENT	W 16-0	T: Miles 2, Eagles, King, Sudlow, C: Nicholas, Walch
Feb 13	Rochdale Hornets	W 4-2	T: A Barrett, Sudlow
Feb 27	BROUGHTON RANGERS	W 4-0	T: T Craven, King
Mar 5	St Helens	L 0-6	
Mar 12	BRADFORD	W 6-2	T: Casey, France, J Roberts
Mar 19	SWINTON	L 0-4	
Mar 26	RUNCORN	W 5-0	T: Miles, C: Manwaring
Apr 2	Manchester	W 13-0	T: Casey, Eagles, Miles, J Roberts, Walch, C: Walch
Apr 4	Broughton	D 5-5	T: A Knowles, C: Walch
Apr 9	Manchester Rangers	W 8-2	T: Eagles, C: Manwaring, PG: Manwaring
Apr 16	Swansea	L 0-9	
Apr 18	Newport	L 0-35	
Apr 23	BROUGHTON RANGERS	W 5-0	T: Miles, C: Manwaring
Apr 30	BROUGHTON	W 14-0	T: Eagles 2, Haslam, D Wilson, C: Manwaring 2

Scoring values: T (try) = 2 points, C (conversion) = 3, DG (drop-goal) = 4, PG (penalty) = 3

1892-93

	Opponent	Result	Scorers
Sep 10	OLDHAM (LCC)	D 2-2	T: Miles
Sep 17	Widnes	W 7-0	T: F Knowles, Miles, C: Walch
Sep 24	BRADFORD	W 7-3	T: Miles 2, C: Walch
Oct 1	RUNCORN	W 7-0	T: A Barrett, Miles, C: Walch
Oct 8	SWINTON (LCC)	D 0-0	
Oct 15	Broughton (LCC)	D 2-2	T: Fox
Oct 22	BROUGHTON RANGERS (LCC)	W 7-0	T: Miles, J Roberts, C: Walch
Oct 29	Liverpool Old Boys	W 17-0	T: A Barrett 2, Casey, Fox, France, F Knowles, Manwaring, C: Walch
Nov 5	LIVERPOOL	W 10-0	T: A Barrett, France, Kent, J Roberts, Walch
Nov 12	Old Leysians (London)	W 11-0	T: Cartwright, T Craven, France, Manwaring, C: Manwaring
Nov 14	Leicester	W 6-0	T: Hindshaw, Kent, Walch
Nov 26	Birkenhead Park	W 12-0	T: A Barrett, Cartwright, Miles, C: Nicholas 2

Salford RU Match Results

1892-93 *continued*

	Opponent	Result	Scorers
Dec 3	ST HELENS RECREATION (LCC)	L 4-9	T: A Barrett, J Roberts
Dec 10	Manchester	W 4-2	T: T Craven, Miles
Dec 17	Manchester Rangers	W 2-0	T: Miles
Dec 24	Rochdale Hornets (LCC)	W 2-0	T: Miles
Dec 26	Bradford*	D 2-33	T: Haslam
Dec 31	LEIGH*	D 0-0	
Jan 14	BIRKENHEAD PARK	W 19-0	T: Cartwright 2, Miles 2, Walch 2, Brierley, J Roberts, C: Walch
Jan 21	Oldham (LCC)	W 8-6	T: Miles, Ward, DG: Ward
Jan 28	St Helens Recreation (LCC)	W 5-0	T: Miles, C: Walch
Feb 4	LIVERPOOL OLD BOYS	W 11-5	T: France, Miles, C: Manwaring, DG: Manwaring
Feb 11	MANCHESTER	W 2-0	T: Harley
Feb 18	BROUGHTON (LCC)	W 5-2	T: A Barrett, PG: Lightfoot
Feb 25	Broughton Rangers (LCC)	W 4-0	T: Brierley, A Knowles
Mar 4	WARRINGTON (LCC)	W 2-0	T: Miles
Mar 11	Swinton (LCC)	W 8-4	T: J Smith, C: Paul, PG: Paul
Mar 18	MANCHESTER RANGERS	W 9-0	T: Ashton, F Knowles, Tewson, C: Paul
Mar 25	Runcorn	L 4-11	DG: Miles
Apr 1	Taunton	W 12-9	T: A Barrett 2, Brierley, C: Paul 2
Apr 3	Exeter	W 15-4	T: A Barrett, Harley, Kent, King, Miles, J Smith, C: Paul
Apr 8	ST HELENS	W 6-2	T: Tewson, DG: J Smith
Apr 12	BARTON	L 0-5	
Apr 15	ROCHDALE HORNETS (LCC)	W 7-0	T: Miles 2, C: Paul
Apr 17	Warrington (LCC)	D 2-2	T: Miles
Apr 22	WIDNES	W 4-2	T: Miles, J Smith
Apr 24	RADCLIFFE	L 3-9	PG: D Wilson
Apr 29	TYLDESLEY (LCC)	W 19-2	T: Miles 2, Brierley, F Knowles, J Smith, C: Paul 3

* *Played on the 'understanding' of a drawn result due to hard, frost-bitten ground*

Lancashire Club Championship winners

Scoring values: T (try) = 2 points, C (conversion) = 3, DG (drop-goal) = 4, PG (penalty) = 3

1893-94

	Opponent	Result	Scorers
Sep 2	HUDDERSFIELD	L 0-6	
Sep 9	HARTLEPOOL ROVERS	W 13-6	T: A Barrett, Miles, J Smith, C: Paul 2

Salford RU Match Results

1893-94 *continued*

	Opponent	Result	Scorers
Sep 16	MANCHESTER RANGERS	W 26-0	T: A Barrett 2, Miles 2, Rangeley 2, Haslam, Hindshaw, C: Paul
Sep 23	WIGAN (LCC)	L 0-5	
Sep 25	Huddersfield	W 3-0	T: Miles
Sep 30	BROUGHTON (LCC)	W 14-0	T: Miles 2, Kent, J Smith, C: Paul
Oct 7	Rochdale Hornets (LCC)	D 7-7	T: France, DG: Rangeley
Oct 14	Swinton (LCC)	L 0-3	
Oct 21	BROUGHTON RANGERS (LCC)	W 3-0	PG: Paul
Oct 28	Warrington (LCC)	L 0-8	
Nov 4	LIVERPOOL OLD BOYS	W 6-5	T: Rowlinson, Walch
Nov 11	TYLDESLEY (LCC)	W 5-0	T: Rangeley, C: Paul
Nov 18	Newport	L 0-29	
Nov 20	Bristol	W 3-0	T: Miles
Nov 25	BIRKENHEAD PARK	W 11-0	T: J Smith 2, D Wilson, C: Manwaring
Dec 2	Barrow (LCC)	W 11-8	T: J Smith 2, Miles, C: King
Dec 9	Oldham (LCC)	L 5-6	T: Rangeley, C: King
Dec 16	MANCHESTER	W 25-0	T: Miles 2, A Barrett, J Smith, T Smith, C: King 3, DG: Rangeley
Dec 23	RUNCORN	L 6-7	T: King, Rangeley
Dec 26	Manchester Rangers	W 27-6	T: Miles 3, A Barrett, Cartwright, King, Rangeley, C: King 2, J Smith
Dec 30	WATSONIANS (Edinburgh)	L 5-13	T: Miles, C: Walch
Jan 1	Leigh	D 6-6	T: Haslam, D Wilson
Jan 13	Wigan (LCC)	D 0-0	
Jan 20	Broughton (LCC)	W 14-5	T: Miles 2, Rangeley, J Smith, C: King
Jan 27	ROCHDALE HORNETS (LCC)	D 0-0	
Feb 3	Liverpool Old Boys	W 3-0	T: T Smith
Feb 10	SWINTON (LCC)	L 6-8	T: Miles, Rangeley
Feb 24	WARRINGTON (LCC)	L 3-8	T: Miles
Mar 3	Tyldesley (LCC)	L 0-23	
Mar 10	BARROW (LCC)	W 18-6	T: Miles 2, King, Rangeley, J Smith, Walch
Mar 17	OLDHAM (LCC)	L 0-6	
Mar 24	Hartlepool Rovers	W 10-7	T: Miles 2, C: King 2
Mar 26	Rockcliff	W 5-0	T: J Smith, C: King
Mar 31	NEWPORT	L 0-3	
Apr 7	Manchester	W 11-3	T: King 2, France, C: Rangeley
Apr 9	Broughton Rangers (LCC)	W 3-0	T: Miles
Apr 14	Runcorn	L 5-16	T: Horrox, C: King

Salford RU Match Results

1893-94 *continued*

	Opponent	Result	Scorers
Apr 21	TYLDESLEY	W 11-10	T: Miles 3, C: Rangeley
Apr 26	LEIGH	L 3-9	T: J Smith
Apr 28	BARTON	L 0-5	

Scoring values: T (try) = 3 points, C (conversion) = 2, DG (drop-goal) = 4, PG (penalty) = 3

1894-95

	Opponent	Result	Scorers
Sep 1	Sale	W 33-0	T: J Roberts 3, A Barrett 2, JJ Jones, Rangeley, C: Chapman 4, DG: Chapman
Sep 8	Manchester Rangers	W 34-3	T: Rangeley 4, Miles 2, A Barrett, Chapman, Haslam, Moss, C: Chapman, Rangeley
Sep 15	Widnes	L 0-8	
Sep 22	Wigan (LCC)	L 0-14	
Sep 29	Tyldesley (LCC)	L 0-6	
Oct 6	ROCHDALE HORNETS (LCC)	W 15-0	T: JJ Jones 2, A Barrett, C: J Smith, DG: Miles
Oct 13	SWINTON (LCC)	D 3-3	PG: Rangeley
Jan 1	MANCHESTER RANGERS	W 21-0	T: Diggle 3, Rangeley, J Roberts, C: Rangeley 2, Manwaring
Jan 5	BIRKENHEAD PARK	W 3-0	T: Diggle
Jan 19	WARRINGTON	W 5-3	T: Brierley, C: Rangeley
Jan 26	MANCHESTER	W 11-0	T: Diggle, Rangeley, J Roberts, C: Manwaring
Feb 2	LIVERPOOL OLD BOYS	W 3-0	T: Deakin
Mar 2	RUNCORN	L 0-3	
Mar 9	BROUGHTON RANGERS	W 6-3	T: Deakin, JJ Jones
Mar 16	ST HELENS	L 6-8	T: Diggle, Moss
Mar 23	Oldham	L 3-6	T: Diggle
Mar 30	LEIGH	D 3-3	T: Diggle
Apr 6	Warrington	W 4-3	DG: Rangeley
Apr 13	Newport	L 0-3	
Apr 15	Gloucester	W 8-0	T: A Barrett, Stephens, C: A Barrett
Apr 20	Swinton	L 0-11	
Apr 27	BROUGHTON	W 7-0	T: Diggle, DG: Manwaring
Apr 30	OLDHAM	L 0-5	

Scoring values: T (try) = 3 points, C (conversion) = 2, DG (drop-goal) = 4, PG (penalty) = 3

Suspended for professionalism Oct 16 to Dec 31 – Lancashire Club Championship results expunged

Salford RU Match Results

1895-96

	Opponent	Result	Scorers
Sep 21	BROUGHTON	L 0-3	
Sep 28	Manchester	W 3-0	T: Ryan
Oct 5	BARROW (LCC)	L 0-4	
Oct 12	Swinton (LCC)	L 0-11	
Oct 19	Blackley Rangers (LCC)	L 0-3	
Oct 26	WALKDEN (LCC)	L 3-8	T: Doran
Nov 2	ST HELENS RECREATION	L 0-5	
Nov 9	Birkenhead Wanderers	L 0-11	
Nov 16	BIRKENHEAD WANDERERS	D 0-0	
Nov 23	LIVERPOOL OLD BOYS	D 3-3	T: J Brown
Nov 30	Lancaster (LCC)	L 0-12	
Dec 7	MORECAMBE (LCC)	L 0-5	
Dec 14	MANCHESTER	W 11-8	T: Jordan, Owen, Wall, C: Fielden
Dec 26	Leicester	D 0-0	
Dec 28	St Helens Recreation*	D 0-0	
Jan 1	Blackley (LCC)	W 6-0	T: Moss, Wall
Jan 4	DEWSBURY	W 10-0	T: Barrington, Moss, C: Cosgrove 2
Jan 11	Liverpool Old Boys	D 3-3	T: King
Jan 18	ROCHDALE ST CLEMENTS (LCC)	L 0-16	
Jan 25	Crompton (LCC)	L 0-7	
Feb 1	BLACKLEY RANGERS (LCC)	W 3-0	T: Moss
Feb 8	ULVERSTON (LCC)	L 0-6	
Feb 15	Walkden (LCC)	L 3-4	T: JJ Jones
Feb 22	SWINTON (LCC)	L 0-10	
Feb 29	Rochdale St Clements (LCC)	D 0-0	
Mar 7	LANCASTER (LCC)	W 3-0	T: Blake
Mar 14	BLACKLEY (LCC)	W 21-0	T: R Smith 2, Harter, Haslam, Vipond, C: Braithwaite 2, Blomley
Mar 21	Morecambe (LCC)	L 0-9	
Mar 28	KENDAL HORNETS	W 6-0	T: Braithwaite, R Smith
Apr 3	SWINTON	L 0-3	
Apr 4	Barrow (LCC)	L 0-8	
Apr 6	Ulverston (LCC)	L 0-8	
Apr 11	CROMPTON (LCC)	W 3-0	T: Harter
Apr 18	Broughton	W 12-0	T: Blake, Braithwaite, C: Braithwaite, DG: Harter
Apr 23	TYLDESLEY**	D 0-0	
Apr 27	Broughton Rangers**	L 0-8	
Apr 30	HALIFAX**	W 14-0	T: Braithwaite, Jack Sunderland (Swinton), C: W Brown, Braithwaite, DG: Braithwaite

Played 15 mins each half due to delayed start through heavy rain
**Friendlies versus NU clubs after Salford's decision on April 16 to leave the Rugby Union*

Scoring values: T (try) = 3 points, C (conversion) = 2, DG (drop-goal) = 4, PG (penalty) = 3

Salford RU Records (1879-1896)

Most appearances

Billy Manwaring	280
Jack Roberts	271
Harry Eagles	268
Alf Barrett	230
Tom King	212
Joe Shaw	196
Tom Kent	172
Sam Williams	170
Frank Miles	161
A. Ottiwell	161
Sam Walch	161
Sam Haslam	114
Joe Newton	111
Tommy Smith	105
Harry Clegg	104
W.H. France	103
Tom Craven	100
Frank Knowles	98
Mick McNally	91
Herbert Cook	89

Most tries

Frank Miles	114
Jack Roberts	100
Harry Eagles	61
Alf Barrett	48
Sam Williams	27
Bob Walmsley	25
Herbert Cook	22
Hugh Williamson	22
Tom Kent	18
Jack Anderton	17
Tom King	17

Most goals

Billy Manwaring	42
W. Sherlock	36
Sam Walch	27
Jack Anderton	25
Joe Shaw	24
Cornie Varley	19
Bob Bullock	18
Vic Slater	18
Arthur Paul	16
Tom King	15
T.L. Nicholas	15

Most tries in a season
27 by Frank Miles, 1890-91

Most tries in a match
5 by Jack Roberts v Manchester Free Wanderers, 15 February 1890

Most goals in a season
24 by W. Sherlock, 1883-84

Most goals in a match
5 by Sam Walch v Dewsbury, 19 April 1890;
Harry Chapman v Sale, 1 September 1894

Club honours board
Lancashire Club Championship, 1892-93

Most consecutive wins
10, January-March 1884;
January-March 1893

Most consecutive matches unbeaten
22 (16 wins, 6 draws),
April 1887-January 1888

1888 RU tour of Australia and New Zealand
Jack Anderton
Harry Eagles
Tom Kent
Sam Williams

England appearances
Tom Kent 6

North (of England) appearances
Harry Eagles 3
Tom Kent 3
Sam Williams 1

Cheshire appearances
Hugh Williamson 1

Salford RU Records (1879-1896)

Lancashire appearances

Tom Kent 33
Harry Eagles 18
Tom Craven 13
JJ Jones 11
Tom King 11
Alf Barrett 10
Billy Manwaring 9
Frank Miles 6
Bob Moss 6

Vic Slater 6
Jack Roberts 5
Sam Williams 4
Sam Walch 2
Jack Anderton 1
Herbert Cook 1
James Jackson 1
Tommy Smith 1

3

Salford Rugby League 1896-97 – 2022

Salford's membership voted overwhelmingly to join the breakaway Northern Union at a meeting that took place at Hope Board School, Liverpool Street, on Thursday, 16th April 1896.

The Northern Union had been founded the previous year at the George Hotel, Huddersfield on the 29th August 1895, resulting in Salford losing the majority of its most attractive fixtures. Salford's resignation was officially accepted by the Lancashire Rugby Union committee on 9th June 1896 at the Grand Hotel, Manchester.

The club moved from New Barnes to The Willows in 1901 and, in 1913-14, won its only major trophy under the Northern Union banner, defeating Huddersfield in the Northern Rugby League Championship Final. The Great War (now known as World War One) of 1914-18 put paid to any further success and the club struggled throughout most of the 1920s. During 1922 the Northern Rugby Football Union (Northern Union) rebranded as the less parochial sounding Rugby Football League (Rugby League) at its annual meeting held at Huddersfield's George Hotel on Wednesday 14th June.

The dismal days of the 1920s ended in the summer of 1928 when Lance Todd was appointed team manager. What followed under his leadership was a decade of unprecedented success that included three Northern Rugby League Championship's and two Wembley appearances. But it all came to an abrupt end at the start of 1939-40 due to the outbreak of World War Two. After initially competing in the Wartime Emergency League, Salford withdrew in January 1942, returning to action in August 1945, after peace resumed.

Salford descended into a mid-table outfit as the 1950s progressed, culminating in a second tier placing when two divisions was briefly experimented with during 1962-63 and 1963-64. Fortunes changed after Brian Snape took over as chairman and Salford enjoyed a revival which saw a return to Wembley in 1969 and, after two divisions had been reintroduced, two First Division Championships were won during the mid-1970s.

John Wilkinson became chairman in 1982, a position he retained for a club record 31 years. His reign saw the team reach two Lancashire Cup finals and appear twice at Old Trafford on Premiership Finals day. The arrival of Super League and summer rugby in 1996, alongside full-time professionalism, presented new tests to be overcome. Having relocated to the new Salford City Stadium (later renamed the AJ Bell Stadium) at Barton in 2012 the team has risen to the challenge, reaching the Super League Grand Final in 2019 and Wembley again in 2020.

The Salford players' records cover all 4,371 official matches played since 1896 under the auspices of the Northern Rugby Football Union and the Rugby Football League up to and including 2022, and is split into two sections: 'Dates' and 'Statistics'. Just five appearances are unidentified, all of them from the match at Stockport on 28th March 1902. Salford were also undermanned on two occasions: at Rochdale Hornets on 14th December 1901 when four short due to players not receiving 'permits' to play under the, then, 'work clause' rule, and at York on 22nd March 1924 when the unfortunate Syd Boyd missed his train!

The number of players per team was reduced from 15 to 13 in 1906-07, and two substitutes allowed from 1964-65, increased to four during the 1996 season. Note that the players' records section does not include friendlies (indicated by 'F' in brackets in the match results section). Also excluded, but covered in separate sections, are players' records in the Salford Royal Hospital Cup, Red Rose Cup, Festival of Sports, and the 1934 tour of France. There is also a separate section focussing on the appearance records of players who participated in the World War One friendly matches.

Where a player has joined Salford on more than one occasion, be it a permanent signing or on loan, a separate entry is shown for each instance, the players name in the 'Name' column being followed by (1) or

(2). This separation also applies when a player appeared as a 'guest' during World War Two in addition to previously or subsequently playing for the club as a registered player during peacetime.

'Debut' and 'Last match' dates refer to official competition matches only. It is possible that a player may have appeared for Salford prior to the debut date shown (for example, in a pre-season friendly) or after his last appearance (for example, Billy Brown appeared in a wartime friendly over nine years after his official finale, and Jim Mills played in two post-season friendlies three months after his last official match). It should also be noted that the debut dates refer only to Northern Union/Rugby League matches even if that player had appeared for Salford prior to the breakaway from the Rugby Football Union in 1896. Where no date appears in the 'Last match' column it indicates the player was still under contract at the time of compiling this information.

Under the 'Previous team' column, where 'loan' appears in brackets after the name of the team, it indicates the player was on loan from the named club, returning to that parent club afterwards. In cases where a player was initially on loan but then transferred to Salford permanently without returning to his parent club in the interim, 'loan' is not indicated. Where 'guest' appears in brackets it highlights players from other clubs who assisted Salford during 'official' World War Two matches.

Also, under the 'Previous team' column, approximately 50 players are listed as being signed from Salford Colts (1970s and 1980s) or Salford Academy (1990s to date). It should be acknowledged that many of those had been nurtured by amateur clubs, past and present, local and further afield, including, amongst others, Cadishead, Eccles, Folly Lane, Irlam Hornets, Langworthy and Leigh Miners Rangers.

The match results section covers all Salford's official and unofficial matches from 1896-97, In the latter category most fixtures are indicated as friendly ('F') and incorporate benefit, charity and testimonial matches, and the non-competitive games played during World War One. The remaining unofficial fixtures cover matches played in the Salford Royal Hospital Cup ('SHC'), Red Rose Cup ('RRC'), Festival of Sports ('FoS'), and Salford's 1934 tour of France.

For the majority of this period tries counted as three points and all goals as two. The exceptions are that in 1896-97 a drop-goal was worth four points and a penalty goal three, from 1974-75 a drop-goal was reduced to one point, and from 1983-84 a try increased to four points.

Attendance figures have been included where available. The period covering 1946-47 to 1966-67 are from official Rugby Football League records held at the Heritage Quay archive, Huddersfield, and those from 1967-68 to date are from the author's records, based on those published by the press. It should be noted that, whereas attendance figures published from 1946-47 are based on official sources and, therefore, generally accurate, the same is not true prior to that. Previously the only source available was the match report and the attendance was usually based on the assessment of the journalist. Therefore most of those attendances appear in rounded numbers usually ending in '000', in other words estimated to the nearest thousand.

There are exceptions where official figures are quoted in reports, usually in the case of Challenge Cup ties or a final. Unfortunately there are gaps where no attendance figure has been quoted.

Salford RL Players – Dates

Name	Pos	Brn	Debut	Last match	Previous team
Ackerman, Rob	F	W	07/10/1992	31/01/1993	Carlisle
Ackers, Andy	H		03/09/2020	-	Toronto Wolfpack (Canada)
Adams, Sid	C	W	04/09/1909	02/04/1910	Tredegar RU
Adamson, Dave	F		07/04/1959	10/03/1962	Latchford Albion (Warrington)
Adamson, Luke	F		11/06/2006	08/09/2012	Leigh East
Adamson, Toby	F		22/08/2010	22/08/2010	Leigh East
Addy, Danny	F		26/03/2021		Leigh
Ainsworth, Arthur	T		01/02/1919	01/03/2019	Salford St Bartholomew's
Aitchison, Alex	W	S	09/09/1905	16/09/1905	Priestfield RU (Edinburgh)
Akauola, Sitaleki	F	NZ	11/02/2022	03/09/2022	Warrington
Alder, Frank	F		04/03/1950	19/11/1960	Leigh
Aldred, James	W		01/09/1900	08/09/1901	Tyldesley
Alexander, Neil	HB		09/08/1998	09/08/1998	Salford Academy
Algie, David	F		29/08/1925	29/08/1925	Warrington
Alker, Malcolm	H		25/08/1997	01/08/2010	Wigan St Patrick's
Allen, Hugh	W		30/01/1904	19/11/1904	Barrow St George's
Allmark, Tommy	HB		12/11/1921	10/12/1921	Swinton Park
Alstead, Peter	FB		20/02/1983	20/02/1983	Leigh (loan)
Ambler, Luke	F		17/08/2008	17/08/2008	Elland (Leeds)
Anderson, Vinnie	F	NZ	02/04/2011	08/09/2012	Warrington
Anderson, W 'Billie'	HB		28/02/1920	28/02/1920	Hull
Anderton, Willie	HB		09/09/1922	05/01/1924	Wigan
Angell, Simon	F	NZ	05/05/1996	14/07/1996	Featherstone Rovers
Argent, Joe	F		29/01/1966	04/09/1967	Widnes
Armitt, Charlie	F		17/10/1959	17/10/1959	Blackpool Borough
Arnold, Danny	W		06/05/2001	05/10/2003	Oldham
Ashall, Bill	F		12/04/1963	29/01/1966	St Helens
Ashall-Bott, Olly	TQ		29/09/2020	23/10/2020	London Broncos (loan)
Ashbridge, Joe	H		06/04/1957	06/04/1957	Broughton Moor (trialist)
Ashcroft, Kevin	H		27/08/1978	02/10/1981	Rochdale Hornets
Ashurst, Matty	F		04/02/2012	12/09/2014	St Helens
Aspey, Connor	H		13/10/2020	17/09/2021	Salford Academy

Salford RL Players – Dates

Name	Pos	Brn	Debut	Last match	Previous team
Aspey, Mal	C		22/08/1982	04/09/1983	Wigan
Aspinall, George	W		29/03/1947	05/04/1952	Hunslet
Atkin, Chris	HB		22/02/2020	-	Hull Kingston Rovers
Austin, Greg (1)	C	A	31/08/1986	28/02/1988	Rochdale Hornets
Austin, Greg (2)			18/03/1994	27/03/1994	Keighley
Ayles, Eric	F		24/03/1956	31/03/1958	St Helens
Ayres, Warren	H		03/05/1999	13/02/2000	Woolston Rovers (Warrington)
Bailey, Gary	FB		13/11/1977	11/02/1979	Salford Colts
Bailey, TJ 'Tommy'	HB	W	04/09/1920	22/10/1921	Pontypool RU
Baines, Albert	W		23/08/1952	03/04/1961	Bedford Recreation (Leigh)
Baker, George	W		17/10/1903	22/04/1905	Adelphi Lads Club (Salford)
Baker, Neil	HB	A	08/09/1985	19/01/1986	South Sydney (Australia)
Baldwin, Simon	F		19/01/2003	05/05/2006	Leigh
Ballard, Andy	W		08/02/2008	20/07/2008	Wigan Academy
Bamford, Darren	T		11/03/2005	13/05/2005	Salford Academy
Banks, Billy	HB	W	31/01/1959	23/04/1960	Whitehaven
Banner, Peter	HB		18/10/1968	31/03/1975	Spotland Rangers (Rochdale)
Bannister, Steve	F		03/02/2008	28/09/2008	Harlequins RL
Bardsley, Barrie	HB		28/10/1961	28/10/1961	Leigh district ARL
Barker, R	W		14/10/1910	15/04/1911	Oldham
Barlow, Albert	HB		01/01/1923	24/03/1923	Old Salfordians RU
Barnes, Tom	HB		11/11/1922	11/11/1922	Dearham Wanderers
Barnes, W 'Billy'	C		11/11/1911	11/11/1911	Seedley Rangers (Salford)
Barnett, Richie	W		21/07/2007	14/09/2007	Warrington
Baron, Matt	W		17/04/1954	23/10/1954	Leigh
Barratt, Mark	FB		26/12/1986	21/01/1990	St Joseph's Folly Lane (Swinton)
Barrington, WH*	F		03/10/1896	25/09/1897	Pendleton

Salford RL Players – Dates

Name	Pos	Brn	Debut	Last match	Previous team
Barry, Dave	H		13/10/1962	19/09/1964	Langworthy Juniors (Salford)
Barton, Roger	FB		26/01/1946	02/02/1946	local ARL (trialist)
Barton, Danny	F		16/09/2001	08/06/2001	Salford Academy
Battersby, William	F	W	01/04/1911	04/11/1911	Llanbradach AFC
Battese, Brian	F	A	06/10/1985	09/02/1986	Canterbury (Australia)
Baxter, Neil	W		22/04/2001	22/04/2001	Salford Academy
Baynes, Neil	F		13/02/1999	05/09/2004	Wigan
Beaver, Bill	W		13/12/1924	26/09/1925	Swinton
Bebbington, Sam	F		05/12/1903	01/10/1904	Stockport
Beckett, Adrian	C		12/11/1982	06/09/1987	Widnes Tigers
Bedford, Alf	W		05/09/1903	09/12/1905	Windhill
Bell, Robert MH	W		28/01/1905	19/04/1906	Broughton Park RU
Bell, Thomas	F		05/12/1903	16/04/1904	Tudhoe RU
Bell, TG 'Tom'	C		06/09/1902	27/04/1903	Maryport
Belshaw, Billy	C		21/12/1940	21/12/1940	Warrington (guest)
Bennett, Jack	W		28/09/1963	12/10/1963	Langworthy Juniors (Salford)
Bennett, Tommy	FB		01/01/1949	03/09/1949	Hindley
Bennion, Gavin	F		04/05/2018	27/07/2018	Rochdale Hornets
Bentley, Keith	W		25/09/1983	14/04/1991	Barrow
Benyon, W	HB		08/04/1898	04/03/1899	-
Berne, Mick	W	A	01/06/2003	13/07/2003	South Sydney (Australia)
Berthezene, David	H	F	25/03/2007	01/06/2007	Catalans Dragons (France, loan)
Bettinson, Les	C		09/03/1957	10/09/1969	Millom RU
Betts, Darren	F		09/01/1991	03/10/1993	Langworthy (Salford)
Bevan, -	F		11/02/1899	11/02/1899	-
Bevan, David William	W	W	04/02/1911	31/10/1914	Llanelli RU
Bevan, William David	FB	W	09/01/1909	09/01/1909	Neath RU
Beverley, Cliff	SO	NZ	19/01/2003	16/09/2005	Barrow
Bevon, Jack	F		11/11/1911	15/02/1919	local NU
Bibby, Jake	T		27/09/2015	12/10/2019	Salford Academy
Birkett, Geoffrey	W		04/02/1939	15/04/1939	Kendal RU

Salford RL Players – Dates

Name	Pos	Brn	Debut	Last match	Previous team
Birkett, Martin	C		07/01/1990	15/03/1995	Frizington
Birkin, Frank	F		02/02/1952	17/04/1954	Halifax
Blacker, Brian	C		13/09/1987	27/09/1987	Barrow (loan)
Blackwood, Bob	F		16/01/1983	25/09/1983	Workington Town
Blakeley, Steve (1)	SO		22/11/1992	05/09/1999	Wigan
Blakeley, Steve (2)			07/05/2000	05/10/2003	Warrington
Blan, Jack	F		27/03/1948	18/09/1948	Wigan
Blease, Ian	F		31/03/1985	18/04/1997	Folly Lane (Swinton)
Bloor Darren (1)	HB		28/08/1983	25/09/1988	Oldham St Annes
Bloor Darren (2)			14/01/1990	14/01/1990	Swinton
Boardman, Frank	H		18/08/1951	03/04/1961	Seedley Rangers (Salford)
Bone, Ernie	W		15/09/1900	13/10/1902	Flixton
Boon, Wilf	F		31/03/1923	19/02/1927	local ARL
Booth, James	HB		29/09/1900	13/10/1900	Radcliffe
Borgese, Chris	H	A	03/02/2008	30/03/2008	Canberra (Australia)
Bott, Charlie	F		19/08/1967	25/04/1971	Oldham
Bourouh, Amir	H		29/04/2022	-	Wigan
Bowden, Colin	H		29/09/1967	29/09/1967	Blackpool Borough
Bowen, Trevor	HB	W	08/04/1935	05/12/1936	Penygraig RU
Bowker, Radney	SO		19/01/2003	08/06/2003	Barrow
Bowker, Vernon	F		29/11/1922	24/03/1923	YMCA
Bowley, JH	F	W	02/09/1899	28/10/1899	Hunslet
Boyd, Denis	F		02/10/1983	21/04/1985	Carlisle
Boyd, Syd	T		29/09/1923	13/12/1933	Wigan
Boyle, Ryan	F		07/02/2010	29/03/2013	Castleford
Bradbourne, Terry	FB		20/08/1955	20/08/1955	Bramley Old Boys RU
Bradbury, David	F		17/08/1997	10/09/1999	Oldham
Bradbury, Joe	F		11/01/1930	12/10/1940	Platt Lane (Wigan)
Bradshaw, Arthur	F		27/09/1989	26/03/1993	Thatto Heath (St Helens)
Bradshaw, Tommy	HB		26/10/1940	26/10/1940	Wigan (guest)
Brady, Billy	HB		05/12/1903	10/02/1912	Adelphi Lads Club (Salford)
Bragger, Ian	C		20/11/1988	04/11/1989	Keighley
Braithwaite, Edwin 'Ted'*	C		05/09/1896	13/02/1897	Kendal Hornets
Breen, Aiden	F		04/09/1965	19/04/1968	Huddersfield
Brennan, Jackie	HB		19/08/1959	20/10/1970	Blackpool Borough

Salford RL Players – Dates

Name	Pos	Brn	Debut	Last match	Previous team
Brennan, Tony	F		06/10/1945	06/10/1945	local ARL
Brereton, Peter	F		03/04/1953	04/01/1958	Vine Tavern (St Helens)
Bridges, Selwyn	HB		09/09/1972	08/10/1972	Castleford district ARL
Brierley, Ryan	FB		11/02/2022	-	Leigh
Briggs, Carl	SH		28/02/1999	04/07/1999	Wakefield Trinity
Brining, Kriss	H		11/02/2017	21/09/2017	York
Broadbent, Gary	FB		06/04/1997	13/09/2002	Widnes
Brockbank, Chris	C		23/09/1922	28/04/1923	Swinton (loan)
Brocklehurst, Andrew	F		08/08/2004	29/05/2008	London Broncos
Brogden, Stan (senior)	C		15/02/1947	15/11/1947	Rochdale Hornets
Brogden, Stan (junior)	W		24/10/1953	24/10/1953	Cleckheaton RU (trialist)
Brokenshire, Mark	F	A	07/10/1984	06/01/1985	Mullumbimby (Australia)
Brooke-Cowden, Mark	F	NZ	03/09/1989	16/04/1990	Leeds
Brookfield, Keri	H		23/09/1992	05/11/1993	Wigan St Patrick's
Brophy, Tom	SO		15/11/1974	09/02/1975	Rochdale Hornets
Broughton, Jodie	W		07/02/2010	06/09/2013	Leeds
Brown, Darren	F	A	13/02/1999	19/08/2001	Penrith (Australia)
Brown, Dennis	C		28/03/1964	25/04/1966	Thames Board Mills (Warrington)
Brown, George	F		19/04/1906	23/04/1906	Egerton (Salford)
Brown, Jack	F		01/09/1945	20/10/1951	Pendlebury Juniors
Brown, John	F		08/04/1898	16/03/1901	local NU
Brown, Kevin	HB		31/01/2020	04/09/2021	Warrington
Brown, Peter	F	NZ	16/10/1988	27/03/1989	Te Atatu (New Zealand)
Brown, R	C		08/04/1898	08/04/1898	
Brown, R 'Bob'	T		12/03/1932	10/12/1938	Wigan
Brown, R 'Dick'	C		16/04/1906	17/09/1910	Broughton Rangers Workshops Comp
Brown, Shaun	H		27/09/1989	01/03/1995	Leigh East
Brown, Walter	F		26/12/1939	26/12/1939	Broughton Rangers (guest)
Brown, W 'Billy'*	F		31/10/1896	26/12/1908	Salford St Bartholomew's

Salford RL Players – Dates

Name	Pos	Brn	Debut	Last match	Previous team
Brownbill, Paul	F		18/03/1984	30/11/1986	St Helens
Bruen, Bob	H		26/01/1980	17/02/1980	Swinton (loan)
Brunning, Tony	C		26/08/1964	13/03/1965	Greetland (Halifax)
Brunt, Ken	W		29/10/1960	25/09/1965	St Helens RU
Bryant, Bill	F		12/09/1969	19/09/1969	Castleford
Buckler, Arthur	F	W	01/10/1904	23/01/1915	Pill Harriers RU (Newport)
Buckler, Herbert	F	W	01/09/1900	30/09/1906	Holbeck
Buckler, William	F	W	18/10/1902	18/10/1902	Newport RU
Bullough, David	F		15/03/1987	09/10/1988	Fulham
Burdell, Bob	H		28/09/1966	27/01/1970	St Helens
Burgess, Andy	F		21/04/1987	12/09/1997	Irlam Hornets
Burgess, Bill	W		20/12/1968	19/04/1970	Barrow
Burgess, Ivan	C		25/04/1955	27/04/1955	Crosfields Recreation (Warrington)
Burgess, Jimmy	F		15/02/1919	09/04/1928	Runcorn
Burgess, Joe	W		11/06/2021	-	Wigan
Burgess, Luke (1)	F		07/08/2016	01/10/2016	Manly (Australia)
Burgess, Luke (2)			02/02/2018	27/09/2018	Catalans Dragons
Burke, Greg	F		14/06/2018	03/09/2022	Widnes
Burness, James	C		19/10/1946	26/10/1946	Yorkshire RU (trialist)
Burns, Martin	F		14/11/1980	19/11/1980	Rochdale Hornets (loan)
Burrell, Cyril	F		06/09/1952	11/10/1952	St Helens district ARL
Burrows, Robert	W		08/02/1919	08/02/1919	Manchester University RU
Burt, Howard	W	W	25/08/1945	28/05/1947	Treorchy RU
Butcher, Tom	F		29/09/1945	26/12/1945	-
Butler, John	C		31/03/1975	26/12/1978	Rochdale Hornets
Butterworth, Frank	F		11/03/1922	11/02/1928	local NU
Byrne, Ged	C		23/08/1981	21/04/1987	Wigan St Patrick's
Byrne, John	HB		04/01/1947	13/12/1947	Tyldesley RU
Cahill, -	W		15/09/1945	22/09/1945	Pendlebury Juniors
Caine, Joel	W	A	22/02/2004	19/09/2004	London Broncos
Cairns, David	HB		04/10/1987	25/03/1990	Barrow
Callender, George	W		13/01/1912	01/01/1920	Fletcher Russell (Warrington)
Camac, Roy	C		25/12/1947	25/12/1947	Army RU

Salford RL Players – Dates

Name	Pos	Brn	Debut	Last match	Previous team
Cambridge, Bert	F		01/01/1937	02/04/1938	Broughton Rangers
Carige, Paul	T	A	13/02/1999	10/09/1999	Parramatta (Australia)
Carney, Justin	W	A	05/02/2016	23/04/2017	Castleford
Carney, Todd	HB	A	24/03/2017	01/09/2017	Catalans Dragons (France)
Cartwright, John	F	A	09/02/1997	12/09/1997	Penrith (Australia)
Cartwright, Les	C		04/04/1953	27/08/1955	Bedford Recreation (Leigh)
Casewell, Aubrey	F	W	25/08/1928	12/01/1935	Salford Juniors
Casey, Garen	C	A	13/02/1999	07/08/1999	Wakefield Trinity
Cashmere, Ray	F	A	14/02/2009	11/09/2011	N Queensland (Australia)
Cassidy, Frank	HB		19/11/1989	02/02/1992	Swinton
Caton-Brown, Mason	W		05/07/2014	19/08/2016	London Broncos
Caudwell, Peter	W		27/09/1950	22/09/1956	Langworthy Juniors (Salford)
Caulfield, John	FB		25/08/1945	29/09/1945	Belle Vue Juniors (Manchester)
Chadderton, John	HB		23/09/1950	13/12/1958	Austerlands (Oldham)
Chadwick, Brian	C		30/04/1960	30/04/1960	Warrington district ARL
Chamberlain, Ed	T		14/06/2018	06/11/2020	Widnes
Chapman, Herbert	FB		23/08/1947	25/12/1948	Featherstone Rovers
Charles, Chris	F		26/01/2003	23/09/2006	Hull Kingston Rovers
Charles, WJ 'Billy'	HB	W	27/08/1921	26/08/1922	Bargoed RU
Charlton, Paul	FB		29/10/1969	29/04/1975	Workington Town
Chase, Moutoa 'Rangi'	SO		16/02/2014	23/08/2015	Castleford
Cherrie, Gavin	C	NZ	30/11/1980	01/01/1981	Ponsonby (NZ)
Cheshire, John	C	W	20/08/1955	09/03/1963	Cross Keys RU
Chick, Stuart	W		04/03/1990	25/03/1990	Leeds (loan)
Churm, Bill	F		24/08/1968	08/11/1968	Warrington
Clare, Jeff	C		25/02/1990	03/10/1990	Wigan
Clare, Mick	F		28/04/1962	24/03/1967	Triangle Valve (Wigan)
Clark, Mick	F		29/09/1962	21/09/1963	Huddersfield
Clarke, Colin	H		03/09/1976	19/12/1976	Wigan

Salford RL Players – Dates

Name	Pos	Brn	Debut	Last match	Previous team
Clarke, Derek	F	W	07/12/1957	26/12/1958	Llanelli RU
Clarke, Derek	H		23/09/1970	24/09/1972	Swinton
Clay, Adam	W		30/04/2011	20/05/2011	Leigh Miners Rangers
Clayton, Val	W		05/11/1904	14/01/1905	Birkenhead Wanderers
Clayton, Ryan	F		11/03/2006	14/07/2006	Huddersfield
Cleary, G	F		05/10/1907	19/10/1907	local NU
Clegg, Walter	FB		22/11/1913	08/01/1927	Weaste (Salford)
Clifford, Reg	W		09/01/1915	04/09/1920	Weaste (Salford)
Clinch, Gavin	SH	A	19/01/2003	05/09/2004	Halifax
Clissold, Walter	C	W	01/09/1906	05/10/1907	Penygraig RU
Clough, John	H		23/03/2003	25/03/2006	Salford Academy
Coates, Jack (1)	F		22/03/1923	10/04/1925	Pendleton
Coates, Jack (2)			10/12/1927	20/12/1930	Leigh
Coates, Tom (senior)	F		03/10/1908	08/03/1919	Egerton (Salford)
Coates, Tom (junior)	F		19/01/1924	26/04/1924	local ARL
Coburn, Chris	W		15/11/1947	14/09/1948	Horden RU (Durham)
Cochrane, Johnny	W		25/11/1905	20/03/1909	Maryport
Coleman, Craig	SH	A	13/09/1992	18/04/1993	South Sydney (Australia)
Coleman, George*	C		05/09/1896	13/02/1897	Kendal Hornets
Coleshill, John	C		28/08/1920	28/08/1920	Runcorn White Star
Coley, Andy	F		11/02/2001	21/08/2007	Swinton
Collier, Frank	F		03/09/1966	20/09/1968	Widnes
Colloby, Tony	C		09/10/1970	20/04/1973	Blackpool Borough
Connor, Joseph	FB		13/04/1925	13/04/1925	Bridgewater Hornets (Wigan)
Conroy, Tony	F		01/04/1990	14/04/1991	Wigan St Patrick's
Cook, Jimmy	W		28/09/1907	18/01/1913	Devonport Albion RU
Coombs, CB 'Bert'	C	W	26/12/1923	26/04/1924	Cardiff West End RU
Coope-Franklin, Joseph	C		03/09/2022	-	Coleg y Cymoedd (Wales)
Cooper, Frank	W		13/12/1919	28/02/1920	Broughton Rangers
Cooper, Harry	F		31/01/1925	06/04/1925	Weaste (Salford)
Corcoran, John	F		08/09/1974	11/01/1978	Wigan St Patrick's

Salford RL 1896-97 to 2022

Salford RL Players – Dates

Name	Pos	Brn	Debut	Last match	Previous team
Corry, Tim	H		18/04/1955	25/04/1955	local ARL
Corvo, Mark	F	A	23/03/2002	04/08/2002	Brisbane Broncos (Australia)
Costello, Matty	C		10/04/2021	-	St Helens
Costigan, Steve	W		04/10/1919	12/03/1921	Stockport County AFC
Coulman, Mike	F		18/10/1968	17/04/1983	Moseley RU
Council, Harry	F		29/01/1955	02/01/1965	Dukinfield RU
Coussons, Phil	W		22/11/1992	28/03/1998	Salford Academy
Crank, Peter	C		29/08/1964	20/03/1970	Langworthy Juniors (Salford)
Critch, Jon	F		29/04/1979	29/04/1979	Salford Colts
Critchley, Ernie	C		27/08/1962	15/09/1967	Halifax
Critchley, Jason	C		30/08/1992	23/04/1995	Widnes
Crocker, Will	C	W	10/10/1896	08/09/1900	Morriston RU
Croft, Brodie	SO	A	11/02/2022	-	Brisbane Broncos (Australia)
Crompton, Martin	SH		14/02/1998	24/04/2000	Oldham
Crook, John	F		08/09/1962	08/09/1962	Leigh (trialist)
Cross, Deon	C		11/02/2022	-	Widnes
Cross, Stephen	F		08/02/1981	22/02/1981	Langworthy (Salford)
Crossley, Jim	F		14/09/1940	21/12/1940	Castleford (guest)
Cruickshank, David	SH	A	01/09/1991	24/01/1993	Fulham
Culshaw, Alec	C		09/01/1915	30/01/1915	Weaste (Salford)
Curran, George	F		19/10/1940	30/09/1950	Platt Lane (Wigan)
Currie, George	F		01/10/1910	16/09/1922	Cadishead and Irlam
Curzon, Ephraime	F		05/09/1908	14/04/1911	Kirkcaldy RU
Dagnan, Harry (1)	C		25/12/1940	25/12/1940	Belle Vue Juniors (Mcr) (guest)
Dagnan, Harry (2)	W		25/08/1945	05/04/1947	Belle Vue Juniors (Manchester)
Dalton, Patrick 'Paddy'	F		01/11/1930	18/05/1940	Harrington (Cumberland)
Danby, Tom	C		24/08/1949	03/04/1954	Harlequins RU
Daniels, J	HB		01/01/1902	28/03/1902	Fletcher Russell (Warrington)
D'Arcy, Tom	W	S	21/10/1905	04/11/1905	Panmure RU (Dundee)

Salford RL Players – Dates

Name	Pos	Brn	Debut	Last match	Previous team
Davidson, Alex	F		18/03/2011	09/08/2013	Salford Academy
Davies, Alan	C		13/11/1965	20/11/1965	Oldham
Davies, Arthur	W		16/03/1901	29/03/1902	Flixton
Davies, Ben	C		11/06/2021	11/07/2021	St Helens (loan)
Davies, D Elwyn	HB	W	28/09/1946	14/12/1946	Maesteg RU
Davies, DJ 'Dai'	HB	W	15/09/1900	01/11/1902	Aberavon RU
Davies, DM 'Dai'	F	W	28/10/1936	04/10/1952	Talywain RU
Davies, Doug	F		26/11/1971	21/04/1974	Huyton
Davies, Eifion 'Jack'	HB	W	01/11/1947	20/04/1955	Harlequins RU
Davies, Harry	F		05/09/1896	21/02/1900	Wakefield Trinity
Davies, Henry	F		03/09/2022	03/09/2022	Leigh Miners Rangers
Davies, Jack	W	W	05/09/1908	05/09/1908	Neath RU
Davies, James E	W		14/01/1905	03/02/1906	Hunslet
Davies, Jordan	F		04/08/2013	06/09/2013	Sale RU
Davies, Wes	W		29/06/2003	07/09/2003	Orrell RU
Davies, William J	W	W	30/01/1926	19/01/1929	Crumlin RU
Davys, Ali	SH	NZ	14/01/1996	25/08/1996	Gold Coast Seagulls (Australia)
Day, HC 'Bert'	H	W	29/08/1931	06/03/1948	Newport RU
Day, Eric	F		07/10/1939	15/04/1949	Langworthy Juniors (Salford)
Deakin, Fred	C		25/09/1920	11/12/1920	Runcorn
Dean, Mick	H		13/03/1991	12/05/1991	Leigh
Derrick, John	F		30/01/1915	30/01/1915	Salford St Bartholomew's
Derrick, Richard	C		09/10/1920	13/11/1920	Army RU
Desborough, C	F		07/09/1940	25/12/1940	Bramley (guest)
Devlin, Ellis	H		06/02/1971	28/09/1976	West Park RU (St Helens)
Dickens, Martin	H		27/08/1968	30/08/1969	Blackpool Borough
Dickens, Steve	F		03/01/1982	22/04/1986	Keighley Cougars
Dickens, Stuart	F		05/03/2005	13/05/2005	Featherstone Rovers
Dignum, John	F		27/10/1951	25/12/1956	Winnington Park RU (Northwich)
Disley, Gary	F		18/11/1984	04/11/1989	Leigh Miners
Dixon, AJ	F		05/02/1898	10/09/1898	-
Dixon, Andrew	F		01/02/2013	31/08/2014	St Helens
Dixon, Colin	F	W	20/12/1968	27/04/1980	Halifax
Dobing, George	C		07/09/1929	14/04/1934	West Hartlepool RU

Salford RL Players – Dates

Name	Pos	Brn	Debut	Last match	Previous team
Dobson, Michael	SH	A	07/02/2015	18/08/2017	Newcastle Knights (Australia)
Dodd, Frank	W		27/11/1954	30/03/1959	local ARL
Doeman, Tom	H	W	20/02/1926	18/08/1926	Blaina RU
Donegan, Austin	F		15/12/1991	08/11/1992	Oldham
Donegan, Joe	F		29/01/1966	29/01/1966	St Helens (loan)
Donoghue, Peter	F		16/08/1958	06/05/1961	Rylands Recreation (Warrington)
Dootson, Ron	F		10/12/1978	20/04/1983	Wigan
Doran, R 'Bobby'*	HB		27/02/1897	25/11/1899	-
Doran, Billy	W		21/12/1929	18/04/1931	Broughton Rangers
Dorn, Luke	SO	A	11/02/2007	14/09/2007	Harlequins RL
Dorning, Alan	W		31/03/1961	31/12/1966	St Helens RU
Downie, James	C		01/04/1911	24/02/1912	Salford St James's
Drake, Frank	HB		29/10/1904	06/10/1906	Egerton (Salford)
Driscoll, Damien	F	A	04/03/2001	16/09/2001	Northern Eagles (Australia)
Driver, David	W		03/04/1979	30/10/1983	Oldham St Annes
Dudson, Gil	F	W	01/02/2019	02/11/2020	Widnes
Duffy, Hugh	F	S	05/02/1955	10/03/1962	Jed-Forest RU
Duffy, John	HB		09/04/2000	30/07/2000	Warrington
Dunemann, Andrew	SO	A	17/02/2006	23/09/2006	Leeds
Dunn, Terry	SH		30/04/1960	21/09/1963	Blackpool Borough
Dupree, Tyler	F		15/05/2022	-	Widnes
Dutton, Charles	F		28/08/1926	09/04/1927	Oldham RU
Dutton, Fred	W		17/11/1906	26/12/1906	Runcorn
Dutton, Les	H		26/12/1955	02/03/1957	Belle Vue Rangers
Dyson, Herbert	W		07/09/1901	21/09/1901	Outwood Church (Wakefield)
Earnshaw, H	F		03/12/1898	10/01/1903	Blackley
Easterbrook, Alan	W		19/04/1950	21/11/1953	Aspatria RU
Eastham, Phil	W		06/10/1972	29/04/1973	Wigan
Ebrill, Greg	F	A	10/02/2002	22/09/2002	Northern Eagles (Australia)
Eccles, Cliff	F		28/08/1994	06/09/1998	Rochdale Hornets

Salford RL Players – Dates

Name	Pos	Brn	Debut	Last match	Previous team
Eden, Greg	FB		27/04/2014	30/05/2014	Hull Kingston Rovers (loan)
Edge, Phil	W		26/12/1983	26/12/1983	Langworthy (Salford) (trialist)
Edmondson, Mark	F		11/02/2007	15/07/2007	Sydney Roosters (Australia)
Edwards, Alan	W	W	21/09/1935	11/05/1946	Aberavon RU
Edwards, Ivor	SH	W	08/01/1949	26/08/1950	Torquay Athletic RU
Edwards, Peter	H	NZ	24/09/1995	27/09/1998	Auckland Warriors (New Zealand)
Egan, Joe	H		21/08/1970	20/09/1970	Blackpool Borough
Elliott, Jack	F		07/04/1906	23/04/1906	Egerton (Salford)
Emmitt, Jake	F		13/04/2013	06/09/2013	Castleford
Enoch, Jack	H	W	08/12/1923	19/09/1925	Ammanford RU
Entwistle, James	W		12/11/1927	03/03/1928	Swinton
Entwistle, W	W		20/09/1924	25/10/1924	Healey Street Adults (Oldham)
Errington, Obadiah	H		11/12/1920	18/02/1922	Aspatria Hornets
Escare, Morgan	FB	F	10/04/2021	03/09/2022	Wigan
Evalds, Niall	FB		09/02/2013	06/11/2020	Salford Academy
Evans, Alf	C		14/04/1958	14/04/1958	Broughton Amateurs AFC
Evans, Cliff (1)	HB	W	04/10/1933	19/09/1936	Neath RU
Evans, Cliff (2)			14/10/1939	12/10/1940	Leeds (guest)
Evans, Dave	FB	W	21/08/1965	24/02/1968	Rochdale Hornets
Evans, Dick	H		03/04/1977	30/04/1978	Swinton
Evans, Emrys	F	W	02/09/1939	31/08/1946	Llanelli RU
Evans, Jim	F	W	31/08/1963	12/09/1964	Aberavon RU
Evans, Sam	HB		03/12/1910	23/01/1915	Prestwich Church Institute
Evans, Tex	W		28/08/1988	23/04/1995	Swinton
Fages, Theo	HB	F	01/02/2013	17/07/2015	Pia (France)
Faimalo, Esene	F	NZ	09/02/1997	20/06/1999	Leeds
Faimalo, Joe	F	NZ	05/04/1998	17/09/2000	Oldham
Fairclough, Andy	HB		22/11/1992	22/11/1992	St Helens
Fairclough, Brian	HB		05/10/1946	07/12/1946	Warrington
Fairhurst, Jim	C		24/01/1953	21/01/1956	St Helens district ARL

Salford RL Players – Dates

Name	Pos	Brn	Debut	Last match	Previous team
Fairhurst, Ray	H		07/12/1963	25/03/1964	Wigan St Patrick's
Farrington, John	W		20/02/1954	20/10/1956	Bedford Recreation (Leigh)
Fawcett, George	W		05/09/1896	13/02/1897	Lancaster
Fazackerley, John	HB		01/09/1985	25/10/1987	Thatto Heath (St Helens)
Fearnley, George	F		09/01/1915	30/01/1915	Cadishead
Fearnley, Jack	F		14/09/1940	14/09/1940	St Helens (guest)
Feetham, Jack	F		21/12/1929	12/04/1947	Hull Kingston Rovers
Fell, David	C		12/11/1989	30/08/1992	Orrell RU
Fiddler, Jim	F		10/01/1975	13/12/1975	Leigh
Fieldhouse, Derek	F		21/01/1956	08/11/1958	Highfield (Wigan)
Fielding, Keith	W		17/08/1973	17/04/1983	Moseley RU
Fields, Fred	F		05/12/1896	30/10/1897	Altrincham
Finnan, Bill	C		18/11/1950	20/03/1954	St Helens
Finnigan, Simon	F		12/02/2006	14/09/2007	Widnes
Fish, Jack	C		07/09/1946	18/01/1947	Rylands Recreation (Warrington)
Fisher, D	F	W	05/12/1896	26/12/1896	Morriston RU
Fisher, George	F		05/09/1896	06/04/1901	Lancaster
Fisher, George H	C		25/10/1930	19/03/1932	Seghill RU (Northumberland)
Fitzpatrick, Karl	FB		23/03/2003	15/08/2010	Swinton
Flanagan, John	F		03/09/1910	28/01/1911	Castner Kellner (Runcorn)
Flanagan, John	HB		14/12/1946	09/04/1955	Warrington district ARL
Flanagan, Mark	F		05/02/2016	06/11/2020	St Helens
Fleming, John	HB		24/03/1906	16/04/1906	Walker's Brewery (Warrington)
Fletcher, J	C		12/10/1901	27/04/1903	Pendleton Britannia
Fletcher, Paul	SH		24/10/1980	21/04/1987	Salford Colts
Flint, Dave	F		08/09/1962	04/05/1963	Huddersfield
Flowers, Jason	FB		19/01/2003	25/07/2004	Halifax
Foley, John	C	W	21/10/1922	23/12/1922	Pill Harriers RU (Newport)
Foran, Liam	SH	NZ	01/03/2013	10/06/2013	Manly (Australia)
Forber, Paul	F		13/01/1993	20/09/1998	St Helens

Salford RL Players – Dates

Name	Pos	Brn	Debut	Last match	Previous team
Ford, Jon	C		21/04/2013	21/04/2013	Salford Academy
Ford, Phil	W	W	30/08/1992	01/10/1995	Leeds
Ford, Steve	W	W	02/02/1986	22/04/1986	Cardiff RU
Forshaw, Jim	F		01/08/1999	01/08/1999	St Helens
Forster, Carl	F		26/03/2015	02/04/2016	St Helens
Foster, Alf	F		10/12/1904	08/02/1908	Runcorn Hornets
Foster, Frank	F		17/09/1910	24/09/1910	Runcorn Hornets
Fox, Kevin	HB		13/04/1988	05/04/1992	Langworthy (Salford)
Fox, Thomas	FB		01/03/1924	04/02/1928	Salford Trinity
Foy, David	HB		17/03/1928	17/03/1928	Rochdale Hornets
Foy, Martin	HB		08/04/1985	26/10/1986	Wigan
Frame, J	C		12/09/1896	26/12/1896	South Shields RU
France, Arthur	W		11/02/1899	04/03/1899	Tyldesley
Francis, Bill	SO		26/12/1980	05/12/1982	Oldham
Fraser, Tom	F		27/04/1957	10/10/1959	Widnes St Marie's
Frodsham, Peter	F		01/05/1971	01/05/1977	West Park RU (St Helens)
Fuller, John	W		25/03/1921	13/10/1923	Seedley Rangers (Salford)
Gagon, Frank	W		15/02/1919	11/09/1920	Weaste (Salford)
Gallagher, J	F		04/04/1925	12/09/1925	Warrington
Garces, Steve	F		10/06/2001	10/06/2001	Leigh
Gardner, Joe	F		04/10/1933	01/05/1946	Higginshaw (Oldham)
Gardner, Len	F	W	10/04/1936	29/08/1936	Usk RU
Gardner, Matt	T		03/02/2008	18/09/2008	Huddersfield
Garland, Sam	C	W	30/01/1926	09/04/1928	Crumlin RU
Garlick, Tommy	F		29/12/1956	02/01/1960	Oldham St Annes
Garner, Charlie	W		19/04/1906	28/09/1907	Prestwich Church Institute
Gaskell, John	H		27/08/1921	05/11/1921	Moss Hall (Wigan)
Gaskell, Lee	FB		29/03/2013	06/09/2013	St Helens (loan)
Gear, Albert	C	W	10/10/1936	24/04/1948	Torquay Athletic RU
Gee, Matty	F		12/04/2015	26/04/2015	Orrell St James

Salford RL Players – Dates

Name	Pos	Brn	Debut	Last match	Previous team
Gee, Peter	F		18/03/1984	25/11/1984	Barrow
Gelling, Bryan	F		30/01/1991	30/01/1991	Swinton
George, Edgar	C	W	18/12/1920	05/03/1921	Maesteg RU
Gerrard, Alex	F		20/02/2022	-	Leigh
Gibson, Ashley	T		07/02/2010	01/09/2013	Leeds
Gibson, Damian	FB	A	10/02/2002	22/09/2002	Halifax
Gibson, Steve	FB	A	13/09/1987	18/04/1993	Brisbane Souths (Australia)
Giedziun, Paul	F		16/09/1973	02/04/1974	Halifax
Gildart, Oliver	T		26/04/2015	08/05/2015	Wigan (loan)
Gilfillan, John	C		16/09/1990	06/02/1994	Wigan
Gill, Ken (1)	SO		11/11/1970	29/01/1978	Pilkington Recs (St Helens)
Gill, Ken (2)			19/08/1979	27/04/1980	Barrow
Gill, Mick	F		07/09/1983	08/04/1990	Oldham St Annes
Gilmore, Tom	HB		29/09/2020	13/10/2020	Halifax (loan)
Gledhill, Ben	F		04/02/2012	21/04/2013	Wakefield Trinity
Gledhill, Miles	F		04/09/1897	13/09/1902	Hull Kingston Rovers
Gleeson, Martin	C		24/02/2013	22/05/2014	Hull
Gleeson, Sean	C		18/03/2011	08/09/2012	Wakefield Trinity
Glynn, Peter	C		21/08/1983	04/09/1988	St Helens
Godwin, Wayne (1)	H		13/02/2011	04/08/2013	Bradford Bulls
Godwin, Wayne (2)			18/04/2015	08/05/2015	Dewsbury (loan)
Goldsmith, Harry	F	NZ	14/09/1912	06/03/1920	Olympic RU (San Francisco, USA)
Gordon, Ernest	H		29/08/1925	29/08/1925	Bradford Northern
Gore, Jack	F	W	28/02/1925	09/04/1928	Blaina RU
Gormley, Ian	H		23/03/1988	16/04/1990	Widnes
Gorski, Andy	F		16/09/2001	01/06/2003	Salford Academy
Goulding, Bobbie	SH		04/03/2001	30/06/2002	Wakefield Trinity
Goulding, Darrell	W		18/04/2009	03/07/2009	Wigan (loan)
Gourley, Tony	F		02/02/1979	27/04/1980	Rochdale Hornets
Gower, David	F	A	22/07/2006	14/09/2007	Penrith (Aus)
Graham, Gordon	C		26/08/1974	10/12/1978	Sale RU
Graham, James	F		08/10/1904	23/04/1906	Wath Brow
Grainger, Jim	F		07/10/1950	02/01/1956	Barrow
Greenwood, Harry	F		17/02/1954	23/04/1955	Batley

Salford RL Players – Dates

Name	Pos	Brn	Debut	Last match	Previous team
Greenwood, James (1)	F		26/04/2015	01/05/2015	Wigan (loan)
Greenwood, James (2)			31/01/2020	-	Hull Kingston Rovers
Greenwood, Tom	F		04/10/1947	20/12/1947	Barrow
Gregory, Andy (1)	SH		17/11/1978	17/11/1978	Wigan St Patrick's (trialist)
Gregory, Andy (2)			21/11/1993	17/09/1995	Leeds
Gregory, Arthur	FB		18/08/1956	30/04/1962	Wigan Old Boys RU
Gregory, Harold	SH		16/08/1958	26/12/1959	Wigan Old Boys RU
Gregory, Mike	F		21/08/1994	01/10/1995	Warrington
Grey, Ivor	HB	W	03/10/1896	19/01/1901	Morriston RU
Gribbin, Vince	C		13/10/1985	03/11/1985	Whitehaven (loan)
Grice, Alan	F		25/09/1970	19/08/1979	Blackbrook (St Helens)
Griffin, Darrell	F		24/02/2013	17/07/2015	Leeds
Griffin, George	F		18/04/2015	12/10/2019	London Broncos
Griffin, Josh	C		28/06/2014	01/10/2016	Batley
Griffiths, Ben	HB	W	03/10/1896	27/04/1903	Morriston RU
Griffiths, Clive	W	W	19/10/1984	01/01/1986	St Helens
Griffiths, David	C		28/02/1982	13/08/1988	Widnes RU
Griffiths, Steve	HB		24/03/1985	22/04/1986	Woolston Rovers (Warrington)
Grimes, Paul	F		09/12/1973	31/03/1975	Leigh
Groves, Paul	H		20/04/1983	27/09/1987	Langworthy (Salford)
Gwilliam, Ken	FB		01/12/1967	29/04/1973	Blackbrook (St Helens)
Hadley, Adrian	W	W	11/09/1988	20/04/1992	Cardiff RU
Hadwen, Herbert	W		02/09/1899	21/09/1901	Morecambe
Haggarty, Matt	F		17/04/2016	17/04/2016	St Helens (loan)
Haggerty, Gareth	F		09/02/2003	10/08/2007	Widnes
Haines, EC 'Teddy'	F		27/08/1921	07/01/1933	Bargoed RU
Hainsworth, Jim	F		31/10/1953	17/03/1956	Crosland Moor Shamrocks (Huddersfield)
Haley, John	FB	W	02/09/1905	11/11/1905	Pill Harriers RU (Newport)
Halford, George	W		08/03/1919	08/03/1919	Warrington
Hall, Clifford	W		09/09/1922	04/02/1928	Wigan
Hall, Walter	C		30/12/1922	23/01/1926	local ARL

Salford RL Players – Dates

Name	Pos	Brn	Debut	Last match	Previous team
Hallas, Dave	F		29/04/1979	13/05/1979	Blackpool Borough
Halliwell, Danny	T		11/02/2007	30/03/2007	Leigh
Halliwell, Ken	F		14/08/1968	06/12/1968	Barrow
Halsall, Albert	F		08/09/1962	08/01/1966	Wigan district ARL
Halton, Fred	HB		06/09/1952	23/04/1953	St Helens district ARL
Halton, Jack	HB		01/11/1924	23/01/1926	St Helens Recreation
Hammond, Karle	HB		25/03/2001	01/07/2001	Widnes
Hampson, Jack	C		23/01/1915	30/01/1915	local NU
Hampson, John	HB		04/11/1911	04/11/1911	Craven Brothers (Salford)
Hampson, Steve	FB		23/08/1995	08/09/1996	Halifax
Hampson, Vernon	W		02/09/1905	19/09/1908	York
Hancock, John	F	W	20/08/1955	07/03/1964	Newport RU
Hancock, Michael	T	A	11/02/2001	09/06/2002	Brisbane Broncos (Australia)
Hanley, Brian	C		25/02/1956	22/03/1958	Manchester RU
Hansen, Harrison	F	NZ	16/02/2014	27/09/2015	Wigan
Hansen, Shane	F	NZ	23/09/1990	29/08/1993	Northcote (New Zealand)
Hanson, Sam	F		05/09/1896	03/04/1897	Altrincham
Hardicre, Jim	F		04/01/1964	21/11/1971	Ferranti (Oldham)
Hardman, Andy	F		03/12/1960	31/10/1964	St Helens
Hare, JH	C		04/10/1919	25/08/1923	Bristol RU
Harmon, Neil	F		17/06/2001	02/09/2001	Bradford Bulls
Harper, Bill	H		14/11/1964	27/08/1966	Warrington
Harris, David	SH		30/01/1977	20/04/1983	Salford Colts
Harris, George	F	W	22/09/1934	20/04/1938	Leicester RU
Harris, Tom	F		07/09/1907	07/11/1908	Llwynypia RU
Harris, William	W	W	29/08/1925	29/01/1927	Aberaman RU
Harrison, Edwin	FB		03/09/1910	30/01/1915	Runcorn
Harrison, FV	W		18/04/1919	18/04/1919	local NU
Harrison, Harold	F		09/01/1915	06/03/1915	Cadishead
Harrison, Tommy	SH		02/04/1938	08/04/1955	Hindley
Harrop, Myles-Dalton	W		03/09/2022	03/09/2022	Kendal RU
Harter, Ezekiel 'Zeke'*	C		05/09/1896	24/09/1904	Crompton
Hartley, Bryn	W		19/08/1950	02/09/1961	Salford Juniors
Hartley, Ralph	F		13/10/1945	31/08/1946	Risedale Old Boys (Barrow)
Hartley, Tim	SO		28/05/2004	14/08/2005	Salford Academy
Harwood, George	H		19/08/1961	31/03/1962	Batley

Salford RL Players – Dates

Name	Pos	Brn	Debut	Last match	Previous team
Haslam, Sam*	F		27/02/1897	03/04/1897	-
Hassan, Phil	C		05/04/1998	13/09/1998	Worcester RU
Hasson, James	F		26/05/2017	23/06/2017	Parramatta (Australia)
Hastings, Jackson	SH	A	27/07/2018	12/10/2019	Manly (Australia)
Hauraki, Weller	F	NZ	07/02/2015	25/05/2018	Castleford
Havard, Keiron	C		21/01/1990	28/01/1990	Wigan St Patrick's
Hawkins, Eynon	F	W	14/02/1948	15/03/1952	Bridgend RU
Hawksley, Roy	H		31/08/1975	02/11/1975	Halifax
Hayes, Arthur	F		03/04/1935	03/04/1935	-
Hayes, DA 'Gus'	C	W	20/09/1924	25/03/1925	St Helens
Hayes, Joey	W		28/02/1999	10/09/1999	St Helens
Hayton, John	W		02/11/1901	28/03/1902	Maryport
Healey, -	C		25/08/1945	20/10/1945	Langworthy Juniors (Salford)
Heaney, Roy	W		08/11/1981	28/02/1982	Wigan
Heath, George	F		05/09/1896	03/12/1904	Pendleton Trinity
Hellewell, Ben	F		17/07/2022	23/07/2022	Featherstone Rovers (loan)
Helliwell, Ricky	F		25/08/1997	09/05/1999	West Bowling (Bradford)
Hemmings, John	H		22/08/1955	02/11/1957	Halifax district ARL
Henighan, Mick	F		25/03/1966	12/12/1970	Folly Lane (Swinton)
Hennessey, Thomas	W		27/11/1912	08/03/1913	Rylands Recreation (Warrington)
Henney, Harold	F		27/11/1977	14/10/1984	Workington Town
Henney, Russell	C		14/01/1981	08/02/1981	Hensingham
Henry, Mark	T	A	14/02/2009	11/09/2011	North Queensland (Australia)
Hepi, Brad	F	NZ	19/03/2000	27/08/2000	Featherstone Rovers
Herbert, Steve	F		15/09/1985	12/11/1989	Barrow
Hesketh, Chris	C		19/08/1967	13/05/1979	Wigan
Hesketh, Eric	SO		20/10/1951	18/10/1952	St Helens
Hewitt, Gareth	C		21/03/1999	09/05/1999	Leeds
Hey, Steve	W		13/11/1977	03/04/1979	Salford Colts
Heyes, J	F		01/11/1924	22/11/1924	St Helens
Heywood, Jim	HB		05/11/1932	05/11/1932	Oldham district ARL

Salford RL Players – Dates

Name	Pos	Brn	Debut	Last match	Previous team
Higgs, Bobby	W		15/03/1947	08/11/1947	Eccles RU
Highton, David	F		05/05/2002	05/10/2003	Warrington
Highton, Paul	F		17/05/1998	28/09/2008	Featherstone Rovers
Hignett, George	FB		08/04/1898	25/10/1902	-
Hill, Doug	C		15/09/1967	11/09/1970	St Helens
Hill, Robert	C		27/09/1919	27/09/1919	Broughton Rangers
Hill, Ron	F W		22/11/1968	27/01/1970	Castleford
Hill, R 'Dicky'	HB		12/09/1896	26/09/1896	Bradford
Hilton, Jack	W		19/11/1938	02/10/1946	Newtown Legion (Wigan)
Hindle, Ray	W		02/12/1950	23/04/1953	Warrington
Hindley, Jim	C		23/09/1961	31/10/1964	Tyldesley RU
Hindshaw, Alex	F		03/09/1904	30/01/1915	Salford St Bartholomew's
Hingano, Ata	HB	NZ	23/07/2021	04/09/2021	Mackay Cutters (Australia)
Hirst, Harry	W		30/08/1924	30/08/1924	Eccles RU
Hobson, Richard	F		09/10/1920	09/10/1920	-
Hock, Gareth	F		16/02/2014	12/02/2015	Wigan
Hodgson, David	W		11/02/2005	14/09/2007	Wigan
Hodkinson, Alan	F		16/11/1968	27/04/1969	Leigh St Thomas'
Holbrook, Sam	F		07/10/1905	23/04/1906	Radcliffe Rangers
Holcroft, Jim	F		15/10/1949	04/11/1950	Warrington
Holding, Billy	FB		05/10/1940	14/12/1940	Warrington (guest)
Holdsworth, Daniel	SO	A	07/02/2010	08/09/2012	Canterbury (Australia)
Holland, -	F		11/02/1899	25/03/1899	-
Holland, Dan	W		07/01/1905	04/03/1905	Highfield (Wigan)
Holland, Ian	W		09/03/1973	16/12/1973	Orrell RU
Holmes, Fred	W		08/09/1945	15/04/1946	local ARL
Holroyd, Graham	SO		04/06/2000	08/09/2002	Halifax
Hood, Liam	H		28/02/2015	27/09/2015	Hunslet
Hope, William	F		06/03/1909	06/03/1909	Egerton (Salford)
Hope, Will	F		21/04/2013	06/09/2013	Salford Academy
Horo, Mark	F	NZ	16/10/1988	27/03/1989	Te Atatu (New Zealand)
Hoskins, Joe	W	W	04/09/1897	03/02/1900	Mountain Ash RU
Hough, Brian	C		20/02/1960	20/02/1960	Folly Lane (Swinton)

Salford RL Players – Dates

Name	Pos	Brn	Debut	Last match	Previous team
Hough, John	W		09/09/1922	30/09/1922	-
Hough, R 'Dick'	C		04/11/1911	04/11/1911	Runcorn
Houghton, Joey	HB		06/03/1954	09/04/1955	Bedford Recreation (Leigh)
Howard, Tony	C		25/02/1990	05/09/1993	Army RU
Howarth, Stuart	H		04/02/2012	17/05/2014	Wakefield Trinity
Howarth, W	F		06/02/1897	10/01/1903	-
Hudson, Bernard 'Barney'	W		06/04/1928	22/04/1946	Hartlepool Rovers RU
Hughes, Fred	FB		17/09/1910	30/11/1910	Seedley Bleach Works (Salford)
Hughes, Arthur	F		21/08/1965	04/09/1967	Widnes
Hughes, Bill	FB		25/08/1951	03/11/1956	Austerlands (Oldham)
Hughes, C*	F		16/01/1897	03/04/1897	Pendleton
Hulme, David	F		09/02/1997	10/09/1999	Leeds
Humpheys, Arthur	C		28/12/1946	18/01/1947	local ARL
Hunte, Alan	T		10/02/2002	05/10/2003	Warrington
Hunter, Brian	SH		06/02/1983	02/10/1983	Ring O' Bells (Widnes)
Hurst, Alex 'Sandy'	HB		14/04/1923	03/04/1926	Wigan Highfield
Hurst, Harry	W		26/02/1921	26/08/1922	-
Hurst, Phil	F		01/05/1971	24/03/1974	Pilkington Recs (St Helens)
Hutchinson, James	W		07/09/1907	26/09/1908	Victoria Park Rangers (Warrington)
Hutson, Bill	W		18/08/1962	14/09/1963	Leigh
Huyte, Patrick	W		08/04/1990	08/04/1990	Combined Services RU
Hyam, William	C		14/12/1907	16/04/1910	Plymouth RU
Ikahihifo, Sebastine	F	NZ	31/01/2020	17/09/2021	Huddersfield (loan)
Ingham, John	F		06/05/1961	19/04/1965	Burnage RU
Ingram, William	H		17/04/1926	17/04/1926	Wigan Old Boys RU
Inu, Krisnan	T	NZ	31/03/2019	17/09/2021	Widnes
Irving, Bob	F		27/11/1977	24/11/1978	Wigan
Irving, R	F		11/11/1950	18/11/1950	Broughton Moor
Irving, WH 'Bill'	FB		05/02/1921	12/02/1921	Bradford Northern
Isherwood, James	FB		18/11/1911	25/11/1911	Walker's Brewery (Warrington)
Jack, Garry (1)	FB	A	04/10/1987	31/01/1988	Balmain (Australia)

Salford RL Players – Dates

Name	Pos	Brn	Debut	Last match	Previous team
Jack, Garry (2)			29/08/1993	17/04/1994	Sheffield Eagles
Jackson, Paul	W		26/09/1966	05/05/1972	Langworthy Juniors (Salford)
James, Jordan	F		04/02/2012	06/09/2013	North Wales Crusaders
Jamieson, Ged	F		07/04/1980	23/03/1986	De La Salle Old Boys RU (Salford)
Jenkins, Emlyn (1)	SO	W	06/12/1930	29/01/1938	Cardiff RU
Jenkins, Emlyn (2)			07/12/1940	07/12/1940	Wigan (guest)
Jenkins, JW 'Jack'	F	W	07/09/1946	04/01/1947	Pontypridd RU
Jenkins, Trevor	W		25/12/1940	25/12/1940	Swinton (guest)
Jewitt, Lee	F		11/02/2007	16/08/2013	Wigan
Jiminez, James	C	A	03/02/2008	08/02/2008	St George-Illawarra (Australia)
John, Richard H	W	W	11/09/1920	02/10/1920	Tonyrefail RU
John, WD 'Dai'	HB	W	21/01/1905	25/02/1922	Penygraig RU
Johns, Graeme	FB		23/01/1979	08/02/1981	Swinton
Johnson, Andy	F		22/02/2004	19/06/2005	Castleford
Johnson, Greg	W		16/02/2014	04/07/2019	Batley
Johnson, Josh	F		12/07/2019	29/04/2022	Barrow
Johnson, Mark	W	SA	21/03/1999	06/08/2000	Hull
Jones, Connor	H	A	08/02/2020	06/11/2020	Featherstone Rovers
Jones, E	F		25/02/1899	25/12/1899	Barton
Jones, Eric	C		18/04/1959	31/08/1960	Army RU
Jones, Graham	W	W	27/11/1954	04/05/1962	Penarth RU
Jones, Graham	F		15/09/1978	25/08/1982	Widnes Tigers
Jones, Henry	F		06/12/1947	07/10/1950	Prestwich RU
Jones, JJ*	F		12/09/1896	14/11/1896	Manchester Rangers
Jones, Joe	FB		26/10/1940	23/11/1940	Wigan (guest)
Jones, Josh	F		05/02/2016	12/10/2019	Exeter RU
Jones, Ken	W		30/08/1987	31/10/1989	Swinton
Jones, Reg	C	W	24/11/1945	17/01/1948	Maesteg RU
Jones-Bishop, Ben	W		07/02/2015	27/09/2015	Leeds
Jonkers, Tim	F	NL	11/07/2004	12/02/2006	St Helens
Joseph, Phil	F		05/02/2016	17/06/2016	Widnes
Jowitt, Warren	F		11/02/2001	21/07/2002	Wakefield Trinity
Kear, Barry	F		28/01/1973	12/01/1974	Featherstone Rovers
Kear, Elliot	TQ	W	07/03/2020	30/04/2021	London Broncos
Keavney, Brian	SH		04/04/1951	16/08/1958	Leigh St Joseph's
Keegan, John	H		03/10/1964	13/02/1965	Rochdale Hornets

Salford RL Players – Dates

Name	Pos	Brn	Debut	Last match	Previous team
Keegan, Bob	C		17/11/1920	12/11/1921	Hull Kingston Rovers
Kelly, Mike	W		03/02/1968	08/11/1968	Bradford Northern
Kenny, Joe	F		15/04/1939	08/03/1952	Seghill RU (Northumberland)
Kenny, Russ	F		07/09/1940	09/04/1949	Pendlebury Juniors
Kenny, Sean	H		01/07/2016	01/10/2016	Warrington Academy
Kenny, Tom	SO		14/01/1939	25/12/1941	Broughton Rangers
Kenward, Shane	SO	A	09/08/1998	09/08/1998	St George (Australia)
Kenyon, Roy	FB		22/08/1964	29/10/1966	Langworthy Juniors (Salford)
Kerry, Steve	SH		11/12/1988	22/03/1992	Preston Grasshoppers RU
Kershaw, AS	F		07/01/1899	07/01/1899	-
Kershaw, Harold	C		27/10/1923	27/10/1923	Stamford Hornets (Oldham)
Kershaw, Stanley	C		12/04/1919	12/04/1919	local NU
Kettle, Bob	H		04/09/1981	28/04/1985	Leigh Miners
Kilgannon, Derek	H		22/03/1958	25/05/1963	Oldham district ARL
King, Tom*	F		07/11/1896	03/04/1897	-
Kinsey, Tom	W		13/02/1904	23/04/1904	North West Manchester
Kirk, Andy	T		23/03/2003	12/09/2004	Leeds
Kirkbride, Bill	F		10/01/1971	29/04/1973	Castleford
Knighton, John	F		24/03/1972	23/04/1978	Heaton Moor RU
Knott, James	F		25/10/1913	01/01/1921	Oldham YMCA
Knowles, Graham	C		26/03/1974	30/08/1974	Salford Colts
Knowles, Phil	T		07/07/1996	25/08/1997	Wigan
Knox, Simon	F		13/09/1998	27/09/1998	Bradford Bulls (loan)
Kopczak, Craig	F		05/02/2016	27/09/2018	Huddersfield
Korkidas, Michael	F	A	11/02/2007	14/09/2007	Wakefield Trinity
Krasniqi, Olsi	F	AL	05/07/2015	01/09/2017	London Broncos
Kyte, Syd	FB		25/12/1940	25/12/1940	Wigan (guest)
Lafai, Tim	C	SM	11/02/2022	-	Canterbury (Australia)
Lamb, Nigel	F		11/12/1983	06/09/1987	Irlam Hornets
Lambert, Roy	W		05/02/1955	03/09/1955	Castleford

Salford RL Players – Dates

Name	Pos	Brn	Debut	Last match	Previous team
Lambert, W 'Billy'	FB		07/11/1903	15/04/1911	Egerton (Salford)
Lancaster, E	W		16/04/1906	30/04/1906	Dewsbury
Landers, Fred	F		01/03/1919	01/03/1919	Weaste (Salford)
Lane, William	HB		25/09/1948	25/09/1948	Wigan district ARL
Lang, David	F		09/03/1979	08/11/1981	Salford Colts
Langi, Junior	W	NZ	03/04/2005	11/08/2006	Parramatta (Australia)
Lannon, Ryan (1)	F		12/04/2015	27/09/2018	Salford Academy
Lannon, Ryan (2)			21/06/2019	03/09/2022	Hull Kingston Rovers
Latham, Keith	C		19/08/1979	04/01/1981	Leigh East
Launce, Harry	FB		02/09/1911	11/12/1920	Camborne RU
Laurence, Jason	FB	A	18/08/1996	28/03/1997	York
Laurie, Mark	F	A	07/02/1993	18/04/1993	Parramatta (Australia)
Lavery, Joe	FB	NZ	28/03/1910	16/04/1910	Leigh
Lawrenson, Johnny	C		26/10/1940	23/11/1940	Wigan (guest)
Lawton, Adam	F		09/03/2019	31/03/2019	West Bank (Widnes)
Leach, Joe	F		11/04/1964	18/09/1965	Greenfield (Oldham)
Leatherbarrow, David	W		31/10/1964	31/10/1964	Hope Rangers (Leigh) (trialist)
Lee, Mark	H		14/01/1990	08/08/2000	St Helens
Lee, Tommy	H		16/02/2014	30/04/2016	London Broncos
Leigh, Matthew	F		13/02/2000	06/08/2000	Warrington
Lendill, Peter	HB		16/08/1960	26/08/1961	Leeds
Leonard, Ken	F	W	23/09/1961	15/09/1962	Pontypridd RU
Leota, Francis	F	NZ	25/11/1990	29/03/1991	Sheffield Eagles
Leuluai, Phil	F	NZ	03/08/2007	05/09/2010	Cronulla (Australia)
Lever, Walter	W		28/08/1920	28/08/1920	Local NU
Lewis, Isaac 'Ike'	F	W	13/02/1904	17/10/1908	Salford St Bartholomew's
Leyland, Fred	W		09/12/1950	18/10/1952	Vine Tavern (St Helens)
Lima, Danny	F	SM	24/06/2006	03/09/2006	Warrington (loan)
Lindley, Jimmy	HB		10/09/1927	26/04/1930	Rochdale district ARL
Littlejohn, Jack	SH	A	02/02/2018	22/09/2018	Wests Tigers (Australia)

Salford RL Players – Dates

Name	Pos	Brn	Debut	Last match	Previous team
Littler, Stuart	C		10/07/1998	05/09/2010	Salford Academy
Livesey, Albert	F		18/01/1919	26/04/1919	Army RU
Livett, Harvey	F		26/03/2021	03/09/2022	Warrington
Llewellyn, William	F	W	05/12/1896	25/11/1899	Morriston RU
Lloyd, John	HB		28/03/1921	23/04/1921	Pendleton
Locke, Kevin	FB	NZ	05/07/2014	01/05/2015	NZ Warriors (New Zealand)
Lolohea, Tuimoala	SO	NZ	28/06/2019	17/09/2021	Leeds
Lomas, Jimmy (1)	C		21/09/1901	31/12/1910	Bramley
Lomas, Jimmy (2)			24/02/1923	29/09/1923	York
Lomas, Jim	F		09/10/1954	03/11/1956	Pendlebury Juniors
Loughlin, Terry 'Paddy'	F		02/12/1961	29/01/1966	Thatto Heath (St Helens)
Love, Henry	F		09/09/1922	09/09/1922	local ARL
Love, William	FB	W	30/01/1926	06/03/1926	Blaina RU
Loveluck, Arthur	C	W	16/09/1911	24/04/1915	Cardiff RU
Lowcock, H	F		23/04/1906	23/04/1906	Egerton (Salford)
Lowdon, Syd	SO		23/11/1957	26/09/1959	Whitehaven
Lowe, Jackie	FB		21/10/1961	11/11/1961	Blackpool Borough
Lowe, Johnny	C		28/04/1954	17/08/1954	Swinton
Lowe, Neil	F		19/01/2003	07/09/2003	Featherstone Rovers
Luckley, Sam	F	S	27/05/2021	17/09/2022	Newcastle Thunder
Lui, Robert	SO	A	05/02/2016	21/06/2019	North Queensland (Australia)
Lussick, Darcy	F	A	10/04/2021	27/05/2021	Toronto Wolfpack (Canada)
Lussick, Joey	H	A	10/08/2018	02/11/2020	Manly (Australia)
Lyons, Peter	HB		13/11/1920	17/11/1920	Widnes
Lyons, J	F		05/09/1896	04/11/1896	Oldham
Mabbett, Thomas	W	W	08/09/1906	29/09/1906	Pontarddulais RU
McAlone, Edwin 'Eddie'	F		02/12/1961	14/09/1963	Whitehaven district ARL
McArthur, Walter 'Wally'	W	A	17/08/1957	20/09/1958	Blackpool Borough
McAtee, John	SH		12/01/1980	24/02/1980	Leigh (loan)
McAvoy, Nathan (1)	C		24/04/1994	10/07/1998	Eccles
McAvoy, Nathan (2)			23/05/2004	16/09/2005	Saracens RU
McCarthy, Bryan	C	A	06/03/1988	23/03/1988	Oldham

Salford RL Players – Dates

Name	Pos	Brn	Debut	Last match	Previous team
McCarthy, Tyrone	F		30/07/2017	06/11/2020	St George-Illawarra (Australia)
McCauley, Kenneth	F		02/09/1950	16/09/1950	United Glass Bottle (St Helens)
McCormick, Stan	W		14/12/1940	14/12/1940	Broughton Rangers (guest)
MacCorquodale, Iain	W		11/11/1970	10/03/1972	Waterloo RU
McGilvray, Dean	W		29/03/2009	12/02/2010	St Helens
McGoldrick, Ryan	HB	A	01/02/2013	06/09/2013	Castleford
McGovern, Terry	HB		19/09/1980	12/10/1980	Swinton (loan)
McGreal, Chris	F		08/04/1975	12/11/1982	Salford Colts
McGuinness, Jack	H		05/11/1958	12/03/1960	St Helens
McGuinness, Kevin	C	A	08/05/2004	14/09/2007	Manly (Aus)
McGuire, James	C		03/04/1924	30/08/1924	Pemberton
McInnes, Alan	C		05/11/1966	11/11/1970	Sale RU
McJennett, Mark	F	W	03/10/1982	06/10/1982	Barrow (loan)
McKay, Graham	F		08/10/1972	20/02/1976	Swinton
McKinney, Tom	H	IR	26/11/1949	27/11/1954	Jed-Forest RU
McPherson, Neil	F		25/08/1997	25/08/1997	Salford Academy
McPherson, Shannan	F	A	10/02/2012	18/04/2014	South Sydney (Australia)
McTigue, Mick	F		17/10/1982	03/09/1989	Leigh
McWhirter, Harry	W		24/09/1904	06/04/1908	Irlam Soap Works
Maddocks, Joe	HB		29/10/1904	02/01/1905	Stockport
Maggs, Keith	W		27/09/1981	18/11/1984	Aspull RU
Mahon, Scott	FB	A	04/09/1994	22/01/1995	Parramatta (Australia)
Mair, James	C		09/11/1946	14/10/1946	Sale RU
Maitua, Reni	F	A	09/08/2015	27/09/2015	Featherstone Rovers
Major, David	F		30/11/1979	02/04/1989	Crosfields (Warrington)
Makin, Craig	F		06/04/1999	16/09/2001	Widnes
Makin, John	HB		17/04/1987	17/04/1987	Wigan St Patrick's
Maloney, Francis	C		11/02/2001	22/09/2002	Wakefield Trinity
Manfredi, Dominic	W		14/03/2014	14/03/2014	Wigan (loan)
Mann, Fred	F		26/02/1927	24/09/1927	Wigan Highfield
Manniex, John	F		27/08/1962	01/09/1962	Warrington
Manning, Dick	C		19/03/1927	18/10/1930	Melbourne Juniors (Salford)
Mannion, Tom	HB		28/08/1926	16/03/1929	Pendlebury Hornets

Salford RL Players – Dates

Name	Pos	Brn	Debut	Last match	Previous team
Mansson, Paul	SO	NZ	31/03/1996	25/08/1996	Canberra (Australia)
Mantle, John	F	W	22/08/1976	01/05/1977	St Helens
Manwaring, W 'Billy'*	FB		12/09/1896	03/04/1897	Broughton
Marland, Lees	FB		18/01/1947	15/03/1947	Waterhead (Oldham)
Marriott, Callum	F		18/03/2011	18/03/2011	Salford Academy
Marsden, Bob	F		31/10/1993	26/03/1995	Rochdale Hornets
Marsden, W 'Bill'	F		03/10/1931	25/12/1940	Platt Lane (Wigan)
Marsh, Iain	W		27/09/1998	27/05/2001	Widnes Tigers
Marsh, Ian	W		23/12/1984	01/11/1987	Wigan St Patrick's
Marsh, Lee	F		30/04/2001	18/05/2003	Salford Academy
Marshall, Wayne	H	A	02/02/1995	12/03/1995	Eastern Suburbs (Australia)
Marston, Peter	F		20/12/1952	18/02/1956	Leigh
Martin, Scott	C		02/04/1995	12/05/1999	Leigh
Mason, Albert	FB	W	17/11/1906	11/04/1908	Llanelli RU
Mateo, Feleti	F	A	07/08/2016	19/08/2016	Manly (Aus)
Mather, Ian	H		09/09/1972	02/02/1973	Thames Board Mills (Warrington)
Matthews, Eddie	HB	W	15/09/1928	25/03/1931	Neath RU
Mauro, Vic	F	A	01/03/2013	10/06/2013	Manly (Aus)
May, Edgar	HB		03/09/1910	15/10/1921	Bramley
Mayor, Graham	C		10/10/1975	05/04/1978	Salford Colts
Meachin, Colin	F		20/04/1983	06/01/1985	Wilmslow RU
Mears, William	H		01/11/1924	31/01/1925	Platt Lane (Wigan)
Meek, Reg	HB	W	29/08/1925	30/09/1933	Ebbw Vale RU
Meli, Francis	W	SM	16/02/2014	28/06/2014	St Helens
Menzies, Luke	F		27/09/2015	27/09/2015	Swinton
Mercer, Andy	W		13/11/1988	19/08/1990	West Park RU (St Helens)
Mesley, Bernard	C		26/09/1908	24/04/1915	Twickenham RU
Messer, Bob	C	W	08/11/1902	31/10/1903	Swinton
Middleton, Alf	F		10/11/1928	28/03/1936	Coventry RU
Miles, Frank*	W		23/01/1897	18/02/1899	Barton
Miller, Jack	F		19/10/1940	19/10/1940	Warrington (guest)
Miller, Sammy	C		18/11/1929	22/12/1945	Blaydon-on-Tyne RU
Mills, Jim	F	W	03/02/1968	01/03/1968	Halifax

Salford RL 1896-97 to 2022

Salford RL Players – Dates

Name	Pos	Brn	Debut	Last match	Previous team
Mills, R	F		06/03/1897	20/03/1897	Stockport
Moana, Martin	F	NZ	03/08/2003	13/06/2004	Halifax
Molyneux, R 'Dick'	FB		27/08/1921	09/09/1922	Platt Lane (Wigan)
Moon, Joel	C	A	04/02/2012	08/07/2012	NZ Warriors (New Zealand)
Moore, John	F		07/10/1961	01/09/1962	Langworthy Juniors (Salford)
Moore, Owen	HB		23/03/1946	11/04/1951	Wigan Juniors
Moran, Dave	HB		21/11/1982	18/12/1982	Widnes (loan)
Moran, Mark	H		26/12/1986	27/02/1991	Simms Cross (Widnes)
Morgan, Joey	HB	W	02/09/1905	07/10/1905	Swinton
Morley, Adrian	F		16/02/2014	27/09/2015	Warrington
Morley, Chris	F		02/04/1999	18/08/1999	Warrington
Morris, Steve	FB		12/10/1986	26/10/1986	Warrington (loan)
Morris, William	F	W	04/09/1897	18/09/1897	Penygraig RU
Morton, Edgar	F		11/09/1909	07/09/1912	Halifax
Morton, Sam	W		24/09/1910	20/01/1915	Swinton Hornets
Moses, Dai	F	W	08/12/1945	11/02/1958	Maesteg RU
Moses, Glyn	C	W	18/12/1948	28/04/1951	Maesteg RU
Moss, Bob*	F		05/09/1896	25/02/1899	Manchester Athletic
Mossop, Lee	F		11/02/2017	16/08/2021	Wigan
Moule, Aaron	C	A	12/02/2006	08/09/2007	Widnes
Moylan, Steve	H		15/11/1985	21/09/1986	Warrington
Muir, Jack	F		16/10/1920	16/09/1933	Army RU
Mullaney, Jake	FB	A	16/02/2014	17/05/2014	Parramatta (Australia)
Muller, Roby	F	NZ	23/09/1984	06/10/1985	Warrington
Murdoch-Masila, Ben	F	NZ	05/02/2016	21/09/2017	Penrith (Australia)
Murdock, Craig	HB		16/04/2000	24/04/2000	Hull
Murphy, Jack	FB		01/02/2013	07/04/2013	Wigan (loan)
Murphy, Paul	W		04/05/1962	08/11/1968	Preston Grasshoppers RU
Murray, Daniel	F		30/04/2017	07/06/2019	Warrington
Murray, Tom	F	NZ	24/01/1982	21/03/1982	Takahiwai (New Zealand)
Myers, David	T		01/11/1995	17/12/1995	Bradford Bulls
Myler, Richie	SH		03/02/2008	31/07/2009	Widnes
Myler, Rob	FB		02/04/1995	23/04/1995	Warrington (loan)
Myler, Stephen	SO		02/04/2006	14/07/2006	Widnes
Myler, Vinny	F		12/04/2004	02/05/2004	Bradford Bulls (loan)

Salford RL Players – Dates

Name	Pos	Brn	Debut	Last match	Previous team
Naidole, Tom	F	FJ	06/03/1988	20/03/1988	Oldham (loan)
Nakubuwai, Ben	F	A	09/02/2018	13/09/2019	Gold Coast Titans (Australia)
Napolitano, Carlo	F		21/05/2000	25/06/2000	Eccles
Nash, Stephen	F		30/03/2007	11/09/2009	Widnes
Nash, Steve	SH		15/08/1975	08/01/1984	Featherstone Rovers
Naylor, Scott (1)	C		29/08/1993	13/09/1998	Wigan
Naylor, Scott (2)			29/02/2004	28/05/2004	Bradford Bulls
Neal, Adam	F		18/07/2010	04/08/2013	Warrington
Neal, Mike	C		28/06/1998	28/06/1998	Oldham
Needham, David	SO		15/03/1987	10/12/1989	Oldham St Annes
Neil, Mike	SH	A	29/08/1993	23/01/1994	Illawarra (Australia)
Nero, Chris	F	A	13/02/2011	17/05/2013	Bradford Bulls
Nestor, Vince	C		26/09/1966	04/09/1967	Oldham
Newton, T	HB		03/11/1945	10/11/1945	(trialist)
Nicholls, George	F		22/08/1982	16/10/1983	Cardiff City
Nicol, Jason	F	A	02/04/2000	22/09/2002	North Queensland (Australia)
Norburn, Peter	F		26/09/1964	04/09/1965	Swinton
Norbury, John	F		08/04/1898	08/04/1898	-
Norman, Dan	F		11/07/2021	22/08/2021	St Helens (loan)
Norrey, Harold (1)	W		27/11/1920	10/11/1923	Swinton
Norrey, Harold (2)			25/12/1925	25/12/1925	St Helens Recreation
Norris, Abraham	W		21/10/1899	17/09/1904	local NU
Nuttall, Alf	F		19/04/1906	06/10/1906	Egerton (Salford)
Nzoungou, Levi	F	C	04/05/2018	21/07/2018	Toulouse Olympique (France)
O'Brien, Gareth	FB		05/02/2016	04/03/2018	Warrington
O'Connor, Terry	F		09/01/1992	24/04/1994	Widnes St Marie's
Offiah, Martin	W		13/02/2000	26/08/2001	London Broncos
Ogden, Terry	F		16/02/1965	31/10/1969	Huddersfield
Okanga-Ajwang, Edwin	C		01/04/2013	07/04/2013	Salford Academy
Oldham, Alan	F		08/01/1978	12/04/1982	Salford Colts
O'Loughlin, Jason	C		13/04/1988	01/04/1991	Wigan St Patrick's
O'Loughlin, Keiron	C		01/09/1985	05/10/1988	Widnes
Olpherts, Derrell	W		22/03/2018	11/08/2019	Newcastle Thunder

Salford RL Players – Dates

Name	Pos	Brn	Debut	Last match	Previous team
O'Neill, Paul	H		18/08/1978	05/02/1984	Wigan St Patrick's
O'Neill, Paul	W		14/10/1990	06/02/1994	Leigh Miners
O'Neill, Steve	F		07/01/1990	08/04/1990	Swinton
Openshaw, Arthur	H		09/03/1957	21/10/1961	Langworthy Juniors (Salford)
Ormondroyd, Jack	F		24/09/2020	-	Featherstone Rovers
Orr, Paul	F		09/10/1970	12/01/1973	Kippax (Castleford)
Osbaldestin, Harold	FB		03/10/1931	06/05/1939	Dewsbury
O'Shea, Terry	F	NZ	26/10/1986	27/03/1988	Te Atatu (New Zealand)
Owen, Gareth	F		20/01/1982	24/01/1982	Oldham (loan)
Owen, Gareth	H		15/08/2010	06/09/2013	Salford Academy
Owen, Tom 'Tot'	HB		10/11/1900	10/11/1900	Wigan
Palea'aesina, Iafeta	F	NZ	13/02/2011	10/08/2012	Wigan
Palmer, H	F	W	07/11/1896	14/11/1896	Llandaff RU
Panapa, Sam	F	NZ	21/08/1994	08/09/1996	Wigan
Parker, Rob	F		14/02/2009	04/03/2011	Warrington
Parkinson, Bill	F		06/05/1961	23/04/1962	Tyldesley RU
Parr, Jim	F		12/11/1955	22/04/1957	Whitehaven
Parry, Bob	W	W	08/10/1904	29/10/1904	Llanelli RU
Parsons, George	F	W	13/12/1958	12/11/1960	Rochdale Hornets
Partridge, Sydney	W	W	25/03/1921	10/12/1921	Bargoed RU
Paterson, Cory	F	A	07/02/2015	20/09/2015	Wests Tigers (Australia)
Patten, Luke	FB	A	13/02/2011	31/08/2012	Canterbury (Australia)
Patton, Dec	HB		26/03/2021	11/07/2021	Warrington
Paul, Robbie	SO	NZ	04/04/2008	11/09/2009	Huddersfield
Pauli, Pauli (1)	F	A	17/05/2019	07/06/2019	Wakefield Trinity (loan)
Pauli, Pauli (2)			31/01/2020	16/08/2021	Wakefield Trinity
Peacock, Charlie	HB		11/04/1925	19/11/1927	Oldham
Pearce, Ray	FB		04/05/1962	25/04/1966	Burtonwood (St Helens)
Pearson, Arthur	W		05/09/1896	06/04/1901	Keighley Cougars
Pearson, Leslie	W		04/10/1933	13/10/1945	Old Salfordians RU
Pemberton, Harold	F		30/10/1926	06/11/1926	Millom
Pemberton, S	W		03/12/1904	14/01/1905	Heyside (Oldham)
Pendlebury, John	F		30/12/1984	26/10/1986	Wigan

Salford RL Players – Dates

Name	Pos	Brn	Debut	Last match	Previous team
Pendlebury, WH	W		09/04/1904	09/04/1904	Eccles
Penni, Julian	W		09/08/1998	09/05/1999	Salford Academy
Philbin, Barry	F		17/10/1978	11/02/1979	Warrington
Phillips, William	HB	W	03/09/1898	02/03/1901	Mountain Ash RU
Pierson, C	FB		05/09/1896	27/02/1897	Radcliffe
Pimblett, Albert	C		02/09/1950	13/01/1951	Warrington
Pinkney, Nick	W		13/02/2000	23/06/2002	Halifax
Platt, Andy	F		09/02/1997	14/06/1998	Auckland Warriors (New Zealand)
Platt, Michael (1)	W		16/09/2001	25/05/2003	Salford Academy
Platt, Michael (2)			21/04/2014	02/06/2014	North Wales Crusaders
Pobjie, Michael	C	A	22/09/1985	15/11/1985	South Sydney (Australia)
Potts, Ian	F		13/04/1988	04/12/1995	Irlam Hornets
Powell, Bryn	W		12/04/2004	02/05/2004	Hunslet
Poynton, John	C		03/12/1910	03/12/1910	Wardley Lane (Swinton)
Preece, Bob	C		29/09/1956	02/12/1961	Army RU
Prescott, Eric (1)	F		15/09/1972	19/09/1980	St Helens
Prescott, Eric (2)			11/03/1984	26/12/1984	Widnes
Preston, Dave	HB		13/12/1902	15/11/1913	Salford Trinity
Price, Gareth	F	W	11/08/2002	17/08/2002	Leigh (loan)
Price, Horace	W	W	07/09/1901	26/04/1902	Wakefield Trinity
Price, Jim	H		26/08/1961	07/09/1963	Blackpool Borough
Price, Malcolm	C	W	28/09/1968	28/09/1968	Rochdale Hornets
Price, W 'Billy'	H		28/08/1926	09/02/1929	Bridgewater Hornets (Wigan)
Prosser, Bob	SH	W	27/01/1968	26/03/1974	St Helens
Pugsley, Joe	F	W	02/09/1911	29/03/1913	Cardiff RU
Puletua, Tony	F	NZ	16/02/2014	12/09/2014	St Helens
Quigley, Jonathan	H		21/03/1991	23/04/1995	Leigh Miners
Quigley, Thomas	C		01/09/1923	13/04/1925	Swinton Park
Quinn, John	F		25/12/1920	08/09/1923	Local NU
Rabbitt, Trevor	SH		17/03/1962	16/08/1969	Cadishead and Irlam
Raistrick, Dean	H		07/12/1975	11/03/1977	Keighley Cougars
Rampling, Tony	F	A	07/10/1989	11/02/1990	South Sydney (Australia)
Ramshaw, Terry	F		19/10/1971	23/04/1973	Wakefield Trinity

Salford RL Players – Dates

Name	Pos	Brn	Debut	Last match	Previous team
Randall, Craig	F		01/01/1992	20/09/1998	Leigh Miners
Rapira, Steve	F	NZ	22/02/2014	15/08/2014	NZ Warriors (New Zealand)
Ratchford, Stefan	SO		30/03/2007	11/09/2011	Salford Academy
Ratcliffe, David	F		13/09/1987	17/04/1988	Leigh Miners
Ratcliffe, Joe	W		09/10/1909	26/04/1919	British Westinghouse (Manchester)
Rawlinson, John	W		05/01/1975	16/05/1976	Salford Colts
Read, Ron	F		20/09/1947	27/09/1947	Langworthy Juniors (Salford)
Reakes, Tom	C	W	14/02/1959	16/03/1959	Workington Town
Reardon, Stuart	W		04/08/2002	02/09/2002	Bradford Bulls (loan)
Redford, Tony	C		22/03/1968	15/12/1974	Blackbrook (St Helens)
Rees, Charlie	F	W	23/10/1909	24/04/1915	Penygraig RU
Rees, Dai	F	W	05/11/1904	13/01/1912	Llwynypia RU
Rees, Graham	F	W	04/02/1961	15/12/1962	Maesteg RU
Rees, Ivor	C	W	11/03/1931	05/12/1931	Treorchy RU
Reeve, Cyril	F		05/12/1936	15/01/1938	Colchester RU
Regan, Dave	F		24/10/1980	09/11/1980	Wigan (loan)
Regan, Peter	F		10/01/1988	15/10/1989	Wigan St Patrick's
Reid, Wayne	SO		15/09/1991	13/11/1993	Wigan
Renninson, Albert	F		30/04/1960	25/08/1962	Vale of Lune RU (Lancaster)
Reynolds, Paul	C		15/09/1991	12/01/1992	Trafford Borough (loan)
Rhapps, Jack	F	W	04/09/1897	06/10/1906	Penygraig RU
Richards, Ken	SO	W	19/08/1961	30/03/1964	Bridgend RU
Richards, Maurice	W	W	15/10/1969	21/08/1983	Cardiff RU
Richards, R 'Bob'	C	W	08/10/1904	26/04/1905	Llanelli RU
Richards, Tom	F		05/02/1949	05/02/1949	-
Rickers, Tom	F		08/09/1906	08/09/1906	Pendlebury
Riley, Fred	SO		29/10/1927	01/09/1928	Swinton Shamrock
Riley, Ike	W		29/10/1921	29/10/1921	Wigan district NU
Riley, Sam	W		06/09/1902	07/02/1903	Irlam
Riley, Todd	SO	A	09/12/1984	30/12/1984	Lakes United (Australia)
Risman, AJ 'Gus'	C	W	31/08/1929	23/03/1946	Cardiff Scottish RU
Ritchie, Bob	F		01/10/1910	24/04/1915	Tynedale RU
Ritter, Neil	SH	A	23/09/1984	06/01/1985	Mullumbimby (Australia)

Salford RL Players – Dates

Name	Pos	Brn	Debut	Last match	Previous team
Roberts, Arthur	F		12/10/1946	25/10/1947	local ARL
Roberts, D	HB		13/03/1897	13/03/1897	Stockport
Roberts, George	F		16/09/1922	01/03/1924	Broughton Rangers
Roberts, Ken	F		29/10/1969	20/10/1970	Rochdale Hornets
Roberts, Luis	W		29/09/2020	13/10/2020	Salford Academy
Roberts, Oliver	F		22/02/2020	17/09/2021	Huddersfield (loan)
Robinson, Frank	H		03/09/1925	16/10/1926	West Liverpool St Old Boys (Salford)
Robinson, Luke	SH		11/02/2005	21/08/2007	Wigan
Robson, Bob	F	S	20/01/1951	19/12/1953	Huddersfield
Robson, Ellis	F		16/08/2021	17/09/2021	Warrington (loan)
Rodgers, George	W		25/10/1902	13/12/1902	Egerton (Salford)
Rogers, Darren	W		27/08/1995	13/09/1998	Dewsbury
Rogers, Jack	F		10/04/1946	23/04/1955	Leeds Juniors
Rogers, Jon	W		09/11/1980	20/04/1984	Widnes Tigers
Roper, Jon	C		20/08/2000	17/09/2000	Warrington (loan)
Rose, C	F		18/01/1947	06/12/1947	Rylands Recreation (Warrington)
Ross, George	F	S	02/09/1899	02/09/1899	Stewartonians RU (Edinburgh)
Rothwell, Frank	F		04/09/1926	04/09/1926	Sandfield (Rochdale)
Roughley, George	C		09/01/1954	25/12/1954	Wigan
Rourke, Josh	FB		03/09/2022	03/09/2022	Leigh Miners Rangers
Roy, Don	C		03/09/1960	22/09/1962	St Helens
Ruddy, Dave	T		21/08/1983	09/11/1986	Orrell RU
Rule, Steve	FB		24/02/1978	24/04/1983	Sale RU
Russell, Robert	W		07/06/1998	04/07/1999	Eccles
Rutgerson, Sean	F	A	22/02/2004	23/09/2006	Canberra (Australia)
Ryan, Tommy	SH		12/09/1953	28/09/1957	Bedford Recreation (Leigh)
Sammon, Joe	W		12/04/1952	14/04/1952	Oldham St Bernard's
Sarginson, Dan	C	A	31/01/2020	29/08/2022	Wigan
Sarsfield, Matt	F		05/02/2016	17/04/2016	Leigh
Sa'u, Junior	C	NZ	16/02/2014	12/07/2019	Melbourne (Australia)

Salford RL Players – Dates

Name	Pos	Brn	Debut	Last match	Previous team
Savage, William	F		23/08/1919	28/08/1920	Swinton
Savelio, Lokeni	F	NZ	01/11/1995	27/09/1998	Hutt Valley (New Zealand)
Saxton, Tom	FB		21/07/2007	14/09/2007	Castleford (loan)
Schofield, Dave	SH		13/12/1933	19/11/1938	Old Salfordians RU
Schubert, Gary	F	A	31/08/1986	12/10/1986	Taree United (Australia)
Scott, John	HB		02/09/1911	18/11/1911	Tynedale RU
Selby, Geoff	F	A	05/10/1986	01/03/1987	St George (Australia)
Sharp, Johnnie	W	S	16/10/1897	01/04/1899	Hawick RU
Shaw, Darren	F	A	10/02/2002	13/09/2002	Castleford
Shaw, David	C		30/08/1987	29/03/1991	Wigan St Patrick's
Shaw, Fred	H		25/08/1928	16/01/1937	Cadishead
Shaw, J	FB		26/01/1898	08/04/1898	-
Shaw, Paul	SO	A	18/09/1988	05/02/1989	Manly (Australia)
Shaw, Robert	F		02/09/1899	22/10/1904	Tudhoe RU
Shaw, Tom	F		08/04/1899	23/01/1904	-
Sheffield, Bill	F		31/03/1975	14/12/1980	Rochdale Hornets
Sheldon, Roland	F		25/11/1911	03/01/1914	Wardley Lane (Swinton)
Sherratt, Ian	F		03/09/1989	27/10/1991	Oldham
Shields, Edwin	F		30/08/1919	01/01/1920	Runcorn
Shipway, Mark	F	A	22/02/2004	16/09/2005	Manly (Australia)
Shore, Hugh	F		16/09/1899	10/09/1904	-
Shore, Jack	FB		10/01/1903	10/01/1903	Salford St Bartholomew's
Shorrocks, Jake	HB		07/04/2018	21/07/2018	Wigan (loan)
Shovelton, Jim	F		25/12/1930	25/12/1930	Tyldesley RU
Shuker, Ray	SO		13/04/1963	26/09/1966	Blackbrook (St Helens)
Shuttleworth, Paul	SO		18/04/1982	03/02/1985	Batley Boys
Sibbit, Ian	F		11/02/2005	05/09/2010	Warrington
Sidlow, Adam	F		04/04/2008	08/09/2012	Widnes
Simcox, Dennis	F		10/10/1959	01/09/1962	Langworthy Juniors (Salford)
Simpkins, Daniel	F	W	27/08/1921	01/03/1922	Llanelli RU
Sims, Geoff	T		20/08/1966	15/09/1967	Oldham
Sini, Fata	W	SM	05/11/1995	12/09/1997	Marist St Joseph RU (Samoa)
Sio, Ken	W	A	01/02/2019	-	Newcastle Knights (Australia)
Slamin, Kevin	HB	W	14/12/1946	22/02/1947	Penarth RU

Salford RL Players – Dates

Name	Pos	Brn	Debut	Last match	Previous team
Sligar, Noel	F	A	07/01/1928	07/01/1928	Sydney University (Australia)
Smart, Geoff	H		13/04/1963	29/10/1966	Widnes
Smethurst, Peter	F		08/09/1967	26/12/1970	Oldham
Smith, Andy	W		02/07/2005	14/08/2005	Bradford Bulls (loan)
Smith, Dan	FB	W	04/09/1897	28/04/1904	Swansea RU
Smith, Derek	F		25/10/1958	17/10/1959	Widnes
Smith, Ernie	W		08/04/1898	17/11/1900	-
Smith, Fred	FB		23/08/1952	13/02/1960	Rylands Recreation (Warrington)
Smith, Hudson	F	A	13/02/1999	10/09/1999	Balmain (Australia)
Smith, James	F	A	27/02/2000	17/09/2000	South Sydney (Australia)
Smith, Jeremy	SO	NZ	14/02/2009	05/09/2010	South Sydney (Australia)
Smith, JH	F	A	13/10/1928	13/10/1928	Cairns (Australia)
Smith, Matty	HB		07/02/2010	29/06/2012	St Helens
Smith, Paul	F		24/04/1994	24/04/1994	Salford Academy
Smith, Richard	W		01/06/1997	08/06/1997	Halifax
Smith, Ron	F		19/04/1979	14/09/1986	Wigan St Patrick's
Smith, TH 'Harry'	HB		27/08/1921	21/03/1925	Teignmouth RU
Smith, Tim	SH	A	16/02/2014	30/05/2014	Wakefield Trinity
Smith, Tom	HB		04/02/1933	15/09/1945	Warrington Rangers
Snell, David	F		27/02/1970	30/03/1970	Langworthy Juniors (Salford)
Sneyd, Marc (1)	HB		04/06/2010	06/09/2013	Salford Academy
Sneyd, Marc (2)	SH		11/02/2022	-	Hull
Snipe, Tom	C		29/09/1945	15/04/1946	Oldham RU
Southern, Paul	F		24/04/1994	17/08/2002	Salford Academy
Southward, Ferguson 'Fergie'	C		22/01/1921	08/04/1933	Brookland Rovers (Maryport)
Southward, Joe	T		16/11/1963	19/08/1969	Workington RU
Sparks, Brian	F	W	03/10/1964	30/10/1965	Halifax
Spencer, Joe	F		07/01/1905	03/04/1909	Flixton
Spencer, Jack	F		21/08/2009	26/04/2011	Salford Academy
Spencer-Tonks, Daniel	F		03/09/2022	03/09/2022	Cheltenham Tigers RU

Above left: Archie Sutherland first played for Cavendish in 1876. It was due to his influence as honorary secretary that the club changed its name to Salford in 1879.

Above right: Former Sale three-quarter Hugh Williamson captained Salford for three seasons from 1881-82 and was its first player accorded representative honours when selected for Cheshire against Yorkshire in 1882.

Above: 1881-82. Wearing the original livery of red, amber and black hoops that were replaced by the more familiar all-red jersey in 1883. Back: WH Allen (secretary), S Williams, H Eagles, WH Buckley, J Clayton, T Heald, G Hulme. Middle: R Bullock, A Ottiwell, E Tomlinson, M McNally, T Thornley, J Jackson (vice-president, seated separate on right). Front: F Butterworth, A Sutton, H Williamson, RG Mackay, T Carrington.

Above: 1887-88. Back: LJ Reynolds (treasurer), A Ottiwell, D Wellwood (chairman), J Roberts, J Higson (secretary), J McVittie, J Horricks (vice-president). Middle: J Shaw, J Anderton, H Eagles, T Kent, G Jackson, AE Ogden. Front: J Newton, H Clegg, S Williams, W Manwaring, H Cook.

Above left: James Jackson became the first of 17 Salford players to represent Lancashire during the club's rugby union era. The Welsh-born forward played against Durham in January 1886 having previously cried off through illness the previous November for the meeting with Yorkshire.

Above right: Salford provided four players for the first ever British rugby tour which visited Australia and New Zealand during 1888. They were Tom Kent (1), Sam Williams (2), Jack Anderton (3) and Harry Eagles (4)

Above: 1888-89. Back: J Horricks (vice-president), J Higson (secretary), J Anderton, T Smith, J Roberts, J McVittie, S Williams, A Smith, D Wellwood (chairman), S Whiteley (treasurer). Middle: B Walmsley, E Austin, W Manwaring, J Mallinson, A Barrett, T King, A Foster. Front: J Newton, H Clegg, H Eagles, H Cook, J Shaw.

Above: 1890-91. Back: H Clegg, T Kent, J Birch, J McVittie, J Tune, F Knowles, J Shaw, S Whiteley (treasurer). Middle: J Horricks, (vice-president), A Barrett, J Roberts, F Miles, D Wellwood (chairman), H Eagles, E Barrett, T King, J Higson (secretary). Front: G Tonge, S Walch

Above: 1896-97. Salford's first season in the Northern Union. Back: F Fields, H Davies, G Heath, JJ Jones, D Fisher, WH Barrington, G Fisher, W Brown. Middle: G Coleman, S Hanson, W Crocker, W Manwaring, W Llewellyn, B Moss. Front: A Pearson, I Grey, B Griffiths, G Fawcett.

Above left: Full-back Billy Manwaring was the Salford captain in 1895-96 (the final season as a rugby union club) and in its inaugural 1896-97 campaign under the auspices of the Northern Union.

Above right: Flying wingman Frank Miles succeeded Manwaring as captain in 1897-98. He had previously held that position in 1892-93 when Salford won the Lancashire Club Championship, the only team honour secured prior to joining the Northern Union.

Above: 1901-02. An early season photograph prior to moving from New Barnes to The Willows in December 1901. Back: R Shore, P Tunney, J Williams, J Rhapps, B Walmsley (director), J Worthington, G Heath, R Shaw, H Dyson, H Buckler. Front: D Smith, R Thomas, DJ Davies, E Mather (chairman), T Williams, B Griffiths, H Price, W Brown.

Above: 1901-02. Salford entertain Batley (in the white jerseys) on 2nd November at New Barnes, its home since 1878-79. The following month Salford moved into The Willows. Taken from the Mitchell and Kenyon archive.

Above: 1902-03. Salford captain Jimmy Lomas (right) looks on as Halifax's Archie Rigg tosses the coin ahead of the 1903 Challenge Cup final at Headingley. Salford appeared in three other Challenge Cup finals (1900, 1902 and 1906) during this period but lost all four.

Above: 1904-05. Back: E Mather (chairman), J Graham, J Williams, J Rhapps, D Rees, P Tunney, R Shaw, S Bebbington, G Cook (trainer). Middle: G Heath (kneeling), W Thomas, J Lomas, A Bedford, B Parry, W Brown, A Norris, I Lewis (kneeling). Front: R Richards, D Preston, E Harter, W Lambert.

Above: 1910–11. Back: T Coates senior, A Ellis (director). Third row (standing): G Bracegirdle (trainer), S Morton, G Thom, E Curzon, H Dawson (director), S Warwick, C Rees, F Foster, F Mattinson (director). Second row (seated): E Morton, W Thomas, J Lomas, F Hampson (chairman), B Mesley, E Harrison. Front: E May, J Cook.

Above: 1913-14. The Northern Union Championship was the first trophy success since leaving Rugby Union in 1896. The players (in kit) are, third row (standing): H Goldsmith, C Rees, G Currie, EJ Thomas, B Ritchie, E Woods, J Bevon, G Thom. Second row (seated): W Clegg, G Callender, W Thomas, A Loveluck, B Mesley, H Launce. Front: WD John, E May.

Above left: Centre Willie Thomas arrived from Aberavon in 1903 and played for Salford for over 18 years, eleven as captain, the longest period as skipper in the club's history. A future chairman of the club, he made 442 'official' appearances plus a further 57 'friendly' matches during World War One.

Above right: Brilliant Welsh half-back Dai John, signed from Penygraig in 1905, was only 5 feet, one inch (1.55m) in height but withstood the rigours of Northern Union for over 17 years, taking part in the finals of the Challenge Cup (1906) and Championship (1914).

Above: 1926-27. Back: E Russell (baggage man), JW Hammond (director), T Coates (assistant trainer), F Mann, EC Haines, W Price, F Butterworth, J Muir, W Taylor (trainer) S Boyd. Middle: L Williams, C Peacock, J Priestley (chairman), J Gore, F Southward, S Garland, unidentified baggage man (standing). Front: R Meek, WJ Davies, T Mannion.

Salford RL Players – Dates

Name	Pos	Brn	Debut	Last match	Previous team
Spruce, Joe	W		01/02/1936	18/04/1938	Pendlebury Juniors
Stacey, Steve	W	A	02/09/1984	10/10/1984	Brisbane Easts (Australia)
Stamper, Joe	F		03/10/1925	29/01/1927	Brookland Rovers (Maryport)
Stapleton, Craig	F	A	03/02/2008	11/09/2009	Cronulla (Australia)
Staveley, Ernest	HB		22/10/1910	28/10/1911	Wardley Lane (Swinton)
Stazicker, Ged	F		01/09/1991	08/01/1994	Wigan
Stead, Frank	FB		05/11/1972	06/10/1982	Widnes RU
Steeden, Phillip	F		21/09/1935	21/09/1935	local ARL
Stephenson, David (1)	C		23/01/1979	29/01/1982	Fylde RU
Stephenson, David (2)			13/03/1991	13/03/1991	Leigh
Stevens, Jack	HB		03/09/2022	03/09/2022	Salford Academy
Stevens, Warren	F		06/05/2001	16/09/2001	Warrington (loan)
Stewart, Anthony	W		22/02/2004	29/05/2006	St Helens
Stewart, James	C		17/11/1920	29/03/1921	Old Salfordians RU
Stirrup, Frank	SO		25/12/1947	11/11/1950	Leigh
Stockley, Trevor	C		08/11/1981	24/04/1983	Wigan
Stoddart, Ray	F		10/12/1955	24/08/1957	Risehow and Gillhead (Maryport)
Storey, Tony	F		16/08/1958	16/03/1959	Warrington
Stott, Roy	F		21/08/1957	01/01/1961	Oldham district ARL
Streets, Geoffrey	W		11/02/1950	11/02/1950	Bradford RU
Stringer, Mitchell	F		18/03/2005	17/04/2006	London Broncos
Subritzky, Peter	F	NZ	03/11/1991	09/02/1992	Huddersfield
Such, William	C		01/10/1904	01/10/1904	Egerton (Salford)
Sulway, Ivor	C	W	04/03/1922	11/03/1922	Aberavon RU
Summerville, Wilf	HB		26/04/1926	12/02/1927	Swinton
Sumner, Phil	F		23/04/1995	23/04/1995	Warrington (loan)
Sutcliffe, James	H		28/08/1926	30/01/1928	Sandfield (Rochdale)
Svabic, Simon	SO		10/07/1998	06/08/2000	Oldham
Swain, Luke	F	A	14/02/2009	05/09/2010	Gold Coast Titans (Australia)
Swift, Phil	W		10/04/1994	24/04/1994	Saddleworth Rangers
Swindells, Charlie	F		10/01/1903	01/09/1906	Adelphi Lads Club (Salford)

Salford RL Players – Dates

Name	Pos	Brn	Debut	Last match	Previous team
Swithenbank, Jimmy	C		22/01/1921	10/12/1921	Healey Street Adults (Oldham)
Sykes, Edward	F		09/01/1915	25/02/1922	Weaste (Salford)
Tabern, Walt	H		22/03/1966	22/03/1966	Workington Town
Talau, Willie	C	SM	14/02/2009	05/09/2010	St Helens
Tamati, Kevin	F	NZ	16/09/1990	01/04/1990	Warrington
Tasi, Lama (1)	F	NZ	16/02/2014	27/09/2015	Brisbane Broncos (Australia)
Tasi, Lama (2)			11/02/2017	14/09/2018	St Helens
Tassell, Kris	C	A	27/02/2000	09/09/2001	North Queensland (Australia)
Tauro, Chris	F	A	24/10/1993	17/04/1994	Manly (Australia)
Taylor, A	F		02/04/1923	07/04/1923	-
Taylor, Elijah	F	NZ	26/03/2021	17/09/2022	Wests Tigers (Australia)
Taylor, John (1)	HB		02/02/1973	24/01/1975	Wigan Colts
Taylor, John (2)			19/02/1984	04/09/1985	Widnes
Taylor, Mark	HB		07/03/1964	30/10/1971	Army RU
Taylor, Peter	W		05/10/1946	08/03/1947	Rylands Recreation (Warrington)
Taylor, R	F		10/09/1927	27/10/1928	Oldham district ARL
Taylor, Scott	F		07/02/2015	20/09/2015	Wigan (loan)
Thom, George	F		08/02/1908	25/12/1913	Broughton Rangers
Thomas, Dai	W	W	03/09/1910	30/11/1910	Hull Kingston Rovers
Thomas, Elvet	W	W	29/08/1931	07/04/1934	Mountain Ash RU
Thomas, Evan J	F	W	02/09/1905	05/04/1915	Pill Harriers RU (Newport)
Thomas, Harold	F	W	09/10/1937	22/12/1945	Neath RU
Thomas, Howard	F	W	03/04/1981	08/11/1981	London Welsh RU
Thomas, Jim	F		09/12/1899	29/09/1900	Swinton
Thomas, Johnnie	HB	W	01/01/1921	12/03/1921	Mountain Ash RU
Thomas, R 'Bob'	F		20/01/1915	01/02/1919	-
Thomas, Radley (1)	C		15/01/1898	15/01/1898	West Hartlepool RU
Thomas, Radley (2)			03/09/1898	21/09/1901	Castleford

Salford RL Players – Dates

Name	Pos	Brn	Debut	Last match	Previous team
Thomas, Willie	C	W	05/09/1903	31/12/1921	Aberavon RU
Thomas, -	W		11/12/1897	11/12/1897	-
Thompson, AJ 'Jack'	FB		26/02/1910	26/02/1910	Mandelberg's (Salford)
Thompson, Bobby	FB	A	13/02/1999	10/09/1999	Penrith (Australia)
Thornburrow, TS	FB		19/01/1924	26/02/1924	Oldham RU
Thornley, Andy	F		13/03/2009	13/03/2009	Wigan (loan)
Thornley, Iain	C		09/08/2015	20/09/2015	Wigan (loan)
Thurlow, Stephen	F		29/01/1921	09/04/1921	Aspatria Hornets
Todd, Peter	C		13/10/1945	04/11/1950	Huddersfield College Old Boys RU
Todd, William	F		29/01/1955	10/12/1955	Widnes
Tomkins, Logan (1)	H		11/04/2014	12/10/2014	Wigan (loan)
Tomkins, Logan (2)			05/06/2015	12/10/2019	Wigan
Treacy, Darren	F	A	10/02/2002	22/09/2002	St George-Illawarra (Australia)
Tunks, Peter	F	A	12/09/1990	18/11/1990	Penrith (Australia)
Tunney, Pat	F	IR	30/10/1897	02/01/1905	Tudhoe RU
Turgut, Jansin	F		14/09/2018	07/04/2019	Hull
Turnbull, Sam	F		17/08/1973	28/04/1985	Salford Colts
Turner, Horace	C	W	02/02/1935	05/12/1936	Pontypool RU
Turner, Joe	W		05/09/1936	29/01/1938	Leigh St Joseph
Turner, Jordan	F		16/09/2006	17/07/2009	Salford Academy
Twist, David	W		25/09/1983	14/10/1984	Salford Colts
Tyrer, Gary	FB		17/04/1994	26/03/1995	Orrell RU
Tyrer, Steve	W		07/02/2010	05/09/2010	St Helens (loan)
Tyson, George	F		21/04/2013	21/04/2013	Salford Academy
Varney, John	W		30/01/1915	30/01/1915	Swinton
Varty, John	C		24/11/1900	08/03/1902	Aspatria
Vatuvei, Manu	W	NZ	30/07/2017	21/09/2017	NZ Warriors (New Zealand)
Veivers, Josh	T		10/03/2012	08/09/2012	Wakefield Trinity
Viane, Gray	W	NZ	30/03/2007	29/07/2007	Castleford
Vibart, Spencer	F		10/04/1939	25/08/1945	Camborne RU
Vidot, Daniel	W	A	07/05/2016	25/09/2016	Brisbane Broncos (Australia)
Vipond, Harry*	F		05/09/1896	13/02/1897	Kendal Hornets
Vuniyayawa, King	F	FJ	11/02/2022	-	Leeds
Wadeson, -	F		25/12/1940	25/12/1940	Wigan district ARL (guest)

Salford RL Players – Dates

Name	Pos	Brn	Debut	Last match	Previous team
Wainwright, Mike (1)	F		13/02/2000	22/09/2002	Warrington
Wainwright, Mike (2)			21/07/2007	03/08/2007	Warrington
Waite, Billy	HB		05/10/1912	26/12/1922	Swinley Hornets (Wigan)
Wakefield, Mark	HB	A	07/09/1986	01/03/1987	Cronulla (Australia)
Walch, Sam*	HB		05/09/1896	26/09/1896	Swinton
Walker, A	HB		24/02/1900	24/02/1900	Seedley Hornets (Salford)
Walker, Adam	F		17/03/2019	12/10/2019	Wakefield Trinity
Walker, James	W		21/01/1933	18/03/1933	-
Walker, Peter	H		29/09/1972	15/08/1975	Bradford Northern
Walker, Ron	W		18/08/1956	10/09/1960	Gus Risman's summer school
Wallwork, W	W		31/10/1906	06/04/1908	Lancashire Dynamo (Manchester)
Walne, Adam	F		20/08/2012	15/09/2017	Salford Academy
Walne, Jordan	F		01/04/2013	21/09/2017	Salford Academy
Walsh, David	SO		06/04/1983	17/04/1983	Huddersfield (loan)
Walsh, Joe	H		22/11/1987	01/04/1991	Wigan St Patrick's
Walsh, Lawrence	C		04/10/1902	13/10/1902	Altrincham
Walton, Colin	W		02/01/1905	26/04/1905	Weaste (Salford)
Walton, Jason (1)	C		07/03/2008	15/08/2009	Salford Academy
Walton, Jason (2)			16/02/2014	14/06/2015	Batley
Wanklyn, Bullig	HB		18/01/1919	23/04/1921	Army RU
Ward, Johnny	F		30/01/1970	23/04/1973	Castleford
Ward, Phil	C		17/12/1971	15/09/1974	Loughborough Colleges RU
Warhurst, Glen	FB		13/04/1988	13/04/1988	Oldham St Annes
Waring, Phil	SH		25/08/1997	22/08/1999	Widnes
Warren, Wayne	SH		24/10/1976	07/11/1978	Salford Colts
Warwick, Silas	F		24/12/1904	09/09/1911	Broughton Rangers
Watkins, David	C	W	20/10/1967	01/04/1979	Newport RU
Watkins, Kallum	F		18/09/2020	-	Toronto Wolfpack (Canada)
Watkins, WE 'Billy'	SH	W	29/08/1931	22/12/1945	Cross Keys RU

Salford RL Players – Dates

Name	Pos	Brn	Debut	Last match	Previous team
Watson, Ian (1)	SH		15/02/1995	25/08/1997	Eccles
Watson, Ian (2)			10/02/2002	22/09/2002	Widnes
Watson, Robert	H		06/10/1923	30/10/1926	Swinton Park
Waugh, Richard	FB		25/11/1905	25/11/1905	Maryport
Webber, Jason	C	A	13/02/2000	17/09/2000	Balmain (Aus)
Webster, Richard	F	W	13/11/1993	23/06/1996	Swansea RU
Welham, Kris	C		16/02/2017	02/11/2020	Bradford Bulls
Wells, Jack	F		26/03/2021	14/04/2022	Wigan
Whalley, Joe	F		21/04/1952	27/11/1954	Westleigh Recreation (Leigh)
Wharton, Alan	W		20/09/1947	15/04/1950	Exeter RU
White, Clarence 'Lofty'	FB	W	14/11/1931	13/04/1936	Cross Keys RU
White, Josh	SH	A	14/02/1998	27/09/1998	London Broncos
White, Paul	W		03/02/2008	29/03/2009	Wakefield Trinity
White, Ted	F		05/03/1960	16/04/1960	Warrington
White, Tom	HB	W	10/10/1903	12/11/1904	Llanelli RU
Whitehead, Harold	C		10/02/1923	10/02/1923	Swinton
Whitehead, JF	F		19/11/1927	08/03/1930	Saddleworth RU
Whitehead, Stuart	F		17/09/1966	21/10/1972	Oldham
Whiteley, Chris	F		31/08/1986	01/04/1991	Wigan St Patrick's
Whitfield, Colin	C		23/01/1979	25/10/1981	Widnes Tigers
Whitney, Harold 'George'	F	W	18/01/1919	01/11/1924	Naval Harlequins RU (Plymouth)
Whittle, Fred	HB		29/10/1921	26/04/1926	Wigan district NU
Wiggins, Richard	H		02/02/1924	09/02/1924	Seedley Rangers (Salford)
Wild, Alfred	C		21/09/1912	31/10/1914	Broughton Rangers
Wild, Stephen	F		13/02/2011	06/09/2013	Huddersfield
Wilkinson, W 'Bill'	F		05/04/1913	28/03/1925	Swinley Hornets (Wigan)
Williams, Connor	C		03/06/2016	03/06/2016	Salford Academy
Williams, Daley	W		24/06/2006	02/05/2008	Keighley
Williams, Danny	W		17/07/2011	30/05/2014	Newcastle RU
Williams, Jack	F	W	04/03/1897	17/11/1906	Swansea RU
Williams, Jack	W		01/03/1930	01/04/1931	Warrington
Williams, Jason	T	NZ	04/11/1994	22/01/1995	Sydney Bulldogs (Australia)
Williams, John	F		16/09/1922	26/12/1925	Broughton Rangers

Salford RL Players – Dates

Name	Pos	Brn	Debut	Last match	Previous team
Williams, Llewellyn	FB	W	20/11/1926	05/04/1930	Crumlin RU
Williams, Owen	C	W	02/02/1946	29/01/1949	Heol-y-Cyw RU (Bridgend)
Williams, Peter	C		23/03/1988	24/04/1994	Orrell RU
Williams, Rhys (1)	T	W	01/02/2013	24/02/2013	Warrington (loan)
Williams, Rhys (2)			31/01/2020	-	London Broncos
Williams, Stewart	F		06/12/1977	23/12/1984	Salford Colts
Williams, Syd	W	W	14/10/1939	20/09/1952	Aberavon RU
Williams, Tom	C	W	04/09/1897	18/10/1902	Llwynypia RU
Williams, WA 'Billy'	F	W	15/10/1927	01/10/1938	Crumlin RU
Wilshere, John	T	PN	12/02/2006	11/09/2009	Leigh
Wilson, Frank	C	W	01/04/1979	20/04/1981	Warrington
Wilson, George	W	S	29/01/1955	18/04/1955	Workington Town
Wilson, Scott	FB	A	01/03/1995	12/03/1995	Canterbury (Australia)
Wilson, Terry	F		30/03/1963	18/11/1966	St Helens
Wiltshire, Roy	W		15/01/1986	13/04/1988	Rochdale Hornets
Winslade, Charlie	F	W	07/10/1967	17/10/1967	Leigh
Winstanley, Jack	W		17/05/1919	03/04/1920	Swinton
Winstanley, John	HB		01/01/1923	06/01/1923	Wardley (Swinton)
Wood, John	F		21/08/1983	08/01/1984	Fulham
Wood, Josh	H		22/05/2015	11/05/2019	Salford Academy
Wood, Mike	H		24/03/1977	27/03/1977	Salford Colts
Wood, Sam	W		16/01/1915	01/02/1919	local NU
Woodhead, Herbert 'Harry'	F		05/09/1896	17/03/1900	Goole RU
Woodhead, Lawrence	C		04/02/1922	30/12/1922	Halifax Old Boys RU
Woods, Ernie	F		10/01/1914	03/01/1925	Weaste (Salford)
Worrall, Mick	F		18/10/1987	29/03/1992	Oldham
Worrall, Tony	F		01/04/1988	14/03/1989	Warrington
Worthington, Joe	F		01/09/1900	01/01/1902	Tyldesley
Wright, Albert	FB		20/09/1924	27/09/1924	Warrington
Wright, Shane	F	A	11/02/2022	-	North Queensland (Australia)
Wynne, Steve	W		20/02/1994	20/02/1994	Widnes
Yates, Luke	F	A	31/01/2020	06/11/2020	London Broncos
Yates, Malcolm	F		19/11/1980	28/08/1983	Leigh
Young, David	F	W	01/09/1991	21/04/1996	Leeds
AN Other	F		08/04/1898	08/04/1898	-
AN Other	F		26/09/1925	26/09/1925	-

Salford RL Players – Dates

Name	Pos	Brn	Debut	Last match	Previous team
AN Other	SH		21/12/1940	21/12/1940	-
AN Other	F		24/11/1945	24/11/1945	-
AN Other	FB		05/01/1946	05/01/1946	-
AN Other	C		25/01/1947	25/01/1947	-
AN Other	W		11/11/1950	25/11/1950	-
AN Other (also 'Gray')	H		13/04/1955	16/04/1955	-
AN Other	W		18/02/1956	25/02/1956	-
AN Other	F		14/04/1956	14/04/1956	-
AN Other	F		16/01/1960	16/01/1960	-
AN Other	FB		29/10/1960	29/10/1960	-
AN Other	W		04/05/1963	04/05/1963	-
AN Other	FB		18/05/1963	18/05/1963	-
AN Other	W		18/10/1968	18/10/1968	-
AN Other	F		20/04/1980	20/04/1980	-
'Davies'	C		29/10/1921	29/10/1921	Yorkshire RU player
'Gallagher'	F		26/09/1966	26/09/1966	-
'Jackson'	C		02/04/1946	02/04/1946	-
'McDonald'	F	S	25/12/1954	25/12/1954	Scottish RU player
'Newman' (also 'Pierce')	SO		13/10/1945	13/10/1945	Royal Navy RU
'Newman'	W		16/04/1954	16/04/1954	-
'Parr'	F		28/12/1954	01/01/1955	-
'SO Else'	C		18/05/1963	18/05/1963	-

*Also played for Salford under Rugby Union prior to 1896 breakaway

Salford RL Players – Statistics

	App	Sub	Tot	Tries	Goals	D-gls	Pts	Representative
Ackerman, Rob	6	7	13	0	0	0	0	W2
Ackers, Andy	44	10	54	7	0	0	28	E1+1
Adams, Sid	31	0	31	10	0	0	30	
Adamson, Dave	17	0	17	3	0	0	9	
Adamson, Luke	101	44	145	20	1	0	82	
Adamson, Toby	0	1	1	0	0	0	0	
Addy, Danny	11	14	25	0	0	0	0	S1
Ainsworth, Arthur	3	0	3	0	0	0	0	
Aitchison, Alex	2	0	2	0	0	0	0	
Akauola, Sitaleki	12	7	19	2	0	0	8	
Alder, Frank	150	0	150	14	0	0	42	
Aldred, James	2	0	2	2	1	0	8	
Alexander, Neil	0	1	1	0	0	0	0	
Algie, David	1	0	1	0	0	0	0	
Alker, Malcolm	356	4	360	75	0	1	301	E2+1
Allen, Hugh	8	0	8	4	0	0	12	
Allmark, Tommy	4	0	4	1	0	0	3	
Alstead, Peter	1	0	1	0	0	0	0	
Ambler, Luke	0	1	1	1	0	0	4	
Anderson, Vinnie	33	4	37	14	0	0	56	
Anderson, W 'Billie'	1	0	1	0	0	0	0	
Anderton, Willie	17	0	17	0	0	0	0	
Angell, Simon	2	3	5	0	0	0	0	
Argent, Joe	20	2	22	4	0	0	12	
Armitt, Charlie	1	0	1	0	0	0	0	
Arnold, Danny	54	14	68	23	0	0	92	S3
Ashall, Bill	37	2	39	1	0	0	3	
Ashall-Bott, Olly	3	0	3	1	0	0	4	
Ashbridge, Joe	1	0	1	0	0	0	0	
Ashcroft, Kevin	55	5	60	4	0	4	16	
Ashurst, Matty	67	8	75	12	0	0	48	
Aspey, Connor	0	2	2	0	0	0	0	
Aspey, Mal	20	3	23	3	0	0	9	
Aspinall, George	173	0	173	79	0	0	237	
Atkin, Chris	28	23	51	11	4	1	53	
Austin, Greg (1)	47	1	48	25	24	1	149	
Austin, Greg (2)	3	0	3	0	0	0	0	
Ayles, Eric	71	0	71	4	0	0	12	
Ayres, Warren	2	10	12	1	2	0	8	
Bailey, Gary	12	0	12	0	0	0	0	
Bailey, TJ 'Tommy'	8	0	8	1	0	0	3	
Baines, Albert	113	0	113	48	0	0	144	
Baker, George	14	0	14	1	0	0	3	
Baker, Neil	19	0	19	11	11	7	73	
Baldwin, Simon	57	31	88	18	0	0	72	
Ballard, Andy	13	0	13	11	63	0	170	
Bamford, Darren	2	2	4	1	0	0	4	

Salford RL Players – Statistics

	App	Sub	Tot	Tries	Goals	D-gls	Pts	Representative
Banks, Billy	50	0	50	4	5	0	22	
Banner, Peter	171	9	180	24	1	0	74	W6, L2
Bannister, Steve	11	14	25	6	8	0	40	
Bardsley, Barrie	1	0	1	0	0	0	0	
Barker, R	8	0	8	2	0	0	6	
Barlow, Albert	4	0	4	0	0	0	0	
Barnes, T	1	0	1	0	0	0	0	
Barnes, W 'Billy'	1	0	1	0	0	0	0	
Barnett, Richie	7	0	7	4	0	0	16	
Baron, Matt	6	0	6	1	1	0	5	
Barratt, Mark	3	1	4	0	0	0	0	
Barrington, WH*	6	0	6	0	0	0	0	
Barry, Dave	17	0	17	1	0	0	3	
Barton, Roger	2	0	2	0	0	0	0	
Barton, Danny	1	2	3	0	0	0	0	
Battersby, William	9	0	9	1	0	0	3	
Battese, Brian	16	1	17	4	0	0	16	
Baxter, Neil	1	0	1	0	0	0	0	
Baynes, Neil	116	28	144	14	0	0	56	
Beaver, Bill	17	0	17	3	0	0	9	
Bebbington, Sam	20	0	20	0	0	0	0	
Beckett, Adrian	4	5	9	1	1	0	5	
Bedford, Alf	43	0	43	15	0	0	45	
Bell, Robert MH	21	0	21	8	0	0	24	
Bell, Thomas	6	0	6	0	0	0	0	DN1
Bell, TG 'Tom'	38	0	38	17	0	0	51	C1
Belshaw, Billy	1	0	1	3	4	0	17	
Bennett, Jack	3	0	3	1	0	0	3	
Bennett, Tommy	19	0	19	0	1	0	2	
Bennion, Gavin	1	1	2	0	0	0		W1+2
Bentley, Keith	88	13	101	28	0	1	113	
Benyon, W	3	0	3	1	0	0	3	
Berne, Mick	4	2	6	2	0	0	8	
Berthezene, David	9	1	10	0	0	0	0	
Bettinson, Les	317	2	319	75	10	0	245	C7
Betts, Darren	0	3	3	0	0	0	0	
Bevan, -	1	0	1	0	0	0	0	
Bevan, David William	20	0	20	4	11	0	34	
Bevan, William David	1	0	1	0	0	0	0	
Beverley, Cliff	86	1	87	53	0	0	212	
Bevon, Jack	112	0	112	2	0	0	6	
Bibby, Jake	75	3	78	36	0	0	144	
Birkett, Geoffrey	2	0	2	0	0	0	0	
Birkett, Martin	113	16	129	35	125	0	390	C2
Birkin, Frank	61	0	61	5	0	0	15	
Blacker, Brian	3	1	4	2	0	0	8	
Blackwood, Bob	6	9	15	1	0	0	3	

Salford RL Players – Statistics

	App	Sub	Tot	Tries	Goals	D-gls	Pts	Representative
Blakeley, Steve (1)	169	7	176	62	573	8	1402	E1+2
Blakeley, Steve (2)	64	23	87	15	207	1	475	
Blan, Jack	7	0	7	0	0	0	0	
Blease, Ian	216	36	252	49	0	0	196	L1
Bloor Darren (1)	123	19	142	46	0	4	188	
Bloor Darren (2)	0	1	1	0	0	0	0	
Boardman, Frank	167	0	167	1	0	0	3	
Bone, Ernie	44	0	44	24	0	0	72	
Boon, Wilf	23	0	23	3	0	0	9	
Booth, James	3	0	3	0	0	0	0	
Borgese, Chris	1	5	6	2	0	0	8	
Bott, Charlie	159	1	160	12	1	0	38	
Bourouh, Amir	3	4	7	0	0	0	0	
Bowden, Colin	1	0	1	0	0	0	0	
Bowen, Trevor	7	0	7	1	0	0	3	
Bowker, Radney	4	2	6	3	0	0	12	
Bowker, Vernon	6	0	6	1	0	0	3	
Bowley, JH	8	0	8	1	0	0	3	
Boyd, Denis	37	2	39	0	0	1	1	
Boyd, Syd	299	0	299	56	0	0	168	
Boyle, Ryan	60	14	74	3	0	0	12	IR2
Bradbourne, Terry	1	0	1	0	0	0	0	
Bradbury, David	26	11	37	7	0	0	28	IR+1
Bradbury, Joe	299	0	299	15	0	0	45	
Bradshaw, Arthur	54	30	84	18	0	0	72	
Bradshaw, Tommy	1	0	1	0	0	0	0	
Brady, Billy	20	0	20	3	0	0	9	
Bragger, Ian	28	0	28	20	0	0	80	
Braithwaite, Edwin 'Ted'*	10	0	10	0	0	0	0	
Breen, Aiden	67	8	75	10	0	0	30	
Brennan, Jackie	317	12	329	70	3	0	216	
Brennan, Tony	1	0	1	0	0	0	0	
Brereton, Peter	31	0	31	0	1	0	2	
Bridges, Selwyn	2	0	2	0	0	0	0	
Brierley, Ryan	25	1	26	12	6	0	60	S1
Briggs, Carl	8	7	15	3	0	1	13	
Brining, Kriss	2	23	25	5	0	0	20	
Broadbent, Gary	135	2	137	25	0	0	100	
Brockbank, Chris	36	0	36	6	1	0	20	
Brocklehurst, Andrew	49	29	78	10	0	0	40	
Brogden, Stan (senior)	20	0	20	3	1	0	11	
Brogden, Stan (junior)	1	0	1	0	0	0	0	
Brokenshire, Mark	4	2	6	0	0	0	0	
Brooke-Cowden, Mark	18	2	20	2	0	0	8	
Brookfield, Keri	3	0	3	0	0	0	0	
Brophy, Tom	13	1	14	2	1	0	8	
Broughton, Jodie	99	0	99	60	0	0	240	

Salford RL Players – Statistics

	App	Sub	Tot	Tries	Goals	D-gls	Pts	Representative
Brown, Darren	53	9	62	12	12	0	72	
Brown, Dennis	45	4	49	8	0	0	24	
Brown, George	2	0	2	0	0	0	0	
Brown, Jack	218	0	218	21	12	0	87	L1
Brown, John	3	0	3	0	0	0	0	
Brown, Kevin	22	0	22	6	1	0	26	
Brown, Peter	14	2	16	1	17	0	38	
Brown, R	1	0	1	0	0	0	0	
Brown, R 'Bob'	251	0	251	136	0	0	408	L9
Brown, R 'Dick'	6	0	6	1	0	0	3	
Brown, Shaun	44	12	56	4	26	5	73	
Brown, Walter	1	0	1	0	0	0	0	
Brown, W 'Billy'*	276	0	276	13	32	0	103	
Brownbill, Paul	7	2	9	0	0	0	0	
Bruen, Bob	2	0	2	0	0	0	0	
Brunning, Tony	9	1	10	3	0	0	9	
Brunt, Ken	36	1	37	9	2	0	31	
Bryant, Bill	2	0	2	0	0	0	0	
Buckler, Arthur	189	0	189	15	0	0	45	W1, L1
Buckler, Herbert	155	0	155	12	3	0	42	ON2, L5
Buckler, William	1	0	1	0	0	0	0	
Bullough, David	20	7	27	1	0	0	4	
Burdell, Bob	115	0	115	6	1	0	20	L3
Burgess, Andy	123	61	184	28	5	0	122	IR3+1
Burgess, Bill	44	0	44	33	0	0	99	GB1, E2, L1
Burgess, Ivan	2	0	2	0	0	0	0	
Burgess, Jimmy	218	0	218	47	89	0	319	
Burgess, Joe	29	0	29	19	0	0	76	
Burgess, Luke (1)	6	2	8	0	0	0	0	
Burgess, Luke (2)	6	9	15	0	1	0	2	
Burke, Greg	37	47	84	4	0	0	16	
Burness, James	2	0	2	0	0	0	0	
Burns, Martin	2	0	2	1	0	0	3	
Burrell, Cyril	7	0	7	3	0	0	9	
Burrows, Robert	1	0	1	0	0	0	0	
Burt, Howard	42	0	42	4	1	0	14	
Butcher, Tom	2	0	2	0	0	0	0	
Butler, John	133	2	135	50	0	0	150	L4
Butterworth, Frank	110	0	110	2	0	0	6	
Byrne, Ged	164	5	169	84	0	0	311	
Byrne, John	7	0	7	1	0	0	3	
Cahill, -	2	0	2	0	0	0	0	
Caine, Joel	24	0	24	8	13	0	58	
Cairns, David	79	0	79	5	0	3	23	C1
Callender, George	113	0	113	33	1	0	101	
Camac, Roy	1	0	1	1	0	0	3	
Cambridge, Bert	31	0	31	1	0	0	3	

Salford RL Players – Statistics

	App	Sub	Tot	Tries	Goals	D-gls	Pts	Representative
Carige, Paul	27	1	28	7	0	0	28	
Carney, Justin	31	0	31	12	0	0	48	
Carney, Todd	10	6	16		7	0	14	
Cartwright, John	16	0	16	3	0	0	12	
Cartwright, Les	29	0	29	5	3	0	21	
Casewell, Aubrey	187	0	187	63	0	0	189	W1
Casey, Garen	16	5	21	5	23	0	66	
Cashmere, Ray	68	4	72	5	0	0	20	
Cassidy, Frank	51	14	65	12	0	5	53	
Caton-Brown, Mason	32	0	32	16	0	0	64	
Caudwell, Peter	27	0	27	4	0	0	12	
Caulfield, John	6	0	6	0	0	0	0	
Chadderton, John	62	0	62	10	0	0	30	
Chadwick, Brian	1	0	1	0	0	0	0	
Chamberlain, Ed	17	1	18	6	50	0	124	
Chapman, Herbert	60	0	60	3	10	0	29	
Charles, Chris	92	20	112	16	231	0	526	E1
Charles, WJ 'Billy'	4	0	4	2	2	0	10	
Charlton, Paul	233	1	234	99	2	0	301	TR1, GB17+1, E1, C13
Chase, Moutoa 'Rangi'	42	0	42	15	13	3	89	
Cherrie, Gavin	4	1	5	1	0	0	3	
Cheshire, John	255	0	255	43	141	0	411	
Chick, Stuart	2	0	2	0	0	0	0	
Churm, Bill	4	0	4	0	0	0	0	
Clare, Jeff	2	4	6	2	0	0	8	
Clare, Mick	77	3	80	2	0	0	6	
Clark, Mick	24	0	24	3	0	0	9	
Clarke, Colin	12	0	12	0	0	0	0	
Clarke, Derek (1957-58)	12	0	12	0	0	0	0	
Clarke, Derek (1970-72)	69	0	69	3	0	0	9	
Clay, Adam	4	0	4	5	0	0	20	
Clayton, Val	5	0	5	1	0	0	3	
Clayton, Ryan	3	10	13	2	0	0	8	
Cleary, G	2	0	2	1	0	0	3	
Clegg, Walter	267	0	267	14	0	0	42	
Clifford, Reg	17	0	17	2	0	0	6	
Clinch, Gavin	56	1	57	13	20	1	93	
Clissold, Walter	2	0	2	0	1	0	2	
Clough, John	1	17	18	1	0	0	4	
Coates, Jack (1)	20	0	20	2	0	0	6	
Coates, Jack (2)	8	0	8	0	0	0	0	
Coates, Tom (senior)	56	0	56	4	1	0	14	
Coates, Tom (junior)	4	0	4	0	0	0	0	
Coburn, Chris	16	0	16	6	0	0	18	
Cochrane, Johnny	75	0	75	12	0	0	36	C2
Coleman, Craig	28	0	28	7	0	0	28	

Salford RL Players – Statistics

	App	Sub	Tot	Tries	Goals	D-gls	Pts	Representative
Coleman, George*	14	0	14	1	0	0	3	
Coleshill, John	1	0	1	0	0	0	0	
Coley, Andy	151	40	191	50	0	0	200	GB1, E3, L1
Collier, Frank	35	4	39	5	0	0	15	
Colloby, Tony	88	1	89	41	3	0	129	C4
Connor, Joseph	1	0	1	0	0	0	0	
Conroy, Tony	6	6	12	0	0	0	0	
Cook, Jimmy	165	0	165	98	0	0	294	MS1
Coombs, CB 'Bert'	15	0	15	1	0	0	3	
Coope-Franklin, Joseph	1	0	1	0	0	0	0	
Cooper, Frank	13	0	13	1	0	0	3	
Cooper, Harry	6	0	6	0	0	0	0	
Corcoran, John	18	22	40	3	0	0	9	
Corry, Tim	3	0	3	0	0	0	0	
Corvo, Mark	7	5	12	0	0	0	0	
Costello, Matty	14	2	16	6	0	0	24	
Costigan, Steve	36	0	36	13	0	0	39	
Coulman, Mike	441	22	463	135	1	1	408	GB2+1, E5, L1, OC1
Council, Harry	262	0	262	20	0	0	60	
Coussons, Phil	33	3	36	15	0	0	60	
Crank, Peter	42	7	49	4	0	0	12	
Critch, Jon	1	0	1	0	0	0	0	
Critchley, Ernie	122	3	125	14	0	0	42	
Critchley, Jason	91	4	95	50	0	0	200	E+1
Crocker, Will	29	0	29	2	0	0	6	
Croft, Brodie	28	0	28	7	0	0	28	CN1
Crompton, Martin	40	6	46	13	6	3	67	IR4
Crook, John	1	0	1	0	0	0	0	
Cross, Deon	28	1	29	13	0	0	52	
Cross, Stephen	3	0	3	1	0	0	3	
Crossley, Jim	7	0	7	0	0	0	0	
Cruickshank, David	26	2	28	3	0	0	12	
Culshaw, Alec	5	0	5	0	1	0	2	
Curran, George	175	0	175	12	1	0	38	TR1, GB6, E12, L7
Currie, George	193	0	193	2	0	0	6	
Curzon, Ephraime	102	0	102	7	0	0	21	TR1, GB1, L3
Dagnan, Harry (1)	1	0	1	0	0	0	0	
Dagnan, Harry (2)	43	0	43	26	0	0	78	
Dalton, Patrick 'Paddy'	291	0	291	58	0	0	174	GB2, E3, C13
Danby, Tom	174	0	174	61	2	0	187	TR1, GB3, E3
Daniels, J	2	0	2	0	0	0	0	
D'Arcy, Tom	2	0	2	2	0	0	6	
Davidson, Alex	0	3	3	0	0	0	0	
Davies, Alan	2	0	2	0	0	0	0	
Davies, Arthur	5	0	5	0	0	0	0	

Salford RL Players – Statistics

	App	Sub	Tot	Tries	Goals	D-gls	Pts	Representative
Davies, Ben	2	1	3	1	0	0	4	
Davies, D Elwyn	2	0	2	0	0	0	0	
Davies, DJ 'Dai'	43	0	43	10	9	0	48	
Davies, DM 'Dai'	370	0	370	39	0	0	117	W9
Davies, Doug	86	15	101	6	0	0	18	
Davies, Eifion 'Jack'	241	0	241	49	470	0	1087	W2
Davies, Harry	27	0	27	0	0	0	0	
Davies, Henry	0	1	1	0	0	0	0	
Davies, Jack	1	0	1	0	0	0	0	
Davies, James E	4	0	4	0	0	0	0	
Davies, Jordan	2	3	5	0	0	0	0	
Davies, Wes	10	0	10	3	0	0	12	
Davies, William J	65	0	65	18	1	0	56	
Davys, Ali	2	10	12	3	0	0	12	
Day, HC 'Bert'	488	0	488	6	0	0	18	W3
Day, Eric	116	0	116	7	0	0	21	
Deakin, Fred	11	0	11	1	0	0	3	
Dean, Mick	9	3	12	1	0	0	4	
Derrick, John	1	0	1	0	0	0	0	
Derrick, Richard	3	0	3	1	0	0	3	
Desborough, C	10	0	10	1	0	0	3	
Devlin, Ellis	78	10	88	16	0	0	48	
Dickens, Martin	28	0	28	3	0	0	9	
Dickens, Steve	75	10	85	5	0	0	20	
Dickens, Stuart	5	5	10	1	4	0	12	
Dignum, John	18	0	18	1	0	0	3	
Disley, Gary	55	13	68	0	0	0	0	
Dixon, AJ	6	0	6	1	0	0	3	
Dixon, Andrew	35	2	37	8	0	0	32	
Dixon, Colin	409	9	418	91	1	0	275	TR1, GB11+2, W13, OC1
Dobing, George	90	0	90	18	14	0	82	
Dobson, Michael	79	1	80	16	118	2	302	
Dodd, Frank	54	0	54	22	13	0	92	
Doeman, Tom	2	0	2	0	0	0	0	
Donegan, Austin	5	8	13	0	0	0	0	
Donegan, Joe	1	0	1	0	0	0	0	
Donoghue, Peter	64	0	64	1	3	0	9	
Dootson, Ron	5	7	12	2	0	0	6	
Doran, R 'Bobby'*	18	0	18	0	4	0	8	
Doran, Billy	26	0	26	4	1	0	14	C1
Dorn, Luke	21	8	29	12	0	0	48	
Dorning, Alan	116	3	119	21	0	0	63	
Downie, James	11	0	11	2	2	0	10	
Drake, Frank	17	0	17	4	0	0	12	
Driscoll, Damien	23	1	24	1	0	0	4	
Driver, David	61	8	69	20	0	0	63	

Salford RL Players – Statistics

	App	Sub	Tot	Tries	Goals	D-gls	Pts	Representative
Dudson, Gil	44	2	46	3	0	0	12	
Duffy, Hugh	240	0	240	51	1	0	155	
Duffy, John	3	11	14	0	1	1	3	
Dunemann, Andrew	27	0	27	1	0	2	6	
Dunn, Terry	82	0	82	27	24	0	129	
Dupree, Tyler	4	10	14	0	0	0	0	
Dutton, Charles	2	0	2	0	0	0	0	
Dutton, Fred	8	0	8	1	0	0	3	
Dutton, Les	5	0	5	0	0	0	0	
Dyson, Herbert	2	0	2	0	0	0	0	
Earnshaw, H	14	0	14	0	0	0	0	
Easterbrook, Alan	22	0	22	5	0	0	15	
Eastham, Phil	4	2	6	4	0	0	12	
Ebrill, Greg	15	7	22	1	0	0	4	
Eccles, Cliff	118	6	124	13	0	0	52	IR1+2
Eden, Greg	5	0	5	1	0	0	4	
Edge, Phil	1	0	1	0	0	0	0	
Edmondson, Mark	10	3	13	0	0	0	0	
Edwards, Alan	199	0	199	128	29	0	442	TR1, GB7, W15
Edwards, Ivor	8	0	8	1	0	0	3	
Edwards, Peter	88	3	91	25	0	0	100	
Egan, Joe	10	0	10	1	1	0	5	
Elliott, Jack	4	0	4	0	0	0	0	
Emmitt, Jake	6	11	17	1	0	0	4	W+1
Enoch, Jack	26	0	26	1	0	0	3	
Entwistle, James	7	0	7	0	0	0	0	
Entwistle, W	6	0	6	1	0	0	3	
Errington, Obadiah	15	0	15	0	0	0	0	C3
Escare, Morgan	17	3	20	8	3	0	38	F3
Evalds, Niall	146	14	160	111	0	0	444	
Evans, Alf	1	0	1	0	0	0	0	
Evans, Cliff (1)	65	0	65	16	4	0	56	
Evans, Cliff (2)	8	0	8	1	16	0	35	
Evans, Dave	86	0	86	2	0	0	6	
Evans, Dick	47	0	47	4	0	0	12	W2
Evans, Emrys	8	0	8	2	0	0	6	W1
Evans, Jim	20	0	20	0	0	0	0	
Evans, Sam	4	0	4	0	0	0	0	
Evans, Tex	142	5	147	69	0	0	276	
Fages, Theo	60	6	66	20	4	0	88	F4+1
Faimalo, Esene	30	32	62	2	0	0	8	
Faimalo, Joe	24	50	74	7	0	0	28	US3
Fairclough, Andy	0	1	1	0	0	0	0	
Fairclough, Brian	9	0	9	1	0	0	3	
Fairhurst, Jim	79	0	79	7	0	0	21	
Fairhurst, Ray	5	0	5	0	0	0	0	

Salford RL Players – Statistics

	App	Sub	Tot	Tries	Goals	D-gls	Pts	Representative
Farrington, John	32	0	32	7	0	0	21	
Fawcett, George	21	0	21	2	2	0	12	
Fazackerley, John	13	4	17	0	11	0	22	
Fearnley, George	4	0	4	0	0	0	0	
Fearnley, Jack	1	0	1	0	0	0	0	
Feetham, Jack	409	0	409	109	0	0	327	TR1, GB7, E1, Y9
Fell, David	61	12	73	29	0	0	116	
Fiddler, Jim	25	3	28	5	43	0	101	
Fieldhouse, Derek	27	0	27	1	0	0	3	
Fielding, Keith	315	4	319	253	133	0	1025	GB4, E7, L3, OC1
Fields, Fred	8	0	8	0	0	0	0	
Finnan, Bill	118	0	118	47	0	0	141	L1
Finnigan, Simon	55	0	55	19	0	0	76	
Fish, Jack	4	0	4	0	0	0	0	
Fisher, D	4	0	4	0	0	0	0	
Fisher, George	123	0	123	1	0	0	3	WM1
Fisher, George H	30	0	30	6	0	0	18	
Fitzpatrick, Karl	122	17	139	49	2	0	200	IR10+3
Flanagan, John (1910-11)	11	0	11	0	0	0	0	
Flanagan, John (1946-55)	60	0	60	10	0	0	30	
Flanagan, Mark	81	30	111	9	0	0	36	
Fleming, John	2	0	2	0	0	0	0	
Fletcher, J	13	0	13	1	0	0	3	
Fletcher, Paul	159	14	173	40	40	1	227	
Flint, Dave	24	0	24	0	0	0	0	
Flowers, Jason	41	1	42	17	0	0	68	
Foley, John	4	0	4	0	0	0	0	
Foran, Liam	12	3	15	1	0	0	4	
Forber, Paul	130	22	152	33	0	0	132	
Ford, Jon	1	0	1	3	0	0	12	
Ford, Phil	93	0	93	55	0	0	220	W6+1
Ford, Steve	9	0	9	1	0	0	4	
Forshaw, Jim	0	1	1	0	0	0	0	
Forster, Carl	6	10	16	1	0	0	4	
Foster, Alf	36	0	36	1	0	0	3	
Foster, Frank	2	0	2	0	0	0	0	
Fox, Kevin	1	1	2	1	0	0	4	
Fox, Thomas	11	0	11	0	0	0	0	
Foy, David	1	0	1	0	0	0	0	
Foy, Martin	6	3	9	3	0	0	12	
Frame, J	10	0	10	1	0	0	3	
France, Arthur	2	0	2	4	0	0	12	
Francis, Bill	34	1	35	6	0	0	18	
Fraser, Tom	3	0	3	0	0	0	0	
Frodsham, Peter	9	7	16	0	0	0	0	

Salford RL Players – Statistics

	App	Sub	Tot	Tries	Goals	D-gls	Pts	Representative
Fuller, John	38	0	38	7	0	0	21	
Gagon, Frank	4	0	4	3	0	0	9	
Gallagher, J	7	0	7	0	0	0	0	
Garces, Steve	0	1	1	0	0	0	0	
Gardner, Joe	110	0	110	1	0	0	3	
Gardner, Len	2	0	2	0	0	0	0	
Gardner, Matt	32	0	32	23	0	0	92	
Garland, Sam	59	0	59	5	0	0	15	
Garlick, Tommy	18	0	18	2	1	0	8	
Garner, Charlie	30	0	30	6	0	0	18	
Gaskell, John	10	0	10	0	0	0	0	
Gaskell, Lee	18	0	18	8	3	0	38	
Gear, Albert	148	0	148	40	3	0	126	
Gee, Matty	0	2	2	0	0	0	0	
Gee, Peter	9	1	10	0	0	0	0	
Gelling, Bryan	1	0	1	1	0	0	4	
George, Edgar	9	0	9	0	0	0	0	
Gerrard, Alex	14	10	24	1	0	0	4	
Gibson, Ashley	83	4	87	43	0	0	172	
Gibson, Damian	29	0	29	3	0	0	12	W1
Gibson, Steve	161	8	169	73	0	0	292	
Giedziun, Paul	0	3	3	0	0	0	0	
Gildart, Oliver	3	0	3	1	0	0	4	
Gilfillan, John	60	15	75	20	0	0	80	
Gill, Ken (1)	240	4	244	60	9	1	199	TR1, GB5+2, E10+2, L7
Gill, Ken (2)	31	0	31	2	0	0	6	
Gill, Mick	7	5	12	0	0	0	0	
Gilmore, Tom	2	0	2	1	0	0	4	
Gledhill, Ben	3	11	14	1	0	0	4	
Gledhill, Miles	99	0	99	5	0	0	15	
Gleeson, Martin	29	1	30	4	0	0	16	
Gleeson, Sean	38	0	38	15	0	0	60	
Glynn, Peter	130	14	144	24	1	6	104	
Godwin, Wayne (1)	44	9	53	6	0	0	24	
Godwin, Wayne (2)	3	0	3	0	0	0	0	
Goldsmith, Harry	95	0	95	4	0	0	12	
Gordon, Ernest	1	0	1	0	0	0	0	
Gore, Jack	125	0	125	29	0	0	87	GB1, W3, GM2, MM1
Gormley, Ian	59	3	62	9	0	0	36	
Gorski, Andy	0	11	11	0	0	0	0	
Goulding, Bobbie	32	1	33	2	59	4	130	
Goulding, Darrell	9	0	9	5	0	0	20	
Gourley, Tony	34	0	34	3	0	0	9	L1
Gower, David	0	18	18	0	0	0	0	
Graham, Gordon	95	19	114	28	0	0	84	

Salford RL Players – Statistics

	App	Sub	Tot	Tries	Goals	D-gls	Pts	Representative
Graham, James	5	0	5	0	0	0	0	
Grainger, Jim	176	0	176	23	0	0	69	L4
Greenwood, Harry	32	0	32	0	0	0	0	
Greenwood, James (1)	1	1	2	1	0	0	4	
Greenwood, James (2)	20	2	22	5	0	0	20	
Greenwood, Tom	10	0	10	0	0	0	0	
Gregory, Andy (1)	1	0	1	0	0	0	0	
Gregory, Andy (2)	31	4	35	4	8	2	34	
Gregory, Arthur	194	0	194	28	0	0	84	
Gregory, Harold	34	0	34	14	0	0	42	
Gregory, Mike	13	5	18	0	0	0	0	
Grey, Ivor	119	0	119	9	0	0	27	
Gribbin, Vince	4	0	4	3	0	0	12	
Grice, Alan	196	49	245	4	0	0	12	
Griffin, Darrell	32	29	61	1	0	0	4	
Griffin, George	88	26	114	23	0	0	92	
Griffin, Josh	55	0	55	34	86	0	308	
Griffiths, Ben	161	0	161	14	65	0	176	L3
Griffiths, Clive	41	1	42	20	151	6	388	
Griffiths, David	3	8	11	0	0	0	0	
Griffiths, Steve	2	9	11	2	0	0	8	
Grimes, Paul	6	3	9	0	0	0	0	
Groves, Paul	92	10	102	15	0	0	60	
Gwilliam, Ken	58	3	61	3	0	0	9	
Hadley, Adrian	97	1	98	63	4	0	260	W+2
Hadwen, Herbert	49	0	49	18	10	0	74	L3
Haggarty, Matt	0	1	1	0	0	0	0	
Haggerty, Gareth	5	120	125	18	0	0	72	IR+3
Haines, EC 'Teddy'	342	0	342	56	0	0	168	E1
Hainsworth, Jim	5	0	5	1	0	0	3	
Haley, John	11	0	11	0	1	0	2	
Halford, George	1	0	1	0	0	0	0	
Hall, Clifford	75	0	75	6	0	0	18	
Hall, Walter	12	0	12	2	0	0	6	
Hallas, Dave	1	1	2	0	0	0	0	
Halliwell, Danny	3	3	6	1	0	0	4	
Halliwell, Ken	17	0	17	3	3	0	15	L1
Halsall, Albert	106	0	106	11	0	0	33	
Halton, Fred	16	0	16	10	0	0	30	
Halton, Jack	30	0	30	7	5	0	31	
Hammond, Karle	2	3	5	1	0	0	4	
Hampson, Jack	2	0	2	0	0	0	0	
Hampson, John	1	0	1	0	0	0	0	
Hampson, Steve	39	0	39	11	11	8	74	
Hampson, Vernon	81	0	81	37	0	0	111	
Hancock, John	149	0	149	2	15	0	36	
Hancock, Michael	13	24	37	7	0	0	28	

Salford RL Players – Statistics

	App	Sub	Tot	Tries	Goals	D-gls	Pts	Representative
Hanley, Brian	29	0	29	4	0	0	12	
Hansen, Harrison	50	2	52	9	0	0	36	
Hansen, Shane	48	13	61	5	0	0	20	
Hanson, Sam	29	0	29	0	0	0	0	
Hardicre, Jim	37	16	53	3	0	0	9	
Hardman, Andy	30	0	30	1	0	0	3	
Hare, JH	44	0	44	1	4	0	11	
Harmon, Neil	6	5	11	0	0	0	0	IR1
Harper, Bill	47	1	48	3	0	0	9	
Harris, David	48	8	56	5	0	0	15	
Harris, George	105	0	105	5	0	0	15	
Harris, Tom	42	0	42	0	0	0	0	
Harris, William	29	0	29	3	3	0	15	
Harrison, Edwin	17	0	17	0	0	0	0	
Harrison, FV	1	0	1	0	0	0	0	
Harrison, Harold	5	0	5	0	0	0	0	
Harrison, Tommy	359	0	359	62	9	0	204	
Harrop, Myles-Dalton	1	0	1	1	0	0	4	
Harter, Ezekiel 'Zeke'*	101	0	101	22	1	0	68	
Hartley, Bryn	231	0	231	89	0	0	267	L1
Hartley, Ralph	29	0	29	4	0	0	12	
Hartley, Tim	6	7	13	5	0	0	20	
Harwood, George	16	0	16	0	0	0	0	
Haslam, Sam*	5	0	5	1	0	0	3	
Hassan, Phil	15	0	15	2	0	0	8	
Hasson, James	4	1	5	0	0	0	0	
Hastings, Jackson	41	0	41	15	15	0	90	GB3
Hauraki, Weller	55	18	73	14	0	0	56	
Havard, Keiron	2	0	2	0	0	0	0	
Hawkins, Eynon	93	0	93	4	0	0	12	W5
Hawksley, Roy	11	0	11	2	0	0	6	
Hayes, Arthur	1	0	1	0	0	0	0	
Hayes, DA 'Gus'	27	0	27	1	0	0	3	
Hayes, Joey	11	0	11	2	0	0	8	
Hayton, John	6	0	6	2	0	0	6	
Healey, -	6	0	6	0	0	0	0	
Heaney, Roy	7	0	7	1	0	0	3	
Heath, George	227	0	227	21	1	0	65	L9
Hellewell, Ben	1	1	2	0	0	0	0	
Helliwell, Ricky	0	2	2	0	0	0	0	
Hemmings, John	24	0	24	1	0	0	3	
Henighan, Mick	66	14	80	11	0	0	33	
Hennessey, Thomas	5	0	5	1	0	0	3	
Henney, Harold	133	20	153	25	0	0	76	C3
Henney, Russell	0	2	2	1	0	0	3	
Henry, Mark	70	0	70	26	0	0	104	
Hepi, Brad	3	5	8	0	0	0	0	

Salford RL Players – Statistics

	App	Sub	Tot	Tries	Goals	D-gls	Pts	Representative
Herbert, Steve	130	3	133	11	0	0	44	C1
Hesketh, Chris	443	9	452	128	0	0	384	TR2, GB21+2, E3, L13+2
Hesketh, Eric	19	0	19	1	1	0	5	
Hewitt, Gareth	2	1	3	0	0	0	0	
Hey, Steve	7	0	7	1	0	0	3	
Heyes, J	3	0	3	0	0	0	0	
Heywood, Jim	1	0	1	0	0	0	0	
Higgs, Bobby	10	0	10	4	0	0	12	
Highton, David	8	37	45	12	0	0	48	
Highton, Paul	154	115	269	24	0	0	96	W4+4
Hignett, George	14	0	14	0	3	0	6	
Hill, Doug	64	2	66	14	170	0	382	
Hill, Robert	1	0	1	0	0	0	0	
Hill, Ron	37	1	38	11	114	0	261	W2
Hill, R 'Dicky'	3	0	3	0	0	0	0	
Hilton, Jack	16	0	16	16	0	0	48	
Hindle, Ray	62	0	62	25	0	0	75	
Hindley, Jim	65	0	65	18	0	0	54	
Hindshaw, Alex	25	0	25	0	0	0	0	
Hingano, Ata	3	2	5	1	0	0	4	
Hirst, Harry	1	0	1	0	0	0	0	
Hobson, Richard	1	0	1	0	0	0	0	
Hock, Gareth	17	1	18	6	0	0	24	
Hodgson, David	88	0	88	36	48	0	240	GB2, E4
Hodkinson, Alan	5	0	5	0	0	0	0	
Holbrook, Sam	19	0	19	0	0	0	0	
Holcroft, Jim	14	0	14	0	0	0	0	
Holding, Billy	7	0	7	0	8	0	16	
Holdsworth, Daniel	75	0	75	18	190	1	453	EX1
Holland, -	3	0	3	0	0	0	0	
Holland, Dan	3	0	3	0	0	0	0	
Holland, Ian	18	2	20	7	2	0	25	
Holmes, Fred	6	0	6	2	0	0	6	
Holroyd, Graham	43	9	52	8	75	5	187	
Hood, Liam	2	20	22	1	0	0	4	S1
Hope, William	1	0	1	0	0	0	0	
Hope, Will	2	2	4	2	0	0	8	
Horo, Mark	20	0	20	4	0	0	16	
Hoskins, Joe	51	0	51	37	1	0	113	L2
Hough, Brian	1	0	1	0	0	0	0	
Hough, John	4	0	4	0	0	0	0	
Hough, R 'Dick'	1	0	1	0	0	0	0	
Houghton, Joey	6	0	6	0	0	0	0	
Howard, Tony	17	1	18	4	0	0	16	
Howarth, Stuart	25	14	39	1	0	0	4	
Howarth, W	23	0	23	0	0	0	0	

Salford RL Players – Statistics

	App	Sub	Tot	Tries	Goals	D-gls	Pts	Representative
Hudson, Bernard 'Barney'	411	0	411	282	58	0	962	TR2, GB9, E5
Hughes, Fred	2	0	2	0	0	0	0	
Hughes, Arthur	68	1	69	8	0	0	24	
Hughes, Bill	13	0	13	2	0	0	6	
Hughes, C*	7	0	7	0	0	0	0	
Hulme, David	65	4	69	8	0	0	32	
Humpheys, Arthur	3	0	3	0	0	0	0	
Hunte, Alan	48	5	53	41	2	0	168	
Hunter, Brian	1	1	2	0	0	0	0	
Hurst, Alex 'Sandy'	93	0	93	7	12	0	45	
Hurst, Harry	6	0	6	1	0	0	3	
Hurst, Phil	0	9	9	0	0	0	0	
Hutchinson, James	17	0	17	9	0	0	27	
Hutson, Bill	15	0	15	3	0	0	9	
Huyte, Patrick	1	0	1	0	0	0	0	
Hyam, William	74	0	74	20	1	0	62	
Ikahihifo, Sebastine	12	20	32	1	0	0	4	
Ingham, John	62	0	62	7	0	0	21	
Ingram, William	1	0	1	0	0	0	0	
Inu, Krisnan	49	3	52	24	195	1	487	
Irving, Bob	39	0	39	7	0	0	21	
Irving, R	2	0	2	0	0	0	0	
Irving, WH 'Bill'	2	0	2	0	0	0	0	
Isherwood, James	2	0	2	0	0	0	0	
Jack, Garry (1)	16	0	16	3	0	0	12	
Jack, Garry (2)	34	0	34	10	0	0	40	
Jackson, Paul	123	11	134	49	3	0	153	
James, Jordan	1	44	45	6	0	0	24	W4+2
Jamieson, Ged	16	12	28	1	0	0	4	
Jenkins, Emlyn (1)	245	0	245	88	43	0	350	TR1, GB11, W4, ON1
Jenkins, Emlyn (2)	1	0	1	0	1	0	2	
Jenkins, JW 'Jack'	14	0	14	2	19	0	44	
Jenkins, Trevor	1	0	1	0	0	0	0	
Jewitt, Lee	40	85	125	7	0	0	28	
Jiminez, James	2	0	2	2	0	0	8	
John, Richard H	2	0	2	0	0	0	0	
John, WD 'Dai'	405	0	405	42	46	0	218	W1
Johns, Graeme	14	2	16	1	16	0	35	W+1
Johnson, Andy	8	28	36	7	0	0	28	
Johnson, Greg	105	0	105	50	1	0	202	
Johnson, Josh	11	17	28	1	0	0	4	
Johnson, Mark	22	12	34	16	0	0	64	SA3
Jones, Connor	7	0	7	1	0	0	4	
Jones, E	17	0	17	1	0	0	3	
Jones, Eric	18	0	18	6	0	0	18	
Jones, Graham (1954-62)	239	0	239	119	0	0	357	

Salford RL Players – Statistics

	App	Sub	Tot	Tries	Goals	D-gls	Pts	Representative
Jones, Graham (1978-82)	3	3	6	1	0	0	3	
Jones, Henry	24	0	24	2	0	0	6	
Jones, JJ*	10	0	10	1	0	0	3	
Jones, Joe	2	0	2	0	0	0	0	
Jones, Josh	110	5	115	19	0	0	76	GB+2
Jones, Ken	48	10	58	15	102	0	264	
Jones, Reg	57	0	57	17	3	0	57	W1
Jones-Bishop, Ben	25	0	25	16	3	0	70	
Jonkers, Tim	5	13	18	0	0	0	0	
Joseph, Phil	2	12	14	0	0	0	0	W2
Jowitt, Warren	19	4	23	4	0	0	16	
Kear, Barry	14	6	20	0	0	0	0	
Kear, Elliot	12	1	13	1	0	0	4	
Keavney, Brian	169	0	169	31	104	0	301	L1
Keegan, John	11	0	11	0	0	0	0	
Keegan, Bob	28	0	28	1	2	0	7	
Kelly, Mike	16	1	17	3	0	0	9	
Kenny, Joe	141	0	141	30	0	0	90	
Kenny, Russ	45	0	45	9	11	0	49	
Kenny, Sean	0	9	9	0	0	0	0	
Kenny, Tom	44	0	44	18	4	0	62	E1
Kenward, Shane	1	0	1	0	0	0	0	
Kenyon, Roy	16	2	18	0	8	0	16	
Kerry, Steve	97	8	105	47	306	12	812	L+1
Kershaw, AS	1	0	1	0	0	0	0	
Kershaw, Harold	1	0	1	0	0	0	0	
Kershaw, Stanley	1	0	1	0	0	0	0	
Kettle, Bob	8	0	8	0	0	0	0	
Kilgannon, Derek	52	0	52	5	0	0	15	
King, Tom*	14	0	14	1	0	0	3	
Kinsey, Tom	5	0	5	0	0	0	0	
Kirk, Andy	46	2	48	29	0	0	116	
Kirkbride, Bill	60	11	71	5	0	0	15	C1
Knighton, John	152	30	182	31	0	0	93	OC2
Knott, James	36	0	36	0	0	0	0	
Knowles, Graham	3	0	3	0	7	0	14	
Knowles, Phil	3	5	8	0	0	0	0	
Knox, Simon	1	1	2	0	0	0	0	S1+1
Kopczak, Craig	44	40	84	13	0	0	52	W5
Korkidas, Michael	28	1	29	1	0	0	4	
Krasniqi, Olsi	11	44	55	2	0	0	8	
Kyte, Syd	1	0	1	0	0	0	0	
Lafai, Tim	25	0	25	6	0	0	24	SM5
Lamb, Nigel	20	5	25	4	0	0	16	
Lambert, Roy	19	0	19	5	0	0	15	
Lambert, W 'Billy'	54	0	54	0	11	0	22	
Lancaster, E	5	0	5	1	0	0	3	

Salford RL Players – Statistics

	App	Sub	Tot	Tries	Goals	D-gls	Pts	Representative
Landers, Fred	1	0	1	0	0	0	0	
Lane, William	1	0	1	0	0	0	0	
Lang, David	8	1	9	1	0	0	3	
Langi, Junior	29	8	37	7	0	0	28	
Lannon, Ryan (1)	28	26	54	10	0	0	40	
Lannon, Ryan (2)	33	17	50	1	0	0	4	
Latham, Keith	14	8	22	3	0	0	9	
Launce, Harry	175	0	175	2	15	0	36	
Laurence, Jason	3	1	4	1	0	0	4	
Laurie, Mark	8	1	9	1	0	0	4	
Lavery, Joe	4	0	4	0	0	0	0	
Lawrenson, Johnny	2	0	2	3	3	0	15	
Lawton, Adam	1	1	2	0	0	0	0	
Leach, Joe	9	1	10	0	0	0	0	
Leatherbarrow, David	1	0	1	0	0	0	0	
Lee, Mark	237	17	254	34	0	35	171	
Lee, Tommy	43	8	51	4	2	0	20	
Leigh, Matthew	1	7	8	0	0	0	0	
Lendill, Peter	29	0	29	2	0	0	6	
Leonard, Ken	26	0	26	1	0	0	3	
Leota, Francis	10	0	10	0	0	0	0	
Leuluai, Phil	16	71	87	7	0	0	28	SM1+2
Lever, Walter	1	0	1	0	0	0	0	
Lewis, Isaac 'Ike'	118	0	118	7	0	0	21	
Leyland, Fred	7	0	7	0	0	0	0	
Lima, Danny	7	2	9	0	0	0	0	SM1
Lindley, Jimmy	67	0	67	5	0	0	15	
Littlejohn, Jack	17	3	20	3	1	0	14	
Littler, Stuart	291	38	329	113	0	0	452	IR12
Livesey, Albert	9	0	9	1	0	0	3	
Livett, Harvey	28	1	29	10	16	0	72	
Llewellyn, William	37	0	37	2	2	0	10	
Lloyd, John	6	0	6	1	0	0	3	
Locke, Kevin	13	0	13	6	11	0	46	
Lolohea, Tuimoala	55	0	55	18	29	1	131	
Lomas, Jimmy (1)	304	0	304	208	464	0	1552	TR1, GB5, E10, C8, L9
Lomas, Jimmy (2)	8	0	8	0	6	0	12	
Lomas, Jim	14	0	14	2	0	0	6	
Loughlin, Terry 'Paddy'	33	5	38	0	0	0	0	
Love, Henry	1	0	1	0	0	0	0	
Love, William	5	0	5	0	0	0	0	
Loveluck, Arthur	128	0	128	33	2	0	103	
Lowcock, H	1	0	1	0	0	0	0	
Lowdon, Syd	72	0	72	41	161	0	445	C4
Lowe, Jackie	3	0	3	0	0	0	0	
Lowe, Johnny	4	0	4	4	0	0	12	

Salford RL Players – Statistics

	App	Sub	Tot	Tries	Goals	D-gls	Pts	Representative
Lowe, Neil	18	8	26	7	0	0	28	
Luckley, Sam	2	25	27	1	0	0	4	S2
Lui, Robert	103	6	109	35	33	0	206	
Lussick, Darcy	0	5	5	1	0	0	4	
Lussick, Joey	34	25	59	18	4	0	80	
Lyons, Peter	2	0	2	0	0	0	0	
Lyons, J	9	0	9	0	0	0	0	
Mabbett, Thomas	2	0	2	0	0	0	0	
McAlone, Edwin 'Eddie'	35	0	35	6	0	0	18	
McArthur, Walter 'Wally'	46	0	46	29	90	0	267	
McAtee, John	2	0	2	0	0	0	0	
McAvoy, Nathan (1)	115	3	118	75	0	0	300	E1
McAvoy, Nathan (2)	22	4	26	3	0	0	12	
McCarthy, Bryan	1	1	2	0	0	0	0	
McCarthy, Tyrone	49	24	73	10	2	0	44	IR5+2
McCauley, Kenneth	2	0	2	1	0	0	3	
McCormick, Stan	1	0	1	0	0	0	0	
MacCorquodale, Iain	14	3	17	4	7	0	26	
McGilvray, Dean	16	0	16	5	0	0	20	
McGoldrick, Ryan	20	1	21	3	0	1	13	
McGovern, Terry	4	0	4	1	0	0	3	
McGreal, Chris	94	25	119	13	3	0	45	
McGuinness, Jack	40	0	40	4	0	0	12	
McGuinness, Kevin	66	4	70	13	0	0	52	
McGuire, James	3	0	3	0	0	0	0	
McInnes, Alan	93	1	94	12	42	0	120	
McJennett, Mark	2	0	2	0	0	0	0	W+1
McKay, Graham	99	16	115	5	0	0	15	C1
McKinney, Tom	148	0	148	0	4	0	8	TR1, GB10, ON6, CN1
McPherson, Neil	0	1	1	0	0	0	0	
McPherson, Shannan	20	12	32	0	0	0	0	
McTigue, Mick	172	9	181	27	0	0	102	
McWhirter, Harry	34	0	34	2	0	0	6	
Maddocks, Joe	9	0	9	1	0	0	3	
Maggs, Keith	24	2	26	4	0	0	14	
Mahon, Scott	17	0	17	6	5	0	34	
Mair, James	6	0	6	0	0	0	0	
Maitua, Reni	6	0	6	0	0	0	0	
Major, David	151	70	221	10	0	0	39	
Makin, Craig	28	20	48	2	0	0	8	W2
Makin, John	1	0	1	0	0	0	0	
Maloney, Francis	46	1	47	26	5	0	114	Y+1
Manfredi, Dominic	1	0	1	2	0	0	8	
Mann, Fred	17	0	17	0	0	0	0	
Manniex, John	2	0	2	0	0	0	0	
Manning, Dick	80	0	80	18	1	0	56	

Salford RL Players – Statistics

	App	Sub	Tot	Tries	Goals	D-gls	Pts	Representative
Mannion, Tom	52	0	52	4	9	0	30	
Mansson, Paul	3	10	13	1	0	0	4	
Mantle, John	37	0	37	6	0	0	18	W1
Manwaring, W 'Billy'*	24	0	24	0	4	0	9	
Marland, Lees	4	0	4	0	2	0	4	
Marriott, Callum		1	1	0	0	0	0	
Marsden, Bob	24	28	52	6	0	0	24	
Marsden, W 'Bill'	20		20	2	0	0	6	
Marsh, Iain	1	4	5	0	0	0	0	
Marsh, Ian	55	1	56	17	0	0	68	
Marsh, Lee	12	10	22	5	19	0	58	
Marshall, Wayne	4	0	4	0	0	0	0	
Marston, Peter	108	0	108	6	0	0	18	
Martin, Scott	70	40	110	32	0	0	128	
Mason, Albert	60	0	60	2	8	0	22	
Mateo, Feleti	2	1	3	0	0	0	0	
Mather, Ian	1	1	2	0	0	0	0	
Matthews, Eddie	78	0	78	34	0	0	102	
Mauro, Vic	2	7	9	2	0	0	8	
May, Edgar	138	0	138	34	2	0	106	
Mayor, Graham	10	7	17	2	0	0	6	
Meachin, Colin	8	6	14	1	0	0	4	
Mears, William	14	0	14	0	0	0	0	
Meek, Reg	260	0	260	32	25	0	146	GM2
Meli, Francis	18	0	18	14	0	0	56	
Menzies, Luke	0	1	1	0	0	0	0	
Mercer, Andy	12	11	23	2	0	0	8	
Mesley, Bernard	215	0	215	87	170	0	601	
Messer, Bob	30	0	30	4	0	0	12	
Middleton, Alf	285	0	285	67	25	0	251	GB1, E1
Miles, Frank*	23	0	23	15	0	0	45	
Miller, Jack	1	0	1	0	0	0	0	
Miller, Sammy	312	0	312	81	57	0	357	C18
Mills, Jim	4	1	5	0	0	0	0	
Mills, R	3	0	3	0	0	0	0	
Moana, Martin	7	11	18	2	0	0	8	
Molyneux, R 'Dick'	39	0	39	0	1	0	2	
Moon, Joel	19	0	19	11	0	0	44	EX1
Moore, John	7	0	7	0	0	0	0	
Moore, Owen	25	0	25	1	0	0	3	
Moran, Dave	4	0	4	0	0	0	0	
Moran, Mark	77	5	82	4	0	0	16	
Morgan, Joey	3	0	3	0	0	0	0	
Morley, Adrian	35	19	54	2	0	0	8	
Morley, Chris	3	5	8	0	0	0	0	W2
Morris, Steve	2	0	2	1	0	0	4	
Morris, William	3	0	3	0	0	0	0	

Salford RL Players – Statistics

	App	Sub	Tot	Tries	Goals	D-gls	Pts	Representative
Morton, Edgar	20	0	20	2	0	0	6	
Morton, Sam	2	0	2	0	0	0	0	
Moses, Dai	328	0	328	29	4	0	95	
Moses, Glyn	78	0	78	4	9	0	30	
Moss, Bob*	60	0	60	2	0	0	6	
Mossop, Lee	79	3	82	7	0	0	28	
Moule, Aaron	48	0	48	19	0	0	76	
Moylan, Steve	21	1	22	2	0	0	8	
Muir, Jack	338	0	338	14	0	0	42	
Mullaney, Jake	13	0	13	2	30	0	68	
Muller, Roby	25	0	25	7	0	0	28	
Murdoch-Masila, Ben	59	1	60	22	0	0	88	T+5
Murdock, Craig	0	2	2	0	0	0	0	
Murphy, Jack	10	0	10	3	1	0	14	
Murphy, Paul	142	1	143	64	70	0	332	
Murray, Daniel	16	16	32	2	0	0	8	
Murray, Tom	10	1	11	1	0	0	3	
Myers, David	2	5	7	0	0	0	0	
Myler, Richie	53	0	53	38	0	0	152	E3
Myler, Rob	4	0	4	1	4	0	12	
Myler, Stephen	4	11	15	1	16	0	36	
Myler, Vinny	0	4	4	0	0	0	0	
Naidole, Tom	1	2	3	0	0	0	0	
Nakubuwai, Ben	8	33	41	3	0	0	12	FJ2
Napolitano, Carlo	0	3	3	1	0	0	4	
Nash, Stephen	13	20	33	2	0	0	8	
Nash, Steve	275	0	275	31	9	17	129	TR1, GB8, E4, Y5
Naylor, Scott (1)	101	9	110	41	0	0	164	
Naylor, Scott (2)	8	0	8	0	0	0	0	
Neal, Adam	18	30	48	1	0	0	4	
Neal, Mike	0	1	1	0	0	0	0	
Needham, David	3	3	6	0	0	0	0	
Neil, Mike	8	1	9	1	0	0	4	
Nero, Chris	34	18	52	9	0	0	36	
Nestor, Vince	15	2	17	2	0	0	6	
Newton, T	2	0	2	0	0	0	0	
Nicholls, George	31	2	33	1	0	0	3	
Nicol, Jason	53	7	60	11	0	0	44	
Norburn, Peter	8	2	10	0	0	0	0	
Norbury, John	1	0	1	0	0	0	0	
Norman, Dan	0	3	3	1	0	0	4	
Norrey, Harold (1)	50	0	50	20	0	0	60	
Norrey, Harold (2)	1	0	1	0	0	0	0	
Norris, Abraham	58	0	58	25	0	0	75	
Nuttall, Alf	3	0	3	0	0	0	0	
Nzoungou, Levi	0	3	3	0	0	0	0	

Salford RL Players – Statistics

	App	Sub	Tot	Tries	Goals	D-gls	Pts	Representative
O'Brien, Gareth	60	5	65	16	142	4	352	
O'Connor, Terry	29	10	39	3	0	0	12	
Offiah, Martin	45	0	45	23	0	2	94	
Ogden, Terry	135	3	138	15	0	0	45	
Okanga-Ajwang, Edwin	2	0	2	0	0	0	0	
Oldham, Alan	7	10	17	0	0	0	0	
O'Loughlin, Jason	6	3	9	4	0	0	16	
O'Loughlin, Keiron	93	1	94	19	0	0	76	L1
Olpherts, Derrell	42	0	42	16	0	0	64	
O'Neill, Paul (1978-84)	140	2	142	42	0	0	127	
O'Neill, Paul (1990-94)	15	4	19	10	0	0	40	
O'Neill, Steve	13	0	13	1	0	0	4	
Openshaw, Arthur	15	0	15	0	0	0	0	
Ormondroyd, Jack	36	16	52	7	0	0	28	
Orr, Paul	14	9	23	4	0	0	12	
Osbaldestin, Harold	271	0	271	25	48	0	171	L4
O'Shea, Terry	29	6	35	10	52	0	144	
Owen, Gareth (1982)	1	1	2	0	0	0	0	
Owen, Gareth (2010-13)	5	32	37	6	0	0	24	
Owen, Tom 'Tot'	1	0	1	0	0	0	0	
Palea'aesina, Iafeta	6	39	45	5	0	0	20	
Palmer, H	2	0	2	0	0	0	0	
Panapa, Sam	71	0	71	36	0	0	144	WS1+1
Parker, Rob	25	15	40	4	0	0	16	
Parkinson, Bill	13	0	13	2	0	0	6	
Parr, Jim	28	0	28	3	0	0	9	
Parry, Bob	4	0	4	1	0	0	3	
Parsons, George	42	0	42	3	0	0	9	
Partridge, Sydney	18	0	18	1	0	0	3	
Paterson, Cory	18	3	21	10	9	0	58	
Patten, Luke	56	0	56	16	0	0	64	
Patton, Dec	7	4	11	2	3	0	14	
Paul, Robbie	20	31	51	9	0	0	36	
Pauli, Pauli (1)	0	3	3	3	0	0	12	
Pauli, Pauli (2)	11	21	32	2	0	0	8	CN+1
Peacock, Charlie	73	0	73	14	0	0	42	
Pearce, Ray	46	0	46	0	91	0	182	
Pearson, Arthur	117	0	117	45	2	0	139	
Pearson, Leslie	51	0	51	16	10	0	68	
Pemberton, Harold	3	0	3	0	0	0	0	
Pemberton, S	2	0	2	0	0	0	0	
Pendlebury, John	55	0	55	7	35	1	99	L1
Pendlebury, WH	1	0	1	0	0	0	0	
Penni, Julian	4	0	4	0	0	0	0	
Philbin, Barry	9	2	11	1	0	0	3	
Phillips, William	40	0	40	13	40	0	119	
Pierson, C	3	0	3	0	0	0	0	

Salford RL Players – Statistics

	App	Sub	Tot	Tries	Goals	D-gls	Pts	Representative
Pimblett, Albert	18	0	18	1	0	0	3	
Pinkney, Nick	69	0	69	32	0	0	128	
Platt, Andy	33	3	36	1	0	0	4	
Platt, Michael (1)	16	0	16	5	0	0	20	
Platt, Michael (2)	2	1	3	0	0	0	0	
Pobjie, Michael	8	1	9	1	0	0	4	
Potts, Ian	3	2	5	1	0	0	4	
Powell, Bryn	1	1	2	0	0	0	0	W2
Poynton, John	1	0	1	0	0	0	0	
Preece, Bob	152	0	152	48	9	0	162	
Prescott, Eric (1)	270	3	273	46	7	1	153	L7+2
Prescott, Eric (2)	18	0	18	5	0	0	20	
Preston, Dave	256	0	256	39	2	0	121	L1
Price, Gareth	0	2	2	0	0	0	0	
Price, Horace	31	0	31	20	0	0	60	
Price, Jim	24	0	24	1	0	0	3	
Price, Malcolm	0	1	1	0	0	0	0	
Price, W 'Billy'	54	0	54	1	1	0	5	
Prosser, Bob	106	22	128	21	0	0	63	W4
Pugsley, Joe	51	0	51	7	0	0	21	W1, WW1
Puletua, Tony	16	11	27	3	0	0	12	
Quigley, Jonathan	19	6	25	4	0	0	16	
Quigley, Thomas	44	0	44	1	3	0	9	
Quinn, John	22	0	22	0	0	0	0	
Rabbitt, Trevor	91	10	101	14	0	0	42	
Raistrick, Dean	36	0	36	0	0	0	0	
Rampling, Tony	11	0	11	2	0	0	8	
Ramshaw, Terry	38	3	41	1	0	0	3	
Randall, Craig	46	54	100	23	0	0	92	
Rapira, Steve	6	14	20	0	0	0	0	
Ratchford, Stefan	84	24	108	40	29	0	218	
Ratcliffe, David	5	1	6	0	0	0	0	
Ratcliffe, Joe	15	0	15	4	0	0	12	
Rawlinson, John	4	1	5	0	0	0	0	
Read, Ron	2	0	2	0	0	0	0	
Reakes, Tom	3	0	3	0	0	0	0	
Reardon, Stuart	7	1	8	3	0	0	12	
Redford, Tony	4	4	8	0	3	0	6	
Rees, Charlie	163	0	163	21	0	0	63	W1
Rees, Dai	196	0	196	14	0	0	42	W2, ON2, L7
Rees, Graham	64	0	64	11	0	0	33	
Rees, Ivor	6	0	6	2	0	0	6	
Reeve, Cyril	19	0	19	0	0	0	0	
Regan, Dave	2	0	2	0	0	0	0	
Regan, Peter	3	1	4	0	0	0	0	
Reid, Wayne	46	15	61	14	0	0	56	
Renninson, Albert	18	0	18	1	4	0	11	

Salford RL Players – Statistics

	App	Sub	Tot	Tries	Goals	D-gls	Pts	Representative
Reynolds, Paul	6	1	7	3	0	0	12	
Rhapps, Jack	286	0	286	3	1	0	11	ON1, L14
Richards, Ken	75	0	75	18	152	0	358	
Richards, Maurice	496	2	498	297	32	0	956	TR1, GB2, W3
Richards, R 'Bob'	25	0	25	2	3	0	12	
Richards, Tom	1	0	1	0	0	0	0	
Rickers, Tom	1	0	1	1	0	0	3	
Riley, Fred	7	0	7	2	0	0	6	
Riley, Ike	1	0	1	0	0	0	0	
Riley, Sam	12	0	12	1	0	0	3	
Riley, Todd	3	0	3	0	0	0	0	
Risman, AJ 'Gus'	427	0	427	144	796	0	2024	TR3, GB18, W18, GM3
Ritchie, Bob	148	0	148	9	0	0	27	
Ritter, Neil	11	2	13	2	0	0	8	
Roberts, Arthur	22	0	22	3	0	0	9	
Roberts, D	1	0	1	0	0	0	0	
Roberts, George	23	0	23	1	0	0	3	
Roberts, Ken	27	2	29	0	0	0	0	
Roberts, Luis	2	0	2	0	0	0	0	
Roberts, Oliver	13	8	21	1	0	0	4	
Robinson, Frank	20	0	20	1	0	0	3	
Robinson, Luke	86	0	86	33	10	2	154	E2
Robson, Bob	58	0	58	5	16	0	47	ON2
Robson, Ellis	4	3	7	1	0	0	4	
Rodgers, George	7	0	7	0	0	0	0	
Rogers, Darren	88	6	94	50	0	0	200	
Rogers, Jack	170	0	170	14	52	0	146	
Rogers, Jon	23	6	29	7	0	0	22	
Roper, Jon	1	4	5	1	3	0	10	
Rose, C	5	0	5	0	0	0	0	
Ross, George	1	0	1	0	0	0	0	
Rothwell, Frank	1	0	1	0	0	0	0	
Roughley, George	36	0	36	8	0	0	24	
Rourke, Josh	1	0	1	0	0	0	0	
Roy, Don	13	0	13	1	0	0	3	
Ruddy, Dave	19	11	30	4	0	0	16	
Rule, Steve	117	6	123	23	384	11	848	W1
Russell, Robert	2	1	3	0	1	0	2	
Rutgerson, Sean	65	9	74	5	0	0	20	
Ryan, Tommy	37	0	37	2	0	0	6	
Sammon, Joe	2	0	2	0	0	0	0	
Sarginson, Dan	28	1	29	6	0	0	24	
Sarsfield, Matt	3	2	5	1	0	0	4	
Sa'u, Junior	142	0	142	59	0	0	236	
Savage, William	2	0	2	0	0	0	0	
Savelio, Lokeni	44	44	88	8	0	0	32	

Salford RL Players – Statistics

	App	Sub	Tot	Tries	Goals	D-gls	Pts	Representative
Saxton, Tom	5	0	5	0	0	0	0	
Schofield, Dave	22	0	22	0	12	0	24	
Schubert, Gary	5	2	7	0	0	0	0	
Scott, John	5	0	5	1	0	0	3	
Selby, Geoff	19	0	19	6	0	0	24	
Sharp, Johnnie	22	0	22	10	0	0	30	
Shaw, Darren	5	10	15	1	0	0	4	
Shaw, David	18	5	23	2	0	0	8	
Shaw, Fred	152	0	152	2	1	0	8	L1
Shaw, J	2	0	2	0	0	0	0	
Shaw, Paul	15	1	16	2	0	0	8	
Shaw, Robert	175	0	175	8	0	0	24	DN4
Shaw, Tom	16	0	16	0	0	0	0	
Sheffield, Bill	68	13	81	3	0	0	9	
Sheldon, Roland	2	0	2	0	0	0	0	
Sherratt, Ian	48	3	51	5	0	0	20	
Shields, Edwin	15	0	15	2	0	0	6	
Shipway, Mark	33	12	45	3	0	0	12	
Shore, Hugh	94	0	94	2	0	0	6	
Shore, Jack	1	0	1	0	0	0	0	
Shorrocks, Jake	11	0	11	0	2	0	4	
Shovelton, Jim	1	0	1	0	0	0	0	
Shuker, Ray	9	0	9	2	12	0	30	
Shuttleworth, Paul	27	7	34	5	18	2	58	
Sibbit, Ian	91	27	118	22	0	0	88	
Sidlow, Adam	48	50	98	17	0	0	68	
Simcox, Dennis	29	0	29	1	0	0	3	
Simpkins, Daniel	20	0	20	0	0	0	0	
Sims, Geoff	45	1	46	6	102	0	222	
Sini, Fata	57	1	58	28	11	0	134	
Sio, Ken	78	1	79	66	13	0	290	CN2
Slamin, Kevin	6	0	6	0	1	0	2	
Sligar, Noel	1	0	1	0	0	0	0	
Smart, Geoff	57	1	58	2	0	0	6	
Smethurst, Peter	121	3	124	10	1	0	32	
Smith, Andy	4	0	4	1	0	0	4	
Smith, Dan	218	0	218	1	14	0	31	ON1, L12
Smith, Derek	33	0	33	4	0	0	12	
Smith, Ernie	3	0	3	1	0	0	3	
Smith, Fred	141	0	141	13	92	0	223	
Smith, Hudson	26	2	28	6	0	0	24	
Smith, James	25	3	28	7	0	0	28	
Smith, Jeremy	28	17	45	2	0	0	8	
Smith, JH	1	0	1	0	0	0	0	
Smith, Matty	71	5	76	14	7	1	71	
Smith, Paul	1	0	1	0	0	0	0	
Smith, Richard	1	1	2	1	0	0	4	

Salford RL Players – Statistics

	App	Sub	Tot	Tries	Goals	D-gls	Pts	Representative
Smith, Ron	64	32	96	22	102	0	271	
Smith, TH 'Harry'	85	0	85	4	1	0	14	
Smith, Tim	13	1	14	2	7	0	22	
Smith, Tom	9	0	9	0	0	0	0	
Snell, David	4	0	4	0	0	0	0	
Sneyd, Marc (1)	37	13	50	7	81	3	193	
Sneyd, Marc (2)	27	0	27	4	105	2	228	E2
Snipe, Tom	13	0	13	2	0	0	6	
Southern, Paul	91	36	127	7	15	0	58	IR2+3
Southward, Ferguson 'Fergie'	350	0	350	90	158	0	586	C26
Southward, Joe	96	4	100	20	37	0	134	C1
Sparks, Brian	37	0	37	2	0	0	6	
Spencer, Joe	99	0	99	6	0	0	18	GB1, E1, L3
Spencer, Jack	0	7	7	0	0	0	0	
Spencer-Tonks, Daniel	0	1	1	0	0	0	0	
Spruce, Joe	11	0	11	3	0	0	9	
Stacey, Steve	7	0	7	6	0	0	24	
Stamper, Joe	50	0	50	0	0	0	0	C1
Stapleton, Craig	57	0	57	9	0	0	36	
Staveley, Ernest	10	0	10	1	0	0	3	
Stazicker, Ged	67	8	75	5	0	0	20	
Stead, Frank	67	12	79	12	0	0	36	
Steeden, Phillip	1	0	1	0	0	0	0	
Stephenson, David (1)	97	0	97	36	2	4	116	L2
Stephenson, David (2)	0	1	1	1	0	0	4	
Stevens, Jack	0	1	1	0	0	0	0	
Stevens, Warren	0	8	8	0	0	0	0	
Stewart, Anthony	54	2	56	16	0	0	64	IR3
Stewart, James	6	0	6	0	0	0	0	
Stirrup, Frank	78	0	78	13	0	0	39	
Stockley, Trevor	47	8	55	13	1	0	41	
Stoddart, Ray	18	0	18	2	0	0	6	
Storey, Tony	8	0	8	0	0	0	0	
Stott, Roy	94	0	94	8	0	0	24	
Streets, Geoffrey	1	0	1	1	0	0	3	
Stringer, Mitchell	12	5	17	1	0	0	4	
Subritzky, Peter	0	2	2	0	0	0	0	
Such, William	1	0	1	0	0	0	0	
Sulway, Ivor	2	0	2	0	0	0	0	
Summerville, Wilf	15	0	15	0	0	0	0	
Sumner, Phil	0	1	1	0	0	0	0	
Sutcliffe, James	21	0	21	0	0	0	0	
Svabic, Simon	14	7	21	3	21	0	54	
Swain, Luke	58	0	58	3	0	0	12	
Swift, Phil	3	0	3	2	0	0	8	
Swindells, Charlie	9	0	9	0	0	0	0	
Swithenbank, Jimmy	21	0	21	0	0	0	0	

Salford RL Players – Statistics

	App	Sub	Tot	Tries	Goals	D-gls	Pts	Representative
Sykes, Edward	70	0	70	2	2	0	10	
Tabern, Walt	1	0	1	0	0	0	0	
Talau, Willie	25	0	25	4	0	0	16	
Tamati, Kevin	5	2	7	0	0	0	0	
Tasi, Lama (1)	32	14	46	5	0	0	20	
Tasi, Lama (2)	36	17	53	3	0	0	12	
Tassell, Kris	37	10	47	13	0	0	52	W4
Tauro, Chris	17	5	22	3	0	0	12	
Taylor, A	2	0	2	0	0	0	0	
Taylor, Elijah	36	5	41	1	0	0	4	
Taylor, John (1)	14	10	24	3	0	0	9	
Taylor, John (2)	30	8	38	5	0	0	20	
Taylor, Mark	73	6	79	5	0	0	15	
Taylor, Peter	6	0	6	2	0	0	6	
Taylor, R	31	0	31	1	0	0	3	
Taylor, Scott	30	0	30	7	0	0	28	
Thom, George	159	0	159	6	2	0	22	
Thomas, Dai	11	0	11	12	1	0	38	
Thomas, Elvet	12	0	12	1	0	0	3	
Thomas, Evan J	306	0	306	25	0	0	75	W2
Thomas, Harold	119	0	119	6	0	0	18	W2
Thomas, Howard	4	6	10	0	0	0	0	
Thomas, Jim	10	0	10	1	0	0	3	
Thomas, Johnnie	8	0	8	0	0	0	0	
Thomas, R 'Bob'	2	0	2	0	0	0	0	
Thomas, Radley (1)	1	0	1	0	0	0	0	
Thomas, Radley (2)	55	0	55	18	0	0	54	
Thomas, Willie	442	0	442	92	62	0	400	W1, ON1, WW1
Thomas, -	1	0	1	0	0	0	0	
Thompson, AJ 'Jack'	1	0	1	0	0	0	0	
Thompson, Bobby	31	0	31	5	2	0	24	
Thornburrow, TS	5	0	5	0	0	0	0	
Thornley, Andy	0	1	1	1	0	0	4	
Thornley, Iain	6	0	6	3	0	0	12	
Thurlow, Stephen	2	0	2	0	0	0	0	
Todd, Peter	142	0	142	38	0	0	114	
Todd, William	31	0	31	1	0	0	3	
Tomkins, Logan (1)	9	9	18	3	0	0	12	
Tomkins, Logan (2)	97	22	119	5	0	0	20	
Treacy, Darren	25	1	26	6	1	0	26	
Tunks, Peter	6	2	8	1	0	0	4	
Tunney, Pat	222	0	222	11	0	0	33	E1, L18
Turgut, Jansin	8	4	12	1	0	0	4	
Turnbull, Sam	118	47	165	30	0	0	92	L1+1
Turner, Horace	6	0	6	0	0	0	0	
Turner, Joe	7	0	7	1	2	0	7	

Salford RL Players – Statistics

	App	Sub	Tot	Tries	Goals	D-gls	Pts	Representative
Turner, Jordan	59	10	69	24	15	0	126	
Twist, David	7	0	7	0	13	0	26	
Tyrer, Gary	12	1	13	5	5	0	30	
Tyrer, Steve	20	0	20	6	9	0	42	
Tyson, George	0	1	1	1	0	0	4	
Varney, John	1	0	1	0	0	0	0	
Varty, John	32	0	32	3	0	0	9	
Vatuvei, Manu	8	0	8	5	0	0	20	T1
Veivers, Josh	6	0	6	3	0	0	12	
Viane, Gray	11	0	11	2	0	0	8	
Vibart, Spencer	8	0	8	0	0	0	0	
Vidot, Daniel	8	2	10	6	0	0	24	
Vipond, Harry*	13	0	13	0	0	0	0	
Vuniyayawa, King	11	6	17	2	0	0	8	FJ3+1
Wadeson, -	1	0	1	0	0	0	0	
Wainwright, Mike (1)	76	4	80	9	0	0	36	S1
Wainwright, Mike (2)	3	0	3	0	0	0	0	
Waite, Billy	78	0	78	4	0	0	12	
Wakefield, Mark	15	5	20	2	0	0	8	
Walch, Sam*	3	0	3	0	0	0	0	
Walker, A	1	0	1	0	0	0	0	
Walker, Adam	10	15	25	4	0	0	16	S1
Walker, James	3	0	3	1	0	0	3	
Walker, Peter	72	2	74	1	1	0	5	
Walker, Ron	74	0	74	32	21	0	138	
Wallwork, W	4	0	4	0	0	0	0	
Walne, Adam	18	58	76	3	0	0	12	
Walne, Jordan	22	34	56	4	0	0	16	
Walsh, David	1	2	3	0	0	0	0	
Walsh, Joe	10	5	15	0	0	0	0	
Walsh, Lawrence	3	0	3	0	0	0	0	
Walton, Colin	7	0	7	1	0	0	3	
Walton, Jason (1)		9	9	2	0	0	8	
Walton, Jason (2)	7	14	21	1	0	0	4	
Wanklyn, Bullig	41	0	41	0	0	0	0	
Ward, Johnny	81	0	81	6	0	0	18	TR1, GB1, E1
Ward, Phil	19	14	33	6	0	0	18	
Warhurst, Glen	1	0	1	0	0	0	0	
Waring, Phil	6	8	14	2	0	0	8	
Warren, Wayne	7	3	10	2	0	0	6	
Warwick, Silas	209	0	209	19	1	0	59	GB2, E1, C9
Watkins, David	405	2	407	147	1225	16	2907	TR1, GB2+4, W16
Watkins, Kallum	36	1	37	16	0	0	64	E5
Watkins, WE 'Billy'	360	0	360	45	8	0	151	TR1, GB7, W6
Watson, Ian (1)	27	15	42	6	30	8	92	W1
Watson, Ian (2)	12	11	23	2	0	1	9	W1

Salford RL Players – Statistics

	App	Sub	Tot	Tries	Goals	D-gls	Pts	Representative
Watson, Robert	44	0	44	0	0	0	0	
Waugh, Richard	1	0	1	0	0	0	0	
Webber, Jason	28	1	29	11	0	0	44	
Webster, Richard	31	20	51	13	0	0	52	W+4
Welham, Kris	100	2	102	31	0	0	124	
Wells, Jack	8	6	14	1	0	0	4	
Whalley, Joe	27	0	27	1	21	0	45	
Wharton, Alan	21	0	21	1	0	0	3	
White, Clarence 'Lofty'	14	0	14	0	15	0	30	
White, Josh	22	3	25	11	7	1	59	
White, Paul	33	0	33	31	0	0	124	
White, Ted	6	0	6	0	0	0	0	
White, Tom	26	0	26	4	1	0	14	
Whitehead, Harold	1	0	1	0	0	0	0	
Whitehead, JF	35	0	35	2	0	0	6	
Whitehead, Stuart	203	20	223	56	0	0	168	L1+1
Whiteley, Chris	28	1	29	0	0	0	0	
Whitfield, Colin	79	10	89	11	101	4	239	L3
Whitney, Harold 'George'	115	0	115	13	0	0	39	W2, ON1
Whittle, Fred	59	0	59	2	0	0	6	
Wiggins, Richard	2	0	2	0	0	0	0	
Wild, Alfred	15	0	15	4	0	0	12	
Wild, Stephen	74	0	74	4	0	0	16	
Wilkinson, W 'Bill'	181	0	181	21	0	0	63	
Williams, Connor	0	1	1	0	0	0	0	
Williams, Daley	11	2	13	4	0	0	16	
Williams, Danny	56	0	56	31	0	0	124	
Williams, Jack (1897-1906)	269	0	269	9	0	0	27	L6
Williams, Jack (1930-31)	26	0	26	4	0	0	12	
Williams, Jason	10	0	10	6	0	0	24	
Williams, John	97	0	97	2	0	0	6	
Williams, Llewellyn	111	0	111	3	126	0	261	GM2, MM1
Williams, Owen	35	0	35	6	0	0	18	
Williams, Peter	146	8	154	35	0	0	140	GB1+1, W1, L1
Williams, Rhys (1)	4	0	4	0	0	0	0	
Williams, Rhys (2)	49	0	49	17	0	0	68	W4
Williams, Stewart	183	40	223	60	0	0	197	
Williams, Syd	222	0	222	81	43	0	329	W5
Williams, Tom	140	0	140	84	14	0	280	L6
Williams, WA 'Billy'	435	0	435	14	0	0	42	TR2, GB2, W3, ON1, GM5
Wilshere, John	108	2	110	51	269	0	742	PN2
Wilson, Frank	66	5	71	17	0	0	51	
Wilson, George	13	0	13	2	2	0	10	
Wilson, Scott	2	0	2	0	0	0	0	
Wilson, Terry	92	3	95	8	0	0	24	

Salford RL Players – Statistics

	App	Sub	Tot	Tries	Goals	D-gls	Pts	Representative
Wiltshire, Roy	32	1	33	10	0	0	40	
Winslade, Charlie	2	0	2	0	0	0	0	
Winstanley, Jack	19	0	19	7	0	0	21	
Winstanley, John	2	0	2	0	0	0	0	
Wood, John	18	0	18	4	0	0	16	
Wood, Josh	27	20	47	5	0	0	20	
Wood, Mike	2	0	2	0	0	0	0	
Wood, Sam	4	0	4	0	0	0	0	
Woodhead, Herbert 'Harry'	80	0	80	6	2	0	22	L1
Woodhead, Lawrence	11	0	11	1	0	0	3	
Woods, Ernie	185	0	185	9	0	0	27	
Worrall, Mick	99	10	109	27	9	2	128	
Worrall, Tony	12	3	15	0	0	0	0	
Worthington, Joe	33	0	33	0	0	0	0	
Wright, Albert	2	0	2	0	0	0	0	
Wright, Shane	10	2	12	2	0	0	8	
Wynne, Steve	1	0	1	0	0	0	0	
Yates, Luke	13	6	19	3	0	0	12	
Yates, Malcolm	89	1	90	28	24	0	132	L+1
Young, David	153	0	153	15	8	0	76	W13
AN Other (1898)	1	0	1	0	0	0	0	
AN Other (1925)	1	0	1	0	0	0	0	
AN Other (1940)	1	0	1	0	0	0	0	
AN Other (1945)	1	0	1	0	0	0	0	
AN Other (1946)	1	0	1	0	0	0	0	
AN Other (1947)	1	0	1	0	0	0	0	
AN Other (1950)	3	0	3	0	0	0	0	
AN Other (1955)	2	0	2	0	0	0	0	
AN Other (Feb 1956)	2	0	2	0	0	0	0	
AN Other (Apr 1956)	1	0	1	0	0	0	0	
AN Other (Jan 1960)	1	0	1	0	0	0	0	
AN Other (Oct 1960)	1	0	1	0	0	0	0	
AN Other (4 May 1963)	1	0	1	0	0	0	0	
AN Other (18 May 1963)	1	0	1	0	0	0	0	
AN Other (1968)	1	0	1	1	0	0	3	
AN Other (1980)	1	0	1	0	0	0	0	
'Davies'	1	0	1	0	0	0	0	
'Gallagher'	1	0	1	0	0	0	0	
'Jackson'	1	0	1	0	0	0	0	
'McDonald'	1	0	1	0	0	0	0	
'Newman' (1945)	1	0	1	0	0	0	0	
'Newman' (1954)	1	0	1	0	0	0	0	
'Parr'	2	0	2	0	0	0	0	
'SO Else'	1	0	1	0	0	0	0	

*Also played for Salford under Rugby Union prior to 1896 breakaway

Billy Williams was the Salford captain during the club's earliest successes under Lance Todd.

Salford RL Match Results

1896-97

	Opponent	Result	Attendance	Scorers
Sep 1	TYLDESLEY (F)	L 6-7	5,000	T: Moss, PG: Fawcett
Sep 5	Widnes	L 0-10	3,000	
Sep 12	OLDHAM	L 0-9	7,000	
Sep 19	ST HELENS	D 0-0	4,000	
Sep 26	Leigh	L 0-14	2,500	
Oct 3	ROCHDALE HORNETS	D 3-3	5,000	T: JJ Jones
Oct 10	Stockport	L 3-6	6,000	T: Fawcett
Oct 17	Warrington	L 0-10	6,000	
Oct 19	Brighouse Rangers (F)	L 3-5	2,000	T: H Davies
Oct 24	Swinton	D 0-0	6,000	
Oct 31	Broughton Rangers	L 0-11	12,000	
Nov 7	WIGAN	W 16-3	5,000	T: Coleman, Crocker, Griffiths, Woodhead, C:Fawcett, Griffiths
Nov 14	Tyldesley	L 10-21	1,500	T: Fawcett, Heath, C: Manwaring 2
Nov 28	ROCHDALE ST CLEMENT'S (F)	L 3-4	5,000	T: Fisher
Dec 5	MORECAMBE	W 13-0	3,000	T: Frame, C: Griffiths, DG: Fawcett, Griffiths
Dec 12	RUNCORN	L 0-3	5,000	
Dec 19	Oldham	L 3-11	6,000	T: Harter
Dec 26	TYLDESLEY	L 0-14	3,000	
Jan 1	Wigan	L 5-6	4,000	T: Harter, C:Griffiths
Jan 2	Morecambe	W 6-3	2,000	T: Moss, Pearson
Jan 4	HUDDERSFIELD (F)	L 6-8	–	T: Brown, Pearson
Jan 9	Rochdale Hornets	L 0-7	–	
Jan 16	Runcorn	D 3-3	2,000	T: Pearson
Jan 23	WIDNES	L 5-7	4,000	T: Griffiths, C: Griffiths
Jan 30	St Helens	L 3-9	1,000	T: Harter
Feb 6	STOCKPORT	L 0-3	8,000	
Feb 13	SWINTON	L 0-12	9,000	
Feb 27	BROUGHTON RANGERS	L 0-15	11,000	
Mar 2	Wigan (F)	W 5-3	2,000	T: Harter, C: Griffiths
Mar 6	WARRINGTON	L 3-8	5,000	T: Llewellyn
Mar 13	LEIGH	D 3-3	4,000	T: Haslam
Mar 20	WARRINGTON ST MARY'S (NUC-1)	W 28-0	3,000	T: Pearson 2, Harter, Llewellyn, Miles, Woodhead, C: Griffiths 3, DG: Griffiths
Mar 27	Werneth (NUC-2)*	W 30-0	3,000	T: Miles 2, Pearson 2, Crocker, Harter, King, C: Doran 2, Manwaring, PG: Manwaring
Apr 3	Stockport (NUC-3)	L 0-8	7,000	

Salford RL Match Results

1896-97 *continued*

	Opponent	Result	Attendance	Scorers
Apr 10	WAKEFIELD TRINITY (F)	W 5-3	–	T: Pearson, C: Manwaring
Apr 16	Manningham (F)	W 12-9	3,000	T: Pearson, C: Griffiths, DG: Griffiths, PG: Fisher
Apr 17	MANNINGHAM (F)**	A 5-0	–	T: Miles, C: Griffiths
Apr 19	BRIGHOUSE RANGERS (F)	W 19-0	3,000	T: Grey, Griffiths, Harter, Pearson, Woodhead, C: Griffiths 2
Apr 20	Huddersfield (F)	L 5-29	–	T: Llewellyn, C: Griffiths
Apr 24	Rochdale St Clement's (F)	W 9-3	–	T: Harter, C: Griffiths, DG: Griffiths
Apr 28	BARTON (F)	W 11-9	–	T: Pearson 2, Worsley, C: Manwaring

* *Away tie played at Rochdale* ** *Abandoned half-time (storm)*

Scoring values: T (try) = 3 points, C (conversion) = 2, DG (drop-goal) = 4, PG (penalty) = 3

1897-98

	Opponent	Result	Attendance	Scorers
Sep 1	WIGAN (F)	W 8-0	4,000	T: Hoskins, T Williams, G: T Williams
Sep 4	ST HELENS	W 8-0	4,000	T: Heath, Hoskins, G: Griffiths
Sep 11	WIDNES	W 8-7	8,000	T: Hoskins 2, G: Griffiths
Sep 18	Morecambe	W 13-4	–	T: Hoskins, Pearson, T Williams, G: Griffiths 2
Sep 25	Oldham	L 6-16	20,000	T: Fisher, Harter
Oct 2	TYLDESLEY	W 32-0	4,000	T: T Williams 4, Hoskins 3, J Williams 2, Pearson, G: Griffiths
Oct 9	STOCKPORT	L 3-6	8,000	T: Hoskins
Oct 16	Rochdale Hornets	W 19-5	6,000	T: T Williams 2, Gledhill, Hoskins, Rhapps, G: Llewellyn 2
Oct 23	BROUGHTON RANGERS	W 11-3	15,000	T: Harter, Hoskins, Sharp, G: W Brown
Oct 30	Wigan	L 0-6	5,000	
Nov 6	SWINTON	D 0-0	20,000	
Nov 13	Stockport	W 19-8	7,000	T: Hoskins 2, Harter, Sharp, Tunney, G: W Brown, D Smith
Nov 20	WARRINGTON	W 13-2	8,000	T: Grey, Harter, Hoskins, G: T Williams 2
Nov 27	Leigh	L 3-20	3,000	T: Hoskins
Dec 4	Runcorn	W 21-8	–	T: T Williams 3, Hoskins 2, G: T Williams 3
Dec 11	Widnes	L 6-25	3,000	T: T Williams 2

Salford RL Match Results

1897-98 *continued*

	Opponent	Result	Attendance	Scorers
Dec 18	ROCHDALE HORNETS*	A 14-3	5,000	T: Pearson, Sharp, T Williams, Woodhead, G: Griffiths
Dec 25	BARTON (F)	W 32-0	4,000	T: Sharp 3, T Williams 3, Gledhill, Pearson, G: T Williams 4
Dec 27	WIGAN	W 8-2	6,000	T: Pearson, T Williams, G: T Williams
Jan 1	Swinton	L 8-12	20,000	T: Hoskins, T Williams, G: W Brown
Jan 8	Tyldesley	L 8-9	1,000	T: Hoskins, T Williams, G: T Williams
Jan 15	RUNCORN	W 20-5	7,000	T: Hoskins 2, T Williams 2, G: Griffiths 3, T Williams
Jan 22	Warrington	D 3-3	7,000	T: Grey
Jan 26	ROCHDALE HORNETS	W 14-11	3,000	T: Grey, Griffiths, Pearson, T Williams, G: T Williams
Jan 29	WALKDEN (F)	L 5-6	1,000	T: Pearson, G: Hignett
Feb 5	OLDHAM	W 10-6	19,000	T: Hoskins, Moss, Griffiths 2
Feb 12	Broughton Rangers	W 6-2	15,000	T: Hoskins 2
Feb 19	MORECAMBE	W 11-3	4,500	T: Pearson 2, Miles, G: Griffiths
Feb 26	MILLOM (NUC-1)**	W 9-2	6,000	T: Hoskins, Miles, T Williams
Mar 5	LEES (NUC-2)	W 65-2	4,000	T: Miles 6, T Williams 5, Hoskins 3, Pearson 2, Griffiths, G: Griffiths 5, Hoskins, T Williams
Mar 12	St Helens	D 14-14	2,000	T: Pearson 2, Heath, Hoskins, G: Griffiths
Mar 19	Altrincham (NUC-3)	W 16-0	6,000	T: T Williams 2, Griffiths, Miles, G: Griffiths 2
Mar 26	BRAMLEY (NUC-4)	W 12-2	7,000	T: T Williams 2, Miles, Pearson
Apr 8	LEIGH	W 11-4	5,000	T: Dixon, Harter, E Smith, G: Doran
Apr 9	Batley (NUC-SF)***	L 0-5	15,000	
Apr 16	Walkden (F)	W 33-5	1,000	T: Miles 4, T Williams 2, Hoskins, G: T Williams 2 *(reported scoring details incomplete)*
Apr 23	LEEDS PARISH CHURCH (F)	W 11-6	3,000	T: Miles 2, Griffiths, G: T Williams
Apr 30	Barton (F)	W 11-0	500	T: Miles 2, Heath, G: Woodhead

* *Abandoned 15 mins after half-time (fog)* ** *Away tie switched to Salford* *** *At Oldham*

Scoring values: All goals (G) count as 2 points from this season

Salford RL Match Results

1898-99

	Opponent	Result	Attendance	Scorers
Sep 1	ST HELENS (F)	L 0-6	8,000	
Sep 3	TYLDESLEY	W 13-3	8,000	T: Hoskins, Phillips, Sharp, G: Phillips 2
Sep 10	LEIGH	W 6-2	10,000	T: Gledhill, J Williams
Sep 17	Runcorn*	W 6-2	4,000	T: R Thomas, T Williams
Sep 24	Tyldesley	W 11-0	3,000	T: Gledhill, Pearson, Phillips, G: Phillips
Oct 1	WARRINGTON	W 9-3	10,000	T: Miles 2, Phillips
Oct 8	Swinton	L 0-2	20,000	
Oct 15	MILLOM (F)	W 12-7	5,000	T: Pearson 2, Miles, T Williams
Oct 22	OLDHAM	W 6-3	12,000	T: R Thomas, T Williams
Oct 29	Broughton Rangers	W 7-0	20,000	T: Heath, G: Woodhead 2
Nov 12	RUNCORN	W 13-10	8,000	T: Hoskins 2, T Williams, G: Phillips 2
Nov 19	Widnes	L 6-9	10,000	T: T Williams 2
Nov 26	Stockport	W 16-4	6,000	T: Sharp 2, Griffiths, Pearson, G: Griffiths 2
Dec 3	ROCHDALE HORNETS	W 17-9	7,000	T: Grey 2, Sharp 2, Pearson, G: Griffiths
Dec 10	STOCKPORT	W 12-8	7,000	T: Pearson 2, T Williams, Woodhead
Dec 17	Leigh	L 0-7	4,000	
Dec 24	ST HELENS	W 13-2	5,000	T Heath, Sharp, T Williams, G: Griffiths, T Williams
Dec 26	Wigan	W 13-5	4,000	T: Heath, Pearson, T Williams, G: T Williams 2
Dec 27	Bradford (F)	W 3-2	2,000	T: Sharp
Dec 31	Rochdale Hornets	D 0-0	5,000	
Jan 2	WIGAN	W 5-0	3,000	T: Woodhead, G: Griffiths
Jan 7	St Helens	D 8-8	–	T: Gledhill, Sharp, G: Griffiths
Jan 14	Morecambe	W 8-0	–	T: Pearson 2, G: Phillips
Jan 21	WIDNES	W 7-3	8,000	T: T Williams, G: Phillips, Rhapps
Feb 4	BROUGHTON RANGERS	L 0-3	16,000	
Feb 11	Warrington	L 6-14	7,000	T: France, Heath
Feb 18	Oldham	L 0-14	22,000	
Feb 25	SWINTON	W 8-2	18,000	T: Pearson, R Thomas, G: Phillips
Mar 4	MORECAMBE	W 16-0	5,000	T: France 3, Benyon, G: W Brown, T Williams

Salford RL Match Results

1898-99 *continued*

	Opponent	Result	Attendance	Scorers
Mar 11	TYLDESLEY (F)	W 24-7	4,000	T: J Hoskins 2, Phillips 2, R Thomas, Woodhead, G: W Brown, Hoskins, R Thomas
Mar 18	LUDDENDENFOOT (NUC-1)	W 63-3	5,000	T: Hoskins 3, R Thomas 3, Phillips 3, T Williams 3, Pearson 2, Gledhill, G: Phillips 9
Mar 20	Millom (F)	W 5-0	–	T: R Thomas, G: Griffiths
Mar 25	WERNETH (NUC-2)	W 31-0	–	T: R Thomas 2, Grey, Hoskins, Pearson, Phillips, T Williams, G: Phillips 4, Pearson
Apr 1	ST HELENS (NUC-3)	W 16-0	6,000	T: Phillips 2, W Brown, Woodhead, G: Phillips 2
Apr 3	BRADFORD (F)	W 15-4	6,000	T: Gledhill, D Smith, R Thomas, G: Griffiths, Phillips, D Smith
Apr 8	HUDDERSFIELD (NUC-4)	W 8-0	12,000	T: R Thomas 2, G: Phillips
Apr 15	Hunslet (NUC-SF)**	L 8-15	7,000	T: E Jones, Tunney, G: Phillips
Apr 22	HALIFAX (F)	W 12-2	5,000	T: T Williams 3, Hignett
Apr 28	SWINTON (F)	W 6-0		T: T Williams 2

* All the Salford backs were Welsh   ** At Bradford

1899-1900

	Opponent	Result	Attendance	Scorers
Sep 2	TYLDESLEY	W 24-3	8,000	T: T Williams 2, Grey, Griffiths, Hadwen, R Thomas, G: Griffiths 3
Sep 9	LANCASTER (F)	W 18-0	5,000	T: Griffiths 2, T Williams 2, Hadwen, R Thomas
Sep 16	Rochdale Hornets	W 14-5	6,000	T: Hadwen 2, Pearson, Tunney, G: Hignett
Sep 23	Tyldesley	W 23-7	700	T: Pearson 3, Shaw, R Thomas, G: Griffiths 4
Sep 24	Leigh	W 12-7	6,000	T: Hadwen 2, G: Griffiths 3
Oct 7	SWINTON	L 6-11	20,000	T: Pearson, T Williams
Oct 14	BROUGHTON RANGERS	L 0-9	14,000	
Oct 21	WARRINGTON	W 10-2	8,000	T: Bowley, Norris, G: Phillips 2
Oct 28	Oldham	L 2-10	15,000	G: Doran
Nov 4	ROCHDALE HORNETS	W 14-3	8,000	T: Pearson 3, T Williams, G: Phillips

Salford RL Match Results

1899-1900 *continued*

	Opponent	Result	Attendance	Scorers
Nov 11	St Helens	L 6-8	–	T: Phillips, T Williams
Nov 18	LEIGH	L 7-9	9,000	T: Hoskins, G: Griffiths, D Smith
Nov 25	Runcorn	L 0-13	4,000	
Dec 9	MILLOM	W 17-10	–	T: Pearson 3, Hadwen, T Williams, G: Pearson
Dec 16	WIDNES	W 11-3	7,000	T: Hadwen, Pearson, Phillips, G: Hadwen
Dec 23	Stockport	W 8-2	4,000	T: Hadwen, Tunney, G: Phillips
Dec 25	WIGAN	L 3-5	7,000	T: Hadwen
Dec 30	BROUGHTON RANGERS (F)	W 9-3	6,000	T: Grey, Pearson, J Thomas
Jan 1	Wigan	L 5-8	3,000	T: Hoskins, G: Phillips
Jan 6	STOCKPORT	L 5-7	4,000	T: R Thomas, G: Hadwen
Jan 13	Broughton Rangers	W 3-2	9,000	T: Harter
Jan 20	Warrington	W 7-2	5,000	T: Grey, G: Phillips 2
Jan 27	OLDHAM	L 0-6	10,000	
Feb 3	Widnes	L 3-10	3,000	T: T Williams
Feb 17	Millom	L 0-2	–	
Feb 21	RUNCORN	L 3-8	8,000	T: W Brown
Feb 24	Swinton	L 5-24	12,000	T: J Thomas, G: Hignett
Mar 3	Lancaster (F)	W 13-2	–	T: Hignett, R Thomas, T Williams, G: Griffiths, D Smith
Mar 10	ST HELENS	W 8-0	8,000	T: T Williams 2, G: Griffiths
Mar 17	YORK (NUC-1)	W 9-0	6,000	T: Griffiths, Pearson, R Thomas
Mar 24	Leigh (NUC-2)	W 9-2	6,000	T: Hadwen, Tunney, T Williams
Mar 31	HUDDERSFIELD (NUC-3)	W 6-5	7,000	T: R Thomas, T Williams
Apr 7	ROCHDALE HORNETS (NUC-4)	W 11-3	14,000	T: Hadwen, Pearson, T Williams, G: W Brown
Apr 14	Widnes (NUC-SF)*	W 11-0	14,000	T: R Thomas 2, Harter, G: W Brown
Apr 17	HULL (F)	W 9-5	4,000	T: Pearson 2, J Thomas
Apr 21	Hull (F)	L 5-32	4,000	T: J Thomas, G: Woodhead
Apr 28	Swinton (NUC-Final)**	L 8-16	17,864	T: Pearson, T Williams, G: Griffiths

*At Oldham   ** At Fallowfield, Manchester

Northern Union Challenge Cup runners-up

Salford RL Match Results

1900-1901

	Opponent	Result	Attendance	Scorers
Sep 1	MILLOM	W 11-2	6,000	T: Aldred, R Thomas, T Williams, G: Griffiths
Sep 8	Warrington	L 7-10	6,000	T: Aldred, G: Aldred, D Smith
Sep 15	LEIGH	L 5-11	10,000	T: T Williams, G: Griffiths
Sep 22	ROCHDALE HORNETS	L 7-11	6,000	T: Bone, G: DJ Davies, D Smith
Sep 29	Barrow	W 14-9	5,000	T: Bone, H Buckler, Griffiths, T Williams, G:Griffiths
Oct 6	WIDNES	W 27-0	5,000	T: Bone 3, Booth, H Buckler, Tunney, T Williams, G: Griffiths 3
Oct 13	Swinton	L 9-12	12,000	T: T Williams, G: H Buckler 3
Oct 20	LANCASTER (F)	W 15-2	3,000	T: Pearson 2, DJ Davies, G: Phillips 3
Oct 27	Broughton Rangers	L 8-9	10,000	T: Bone, Phillips, G: Hadwen
Nov 10	OLDHAM	L 0-10	12,000	
Nov 17	St Helens	W 13-2	4,000	T: Hadwen, Heath, T Williams, G: Hadwen, Phillips
Nov 24	RUNCORN	W 11-10	8,000	T: Bone, Hadwen, T Williams, G: Hadwen
Dec 1	Leigh	W 10-6	4,000	T: Bone, Griffiths, G: Hadwen, D Smith
Dec 8	MORECAMBE (F)	W 15-0	1,500	T: H Buckler, Griffiths, Heath, G: Griffiths 2, Hadwen
Dec 15	WARRINGTON	W 13-0	6,000	T: Bone, Grey, Griffiths, G: Phillips 2
Dec 22	Stockport	W 8-5	3,000	T: DJ Davies, Hadwen, G: Hadwen
Dec 25	Wigan	L 3-10	5,000	T: H Buckler
Dec 29	SWINTON	L 0-3	15,000	
Jan 1	WIGAN	W 5-0	4,000	T: Varty, G: Phillips
Jan 5	Lancaster (F)	W 11-5	3,000	T: DJ Davies, Hadwen, Heath, G: DJ Davies
Jan 12	STOCKPORT	W 7-0	6,000	T: H Buckler, G: Phillips, D Smith
Jan 19	BROUGHTON RANGERS	L 2-8	8,000	G: Griffiths
Jan 26	Runcorn	L 0-4	3,000	
Feb 9	Rochdale Hornets	W 13-5	6,000	T: DJ Davies, Shaw, T Williams, G: Phillips 2
Feb 23	Widnes	W 17-5	2,000	T: T Williams 3, Hadwen, Phillips, G: Phillips

Salford RL Match Results

1900-1901 *continued*

	Opponent	Result	Attendance	Scorers
Mar 2	Hull Kingston Rovers (NUC-1)	L 0-4	6,000	
Mar 16	Millom	W 9-3	–	T: Hadwen, G: Hadwen 3
Mar 23	Halifax (F)	L 2-8	3,000	G: Hadwen
Mar 30	BARROW	W 14-2	5,000	T: T Williams 2, Hadwen, Heath, G: D Smith
Apr 5	ST HELENS	W 16-7	8,000	T: H Buckler, DJ Davies, Hadwen, T Williams, G: DJ Davies 2
Apr 6	Oldham	L 0-5	15,000	
Apr 8	Morecambe (F)	W 8-5	3,000	T: Heath, Pearson, G: Hadwen
Apr 20	HALIFAX (F)	W 16-12	3,000	T: Harter, Pearson, Shore, E Smith, G: D Smith 2

1901-1902

	Opponent	Result	Attendance	Scorers
Sep 7	BRIGHOUSE RANGERS	W 16-0	8,000	T: Price 2, W Brown, T Williams, G: DJ Davies, Griffiths
Sep 14	SOUTH SHIELDS (F)	W 25-0	3,000	T: T Williams 4, DJ Davies, Dyson, Hadwen, G: DJ Davies 2
Sep 21	Leigh	L 2-11	5,000	G: Lomas
Sep 28	Huddersfield	W 11-3	4,000	T: Lomas 2, Price, G: Lomas
Oct 5	BRADFORD	L 10-14	5,000	T: Lomas, T Williams, G: Lomas 2
Oct 12	HALIFAX	W 9-4	8,000	T: T Williams, G: Lomas 3
Oct 19	Broughton Rangers*	L 2-3	15,000	G: Lomas
Oct 26	Hull	L 5-14	8,000	T: Bone, G: Griffiths
Nov 2	BATLEY	W 14-6	8,000	T: T Williams 2, Lomas, Varty, G: Lomas
Nov 9	Brighouse Rangers	W 24-8	2,000	T: Lomas 2, Price 2, Griffith, D Smith, G: Lomas 3
Nov 23	LEIGH	W 11-3	7,000	T: Griffiths, Lomas, Varty, G: Lomas
Nov 30	HULL	W 11-5	9,000	T: Bone, Heath, Price, G: Lomas
Dec 7	Halifax	D 0-0	8,000	
Dec 14	Rochdale Hornets (SELL)	D 0-0	3,000	
Dec 21	SWINTON*	W 2-0	16,981	G: Lomas
Dec 25	BROUGHTON RANGERS*	L 0-3	9,000	
Dec 26	STOCKPORT (SELL)	W 7-0	2,000	T: Hayton, G: Lomas 2
Dec 28	Runcorn	L 2-6	5,000	G: Lomas
Jan 1	HUNSLET	L 0-7	5,000	
Jan 4	Oldham*	D 0-0	5,000	

Salford RL Match Results

1901-1902 *continued*

	Opponent	Result	Attendance	Scorers
Jan 11	South Shields (F)	W 13-8	3,000	T: Bone, Gledhill, Price, G: DJ Davies, Lomas
Jan 18	Hunslet	W 11-3	5,000	T: Lomas, G: Lomas 4
Jan 25	OLDHAM*	W 6-0	12,000	T: Bone, Varty
Feb 11	Bradford	W 2-0	4,000	G: Lomas
Feb 22	Swinton*	L 5-13	15,000	T: Bone, G: Lomas
Feb 25	Batley	W 11-9	–	T: Heath, Price, T Williams, G: Lomas
Mar 1	WARRINGTON	W 16-6	8,000	T: Lomas 2, Bone, Price, G: Lomas 2
Mar 3	ROCHDALE HORNETS (SELL)	W 19-3	2,000	T: Lomas 2, Hayton, Price, T Williams, G: Griffiths, Lomas
Mar 8	RUNCORN	D 0-0	5,000	
Mar 15	PONTEFRACT (NUC-1)	W 28-2	4,000	T: Bone 2, Price 2, Lomas, T Williams, G: Lomas 5
Mar 22	Dewsbury (NUC-2)	W 2-0	6,000	G: Lomas
Mar 28	Stockport (SELL)	W 8-3	2,000	T: Price 2, G: Hignett
Mar 29	GOOLE (NUC-3)	W 67-0	1,500	T: Bone 6, Lomas 3, T Williams 3, DJ Davies 2, Heath, G: Lomas 11
Mar 31	HUDDERSFIELD	W 57-0	3,000	T: Price 5, DJ Davies 2, Lomas 2, T Williams 2, Bone, H Buckler, G: Lomas 5, DJ Davies 4
Apr 5	Huddersfield (NUC-4)	W 9-6	6,000	T: DJ Davies, Lomas, Price
Apr 12	Batley (NUC-SF)**	W 8-0	13,000	T: DJ Davies, Lomas, G: Lomas
Apr 14	Warrington	W 8-7	4,000	T: DJ Davies, Price, G: Lomas
Apr 26	Bradford (NUC-Final)***	L 0-25	15,006	

* *Also counted in the SELL*   ** *At Oldham*   *** *At Rochdale*

Home matches played at The Willows from Dec 21 (previously at New Barnes)
Northern Rugby League Championship runners-up
Northern Union Challenge Cup runners-up

1902-1903

	Opponent	Result	Attendance	Scorers
Sep 6	HUNSLET	W 11-7	8,000	T: T Williams 2, Shore, G: DJ Davies
Sep 13	Wigan	W 5-0	8,000	T: Riley, G: Griffiths
Sep 20	WIDNES	W 5-0	6,000	T: Lomas, G: Lomas
Sep 27	Bradford	D 2-2	10,000	G: Lomas

Salford RL Match Results

1902-1903 *continued*

	Opponent	Result	Attendance	Scorers
Oct 4	HUDDERSFIELD	W 4-0	7,000	G: W Brown, Lomas
Oct 11	WARRINGTON	W 9-5	8,000	T: Bone, Lomas, T Williams
Oct 13	Brighouse Rangers	L 0-4	1,000	
Oct 18	BROUGHTON RANGERS	L 0-5	14,710	
Oct 25	St Helens	L 5-9	–	T: Norris, G: Lomas
Nov 1	RUNCORN	W 10-6	7,000	T: TG Bell 2, G: W Brown, Griffiths
Nov 8	Batley	L 2-5	2,000	G: D Smith
Nov 22	HALIFAX	W 12-0	7,000	T: TG Bell, Shore, G: Lomas 3
Nov 29	Leigh	W 5-0	5,000	T: Lomas, G: Griffiths
Dec 6	HULL	D 3-3	5,000	T: TG Bell
Dec 13	Oldham	W 2-0	5,000	G: D Smith
Dec 25	Broughton Rangers	D 0-0	18,000	
Dec 27	HULL KINGSTON ROVERS	W 17-0	5,000	T: Heath, Norris, Preston, G: Lomas 3, D Smith
Jan 1	Swinton	D 6-6	15,000	T: TG Bell, H Buckler
Jan 3	Hunslet	W 16-2	7,000	T: Lomas 2, TG Bell, Norris, G: W Brown, Lomas
Jan 10	WIGAN	L 0-13	4,000	
Jan 24	BRADFORD	W 14-0	5,000	T: TG Bell, Lomas, Preston, Shaw, G: Lomas
Jan 31	Huddersfield	W 12-6	5,000	T: Norris 2, TG Bell, Lomas
Feb 5	Widnes	L 3-7	2,000	T: Harter
Feb 7	Warrington	W 11-2	5,000	T: TG Bell, Messer, J Williams, G: Lomas
Feb 14	ALTRINCHAM (NUC-1)	W*	–	
Feb 21	LEIGH (NUC-2)	W 11-0	6,000	T: TG Bell, Harter, Lomas, G: W Brown
Feb 24	BRIGHOUSE RANGERS	W 14-0	3,000	T: Harter, Lomas, Messer, Shore, G: Lomas
Feb 28	Runcorn	L 0-4	3,000	
Mar 7	Rochdale Hornets (NUC-3)	W 15-0	10,000	T: Lomas 3, TG Bell, Norris
Mar 14	SWINTON	W 10-0	17,312	T: Harter, Lomas, G: Griffiths, Lomas
Mar 16	BATLEY	W 28-8	2,000	T: TG Bell 3, Lomas 2, Norris 2, Harter, G: Griffiths, Lomas
Mar 21	York (NUC-4)	W 25-2	10,000	T: TG Bell 2, Norris 2, Lomas, Messer, Shaw, G: Harter, Lomas
Mar 28	LEIGH	W 14-0	6,000	T: Norris 2, Fletcher, Lomas, G: Lomas
Apr 4	Oldham (NUC-SF)**	D 0-0	19,000	

Salford RL Match Results

1902-1903 *continued*

	Opponent	Result	Attendance	Scorers
Apr 8	Oldham (NUC-SF Replay)**	W 8-0	12,000	T: Lomas, Norris, G: Griffiths
Apr 11	OLDHAM	W 3-0	9,000	T: Griffiths
Apr 13	ST HELENS	W 11-3	5,000	T: TG Bell, W Brown, Messer, G: Griffiths
Apr 16	Halifax	D 5-5	14,000	T: Lomas, G: Lomas
Apr 20	Hull	L 5-12		T: Norris, G: Lomas
Apr 25	Halifax (NUC-Final)***	L 0-7	32,507	
Apr 27	Hull Kingston Rovers	L 0-16	1,000	

*Walkover, Altrincham disbanded   ** Both at Broughton   *** At Leeds*

First Division Championship runners-up
Northern Union Challenge Cup runners-up

1903-1904

	Opponent	Result	Attendance	Scorers
Sep 5	Batley	W 13-3	5,000	T: W Thomas 2, Norris, G: Lomas 2
Sep 12	KEIGHLEY	W 24-2	8,000	T: Bedford 2, Norris 2, Lomas, W Thomas, G: Lomas 2, D Smith
Sep 19	Broughton Rangers	W 20-6	17,000	T: Lomas 2, H Buckler, W Brown, G: W Brown 2, Lomas 2
Sep 26	HUNSLET	W 18-2	10,000	T: Harter, Heath, Lomas, W Thomas, G: Lomas 2, D Smith
Oct 3	Widnes	W 13-0	3,000	T: Harter, Lomas, Norris, G: Lomas 2
Oct 10	SWINTON	W 8-0	15,111	T: H Buckler, Heath, G: Lomas
Oct 17	Hull Kingston Rovers	D 7-7	10,000	T: Preston, G: Lomas 2
Oct 24	OLDHAM	L 2-8	12,000	G: D Smith
Oct 31	Halifax	L 3-6	12,000	T: Tunney
Nov 7	HUDDERSFIELD	W 16-3	6,000	T: H Buckler, Lomas, Preston, J Williams, G: Lomas 2
Nov 21	WIGAN	W 5-0	4,000	T: Baker, G: W Brown
Nov 28	Leeds	L 0-6	7,000	
Dec 5	RUNCORN*	A 5-0	3,000	T: Preston, G: Lomas
Dec 12	HULL	W 11-0	4,000	T: Norris, G: Lomas 4
Dec 19	Leigh	W 5-0	2,000	T: Heath, G: Lomas
Dec 25	Bradford	L 0-9	20,000	
Dec 26	WARRINGTON	L 3-11	8,000	T: Bedford
Dec 28	RUNCORN	W 19-0	4,000	T: Heath, Lomas, Norris, W Thomas, Tunney, G: Lomas, White

Salford RL Match Results

1903-1904 *continued*

	Opponent	*Result*	*Attendance*	*Scorers*
Jan 2	BATLEY	W 39-0	7,000	T: Lomas 4, White 2, Bedford, Heath, Tunney, G: Lomas 6
Jan 9	Keighley	D 2-2	3,000	G: Lomas
Jan 16	BROUGHTON RANGERS	W 5-3	12,000	T: Lomas, G: Lomas
Jan 23	Hunslet	L 2-12	9,000	G: Lomas
Jan 30	WIDNES	W 17-2	5,000	T: Allen 2, Lomas, W Thomas, Tunney, G: Lomas
Feb 6	Swinton	W 11-0	8,000	T: Bedford, Heath, Lomas, G: Lomas
Feb 13	HULL KINGSTON ROVERS	W 16-0	4,000	T: Heath, Lomas, Rhapps, W Thomas, G: Lomas 2
Feb 20	Oldham	W 2-0	7,000	G: Lomas
Feb 27	HALIFAX	W 5-0	6,000	T: J Williams, G: Lomas
Mar 5	Huddersfield	W 21-0	4,000	T: Lomas 2, Harter, Shaw, W Thomas, G: Lomas 2, W Brown
Mar 12	BROOKLAND ROVERS (NUC-1)**	W 57-0	–	T: W Thomas 4, Lomas 3, Norris 3, Bedford 2, Preston 2, Shaw, G: Lomas 5, Lambert
Mar 19	Hull (NUC-2)	W 23-5	12,000	T: W Brown 2, Shaw 2, Lomas, G: Lomas 4
Mar 26	LEEDS	W 12-3	10,000	T: Bedford, H Buckler, Preston, White
Mar 28	BRADFORD	W 4-2	5,000	G: Heath, Lomas
Apr 2	HUNSLET (NUC-3)	L 2-5	8,108	G: Lomas
Apr 4	Wigan	W 5-2	15,000	T: Preston, G: Lomas
Apr 9	Hull	L 0-7	6,000	
Apr 11	Runcorn	W 11-3	–	T: Lomas 2, White, G: W Brown
Apr 16	LEIGH	W 28-6	4,000	T: W Thomas 2, Bedford, Harter, Lomas, Preston, G: Lomas 4, D Smith
Apr 23	Warrington	W 19-3	5,000	T: Bedford 2, Harter, Lomas, Preston, G: Lomas 2
Apr 28	Bradford (NRL-Play off)***	L 0-5	10,154	

* Abandoned 19 mins after half-time (fog)   ** Away tie switched to Salford   *** At Halifax

First Division Championship runners-up

Salford RL Match Results

1904-1905

	Opponent	Result	Attendance	Scorers
Sep 3	Halifax	W 5-3	10,000	T: Lomas, G: Lomas
Sep 10	HULL	W 13-7	7,000	T: Bedford, Lewis, Norris, G: Lomas 2
Sep 17	Bradford	L 3-11	10,000	T: Lomas
Sep 24	LEEDS	L 3-9	7,000	T: Preston
Oct 1	Runcorn	L 3-10	2,000	T: H Buckler
Oct 8	OLDHAM	W 10-3	7,000	T: Heath, Preston, G: Lomas 2
Oct 15	Wigan	W 10-3	15,000	T: Allen, Parry, G: Lomas 2
Oct 22	SWINTON	L 3-8	14,000	T: W Brown
Oct 29	St Helens	L 11-13	4,000	T: Maddocks, G: Lomas 4
Nov 5	HULL KINGSTON ROVERS	W 15-4	7,000	T: Clayton, Richards, W Thomas, G: Lomas 2, W Brown
Nov 12	Batley	W 7-3	2,000	T: Tunney, G: W Brown 2
Nov 19	HUNSLET	W 12-6	5,000	T: Allen, Lomas, G: Lomas 3
Dec 3	Broughton Rangers	L 5-20	12,000	T: Tunney, G: Lomas
Dec 10	WARRINGTON	W 5-0	5,000	T: Lomas, G: Lomas
Dec 17	Wakefield Trinity	W 10-0	5,000	T: Lomas, W Thomas, G: Lomas, Richards
Dec 24	LEIGH	L 6-11	3,000	T: Lomas 2
Dec 31	HALIFAX	W 7-3	4,000	T: Lomas, G: Lomas, Richards
Jan 2	Widnes	L 0-2	3,000	
Jan 7	Hull	L 0-18	6,000	
Jan 14	BRADFORD	L 3-14	5,000	T: Bedford
Jan 21	Leeds	L 10-15	7,000	T: Lewis, Lomas, G: Lomas 2
Jan 28	RUNCORN	W 8-0	4,000	T: Lomas 2, G: Lomas
Feb 4	Oldham	D 0-0	8,000	
Feb 11	WIGAN	W 14-2	6,000	T: RMH Bell, John, Lomas, J Williams, G: Lomas
Feb 18	Swinton	W 8-3	8,000	T: A Buckler, Lomas, G: Lomas
Feb 25	ST HELENS	W 19-2	7,000	T: Preston 2, RMH Bell, Lewis, Lomas, G: Lomas 2
Mar 4	Keighley (NUC-1)	L 0-8	6,000	
Mar 11	BATLEY	D 0-0	3,000	
Mar 25	WIDNES	W 23-2	2,000	T: Lomas 3, RMH Bell, Richards, G: Lomas 4
Apr 8	Warrington	L 0-5	4,000	
Apr 15	WAKEFIELD TRINITY	W 21-0	2,000	T: RMH Bell 2, Lewis, Lomas, W Thomas, G: Lomas 2, W Brown

Salford RL Match Results

1904-1905 *continued*

	Opponent	Result	Attendance	Scorers
Apr 21	BROUGHTON RANGERS	W 7-0	14,000	T: W Thomas, G: W Brown, Lomas
Apr 22	Leigh	W 16-2	1,800	T: Preston 2, D Rees, W Thomas, G: W Brown, Richards
Apr 25	Hunslet	W 16-11	3,000	T: Lomas 2, Preston, Walton, G: Lomas 2
Apr 26	Hull Kingston Rovers	L 3-14	4,000	T: W Thomas

1905-1906

	Opponent	Result	Attendance	Scorers
Sep 2	HULL	W 12-3	6,000	T: Hampson 2, Bedford, Lomas
Sep 9	Swinton	W 8-0	5,000	T: Hampson, Lomas, G: Lomas
Sep 16	BATLEY	W 21-6	6,000	T: Hampson, John, Spencer, EJ Thomas, W Thomas, G: Lomas 3
Sep 23	Leigh	L 5-8	3,000	T: W Thomas, G: Lomas
Sep 30	ST HELENS	W 25-5	6,000	T: Lomas 2, A Buckler, RMH Bell, Hampson, G: Lomas 3, Morgan, W Thomas
Oct 7	Runcorn	L 3-4	1,000	T: RMH Bell
Oct 14	SWINTON (LC-1)	W 3-0	10,000	T: Hampson
Oct 21	Rochdale Hornets	W 19-0	5,000	T: D'Arcy 2, Lomas 2, Preston, G: Lomas 2
Oct 28	OLDHAM (LC-2)	L 0-10	12,000	
Nov 4	HULL KINGSTON ROVERS	L 5-8	8,000	T: W Thomas, G: Haley
Nov 11	OLDHAM	W 2-0	7,000	G: Lomas
Nov 18	LEEDS (F)*	A 0-5	4,000	
Nov 25	BARROW	W 26-5	4,000	T: Hampson 2, Cochrane, Lomas, W Thomas, D Rees, G: Lomas 4
Dec 2	Hull Kingston Rovers	L 10-13	8,000	T: Hampson, Lomas, G: Lomas 2
Dec 9	WIDNES	W 25-3	5,000	T: Hampson 2, Lomas 2, Bedford, Preston, W Thomas, G: Lomas 2
Dec 16	Batley	W 13-2	4,000	T: Lomas 2, Hampson, G: Lomas 2
Dec 23	SWINTON	W 10-0	10,000	T: RMH Bell, Warwick, G: Lomas 2
Dec 25	Broughton Rangers	L 5-11	15,000	T: Lomas, G: Lomas
Dec 26	Warrington	W 5-4	6,000	T: D Rees, G: Lomas
Dec 30	BRADFORD	W 13-0	7,000	T: Hampson, Lomas, Spencer, G: Lomas 2

Salford RL Match Results

1905-1906 *continued*

	Opponent	Result	Attendance	Scorers
Jan 1	LEIGH	L 0-9	3,000	
Jan 6	Wigan	D 0-0	4,000	
Jan 13	BROUGHTON RANGERS	D 0-0	7,000	
Jan 20	Hunslet	L 5-9	4,000	T: Lomas, G: Lomas
Jan 27	WARRINGTON	L 6-8	5,000	T: Lomas 2
Feb 3	ROCHDALE HORNETS	W 8-0	4,000	T: W Brown, Hampson, G: W Brown
Feb 10	Oldham	D 0-0	5,000	
Feb 17	Swinton (F, at Liverpool)	L 6-8	3,000	T: Hampson, John
Feb 24	Hull	L 2-13	4,000	G: W Brown
Mar 3	Rochdale Hornets (NUC-1)	W 6-0	5,300	T: Hampson, Lomas
Mar 10	Halifax	L 5-10	7,000	T: A Buckler, G: Lomas
Mar 14	WIGAN	L 6-8	2,000	T: Hampson, W Thomas
Mar 17	EGERTON (NUC-2)	W 38-5	3,000	T: Lomas 3, McWhirter 2, W Thomas 2, Drake, Hampson, D Rees, G: Lomas 4
Mar 24	Bradford	L 0-33	2,000	
Mar 31	BROUGHTON RANGERS (NUC-3)	D 2-2	16,000	G: Lomas
Apr 4	Broughton R (NUC-3 Replay)	D 3-3	8,242	T: John
Apr 6	Broughton R (NUC-3 2nd Replay)**	W 5-3	5,367	T: Drake, G: W Brown
Apr 7	Barrow	L 0-24	6,000	
Apr 14	Keighley (NUC-SF)***	W 6-3	8,500	T: John, Preston
Apr 16	RUNCORN	L 0-33	2,500	
Apr 19	Widnes	L 0-11	500	
Apr 21	HALIFAX	W 21-3	3,000	T: Hampson, John, Lancaster, Preston, Rhapps, G: John 3
Apr 23	HUNSLET	L 12-26	1,000	T: Brady, R Brown, Drake, Garner
Apr 28	Bradford (NUC-Final)****	L 0-5	15,834	
Apr 30	St Helens	L 0-11	-	

* Abandoned just before half-time (fog)   ** At Wigan   *** At Warrington   **** At Leeds

Northern Union Challenge Cup runners-up

1906-1907

	Opponent	Result	Attendance	Scorers
Sep 1	BATLEY	W 12-7	5,000	T: Hampson, Lomas, G: Lomas 3
Sep 8	Liverpool City	W 28-3	500	T: Drake, Hampson, Lomas, Rickers, W Thomas, J Williams, G: Lomas 4, John

Salford RL Match Results

1906-1907 *continued*

	Opponent	Result	Attendance	Scorers
Sep 15	LEEDS	W 22-4	5,000	T: Hampson, Preston, D Rees, Spencer, G: Lomas 5
Sep 22	Hunslet	L 5-17	7,000	T: W Thomas, G: Lomas
Sep 29	Bradford	L 5-35	4,000	T: Lomas, G: Lomas
Oct 6	Warrington	L 3-33	5,000	T: Hampson
Oct 13	WIGAN (LC-1)	W 12-3	5,000	T: Foster, John, G: Lomas 3
Oct 20	Broughton Rangers	L 3-26	14,673	T: W Brown
Oct 27	RUNCORN (LC-2)	L 2-3	5,000	G: Lomas
Oct 31	WARRINGTON	W 8-5	2,000	T: Lomas 2, G: Lomas
Nov 3	Runcorn	L 2-17	2,000	G: W Brown
Nov 10	ST HELENS	W 26-13	4,000	T: Hampson 4, A Buckler, EJ Thomas, G: Lomas 4
Nov 17	LEIGH	W 17-8	6,000	T: A Buckler, Dutton, John, G: Lomas 4
Nov 24	Oldham*	A 7-0	10,000	T: Lomas, G: Lomas 2
Dec 1	WIGAN	W 7-2	5,000	T: Preston, G: Lomas 2
Dec 3	Oldham	L 6-10	3,000	T: Cochrane, Warwick
Dec 8	BRADFORD	W 16-0	4,000	T: John, Lewis, Lomas, Preston, G: Lomas 2
Dec 15	Barrow	L 5-11	5,000	T: Lomas, G: Lomas
Dec 22	Swinton	L 6-15	6,000	G: Lomas 3
Dec 25	BROUGHTON RANGERS	W 7-5	14,000	T: Lomas, G: Lomas 2
Dec 26	Leeds	L 6-14	5,000	T: Lomas 2
Jan 1	HUNSLET	L 10-11	2,000	T: John, Mason, G: Lomas, Preston
Jan 5	SWINTON	W 27-0	6,000	T: Lomas 4, W Thomas 2, Cochrane, G: Lomas 3
Jan 12	OLDHAM	W 17-15	6,000	T: Garner 2, Hampson, Lewis, Preston, G: W Brown
Jan 16	Leigh	W 22-4	1,100	T: W Brown, Lewis, Lomas, Preston, D Rees, W Thomas, G: Lomas 2
Jan 19	Halifax	L 9-11	8,000	T: John, G: Lomas 3
Feb 2	LIVERPOOL CITY	W 78-0	3,000	T: Lomas 5, A Buckler 2, Hampson 2, John 2, Preston 2, Brown, Cochrane, Garner, W Thomas, Warwick, G: Lomas 12
Feb 9	Batley	W 11-7	3,000	T: Lomas 2, John, G: Lomas
Feb 13	BARROW	W 49-0	2,000	T: Lomas 4, EJ Thomas 2, W Thomas 2, A Buckler, W Brown, Cochrane, Hampson, D Rees, G: Lomas 5

Salford RL Match Results

1906-1907 *continued*

	Opponent	Result	Attendance	Scorers
Feb 16	WAKEFIELD TRINITY	W 26-2	4,000	T: Cochrane 2, Lomas 2, Warwick 2, G: Lomas 4
Feb 23	HALIFAX	W 9-5	14,000	T: A Buckler, G: Lomas 3
Mar 2	Wigan	L 5-10	14,000	T: W Thomas, G: W Brown
Mar 16	LEIGH (NUC-1)	W 10-5	3,729	T: Cochrane, Preston, G: W Brown 2
Mar 23	WIGAN (NUC-2)	W 18-5	14,000	T: Lomas 3, W Thomas, G: Lomas 3
Mar 29	RUNCORN	W 5-0	7,000	T: John, G: Lomas
Mar 30	LEEDS (NUC-3)	W 12-3	10,933	T: Hampson, Lomas, G: Lomas 2, W Brown
Apr 1	St Helens	L 5-30	3,000	T: Lomas, G: Lomas
Apr 6	Wakefield Trinity	L 5-29	2,000	T: Cochrane, G: Lomas
Apr 13	Oldham (NUC-SF)**	L 0-6	16,000	

* Abandoned 18 mins after half-time (failing light due to delayed start)   ** At Rochdale

1907-1908

	Opponent	Result	Attendance	Scorers
Sep 7	ROCHDALE HORNETS	W 12-8	5,000	T: Hampson 2, G: Lomas 3
Sep 9	Halifax	L 7-12	9,000	T: D Rees, G: Lomas 2
Sep 14	Ebbw Vale	W 29-0	5,000	T: Lomas 3, Hampson 2, Hutchinson 2, G: Lomas 4
Sep 21	ST HELENS	W 21-2	4,000	T: Hampson 2, A Buckler, Garner, Lomas, G: Lomas 3
Sep 28	Leeds	L 2-23	4,000	G: Lomas
Oct 5	LEIGH	W 16-8	4,000	T: John 2, Cleary, EJ Thomas, G: Clessold, W Thomas
Oct 12	Hunslet	D 12-12	5,000	T: Hutchinson, EJ Thomas, G: Lomas 3
Oct 19	Barrow	L 2-6	4,000	G: Mason
Oct 26	WIGAN (LC-2)	W 10-8	10,000	T: Spencer, EJ Thomas, G: Lomas 2
Nov 2	WARRINGTON	D 8-8	5,000	T: A Buckler, Warwick, G: Mason
Nov 9	BROUGHTON RANGERS	W 8-5	10,000	T: Hutchinson 2, G: Lomas
Nov 16	OLDHAM (LC-SF)	L 7-8	10,000	T: Lomas, G: Lomas 2
Nov 23	WIGAN	L 10-13	3,000	T: John, Lomas, G: Lomas 2
Dec 7	St Helens	W 18-0	3,000	T: Lomas 2, Cook, John, G: Lomas 3
Dec 11	WIDNES	W 26-0	2,000	T: Hutchinson 4, A Buckler, Cook, John, Mason, G: Lomas

Salford RL Match Results

1907-1908 *continued*

	Opponent	Result	Attendance	Scorers
Dec 14	SWINTON	W 11-0	6,000	T: Cook 2, Hyam, G: Lomas
Dec 21	Oldham	L 5-6	14,000	T: John, G: Mason
Dec 25	Broughton Rangers	L 10-14	16,000	T: Preston, Warwick, G: Lomas 2
Dec 26	LEEDS	W 20-2	–	T: Lomas 2, Cook, Hyam, W Thomas, Warwick, G: Lomas
Dec 28	NEW ZEALAND (Tour)	L 2-9	12,000	G: Lomas
Jan 1	WAKEFIELD TRINITY	W 18-12	2,000	T: Cook, Hyam, Spencer, Warwick, G: Lomas 3
Jan 11	EBBW VALE	W 15-2	3,000	T: Brady, Cook, Spencer, G: Mason 2, Hyam
Jan 15	Runcorn	W 14-6	1,000	T: Cook, Hyam, Lomas, W Thomas, G: Lomas
Jan 18	Widnes	W 8-5	2,000	T: Cook, Hyam, G: Lomas
Jan 25	HUNSLET	W 7-6	5,000	T: W Thomas, G: Lomas 2
Feb 1	RUNCORN	W 12-0	5,000	T: Lomas 3, Cook
Feb 3	Warrington	D 0-0	4,000	
Feb 8	Swinton	W 2-0	5,000	G: Lomas
Feb 15	Leigh	W 13-5	3,000	T: Cook, Lomas, Warwick, G: Lomas 2
Feb 22	OLDHAM	W 5-0	12,000	T: EJ Thomas, G: Lomas
Feb 29	WIDNES (NUC-1)	W 15-2	3,000	T: Cook, John, EJ Thomas, G: Lomas 3
Mar 7	HALIFAX	L 10-11	10,000	T: Hyam, EJ Thomas, G: Lomas 2
Mar 14	Hull (NUC-2)	L 9-15	12,000	T: W Thomas, G: Lomas 3
Mar 21	Wigan	L 0-2	16,000	
Apr 4	Rochdale Hornets	L 5-6	3,000	T: Hyam, G: W Thomas
Apr 6	BARROW	W 15-2	1,500	T: Cochrane 2, Warwick, G: Mason 3
Apr 11	Wakefield Trinity	L 3-11	2,000	T: Lomas
Apr 20	Barrow (F)	L 0-14	–	

1908-1909

	Opponent	Result	Attendance	Scorers
Sep 5	RUNCORN	L 7-18	5,000	T: Lomas, G: Lomas 2
Sep 12	Oldham	L 5-20	23,000	T: A Buckler, G: W Thomas
Sep 19	WIGAN	L 7-36	6,000	T: Lomas, G: Lomas 2
Sep 26	Broughton Rangers	W 14-5	10,000	T: Cook, Lomas, G: Lomas 3, Mesley
Oct 3	WARRINGTON	W 14-7	8,000	T: Cook, Mesley, G: Mesley 3, W Brown
Oct 10	Widnes	W 15-2	3,000	T: Cook 2, Cochrane, G: W Brown, Lomas, Mesley

Salford RL Match Results

1908-1909 *continued*

	Opponent	Result	Attendance	Scorers
Oct 17	AUSTRALIA (Tour)	D 9-9	6,100	T: Cook, G: Mesley 2, Preston
Oct 24	Rochdale Hornets	W 13-2	4,000	T: Cook, Curzon, W Thomas, G: Lomas 2
Oct 31	St Helens	W 13-8	3,000	T: W Thomas 2, Cook, G: Lomas 2
Nov 7	Oldham (LC-1)	L 5-20	16,000	T: Lomas, G: Lomas
Nov 14	LEEDS	W 20-2	6,000	T: Lomas 3, Hyam, G: Lomas 3, Mesley
Nov 18	HALIFAX	L 8-11	3,000	T: Cook, Lomas, G: Lomas
Nov 21	Broughton Rangers (F)	L 21-24	6,000	T: Cook 2, A Buckler, Mesley, W Thomas, G: Lomas 3
Nov 28	Wigan	L 2-5	12,000	G: Lomas
Dec 5	SWINTON	W 17-0	7,000	T: W Thomas 2, Lomas, G: Lomas 4
Dec 12	Runcorn	L 4-16	2,000	G: Lomas 2
Dec 16	HUNSLET	W 17-6	2,000	T: Cook 3, Hyam, W Thomas, G: Lomas
Dec 19	ST HELENS	W 15-14	2,500	T: Cook, Hyam, Lomas, G: Lomas 3
Dec 25	BROUGHTON RANGERS	W 19-10	9,000	T: Mesley 2, Lomas, G: Lomas 3, Mesley 2
Dec 26	Leigh	L 3-5	3,000	T. Hyam
Jan 2	Barrow	W 16-6	2,000	T: Cook 2, Hyam, Preston, G: W Thomas 2
Jan 9	ROCHDALE HORNETS	W 18-3	5,000	T: Lomas 2, John, W Thomas, G: Lomas 3
Jan 16	LEIGH	W 27-5	4,000	T: A Buckler, Coates, Hyam, Lomas, Mesley, EJ Thomas, Warwick, G: Lomas 3
Jan 30	WIDNES	W 14-8	4,000	T: Mesley 3, Lomas, G: Lomas
Feb 6	Wakefield Trinity	W 10-7	3,000	T: Cook, Lomas, G: Lomas 2
Feb 8	Ebbw Vale	W 20-6	2,000	T: Cook 2, Lomas, W Thomas, G: Lomas 4
Feb 13	BARROW	W 29-2	6,000	T: Hyam 3, Cook, Lomas, Mesley, EJ Thomas, G: Lomas 4
Feb 20	Leeds	L 7-13	7,000	T: Warwick, G: Lomas 2
Feb 27	DEWSBURY (NUC-1)	W 28-0	6,000	T: Cook 3, Lomas 2, Preston, G: Lomas 5
Mar 6	Swinton	W 11-6	8,000	T: A Buckler, Cook, Mesley, G: Mesley

Salford RL Match Results

1908-1909 *continued*

	Opponent	Result	Attendance	Scorers
Mar 13	Broughton Rangers (NUC-2)	W 4-0	18,000	G: Lomas 2
Mar 17	EBBW VALE	W 19-4	2,000	T: Lomas 3, Coates, Curzon, G: Lomas 2
Mar 20	Halifax	L 2-22	14,000	G: Lomas
Mar 27	HALIFAX (NUC-3)	L 7-12	13,976	T: D Rees, G: Mesley 2
Apr 3	Hunslet	L 8-16	4,000	T: Lomas, W Thomas, G: Lomas
Apr 9	WAKEFIELD TRINITY	W 53-0	4,000	T: W Thomas 3, Lomas 2, Mesley 2, Cook, Curzon, EJ Thomas, Warwick, G: Lomas 6, Mesley 3, John
Apr 10	Warrington	D 15-15	3,000	T: Lomas 2, Mesley, G: Lomas 3
Apr 12	OLDHAM	L 13-19	5,000	T: Mesley 2, EJ Thomas, G: Lomas, Mesley
Apr 13	Merthyr Tydfil (F)	D 8-8	4,000	T: Curzon, Lomas, G: Mesley

1909-1910

	Opponent	Result	Attendance	Scorers
Sep 4	Runcorn	L 5-13	2,000	T: Lomas, G: Lomas
Sep 11	OLDHAM	W 9-8	12,000	T: Adams, G: Lomas 3
Sep 18	Wigan	L 11-22	15,000	T: Lomas 2, W Thomas, G: Lomas
Sep 25	BROUGHTON RANGERS	W 20-7	15,000	T: W Thomas 2, Curzon, Morton, G: Lomas 3, Mesley
Oct 2	Warrington	L 5-8	6,000	T: Warwick, G: Lomas
Oct 9	HUNSLET	W 17-12	10,000	T: Cook 2, Adams, G: Lomas 4
Oct 23	WIDNES	W 11-5	–	T: Ratcliffe 2, Adams, G: Mesley
Oct 30	Leigh (LC-2)	L 6-13	8,000	G: Lomas 2, John
Nov 6	BARROW	W 25-6	2,000	T: Cook 2, Adams, Coates, W Thomas, G: Mesley 4, W Thomas
Nov 13	Hull Kingston Rovers	W 3-2	8,000	T: W Thomas
Nov 18	Treherbert	W 19-2	–	T: Lomas 2, Adams, Mesley, Preston, G: Lomas 2
Nov 20	YORK	W 27-10	2,000	T: Mesley 2, Adams, Cook, Curzon, D Rees, Thom, G: Lomas 3
Nov 27	Swinton	W 11-3	6,000	T: Cook, Mesley, Warwick, G: Lomas

Salford RL Match Results

1909-1910 *continued*

	Opponent	Result	Attendance	Scorers
Dec 4	LEIGH	W 23-8	4,000	T: Cook, Mesley, Preston, W Thomas, Warwick, G: Mesley 4
Dec 11	St Helens	L 3-7	4,000	T: Preston
Dec 18	RUNCORN	W 20-0	4,000	T: Adams, Lomas, Preston, Warwick, G: Lomas 4
Dec 25	Broughton Rangers	W 10-5	16,000	T: Mesley, EJ Thomas, G: Lomas 2
Dec 27	SWINTON	W 10-3	10,000	T: Cook, Lomas, G: Lomas 2
Jan 1	Barrow	W 15-0	1,000	T: Cook, Lomas, Warwick, G: Lomas 2, Mesley
Jan 8	ST HELENS	W 24-5	6,000	T: Cook 3, Hyam 2, W Thomas, G: Lomas 3
Jan 15	WARRINGTON	W 8-0	4,000	T: Lomas 2, G: Lomas
Feb 5	Rochdale Hornets	W 8-3	4,000	T: Cook, Lomas, G: Lomas
Feb 12	HALIFAX	W 12-8	7,000	T: Lomas 2, G: Lomas 3
Feb 16	WIGAN	L 2-12	7,000	G: Lomas
Feb 19	Leigh	W 14-8	4,000	T: Cook 3, Lomas, G: Lomas
Feb 26	YORK IRISH NATIONAL LEAGUE (NUC-1)*	W 64-0	3,200	T: Cook 4, Lomas 4, Mesley 3, Hyam 2, John, Thom, W Thomas, G: Lomas 3, Coates, John, Mesley, W Thomas, Warwick
Mar 5	Oldham	D 3-3	25,000	T: Mesley
Mar 12	WIGAN (NUC-2)	W 12-5	25,000	T: Cook, Mesley, G: Lomas 3
Mar 16	Widnes	L 0-8	1,500	
Mar 19	EBBW VALE (NUC-3)*	W 8-2	10,000	T: Adams, Cook, G: Lomas
Mar 25	York	W 21-17	4,500	T: Adams, Cook, Lomas, Preston, C Rees, G: Lomas 3
Mar 26	HULL KINGSTON ROVERS	W 19-11	8,000	T: Lomas 2, Cook, Mesley, D Rees, G: Lomas 2
Mar 28	ROCHDALE HORNETS	W 23-12	6,000	T: Cook 2, Adams, Mesley, Thom, G: Mesley 4
Apr 2	Hull (NUC-SF)**	L 6-20	11,000	G: Mesley 2, Lomas
Apr 4	Halifax	W 6-0	3,000	G: Lomas 3
Apr 9	Hunslet	W 3-2	2,500	T: C Rees
Apr 16	WIGAN (NRL-SF)	L 6-17	9,000	T: Lomas 2

* *Away ties switched to Salford*   ** *At Wakefield*

Salford RL Match Results

1910-1911

	Opponent	Result	Attendance	Scorers
Sep 3	MERTHYR TYDFIL	W 34-2	6,000	T: D Thomas 5, Cook, Morton, W Thomas, G: Mesley 2, W Thomas 2, John
Sep 10	Halifax	L 8-29	9,000	T: Cook, D Thomas, G: Mesley
Sep 17	St Helens	L 14-19	8,000	T: Cook 2, Mesley, C Rees, G: W Thomas
Sep 24	BROUGHTON RANGERS	L 6-11	8,000	T: Cook, Mesley
Oct 1	Hunslet	W 18-12	8,000	T: Cook, Lomas, May, D Thomas, G: Lomas 2, Mesley
Oct 8	LEIGH	W 18-8	7,000	T: Cook 2, Lomas, Mesley, D Thomas, W Thomas
Oct 15	Widnes	L 2-15	3,000	G: John
Oct 22	COVENTRY	W 37-10	4,000	T: Cook 3, Mesley 2, D Thomas 2, W Thomas 2, G: Mesley 2, W Thomas 2, D Thomas
Oct 29	Oldham	L 2-20	15,000	G: Lomas
Nov 5	Warrington (LC-2)	L 5-14	5,000	T: D Thomas, G: Lomas
Nov 12	Swinton	L 3-14	8,000	T: W Thomas
Nov 26	WARRINGTON	D 3-3	5,000	T: Cook
Nov 30	HULL KINGSTON ROVERS	L 5-9	2,000	T: D Thomas, G: W Thomas
Dec 3	Merthyr Tydfil	L 2-7	500	G: W Thomas
Dec 10	RUNCORN	W 19-8	5,000	T: Cook 2, May 2, C Rees, G: John, W Thomas
Dec 17	Rochdale Hornets	L 3-15	3,000	T: Preston
Dec 24	Broughton Rangers	W 3-2	10,000	T: Ritchie
Dec 26	Coventry	L 5-14	3,000	T: Mesley, G: Lambert
Dec 27	SWINTON	W 11-5	10,000	T: Mesley, G: Mesley 2, Lambert, W Thomas
Dec 31	BARROW	W 19-9	8,000	T: John 2, Cook, Lomas, EJ Thomas, G: Lomas, W Thomas
Jan 7	Wigan	L 0-17	8,000	
Jan 14	HUNSLET	W 16-8	2,000	T: Cook 3, Staveley, G: Lambert 2
Jan 28	Runcorn	W 16-3	1,000	T: Barker 2, Cook, Curzon, G: Lambert 2
Feb 4	OLDHAM	L 11-16	10,000	T: Cook 3, G: Lambert
Feb 11	Leigh	L 7-9	4,000	T: C Rees, G: DW Bevan, Lambert
Feb 18	Keighley (NUC-1)	W 5-0	5,000	T: Mesley, G: Lambert
Feb 25	WIDNES	W 9-3	9,000	T: John, May, Mesley

Salford RL Match Results

1910-1911 *continued*

	Opponent	Result	Attendance	Scorers
Mar 4	Barrow (NUC-2)	W 6-5	7,000	T: Cook, W Thomas
Mar 11	Warrington	L 0-6	6,000	
Mar 18	BATLEY (NUC-3)	L 3-18	8,000	T: Cook
Mar 22	ST HELENS	W 19-6	2,000	T: DW Bevan, May, C Rees, Ritchie, W Thomas, G: DW Bevan, Lambert
Mar 25	HALIFAX	W 5-2	4,000	T: Curzon, G: W Thomas
Apr 1	Barrow	L 4-18	4,000	G: DW Bevan 2
Apr 12	WIGAN	D 12-12	3,000	T: Cook, C Rees, G: DW Bevan 2, W Thomas
Apr 14	Hull Kingston Rovers	L 6-25	7,000	T: May, C Rees
Apr 15	ROCHDALE HORNETS	W 18-0	4,000	T: Cook, Mesley, Ritchie, EJ Thomas, G: DW Bevan 3

1911-1912

	Opponent	Result	Attendance	Scorers
Sep 2	ROCHDALE HORNETS	L 8-19	6,000	T: Battersby, Cook, G: May
Sep 9	Broughton Rangers	L 0-5	8,000	
Sep 16	BARROW	W 16-11	5,000	T: DW Bevan, Cook, Loveluck, Mesley, G: Mesley 2
Sep 23	Leigh	W 8-5	2,000	T: Pugsley, Ratcliffe, G: W Thomas
Sep 30	Wigan	L 0-16	9,000	
Oct 7	COVENTRY	W 21-2	3,000	T: Mesley 2, D Rees 2, Loveluck, Ritchie, W Thomas
Oct 14	HUNSLET	D 15-15	6,000	T: Mesley 2, Loveluck, G: Mesley 2, W Thomas
Oct 21	St Helens (LC-1)	L 7-18	5,000	T: D Rees, G: Mesley, W Thomas
Oct 28	RUNCORN	W 13-7	4,000	T: Loveluck, Pugsley, W Thomas, G: Mesley 2
Nov 4	Barrow	L 5-16	3,000	T: W Thomas, G: Mesley
Nov 11	Widnes	L 5-10	2,000	T: Cook, G: Mesley
Nov 18	ST HELENS	L 13-15	5,000	T: Loveluck, Pugsley, Scott, G: Mesley, W Thomas
Nov 25	Coventry	W 12-5	3,000	T: John, W Thomas, G: Mesley 3
Dec 2	WARRINGTON	W 12-0	3,000	T: Brady, Mesley, G: Mesley 3
Dec 9	AUSTRALIA (Tour)	L 3-6	4,000	T: Mesley
Dec 16	Hunslet	L 9-11	4,000	T: Pugsley, G: Mesley 3
Dec 23	Hull Kingston Rovers	L 10-17	-	T: Downie, C Rees, G: Downie 2

Salford RL Match Results

1911-1912 *continued*

	Opponent	Result	Attendance	Scorers
Dec 25	BROUGHTON RANGERS	D 3-3	8,000	T: John
Dec 26	SWINTON	D 0-0	7,000	
Dec 30	Rochdale Hornets	L 5-10	5,000	T: Thom, G: John
Jan 1	Swinton	L 0-14	12,000	
Jan 6	OLDHAM	L 0-8	3,000	
Jan 13	WIGAN	W 7-2	5,000	T: Downie, G: Mesley 2
Jan 27	LEIGH	L 5-9	5,000	T: Loveluck, G: Mesley
Feb 10	YORK	D 7-7	3,000	T: Loveluck, G: John, Mesley
Feb 17	Widnes (NUC-1)	W 8-3	4,000	T: Loveluck, May, G: John
Feb 24	Batley	L 5-9	4,000	T: Cook, G: Mesley
Mar 2	DEWSBURY (NUC-2)	L 8-9	5,855	T: Cook, Mesley, G: Thom
Mar 9	WIDNES	W 22-3	4,000	T: Pugsley 2, Loveluck, W Thomas, G: Mesley 4, W Thomas
Mar 16	St Helens	L 6-19	5,000	T: Pugsley, C Rees
Mar 23	Runcorn	W 10-4	5,000	T: Loveluck 2, G: Mesley 2
Mar 30	York	L 5-21	3,000	T: Launce, G: Mesley
Apr 5	BATLEY	W 22-5	4,000	T: Cook 2, Loveluck 2, Thom 2, G: John, Thom
Apr 6	Oldham	L 5-9	8,000	T: C Rees, G: Mesley
Apr 8	Warrington	L 0-34	3,000	
Apr 13	HULL KINGSTON ROVERS	W 20-13	3,000	T: Cook, John, Mesley, EJ Thomas, G: Mesley 3, W Thomas

1912-1913

	Opponent	Result	Attendance	Scorers
Sep 7	Rochdale Hornets	W 3-2	7,000	T: Callender
Sep 14	WIDNES	W 16-11	5,000	T: Loveluck, Mesley, G: Mesley 5
Sep 21	Warrington	W 15-2	5,000	T: Mesley 2, Wild, G: John 2, Mesley
Sep 28	BROUGHTON RANGERS	L 5-6	8,000	T: Mesley, G: W Thomas
Oct 5	Leigh	W 5-3	3,000	T: Mesley, G: Loveluck
Oct 12	WIGAN	L 8-17	8,000	T: C Rees, Wild, G: W Thomas
Oct 19	Barrow (LC-1)	W 18-0	4,000	T: Loveluck 2, May, Mesley, G: W Thomas 2, Mesley
Nov 2	WIDNES (LC-2)	W 16-3	6,000	T: Mesley, EJ Thomas, W Thomas, Wild, G: Launce, Mesley
Nov 6	Runcorn	W 12-5	1,000	T: Mesley 2, G: Mesley 2, W Thomas
Nov 9	BARROW	W 11-0	3,000	T: Mesley, C Rees, Ritchie, G: Mesley

Salford RL Match Results

1912-1913 *continued*

	Opponent	Result	Attendance	Scorers
Nov 16	WIGAN (LC-SF)	L 5-13	8,764	T: Loveluck, G: Mesley
Nov 23	Oldham	L 5-11	8,000	T: Wild, G: Mesley
Nov 27	HUNSLET	L 3-8	2,000	T: Mesley
Dec 7	Batley	W 8-6	2,000	T: Callender, Loveluck, G: W Thomas
Dec 14	ST HELENS	W 11-3	–	T: Mesley 2, Loveluck, G: Mesley
Dec 21	Barrow	W 15-8	4,000	T: Goldsmith, John, C Rees, G: John 3
Dec 25	Broughton Rangers	L 0-13	12,000	
Dec 26	SWINTON	W 7-3	4,000	T: Loveluck, G: May, Mesley
Jan 1	Swinton	L 0-2	6,000	
Jan 4	LEIGH	W 11-3	2,000	T: Callender, Loveluck, W Thomas, G: John
Jan 11	BRADFORD NORTHERN	W 18-3	1,300	T: Callender 2, Cook 2, John, May
Jan 18	BATLEY	W 8-3	5,000	T: Loveluck, EJ Thomas, G: Mesley
Jan 25	Hunslet	W 6-0	7,000	T: Callender, May
Feb 1	Widnes	L 4-8	3,000	G: Mesley 2
Feb 8	ROCHDALE HORNETS	W 18-0	5,000	T: C Rees 2, Callender, EJ Thomas, G: Mesley 3
Feb 15	Bradford Northern	L 0-7	4,000	
Feb 22	WARRINGTON	W 2-0	7,000	G: Mesley
Mar 1	Wigan	L 0-23	15,000	
Mar 8	COVENTRY (NUC-1)	W 34-14	2,355	T: Mesley 3, Hennessey, John, Launce, May, W Thomas, G: W Thomas 3, John, Mesley
Mar 15	Broughton Rangers (NUC-2)	W 2-0	12,000	G: Mesley
Mar 21	KEIGHLEY	W 16-3	8,000	T: Callender 2, Goldsmith, Mesley, G: Mesley 2
Mar 22	St Helens	L 0-6	2,000	
Mar 24	Keighley	L 5-13	5,000	T: Callender, G: W Thomas
Mar 29	WARRINGTON (NUC-3)	L 4-7	11,000	G: Mesley 2
Apr 5	RUNCORN	W 17-8	3,000	T: Mesley 2, W Thomas 2, Callender, G: W Thomas
Apr 7	OLDHAM	W 16-5	2,000	T: May, Mesley, C Rees, EJ Thomas, G: Mesley 2

Salford RL Match Results

1913-1914

	Opponent	Result	Attendance	Scorers
Sep 6	ROCHDALE HORNETS	W 13-6	6,000	T: Callender, May, W Thomas, G: John, Mesley
Sep 13	Hunslet	L 8-9	10,000	T: Callender, Mesley, G: Loveluck
Sep 20	ST HELENS	W 17-4	6,000	T: Mesley 2, John, G: Mesley 2, W Thomas 2
Sep 27	Leigh	W 8-0	3,000	T: Loveluck, Ritchie, G: Mesley
Oct 4	Broughton Rangers	W 15-2	11,000	T: Mesley 2, EJ Thomas, G: Mesley 3
Oct 11	BARROW	W 23-6	5,000	T: W Thomas 2, Loveluck, May, Ritchie, G: Mesley 3, W Thomas
Oct 18	Hull Kingston Rovers	L 2-5	8,000	G: W Thomas
Oct 25	BATLEY	W 5-3	6,000	T: Mesley, G: Mesley
Nov 1	WIGAN (LC-1)	L 7-9	14,000	T: Loveluck, G: Mesley 2
Nov 8	WIDNES	W 5-3	4,000	T: Goldsmith, G: Mesley
Nov 15	Barrow	L 0-7	4,000	
Nov 22	HUNSLET	W 13-0	5,000	T: May 2, Callender, G: Mesley 2
Nov 29	Batley	W 10-2	2,000	T: May, Mesley, G: Mesley 2
Dec 6	WARRINGTON	W 5-2	4,000	T: May, G: Mesley
Dec 20	Oldham	W 10-6	10,000	T: J Bevon, EJ Thomas, G: Mesley 2
Dec 25	BROUGHTON RANGERS	L 3-5	8,000	T: Callender
Dec 26	SWINTON	W 10-0	6,500	T: Callender, May, G: Mesley 2
Dec 27	Warrington	D 10-10	5,000	T: Callender, May, G: Mesley, W Thomas
Jan 3	LEEDS	W 10-0	5,000	T: Callender, Loveluck, G: John, Mesley
Jan 10	OLDHAM	W 6-5	8,000	G: Mesley 3
Jan 17	Swinton	W 7-2	6,000	T: W Thomas, G: Mesley 2
Jan 24	LEIGH	W 15-5	4,000	T: Callender, May, EJ Thomas, G: W Thomas 2, Launce
Jan 31	Widnes	L 0-17	4,000	
Feb 7	Runcorn	W 17-6	2,000	T: May 2, Loveluck, G: Mesley 3, John
Feb 14	HULL KINGSTON ROVERS	W 8-3	8,000	T: Callender, John, G: John
Feb 21	Leeds	W 12-3	10,000	T: May 2, Mesley, E Woods
Feb 28	Hull (NUC-1)	L 5-8	15,000	T: May, G: John
Mar 7	RUNCORN	W 27-0	4,000	T: May 2, E Woods 2, Mesley, Ritchie, W Thomas, G: Mesley 2, W Thomas
Mar 11	Wigan	L 0-14	13,000	

Salford RL Match Results

1913-1914 *continued*

	Opponent	Result	Attendance	Scorers
Mar 14	Bradford Northern	W 17-3	2,000	T: Loveluck 2, Mesley 2, May, G: Mesley
Mar 28	St Helens	W 8-2	5,000	T: May, Mesley, G: W Thomas
Apr 7	Rochdale Hornets	W 3-0	5,000	T: Loveluck
Apr 10	BRADFORD NORTHERN	W 22-7	8,000	T: Clegg, Goldsmith, John, Mesley, EJ Thomas, W Thomas, G: Mesley 2
Apr 11	WIGAN	W 11-3	17,000	T: John, G: Mesley 3, John
Apr 18	WIGAN (NRL-SF)	W 16-5	16,500	T: W Thomas 2, Mesley, E Woods, G: John, Mesley
Apr 25	Huddersfield (NRL-Final)*	W 5-3	8,091	T: C Rees, G: Mesley

* At Leeds

Northern Rugby League Championship winners
Lancashire League Championship runners-up

1914-1915

	Opponent	Result	Attendance	Scorers
Sep 5	Rochdale Hornets	L 0-7	4,000	
Sep 12	HUNSLET	W 19-5	3,000	T: Mesley 3, Callender, John, G: Mesley 2
Sep 19	Hull Kingston Rovers	D 5-5	6,000	T: Loveluck, G: W Thomas
Sep 26	BROUGHTON RANGERS	W 7-0	7,000	T: Loveluck, G: Mesley 2
Oct 3	Warrington	L 0-5	5,000	
Oct 10	LEIGH	W 9-0	6,000	T: John, G: Mesley 3
Oct 17	Widnes	L 0-7	2,000	
Oct 24	HULL KINGSTON ROVERS	W 3-0	5,000	T: DW Bevan
Oct 31	Warrington (LC-2)	L 10-22	5,000	T: DW Bevan, C Rees, G: DW Bevan 2
Nov 7	BARROW	W 7-3	4,000	T: C Rees, G: John, Mesley
Dec 12	Wigan	L 0-36	6,000	
Dec 19	OLDHAM	L 0-8	3,000	
Dec 26	SWINTON	W 5-3	8,000	T: Ritchie, G: Mesley
Jan 1	Swinton	D 2-2	5,000	G: Mesley
Jan 2	Hull	D 10-10	8,000	T: Callender, Mesley, G: Launce, Mesley
Jan 9	ST HELENS	L 3-9	-	T: Waite
Jan 16	Batley	L 3-11	2,000	T: A Buckler
Jan 20	ROCHDALE HORNETS	L 0-11	1,000	
Jan 23	WARRINGTON	L 0-11	3,000	
Jan 30	Hunslet	L 2-32	3,000	G: Culshaw
Feb 6	St Helens	L 2-23	4,000	G: Mesley
Feb 10	Huddersfield	L 2-38	2,817	G: Mesley
Feb 13	WIGAN	L 0-9	3,000	

Salford RL Match Results

1914-1915 *continued*

	Opponent	Result	Attendance	Scorers
Feb 20	WIDNES	W 11-3	3,000	T: Callender, May, E Woods, G: John
Feb 27	Brighouse Rangers (NUC-1)	W 26-0	2,000	T: Callender 2, Waite 2, May, Wilkinson, G: W Thomas 4
Mar 6	Leigh	L 0-14	1,200	
Mar 13	Warrington (NUC-2)	W 11-2	6,200	T: Mesley 2, May, G: John
Mar 17	HULL	L 10-17	2,000	T: John, C Rees, G: Mesley 2
Mar 27	Huddersfield (NUC-3)	L 0-33	12,886	
Apr 2	BATLEY	W 10-0	4,000	T: J Bevon, Currie, G: Mesley 2
Apr 3	HUDDERSFIELD	L 6-10	7,000	T: Loveluck, W Thomas
Apr 5	Oldham	L 8-19	5,000	T: Clegg, EJ Thomas, G: W Thomas
Apr 17	Broughton Rangers	L 3-11	7,000	T: Mesley
Apr 24	Barrow	D 7-7	4,000	T: Mesley, G: Mesley 2

1915-1916

	Opponent	Result	Attendance	Scorers
Sep 4	ROCHDALE HORNETS (F)	W 14-3	4,000	T: Greatorex, C Rees, Ritchie, W Thomas, G: W Thomas
Sep 11	Oldham (F)	L 3-9	5,000	T: E Woods
Sep 18	BARROW (F)	W 19-3	3,000	T: John 2, DW Bevan, Clegg, C Rees, G: John, Ritchie
Sep 25	Rochdale Hornets (F)	W 7-0	2,000	T: Clifford, G: John, Ritchie
Oct 2	Broughton Rangers (F)	W 6-5	4,000	T: Clifford, W Thomas
Oct 9	St Helens (F)	L 8-27	1,000	T: Goldsmith, C Rees, G: W Thomas
Oct 16	SWINTON (F)	L 3-4	6,000	T: Greatorex
Oct 23	Leigh (F)	W 9-8	1,000	T: Clegg, G: John 2, Launce
Oct 30	ST HELENS RECREATION (F)	L 5-11	2,500	T: Loveluck, G: John
Nov 6	Halifax (F)	W 10-3	1,000	T: Clegg, John, G: John 2
Nov 13	ST HELENS (F)	W 18-5	2,500	T: Burgess, Clegg, Goldsmith, Loveluck, G: W Thomas 2, Burgess
Dec 4	Swinton (F)	L 0-6	1,500	
Dec 11	OLDHAM (F)	D 3-3	1,200	T: Burgess
Dec 18	RUNCORN (F)	W 12-2	–	T: Clifford 2, Clegg, E Woods
Dec 25	Broughton Rangers (F)	W 10-0	8,000	T: Goldsmith, W Thomas, G: John, Ritchie
Dec 27	SWINTON (F)	D 8-8	5,000	T: Banks, John, G: John
Jan 1	Swinton (F)*	A 0-0	5,000	
Jan 8	LEIGH (F)	L 0-5	3,000	

Above: 1929-30. Back: B Hudson, EC Haines, J Muir, A Casewell, F Shaw. Front: WA Williams, D Manning, R Meek, S Boyd, A Middleton, AJ Risman, G Dobing, E Matthews.

Above: 1931-32. Salford with the Lancashire Cup, the first trophy won under Lance Todd. Back: F Shaw, EC Haines, B Hudson, J Feetham. Third row: AJ Risman, E Jenkins, F Southward, S Miller, J Bradbury. Second row (seated): LB Todd (team manager), WA Williams, CB Riley (chairman), A Middleton, T Coates (trainer). Front: WE Watkins, R Meek.

Above: 1933-34. Back: HC Day, H Osbaldestin, B Hudson, A Casewell, A Middleton, P Dalton, J Feetham, J Bradbury, C Evans. Middle (seated): AJ Risman, CB Riley (chairman), WA Williams, LB Todd (team manager), R Brown. Front: E Jenkins (kneeling), L Pearson, S Miller, WE Watkins (kneeling). The three trophies are: Salford Royal Hospital Cup, Lancashire League Championship Trophy, Broughton Rangers Sevens Trophy.

Above: 1935-36. Back: G Harris, J Bradbury, R Brown, WA Williams, J Feetham, HC Day, A Middleton, H Osbaldestin, B Hudson. Front: A Edwards, WE Watkins, AJ Risman, E Jenkins.

Above: 1936-37. Bob Brown releases winger Joe Turner on a scoring run against visitors Rochdale Hornets whilst team-mate Sammy Miller provides support in the background

Above: 1937-38. The pivotal moment of the 1938 Rugby League Challenge Cup final at Wembley as Albert Gear scores the only try of the match, Salford beating Barrow 7-4. Back-row forward Paddy Dalton (leaning over Gear) adds his congratulations.

Above: 1937-38. Salford with the Challenge Cup following their first Wembley visit. Back: J Feetham, DM Davies, H Thomas, R Brown, J Bradbury. Third row (standing): A Edwards, P Dalton, H Osbaldestin, WA Williams, B Hudson, HC Day, A Gear. Second row (seated): LB Todd (team manager), CB Riley (chairman), AJ Risman, JB Goldstraw (vice-chairman), J Dawson (trainer). Front: S Miller, WE Watkins.

Above: 1938-39. A unique occasion on a snow-covered Headingley cricket ground on 24th December 1938 as Salford's Paddy Dalton, Sammy Miller and Billy Watkins emerge from the pavilion alongside Leeds' players, the adjoining rugby ground having frozen over.

Above: 1946-47. Harry Dagnan (right) tries to outflank the Warrington cover as he heads towards the Willows Road end during a Lancashire Cup match.

Above: 1947-48. Back: G Aspinall, J Kenny, HC Day, J Brown, E Day, A Gear, H Chapman. Front: J Flanagan, G Curran, DM Davies, J Byrne, E Davies, C Coburn.

Above: 1948-49. A spectacular shot of George Aspinall as he appears to have stepped into touch in an effort to evade Wigan's defence watched by a huge crowd gathered at the cricket ground end.

Above: 1949-50. Back: T Danby, G Curran, E Hawkins, J Brown, J Holcroft, DM Davies. Middle: D Moses, G Moses, E Davies, S Williams, G Aspinall. Front: T Harrison, F Stirrup.

Above: 1950-51. Back: J Flanagan, F Alder, B Hartley, D Moses, A Pimblett, T McKinney. Middle: E Hawkins, G Curran, T Harrison, E Davies, G Moses. Front: G Aspinall, F Stirrup.

Above: 1952-53. Back: J Rogers, F Alder, J Grainger, D Moses, B Hartley, F Birkin. Front: E Hesketh (kneeling), E Davies, S Williams, T Danby, T Harrison, T McKinney, F Smith (kneeling).

Above: 1957-58. Back: R Stott, T Garlick, H Duffy, F Boardman, F Alder, J Cheshire. Middle: R Walker, B Preece, E Ayles, F Smith, W McArthur. Front: T Ryan, B Keavney.

Above: 1959-60. Bob Preece scores against the Australian tourists with Graham Jones (right) in support. Salford lost a thrilling match 22-20.

Salford RL Match Results

1915-1916 *continued*

	Opponent	Result	Attendance	Scorers
Jan 15	St Helens Recreation (F)	L 6-18	500	T: Clegg, Greatorex
Jan 22	DEWSBURY (F)	W 7-5	6,000	T: E Woods, G: John 2
Jan 29	Wigan (F)	L 3-9	3,000	T: Gagon
Feb 5	BROUGHTON RANGERS (F)	W 4-2	6,000	G: J Hampson, John
Feb 12	HUDDERSFIELD (F)	L 6-23	7,000	T: Burgess, May
Feb 19	Runcorn (F)	W 7-4	1,000	T: Goldsmith, G: John 2
Feb 26	WIGAN (F)	W 7-6	900	T: Clegg, G: John 2
Mar 4	Barrow (F)	D 5-5	3,000	T: Clifford, G: John
Mar 11	HUNSLET (F)	W 21-0	–	T: Goldsmith, John, Ratcliffe, C Rees, E Woods, G: John 3
Mar 18	Hunslet (F)	L 0-8	4,500	
Mar 25	Huddersfield (F)	L 7-20	3,000	T: Loveluck, G: Launce 2
Apr 1	HULL KINGSTON ROVERS (F)	L 7-23	5,000	T: Burgess, G: John, Launce
Apr 8	Dewsbury (F)	L 2-17	3,000	G: John
Apr 15	HALIFAX (F)	W 17-5	–	T: Boardman 2, W Thomas, G: John 3, W Thomas
Apr 21	Swinton (F)	W 5-2	4,000	T: Goldsmith, G: John
Apr 24	Hull Kingston Rovers (F)	D 10-10	3,000	T: Ainsworth, Goldsmith, G: John 2
Apr 29	BROUGHTON RANGERS (F)	W 23-3	6,000	T: Clifford 2, Clegg, John, W Thomas, G: John 4

* Abandoned 30 mins (heavy rain)

1916-1917

	Opponent	Result	Attendance	Scorers
Sep 9	BRIGHOUSE RANGERS (F)	W 28-8	1,000	T: Clegg 2, Clifford 2, Ainsworth, Sykes, G: John 5
Sep 16	BARROW (F)	W 8-0	3,000	T: Clegg, Sykes, G: John
Sep 23	Wigan (F)	L 3-20	4,000	T: Whitney
Sep 30	Rochdale Hornets (F)	L 2-7	1,500	G: Launce
Oct 7	BROUGHTON RANGERS (F)	W 3-0	3,000	T: Mesley
Oct 14	Swinton (F)	W 5-2	4,000	T: Burgess, G: John
Oct 21	RUNCORN (F)	W 25-0	3,000	T: Clifford 4, Robinson 2, Coates, G: John 2
Oct 28	ROCHDALE HORNETS (F)	W 13-0	1,500	T: Ainsworth, Robinson, Whitney, G: John 2
Nov 4	Warrington (F)	W 5-0	3,000	T: John, G: John
Nov 11	WIGAN (F)	W 3-0	5,000	T: Clifford
Nov 18	ST HELENS (F)	W 8-0	3,000	T: Burgess, Clifford, G: John
Nov 25	Broughton Rangers (F)*	A 0-0	3,000	
Dec 2	WIDNES (F)	W 4-0	–	G: John 2
Dec 9	Leigh (F)	L 5-18	2,000	T: John, G: John
Dec 25	Broughton Rangers (F)	L 2-3	3,000	G: John

Salford RL Match Results

1916-1917 *continued*

	Opponent	*Result*	*Attendance*	*Scorers*
Dec 26	SWINTON (F)	W 6-2	5,000	T: Ainsworth, Clegg
Jan 1	Swinton (F)	L 0-8	3,500	
Jan 13	St Helens Recreation (F)	L 5-20	–	T: H Harrison, G: Launce
Jan 20	LEIGH (F)	L 0-8	3,000	
Feb 17	Widnes (F)	L 0-6	200	
Feb 24	SWINTON (F)	L 6-7	4,000	T: Burgess, Wanklyn
Mar 3	Barrow (F)	L 0-17	3,000	
Mar 17	Runcorn (F)	L 2-7	600	G: Launce
Mar 24	WARRINGTON (F)	D 12-12	2,000	T: Burgess 2, Ainsworth, Dixon
Mar 31	St Helens (F)	L 6-8	2,000	T: Burgess, Costigan
Apr 6	Warrington (F)	L 5-17	4,000	T: Burrows, G: Burgess
Apr 7	ST HELENS RECREATION (F)	L 0-14	4,000	
Apr 14	OLDHAM (F)	L 9-10	4,000	T: Ainsworth, Burgess, Burrows
Apr 21	Oldham (F)	L 3-13	7,000	T: May
Apr 28	BROUGHTON RANGERS (F)	W 20-5	3,000	T: Burgess 2, Lomas 2, W Thomas, S Wood, G: Lomas
May 12	Broughton Rangers (F)	L 6-13	2,500	T: Burgess, W Thomas

* Abandoned 24 mins (rainstorm)

1917-1918

	Opponent	*Result*	*Attendance*	*Scorers*
Sep 15	BROUGHTON RANGERS (F)	L 8-19	4,000	T: Clegg, Sykes, G: Launce
Sep 22	Leigh (F)	L 5-24	1,200	T: Ainsworth, G: Spencer
Sep 29	Wigan (F)	L 6-41	4,000	T: Coates, Spencer
Oct 6	BARROW (F)	L 0-31	2,000	
Oct 13	Swinton (F)	L 0-24	1,500	
Oct 20	WARRINGTON (F)	L 0-13	2,000	
Oct 27	Barrow (F)	L 5-52	4,000	T: Sykes, G: Clegg
Nov 3	Leigh (F)	L 0-10	1,000	
Nov 24	Broughton Rangers (F)	L 0-8	1,500	
Dec 1	WIGAN (F)	L 3-18	500	T: Landers
Dec 25	Broughton Rangers (F)	L 0-21	4,000	
Dec 26	SWINTON (F)	L 0-12	–	
Dec 29	LEIGH (F)	D 0-0	1,000	
Jan 1	Swinton (F)	L 0-13	2,500	
Jan 12	Leigh (F)	L 0-41	700	
Jan 19	RUNCORN (F)	W 2-0	–	G: Launce
Feb 9	BROUGHTON RANGERS (F)	L 2-11	1,000	G: Burgess
Feb 16	Barrow (F)	L 0-29	4,000	
Feb 23	SWINTON (F)	L 2-6	2,000	G: W Thomas
Mar 2	Wigan (F)	L 0-32	3,000	

Salford RL Match Results

1917-1918 *continued*

	Opponent	Result	Attendance	Scorers
Mar 9	WARRINGTON (F)	L 6-16	1,000	T: Burgess 2
Mar 16	Runcorn (F)	L 3-8	600	T: Wanklyn
Mar 23	WIGAN (F)	L 3-13	2,000	T: Campbell
Mar 29	Warrington (F)	L 2-8	5,000	G: Launce
Mar 30	LEIGH (F)	L 0-6	800	
Apr 1	St Helens Recreation (F)	L 0-24	1,000	
Apr 13	LEIGH (F)	L 3-7	500	T: Campbell
Apr 27	ST HELENS RECREATION (F)	L 4-12	1,000	G: Burgess 2

1918-1919

	Opponent	Result	Attendance	Scorers
Nov 2	WIGAN (F)	L 0-11	1,000	
Nov 23	Swinton (F)	D 5-5	1,000	T: Livesey, G: Launce
Dec 7	Wigan (F)	L 2-9	2,000	G: Burgess
Dec 14	Broughton Rangers (F)	L 0-5	5,000	
Dec 25	Broughton Rangers (F)	D 5-5	–	T: Brockbank, G: unreported
Dec 26	Swinton (F)	L 0-8	–	
Dec 28	Barrow (F)	L 3-18	4,000	T: Clegg
Jan 1	SWINTON (F)	L 0-8	2,000	
Jan 18	BROUGHTON RANGERS	W 12-0	5,000	T: Clegg, Coates, May, Sykes
Jan 25	Leigh	L 2-5	1,200	G: Launce
Feb 1	Barrow	L 2-17	3,500	G: Launce
Feb 8	Rochdale Hornets	L 0-3	3,000	
Feb 15	SWINTON	W 3-0	6,000	T: Clifford
Mar 1	Widnes	L 0-13	1,500	
Mar 8	ROCHDALE HORNETS	L 0-6	3,000	
Mar 15	BROUGHTON RANGERS (F)	W 9-2	3,000	T: Callender 2, Sykes
Mar 22	WARRINGTON	L 2-7	3,000	G: John
Apr 5	Rochdale Hornets (LC-1)	L 5-7	9,500	T: Callender, G: Launce
Apr 12	Broughton Rangers	W 13-7	4,000	T: Callender, Clegg, Livesey, G: John 2
Apr 18	Warrington	L 0-11	3,000	
Apr 19	LEIGH	L 0-8	5,000	
Apr 26	WIDNES	W 16-4	4,000	T: Burgess, Callender, Clegg, Ratcliffe, G: Callender, Launce
May 3	BARROW	W 35-7	5,000	T: Callender 4, Burgess 2, Gagon 2, W Thomas, G: W Thomas 3, Launce
May 17	Swinton	W 13-5	4,000	T: Gagon, Whitney, Winstanley G: Lounce, W Thomas

Salford RL Match Results

1919-1920

	Opponent	Result	Attendance	Scorers
Aug 23	BRAMLEY	D 8-8	4,000	T: Burgess, Winstanley, G: W Thomas
Aug 30	Barrow	L 3-19	5,000	T: Winstanley
Sep 6	ST HELENS RECREATION	W 8-3	4,000	T: Callender, Clegg, G: Burgess
Sep 13	Hunslet	W 2-0	–	G: Launce
Sep 20	Bradford Northern	L 0-11	4,000	
Sep 27	WIGAN	L 5-8	5,000	T: Winstanley, G: Burgess
Oct 4	Bramley	L 8-18	3,000	T: Clegg, Shields, G: Launce
Oct 11	WIDNES	W 8-0	12,000	T: Wilkinson, Winstanley, G: Launce
Oct 18	BARROW (LC-1)	L 0-15	7,000	
Oct 25	Leigh	L 6-11	3,000	T: Clegg, Winstanley
Nov 1	Halifax (F)	W 3-0	6,000	T: Costigan
Nov 8	Hull	L 2-30	12,000	G: John
Nov 15	BARROW	L 6-8	4,000	T: Costigan 2
Nov 22	St Helens Recreation	L 2-12	10,000	G: W Thomas
Nov 29	Warrington (F)	L 3-8	4,000	T: Cooper
Dec 13	YORK	W 14-0	4,000	T: Costigan, W Thomas, Whitney, E Woods, G: Launce
Dec 20	York	W 11-8	–	T: Burgess, Costigan, Shields, G: Burgess
Dec 25	Broughton Rangers	L 0-6	6,000	
Dec 26	SWINTON	W 13-9	–	T: Burgess, Waite, Wilkinson, G: Burgess, John
Jan 1	Swinton	W 6-2	7,000	T: Burgess, John
Jan 3	ROCHDALE HORNETS	L 0-8	6,000	
Jan 10	St Helens	W 13-6	4,000	T: Wilkinson, Winstanley, E Woods, G: Burgess, John
Jan 17	HULL	L 5-13	6,000	T: Cooper, G: Burgess
Jan 24	Rochdale Hornets	W 5-4	7,000	T: Whitney, G: Burgess
Jan 31	BRADFORD NORTHERN*	W 8-0	4,000	T: Burgess 2, G: John
Feb 7	BROUGHTON RANGERS	W 13-5	8,000	T: Burgess, Clegg, Wilkinson, G: John 2
Feb 14	Wigan	L 5-13	10,000	T: John, G: John
Feb 21	Batley (NUC-1)	L 0-19	10,000	
Feb 28	HUNSLET	W 12-3	5,000	T: Burgess 2, Costigan, Whitney
Mar 6	OLDHAM	L 3-9	8,000	T: Costigan
Mar 20	WARRINGTON	W 14-12	10,000	T: Costigan, Currie, Sykes, Whitney, G: John
Mar 24	Widnes	L 6-10	4,000	T: Clegg, Wilkinson
Apr 2	Warrington	L 6-22	6,000	T: Clifford, Wilkinson
Apr 3	Oldham	L 3-7	7,000	T: Burgess

Salford RL Match Results

1919-1920 continued

	Opponent	Result	Attendance	Scorers
Apr 10	ST HELENS	W 7-5	4,000	T: John, G: Hare, John
Apr 17	LEIGH	L 0-2	4,000	

* Abandoned 25 mins after half-time (failing light due to delayed start) – result stands

1920-1921

	Opponent	Result	Attendance	Scorers
Aug 28	Barrow	L 2-45	6,000	G: Sykes
Sep 4	LEIGH	D 6-6	4,000	T: Bailey, Whitney
Sep 11	ROCHDALE HORNETS	L 2-13	10,000	G: Burgess
Sep 25	Warrington	L 3-10	6,000	T: Costigan
Oct 2	Broughton Rangers	L 0-11	10,000	
Oct 9	WAKEFIELD TRINITY	L 11-17	9,000	T: Costigan 2, Wilkinson, G: Hare
Oct 16	Rochdale Hornets (LC-1)	L 5-11	8,000	T: Deakin, G: Launce
Oct 23	Leigh	L 7-13	8,000	T: Burgess, G: W Thomas 2
Nov 6	Wakefield Trinity	W 5-3	4,000	T: Derrick, G: W Thomas
Nov 13	BRAMLEY	L 0-8	5,000	
Nov 17	ST HELENS RECREATION	L 5-13	3,000	T: Wilkinson, G: Launce
Nov 20	WIGAN	L 0-21	7,000	
Nov 27	St Helens	L 5-14	6,000	T: Muir, G: Sykes
Dec 4	Wigan	L 0-26	10,000	
Dec 11	HULL KINGSTON ROVERS	L 3-8	5,000	T: Costigan
Dec 18	Hull Kingston Rovers	L 0-5	6,000	
Dec 25	BROUGHTON RANGERS	L 0-10	8,000	
Dec 27	SWINTON	L 6-18	8,000	T: Costigan, Norrey
Jan 1	Swinton	L 3-18	10,000	T: Clegg
Jan 8	Oldham	L 3-14	10,000	T: Burgess
Jan 22	BARROW	L 0-5	6,000	
Jan 29	OLDHAM	L 3-12	4,000	T: Whitney
Feb 5	Widnes	W 5-2	–	T: T: Burgess, G: W Thomas
Feb 12	Bramley	L 0-10	2,656	
Feb 19	WARRINGTON	L 7-13	7,000	T: Costigan, G: Burgess, John
Feb 26	BARROW (NUC-1)	W 4-0	8,000	G: Burgess, John
Mar 5	Rochdale Hornets	L 0-31	8,000	
Mar 12	LEEDS (NUC-2)	L 0-21	13,000	
Mar 25	St Helens Recreation	L 0-29	6,000	
Mar 28	Hunslet	D 3-3	3,000	T: Lloyd
Mar 29	Dewsbury	L 3-27	4,000	T: Burgess
Apr 2	ST HELENS	L 5-10	4,500	T: Whitney, G: Hare
Apr 9	HUNSLET	L 6-12	4,000	T: Fuller 2
Apr 16	DEWSBURY	L 13-15	4,000	T: Partridge, G: Burgess 5
Apr 23	WIDNES	L 5-21	4,000	T: Fuller, G: Burgess

Salford RL Match Results

1921-1922

	Opponent	*Result*	*Attendance*	*Scorers*
Aug 27	YORK	W 5-3	10,000	T: Burgess, G: Burgess
Sep 3	BRADFORD NORTHERN	W 18-3	8,000	T: Charles 2, W Thomas, Wilkinson, G: Burgess 2, W Thomas
Sep 10	St Helens	L 6-16	–	G: Charles 2, TH Smith
Sep 17	AUSTRALIA (Tour)	L 3-48	9,000	T: W Thomas
Sep 24	Keighley	W 6-0	3,000	T: Fuller, Whitney
Oct 1	LEIGH	L 5-17	8,000	T: Burgess, G: Burgess
Oct 8	Oldham	L 9-14	10,000	T: Burgess, G: Burgess 3
Oct 15	Rochdale Hornets	L 5-24	8,000	T: Fuller, G: Burgess
Oct 22	Widnes (LC-1)	L 0-6	1,000	
Oct 29	HUNSLET	D 0-0	5,000	
Nov 5	FEATHERSTONE ROVERS	W 21-6	4,000	T: Fuller, Keegan, Muir, Southward, Wilkinson, G: Keegan 2, Molyneux
Nov 12	St Helens Recreation	L 10-15	4,000	T: Allmark, Wilkinson, G: Southward 2
Nov 19	WIGAN (F)	L 5-13	5,000	T: Wilkinson, G: Southward
Nov 26	WARRINGTON	L 2-8	5,000	G: Southward
Dec 7	OLDHAM	L 0-23	3,000	
Dec 10	Widnes	L 3-19	–	T: Haines
Dec 17	WIGAN	L 4-6	4,000	G: Burgess 2
Dec 24	Broughton Rangers	L 4-5	5,000	G: Burgess 2
Dec 26	SWINTON	W 4-2	10,000	G: Burgess 2
Dec 27	Hunslet	W 5-3	6,000	T: Fuller, G: Burgess
Dec 31	WIDNES	D 0-0	4,000	
Jan 2	Swinton	L 0-9	10,000	
Jan 7	ST HELENS	W 5-3	3,000	T: TH Smith, G: Southward
Jan 21	BARROW	L 2-11	3,000	G: Burgess
Jan 28	Bradford Northern	L 2-8	200	G: Burgess
Feb 4	ROCHDALE HORNETS	D 0-0	1,500	
Feb 11	Featherstone Rovers	L 5-13	2,500	T: Hare, G: Burgess
Feb 18	ST HELENS RECREATION	L 2-7	5,500	G: Burgess
Feb 25	Barrow (NUC-1)	L 2-20	4,800	G: Hare
Mar 1	Wigan	L 3-22	2,000	T: Wilkinson
Mar 4	KEIGHLEY	W 10-7	5,000	T: Burgess 2, G: Southward 2
Mar 11	Leigh	L 3-12	3,000	T: Southward
Mar 18	BROUGHTON RANGERS	D 0-0	6,000	
Mar 25	Warrington	L 2-14	4,000	G: Burgess
Apr 8	York	L 3-15	3,000	T: Wilkinson
Apr 14	Barrow	L 0-6	2,000	
Apr 17	Dewsbury	L 7-18	–	T: H Hurst, G: Southward 2
Apr 18	DEWSBURY	W 13-3	3,000	T: Butterworth Wilkinson, Woodhead, G: Burgess 2

Salford RL Match Results

1922-1923

	Opponent	Result	Attendance	Scorers
Aug 26	Wigan	L 6-46	10,000	T: Southward, E Woods
Sep 9	LEIGH	L 5-12	5,000	T: Wilkinson, G: Southward
Sep 16	Featherstone Rovers	L 3-17	3,000	T: TH Smith
Sep 23	WARRINGTON	L 5-13	6,000	T: C Hall, G: Southward
Sep 30	Leigh	L 6-17	6,000	T: Roberts, Southward
Oct 7	Broughton Rangers	D 0-0	7,000	
Oct 14	St Helens (LC-1)	L 8-25	12,000	T: Muir, Norrey, G: Southward
Oct 21	WIGAN HIGHFIELD	W 14-0	4,000	T: Southward, J Williams, G: Southward 4
Oct 28	Keighley	L 0-10	3,000	
Nov 4	BARROW	W 9-3	1,500	T: Brockbank, Burgess, C Hall
Nov 11	BRADFORD NORTHERN	W 20-7	3,500	T: Burgess, C Hall, Muir, Norrey, G: Burgess 2, Southward 2
Nov 18	Oldham	W 7-4	10,000	T: Burgess, G: Burgess 2
Nov 29	WIDNES	W 16-2	2,000	T: Burgess, Norrey, G: Burgess 5
Dec 2	St Helens Recreation	L 9-19	4,000	T: Norrey 2, Bowker
Dec 9	ROCHDALE HORNETS	W 14-6	6,000	T: Brockbank, Haines, Norrey, Southward, G: Burgess
Dec 16	Rochdale Hornets	L 2-12	6,000	G: Burgess
Dec 23	Barrow	L 8-39	2,500	T: Norrey 2, G: Burgess
Dec 25	BROUGHTON RANGERS	L 3-7	–	T: Southward
Dec 26	SWINTON	L 0-27	–	
Dec 30	Bradford Northern	L 9-14	2,000	T: Norrey, G: Burgess 3
Jan 1	Swinton	L 5-14	10,000	T: Haines, G: Southward
Jan 6	BRAMLEY	W 13-3	2,000	T: Burgess, Norrey, Southward, G: Burgess, Southward
Jan 13	HUNSLET	W 6-3	2,500	G: Burgess 2, Southward
Jan 20	Bramley	L 0-15	2,000	
Jan 27	St Helens	L 5-17	2,000	T: Norrey, G: Southward
Feb 3	ST HELENS RECREATION	W 3-0	3,000	T: Norrey
Feb 10	Wigan Highfield	L 5-7	1,000	T: Southward, G: Burgess
Feb 17	CASTLEFORD (RLC-1)	W 16-0	3,000	T: Brockbank, Norrey, Smith, Southward, G: Southward 2
Feb 24	ST HELENS	W 11-3	6,000	T: Norrey 2, Burgess, G: Lomas
Mar 3	WAKEFIELD TRINITY (RLC-2)	W 6-0	5,000	T: Norrey, E Woods
Mar 10	WIGAN	D 0-0	10,000	
Mar 17	HULL (RLC-3)	L 0-24	18,000	
Mar 22	Widnes	L 5-12	–	T: Norrey, G: Lomas

Salford RL Match Results

1922-1923 continued

	Opponent	Result	Attendance	Scorers
Mar 24	Hunslet	L 2-41	7,000	G: Burgess
Mar 31	OLDHAM	W 10-0	5,000	T: Whitney, Whittle, G: Southward 2
Apr 2	York	L 9-14	5,000	T: Boon, Norrey, Whitney
Apr 4	YORK	W 20-8	3,000	T: Brockbank 2, Norry, Whitney, G: Burgess 3, Southward
Apr 7	Warrington	L 5-11	6,000	T: Southward, G: Southward
Apr 14	KEIGHLEY	W 12-10	4,000	T: Haines, Southward, G: Southward 2, Brockbank
Apr 28	FEATHERSTONE ROVERS	W 16-8	4,000	T: Southward 2, Brockbank, C Hall, G: Burgess, Southward

1923-1924

	Opponent	Result	Attendance	Scorers
Aug 25	ST HELENS RECREATION	L 2-8	7,000	G: Southward
Sep 1	Hunslet	L 3-10	5,000	T: Southward
Sep 8	WIGAN	L 0-19	5,000	
Sep 15	Oldham	L 5-33	9,000	T: Wilkinson, G: Burgess
Sep 22	WIDNES	W 19-6	4,000	T: Boon, Southward, Wilkinson, G: Lomas 4, Burgess
Sep 29	Wakefield Trinity	L 3-26	5,000	T: Burgess
Oct 6	BROUGHTON RANGERS	W 7-0	7,000	T: Boon, G: Southward 2
Oct 13	St Helens (LC-1)	L 0-5	6,000	
Oct 20	St Helens Recreation	L 0-21	2,000	
Oct 27	WIGAN HIGHFIELD	L 0-5	4,000	
Nov 10	Leigh	L 5-24	5,000	T: Southward, G: Quigley
Nov 17	HUNSLET	D 4-4	2,000	G: Burgess, Southward
Nov 24	Batley	L 7-17	5,000	T: Whitney, G: Quigley, Southward
Dec 1	ST HELENS	W 6-0	3,000	T: Southward 2
Dec 8	Wigan	L 0-49	7,000	
Dec 15	WARRINGTON	L 7-9	2,000	T: Enoch, G: Quigley, Southward
Dec 26	SWINTON	L 3-5	6,000	T: Southward
Dec 29	HALIFAX	W 17-0	3,500	T: Coombes, Haines, Southward, G: Southward 4
Jan 1	Swinton	L 3-12	12,000	T: Southward
Jan 5	Wigan Highfield	W 5-3	1,000	T: Wilkinson, G: Southward
Jan 12	BARROW	L 2-3	–	G: Burgess
Jan 19	WAKEFIELD TRINITY	L 3-8	–	T: Clegg
Jan 26	Warrington	L 3-5	5,000	T: Boyd
Feb 2	ROCHDALE HORNETS	L 0-15	5,000	

Salford RL Match Results

1923-1924 *continued*

	Opponent	Result	Attendance	Scorers
Feb 9	Barrow	L 10-23	2,000	T: Boyd, Clegg, G: Southward 2
Feb 16	HUNSLET (RLC-1)	L 6-8	6,000	T: Southward, Wilkinson
Mar 1	LEIGH	L 0-6	6,000	
Mar 15	BATLEY	L 2-7	6,000	G: Southward
Mar 22	York	L 7-49	3,500	T: Southward, G: Southward 2
Apr 3	OLDHAM	L 8-18	2,000	T: Southward, J Williams, G: Burgess
Apr 12	Widnes	L 0-21	3,000	
Apr 18	Broughton Rangers	W 5-0	7,000	T: Wilkinson, G: Southward
Apr 19	Rochdale Hornets	L 3-24	4,000	T: A Hurst
Apr 21	Halifax	W 8-5	–	T: Burgess, Haines, G: Southward
Apr 23	YORK	W 13-3	–	T: Haines, Quigley, Whittle, G: Southward 2
Apr 26	St Helens	L 15-37	5,000	T: Burgess, Haines, Southward, G: Southward 3

1924-1925

	Opponent	Result	Attendance	Scorers
Aug 30	St Helens Recreation	L 4-25	8,000	G: Southward 2
Sep 13	BRADFORD NORTHERN	L 0-10	4,000	
Sep 20	OLDHAM	L 0-5	7,000	
Sep 27	Broughton Rangers	L 0-11	10,000	
Oct 4	WIDNES	W 8-3	5,000	T: Burgess, A Hurst, G: Burgess
Oct 11	WIGAN HIGHFIELD (LC-1)	W 5-3	5,000	T: Entwistle, G: Burgess
Oct 18	Leigh	L 0-26	5,000	
Oct 25	St Helens Recreation (LC-2)	L 5-36	4,000	T: Southward, G: Burgess
Nov 1	Keighley	L 2-7	3,000	G: Southward
Nov 8	Featherstone Rovers	W 6-0	2,000	T: Burgess 2
Nov 15	ST HELENS	W 13-3	5,000	T: Southward 2, Halton, G: Burgess, Southward
Nov 22	Bramley	D 3-3	–	T: Boyd
Nov 29	WARRINGTON	L 3-5	3,000	T: Halton
Dec 6	Rochdale Hornets	W 10-9	3,000	T: Boyd, Hayes, G: Burgess, Southward
Dec 13	WIGAN HIGHFIELD	W 8-5	3,000	T: Burgess, Southward, G: Southward
Dec 17	ST HELENS RECREATION	W 3-0	–	T: Burgess
Dec 20	Widnes	L 0-18	–	
Dec 25	BROUGHTON RANGERS	W 14-7	9,000	T: Boyd, Burgess, Halton, Southward, G: Southward
Dec 26	SWINTON	L 3-8	14,000	T: C Hall

Salford RL Match Results

1924-1925 *continued*

	Opponent	Result	Attendance	Scorers
Jan 1	Swinton	L 2-16	10,000	G: Southward
Jan 3	LEIGH	L 0-7	4,000	
Jan 10	Barrow	D 0-0	3,000	
Jan 17	WIGAN	L 5-63	10,000	T: A Hurst, G: Southward
Jan 31	St Helens*	A 0-14	500	
Feb 7	BRAMLEY	W 6-5	2,000	T: Beaver, Halton
Feb 14	Wakefield Trinity (RLC-1)	L 3-14	11,000	T: J Coates
Feb 21	BARROW	W 5-0	–	T: C Hall, G: Southward
Feb 28	St Helens	L 0-17	3,000	
Mar 7	Wigan Highfield	W 11-5	1,000	T: Beaver 2, Boyd, G: Southward
Mar 21	Oldham	L 3-32	8,000	T: TH Smith
Mar 25	KEIGHLEY	D 2-2	2,000	G: Southward
Mar 28	Warrington	L 0-15	6,000	
Apr 4	FEATHERSTONE ROVERS	W 5-3	3,000	T: Halton, G: Southward
Apr 6	Bradford Northern	L 3-15	1,000	T: J Coates
Apr 10	York	L 3-8	1,000	T: Southward
Apr 11	YORK	W 9-6	4,000	T: Southward, G: Halton 2, Burgess
Apr 13	Wigan	L 19-57	4,000	T: Halton 2, Haines, W Hall, Southward, G: Halton 2
Apr 20	ROCHDALE HORNETS	W 10-3	3,000	T: Haines, Southward, G: Halton, Southward
Apr 25	BROUGHTON RANGERS (SHC-SF)	W 11-3	–	T: Boyd, Haines, Southward, G: Burgess
May 9	Swinton (SHC-Final)**	L 0-8	6,000	

*Abandoned half-time (heavy rain, waterlogged pitch)   ** At Broughton*

1925-1926

	Opponent	Result	Attendance	Scorers
Aug 29	HULL	W 8-0	5,000	T: Peacock, Southward, G: Southward
Sep 3	Barrow	W 6-0	4,500	T: W Harris, Haines
Sep 5	Oldham	L 2-32	8,000	G: Southward
Sep 12	BROUGHTON RANGERS	W 10-9	10,000	T: Haines, Southward, G: Southward 2
Sep 19	Wakefield Trinity	L 0-3	2,000	
Sep 26	ST HELENS RECREATION	L 0-5	3,000	
Oct 3	Wigan	L 5-18	8,000	T: Boyd, G: Meek
Oct 10	Wigan Highfield (LC-1)	W 7-6	500	T: Peacock, G: Southward 2
Oct 17	LEIGH	W 25-10	3,000	T: Meek 2, Peacock 2, Burgess, G: Burgess 5
Oct 19	Oldham (LC-2)	L 5-8	5,000	T: Peacock, G: Burgess

Salford RL Match Results

1925-1926 *continued*

	Opponent	Result	Attendance	Scorers
Oct 24	York	L 2-17	–	G: Southward
Oct 31	Featherstone Rovers	L 15-22	–	T: A Hurst 2, Southward, G: Southward 3
Nov 7	WARRINGTON	L 2-7	2,000	G: Southward
Dec 12	ST HELENS	W 17-3	5,000	T: Gore 2, A Hurst, G: W Harris 3, A Hurst
Dec 19	BARROW	D 8-8	–	T: Boyd, Gore, G: A Hurst
Dec 25	Broughton Rangers	W 5-0	5,000	T: Meek, G: Southward
Dec 26	SWINTON	L 3-13	15,000	T: Burgess
Jan 1	Swinton	W 11-10	12,000	T: Burgess 2, Peacock, G: A Hurst
Jan 2	Rochdale Hornets	L 6-7	3,000	T: Burgess, Haines
Jan 9	WAKEFIELD TRINITY	L 0-8	7,000	
Jan 16	WIDNES	L 12-21	3,000	T: Butterworth, Haines, G: A Hurst 3
Jan 23	St Helens*	V 10-13	3,000	T: W Hall, Meek, G: A Hurst 2
Jan 30	WIGAN HIGHFIELD	D 8-8	3,000	T: Boyd 2, G: Southward
Feb 6	Wigan Highfield	L 0-3	500	
Feb 13	LEEDS (RLC-1)	L 2-3	7,000	G: Southward
Feb 20	FEATHERSTONE ROVERS	D 5-5	3,000	T: Southward, G: A Hurst
Feb 27	KEIGHLEY	W 11-2	2,000	T: Haines, G: Southward 4
Mar 6	WIGAN	L 3-16	6,000	T: Gore
Mar 13	St Helens Recreation	L 5-14	4,500	T: Gore, G: Southward
Mar 20	ROCHDALE HORNETS	W 14-9	4,000	T: WJ Davies, A Hurst, G: Burgess 4
Apr 2	Leigh	D 10-10	3,000	T: Burgess, Garland, G: A Hurst, Southward
Apr 3	YORK	W 27-14	2,000	T: Gore 3, Burgess 2, WJ Davies, Haines, G: A Hurst 2, Southward
Apr 5	Hull	L 8-23	8,000	T: Burgess, W Harris, G: Burgess
Apr 10	Keighley	W 6-5	–	T: Haines, Southward
Apr 17	Warrington	L 4-34	7,000	G: Burgess 2
Apr 21	OLDHAM	L 0-10	3,000	
Apr 24	Widnes	L 8-24	–	T: Boyd, Robinson, G: Burgess
Apr 26	St Helens	L 0-23	3,000	

* Declared void after Salford protested a St Helens try – replay ordered

Salford RL Match Results

1926-1927

	Opponent	Result	Attendance	Scorers
Aug 28	St Helens Recreation	L 0-58	3,000	
Sep 1	SWINTON (SHC-SF)*	L 2-10	4,000	G: Southward
Sep 4	BARROW	L 0-15	4,000	
Sep 11	Bramley	D 5-5	2,000	T: Meek, G: Southward
Sep 18	PONTYPRIDD	W 20-7	5,000	T: Southward 3, Meek, G: Mannion 4
Sep 25	Bradford Northern	W 15-9	2,000	T: Gore 2, WJ Davies, G: Southward 2, Meek
Oct 2	WARRINGTON	L 9-10	5,000	T: Clegg, Meek, Peacock
Oct 9	Oldham (LC-1)	W 3-2	6,000	T: Peacock
Oct 16	Widnes	L 0-8	–	
Oct 20	BARROW (LC-2)	W 6-5	2,500	G: Southward 2, Meek
Oct 23	HUNSLET	L 5-8	4,000	T: Southward, G: Southward
Oct 30	Broughton Rangers	L 0-8	7,000	
Nov 3	NEW ZEALAND (Tour)	L 10-18	3,500	T: Gore, Meek, G: Southward 2
Nov 6	Castleford	L 3-10	5,000	T: Boyd
Nov 10	St Helens Recreation (LC-SF)	D 8-8	3,000	T: Boyd, Gore, G: Southward
Nov 12	ST HELENS RECREATION (LC-SF Replay)	L 0-14	3,000	
Nov 13	ST HELENS	W 8-5	4,000	T: Muir, Peacock, G: Burgess
Nov 20	KEIGHLEY	W 10-3	2,000	T: Gore, Haines, G: Meek, Price
Dec 4	Hunslet	W 15-13	–	T: Peacock, G: Southward 3, L Williams 3
Dec 11	WIGAN HIGHFIELD	W 15-0	4,000	T: Haines 2, J Harris, G: L Williams 2, Southward
Dec 18	Rochdale Hornets	L 0-5	6,000	
Dec 25	BROUGHTON RANGERS	W 6-5	10,000	T: Southward 2
Dec 27	Swinton	L 5-11	15,000	T: Southward, G: L Williams
Jan 1	SWINTON	L 0-8	14,342	
Jan 8	Barrow	L 3-13	4,000	T: Boyd
Jan 15	OLDHAM	D 5-5	4,000	T: Mannion, G: L Williams
Jan 29	ST HELENS RECREATION	L 3-8	3,000	T: Southward
Feb 12	Oldham (RLC-1)	L 0-8	13,512	
Feb 19	Warrington	L 10-13	6,000	T: Haines, Peacock, G: Mannion, L Williams
Feb 26	LEIGH	W 17-10	5,000	T: Boyd, Mannion, Southward, G: L Williams 2, Mannion, Meek
Mar 5	WIGAN	W 18-10	7,000	T: Boyd, WJ Davies, Gore, Peacock, G: Mannion 2, L Williams

Salford RL Match Results

1926-1927 *continued*

	Opponent	Result	Attendance	Scorers
Mar 9	Wigan Highfield	L 0-8	1,000	
Mar 12	Pontypridd	L 5-13	3,000	T: Boyd, G: L Williams
Mar 19	Keighley	L 11-12	4,000	T: WJ Davies, Gore, Manning, G: WJ Davies
Mar 21	Oldham	L 12-18	5,000	T: Southward 2, Boyd, Garland
Mar 26	BRAMLEY**	W 18-0	3,000	T: Southward 2, Boyd, Haines, G: Southward 2, Mannion
Apr 2	St Helens	L 3-8	3,000	T: Burgess
Apr 9	BRADFORD NORTHERN	W 13-0	3,000	T: Gore 3, G: Southward 2
Apr 15	Leigh	L 8-12	6,000	T: Haines, Peacock, G: Southward
Apr 16	WIDNES	W 12-8	3,000	T: Gore, Mannion, G: L Williams 3
Apr 18	ROCHDALE HORNETS	W 28-0	6,000	T: WJ Davies 2, Haines 2, Boyd, Gore, G: L Williams 5
Apr 19	Wigan	L 15-20	4,000	T: Gore, Mannion, Southward, G: L Williams 3
Apr 23	CASTLEFORD	W 9-7	3,000	T: Garland, Gore, Southward
May 9	Broughton Rangers (SHC-SF)	W 18-0	3,000	T: Boyd, Gore, Peacock, Southward, G: L Williams 2, Mannion
May 14	Swinton (SHC-Final)***	W 8-6	7,000	T: Haines 2, G: L Williams

* Held over from previous season
** Abandoned 35 min (pitch waterlogged) – result stands
*** At Broughton

1927-1928

	Opponent	Result	Attendance	Scorers
Aug 27	OLDHAM	L 4-8	8,000	G: L Williams 2
Sep 3	St Helens Recreation	L 3-37	4,000	T: Haines
Sep 10	BROUGHTON RANGERS	W 13-10	7,000	T: WJ Davies 2, Boyd, G: L Williams 2
Sep 17	Wigan	L 3-15	7,000	T: Lindley
Sep 24	ROCHDALE HORNETS	L 0-5	4,000	
Oct 8	Warrington	D 12-12	8,000	T: Garland, Meek, G: L Williams 3
Oct 15	St Helens	L 10-44	–	T: Meek, Peacock, G: L Williams 2
Oct 17	BARROW (LC-2)	D 0-0	2,000	
Oct 20	Barrow (LC-2 Replay)	W 5-2	–	T: Haines, G: L Williams
Oct 22	HUDDERSFIELD	L 2-12	4,000	G: L Williams
Oct 29	Oldham	L 9-22	9,500	T: Riley 2, Gore
Nov 2	Swinton (LC-SF)	L 3-10	7,000	T: WJ Davies

Salford RL Match Results

1927-1928 *continued*

	Opponent	Result	Attendance	Scorers
Nov 5	BARROW	W 6-0	2,000	T: Boyd, Meek
Nov 12	Wigan Highfield	L 0-5	2,000	
Nov 19	LEIGH	L 8-16	4,000	T: WJ Davies, Gore, G: L Williams
Nov 26	WIGAN	L 13-23	5,000	T: Boyd, Southward, L Williams, G: L Williams 2
Dec 3	Keighley	L 8-13	4,000	T: WJ Davies, Meek, G: L Williams
Dec 10	BATLEY	W 22-2	3,000	T: Manning 2, Southward 2, Gore, Haines, G: L Williams 2
Dec 24	WARRINGTON	W 3-0	4,000	T: Meek
Dec 26	Broughton Rangers	W 14-13	–	T: WJ Davies, Manning, Southward, R Taylor, G: Southward
Dec 27	SWINTON	L 0-18	12,000	
Jan 2	Swinton	L 2-11	14,000	G: L Williams
Jan 7	WIDNES	W 8-5	3,000	T: Gore, Meek, G: Southward
Jan 14	Widnes	L 5-6	–	T: WJ Davies, G: Southward
Jan 28	Batley	L 5-24	3,000	T: Boyd, G: Southward
Jan 30	Featherstone Rovers	L 0-18	2,000	
Feb 4	Rochdale Hornets	L 0-13	3,000	
Feb 11	CASTLEFORD (RLC-1)	L 3-7	2,945	T: Haines
Feb 18	FEATHERSTONE ROVERS	L 7-11	3,000	T: Garland, G: Southward 2
Feb 25	ST HELENS	W 14-5	3,000	T: Boyd, Gore, Manning, Meek, G: Southward
Mar 3	Huddersfield	L 11-26	5,000	T: Gore, G: L Williams 4
Mar 10	Leigh	L 2-21	4,000	G: Southward
Mar 17	ST HELENS RECREATION	L 5-15	5,000	T: Haines, G: Southward
Apr 6	WIGAN HIGHFIELD	L 10-14	6,000	T: Price, Southward, G: Southward 2
Apr 7	KEIGHLEY	W 13-3	3,000	T: Gore, Haines, WA Williams, G: Burgess, Southward
Apr 9	Barrow	W 8-7	–	T: Hudson 2, G: Southward
Apr 25	Broughton Rangers (SHC-SF)	L 5-12	3,000	T: Southward, G: Southward

Salford RL Match Results

1928-1929

Date	Opponent	Result	Attendance	Scorers
Aug 25	Oldham	W 20-0	–	T: Boyd, Casewell, Hudson, Muir, G: L Williams 3, Southward
Sep 1	ST HELENS RECREATION	L 9-10	7,000	T: Casewell, G: Southward 2, L Williams
Sep 8	Hull	L 2-6	4,000	G: Southward
Sep 15	BARROW	W 25-9	6,000	T: Casewell, WJ Davies, Hudson, Matthews, Muir, G: L Williams 5
Sep 22	Keighley	W 10-2	–	T: Matthews, Muir, G: L Williams 2
Sep 29	YORK	W 12-4	–	T: Hudson, L Williams, G: L Williams 3
Oct 6	St Helens Recreation	L 6-18	8,000	T: Hudson, WJ Davies
Oct 13	Carlisle City*	W 12-3	650	T: Matthews 2, G: L Williams 3
Oct 20	HULL	D 5-5	5,000	T: Meek, G: L Williams
Oct 24	Oldham (LC-2)	L 2-12	2,753	G: L Williams
Oct 27	WIGAN HIGHFIELD	W 16-0	6,000	T: WJ Davies 2, Boyd, Matthews, G: L Williams 2
Nov 10	Widnes	L 0-5	5,000	
Nov 17	OLDHAM	W 10-0	5,000	T: Matthews, Middleton, G: Middleton, L Williams
Nov 24	Leigh	L 2-6	5,000	G: Middleton
Dec 1	WIDNES	W 5-0	6,000	T: Hudson, G: Middleton
Dec 8	Wigan	L 6-42	4,000	T: Hudson, Matthews
Dec 25	BROUGHTON RANGERS	W 17-7	9,500	T: Casewell 2, Manning, G: L Williams 4
Dec 26	Wigan Highfield	W 5-3	1,500	T: Middleton, G: L Williams
Dec 29	BATLEY	W 16-0	5,000	T: Hudson 2, Lindley, Meek, G: L Williams 2
Jan 1	Swinton	L 3-14	16,000	T: Lindley
Jan 5	Broughton Rangers	W 10-4	6,000	T: Whitehead 2, G: Southward, L Williams
Jan 12	ST HELENS	W 10-7	6,000	T: Haines, Matthews, G: L Williams 2
Jan 19	Batley	L 7-12	–	T: Hudson, G: L Williams 2
Jan 26	ROCHDALE HORNETS	W 29-10	6,000	T: Casewell, Haines, Hudson, Manning, Matthews, Southward, L Williams, G : L Williams 4
Feb 2	St Helens	D 11-11	3,000	T: Hudson, Matthews, Meek, G: L Williams
Feb 9	KEIGHLEY (RLC-1)	L 5-9	6,744	T: Southward, G: L Williams
Mar 2	Warrington	W 13-11	8,000	T: Casewell, Muir, Southward, G: L Williams 2

Salford RL Match Results

1928-1929 *continued*

	Opponent	Result	Attendance	Scorers
Mar 9	LEIGH	W 10-0	8,000	T: Hudson, WA Williams, G: L Williams 2
Mar 16	Rochdale Hornets	W 6-3	5,000	T: Hudson, Matthews
Mar 23	BRADFORD NORTHERN	W 20-5	–	T: Boyd, Hudson, Manning, Matthews, G: L Williams 4
Mar 29	York	W 23-0	5,000	T: Hudson 2, Haines, Meek, Southward, G: L Williams 4
Mar 30	SWINTON	L 5-10	20,000	T: Haines, G: L Williams
Apr 3	WARRINGTON	W 18-5	6,000	T: Southward 2, Hudson, Manning, G: L Williams 2, Meek
Apr 6	Bradford Northern	W 21-13	2,000	T: Southward 2, Casewell, Matthews, Middleton, G: L Williams 3
Apr 11	Barrow	W 8-0	3,000	T: Matthews, Middleton, G: L Williams
Apr 13	KEIGHLEY	W 20-0	8,000	T: Haines 2, Meek, Middleton, G: L Williams 4
Apr 17	WIGAN	W 15-0	20,000	T: Boyd, Haines, Hudson, G: L Williams 3
Apr 27	Huddersfield (NRL-SF)	L 5-13	19,000	T: Hudson, G: L Williams

* Result expunged from league table after Carlisle City withdrew

1929-1930

	Opponent	Result	Attendance	Scorers
Aug 31	BARROW	W 16-13	7,039	T: Casewell, Matthews, Middleton, Risman, G: Middleton 2
Sep 7	St Helens Recreation	L 2-13	6,000	G: L Williams
Sep 14	HULL KINGSTON ROVERS	W 11-0	9,000	T: Matthews 2, Manning, G: Meek
Sep 21	Bradford Northern	W 5-2	1,000	T: Hudson, G: Dobing
Sep 28	WIGAN HIGHFIELD	W 18-8	6,000	T: Dobing, Hudson, Manning, Muir, G: Middleton 2, Dobing
Oct 2	BROUGHTON RANGERS (SHC-SF)	W 19-5	2,648	T: Southward 2, Hudson, Manning, Matthews, G: Meek 2
Oct 5	Widnes	W 2-0	3,000	G: Dobing
Oct 19	St Helens	L 12-18	8,500	T: Matthews, Middleton, G: Middleton 2, Meek

Salford RL Match Results

1929-1930 *continued*

	Opponent	Result	Attendance	Scorers
Oct 23	St Helens (LC-2)	D 8-8	8,000	T: Haines, Matthews, G: Dobing
Oct 26	LEEDS	W 4-0	9,419	G: Middleton 2
Oct 30	ST HELEN (LC-2 Replay)	W 13-3	8,000	T: Matthews 2, Casewell, G: Middleton, Southward
Nov 2	Wigan	L 3-18	10,000	T: Casewell
Nov 9	WIDNES	W 6-0	6,000	T: Middleton 2
Nov 13	SWINTON (LC-SF)	D 3-3	9,000	T: Manning
Nov 16	ST HELENS RECREATION	W 13-6	7,000	T: Dobing, Manning, Matthews, G: Middleton 2
Nov 18	Swinton (LC-SF Replay)	D 0-0	6,000	
Nov 20	Swinton (LC-SF 2nd Replay)*	W 8-0	7,509	T: Hudson, Manning, G: Dobing
Nov 23	Warrington (LC-Final)**	L 2-15	21,012	G: Dobing
Nov 30	Wakefield Trinity	L 8-12	4,000	T: Hudson, Meek, G: L Williams
Dec 7	LEIGH	W 11-2	3,000	T: Hudson 2, Matthews, G: L Williams
Dec 14	Oldham	L 3-18	5,000	T: Casewell
Dec 21	YORK	D 0-0	6,000	
Dec 25	Broughton Rangers	W 21-2	9,000	T: Boyd, Casewell, Dobing, Manning, Middleton, G: Middleton 3
Dec 26	SWINTON	L 3-8	18,000	T: Casewell
Dec 28	Warrington	W 8-0	5,000	T: Hudson, Middleton, G: L Williams
Jan 1	Swinton	D 0-0	10,000	
Jan 11	AUSTRALIA (Tour)	L 5-21	8,000	T: Lindley, G: L Williams
Jan 18	WAKEFIELD TRINITY	L 2-8	6,000	G: Dobing
Jan 25	Wigan Highfield	W 15-0	1,000	T: Casewell, Dobing, Middleton, G: Meek 2, Dobing
Feb 1	OLDHAM	W 5-2	10,000	T: Hudson, G: Middleton
Feb 8	Wigan Highfield (RLC-1)	L 0-5	8,111	
Feb 15	Leigh	L 0-5	4,000	
Feb 22	Rochdale Hornets	W 13-2	3,000	T: Dobing, Feetham, Middleton, G: L Williams 2
Mar 1	ROCHDALE HORNETS	W 15-3	6,000	T: Hudson, Risman, WA Williams, G: L Williams 3
Mar 8	York	L 0-7	5,270	
Mar 15	ST HELENS	W 11-2	5,000	T: Hudson 2, Feetham, G: Meek
Mar 22	WARRINGTON	W 26-11	8,000	T: Feetham, Hudson, Manning, Matthews, Middleton, Risman, G: L Williams 4
Apr 2	Leeds	D 8-8	–	T: Hudson 2, G: Miller

Salford RL Match Results

1929-1930 *continued*

	Opponent	Result	Attendance	Scorers
Apr 5	Huddersfield	L 3-15	8,000	T: Hudson
Apr 12	BRADFORD NORTHERN	W 46-5	–	T: Hudson 4, Casewell, Feetham, Haines, Lindley, Meek, Middleton, G: Miller 8
Apr 14	Hull Kingston Rovers	W 15-8	5,000	T: Haines 2, Matthews 2, Feetham
Apr 18	Barrow	W 8-0	–	T: Dobing 2, G: Middleton
Apr 19	HUDDERSFIELD	W 11-2	12,000	T: Boyd, Haines, Middleton, G: Manning
Apr 21	BROUGHTON RANGERS	W 53-8	11,000	T: Casewell 2, Feetham 2, Hudson 2, Manning 2, Middleton 2, Boyd, Dobing, Muir, G: Hudson 2, Middleton 2, Doran, Meek, Shaw
Apr 22	WIGAN	W 20-8	12,000	T: Feetham 2, Hudson, Middleton, G: Hudson 2, Meek, Middleton
Apr 26	Huddersfield (NRL-SF)	L 10-15	16,000	T: Casewell, Hudson, G: Hudson 2
Apr 30	Swinton (SHC-Final)*	L 3-15	6,000	T: Hudson

* At Broughton ** At Wigan

Lancashire League Championship runners-up
Lancashire Cup runners-up

1930-1931

	Opponent	Result	Attendance	Scorers
Aug 30	Leigh	W 11-0	4,500	T: Haines 2, Hudson, G: Hudson
Sep 6	HUNSLET	W 15-3	6,000	T: Haines, Matthews, J Williams, G: Hudson 3
Sep 10	ST HELENS	W 11-5	8,000	T: Hudson 2, J Williams, G: Hudson
Sep 13	Widnes	W 3-0	6,000	T: Matthews
Sep 20	ST HELENS RECREATION	W 17-7	8,000	T: Hudson 2, Feetham, Matthews, WA Williams, G: Hudson
Sep 22	Oldham	L 0-4	6,000	
Sep 27	Broughton Rangers	W 20-2	14,000	T: Hudson 2, Dobing, Feetham, G: Hudson 3, Meek
Oct 4	HALIFAX	W 3-2	10,000	T: Hudson
Oct 11	Oldham (LC-1)	L 2-7	17,000	G: Hudson
Oct 18	Warrington	L 3-4	7,000	T: Hudson

Salford RL Match Results

1930-1931 *continued*

	Opponent	Result	Attendance	Scorers
Oct 25	LEIGH	W 14-5	10,000	T: Haines, Hudson, Matthews, J Williams, G: Hudson
Nov 1	Wigan Highfield*	A 6-2	2,000	T: Matthews, Muir
Nov 8	WARRINGTON	W 17-7	7,000	T: Feetham, Haines, Hudson, G: Hudson 2, Meek 2
Nov 15	St Helens	L 0-7	10,000	
Nov 29	Halifax	L 0-10	9,000	
Dec 3	KEIGHLEY	W 44-7	5,000	T: Matthews 2, Middleton 2, Southward 2, Dalton, Meek, Miller, WA Williams, G: Meek 6, Miller
Dec 6	DEWSBURY	W 8-0	6,000	T: Dalton, Southward, G: Meek
Dec 13	Dewsbury	W 9-0	–	T: Jenkins, Middleton, Southward
Dec 20	Barrow	D 0-0	4,500	
Dec 25	BROUGHTON RANGERS	W 5-0	13,000	T: Boyd, G: Hudson
Dec 27	WIGAN HIGHFIELD	D 0-0	5,000	
Jan 1	Swinton	W 8-4	18,000	T: Hudson 2, G: Southward
Jan 3	LEEDS	W 19-7	8,000	T: Southward 2, Dalton, Jenkins, Miller, G: Hudson, Meek
Jan 10	Wigan	L 2-19	10,000	G: Middleton
Jan 13	Keighley	L 6-7	1,800	T: Hudson, Muir
Jan 17	WIGAN	W 6-3	13,000	T: Middleton, J Williams
Jan 24	St Helens Recreation	W 11-0	6,000	T: Boyd, Dobing, Hudson, G: Middleton
Jan 31	CASTLEFORD**	W 32-4	5,000	T: Hudson 3, Boyd, Dobing, Haines, Muir, Risman, G: Hudson 4
Feb 7	BATLEY (RLC-1)	W 16-3	12,000	T: Dalton, Doran, Haines, Meek, G: Hudson 2
Feb 14	Rochdale Hornets	W 5-3	7,000	T: Dalton, G: Hudson
Feb 21	LEEDS (RLC-2)	W 9-0	23,000	T: Boyd, Hudson, WA Williams
Mar 7	YORK (RLC-3)	L 2-12	18,300	G: Hudson
Mar 11	WIDNES	W 26-0	–	T: Boyd, Doran, Hudson, Matthews, Middleton, Risman, G: Hudson 4
Mar 14	BARROW	W 45-20	–	T: Fisher 4, Boyd 3, Doran 2, Rees, Shaw, G: Miller 3, Risman 3

Salford RL Match Results

1930-1931 *continued*

	Opponent	Result	Attendance	Scorers
Mar 21	Huddersfield	L 9-14	11,000	T: Hudson, G: Hudson 3
Mar 25	Hunslet	L 8-35	4,000	T: Feetham, Hudson, G: Hudson
Mar 28	Castleford	W 22-10	2,000	T: Hudson 2, Boyd, Dalton, Feetham, Middleton, G: Hudson 2
Apr 1	Wigan Highfield	L 5-17	1,500	T: Jenkins, G: Hudson
Apr 4	SWINTON	D 0-0	18,500	
Apr 6	Leeds	L 3-18	16,000	T: Bradbury
Apr 11	HUDDERSFIELD	L 9-19	10,000	T: Hudson 2, Middleton
Apr 13	OLDHAM	L 3-8	7,000	T: Fisher
Apr 18	ROCHDALE HORNETS	W 18-3	4,000	T: Feetham, Hudson, Middleton, Miller, G: Hudson 2, Risman
Apr 29	BROUGHTON RANGERS (SHC)	W 8-5	6,500	T: Doran, Hudson, G: Hudson

Abandoned half-time (heavy rain, muddy pitch)
**Abandoned 73 min (snow blizzard, muddy pitch) – result stands*

1931-1932

	Opponent	Result	Attendance	Scorers
Aug 29	OLDHAM	L 5-7	12,000	T: Middleton, G: Hudson
Sep 5	Rochdale Hornets	L 6-7	6,000	T: Feetham, Hudson
Sep 12	Broughton Rangers	W 14-2	8,000	T: Hudson 3, Haines, G: Southward
Sep 19	LEIGH	W 21-4	8,000	T: Southward 2, Hudson, Feetham, Meek, G: Hudson 3
Sep 23	WIGAN HIGHFIELD	W 34-0	6,000	T: Feetham 2, Hudson 2, Watkins 2, Dobing, Southward, G: Southward 4, Hudson
Sep 26	Widnes	W 14-7	6,000	T: Bradbury, Hudson, Meek, Watkins, G: Southward
Oct 3	CASTLEFORD	W 36-6	8,000	T: Boyd 2, Hudson 2, Risman 2, Dobing, Meek, Watkins, WA Williams, G: Hudson 3
Oct 10	ST HELENS (LC-1)	W 16-5	14,000	T: Risman 2, Feetham, Hudson, G: Hudson, Southward
Oct 17	York	D 2-2	6,000	G: Osbaldestin

Salford RL Match Results

1931-1932 *continued*

	Opponent	Result	Attendance	Scorers
Oct 21	Warrington (LC-2)	W 17-7	8,000	T: Haines, Hudson, Middleton, G: Southward 3, Osbaldestin
Oct 24	Hull Kingston Rovers	W 17-7	–	T: Feetham 2, Risman, Southward, E Thomas, G: Osbaldestin
Oct 31	HALIFAX	W 10-2	10,000	T: Boyd, Southward, G: Hudson, Southward
Nov 7	WAKEFIELD TRINITY	W 19-7	–	T: Feetham 2, Southward 2, Hudson, G: Hudson 2
Nov 11	BARROW (LC-SF)	W 21-0	8,000	T: Boyd, Meek, Middleton, Rees, Risman, G: Southward 3
Nov 14	St Helens	L 2-10	5,000	G: White
Nov 21	Swinton (LC-Final)*	W 10-8	26,471	T: Jenkins 2, G: Southward 2
Nov 28	Wakefield Trinity	L 3-7	3,000	T: Hudson
Dec 5	BATLEY	W 13-6	5,000	T: Feetham 2, Boyd, G: Hudson, Southward
Dec 12	Castleford	W 13-8	5,000	T: Feetham 2, Risman, G: Southward 2
Dec 19	ST HELENS RECREATION	W 34-18	4,000	T: Risman 3, Haines 2, Dalton, Feetham, Southward, G: Southward 3, Hudson 2
Dec 25	Wigan	L 3-13	14,000	T: Risman
Dec 26	BROUGHTON RANGERS	W 10-9	15,000	T: Hudson, Watkins, G: Southward 2
Jan 1	Swinton	L 0-3	22,000	
Jan 2	ROCHDALE HORNETS	W 8-0	5,000	T: Casewell, Watkins, G: Southward
Jan 9	Wigan Highfield	W 22-5	1,500	T: Feetham 2, Boyd, Fisher, Middleton, Watkins, G: Southward 2
Jan 13	ST HELENS	W 9-3	5,000	T: Boyd, Feetham, WA Williams
Jan 16	YORK	L 0-8	5,000	
Jan 23	Oldham	W 18-10	10,000	T: Hudson 2, Feetham, Risman, G: Southward 3
Jan 30	Batley	L 3-4	–	T: Risman
Feb 6	St Helens Recreation (RLC-1)	L 6-10	14,000	T: Hudson 2
Feb 13	KEIGHLEY	W 40-0	5,000	T: Feetham 2, Hudson 2, Jenkins 2, Bradbury, Casewell, Haines, Risman, G: Miller 4, Meek
Feb 27	St Helens Recreation	W 28-8	7,000	T: Hudson 3, Casewell, Feetham, Risman, G: Miller 5

Salford RL Match Results

1931-1932 *continued*

	Opponent	Result	Attendance	Scorers
Mar 5	Warrington	W 12-10	7,000	T: Jenkins, Watkins, G: White 3
Mar 12	HULL KINGSTON ROVERS	W 34-2	–	T: Brown 2, Jenkins 2, Middleton 2, Casewell, Hudson, Risman, Southward, G: Southward 2
Mar 19	BARROW	W 24-8	5,000	T: Hudson 3, Brown 2, Southward, G: Risman 3
Mar 25	Barrow	W 18-5	10,565	T: Brown, Hudson, Southward, Watkins, G: Risman 3
Mar 26	SWINTON	L 4-5	23,500	G: Risman 2
Mar 28	WIGAN	W 21-9	12,000	T: Bradbury, Hudson, Jenkins, Miller, Watkins, G: Risman 3
Apr 2	Leigh	D 5-5	5,000	T: Boyd, G: Risman
Apr 9	Halifax	L 2-4	8,000	G: Risman
Apr 16	WIDNES	W 15-0	5,000	T: Dalton, Marsden, Miller, G: White 3
Apr 20	WARRINGTON	W 22-0	6,000	T: Dalton 2, Brown, Jenkins, Southward, Watkins, G: White 2
Apr 23	Keighley	W 10-0	2,000	T: Dalton, Watkins, G: White 2

* At Broughton

Lancashire Cup winners
Lancashire League Championship runners-up

1932-1933

	Opponent	Result	Attendance	Scorers
Aug 27	Wigan	W 23-5	5,000	T: Casewell 2, Haines, Meek, Watkins, G: Miller 4
Sep 3	HUDDERSFIELD	W 28-3	10,000	T: Jenkins 3, Brown, Dalton, Southward, G: Osbaldestin 5
Sep 7	Bramley	W 12-0	3,000	T: Bradbury, Dalton, G: Osbaldestin 3
Sep 10	St Helens Recreation	D 12-12	8,000	T: Bradbury, Jenkins, G: Osbaldestin 3
Sep 17	HALIFAX	W 7-5	14,000	T: Meek, G: Osbaldestin 2
Sep 24	Widnes	L 6-7	7,500	T: Hudson, Miller
Oct 1	Broughton Rangers	L 7-9	15,000	T: Hudson, G: Risman 2
Oct 8	Rochdale Hornets (LC-1)	D 8-8	5,000	G: Risman 3, Osbaldestin

Salford RL Match Results

1932-1933 *continued*

Date	Opponent	Result	Attendance	Scorers
Oct 12	ROCHDALE HORNETS (LC-1 Replay)	W 26-13	7,000	T: Hudson 3, Brown, Casewell, Risman, G: Risman 4
Oct 15	WIGAN HIGHFIELD	W 32-4	6,000	T: Middleton 2, Casewell, Dobing, Feetham, Hudson, Jenkins, Risman, G: Risman 4
Oct 19	SWINTON (LC-2)	W 25-11	12,000	T: Jenkins 2, Brown, Feetham, Hudson, G: Osbaldestin 5
Oct 22	Warrington	W 12-8	8,000	T: Feetham, Jenkins, G: Osbaldestin 3
Oct 29	WAKEFIELD TRINITY*	W 35-0	–	T: Hudson 2, Middleton 2, Miller 2, Boyd, HC Day, Watkins, G: Miller 4
Nov 2	ST HELENS (LC-SF)	D 2-2	10,000	G: Osbaldestin
Nov 5	ROCHDALE HORNETS	W 16-11	6,000	T: Hudson 2, Feetham, Middleton, G: Osbaldestin 2
Nov 7	St Helens (LC-SF Replay)	L 10-17	10,000	T: Casewell 2, G: Osbaldestin 2
Nov 12	Huddersfield	W 6-0	–	T: Southward 2
Nov 19	BARROW	L 0-12	6,000	
Nov 26	Rochdale Hornets	L 5-8	3,000	T: Hudson, G: Risman
Dec 3	Wakefield Trinity	W 8-2	–	T: Casewell, Feetham, G: Risman
Dec 10	LEEDS	W 12-7	8,500	T: Hudson, Miller, G: Risman 3
Dec 17	ST HELENS	W 13-5	8,000	T: Risman 2, Hudson, G: Risman 2
Dec 24	Featherstone Rovers	W 24-3	–	T: Middleton 2, Boyd, Casewell, Hudson, Jenkins, G: Osbaldestin 3
Dec 26	BROUGHTON RANGERS	W 21-10	12,000	T: Boyd 2, Casewell, Miller, Risman, G: Risman 2, Osbaldestin
Dec 27	Leigh	W 20-0	5,000	T: Jenkins 3, Risman, G: Risman 4
Dec 31	FEATHERSTONE ROVERS	W 23-6	6,000	T: Meek 2, Brown, Feetham, Jenkins, Shaw, Southward, G: Risman
Jan 2	Swinton	W 11-3	20,000	T: Brown, Jenkins, Middleton, G: Risman
Jan 7	St Helens	L 5-12	9,000	T: Jenkins, G: Risman

Salford RL Match Results

1932-1933 *continued*

	Opponent	Result	Attendance	Scorers
Jan 14	HUNSLET	W 34-8	6,000	T: Brown 3, Miller 2, Jenkins, Risman, Watkins, G: Risman 5
Jan 21	Hunslet	W 17-0	–	T: Hudson, Middleton, Miller, G: Risman 4
Feb 4	WARRINGTON	W 8-0	8,000	T: Brown, Hudson, G: Risman
Feb 11	CASTLEFORD (RLC-1)	W 11-0	13,800	T: Boyd, Casewell, Hudson, G: Risman
Feb 18	Leeds	W 16-0	8,000	T: Hudson 4, G: Risman 2
Mar 1	LEEDS (RLC-2)	L 3-4	21,000	T: Jenkins
Mar 4	Oldham	D 3-3	8,000	T: Brown
Mar 11	OLDHAM	W 44-0	9,000	T: Feetham 2, Miller 2, Brown, Casewell, Jenkins, Middleton, Watkins, WA Williams, G: Risman 7
Mar 18	Wigan Highfield	W 40-0	2,000	T: Casewell 3, Brown, Feetham, Jenkins, Middleton, Miller, Risman, Walker, G: Risman 5
Mar 22	LEIGH	W 40-0	5,000	T: Jenkins 2, Boyd, Brown, Casewell, Feetham, Risman, Watkins, G: Risman 8
Mar 25	WIDNES	W 32-7	6,000	T: Brown 3, Miller 2, Casewell, Middleton, Risman, G: Risman 4
Apr 1	Halifax	W 3-0	9,000	T: Middleton
Apr 5	BRAMLEY	W 74-3	5,000	T: Jenkins 4, Brown 3, Hudson 2, Miller 2, Risman 2, Feetham, Middleton, Osbaldestin, G: Risman 13
Apr 8	ST HELENS RECREATION	W 46-0	12,000	T: Hudson 4, Risman 2, Brown, Casewell, Feetham, Jenkins, G: Risman 8
Apr 14	Barrow	W 20-6	21,555	T: Brown 2, Middleton, Watkins, G: Risman 4
Apr 15	SWINTON	W 17-2	20,000	T: Bradbury, Miller, Watkins, G: Risman 3, Osbaldestin
Apr 17	WIGAN	W 19-4	19,000	T: Boyd, Brown, Hudson, Middleton, Risman, G: Risman 2
Apr 22	WIGAN (NRL-SF)	W 14-2	21,000	T: Brown, Casewell, Miller, Risman, G: Risman

Salford RL Match Results

1932-1933 *continued*

	Opponent	Result	Attendance	Scorers
Apr 29	Swinton (NRL-Final)**	W 15-5	18,000	T: Brown, Feetham, Jenkins, G: Risman 3

* Abandoned 63 min (waterlogged) – result stands   ** At Wigan

Northern Rugby League Championship winners
Lancashire League Championship winners

1933-1934

	Opponent	Result	Attendance	Scorers
Aug 26	HUDDERSFIELD	W 19-2	17,000	T: Brown 2, Hudson, Miller, Risman, G: Risman 2
Sep 2	York	W 30-5	11,000	T: Casewell 2, Brown, Hudson, Miller, Watkins, G: Risman 6
Sep 9	DEWSBURY	W 17-5	–	T: Brown, Casewell, Risman, G: Risman 4
Sep 13	Warrington	W 13-10	15,000	T: Hudson, Middleton, Miller, G: Risman 2
Sep 16	Leigh	W 28-20	8,000	T: Risman 3, Hudson 2, Brown, G: Risman 5
Sep 20	HALIFAX	W 23-5	9,000	T: Brown 2, Casewell, Hudson, Jenkins, G: Risman 4
Sep 23	Broughton Rangers	W 7-2	25,000	T: Hudson, G: Dobing 2
Sep 30	St Helens (LC-1)	L 8-12	12,000	G: Risman 4
Oct 4	WAKEFIELD TRINITY	W 21-9	–	T: Brown 3, Osbaldestin, Pearson, G: C Evans 2, Pearson
Oct 7	Wakefield Trinity	L 3-4	6,000	T: Dalton
Oct 14	OLDHAM	W 18-8	10,000	T: Brown 2, Miller, Pearson, G: Risman 3
Oct 21	AUSTRALIA (Tour)	W 16-9	15,761	T: Feetham, Miller, G: Risman 4, Miller
Oct 28	St Helens	W 17-2	7,500	T: Brown, Casewell, Feetham, Pearson, WA Williams, G: Risman
Nov 11	ROCHDALE HORNETS	W 27-7	6,000	T: Brown 2, Casewell 2, Dobing, Middleton, Watkins, G: Pearson 3
Nov 25	WIDNES	W 46-5	6,000	T: Casewell 3, Hudson 2, Miller 2, Feetham, Jenkins, Risman, G: Risman 8
Dec 2	Huddersfield	W 16-10	12,000	T: Brown 2, Hudson, Risman, G: Risman 2

Salford RL Match Results

1933-1934 *continued*

	Opponent	Result	Attendance	Scorers
Dec 9	LEIGH	W 34-0	6,000	T: Hudson 2, Brown, Dobing, Feetham, Jenkins, Middleton, Watkins, G: Risman 5
Dec 13	London Highfield	L 10-15	2,000	T: Middleton 2, G: Pearson 2
Dec 23	ST HELENS	W 17-10	8,000	T: Dalton, Dobing, Risman, G: Risman 3, Osbaldestin
Dec 25	Wigan	L 9-15	18,000	T: Brown, G: Risman 3
Dec 26	BROUGHTON RANGERS	W 24-7	14,000	T: Casewell, Feetham, Middleton, Miller, Risman, Watkins, G: Risman 3
Dec 30	Barrow	L 6-9	6,451	T: Miller, Osbaldestin
Jan 1	Swinton	D 8-8	14,000	T: Brown, Hudson, G: Risman
Jan 6	BARROW	W 34-5	–	T: Miller 2, Brown, Casewell, Dalton, Feetham, Hudson, Risman, G: Risman 5
Jan 13	Halifax	W 16-8	16,000	T: Brown 2, Casewell, Risman, G: Risman 2
Jan 20	ST HELENS RECREATION	W 22-5	9,000	T: Casewell, Jenkins, Miller, Risman, G: Risman 4, Osbaldestin
Jan 27	HUNSLET	W 19-17	14,800	T: Hudson 3, Brown, C Evans, G: Miller, Osbaldestin
Feb 3	Rochdale Hornets	W 21-7	5,000	T: C Evans 2, Brown, Jenkins, Middleton, G: Osbaldestin 2, Miller
Feb 10	BARROW (RLC-1)	W 15-2	17,200	T: Brown 2, Jenkins, G: Risman 3
Feb 17	WARRINGTON	W 30-2	10,000	T: Brown 2, Casewell, Hudson, Miller, Watkins, G: Risman 6
Feb 24	HALIFAX (RLC-2)	L 5-9	24,442	T: Brown, G: Risman
Mar 3	LONDON HIGHFIELD	W 26-5	8,000	T: Brown, Casewell, Hudson, Jenkins, Miller, Risman, G: Risman 4
Mar 7	Dewsbury	W 35-5	2,000	T: Hudson 4, Casewell 2, Brown, Miller, Risman, G: Risman 4
Mar 10	Castleford	W 19-5	2,000	T: Brown 2, Hudson, G: Risman 5
Mar 14	Oldham	W 25-13	3,663	T: Brown, Dalton, Hudson, Middleton, Miller, G: Risman 5

Salford RL Match Results

1933-1934 *continued*

	Opponent	Result	Attendance	Scorers
Mar 17	Hunslet	W 9-3	12,000	T: Miller, G: Risman 2, Miller
Mar 24	YORK	W 21-0	12,000	T: Brown, Feetham, Hudson, Risman, Watkins, G: Risman 3
Mar 26	FRANCE (Tour)	W 35-0	7,000	T: Brown 4, HC Day, Dobing, Feetham, Hudson, Jenkins, G: Risman 4
Mar 30	St Helens Recreation	W 7-5	10,000	T: Brown, G: Risman 2
Mar 31	SWINTON	W 7-5	22,000	T: Jenkins, G: Dobing, Osbsaldestin
Apr 2	WIGAN	L 10-21	20,000	T: Jenkins, Middleton, G: Risman 2
Apr 7	Widnes	L 3-17	7,000	T: WA Williams
Apr 14	CASTLEFORD	W 18-0	3,000	T: Brown 4, G: Dobing 3
Apr 21	HALIFAX (NRL-SF)	W 28-3	20,000	T: Miller 2, Casewell, Feetham, Middleton, Pearson, G: Risman 4, Osbaldestin
Apr 28	Wigan (NRL-Final)*	L 3-15	31,564	T: Jenkins
May 2	SWINTON (SHC)	W 25-8	7,800	T: Brown, Dalton, Miller, Risman, WA Williams, G: Risman 4, Osbaldestin

* At Warrington

Lancashire League Championship winners
Northern Rugby League Championship runners-up

1934-1935

	Opponent	Result	Attendance	Scorers
Aug 25	Hull Kingston Rovers	W 24-9	8,000	T: Jenkins 3, Feetham, Hudson, Risman, G: Risman 3
Aug 27	Hunslet	W 23-9	9,000	T: Risman 3, Brown, Hudson, G: Risman 3, Osbaldestin
Sep 1	DEWSBURY	W 32-3	14,000	T: C Evans 2, Hudson 2, Bradbury, Casewell, G: Risman 7
Sep 8	LEIGH (LC-1)	W 34-0	10,300	T: Hudson 2, Casewell, Jenkins, Risman, WA Williams, G: Risman 8
Sep 15	Halifax	L 12-13	15,000	T: Dalton, Risman, G: Risman 3
Sep 19	Warrington (LC-2)	W 23-5	12,000	T: Feetham 2, Hudson 2, Brown, G: Risman 4

Salford RL Match Results

1934-1935 *continued*

	Opponent	*Result*	*Attendance*	*Scorers*
Sep 22	OLDHAM	W 25-2	6,000	T: Hudson 2, Jenkins 2, Pearson 2, Bradbury, G: Risman 2
Sep 29	Widnes	W 14-9	4,500	T: Brown, Hudson, G: Risman 4
Oct 3	Swinton (LC-SF)	W 12-5	12,896	T: Feetham, Hudson, G: Risman 3
Oct 6	ST HELENS RECREATION	W 5-2	7,000	T: Brown, G: Risman
Oct 13	Oldham	W 10-4	6,500	T: HC Day, Middleton, G: Risman 2
Oct 20	Wigan (LC-Final)*	W 21-12	33,544	T: Hudson, Jenkins, Middleton, G: Risman 6
Oct 21	Paris XIII (Tour)	W 51-36	3,000	T: Brown 2, C Evans 2, Hudson 2, Casewell, Feetham, Jenkins, Risman, Watkins, G: Risman 9
Oct 27	Lyons-Villeurbanne (Tour)	W 34-17	7,000	T: Brown 2, Osbaldestin 2, C Evans, Hudson, Jenkins, Middleton, G: Risman 5
Oct 28	Beziers (Tour)	W 41-8	6,000	T: Brown 3, C Evans 2, WA Williams 2, Dalton, Feetham, G: Jenkins 5, Pearson 2
Nov 1	Albi (Tour)	W 44-5	–	T: Hudson 3, Feetham 2, Brown, Middleton, Risman, Watkins, WA Williams, G: Risman 6, Watkins
Nov 2	XIII Catalans (Tour)	W 41-16	–	T: Hudson 4, Osbaldestin 2, HC Day, Jenkins, Middleton, Miller, Watkins, G: Jenkins 3, G Harris
Nov 4	Villeneuve (Tour)	W 34-10	–	T: Osbaldestin 3, Middleton 2, Dalton, Feetham, Jenkins, G: Risman 5
Nov 10	Rochdale Hornets	W 14-3	7,000	T: Osbaldestin 2, Jenkins, Pearson, G: Risman
Nov 17	SWINTON	W 19-7	18,000	T: Hudson 2, Brown, G: Risman 5
Nov 24	Leeds	L 3-12	21,000	T: Dalton
Dec 1	HALIFAX	W 17-5	7,000	T: Casewell, Pearson, Risman, G: Risman 4
Dec 8	Liverpool Stanley	W 15-5	10,000	T: Brown, Feetham, Hudson, G: Risman 3

Salford RL Match Results

1934-1935 *continued*

	Opponent	Result	Attendance	Scorers
Dec 15	BARROW	W 14-10	–	T: Brown, Feetham, Pearson, Risman, G: Risman
Dec 22	St Helens Recreation	L 0-20	8,000	
Dec 25	Wigan	L 6-18	18,000	G: Risman 3
Dec 26	BROUGHTON RANGERS	W 14-5	18,000	T: Brown, Dalton, C Evans, Miller, G: Risman
Dec 29	Hull	L 3-20	8,000	T: Hudson
Jan 1	Swinton**	A 0-0	8,000	
Jan 5	LEIGH	W 29-7	6,000	T: Hudson 4, Feetham, Middleton, Miller, G: Risman 4
Jan 12	LEEDS	L 5-10	14,000	T: Jenkins, G: Pearson
Jan 19	Leigh	W 14-10	5,000	T: Feetham, Miller, Osbaldestin, Watkins, G: Jenkins
Jan 26	Warrington	W 10-2	15,000	T: Dalton, Jenkins, G: Jenkins, Osbaldestin
Feb 2	ROCHDALE HORNETS	W 25-10	10,000	T: Brown 2, Feetham 2, Hudson 2, Jenkins, G: Jenkins 2
Feb 9	HALIFAX (RLC-1)	W 16-11	17,670	T: Hudson, Miller, G: Risman 5
Feb 16	York	L 0-5	6,000	
Feb 23	Hunslet (RLC-2)	L 2-22	20,451	G: Risman
Feb 27	WIDNES	W 7-2	3,000	T: Brown, G: Risman 2
Mar 9	Swinton	L 3-7	14,980	T: Feetham
Mar 16	St Helens	W 26-8	6,500	T: Feetham 2, Risman 2, Jenkins, Middleton, G: Risman 4
Mar 20	HULL	W 26-4	10,000	T: Hudson 2, Bradbury, Brown, C Evans, Miller, G: Jenkins 3, Middleton
Mar 23	ST HELENS	W 9-5	6,000	T: Brown, C Evans, Hudson
Mar 27	Broughton Rangers	L 0-11	6,000	
Mar 30	Dewsbury	L 0-9	3,500	
Apr 3	HUNSLET	W 4-3	7,000	G: Jenkins, White
Apr 6	YORK	W 16-7	–	T: Brown, Dalton, C Evans, Hudson, G: Jenkins, White
Apr 8	WARRINGTON	W 9-0	10,000	T: Bowen, G: Risman 3
Apr 13	LIVERPOOL STANLEY	W 9-3	–	T: Brown, C Evans, Jenkins
Apr 19	Barrow	W 8-5	11,744	T: Brown, Miller, G: Jenkins

Salford RL Match Results

1934-1935 *continued*

	Opponent	Result	Attendance	Scorers
Apr 20	HULL KINGSTON ROVERS	W 20-0	8,000	T: Brown 3, G Harris, G: Risman 4
Apr 22	WIGAN	D 8-8	25,000	T: Miller, Pearson, G: Risman
Apr 27	Swinton (NRL-SF)	L 2-10	20,207	G: Risman

* At Swinton   ** Abandoned 50 mins (heavy rain, muddy pitch)

Lancashire League Championship winners
Lancashire Cup winners

1935-1936

	Opponent	Result	Attendance	Scorers
Aug 31	ST HELENS RECREATION	W 33-0	12,000	T: Hudson 2, Miller 2, Dalton, Jenkins, Risman, G: Risman 6
Sep 5	Hull	L 5-7	12,000	T: Risman, G: Risman
Sep 7	Huddersfield	W 25-12	11,354	T: Feetham 2, Brown, Hudson, Watkins, G: Risman 5
Sep 14	Liverpool Stanley (LC-1)	W 14-7	5,000	T: Feetham, Risman, G: Risman 4
Sep 21	Broughton Rangers	L 10-12	25,000	T: Middleton, Risman, G: Risman 2
Sep 25	WARRINGTON (LC-2)	W 11-0	15,000	T: Brown, Hudson, Watkins, G: Risman
Sep 28	HULL	W 33-7	18,000	T: Hudson 2, Edwards, G Harris, Jenkins, Miller, Watkins, G: Risman 6
Oct 5	LEIGH	W 17-5	8,000	T: Brown 2, Risman 2, Feetham, G: Risman
Oct 9	ST HELENS (LC-SF)	W 19-6	3,500	T: Feetham, Jenkins, Risman, G: Risman 4, Jenkins
Oct 12	Warrington	W 13-6	12,000	T: Jenkins, Middleton, Miller, G: Risman 2
Oct 19	Wigan (LC-Final)*	W 15-7	16,500	T: Bradbury, Feetham, Middleton, G: Risman 3
Oct 24	St Helens	L 2-9	8,000	G: Risman
Oct 26	HALIFAX	W 10-2	9,000	T: Edwards, Hudson, G: Risman 2
Nov 2	Liverpool Stanley	L 5-6	7,000	T: Hudson, G: Risman
Nov 9	OLDHAM	W 23-7	10,000	T: Edwards 2, Hudson 2, Dalton, G: Risman 4
Nov 16	Leeds	W 15-13	18,000	T: Edwards, Hudson, Watkins, G: Risman 3

Salford RL Match Results

1935-1936 *continued*

	Opponent	Result	Attendance	Scorers
Nov 23	CASTLEFORD	L 2-9	8,000	G: White
Nov 30	Streatham & Mitcham	W 9-3	10,000	T: Edwards, G Harris, Miller
Dec 7	WARRINGTON	W 17-10	10,000	T: Bradbury, Jenkins, Risman, G: Risman 3, White
Dec 14	Halifax	L 3-13	8,000	T: Edwards
Dec 26	BROUGHTON RANGERS	W 18-0	–	T: Edwards 2, HC Day, Miller, G: Risman 3
Dec 28	LIVERPOOL STANLEY	W 8-4	12,000	T: Edwards, Hudson, G: Risman
Jan 1	Swinton	W 10-5	17,805	T: Brown, Hudson, G: Risman 2
Jan 4	YORK	W 8-0	12,000	T: Feetham, Risman, G: Risman
Jan 11	Widnes	W 6-2	9,500	T: Edwards, Hudson
Jan 25	STREATHAM & MITCHAM	W 35-11	6,000	T: Dalton 2, Risman 2, Edwards, Feetham, Jenkins, G: Jenkins 4, Risman 3
Feb 1	Oldham	W 9-4	9,141	T: Jenkins, Miller, Spruce
Feb 8	ST HELENS RECREATION (RLC-1)	W 20-3	12,000	T: Edwards 2, Risman 2, G: Risman 4
Feb 15	Leigh	W 14-0	4,000	T. Brown 2, Edwards, C Evans, G: Miller
Feb 22	Hunslet (RLC-2)	D 2-2	16,600	G: Risman
Feb 26	HUNSLET (RLC-2 Replay)	W 20-2	13,000	T: Edwards 2, Hudson, Middleton, G: Risman 4
Feb 29	BARROW	L 3-6	8,000	T: Hudson
Mar 7	CASTLEFORD (RLC-3)	W 5-4	24,000	T: Edwards, G: Risman
Mar 11	WIDNES	W 9-8	5,000	T: Risman, G: Risman 3
Mar 14	LEEDS	W 27-2	16,000	T: Brown 2, Jenkins 2, Edwards, G: Risman 6
Mar 21	Warrington (RLC-SF)**	L 2-7	41,670	G: Risman
Mar 25	ROCHDALE HORNETS	W 30-7	8,000	T: Edwards 2, Jenkins 2, Miller, Risman, G: Risman 6
Mar 28	Castleford	W 15-11	10,000	T: Hudson, Jenkins, Watkins, G: Jenkins 3
Apr 1	Wigan	L 5-9	10,000	T: Brown, G: Risman
Apr 4	ST HELENS	W 21-7	7,000	T: Risman 2, Feetham, Hudson, Osbaldestin, G: Risman 3
Apr 6	St Helens Recreation	L 2-7	3,000	G: Risman
Apr 10	Barrow	L 5-10	14,334	T: Brown, G: Risman
Apr 11	SWINTON	L 2-9	–	G: Risman

Salford RL Match Results

1935-1936 *continued*

	Opponent	Result	Attendance	Scorers
Apr 13	WIGAN	L 3-16	17,000	T: Brown
Apr 22	Rochdale Hornets	W 8-4	2,500	T: C Evans 2, G: Schofield
Apr 25	HUDDERSFIELD	W 16-8	–	T: Miller 2, Pearson, Spruce, G: Schofield 2
Apr 29	York	L 5-10	7,000	T: Miller, G: Schofield
May 9	SWINTON (SHC)	W 4-2	3,500	G: Schofield 2

* At Warrington ** At Wigan

Lancashire Cup winners

1936-1937

	Opponent	Result	Attendance	Scorers
Aug 29	St Helens Recreation	L 7-16	4,000	T: Spruce, G: Schofield 2
Sep 5	ROCHDALE HORNETS	W 21-0	5,000	T: C Evans 2, Brown, Miller, Turner, G: C Evans 2, Turner
Sep 12	OLDHAM (LC-1)	W 8-4	6,000	T: Miller, Pearson, G: Schofield
Sep 16	Castleford	L 7-11	6,500	T: Pearson, G: Schofield 2
Sep 19	Halifax	W 12-8	12,000	T: Hudson 2, Brown, C Evans
Sep 23	SWINTON (LC-2)	W 11-3	14,000	T: Feetham 2, Edwards, G: Risman
Sep 26	ST HELENS	W 34-12	9,000	T: Hudson 3, Dalton, Edwards, Feetham, Jenkins, WA Williams, G: Jenkins 5
Sep 30	BARROW (LC-SF)	D 15-15	10,000	T: Dalton, Edwards, Risman, G: Risman 2, Jenkins
Oct 3	Oldham	W 17-13	10,000	T: Edwards, Hudson, Risman, G: Jenkins 3, Risman
Oct 8	Barrow (LC-SF Replay)	W 19-13	15,489	T: Brown, Miller, Risman, G: Jenkins 4, Osbaldestin
Oct 10	BARROW	W 38-0	10,000	T: Jenkins 4, Brown, Feetham, Gear, Marsden, G: Risman 7
Oct 17	Wigan (LC-Final)*	W 5-2	17,500	T: Osbaldestin, G: Risman
Oct 24	Widnes	W 22-16	4,000	T: Hudson 2, Dalton, Edwards, G: Jenkins 3, Schofield 2
Oct 28	HULL	W 14-2	3,000	T: Edwards 3, Gear, G: Risman
Oct 31	Hull	W 12-7	5,000	T: Pearson 2, G: Risman 2, Osbaldestin

Salford RL Match Results

1936-1937 *continued*

	Opponent	Result	Attendance	Scorers
Nov 7	CASTLEFORD	W 2-0	6,000	G: Pearson
Nov 14	LIVERPOOL STANLEY	L 2-15	5,000	G: Risman
Nov 21	St Helens	W 20-0	2,000	T: Brown, Gear, Jenkins, Osbaldestin, G: Risman 4
Nov 28	WARRINGTON	W 11-5	7,000	T: Risman 2, Edwards, G: Risman
Dec 5	Liverpool Stanley	L 2-7	4,000	G: Pearson
Dec 12	LEEDS	W 10-8	8,000	T: Brown, Dalton, G: Risman 2
Dec 19	Rochdale Hornets	W 10-0	5,000	T: Dalton, Edwards, G: Risman 2
Dec 25	Wigan	W 17-10	24,200	T: Hudson 2, Jenkins, G: Risman 4
Dec 26	BROUGHTON RANGERS	W 9-6	12,000	T: Jenkins, G: Risman 3
Dec 28	Leeds	L 3-7	24,000	T: Hudson
Jan 1	Swinton	W 13-2	15,000	T: Hudson 2, Edwards, G: Risman 2
Jan 2	OLDHAM	W 5-2	6,000	T: Risman, G: Risman
Jan 9	Bradford Northern	W 3-0	16,000	T: Brown
Jan 16	Leigh	W 26-2	2,500	T: Dalton, Gear, Hudson, Jenkins, Pearson, WA Williams, G: Risman 4
Jan 23	STREATHAM & MITCHAM	W 33-0	5,000	T: Risman 4, Brown, Miller, Osbaldestin, G: Risman 6
Jan 30	Warrington	L 0-11	12,000	
Feb 6	BRADFORD NORTHERN	D 8-8	13,000	T: Dalton, Feetham, G: Risman
Feb 13	WARRINGTON (RLC-1)	L 4-10	26,470	G: Risman 2
Feb 20	York	W 8-6	7,000	T: Brown 2, G: Miller
Mar 6	Broughton Rangers	D 0-0	–	
Mar 13	ST HELENS RECREATION	W 10-0	5,000	T: Edwards, Osbaldestin, G: Risman 2
Mar 20	LEIGH	W 31-8	6,000	T: Risman 3, Hudson 2, Brown, Feetham, Miller, Osbaldestin, G: Risman 2
Mar 26	Barrow	D 3-3	16,193	T: Risman
Mar 27	SWINTON	W 13-0	16,000	T: Edwards, Gear, Jenkins, G: Risman 2
Mar 29	WIGAN	W 15-5	25,000	T: Brown, Dalton, Feetham, Gear, Risman
Apr 7	WIDNES	W 35-0	6,000	T: Hudson 3, Osbaldestin 2, Dalton, Edwards, Feetham, Gear, G: Risman 4

Salford RL Match Results

1936-1937 *continued*

	Opponent	Result	Attendance	Scorers
Apr 10	YORK	W 40-6	8,000	T: Dalton 2, Hudson 2, Bradbury, Cambridge, Edwards, Jenkins, Osbaldestin, Risman, G: Risman 5
Apr 17	HALIFAX	W 16-0	8,000	T: Dalton, Feetham, Hudson, Watkins, G: Risman 2
Apr 24	LIVERPOOL STANLEY (NRL-SF)	W 15-7	14,000	T: Hudson 2, Osbaldestin, G: Risman 3
May 1	Warrington (NRL-Final)**	W 13-11	31,500	T: Hudson, G: Risman 5
May 12	Leeds (F)***	L 9-15	6,000	T: Hudson, G: Risman 3

*At Warrington　　**At Wigan　　***Experimental 12-a-side match

Northern Rugby League Championship winners
Lancashire League Championship winners
Lancashire Cup winners

1937-1938

	Opponent	Result	Attendance	Scorers
Aug 28	Leigh	W 17-0	2,500	T: Dalton, Feetham, Hudson, G: Jenkins 4
Sep 1	WARRINGTON	L 5-11	12,000	T: Gear, G: Jenkins
Sep 4	BARROW	L 5-10	–	T: Miller, G: Jenkins
Sep 11	WIDNES (LC-1)	L 2-3	12,000	G: Risman
Sep 18	Rochdale Hornets	W 41-10	4,000	T: Edwards 2, Risman 2, Feetham, Hudson, Jenkins, G: Risman 10
Sep 25	Castleford	L 4-21	8,600	G: Risman 2
Oct 2	HUDDERSFIELD	W 38-8	15,000	T: Risman 4, Edwards, Gear, Hudson, Watkins, G: Risman 7
Oct 9	ST HELENS RECREATION	W 32-5	8,000	T: Brown 3, Edwards 2, Dalton, Osbaldestin, Risman, G: Risman 4
Oct 16	Liverpool Stanley	W 11-6	3,000	T: Feetham, Hudson, Miller, G: Turner
Oct 23	HALIFAX	W 24-2	8,000	T: Brown 2, Hudson 2, Risman 2, G: Risman 3
Oct 30	AUSTRALIA (Tour)	W 11-8	12,000	T: Edwards, Feetham, Hudson, G: Risman
Nov 6	Hull	W 5-2	7,000	T: Jenkins, G: Risman
Nov 13	Wakefield Trinity	L 5-12	3,000	T: Dalton, G: Schofield
Nov 20	LEEDS	L 0-10	–	

Salford RL Match Results

1937-1938 *continued*

	Opponent	Result	Attendance	Scorers
Nov 27	St Helens	W 31-0	4,000	T: Gear 4, DM Davies, Miller, Edwards, G: Risman 5
Dec 4	HULL	W 20-6	7,000	T: DM Davies, G Harris, Hudson, Miller, G: Risman 4
Dec 11	Widnes	W 7-5	4,500	T: Gear, G: Jenkins 2
Dec 27	BROUGHTON RANGERS	W 10-5	10,000	T: Dalton, Hudson, G: Risman 2
Dec 28	Leeds	L 2-26	24,000	G: Risman
Jan 1	Swinton	W 11-2	18,500	T: Edwards 2, Gear, G: Risman
Jan 3	ST HELENS	W 12-5	3,000	T: Gear, Risman, G: Risman 2, Osbaldestin
Jan 15	OLDHAM	L 5-16	3,000	T: DM Davies, G: Risman
Jan 22	LIVERPOOL STANLEY	W 34-6	5,000	T: Gear 3, Risman 3, Hudson, Osbaldestin, G: Risman 5
Jan 29	Broughton Rangers	L 3-7	–	T: Jenkins
Feb 5	CASTLEFORD	W 8-5	12,000	T: Edwards, Osbaldestin, G: Risman
Feb 12	St Helens Recreation	W 7-0	4,000	T: Edwards, G: Risman 2
Feb 19	HULL (RLC-1)	W 38-2	16,000	T: Edwards 4, Brown 2, Feetham, Hudson, Osbaldestin, Risman, G: Risman 4
Feb 26	Oldham	W 19-5	7,000	T: Watkins 2, Edwards, G: Risman 4, Gear
Mar 5	WAKEFIELD TRINITY	W 38-13	7,000	T: Brown 2, Edwards 2, Gear 2, Dalton, Feetham, Risman, Watkins, G: Risman 4
Mar 12	Liverpool Stanley (RLC-2)	W 11-3	13,500	T: Brown, Edwards, Feetham, G: Risman
Mar 19	LEIGH	W 31-0	8,000	T: DM Davies, Edwards, Gear, G Harris, Watkins, G: Risman 8
Mar 26	ST HELENS RECREATION (RLC-3)	W 19-0	15,500	T: Brown, Hudson, H Thomas, G: Risman 5
Mar 30	Wigan	L 11-17	18,000	T: Osbaldestin, G: Risman 4
Apr 2	Halifax	W 5-2	6,000	T: Osbaldestin, G: Pearson
Apr 4	Huddersfield	L 10-11	4,000	T: Brown, Edwards, G: Risman 2
Apr 9	Swinton (RLC-SF)*	W 6-0	31,664	T: Dalton, Feetham
Apr 11	Warrington	L 0-19	14,000	

Salford RL Match Results

1937-1938 *continued*

	Opponent	Result	Attendance	Scorers
Apr 13	ROCHDALE HORNETS	W 20-8	6,000	T: Hudson 2, Risman 2, G: Risman 4
Apr 15	Barrow	L 0-31	21,651	
Apr 16	SWINTON	W 9-5	19,000	T: Brown, G: Risman 3
Apr 18	WIGAN	W 13-2	15,000	T: Brown 2, Feetham, G: Risman 2
Apr 20	WIDNES	D 0-0	6,500	
May 7	Barrow (RLC-Final)**	W 7-4	51,243	T: Gear, G: Risman 2
May 14	BROUGHTON RANGERS (SHC)	W 29-23	13,000	T: Hudson 3, Risman 2, Brown, Thomas, G: Risman 3, Thomas

* At Belle Vue, Manchester   ** At Wembley

Rugby League Challenge Cup winners

1938-1939

	Opponent	Result	Attendance	Scorers
Aug 27	OLDHAM	W 14-4	14,000	T: Edwards 3, Hudson, G: Risman
Aug 31	Batley	W 27-0	6,000	T: Hudson 3, Brown, Dalton, Edwards, Feetham, G: Risman 3
Sep 3	Broughton Rangers	L 5-10	–	T: T: Hudson, G: Risman
Sep 6	LEEDS (F)*	L 6-8	7,000	T: Brown, DM Davies
Sep 10	BROUGHTON RANGERS (LC-1)	W 8-4	15,000	T: Hudson, H Thomas, G: Risman
Sep 17	Hunslet	L 2-10	10,000	G: Risman
Sep 24	LIVERPOOL STANLEY	W 12-0	5,000	T: Feetham, Risman, G: Risman 3
Sep 29	Warrington (LC-SF)	W 12-6	12,000	T: Brown, Harrison, G: Risman 3
Oct 1	Hull	W 12-7	–	T: Risman, Watkins, G: Risman 3
Oct 8	CASTLEFORD	W 17-0	8,000	T: Edwards, Hudson, Osbaldestin, G: Risman 4
Oct 12	WIDNES	W 11-0	5,000	T: Edwards, G: Risman 4
Oct 15	Liverpool Stanley	W 13-2	3,000	T: Dalton, Edwards, Risman, G: Risman 2
Oct 22	Wigan (LC-Final)**	L 7-10	27,940	T: Gear, G: Osbaldestin, Risman
Oct 29	St Helens Recreation	W 20-6	4,000	T: Dalton, Edwards, Harrison, H Thomas, G: Risman 4

Salford RL Match Results

1938-1939 *continued*

	Opponent	Result	Attendance	Scorers
Nov 5	HUNSLET	W 18-0	6,000	T: Feetham, Gear, Hudson, Osbaldestin, G: Miller 2, Osbaldestin
Nov 12	Castleford	L 5-12	6,000	T: Edwards, G: Risman
Nov 19	ROCHDALE HORNETS	W 48-12	6,000	T: Hilton 4, Feetham 2, Dalton, DM Davies, Edwards, Gear, G: Risman 9
Nov 26	Widnes	D 0-0	5,000	
Dec 3	BRADFORD NORTHERN	W 10-7	10,000	T: Dalton, Hudson, G: Risman 2
Dec 10	Rochdale Hornets	W 8-5	3,000	T: Edwards, Risman, G: Risman
Dec 17	ST HELENS RECREATION	W 23-5	6,000	T: Miller 3, DM Davies, Osbaldestin, G: Risman 4
Dec 24	Leeds	L 0-5	12,000	
Dec 26	Wigan	W 11-0	8,000	T: Dalton, Hudson, Miller, G: Risman
Dec 27	WARRINGTON	W 12-5	17,000	T: Gear, Watkins, G: Risman 3
Dec 31	Bradford Northern	W 7-5	13,000	T: Edwards, G: Risman 2
Jan 2	Swinton	W 7-4	14,000	T: Harrison, G: Risman 2
Jan 14	ST HELENS	W 37-0	6,000	T: T Kenny 4, Edwards 2, Risman 2, Bradbury, Feetham, Hudson, G: Risman 2
Jan 21	St Helens	W 32-5	2,000	T: Edwards 2, Hudson 2, Risman 2, Feetham, H Thomas, G: Risman 4
Jan 28	HULL	W 8-5	12,000	T: Edwards, T Kenny, G: Risman
Feb 4	ST HELENS (RLC-1)	W 11-0	12,500	T: Edwards, Gear, Risman, G: Risman
Feb 11	Oldham	W 3-0	11,306	T: Edwards
Feb 18	HUNSLET (RLC-2)	W 18-2	23,000	T: T Kenny 2, Dalton, DM Davies, G: Risman 3
Feb 22	LEIGH	W 17-5	4,000	T: T Kenny 2, Hudson, Miller, Risman, G: Risman
Feb 25	BARROW	W 19-0	5,000	T: Edwards 3, T Kenny, Watkins, G: Risman 2
Mar 1	WAKEFIELD TRINITY	D 10-10	–	T: Edwards, Hudson, G: Risman 2
Mar 4	Leigh	W 19-2	4,000	T: Risman 2, Edwards, Hudson, H Thomas, G: Risman 2
Mar 11	BRAMLEY (RLC-3)	W 20-0	14,000	T: Dalton, Gear, Hudson, Watkins, G: Risman 4

Salford RL Match Results

1938-1939 *continued*

	Opponent	Result	Attendance	Scorers
Mar 18	BATLEY	W 29-0	6,000	T: Edwards 3, Gear 2, DM Davies, Miller, G: Risman 4
Mar 25	Wakefield Trinity	W 8-4	6,200	T: Edwards, T Kenny, G: Risman
Apr 1	Wigan (RLC-SF)***	W 11-2	31,212	T: Risman, G: Risman 4
Apr 7	Warrington	W 13-5	22,000	T: Risman 3, G: Risman 2
Apr 8	SWINTON	L 0-5	17,000	
Apr 10	WIGAN	W 17-12	19,000	T: Harrison, Hudson, Watkins, G: Risman 4
Apr 11	Halifax	L 10-11	22,000	T: Hudson, Watkins, G: Risman, Watkins
Apr 15	Barrow	L 0-3	8,205	
Apr 19	LEEDS	W 14-10	20,000	T: DM Davies, Edwards, Feetham, Hudson, G: Risman
Apr 22	HALIFAX	W 31-13	18,000	T: Risman 2, Dalton, Edwards, Gear, T Kenny, Miller, G: Risman 5
Apr 24	BROUGHTON RANGERS	D 2-2	–	G: Risman
Apr 29	HUDDERSFIELD (NRL-SF)	W 15-0	22,000	T: Edwards, Gear, Miller, G: Risman 2, Gear
May 6	Halifax (RLC-Final)****	L 3-20	55,453	T: Risman
May 13	Castleford (NRL-Final)*****	W 8-6	69,504	T: Edwards, T Kenny, G: Risman

* *Lance Todd benefit match – played with experimental line-out*
** *At Swinton*
*** *At Rochdale, estimated 40,000 attended due to break-ins*
**** *At Wembley*
***** *At Maine Road, Manchester*

Northern Rugby League Championship winners
Lancashire League Championship winners
Rugby League Challenge Cup runners-up
Lancashire Cup runners-up

1939-1940

	Opponent	Result	Attendance	Scorers
Aug 26	Hunslet*	W 10-8	7,000	T: Harrison, Hudson, G: Risman, Watkins
Aug 30	OLDHAM*	W 15-4	8,000	T: Edwards, Gear, J Kenny, G: Miller 2, Watkins
Sep 2	ROCHDALE HORNETS*	W 39-8	6,000	T: E Evans 2, Hudson 2, Dalton, DM Davies, Harrison, G: Miller 9

Salford RL Match Results

1939-1940 *continued*

	Opponent	Result	Attendance	Scorers
Sep 16	Swinton (F)	L 10-27	8,000	T: Edwards, Hilton, G: Miller 2
Sep 23	Halifax (F)	W 13-11	4,000	T: Miller 2, Gear, G: Miller 2
Sep 30	Oldham (WEL)	W 16-13	3,853	T: Edwards, Hilton, T Kenny, Risman, G: Risman 2
Oct 7	LEIGH (WEL)	W 35-5	2,870	T: Hilton 6, J Kenny, T Kenny, Risman, G: T Kenny 4
Oct 14	Broughton Rangers (WEL)**	W 31-12	2,000	T: Edwards 2, S Williams 2, DM Davies, C Evans, Risman, G: Miller 5
Oct 21	Barrow (WEL)	W 14-5	5,689	T: Harrison 2, G: Risman 4
Oct 28	LIVERPOOL STANLEY (WEL)	W 26-4	3,000	T: Dalton, Edwards, Harrison, Hilton, Miller, S Williams, G: Risman 3, Miller
Nov 4	OLDHAM (WEL)	W 21-14	8,000	T: Harrison 3, G: Risman 6
Nov 11	St Helens (WEL)	W 15-10	4,000	T: Edwards, Harrison, S Williams, G: Risman 3
Nov 18	BROUGHTON RANGERS (WEL)	W 18-11	5,000	T: Edwards 2, DM Davies, W Williams, G: Risman 2, Watkins
Nov 25	Leigh (WEL)	W 2-0	1,000	G: Risman
Dec 2	ST HELENS (WEL)	W 10-5	4,000	T: Feetham, Harrison, G: Risman 2
Dec 9	Widnes (WEL)	L 3-5	1,000	T: T Kenny
Dec 16	WIDNES (WEL)	W 17-3	3,000	T: Edwards, Watkins, S Williams, G: Risman 4
Dec 25	Wigan (WEL)	L 5-12	10,000	T: Risman, G: Risman
Dec 26	WARRINGTON (WEL)	W 30-4	5,000	T: Miller 2, Edwards, Hudson, T Kenny, Risman, G: Risman 6
Jan 1	Swinton (WEL)	L 6-16	5,000	G: Risman 3
Feb 24	Warrington (F)	W 12-8	5,000	T: Watkins, S Williams, G: Risman 3
Mar 2	Swinton (LC-1)	L 0-7	7,945	
Mar 9	SWINTON (LC-1)	D 6-6	5,900	G: Risman 3
Mar 22	Warrington (WEL)	W 14-12	7,000	T: Edwards, Harrison, G: Risman 4
Mar 23	SWINTON (WEL)	L 0-6	–	
Mar 25	WIGAN (WEL)	D 9-9	7,000	T: S Williams, G: Risman 3
Mar 30	BARROW (WEL)	W 12-9	4,000	T: Hilton, Hudson, G: Risman 2, Watkins
Apr 6	Broughton Rangers (F)	W 6-2	4,000	T: Hilton, S Williams

Salford RL Match Results

1939-1940 *continued*

	Opponent	Result	Attendance	Scorers
Apr 13	Liverpool Stanley (WEL)	D 7-7	2,000	T: Risman, G: Risman 2
Apr 27	Oldham (F)	L 4-7	3,000	G: Risman 2
May 1	ROCHDALE HORNETS (WEL)	W 25-5	2,000	T: Edwards 2, S Williams 2, DM Davies, G: Risman 5
May 11	Rochdale Hornets (WEL)	W 12-4	1,405	T: Edwards 2, G: Risman 2, Watkins
May 13	BROUGHTON RANGERS (WSL)	W 13-0	–	T: Edwards, Risman, S Williams, G: Risman 2
May 18	Broughton Rangers (WSL)	W 65-15	–	T: Miller 3, J Kenny 2, Risman 2, Dalton, E Day, Feetham, Harrison, Hudson, Watkins, G: Risman 13
May 25	LEIGH (WSL)	W 60-8	–	T: Edwards 4, Hudson 3, Risman 2, S Williams 2, Harrison, Miller, H Thomas, G: Risman 7, Hudson, Watkins

* *Northern Rugby League Championship (abandoned due to World War II)*
** *Away match played at Salford*

War Emergency League (Lancashire) runners-up

1940-1941

	Opponent	Result	Attendance	Scorers
Sep 7	LEIGH (WEL)	W 30-5	1,100	T: Bradbury, HC Day, Desborough, Gear, R Kenny, S Williams, G: C Evans 4, Gear, Miller
Sep 14	Swinton (WEL)*	W 16-0	3,000	T: Hudson 2, Harrison, S Williams, G: C Evans 2
Sep 21	WARRINGTON (WEL)	L 0-12	1,000	
Sep 28	Liverpool Stanley (WEL)	W 41-3	500	T: S Williams 4, Hudson, T Kenny, R Kenny, G: C Evans 10
Oct 5	Warrington (WEL)	L 0-13	1,000	
Oct 12	WIGAN (WEL)	L 9-13	3,000	T: S Williams, G: Holding 3
Oct 19	St Helens (WEL)	L 0-6	1,000	
Oct 26	ST HELENS (WEL)	W 15-13	2,000	T: Lawrenson 2, Hudson, G: J Jones, Lawrenson, Miller
Nov 23	Oldham (WEL)	W 7-6	2,000	T: Lawrenson, G: Lawrenson 2
Nov 30	OLDHAM (WEL)	W 3-2	–	T: Harrison

Salford RL Match Results

1940-1941 *continued*

	Opponent	Result	Attendance	Scorers
Dec 7	Leigh (WEL)*	W 38-0	800	T: Edwards 2, Hudson 2, R Kenny 2, S Williams 2, HC Day, Miller, G: Holding 3, E Jenkins
Dec 14	LIVERPOOL STANLEY (WEL)	W 25-2	–	T: Hudson 3, S Williams 3, R Kenny, G: Holding 2
Dec 21	Broughton Rangers (WEL)*	W 32-8	–	T: Belshaw 3, Hudson 2, S Williams 2, R Kenny, G: Belshaw 4
Dec 25	Wigan (WEL)	L 0-12	7,000	

*Away matches played at Salford

Salford withdrew for duration of World War II

1945-1946

	Opponent	Result	Attendance	Scorers
Aug 25	CASTLEFORD	W 10-0	10,000	T: Dagnan 2, Risman 2
Sep 1	Warrington	L 3-13	8,000	T: A Edwards
Sep 8	HULL	W 17-5	8,000	T: Brown, Holmes, Risman, G: Risman 4
Sep 15	Dewsbury	L 2-9	4,000	G: Risman
Sep 22	Widnes (LC-1)	L 0-37	6,000	
Sep 29	WIDNES (LC-1)	L 2-15	8,000	G: Risman
Oct 6	Oldham	L 7-10	5,500	T: Brown, G: Risman 2
Oct 13	WORKINGTON TOWN	W 23-4	6,000	T: Burt 2, A Edwards 2, Dagnan, J Gardner, Todd, G: Harrison
Oct 20	Wakefield Trinity	L 11-16	5,000	T: Dagnan 2, A Edwards, G: Brown
Nov 3	Barrow	W 3-0	7,901	T: A Edwards
Nov 10	Halifax	W 9-5	6,000	T: Dagnan, G: Brown 2, Harrison
Nov 17	HUDDERSFIELD	L 10-14	8,584	T: Dagnan, Hilton, G: Brown 2
Nov 24	Castleford	L 5-15	4,000	T: Todd, G: Brown
Dec 1	LIVERPOOL STANLEY	W 37-6	5,340	T: R Jones 4, A Edwards 2, Hilton 2, Todd, G: Brown 5
Dec 8	Wigan	L 8-24	7,000	T: A Edwards, Todd, G: Brown
Dec 15	BARROW	L 5-17	5,000	T: R Kenny, G: Watkins
Dec 22	Broughton Rangers	L 0-17	6,000	
Dec 25	BROUGHTON RANGERS	L 7-12	8,576	T: R Jones, G: Risman 2
Dec 26	Swinton	W 16-3	12,000	T: D Moses 2, A Edwards, R Jones, G: Risman 2
Dec 29	SWINTON	W 9-4	9,000	T: A Edwards 2, R Jones

Salford RL Match Results

1945-1946 *continued*

	Opponent	Result	Attendance	Scorers
Jan 5	LEEDS	W 17-3	4,500	T: Curran 2, Dagnan, Harrison, R Jones, G: R Jones
Jan 12	St Helens	W 13-6	4,500	T: Curran, A Edwards, R Jones, G: A Edwards, R Jones
Jan 26	Leeds	W 6-5	7,000	G: Risman 3
Feb 2	WARRINGTON	W 3-0	5,800	T: A Edwards
Feb 9	OLDHAM (RLC-1)	W 8-3	11,400	T: Harrison, R Jones, G: Risman
Feb 16	Oldham (RLC-1)	W 3-2	11,958	T: Harrison
Mar 2	Hull Kingston Rovers (RLC-2)	D 0-0	9,000	
Mar 6	HULL KINGSTON ROVERS (RLC-2 replay)	W 38-6	8,000	T: Dagnan 5, A Edwards, Harrison, R Hartley, R Jones, D Moses, G: Risman 4
Mar 9	Liverpool Stanley	W 18-0	1,000	T: Snipe 2, R Hartley, Risman, G: Risman 3
Mar 16	HUNSLET (RLC-3)	L 8-15	21,000	T: R Jones, Todd, G: Risman
Mar 23	ROCHDALE HORNETS	W 13-6	6,000	T: Dagnan 2, Todd, G: Risman 2
Mar 30	Hull	L 9-19	9,000	T: DM Davies, G: A Edwards 3
Apr 2	Rochdale Hornets	W 19-15	2,000	T: Dagnan 2, DM Davies, A Edwards, R Hartley, G: A Edwards 2
Apr 6	HALIFAX	W 18-3	6,200	T: Dagnan, DM Davies, D Moses, Todd, G: A Edwards 3
Apr 10	ST HELENS	W 6-5	5,000	T: DM Davies, Holmes
Apr 13	WAKEFIELD TRINITY	W 26-18	9,000	T: Dagnan, Feetham, Harrison, R Hartley, R Jones, Todd, G: A Edwards 4
Apr 15	Widnes	W 16-9	6,000	T: Harrison 2, Dagnan, A Edwards, G: A Edwards 2
Apr 19	Workington Town	W 13-8	14,839	T: Dagnan, DM Davies, D Moses, G: A Edwards 2
Apr 20	DEWSBURY	W 6-4	9,400	G: A Edwards 3
Apr 22	WIGAN	W 16-13	21,500	T: Dagnan, D Moses, G: A Edwards 4, Burt
Apr 27	Huddersfield	L 15-22	13,000	T: Dagnan, D Moses, S Williams, G: A Edwards 3
May 1	WIDNES	W 11-7	6,900	T: Dagnan, A Edwards, Moore, G: A Edwards
May 11	OLDHAM	L 8-25	9,000	T: Burt 2, G: A Edwards

Salford RL 1896-97 to 2022

Salford RL Match Results

1946-1947

	Opponent	Result	Attendance	Scorers
Aug 31	Barrow	L 8-20	8,000	T: Harrison, R Jones, G: R Jones
Sep 7	WARRINGTON (LC-1)	W 10-3	13,431	T: Harrison, S Williams, G: JW Jenkins 2
Sep 14	Warrington (LC-1)	L 5-10	15,500	T: Dagnan, G: JW Jenkins
Sep 21	BARROW	W 23-5	8,000	T: Harrison 2, JW Jenkins, Todd, O Williams, G: JW Jenkins 4
Sep 25	Wigan (LC-2)	L 0-31	27,000	
Sep 28	Belle Vue Rangers	L 5-13	12,000	T: D Moses, G: JW Jenkins
Oct 2	WIGAN (LC-2)	L 0-19	11,000	
Oct 5	HALIFAX	L 0-23	8,000	
Oct 12	Huddersfield	L 18-29	8,129	T: Taylor 2, R Jones, Todd, G: R Kenny 2, JW Jenkins
Oct 19	ST HELENS	L 2-11	8,000	G: R Kenny
Oct 26	Batley	L 11-27	4,000	T: JW Jenkins, G: JW Jenkins 4
Nov 2	Leigh	L 7-13	9,000	T: S Williams, G: JW Jenkins, Rogers
Nov 9	WIDNES	L 6-10	6,500	G: JW Jenkins 3
Nov 16	Halifax	L 3-5	5,000	T: Harrison
Nov 23	ROCHDALE HORNETS	W 13-8	6,000	T: DM Davies 2, O Williams, G: Rogers 2
Nov 30	Warrington	L 7-14	7,000	T: Fairclough, G: Rogers 2
Dec 7	WARRINGTON	L 0-23	6,000	
Dec 14	St Helens	L 8-9	5,000	T: O Williams, S Williams, G: Rogers
Dec 25	Wigan	L 9-24	18,000	T: D Moses, G: Rogers 3
Dec 26	OLDHAM	L 5-14	12,000	T: D Moses, G: Rogers
Dec 28	BRADFORD NORTHERN	L 8-12	10,000	T: Todd, S Williams, G: JW Jenkins
Jan 1	Swinton	L 2-10	11,000	G: Slamin
Jan 4	HUDDERSFIELD	W 8-7	10,000	T: O Williams, S Williams, G: JW Jenkins
Jan 11	Workington Town	L 3-9	7,000	T: S Williams
Jan 18	Bradford Northern	L 7-23	7,000	T: R Kenny, G: Marland 2
Jan 25	BATLEY	W 6-3	7,000	T: Curran, Flanagan
Feb 15	WAKEFIELD TRINITY	D 0-0	8,000	
Feb 22	BRADFORD NORTHERN (RLC-1)	W 5-2	12,100	T: Gear, G: Rogers
Mar 12	Bradford Northern (RLC-1)	L 0-10	4,127	
Mar 15	LIVERPOOL STANLEY	W 6-0	8,000	T: Gear, R Kenny
Mar 22	Oldham	L 6-16	8,000	T: Higgs, S Williams
Mar 29	BRAMLEY	W 26-7	5,000	T: Aspinall, Brogden, Curran, Dagnan, E Day, Higgs, G: R Kenny 4
Apr 4	Liverpool Stanley	W 6-4	2,000	T: Aspinall 2

Salford RL Match Results

1946-1947 *continued*

	Opponent	Result	Attendance	Scorers
Apr 5	SWINTON	W 9-3	13,000	T: Aspinall, Curran, S Williams
Apr 7	WIGAN	L 5-21	21,000	T: Higgs, G: Rogers
Apr 8	Wakefield Trinity*	D 3-3	4,000	T: Brown
Apr 12	Bramley	W 10-6	3,000	T: Higgs, S Williams, G: Brogden, Rogers
Apr 26	Rochdale Hornets	W 7-4	4,000	T: Flanagan, G: S Williams 2
May 10	Widnes	L 3-4	8,000	T: S Williams
May 17	Barrow (F)**	W 28-19	4,000	T: Harrison 2, Aspinall, Brogden, R Kenny, S Williams, G: S Williams 5
May 24	WORKINGTON TOWN	L 8-17	8,000	T: Aspinall, Flanagan, G: S Williams
May 26	LEIGH	W 21-10	8,000	T: Aspinall 2, Roberts 2, DM Davies, G: S Williams 3
May 28	BELLE VUE RANGERS	L 11-15	7,000	T: Brogden 2, S Williams, G: S Williams

* Abandoned half-time (heavy rain, muddy pitch) – result stands due to fixture congestion
** At Lancaster (charity match)

1947-1948

	Opponent	Result	Attendance	Scorers
Aug 9	LEIGH (SHC-SF)	W 34-8	9,800	T: Aspinall, Brown, DM Davies, Flanagan, Harrison, R Jones, R Kenny S Williams, G: S Williams 5
Aug 16	SWINTON (SHC-Final)	W 18-10	10,000	T: R Jones 2, E Day, S Williams, G: S Williams 3
Aug 23	Hunslet	W 13-6	9,000	T: Brown, Flanagan, Gear, G: S Williams 2
Aug 30	Widnes (LC-1)	W 8-4	8,400	T: Harrison, Roberts, G: S Williams
Sep 3	WIDNES (LC-1)	W 9-4	12,000	T: Aspinall, Gear, D Moses
Sep 6	ST HELENS	L 5-12	10,000	T: D Moses, G: S Williams
Sep 15	Oldham	L 0-26	12000	
Sep 20	Liverpool Stanley	W 23-5	1,500	T: Aspinall 3, R Jones, Todd, G: R: Kenny 4
Sep 27	Keighley	W 9-8	3,500	T: Aspinall, Wharton, O Williams
Oct 1	Belle Vue Rangers (LC-2)	L 5-10	8,000	T: D Moses, G: S Williams
Oct 4	HUNSLET	W 10-7	7,000	T: Aspinall, R Jones, G: Chapman 2
Oct 11	Bramley	W 16-11	3,586	T: Aspinall 2, S Williams 2, G: Chapman 2

Salford RL Match Results

1947-1948 *continued*

	Opponent	Result	Attendance	Scorers
Oct 18	WAKEFIELD TRINITY	W 10-9	10,000	T: Aspinall, Brown, G: Chapman 2
Oct 25	Wakefield Trinity	L 8-15	13,000	T: Aspinall, O Williams, G: Chapman
Nov 1	KEIGHLEY	W 13-10	8,000	T: Aspinall 3, G: E Davies 2
Nov 8	Hull Kingston Rovers	L 5-13	8,000	T: E Day, G: E Davies
Nov 15	Rochdale Hornets	L 2-13	5,000	G: Chapman
Nov 22	ROCHDALE HORNETS	W 5-3	5,000	T: Flanagan, G: S Williams
Nov 29	St Helens	L 10-31	10,000	T: E Day, Flanagan, G: E Davies 2
Dec 6	HALIFAX	W 12-5	8,000	T: Byrne, Flanagan, G: E Davies 3
Dec 13	Warrington	L 13-45	8,000	T: Coburn 2, J Kenny, G: E Davies 2
Dec 20	Workington Town	L 0-19	8,000	
Dec 25	Wigan	L 10-55	22,000	T: Camac, S Williams, G: E Davies 2
Dec 26	OLDHAM	W 9-0	10,000	T: Aspinall, Gear, S Williams
Dec 27	LIVERPOOL STANLEY	W 30-2	5,000	T: S Williams 2, Aspinall, Curran, E Davies, E Day, Flanagan, J Kenny, G: S Williams 2, E Davies
Jan 1	Swinton	D 0-0	7,000	
Jan 3	BRAMLEY	W 19-8	6,000	T: Aspinall 2, Brown, J Kenny, S Williams, G: E Davies, S Williams
Jan 10	HULL KINGSTON ROVERS	W 8-0	8,000	T: Aspinall 2, G: E Davies
Jan 17	Leigh*	L 3-15	6,000	T: Aspinall
Jan 24	WORKINGTON TOWN	W 16-3	8,000	T: Aspinall, Coburn, E Davies, Flanagan, G: E Davies 2
Jan 31	Barrow	W 11-10	7,000	T: Todd 2, Chapman, G: Chapman
Feb 7	WAKEFIELD TRINITY (RLC-1)	L 2-13	14,000	G: E Davies
Feb 14	Wakefield Trinity (RLC-1) (AET)	L 15-20	14,500	T: Brown, Coburn, E Day, G: E Davies 3
Feb 21	BARROW	W 21-5	5,000	T: Curran 3, Coburn 2, G: E Davies 3
Mar 6	Widnes	L 0-13	6,000	
Mar 13	BELLE VUE RANGERS	W 7-2	7,000	T: Aspinall, G: E Davies 2
Mar 20	WARRINGTON	L 5-13	18,000	T: Brown, G: E Davies
Mar 27	SWINTON	W 21-8	16,000	T: Aspinall 2, Chapman, DM Davies, Stirrup, G: E Davies 3

Salford RL Match Results

1947-1948 *continued*

	Opponent	Result	Attendance	Scorers
Mar 29	WIGAN	L 9-27	20,000	T: Chapman, G: E Davies 3
Mar 30	Halifax	L 8-17	8,000	T: Aspinall 2, G: E Davies
Apr 5	Belle Vue Rangers	L 3-20	5,000	T: Aspinall
Apr 14	WIDNES	W 4-2	6,000	G: E Davies 2
Apr 24	LEIGH	W 9-7	3,500	T: Harrison, G: E Davies 3
May 15	Oldham (F)**	L 10-27	6,000	T: Blan, J Kenny, G: E Davies 2

* Abandoned 70 min (torrential rain, pitch flooded) – result stands
** At Lancaster (charity match)

1948-1949

	Opponent	Result	Attendance	Scorers
Aug 21	LEIGH	W 10-2	8,000	T: Aspinall, S Williams, G: S Williams 2
Aug 26	Widnes	L 0-2	9,000	
Aug 28	Bramley	W 13-5	6,500	T: Aspinall, Todd, S Williams, G: S Williams 2
Sep 1	BARROW	W 8-0	7,000	T: Hawkins, Stirrup, G: S Williams
Sep 4	Workington Town (LC-1)	L 5-7	16,000	T: Harrison, G: Chapman
Sep 8	WORKINGTON TOWN (LC-1)	W 14-0	10,000	T: Aspinall, Brown, Stirrup, S Williams, G: S Williams
Sep 11	OLDHAM	W 20-9	12,000	T: Aspinall, Harrison, J Kenny, Stirrup, G: S Williams 4
Sep 14	Rochdale Hornets	L 3-8	3,500	T: Aspinall
Sep 18	Hunslet	L 0-15	9,000	
Sep 25	WHITEHAVEN	W 22-11	6,000	T: Aspinall, DM Davies, D Moses, S Williams, G: E Davies 3, S Williams 2
Sep 29	WIGAN (LC-2)	L 5-18	14,000	T: Aspinall, G: S Williams
Oct 2	AUSTRALIA (Tour)	L 2-13	16,627	G: E Davies
Oct 9	Workington Town	L 0-18	13,000	
Oct 16	BRADFORD NORTHERN	W 4-3	12,000	G: E Davies 2
Oct 23	Hull	L 5-12	10,000	T: Stirrup, G: E Davies
Oct 30	LIVERPOOL STANLEY	W 35-7	4,000	T: Brown 2, E Davies 2, D Moses, Stirrup, S Williams, G: E Davies 7
Nov 6	St Helens	L 12-17	12,000	T: E Davies, Stirrup, G: E Davies 3
Nov 13	HUNSLET	W 13-0	4,000	T: E Davies, Harrison, Hawkins, G: E Davies 2
Nov 20	Warrington	L 12-15	16,680	T: Harrison, Stirrup, G: E Davies 2, Curran

Salford RL Match Results

1948-1949 *continued*

	Opponent	Result	Attendance	Scorers
Nov 27	Liverpool Stanley	W 10-8	500	T: Aspinall, S Williams, G: E Davies 2
Dec 4	ROCHDALE HORNETS	W 11-0	8,000	T: Brown, DM Davies, Harrison, G: E Davies
Dec 11	Belle Vue Rangers	W 17-5	6,000	T: Aspinall, Todd, S Williams, G: E Davies 4
Dec 18	HALIFAX	W 6-5	4,839	T: Todd, S Williams
Dec 25	Wigan	L 5-24	23,000	T: DM Davies, G: E Davies
Jan 1	SWINTON	D 0-0	12,098	
Jan 8	HULL	W 10-2	7,000	T: J Kenny, S Williams, G: E Davies 2
Jan 15	Bradford Northern	W 7-2	8,500	T: J Kenny, G: E Davies 2
Jan 22	WIDNES	D 5-5	10,000	T: J Kenny, G: E Davies
Jan 29	WORKINGTON TOWN	W 12-5	11,000	T: Brown, J Kenny, G: E Davies 3
Feb 5	Halifax	L 4-13	10,000	G: Bennett, S Williams
Feb 12	Hunslet (RLC-1)	L 0-22	9,000	
Feb 19	HUNSLET (RLC-1)	W 11-10	10,000	T: S Williams 2, Todd, G: E Davies
Feb 26	BELLE VUE RANGERS	W 12-2	7,000	T: Aspinall, Harrison, G: E Davies 2, S Williams
Mar 12	Leigh	D 0-0	9,000	
Mar 19	ST HELENS	W 7-6	9,000	T: I Edwards, G: E Davies 2
Apr 2	WARRINGTON	L 2-18	12,000	G: E Davies
Apr 4	Oldham	D 2-2	8,000	G: E Davies
Apr 9	Whitehaven	W 20-12	7,000	T: Aspinall, E Day, Harrison, H Jones, G Moses, Todd, G: S Williams
Apr 15	Barrow	L 7-12	14,597	T: Todd, G: E Davies, S Williams
Apr 16	Swinton	W 34-5	15,000	T: Aspinall 4, Harrison, J Kenny, Todd, S Williams, G: E Davies 5
Apr 18	WIGAN	D 9-9	18,500	T: Todd, G: E Davies 3
Apr 23	BRAMLEY	W 34-8	5,000	T: J Kenny 2, S Williams 2, Aspinall, DM Davies, G: E Davies 8

1949-1950

	Opponent	Result	Attendance	Scorers
Aug 24	LIVERPOOL STANLEY	W 41-7	8,000	T: Aspinall 2, J Kenny 2, Danby, DM Davies, Harrison, H Jones, S Williams, G: E Davies 7
Aug 27	WARRINGTON (LC-1)	L 9-22	17,000	T: J Kenny, G: E Davies 3
Aug 31	Warrington (LC-1)	L 2-17	15,000	G: E Davies
Sep 3	Bradford Northern	W 17-12	13,500	T: Danby, DM Davies, E Davies, G: E Davies 4

Salford RL Match Results

1949-1950 *continued*

	Opponent	Result	Attendance	Scorers
Sep 7	HUDDERSFIELD	W 29-8	17,500	T: Curran 2, J Kenny, G Moses, S Williams, G: E Davies 6, S Williams
Sep 10	WHITEHAVEN	W 14-13	5,000	T: E Davies, J Kenny, Todd, S Williams, G: S Williams
Sep 17	Widnes	W 13-7	3,000	T: Aspinall, Danby, J Kenny, G: E Davies 2
Sep 24	Hunslet	W 10-4	10,000	T: J Kenny 2, G: E Davies 2
Oct 1	BELLE VUE RANGERS	W 16-2	11,500	T: Aspinall, Brown, E Davies, Todd, G: E Davies 2
Oct 8	Leigh	L 9-10	16,000	T: E Davies, G: E Davies 3
Oct 15	YORK	W 36-9	8,000	T: Aspinall 2, Todd 2, DM Davies, E Davies, Harrison, Stirrup, G: E Davies 6
Oct 22	Barrow	L 2-3	9,829	G: Rogers
Oct 29	BARROW	W 16-7	8,000	T: Brown, E Davies, Harrison, Stirrup, G: E Davies 2
Nov 5	York	W 19-9	3,763	T: Danby 2, Todd 2, Brown, G: E Davies 2
Nov 12	WIDNES	W 13-0	5,000	T: Aspinall, Harrison, J Kenny, G: S Williams 2
Nov 19	Workington Town	W 20-7	13,000	T: Aspinall, Stirrup, Todd, S Williams, G: E Davies 4
Nov 26	HUNSLET	W 24-5	8,000	T: Aspinall, Danby, Todd, S Williams, G: E Davies 6
Dec 3	Huddersfield	D 4-4	15,647	G: E Davies 2
Dec 10	ST HELENS	W 8-4	19,500	T: Danby, Hawkins, G: E Davies
Dec 17	HULL KINGSTON ROVERS	W 3-0	6,000	T: Danby
Dec 23	Wigan	L 7-22	32,000	T: S Williams, G: E Davies 2
Dec 26	WORKINGTON TOWN	L 0-7	14,000	
Dec 27	OLDHAM	W 11-2	20,000	T: Danby, DM Davies, Todd, G: E Davies
Dec 31	Rochdale Hornets	W 8-2	4,500	T: Aspinall, G Moses, G: S Williams
Jan 2	SWINTON	D 2-2	16,000	G: S Williams
Jan 7	Belle Vue Rangers	W 5-3	8,000	T: Aspinall, G: E Davies
Jan 14	BRADFORD NORTHERN	W 14-10	12,000	T: Danby 2, G: E Davies 4
Jan 21	Hull Kingston Rovers	L 2-16	8,000	G: E Davies
Feb 4	Cardiff (RLC-1)	W 15-10	5,000	T: Brown, Harrison, J Kenny, G: E Davies 3
Feb 11	CARDIFF (RLC-1)	W 20-5	6,000	T: Aspinall 2, Danby, Harrison, J Kenny, Streets, G: E Davies

Salford RL Match Results

1949-1950 *continued*

	Opponent	Result	Attendance	Scorers
Feb 18	Warrington	L 7-11	21,127	T: E Davies, G: E Davies 2
Feb 25	ST HELENS (RLC-2)	L 2-9	26,000	G: E Davies
Mar 4	LEIGH	W 8-2	10,000	T: Harrison, Todd, G: E Davies
Mar 18	Liverpool Stanley	W 12-5	4,000	T: DM Davies, E Davies, G: E Davies 3
Mar 25	WARRINGTON	W 23-11	12,498	T: Brown, DM Davies, E Davies, D Moses, Todd, G: E Davies 4
Apr 7	Oldham	W 8-5	18,182	T: Danby, Harrison, G: E Davies
Apr 8	Swinton	L 0-3	20,000	
Apr 10	WIGAN	L 5-26	17,000	T: Aspinall, G: E Davies
Apr 15	Whitehaven	L 3-20	8,000	T: D Moses
Apr 19	St Helens	L 3-38	17,000	T: D Moses
Apr 22	ROCHDALE HORNETS	W 15-10	5,000	T: Todd 2, Easterbrook, G: E Davies 3

1950-1951

	Opponent	Result	Attendance	Scorers
Aug 12	BLAINA (F)	W 53-0	–	T: Brown 2, I Edwards 2, Stirrup 2, Aspinall, Curran, E Davies, Easterbrook, B Hartley, R Kenny, 'Trialist', G: I Edwards 4, E Davies 3
Aug 19	Huddersfield	L 8-29	15,607	T: Alder, Easterbrook, G: E Davies
Aug 26	HUDDERSFIELD	L 8-25	12,000	T: E Davies, Todd, G: E Davies
Sep 2	Widnes (LC-1)	L 13-15	6,000	T: Hawkins, McCauley, Stirrup, G: E Davies 2
Sep 9	LEEDS	L 9-10	12,000	T: Flanagan, G: E Davies 3
Sep 13	WIDNES (LC-1)	W 7-0	6,000	T: Todd, G: E Davies 2
Sep 16	Widnes	L 0-17	5,000	
Sep 23	CASTLEFORD	L 9-11	6,000	T: Danby, G: E Davies 3
Sep 27	St Helens (LC-2)	L 3-20	17,673	T: Stirrup
Sep 30	Keighley	L 8-11	6,000	T: Danby 2, G: Danby
Oct 7	Oldham	L 10-16	11,000	T: B Hartley, Pimblett, G: G Moses 2
Oct 14	ST HELENS	W 25-3	10,000	T: Aspinall 2, Chadderton, DM Davies, Grainger, G: G Moses 5
Oct 21	Warrington	L 2-17	18,332	G: G Moses
Oct 28	BELLE VUE RANGERS	L 10-27	10,000	T: Danby, E Davies, G: E Davies 2
Nov 4	Whitehaven	L 3-15	9,000	T: Todd

Salford RL Match Results

1950-1951 *continued*

	Opponent	Result	Attendance	Scorers
Nov 11	BARROW	L 12-18	10,000	T: DM Davies, Grainger, G: E Davies 3
Nov 18	Workington Town	L 2-15	10,000	G: E Davies
Nov 25	OLDHAM	W 12-9	8,000	T: Brown, Harrison, G: E Davies 3
Dec 2	Barrow	L 0-5	8,149	
Dec 9	WORKINGTON TOWN	W 9-8	8,000	T: Alder, G: E Davies 2, Rogers
Dec 23	Wakefield Trinity	L 9-16	5,350	T: E Davies, G: E Davies 3
Dec 25	Wigan	L 5-17	20,000	T: Aspinall, G: E Davies
Jan 6	KEIGHLEY	D 2-2	5,000	G: G Moses
Jan 13	Rochdale Hornets	L 3-6	6,000	T: Hindle
Jan 20	LIVERPOOL STANLEY	W 19-3	7,000	T: Hindle 2, Danby, G: E Davies 5
Jan 27	Leeds	L 14-17	15,000	T: Hindle 2, G: E Davies 4
Feb 3	St Helens	L 0-10	14,000	
Feb 10	WAKEFIELD TRINITY (RLC-1)	W 16-10	12,000	T: Aspinall, S Williams, G: E Davies 5
Feb 17	Wakefield Trinity (RLC-1)	W 6-2	10,000	T: E Davies, Hindle
Feb 24	WIDNES	W 18-0	9,000	T: Aspinall, Danby, J Kenny, G Moses, G: E Davies 3
Mar 3	DEWSBURY (RLC-2)	W 6-0	16,500	G: E Davies 3
Mar 10	WHITEHAVEN	W 20-5	5,000	T: Aspinall 2, Grainger, S Williams, G: E Davies 4
Mar 17	WARRINGTON (RLC-3)	L 4-8	26,327	G: E Davies 2
Mar 24	Castleford	W 12-9	3,000	T: Brown, S Williams, G: E Davies 3
Mar 26	WIGAN	W 16-3	8,000	T: E Davies, S Williams, G: E Davies 5
Mar 31	SWINTON	W 6-0	10,000	G: E Davies 3
Apr 4	ROCHDALE HORNETS	W 20-7	8,000	T: Danby, E Davies, Finnan, Grainger, G: E Davies 4
Apr 7	Belle Vue Rangers	W 9-4	5,000	T: J Kenny, G: E Davies 3
Apr 11	LEIGH	W 28-8	8,000	T: Aspinall 3, DM Davies, E Davies, S Williams, G: E Davies 5
Apr 14	Leigh	L 5-7	11,500	T: S Williams, G: E Davies
Apr 18	Swinton	W 20-14	13,071	T: Danby, E Davies, Finnan, S Williams, G: E Davies 4
Apr 21	WARRINGTON	L 0-19	11,901	
Apr 25	WAKEFIELD TRINITY	W 24-21	–	T: E Davies 2, Alder, Finnan, G: E Davies 6
Apr 28	Liverpool Stanley	W 23-5	700	T: Danby 2, Aspinall, DM Davies, Rogers, G: E Davies 4

Salford RL Match Results

1951-1952

	Opponent	Result	Attendance	Scorers
Aug 18	BATLEY	W 17-7	8,000	T: Aspinall, Finnan, Hindle, G: E Davies 4
Aug 23	Liverpool City	L 4-8	1,200	G: E Davies 2
Aug 25	Belle Vue Rangers	W 15-6	5,000	T: Danby 2, Hindle, G: E Davies 3
Aug 29	WARRINGTON	W 28-19	11,487	T: J Kenny 2, Aspinall, Harrison, Hindle, Robson, G: E Davies 5
Sep 1	LEIGH (LC-1)	L 7-14	14,000	T: Robson, G: E Davies 2
Sep 8	Whitehaven	L 5-14	7,000	T: Harrison, G: S Williams
Sep 12	Leigh (LC-1)	L 9-15	15,000	T: S Williams, G: E Davies 3
Sep 15	ROCHDALE HORNETS	W 31-10	7,000	T: Danby 3, Finnan, Hughes, Rogers, S Williams, G: Harrison 5
Sep 22	HULL KINGSTON ROVERS	W 36-11	7,000	T: DM Davies 2, E Davies 2, Finnan, Hughes, Rogers, S Williams, G: E Davies 6
Sep 29	Dewsbury	W 21-9	5,000	T: Finnan, Hindle, S Williams, G: E Davies 6
Oct 6	Featherstone Rovers	L 22-23	3,500	T: Finnan 2, Hindle, Grainger, G: E Davies 5
Oct 13	LEIGH	L 8-14	14,000	G: E Davies 4
Oct 20	Batley	L 11-17	6,800	T: Brown, Danby, Grainger, G: E Davies
Oct 27	OLDHAM	L 5-19	10,000	T: B Hartley, G: E Davies
Nov 3	Warrington	L 4-5	7,821	G: E Davies 2
Nov 10	Widnes	D 5-5	6,000	T: E Davies, G: E Davies
Nov 17	FEATHERSTONE ROVERS	W 29-12	5,000	T: Finnan 3, Hindle, S Williams, G: E Davies 7
Nov 24	Rochdale Hornets	W 9-2	2,000	T: Danby, G: E Davies 2, Rogers
Dec 1	NEW ZEALAND (Tour)	L 12-27	10,000	T: Finnan, Hindle, G: E Davies 3
Dec 8	WHITEHAVEN	W 6-3	3,000	T: Finnan, Hindle
Dec 15	St Helens	W 14-6	12,000	T: Finnan, Hindle, G: E Davies 4
Dec 22	ST HELENS	W 5-0	4,000	T: E Davies, G: E Davies
Dec 25	Wigan	L 5-8	19,468	T: Finnan, G: E Davies
Dec 26	BARROW	L 0-13	8,000	
Dec 29	Hull Kingston Rovers	L 8-13	4,000	T: Danby, S Williams, G: E Davies
Jan 5	HALIFAX	W 12-7	8,177	T: Danby, D Moses, G: E Davies 3
Jan 12	Oldham	D 9-9	11,052	T: B Hartley, G: E Davies 2, S Williams
Jan 19	Leigh	L 6-14	14,000	G: E Davies 3

Salford RL Match Results

1951-1952 *continued*

	Opponent	Result	Attendance	Scorers
Feb 2	Barrow	W 10-8	7,000	T: Grainger, Harrison, G: Rogers 2
Feb 9	HUNSLET (RLC-1)	W 13-6	16,000	T: Danby, Grainger, D Moses, G: Hesketh, S Williams
Feb 16	Hunslet (RLC-1)	L 3-6	13,000	T: Finnan
Feb 23	WORKINGTON TOWN	L 7-13	12,000	T: Danby, G: Harrison, S Williams
Mar 1	BARROW (RLC-2)	L 6-11	17,000	T: Hindle 2
Mar 8	LIVERPOOL CITY	W 30-8	5,000	T: Aspinall 2, B Hartley 2, S Williams 2, Harrison, D Moses, G: E Davies 3
Mar 15	SWINTON	W 22-9	12,000	T: Danby, Grainger, B Hartley, Hindle, G: E Davies 5
Mar 22	WIDNES	W 14-11	8,000	T: Danby, DM Davies, Grainger, B Hartley, G: E Davies
Apr 2	BELLE VUE RANGERS	W 14-9	8,000	T: Grainger, Harrison, B Hartley, Hesketh, G: Harrison
Apr 5	DEWSBURY	L 3-9	5,000	T: Finnan
Apr 11	Workington Town	L 11-21	11,072	T: Danby, E Davies, Finnan, G: E Davies
Apr 12	Swinton	L 10-11	10,000	T: Danby, B Hartley, G: E Davies 2
Apr 14	WIGAN	L 8-25	13,000	T: Alder, Danby, G: E Davies
Apr 21	Halifax	W 10-8	7,961	T: Danby, Grainger, G: E Davies 2
Jun 23	Barrow (FoS-SF)*	W 19-12	–	T: Alder, Birkin, Danby, G: E Davies 5
Jun 27	Doncaster (FoS-Final)*	W 26-7	–	T: B Hartley 4, E Davies, Finnan, G: E Davies 3, Harrison

* At Blackpool

1952-1953

	Opponent	Result	Attendance	Scorers
Aug 23	Whitehaven	L 10-17	7,564	T: Baines, Finnan, G: E Davies 2
Aug 27	ST HELENS	L 9-15	10,005	T: D Moses, G: Rogers 2, E Davies
Aug 30	WARRINGTON (LC-1)	L 17-19	15,000	T: Harrison, B Hartley, Rogers, G: E Davies 4
Sep 3	Warrington (LC-1)	L 8-30	14,535	T: Grainger, S Williams, G: E Davies

Salford RL Match Results

1952-1953 *continued*

	Opponent	Result	Attendance	Scorers
Sep 6	DONCASTER	W 35-11	5,789	T: Halton 2, Alder, Baines, Danby, Finnan, F Smith, G: F Smith 4, Rogers 3
Sep 8	Workington Town	L 14-23	7,623	T: Baines, Easterbrook, Finnan, Rogers, G: Danby
Sep 13	BRAMLEY	W 20-9	5,278	T: Burrell, Danby, Finnan, Hindle, G: F Smith 3, Rogers
Sep 20	Dewsbury	W 14-7	2,907	T: Baines 2, Danby, B Hartley, G: Rogers
Sep 27	LIVERPOOL CITY	W 18-5	2,839	T: Burrell 2, B Hartley 2, G: McKinney 3
Oct 4	Leigh	L 7-10	7,815	T: B Hartley, G: F Smith 2
Oct 11	DEWSBURY	L 5-15	5,896	T: Finnan, G: McKinney
Oct 18	St Helens	L 6-14	14,327	G: Whalley 3
Oct 25	WHITEHAVEN	W 35-10	4,918	T: Halton 2, B Hartley 2, Finnan, Harrison, Robson, G: Whalley 7
Nov 1	Hunslet	L 13-15	6,000	T: Danby 2, B Hartley, G: Whalley 2
Nov 15	BARROW	L 8-10	4,754	T: Danby, Halton, G: Rogers
Nov 22	Oldham	L 3-32	11,765	T: Grainger
Dec 13	Bramley	W 16-6	1,378	T: Finnan 2, Halton, B Hartley, G: Whalley 2
Dec 20	BELLE VUE RANGERS	W 32-0	2,724	T: B Hartley 3, Halton 2, Danby, Finnan, Robson, G: Robson 4
Dec 25	Wigan	L 8-34	14,076	T: Halton, B Hartley, G: Robson
Dec 26	WIDNES	W 8-0	6,339	T: B Hartley, F Smith, G: E Davies
Dec 27	Barrow	L 0-41	11,246	
Jan 1	Swinton	W 7-3	7,000	T: B Hartley, G: E Davies 2
Jan 3	KEIGHLEY	W 11-7	4,830	T: Danby, B Hartley, Whalley, G: E Davies
Jan 10	Doncaster	W 8-5	729	T: B Hartley, Hindle, G: Robson
Jan 17	OLDHAM	L 4-8	11,636	G: Robson 2
Jan 24	Liverpool City	W 37-4	366	T: Finnan, B Hartley, Keavney, D Moses, Robson, Rogers, F Smith, G: Robson 8
Jan 31	HUNSLET	W 8-7	3,884	T: Harrison, Hindle, G: E Davies
Feb 7	YORK (RLC-1)	W 24-14	6,735	T: Hindle 2, Finnan, Grainger, B Hartley, Rogers, G: E Davies 3

Salford RL Match Results

1952-1953 *continued*

	Opponent	Result	Attendance	Scorers
Feb 18	York (RLC-1)	W 8-3	5,323	T: Grainger, Hindle, G: E Davies
Feb 21	Keighley	W 16-5	4,278	T: Keavney 2, Finnan, B Hartley, G: E Davies 2
Feb 28	Bradford Northern (RLC-2)	L 4-18	23,413	G: E Davies, Whalley
Mar 7	Belle Vue Rangers	W 17-9	3,766	T: Caudwell, Danby, E Davies, G: E Davies 4
Mar 21	LEIGH	W 24-10	9,731	T: Birkin, E Davies, Finnan, Rogers, G: E Davies 5, Keavney
Mar 28	Rochdale Hornets	W 30-12	2,926	T: Danby 3, Birkin, E Davies, Finnan, Grainger, B Hartley, G: Rogers 2, E Davies
Mar 30	Warrington	W 13-10	4,637	T: Birkin, Danby, Harrison, G: E Davies 2
Apr 3	ROCHDALE HORNETS	L 8-22	7,666	T: Danby 2, G: E Davies
Apr 4	SWINTON	W 13-5	8,716	T: B Hartley, G: Rogers 4, E Davies
Apr 6	WIGAN	L 5-8	9,313	T: Danby, G: E Davies
Apr 11	WORKINGTON TOWN	W 27-8	6,247	T: E Davies 2, Finnan, B Hartley, Rogers, G: E Davies 5, Rogers
Apr 18	WARRINGTON	L 11-33	8,113	T: Birkin, B Hartley, Rogers, G: Rogers
Apr 23	Widnes	L 8-11	5,588	T: Halton, Hindle, G: Rogers
Jun 15	Barrow (FoS-SF)*	L 10-25	–	T: Baines, E Davies, G: E Davies 2

* At Blackpool

1953-1954

	Opponent	Result	Attendance	Scorers
Aug 15	Warrington	L 4-17	12,290	G: E Davies, Whalley
Aug 22	WAKEFIELD TRINITY	L 3-13	3,189	T: Baines
Aug 29	Bramley	L 13-15	2,155	T: Birkin, E Davies, Finnan, G: Rogers 2
Sep 2	YORK	L 15-19	3,392	T: E Davies 2, B Hartley 2, Marston
Sep 5	WIGAN (LC-1)	W 12-7	10,000	T: E Davies, Finnan, G: E Davies 3
Sep 7	Wigan (LC-1)	L 2-28	21,489	G: E Davies
Sep 12	HUNSLET	W 13-7	5,552	T: Danby, E Davies, B Hartley, G: E Davies 2
Sep 19	York	L 20-22	5,685	T: Finnan 2, E Davies, B Hartley, G: E Davies 4

Salford RL Match Results

1953-1954 *continued*

	Opponent	Result	Attendance	Scorers
Sep 26	WORKINGTON TOWN	W 14-9	7,944	T: Fairhurst, Finnan, G: E Davies 3, Rogers
Oct 3	Barrow	L 11-17	9,944	T: Danby, E Davies, Marston, G: E Davies
Oct 10	Wakefield Trinity	L 6-34	5,573	T: B Hartley, F Smith
Oct 17	OLDHAM	D 11-11	12,114	T: Baines, G: E Davies 3, Rogers
Oct 24	Widnes	L 0-18	4,530	
Oct 31	BELLE VUE RANGERS	W 22-0	4,637	T: Baines 2, B Hartley 2, E Davies, Hainsworth, G: E Davies, Rogers
Nov 7	Keighley	W 13-4	2,009	T: Easterbrook 2, E Davies, G: E Davies 2
Nov 14	KEIGHLEY	W 18-9	3,419	T: Finnan 2, B Hartley, F Smith, G: E Davies 2, Rogers
Nov 21	WARRINGTON	L 8-10	7,252	T: Baines, E Davies, G: Rogers
Nov 28	Hunslet	L 6-19	5,800	T: Finnan, F Smith
Dec 5	BRAMLEY	W 52-13	3,623	T: B Hartley 4, Rogers 2, Danby, E Davies, Finnan, Keavney, Marston, F Smith, G: E Davies 7, F Smith
Dec 12	Rochdale Hornets	L 2-27	10,848	G: F Smith
Dec 19	ST HELENS	L 7-11	7,158	T: B Hartley, G: Keavney, F Smith
Dec 25	Wigan	L 0-5	13,249	
Dec 26	LIVERPOOL CITY	W 13-0	3,244	T: Finnan 2, B Hartley, G: F Smith 2
Jan 9	Oldham	D 2-2	7,902	G: E Davies
Jan 16	Belle Vue Rangers	L 4-6	2,603	G: E Davies 2
Jan 23	WHITEHAVEN	W 3-2	4,962	T: Finnan
Jan 30	St Helens	L 0-29	10,321	
Feb 17	HUNSLET (RLC-1)	L 3-18	3,639	T: Danby
Feb 20	BARROW	W 8-0	5,308	T: Fairhurst, Farrington, G: D Moses
Feb 22	Hunslet (RLC-1)	L 5-20	5,216	T: Danby, G: Rogers
Mar 6	Liverpool City	L 0-10	645	
Mar 13	Leigh	L 3-22	4,430	T: Cartwright
Mar 30	ROCHDALE HORNETS	W 9-3	6,233	T: Finnan, Grainger, Harrison
Apr 3	Workington Town	L 5-10	5,520	T: D Moses, G: E Davies
Apr 10	WIDNES	W 20-3	4,482	T: Alder, Cartwright, D Moses, F Smith, G: E Davies 3, Cartwright
Apr 16	Whitehaven	L 8-15	5,177	T: Alder, F Smith, G: Cartwright

Salford RL Match Results

1953-1954 *continued*

	Opponent	Result	Attendance	Scorers
Apr 17	Swinton	W 13-2	7,000	T: Cartwright, Grainger, Roughley, G: Cartwright, E Davies
Apr 19	WIGAN	L 10-14	9,717	T: Baines, Roughley, G: Baron, E Davies
Apr 28	LEIGH	L 8-34	4,819	T: E Davies, Lowe, G: E Davies
May 1	SWINTON	W 26-6	2,000	T: Lowe 3, Baines, Grainger, Roughley, G: Whalley 4

1954-1955

	Opponent	Result	Attendance	Scorers
Aug 7	SWINTON (RRC)	L 3-12	4,500	T: Lowe
Aug 14	BLACKPOOL BOROUGH	W 40-3	4,000	T: B Hartley 4, Baines, E Davies, Grainger, Roughley, G: E Davies 8
Aug 17	Dewsbury	W 7-0	395	T: Baines, G: Rogers 2
Aug 21	Castleford	L 0-19	2,321	
Aug 25	OLDHAM	W 11-2	7,903	T: Baines, G: E Davies 4
Aug 28	BARROW	L 6-16	6,340	G: E Davies 3
Sep 4	Rochdale Hornets	D 5-5	8,974	T: Baines, G: E Davies
Sep 11	Liverpool City (LC-1)	L 3-6	2,500	T: B Hartley
Sep 25	CASTLEFORD	W 23-0	2,903	T: Harrison 2, B Hartley 2, Baron, Rogers, Roughley, G: E Davies
Oct 2	DEWSBURY	W 25-12	4,770	T: B Hartley 3, Grainger, Roughley, G: E Davies 4, Rogers
Oct 9	Featherstone Rovers	L 5-32	4,500	T: Baines, G: Rogers
Oct 16	ST HELENS	L 2-19	7,564	G: E Davies
Oct 23	Workington Town	L 0-7	3,550	
Oct 30	FEATHERSTONE ROVERS	W 13-6	2,593	T: Cartwright, Farrington, Roughley, G: Rogers 2
Nov 6	Warrington	L 15-18	9,398	T: Roughley 2, D Moses, G: Rogers 3
Nov 13	ROCHDALE HORNETS*	A 0-10	2,482	
Nov 20	Liverpool City	L 5-18	1,234	T: Baines, G: E Davies
Nov 27	LEIGH	L 8-11	5,700	T: Dodd, Fairhurst, G: Whalley
Dec 11	WIDNES	L 3-10	3,200	T: Farrington
Dec 25	Wigan	L 7-50	11,085	T: Rogers, G: E Davies 2
Dec 27	WHITEHAVEN	D 6-6	2,967	T: Farrington, G Jones
Dec 28	Oldham	L 0-27	15,485	
Jan 1	Swinton	L 4-6	5,300	G: E Davies 2
Jan 8	WORKINGTON TOWN	L 0-36	1,684	

Salford RL Match Results

1954-1955 *continued*

	Opponent	Result	Attendance	Scorers
Jan 29	BELLE VUE RANGERS	W 10-7	3,684	T: Farrington, D Moses, G: E Davies 2
Feb 5	LIVERPOOL CITY	D 7-7	4,400	T: Lambert, G: Keavney 2
Feb 12	CASTLEFORD (RLC-1)	W 13-5	5,296	T: B Hartley 2, Lambert, G: Keavney 2
Mar 5	BARROW (RLC-2)	L 0-13	8,373	
Mar 12	Hull Kingston Rovers	L 3-8	2,294	T: G Jones
Mar 26	St Helens	L 8-16	4,279	T: G Jones, Lambert, G: F Smith
Mar 30	Whitehaven	L 5-11	4,052	T: Baines, G: F Smith
Apr 2	WARRINGTON	L 10-26	6,015	T: Lambert, G Wilson, G: F Smith 2
Apr 8	Leigh	L 0-26	5,788	
Apr 9	SWINTON	L 0-22	6,840	
Apr 11	WIGAN	L 2-24	6,966	G: Keavney
Apr 13	Blackpool Borough	L 9-11	1,615	T: Cartwright, G: Keavney 2, G Wilson
Apr 16	Widnes	L 5-10	3,321	T: E Davies, G: Keavney
Apr 18	Belle Vue Rangers	L 7-13	695	T: G Wilson, G: E Davies, G Wilson
Apr 23	ROCHDALE HORNETS	L 7-10	3,686	T: Baines, G: Keavney 2
Apr 25	Barrow	L 15-19	4,625	T: G Jones 3, G: B Keavney 3
Apr 27	HULL KINGSTON ROVERS	L 6-14	1,277	T: Dodd, Lambert

* Abandoned 53 mins (bad light due to heavy rainfall)

1955-1956

	Opponent	Result	Attendance	Scorers
Aug 13	Swinton (RRC)	W 10-8	4,000	T: Lambert, Marston, G: Bradbourne, Rogers
Aug 20	DONCASTER	W 20-18	4,257	T: Duffy, Fairhurst, Hancock, Todd, G: Hancock 4
Aug 22	Workington Town	L 17-31	5,400	T: Fairhurst 2, G Jones, G: Keavney 3, Dodd
Aug 27	WIDNES (LC-1)	L 8-23	5,000	T: B Hartley, G Jones, G: Hancock
Aug 31	ST HELENS	W 11-10	6,946	T: Duffy, G: Keavney 4
Sep 3	Keighley	L 11-13	2,798	T: Cheshire, G: Keavney 4
Sep 8	Barrow	L 13-30	6,174	T: Chadderton, Fairhurst, Lomas, G: Keavney 2
Sep 10	HULL KINGSTON ROVERS	L 10-17	3,764	T: Dodd, Marston, G: Keavney 2
Sep 17	Liverpool City	W 20-9	1,349	T: G Jones 2, Dodd, Marston, G: Hancock 3, Keavney

Salford RL Match Results

1955-1956 *continued*

	Opponent	Result	Attendance	Scorers
Sep 24	KEIGHLEY	L 8-10	3,919	G: Keavney 4
Oct 1	Doncaster	D 13-13	1,400	T: Dodd, Duffy, Keavney, G: Hancock 2
Oct 8	Blackpool Borough	W 15-13	1,776	T: Dodd, G Jones, Ryan, G: Hancock 3
Oct 15	WHITEHAVEN	W 16-6	3,370	T: Dodd 2, G Jones, Keavney, G: Hancock 2
Oct 22	Hull Kingston Rovers	L 9-13	3,000	T: Dodd 2, Cheshire
Oct 29	LEIGH	L 12-21	5,898	T: Baines, Cheshire, Duffy, G Jones
Nov 5	Whitehaven	W 6-2	2,899	T: Baines, Chadderton
Nov 12	DEWSBURY	W 24-5	3,543	T: Dodd 3, Cheshire, Duffy, Hancock, G: Keavney 2, Brereton
Nov 26	NEW ZEALAND (Tour)	L 5-21	4,000	T: Grainger, G: Keavney
Dec 3	Widnes	L 7-8	3,043	T: Dodd, G: Keavney, D Moses
Dec 10	OLDHAM	L 0-24	4,827	
Dec 17	Oldham	L 14-27	9,591	T: Dodd 2, Cheshire, Parr, G: Keavney
Dec 24	WARRINGTON	L 0-24	4,741	
Dec 26	WIGAN	L 6-21	4,198	T: Cheshire, B Hartley
Dec 27	Rochdale Hornets	L 4-31	3,118	G: F Smith 2
Jan 2	Swinton	W 16-11	7,500	T: Chadderton, D Moses, G: F Smith 5
Jan 7	St Helens	L 2-48	5,617	G: F Smith
Jan 14	BLACKPOOL BOROUGH	L 12-20	2,570	T: Cheshire, Parr, G: F Smith 2, D Moses
Jan 21	WORKINGTON TOWN*	W 11-0	1,789	T: G Jones, Marston, F Smith, G: F Smith
Jan 28	Wigan (F)	L 22-28	6,446	T: Baines, Farrington, Fieldhouse, D Moses, G: F Smith 5
Feb 11	Workington Town (RLC-1)	L 0-16	7,032	
Feb 18	Leigh	L 8-14	5,986	T: Farrington, G Jones, G: Duffy
Feb 25	LIVERPOOL CITY	L 10-12	2,848	T: Hanley, G Jones, G: F Smith 2
Mar 17	Warrington	L 10-41	10,599	T: Dodd, Hanley, G: F Smith 2
Mar 24	Dewsbury	W 15-10	993	T: Keavney 2, Baines, G: F Smith 3
Mar 31	SWINTON	W 23-9	8,025	T: G Jones 2, Council, Duffy, Ryan, G: Dodd 3, F Smith
Apr 2	Wigan	L 7-39	12,990	T: Dodd, G: Dodd 2

Salford RL Match Results

1955-1956 *continued*

	Opponent	Result	Attendance	Scorers
Apr 11	ROCHDALE HORNETS	W 13-0	3,060	T: Caudwell 2, Farrington, G: Dodd 2
Apr 14	WIDNES	W 18-12	4,028	T: Baines, Caudwell, Cheshire, Duffy, G: Dodd 3
Apr 17	BARROW	L 10-13	2,967	T: Cheshire, Keavney, G: Dodd 2

* Abandoned 76 min (snowstorm) – result stands

1956-1957

	Opponent	Result	Attendance	Scorers
Aug 11	SWINTON (RRC)	L 4-15	5,000	G: Hancock 2
Aug 18	Dewsbury	W 13-2	811	T: Dodd, G Jones, Walker, G: Keavney 2
Aug 22	WARRINGTON	L 11-12	7,233	T: Ayles, G: Keavney 4
Aug 25	BLACKPOOL BOROUGH	L 9-12	3,299	T: Walker, G: Keavney 3
Aug 29	St Helens	L 0-40	12,600	
Sep 1	WORKINGTON TOWN (LC-1)	W 17-9	4,791	T: Alder 2, Fieldhouse, G: Keavney 3, F Smith
Sep 8	CASTLEFORD	W 22-15	4,498	T: Dodd, Keavney, Lomas, Parr, G: F Smith 5
Sep 11	OLDHAM (LC-2)	L 0-31	13,589	
Sep 15	Halifax	L 13-41	9,055	T: Ayles, F Smith, Walker, G: F Smith 2
Sep 22	Warrington	W 15-11	8,945	T: Boardman, G: F Smith 6
Sep 29	DEWSBURY	W 25-8	3,307	T: G Jones 2, Cheshire, Dodd, Duffy, Keavney, Stoddart, G: F Smith 2
Oct 6	Workington Town	L 4-7	3,783	G: F Smith 2
Oct 13	ST HELENS	L 11-27	8,410	T: Duffy, G: F Smith 4
Oct 20	Barrow	L 5-30	5,273	T: Dignum, G: Preece
Oct 27	HULL KINGSTON ROVERS	W 34-7	3,700	T: Chadderton 3, B Hartley 2, Keavney 2, Preece, G: Keavney 4, D Moses
Nov 3	Liverpool City	W 19-6	1,168	T: Preece 2, Cheshire, G: Keavney 5
Nov 10	HALIFAX	L 5-6	5,496	T: Council, G: Keavney
Nov 17	Batley	W 29-23	3,000	T: Keavney 2, Duffy, B Hartley, Preece, G: Walker 4, Keavney 3
Nov 24	BARROW	W 9-8	5,439	T: Chadderton, G: Keavney 3
Dec 1	Widnes	L 7-17	2,867	T: Preece, G: Keavney 2

Salford RL Match Results

1956-1957 *continued*

	Opponent	Result	Attendance	Scorers
Dec 8	DONCASTER	W 22-2	3,677	T: Baines 3, Chadderton, Council, B Hartley, G: Keavney 2
Dec 25	Wigan	L 10-13	6,692	T: Keavney, Walker, G: Keavney 2
Dec 29	LEIGH	W 32-8	6,863	T: Cheshire 2, G Jones 2, Garlick, Keavney, G: Keavney 7
Jan 1	SWINTON	L 7-16	7,988	T: G Jones, G: Keavney 2
Jan 5	Leigh	L 7-19	3,597	T: G Jones, G: Keavney 2
Jan 12	Oldham	L 3-17	12,038	T: Ayles
Jan 19	WORKINGTON TOWN	W 13-5	3,707	T: Duffy, G Jones, Preece, G: Walker 2
Jan 26	Hull Kingston Rovers	D 4-4	3,814	G: Walker 2
Feb 2	OLDHAM	L 3-27	12,222	T: Garlick
Feb 9	Hull Kingston Rovers (RLC-1)	W 10-2	4,653	T: B Hartley, G Jones, G: Keavney 2
Feb 16	Rochdale Hornets	L 0-3	2,917	
Feb 23	HUDDERSFIELD (RLC-2)	L 2-6	7,762	G: F Smith
Mar 2	Castleford	D 9-9	2,688	T: Baines, G: F Smith 3
Mar 9	BATLEY	W 16-5	3,349	T: A Gregory, Keavney, G: F Smith 5
Mar 16	WIDNES	W 16-0	4,123	T: Duffy, B Hartley, Keavney, Stoddart, G: F Smith 2
Mar 23	WHITEHAVEN	W 22-14	5,037	T: Baines, A Gregory, G Jones, Keavney, G: F Smith 5
Mar 30	Doncaster	W 22-9	728	T: Cheshire, Duffy, A Gregory, G Jones, G: F Smith 4, Keavney
Apr 6	Whitehaven	L 5-12	4,700	T: G Jones, G: Keavney
Apr 13	LIVERPOOL CITY	W 25-7	3,983	T: Baines 2, Council, Duffy, G Jones, G: Keavney 5
Apr 19	Blackpool Borough	L 11-22	3,196	T: Keavney 2, B Hartley, G: Keavney
Apr 20	Swinton	W 35-19	7,000	T: B Hartley 3, Baines 2, Cheshire, Duffy, Keavney, Preece, G: Keavney 4
Apr 22	WIGAN	W 15-10	8,412	T: Cheshire, B Hartley, Preece, G: Keavney 2, Preece
Apr 27	ROCHDALE HORNETS	W 10-9	5,401	T: Cheshire, Keavney, G: Keavney 2

Salford RL Match Results

1957-1958

	Opponent	Result	Attendance	Scorers
Aug 10	Swinton (RRC)	L 6-25	6,000	G: McArthur 3
Aug 17	Castleford	L 8-21	3,047	T: G Jones, Walker, G: McArthur
Aug 21	DEWSBURY	W 40-9	4,658	T: Duffy 2, A Gregory 2, Preece 2, Keavney, McArthur, G: McArthur 7, F Smith
Aug 24	WIDNES	L 5-16	5,375	T: Walker, G: McArthur
Aug 27	Dewsbury	L 5-8	1,399	T: Walker, G: McArthur
Aug 31	ROCHDALE HORNETS (LC-1)	L 6-12	10,000	G: McArthur 3
Sep 4	ROCHDALE HORNETS	W 15-4	4,063	T: Keavney, Preece, Walker, G: McArthur 3
Sep 7	Whitehaven	L 13-16	4,146	T: Walker 2, Duffy, G: McArthur 2
Sep 14	BATLEY	W 17-5	3,728	T: Preece 2, Duffy, Keavney, Walker, G: McArthur
Sep 21	Doncaster	W 10-0	631	T: McArthur 2, G: McArthur 2
Sep 28	LIVERPOOL CITY	W 16-3	2,070	T: Cheshire, B Hartley, McArthur, Walker, G: McArthur 2
Oct 5	Leeds	D 25-25	12,477	T: McArthur 2, Alder, Keavney, Stott, G: McArthur 5
Oct 12	WARRINGTON	W 10-8	7,445	T: Cheshire, McArthur, G: Keavney, McArthur
Oct 19	Leigh	L 7-12	4,312	T: McArthur, G: McArthur 2
Oct 26	HULL KINGSTON ROVERS	W 24-10	4,444	T: McArthur 2, Walker 2, D Moses, Preece, G: McArthur 3
Nov 2	Liverpool City	W 24-19	998	T: G Jones 2, Cheshire, Stott, G: McArthur 6
Nov 9	OLDHAM	L 5-14	15,207	T: G Jones, G: McArthur
Nov 16	Widnes	L 3-12	4,900	T: B Hartley
Nov 23	BARROW	W 18-15	6,409	T: McArthur 2, Hanley, G Jones, G: Lowdon 2, McArthur
Nov 30	Oldham	L 12-34	14,652	T: McArthur 2, G: Lowdon 2, McArthur
Dec 7	DONCASTER	W 31-4	3,010	T: Lowdon 2, McArthur 2, Council, G Jones, Preece, G: McArthur 4, Lowdon
Dec 14	Warrington	L 16-20	5,697	T: G Jones 2, G: Lowdon 3, McArthur 2

Salford RL Match Results

1957-1958 *continued*

	Opponent	Result	Attendance	Scorers
Dec 21	BLACKPOOL BOROUGH	W 10-9	4,044	T: G Jones, Lowdon, G: McArthur 2
Dec 25	WIGAN	L 7-14	6,737	T: Ayles, G: Lowdon, McArthur
Dec 26	Rochdale Hornets	W 16-10	6,361	T: Lowdon 2, Hancock, McArthur, G: McArthur 2
Dec 28	ST HELENS	W 12-7	13,039	T: G Jones, McArthur, G: McArthur 2, Lowdon
Jan 1	Swinton	W 7-6	8,000	T: McArthur, G: McArthur 2
Jan 4	Barrow	L 12-22	6,227	T: Keavney, McArthur, G: McArthur 2, Lowdon
Jan 11	CASTLEFORD	W 8-2	4,352	T: G Jones, McArthur, G: Lowdon
Feb 1	WHITEHAVEN	W 18-3	4,749	T: G Jones 2, A Gregory, Lowdon, G: McArthur 3
Feb 11	Keighley (RLC-1)	L 6-12	3,192	T: Hanley, B Hartley
Feb 15	Blackpool Borough	W 14-5	726	T: A Gregory, G Jones, G: McArthur 3, Lowdon
Feb 22	LEIGH	L 12-24	4,485	T: Preece 2, G: Lowdon 3
Mar 15	Batley	L 10-12	3,000	T: Lowdon, McArthur, G: Lowdon, McArthur
Mar 22	Hull Kingston Rovers	L 2-25	4,228	G: McArthur
Mar 31	WORKINGTON TOWN	L 7-15	2,850	T: Walker, G: Lowdon 2
Apr 4	Workington Town	L 2-32	6,182	G: Lowdon
Apr 5	SWINTON	L 5-10	4,825	T: A Gregory, G: McArthur
Apr 7	LEEDS	W 15-7	5,117	T: A Gregory 2, Keavney, G: McArthur 3
Apr 12	Wigan	L 2-42	14,095	G: McArthur
Apr 14	St Helens	L 8-42	14,748	T: Chadderton, Keavney, G: Garlick

1958-1959

	Opponent	Result	Attendance	Scorers
Aug 9	SWINTON (RRC)	L 18-23	6,471	T: G Jones 2, B Hartley, Lowdon, G: Lowdon 2, Keavney
Aug 16	BRADFORD NORTHERN	L 13-15	5,473	T: Cheshire 2, H Gregory, G: Lowdon, McArthur
Aug 23	Workington Town	L 12-19	5,792	T: McArthur 2, G: Lowdon 2, McArthur
Aug 27	BLACKPOOL BOROUGH	W 44-5	4,284	T: G Jones 2, McArthur 2, Cheshire, A Gregory, H Gregory, B Hartley, Lowdon, Preece, G: McArthur 7

Salford RL Match Results

1958-1959 continued

Date	Opponent	Result	Attendance	Scorers
Aug 30	Widnes (LC-1)	L 13-44	6,897	T: Alder, B Hartley, G Jones, G: McArthur 2
Sep 6	Rochdale Hornets	W 26-16	5,363	T: McArthur 2, Council, B Hartley, G Jones, Lowdon, G: McArthur 3, Lowdon
Sep 13	YORK	L 21-37	4,366	T: H Gregory 4, G Jones, G: McArthur 3
Sep 20	Hull Kingston Rovers	W 21-13	4,600	T: B Hartley, Lowdon, McArthur, G: Lowdon 6
Sep 27	WARRINGTON	L 16-22	6,363	T: H Hartley, G Jones, Lowdon, Preece, G: Lowdon, F Smith
Oct 4	HUDDERSFIELD	W 26-6	4,552	T: G Jones 2, Baines, Cheshire, H Gregory, B Hartley, G: Lowdon 4
Oct 11	Widnes	L 10-35	5,964	T: Lowdon 2, G: Lowdon 2
Oct 25	Whitehaven	L 10-19	4,433	T: G Jones, Lowdon, G: Lowdon 2
Nov 1	ST HELENS	L 12-28	9,674	T: Baines, H Gregory, G: Lowdon 3
Nov 5	LEEDS*	L 17-22	8,693	T: Baines, Cheshire, Duffy, G: Lowdon 4
Nov 8	Leigh	W 20-15	4,649	T: Cheshire, Lowdon, Preece, Walker, G: Lowdon 4
Nov 15	OLDHAM	W 14-9	5,481	T: McGuinness, Preece, G: Lowdon 4
Nov 29	LIVERPOOL CITY	W 8-6	1,878	T: A Gregory, Walker, G: Lowdon
Dec 6	Barrow	L 8-28	3,269	T: H Gregory, G Jones, G: Lowdon
Dec 13	LEIGH	L 12-16	3,537	T: Lowdon, Walker, G: Lowdon 3
Dec 20	Keighley	L 16-20	3,428	T: G Jones 2, H Gregory, Preece, G: Lowdon 2
Dec 25	Wigan	L 14-31	17,606	T: B Hartley, Lowdon, G: Lowdon 4
Dec 26	WHITEHAVEN	W 19-15	2,839	T: Preece 2, Baines, A Gregory, G Jones, G: Lowdon 2
Dec 27	BARROW	W 19-10	3,663	T: Baines 2, A Gregory, Gregory, Walker, G: Lowdon 2
Jan 1	SWINTON**	L 0-3	7,509	
Jan 3	Bradford Northern	W 15-9	2,764	T: Cheshire, Duffy, H Gregory, G: F Smith 3

Salford RL Match Results

1958-1959 *continued*

	Opponent	Result	Attendance	Scorers
Jan 31	HULL KINGSTON ROVERS	W 29-7	3,126	T: Lowdon 2, Parsons, Preece, D Smith, F Smith, Walker, G: F Smith 4
Feb 7	Huddersfield	L 14-17	2,823	T: G Jones 2, Stott, Walker, G: Lowdon
Feb 14	ROCHDALE HORNETS	W 16-4	3,781	T: Council, G Jones, G: Lowdon 5
Feb 21	BARROW (RLC-1)	W 15-0	4,370	T: A Gregory, Preece, Walker, G: Lowdon 3
Feb 28	Liverpool City	W 18-7	649	T: H Gregory, Lowdon, Preece, Walker, G: Lowdon 3
Mar 7	HUDDERSFIELD (RLC-2)	W 15-2	9,749	T: Baines, Cheshire, Lowdon, G: Lowdon 3
Mar 14	KEIGHLEY	W 29-9	3,564	T: Baines 2, Lowdon 2, Duffy, Preece, Stott, G: Lowdon 4
Mar 16	St Helens	L 4-44	13,599	G: Lowdon 2
Mar 21	Leigh (RLC-3)	D 6-6	16,216	G: Lowdon 3
Mar 25	LEIGH (RLC-3 Replay)	L 4-6	16,656	G: Lowdon 2
Mar 27	Blackpool Borough	L 10-11	1,412	T: Bettinson, Cheshire, G: Lowdon 2
Mar 28	Swinton	D 11-11	7,000	T: Lowdon, G: Lowdon 4
Mar 30	WIGAN	L 15-38	13,616	T: Dodd, D Smith, Stott, G: F Smith 3
Apr 4	Warrington	L 21-27	5,839	T: Lowdon 3, Council, F Smith, G: Lowdon 2, F Smith
Apr 7	Oldham	L 10-25	8,177	T: Bettinson, Preece, G: Lowdon 2
Apr 11	WORKINGTON TOWN	W 19-18	1,806	T: Bettinson 2, Cheshire, A Gregory, G Jones, G: Lowdon 2
Apr 15	WIDNES	L 5-20	3,110	T: Lowdon, G: Lowdon
Apr 18	Leeds	W 19-18	8,512	T: Duffy 2, Lowdon 2, A Gregory, G: Lowdon 2
Apr 25	York	L 10-25	2,352	T: Baines, G Jones, G: Lowdon 2

* Home match at Old Trafford, Manchester, under floodlight
** Abandoned 73 min – result stands

Above: 1959-60. Loose-forward Hugh Duffy (light jersey) gets to grips with a Rochdale Hornets player whilst colleague John Cheshire (poised behind him) prepares to give assistance.

Above: 1961-62. Back: H Council, J Cheshire, H Duffy, B Hartley, J Hancock, G Rees, G Harwood. Front: G Jones, J Brennan, T Dunn, L Bettinson, K Brunt, A Gregory.

Above: 1963-64. Back: T Dunn, L Bettinson, A Dorning, J Hindley, J Hancock, A Halsall, T Wilson, E McAlone. Front: B Hutson, R Pearce, M Clark, J Brennan, G Smart.

Above: 1964-65. Action stations for Salford's defence during a Challenge Cup tie at Warrington. The Salford players, left to right, are Paul Murphy, Jackie Brennan, Ernie Critchley (behind Brennan) and Terry Wilson.

Above: 1967-68. Back: A Breen, D Hill, C Bott, S Whitehead, T Ogden, M Kelly, L Bettinson, K Gwilliam. Front: P Smethurst, B Prosser, A McInnes, C Hesketh, J Brennan, D Watkins, B Burdell.

Above left: 1966-67. Salford showed dramatic signs of improvement during February 1967 through winning at Wigan and St Helens in the opening rounds of the Challenge Cup. However, they came unstuck at Dewsbury in the quarter final losing 9-7 despite this opening try from Les Bettinson who is supported by prop Terry Ogden.

Above right: 1968-69. Wembley at last after a thirty-year absence as Salford's international winger Bill Burgess takes on the Castleford defence.

Above: 1969-70. Back: C Evans (coach), C Bott, M Richards, M Henighan, K Roberts, C Dixon, J Egan, P Smethurst, C Hesketh, J Brennan, S Whitehead, GB Snape (chairman). Front: P Crank, M Taylor, M Coulman, P Charlton, D Watkins, B Prosser, D Hill, P Jackson.

Above: 1969-70. Colin Dixon attempts to halt an attack in a Rugby League Challenge Cup tie at Castleford. The supporting player is Bob Prosser.

Above left: 1972-73. Silverware at last as David Watkins shows off the Lancashire Cup after defeating Swinton in the final. It was the first major trophy won by Salford since the 1930s.

Above right: 1972-73. The Player's No.6 Trophy final was less fruitful, losing to Leeds at Fartown, Huddersfield. Salford's Bill Kirkbride and Ken Gill (6) are seen making the tackle.

Above: 1973-74. The Championship Trophy is regained after a gap of 35 years. Back: M Coulman, E Prescott, A Grice, G McKay, L Bettinson (coach), C Dixon, J Knighton, D Davies, K Fielding, M Richards, C Evans (former coach). Front: P Walker, K Gill, P Charlton, C Hesketh, GB Snape (chairman), D Watkins, JW Hammond (president), P Banner, J Taylor.

Above left: 1974-75. A muddied Chris Hesketh lifts the BBC2 Floodlit Trophy after Salford had defeated Warrington at Wilderspool in the replayed final.

Above right: 1975-76. The Premiership Trophy final at Swinton. David Watkins kicks for touch as Keith Fielding looks on. Salford eventually lost 15-2 to St Helens.

Above: 1975-76. Salford's second Championship success in three seasons. Back: M Coulman, J Corcoran, B Sheffield, C Dixon, S Turnbull, E Prescott, A Grice, J Knighton, F Stead, P Frodsham, M Richards. Front: D Watkins, J Butler, S Nash, C Hesketh, GB Snape (chairman), L Bettinson (coach), G Graham, K Fielding, D Raistrick.

Above: 1979-80. Salford line-up in red, amber and black hoops for the Centenary clash with Widnes, celebrating 100 years since the club was renamed as Salford in 1879. Back: M Coulman, S Turnbull, S Williams, C Dixon, C McGreal, E Prescott, D Stephenson, F Wilson, M Richards. Front: D Harris, K Gill, K Fielding, P O'Neill, C Whitfield, S Rule.

Above: 1982-83. Back: M Coulman, M Yates, T Stockley, S Turnbull, G Nicholls, R Smith, H Henney, D Major, M Richards. Front: M Aspey, G Byrne, P O'Neill, S Nash, K Fielding, D Driver.

Above: 1987-88. Salford's forwards attack the Wigan line as Mick Worrall (right) transfers the ball to Steve Herbert supported by David Major (centre).

Above: 1987-88. Back: T Grainey (coach), G Austin, G Jack, S Gibson, M Worrall, I Blease, S Herbert, T O'Shea, K Ashcroft (team manager). Front: D Major, K Bentley, J Fazackerley, M Moran, D Bloor, D Cairns, D Bullough, P Glynn, M McTigue.

Salford RL Match Results

1959-1960

	Opponent	Result	Attendance	Scorers
Aug 8	Swinton (RRC)	L 5-32	5,000	T: Baines, G: Preece
Aug 15	Leigh	L 12-25	6,866	T: Council, Lowdon, G: Lowdon 3
Aug 19	WHITEHAVEN	W 23-14	5,383	T: Duffy 2, G Jones 2, Lowdon, G: Lowdon 4
Aug 22	OLDHAM	D 12-12	8,774	T: G Jones 2, G: Lowdon 3
Aug 29	LIVERPOOL CITY (LC-1)	W 45-8	4,153	T: Brennan 2, G Jones 2, Lowdon 2, Adamson, Banks, Duffy, G: Lowdon 9
Sep 2	BATLEY	W 34-2	4,957	T: E Jones 2, Preece 2, Brennan, Cheshire, Duffy, A Gregory, G: Lowdon 5
Sep 5	KEIGHLEY	W 50-14	5,388	T: Preece 3, D Smith 2, Council, Duffy, G Jones, Lowdon, McGuinness, G: Lowdon 9, Banks
Sep 7	Wigan (LC-2)	L 15-39	19,963	T: Duffy, H Gregory, E Jones, G: Lowdon 3
Sep 12	Doncaster	W 26-11	675	T: Lowdon 3, Baines, Duffy, G Jones, G: Lowdon 4
Sep 19	BRAMLEY	W 34-14	4,041	T: Lowdon 2, McGuinness 2, Cheshire, Duffy, G Jones, Preece, G: Lowdon 5
Sep 26	AUSTRALIA (Tour)	L 20-22	11,088	T: Brennan, G Jones, Lowdon, Preece, G: Lowdon 4
Oct 3	St Helens	L 11-40	15,564	T: Duffy, G Jones, Parsons, G: Preece
Oct 10	WARRINGTON	L 7-15	7,467	T: Brennan, G: Banks, Preece
Oct 17	Liverpool City	W 18-6	600	T: Cheshire, E Jones, G Jones, Parsons, G: Preece 3
Oct 24	DEWSBURY	W 26-0	2,017	T: Cheshire 2, Duffy, A Gregory E Jones, G Jones, G: Donoghue 3, Banks
Oct 31	Keighley	L 7-36	5,177	T: Adamson, G: Brennan, Preece
Nov 7	CASTLEFORD	W 25-12	2,671	T: Adamson, Banks, Brennan, Cheshire, Preece, G: Walker 5
Nov 14	Whitehaven	L 10-34	2,868	T: Brennan, Walker, G: Banks, Walker
Nov 21	Batley	L 13-23	2,300	T: Brennan 2, Banks, G: Walker 2

Salford RL Match Results

1959-1960 *continued*

	Opponent	Result	Attendance	Scorers
Nov 28	BARROW	W 13-5	3,211	T: G Jones, G: Walker 4, Banks
Dec 5	Castleford	W 23-10	1,750	T: Alder 2, G Jones 2, Cheshire, G: Cheshire 3, Preece
Dec 12	WIDNES	W 23-6	1,621	T: Walker 2, Banks, Cheshire, Duffy, G: Cheshire 4
Dec 19	Barrow	W 21-6	1,960	T: G Jones 3, Preece, Walker, G: Cheshire 3
Dec 26	Rochdale Hornets	W 8-7	3,528	G: Cheshire 4
Dec 28	WIGAN	L 13-20	8,337	T: Stott, G: Cheshire 5
Jan 1	Swinton	L 5-12	11,338	T: Brennan, G: Cheshire
Jan 2	LEIGH	L 10-30	5,492	T: Preece, Walker, G: Cheshire 2
Jan 9	Dewsbury	W 14-13	1,000	T: Baines, A Gregory, G Jones, Walker, G: Walker
Jan 16	BLACKPOOL BOROUGH	W 26-5	2,431	T: Brennan 2, A Gregory, Walker, G: Cheshire 7
Jan 30	ST HELENS	D 2-2	5,231	G: Cheshire
Feb 6	Oldham	L 15-20	10,591	T: Duffy 2, G Jones, G: Cheshire 3
Feb 13	HALIFAX (RLC-1)	L 0-5	6,711	
Feb 20	Bramley	L 5-7	1,650	T: Preece, G: Cheshire
Feb 27	Workington Town	L 8-15	1,854	T: Duffy, G Jones, G: Cheshire
Mar 5	LIVERPOOL CITY	W 19-3	2,743	T: Duffy 2, E Jones, G Jones, Preece, G: Cheshire 2
Mar 12	Warrington	L 5-37	7,640	T: Brennan, G: Cheshire
Mar 19	WORKINGTON TOWN	W 31-5	1,692	T: Preece 2, Brennan, Council, Duffy, A Gregory, Stott, G: Cheshire 5
Apr 2	ROCHDALE HORNETS	W 13-5	3,017	T: Preece, G: Cheshire 5
Apr 15	Blackpool Borough	L 8-17	2,150	T: Bettinson, A Gregory, G: Cheshire
Apr 16	SWINTON	L 5-25	6,562	T: A Gregory, G: Cheshire
Apr 18	Wigan	L 13-38	15,955	T: G Jones 2, Bettinson, G: Cheshire 2
Apr 23	Widnes	L 13-32	3,559	T: Baines, Bettinson, G Jones, G: Cheshire 2
Apr 30	DONCASTER	W 28-5	2,473	T: Bettinson 2, Dunn, B Hartley, G Jones, Preece, G: Cheshire 5

Salford RL Match Results

1960-1961

Date	Opponent	Result	Attendance	Scorers
Aug 6	SWINTON (RRC)	L 9-22	3,000	T: Dunn, G: Cheshire 3
Aug 13	LEIGH	L 4-17	10,759	G: Cheshire 2
Aug 16	Doncaster	W 20-6	850	T: Dunn 2, G Jones 2, Alder, Walker, G: Cheshire
Aug 20	Castleford	W 16-14	3,550	T: B Hartley 2, Cheshire, Council, G: Cheshire 2
Aug 24	BARROW	W 9-0	1,329	T: Lendill, G: Cheshire 3
Aug 31	ROCHDALE HORNETS (LC-1)	W 11-3	4,000	T: Council, Duffy, Walker, G: Cheshire
Sep 3	YORK	W 18-15	3,197	T: Dunn 2, Duffy, Lendill, G: Cheshire 3
Sep 7	SWINTON (LC-2)	L 6-9	6,000	G: Cheshire 3
Sep 10	Liverpool City	W 26-22	630	T: G Jones 2, Cheshire, Donoghue, B Hartley, Preece, G: Cheshire 4
Sep 17	HALIFAX	L 11-17	5,166	T: Dunn, G: Cheshire 4
Sep 21	Leigh	L 3-18	4,526	T: G Jones
Sep 28	WIDNES	W 18-9	2,395	T: Preece 2, Duffy, G Jones, G: Dunn 3
Oct 15	BATLEY	L 13-15	2,681	T: Baines, Dunn, G Jones, G: Dunn 2
Oct 22	Warrington	L 4-48	5,891	G: Cheshire 2
Oct 29	CASTLEFORD	L 7-19	1,998	T: Stott, G: Cheshire 2
Nov 5	Batley	L 8-19	2,100	T: Dunn, B Hartley, G: Cheshire
Nov 12	WORKINGTON TOWN	W 20-8	1,961	T: Kilgannon 2, Bettinson, G Jones, G: Cheshire 4
Nov 19	Oldham	L 0-37	8,184	
Dec 3	DONCASTER	W 16-10	999	T: Cheshire, Duffy, Dunn, Roy, G: Brunt, Cheshire
Dec 10	Whitehaven	L 0-13	2,118	
Dec 17	ROCHDALE HORNETS	W 20-9	1,385	T: Baines, Bettinson, Brunt, Hardman, G: Cheshire 4
Dec 24	ST HELENS	L 5-17	3,671	T: Dunn, G: Cheshire
Dec 26	Wigan	L 6-47	13,687	T: Cheshire, Dunn
Jan 2	SWINTON	L 5-24	10,867	T: Dunn, G: Cheshire
Jan 21	Barrow	L 0-15	1,565	
Feb 4	BLACKPOOL BOROUGH	L 5-12	1,772	T: Dunn, G: Cheshire
Feb 11	DEWSBURY (RLC-1)	W 22-8	2,261	T: Brunt 2, G Jones 2, Bettinson, A Gregory, G: Cheshire 2
Feb 18	Workington Town	L 0-21	2,800	
Feb 25	HUDDERSFIELD (RLC-2)	W 13-5	5,491	T: Brennan, Brunt, G Jones, G: Cheshire 2
Mar 4	OLDHAM	L 7-26	7,121	T: Rees, G: Cheshire 2
Mar 11	Wigan (RLC-3)	L 5-22	29,110	T: Brennan, G: Cheshire

Salford RL Match Results

1960-1961 *continued*

	Opponent	Result	Attendance	Scorers
Mar 18	WARRINGTON	D 13-13	4,891	T: Brunt, Dunn, B Hartley, G: Brunt, Dunn
Mar 25	St Helens	L 2-45	13,579	G: Dunn
Mar 31	Blackpool Borough	W 15-7	1,300	T: Brunt, Council, Dunn, G: Dunn 2, Cheshire
Apr 1	Swinton	L 5-13	7,441	T: Duffy, G: Cheshire
Apr 3	WIGAN	L 5-32	7,600	T: Council, G: Renninson
Apr 8	Widnes	L 9-30	3,188	T: Council, G: Renninson 3
Apr 11	Rochdale Hornets	L 8-17	1,734	T: B Hartley, Renninson, G: Dunn
Apr 22	LIVERPOOL CITY	W 20-10	1,651	T: Dorning 2, Kilgannon, Rees, G: Dunn 4
Apr 26	WHITEHAVEN	D 9-9	492	T: Bettinson, Dorning, Kilgannon
Apr 29	Halifax	L 8-33	3,983	T: Bettinson, Dunn, G: Cheshire
May 6	York	L 6-22	537	G: Cheshire 3

1961-1962

	Opponent	Result	Attendance	Scorers
Aug 12	Swinton (RRC)	L 5-21	–	T: G Jones, G: Cheshire
Aug 19	DEWSBURY	W 10-9	3,181	T: Rees, K Richards, G: K Richards 2
Aug 26	Warrington	L 11-32	7,144	T: Brennan, Dunn, G Jones, G: Dunn
Sep 2	Liverpool City (LC-1)	W 16-14	600	T: G Jones 2, Brennan, A Gregory, G: K Richards 2
Sep 6	Widnes	L 2-15	4,789	G: Cheshire
Sep 9	ST HELENS	L 7-24	6,431	T: Simcox, G: K Richards 2
Sep 16	Castleford	L 8-53	2,650	T: A Gregory, K Richards, G: K Richards
Sep 18	BLACKPOOL BOROUGH (LC-2)	W 22-10	3,000	T: K Richards 2, Duffy, G Jones, G: K Richards 5
Sep 23	DONCASTER	W 33-8	2,500	T: Bettinson 2, Brennan, Brunt, Duffy, A Gregory, Rees, G: K Richards 6
Sep 30	Liverpool City	W 22-11	479	T: Bettinson, Brennan, Rees, K Richards, G: K Richards 5
Oct 7	BRADFORD NORTHERN	W 35-7	3,150	T: Brunt 2, Duffy 2, Bettinson, G Jones, K Richards, G: K Richards 7
Oct 10	St Helens (LC-SF)	L 2-21	11,000	G: Bettinson
Oct 14	Leigh	L 10-33	6,634	T: Duffy, Rees, G: K Richards 2

Salford RL Match Results

1961-1962 *continued*

	Opponent	Result	Attendance	Scorers
Oct 21	HUDDERSFIELD	L 8-26	4,350	T: Bettinson, Cheshire, G: Cheshire
Oct 28	Workington Town	L 0-52	4,200	
Nov 11	LIVERPOOL CITY	W 8-5	1,305	T: Brennan, G Jones, G: K Richards
Nov 25	OLDHAM	L 4-50	4,017	G: K Richards 2
Dec 2	Dewsbury	D 2-2	500	G: K Richards
Dec 9	Barrow	W 13-7	2,483	T: Hindley 2, Rees, G: K Richards 2
Dec 16	CASTLEFORD	W 8-3	1,947	T: Hindley, K Richards, G: K Richards
Jan 6	ROCHDALE HORNETS	W 28-10	2,087	T: G Jones 3, Dunn 2, K Richards, G: K Richards 5
Jan 13	Rochdale Hornets	L 6-8	1,870	T: Cheshire, Leonard
Jan 20	BARROW	W 16-15	1,781	T: Dunn 2, G Jones 2, G: Dunn 2
Jan 27	Doncaster	L 7-10	1,000	T: Hindley, G: Dunn 2
Feb 3	WARRINGTON	W 16-0	3,871	T: Hindley 2, Council, Dunn, G: Cheshire 2
Feb 10	ST HELENS (RLC-1)	L 2-15	11,004	G: Dunn
Feb 17	St Helens	L 12-17	7,450	T: Brennan, Rees, G: Dunn 3
Feb 24	WHITEHAVEN	W 16-3	2,450	T: Parkinson 2, G: Cheshire 4, Dunn
Mar 3	Swinton	L 10-34	6,600	T: Bettinson, Brennan, G: Cheshire 2
Mar 10	BLACKPOOL BOROUGH	L 2-11	2,560	G: Cheshire
Mar 17	Bradford Northern	W 20-6	1,323	T: Council 2, Hindley, McAlone, G: Cheshire 4
Mar 31	Huddersfield	L 13-26	3,599	T: G Jones 3, G: Cheshire 2
Apr 5	Oldham	L 10-37	3,455	T: G Jones, McAlone, G: Cheshire 2
Apr 11	WIDNES	L 2-15	3,518	G: K Richards
Apr 14	Whitehaven	L 3-40	1,796	T: Cheshire
Apr 20	Blackpool Borough	L 6-10	1,600	G: K Richards 3
Apr 21	SWINTON	L 2-32	3,550	G: K Richards
Apr 23	Wigan	L 12-46	15,095	T: G Jones, Price, G: Cheshire 3
Apr 28	WORKINGTON TOWN	L 10-18	2,150	T: G Jones 2, G: K Richards 2
Apr 30	WIGAN	L 8-49	4,700	T: Bettinson, Dunn, G: K Richards
May 4	LEIGH	L 5-16	2,450	T: Bettinson, G: Pearce

Salford RL Match Results

1962-1963

Date	Opponent	Result	Attendance	Scorers
Aug 11	SWINTON (RRC)	L 12-25	2,200	T: Dunn, Rees, G: K Richards 3
Aug 18	ST HELENS (WD)	L 24-35	5,893	T: Bettinson, Dunn, Kilgannon, Rees, G: K Richards 6
Aug 22	Swinton (WD)	L 7-34	7,500	T: Rees, G: K Richards 2
Aug 25	Warrington (WD)	L 4-20	5,572	G: K Richards 2
Aug 27	WORKINGTON TOWN (WD)	L 5-23	2,276	T: Hindley, G: K Richards
Sep 1	St Helens (WD)	L 0-59	10,643	
Sep 8	Blackpool Borough (LC-1)	L 9-23	3,000	T: Dunn, G: K Richards 3
Sep 15	SWINTON (WD)	L 13-24	4,942	T: Dorning 2, Brennan, G: Cheshire, K Richards
Sep 22	Workington Town (WD)	L 5-60	4,400	T: Rees, G: K Richards
Sep 29	WARRINGTON (WD)	L 13-40	3,789	T: Murphy 3, G: K Richards 2
Oct 6	BATLEY	W 16-8	2,821	T: Bettinson 2, Dunn, Murphy, G: Cheshire 2
Oct 13	Hunslet	L 5-46	4,200	T: Dorning, G: Cheshire
Oct 20	BRADFORD NORTHERN	W 16-5	2,076	T: Bettinson, Clark, Dorning, Hutson, G: K Richards 2
Oct 26	Leigh	W 10-9	5,268	T: Bettinson, Hindley, G: K Richards 2
Nov 3	BARROW	L 13-20	3,020	T: Hindley, G: K Richards 5
Nov 10	Batley	L 0-43	1,000	
Nov 17	HUNSLET	L 6-9	1,987	T: Bettinson, Hindley
Nov 24	Bradford Northern	L 13-20	744	T: Bettinson, McAlone, K Richards, G: K Richards 2
Dec 1	LEIGH	L 15-18	3,103	T: Brennan 2, Hutson, G: K Richards 3
Dec 8	Barrow	L 7-14	2,235	T: Bettinson, G: Cheshire 2
Dec 15	WHITEHAVEN	W 10-0	1,002	T: McAlone, Murphy, G: Pearce 2
Mar 2	YORK (RLC-1)	L 11-29	3,681	T: Critchley, Halsall, Murphy, G: K Richards
Mar 9	Doncaster	L 11-17	875	T: Ingham, McAlone, Murphy, G: K Richards
Mar 16	ROCHDALE HORNETS	D 5-5	1,703	T: Bettinson, G: K Richards
Mar 23	Rochdale Hornets	L 11-20	2,652	T: Murphy 3, G: K Richards
Mar 30	DEWSBURY	W 13-12	1,340	T: Clark, Ingham, K Richards, G: K Richards 2
Apr 6	KEIGHLEY	L 12-15	2,096	T: Bettinson, Clark, G: K Richards 3
Apr 12	Blackpool Borough	L 8-11	1,500	T: Bettinson, Ingham, G: K Richards
Apr 13	Liverpool City	W 10-3	513	T: Bettinson, T Wilson, G: Shuker 2

Salford RL Match Results

1962-1963 *continued*

	Opponent	Result	Attendance	Scorers
Apr 15	YORK	L 3-11	2,197	T: Murphy
Apr 19	LIVERPOOL CITY	L 11-16	1,873	T: Dorning, Ingham, K Richards, G: K Richards
Apr 27	York	L 11-30	3,535	T: Murphy 2, Rabbitt, G: K Richards
May 4	Dewsbury	L 4-29	1,000	G: K Richards 2
May 8	Whitehaven	W 19-9	2,185	T: Murphy 2, Bettinson, G: Pearce 5
May 18	BLACKPOOL BOROUGH	L 3-14	1,298	T: K Richards
May 22	Keighley	L 5-32	2,860	T: Ashall, G: K Richards
May 25	DONCASTER	W 34-26	1,376	T: Hindley 2, Murphy 2, Clare, K Richards, G: K Richards 8

1963-1964

	Opponent	Result	Attendance	Scorers
Aug 17	Swinton (RRC)	L 5-31	5,250	T: Halsall, G: Pearce
Aug 24	YORK	W 23-21	1,512	T: Hindley 2, Bettinson, Brennan, Murphy, G: Pearce 4
Aug 27	Dewsbury	L 7-17	2,200	T: Dorning, G: Pearce 2
Aug 31	Blackpool Borough	L 16-36	6,075	T: K Richards 2, Brennan, Murphy, G: Pearce, K Richards
Sep 4	BARROW	L 15-23	2,390	T: Dunn, McAlone, K Richards, G: K Richards 3
Sep 7	WARRINGTON (LC-1)	L 0-31	2,900	
Sep 14	Bradford Northern*	L 6-27	1,044	T: Hutson, Murphy
Sep 21	ROCHDALE HORNETS	L 4-20	2,655	G: K Richards 2
Sep 28	Whitehaven	L 7-10	1,891	T: Rabbitt, G: K Richards 2
Oct 5	WARRINGTON (WD)	L 18-22	2,309	T: Brennan 2, Bennett, K Richards, G: K Richards 3
Oct 12	Leigh	L 9-25	6,516	T: K Richards, G: K Richards 3
Oct 19	DEWSBURY	L 4-6	2,369	G: K Richards 2
Nov 2	BATLEY	W 15-3	2,259	T: Dorning, Murphy, Rabbitt, G: K Richards 3
Nov 9	Liverpool City	W 8-7	453	T: Bettinson, Dorning, G: K Richards
Nov 16	BLACKPOOL BOROUGH**	A 5-7	1,500	T: Rabbitt, G: K Richards
Nov 23	Bramley	L 3-4	800	T: Brennan
Dec 7	Batley	W 3-2	1,250	T: Brennan
Dec 14	LIVERPOOL CITY	L 2-15	1,419	G: Southward
Dec 28	WHITEHAVEN	W 5-0	1,710	T: Bettinson, G: K Richards
Jan 1	LEIGH	W 9-6	5,789	T: Council, G: Southward 3
Jan 4	ST HELENS (WD)	L 5-15	3,491	T: T Wilson, G: Southward

Salford RL Match Results

1963-1964 *continued*

	Opponent	Result	Attendance	Scorers
Jan 11	York	L 8-14	2,295	T: Dorning, Murphy, G: Bettinson
Jan 25	Oldham	L 20-37	4,657	T: Bettinson, Critchley, Halsall, Southward, G: K Richards 4
Feb 8	LEEDS (RLC-1)	W 10-6	5,884	T: Critchley, Southward, G: K Richards 2
Feb 15	WIDNES (WD)	L 9-15	3,359	T: Bettinson, G: K Richards 3
Feb 22	BRAMLEY	L 12-23	2,187	G: K Richards 6
Feb 29	BARROW (RLC-2)	L 4-10	5,745	G: K Richards 2
Mar 7	Barrow	L 3-33	2,735	T: Dorning
Mar 21	Warrington (WD)	L 4-13	3,153	G: K Richards 2
Mar 25	Widnes (WD)	L 10-11	4,907	T: Bettinson, Dorning, G: K Richards 2
Mar 28	St Helens (WD)	L 13-24	6,843	T: Critchley, Dorning, T Wilson, G: K Richards 2
Mar 30	OLDHAM	L 8-43	3,780	T: Dorning 2, G: K Richards
Apr 4	Doncaster	W 10-9	675	T: Halsall, Hindley, G: Bettinson 2
Apr 8	Swinton (WD)	L 0-47	6,395	
Apr 11	BLACKPOOL BOROUGH	W 25-8	1,158	T: Bettinson 2, Brennan, Brown, Murphy, G: Bettinson 5
Apr 14	Rochdale Hornets	L 0-25	1,579	
Apr 18	DONCASTER	L 2-5	1,498	G: Bettinson
Apr 22	SWINTON (WD)	L 0-43	4,010	

* Result expunged from league table after Bradford Northern withdrew
** Abandoned 32 mins (fog)

1964-1965

	Opponent	Result	Attendance	Scorers
Aug 22	Rochdale Hornets	L 4-10	2,641	G: Southward 2
Aug 26	WHITEHAVEN	W 24-9	2,679	T: Brunning 2, Barry, Ingham, G: Southward 6
Aug 29	LEIGH	W 19-9	3,826	T: Ingham, Murphy, M Taylor, G: Kenyon 3, Southward 2
Sep 2	Bradford Northern	L 12-20	10,002	T: Brown, Brunning, G: Kenyon 3
Sep 5	Wigan (LC-1)	L 6-36	8,135	G: Pearce 3
Sep 12	Batley	L 13-15	1,500	T: Halsall 2, Murphy, G: Kenyon 2
Sep 19	WARRINGTON	L 7-21	4,032	T: Southward, G: Southward 2

Salford RL Match Results

1964-1965 *continued*

	Opponent	Result	Attendance	Scorers
Sep 26	Liverpool City	D 5-5	613	T: Murphy, G: Southward
Oct 3	DONCASTER	W 13-5	3,005	T: Bettinson, Hindley, Ingham, G: Southward 2
Oct 10	Whitehaven	L 7-32	1,347	T: Sparks, G: Southward 2
Oct 17	BATLEY	W 20-8	2,091	T: Halsall 3, Hindley, G: Southward 4
Oct 24	Doncaster	L 13-18	650	T: Bettinson, Halsall, Murphy, G: Murphy 2
Oct 31	BLACKPOOL BOROUGH	W 7-4	2,355	T: Crank, G: Leatherbarrow 2
Nov 7	Widnes	W 12-4	4,699	T: Bettinson, T Wilson, G: Pearce 3
Nov 14	BRADFORD NORTHERN	W 12-2	2,499	T: Bettinson, Dorning, G: Pearce 3
Nov 21	Leigh	L 7-31	5,284	T: Brown, G: Pearce 2
Nov 28	OLDHAM	L 5-9	3,027	T: Critchley, G: Pearce
Dec 5	Workington Town	L 12-19	1,208	T: Dorning, Southward, G: Southward 3
Dec 19	Barrow	L 7-32	2,257	T: Critchley, G: Southward 2
Jan 2	ROCHDALE HORNETS	W 21-5	1,865	T: Murphy 4, Brown, G: Shuker 3
Jan 9	Huddersfield	L 2-9	2,567	G: Shuker
Jan 16	WORKINGTON TOWN	D 7-7	1,149	T: Crank, G: Southward 2
Jan 30	WIDNES	L 10-16	2,801	T: Murphy, M Taylor, G: Southward 2
Feb 6	Keighley (RLC-1)	W 11-8	2,546	T: Dorning, G: Pearce 4
Feb 13	Wigan	L 4-16	8,544	G: Pearce 2
Feb 16	St Helens	L 6-12	12,848	G: Pearce 3
Feb 20	LIVERPOOL CITY	L 0-9	2,012	
Feb 27	Warrington (RLC-2)	L 2-16	4,278	G: Pearce
Mar 13	BARROW	L 9-10	1,813	T: Crank, G: Pearce 3
Mar 20	SWINTON	W 12-2	4,278	T: Murphy, Rabbitt, G: Pearce 3
Mar 27	ST HELENS	W 11-8	3,652	T: Ogden, G: Pearce 4
Mar 31	Warrington	L 0-18	6,735	
Apr 7	HUDDERSFIELD	L 7-8	2,439	T: Critchley, G: Pearce 2
Apr 13	Oldham	L 3-21	5,347	T: Murphy
Apr 16	Blackpool Borough	W 14-3	1,365	T: Brennan, Brown, G: Pearce 4
Apr 17	Swinton	L 0-6	5,200	
Apr 19	WIGAN	L 2-17	6,853	G: Pearce

Salford RL Match Results

1965-1966

	Opponent	Result	Attendance	Scorers
Aug 21	DEWSBURY	W 21-11	3,126	T: Brennan, Harper, Murphy, Shuker, Sparks, G: Shuker 3
Aug 25	Keighley	L 10-20	1,625	T: Bettinson, Shuker, G: Shuker 2
Aug 28	Warrington	L 9-13	5,209	T: Harper, G: Pearce 3
Aug 30	SWINTON	L 10-44	8,009	T: Brennan, T Wilson, G: Pearce 2
Sep 4	LEIGH	W 12-5	2,918	T: Bettinson, Hughes, G: Pearce 3
Sep 11	WORKINGTON TOWN (LC-1)	W 14-5	4,900	T: Bettinson, Brennan, G: Pearce 4
Sep 15	LEIGH (LC-2)	L 5-8	4,008	T: Murphy, G: Pearce
Sep 18	Dewsbury	L 15-16	1,300	T: Bettinson, Halsall, Murphy, G: Pearce 3
Sep 25	Oldham	L 8-12	4,888	G: Pearce 4
Oct 2	HUDDERSFIELD	L 10-27	3,140	T: Brennan, Murphy, G: Pearce 2
Oct 9	Liverpool City	L 16-20	661	T: Bettinson, T Wilson, G: Pearce 5
Oct 16	ST HELENS	L 11-15	4,022	T: Brown, Harper, Southward, G: Southward
Oct 23	Leigh	L 8-23	4,215	T: Critchley, Evans, G: Murphy
Oct 30	WHITEHAVEN	W 16-10	2,109	T: Murphy 2, Evans, Hughes, G: Murphy 2
Nov 4	Widnes	W 12-11	5,716	T: Bettinson, Brown, G: Murphy 3
Nov 13	OLDHAM	W 12-11	3,002	T: Murphy, T Wilson, G: Murphy 3
Nov 20	LIVERPOOL CITY	W 11-9	1,516	T: Murphy, G: Murphy 4
Dec 4	ROCHDALE HORNETS	W 10-9	2,452	T: Bettinson, T Wilson, G: Murphy 2
Dec 11	Workington Town	W 10-8	1,700	T: Murphy, M Taylor, G Murphy 2
Dec 18	YORK	W 8-0	1,720	G: Murphy 4
Jan 1	St Helens	L 3-16	9,801	T: Murphy
Jan 8	Blackpool Borough	W 14-6	950	T: Breen, Critchley, Halsall, Southward, G: Murphy
Jan 29	WORKINGTON TOWN	L 7-8	2,792	T: Critchley, G: Murphy 2
Feb 12	KEIGHLEY	W 20-2	2,167	T: Critchley, Hughes, Murphy, Ogden, G: Murphy 4
Feb 19	Rochdale Hornets	W 13-4	2,059	T: Breen 2, Rabbitt, G: Murphy 2
Feb 26	Hull (RLC-1)	L 2-11	3,401	G: Murphy

Salford RL Match Results

1965-1966 *continued*

	Opponent	Result	Attendance	Scorers
Mar 11	WIDNES	W 7-5	5,101	T: Murphy, G: Murphy 2
Mar 15	WIGAN	L 8-36	8,337	T: Argent, Brennan, G: Murphy
Mar 22	BARROW	L 4-17	3,427	G: Murphy 2
Mar 25	WARRINGTON	W 22-2	5,433	T: Bettinson, Brown, Hughes, Rabbitt, G: Pearce 5
Mar 30	BLACKPOOL BOROUGH	W 13-5	2,590	T: Murphy 2, Southward, G: Murphy, Pearce
Apr 8	Barrow	L 12-18	3,887	T: Bettinson, Brennan, G: Murphy 3
Apr 11	Wigan	L 7-15	10,024	T: Smart, G: Murphy 2
Apr 13	Swinton	L 7-12	6,000	T: Smart, G: Murphy, Southward
Apr 16	York	L 2-7	950	G: Pearce
Apr 23	Whitehaven	D 4-4	378	G: Pearce 2
Apr 25	Huddersfield	L 8-17	2,193	T: Bettinson, Critchley, G: Pearce

1966-1967

	Opponent	Result	Attendance	Scorers
Aug 13	WAKEFIELD TRINITY (RRC)	W 18-10	–	T: Bettinson, Evans, M Taylor, Southward, G: Sims 2, Southward
Aug 20	LEIGH	W 38-5	4,296	T: Argent 3, Bettinson 2, Critchley, Rabbitt, M Taylor, G: Sims 7
Aug 24	Widnes	W 9-7	5,643	T: Rabbitt, G: Sims 3
Aug 27	St Helens	L 7-42	7,683	T: Southward, G: Sims 2
Aug 29	SWINTON	L 2-7	5,228	G: Sims
Sep 3	Workington Town (LC-1)	W 17-9	2,201	T: Ogden 2, Critchley, G: Sims 4
Sep 6	ST HELENS (FT-Preliminary)	L 10-19	4,953	G: Sims 5
Sep 9	OLDHAM	W 15-13	6,019	T: Brennan 2, Southward, G: Sims 3
Sep 15	OLDHAM (LC-2)	L 2-7	6,000	G: Sims
Sep 17	Workington Town	L 13-30	2,000	T: Brennan, G: Sims 5
Sep 19	Whitehaven	L 9-11	1,755	T: Rabbitt, G: Sims 3
Sep 23	WARRINGTON	L 6-12	5,495	T: Bettinson, Dorning
Sep 26	St Helens (FT-Preliminary)	L 5-40	7,872	T: Whitehead, G: Shuker
Sep 28	LIVERPOOL CITY	W 25-7	3,595	T: Bettinson, Brennan, Collier, Hughes, M Taylor, G: Sims 5
Oct 1	Huddersfield	W 7-3	2,031	T: Sims, G: Sims 2
Oct 7	BARROW	W 12-7	4,003	T: Breen, Hughes, G: Sims 3

Salford RL Match Results

1966-1967 *continued*

	Opponent	Result	Attendance	Scorers
Oct 12	BLACKPOOL BOROUGH	W 10-8	3,916	G: Sims 5
Oct 17	Leigh	W 9-6	4,345	T: Breen, G: Sims 3
Oct 22	ST HELENS	L 3-30	4,567	T: Nestor
Oct 29	Hunslet	L 6-21	1,450	G: Sims 3
Nov 5	BRAMLEY	W 15-11	3,389	T: Breen, G: Sims 6
Nov 12	Hull	W 16-10	3,100	T: Brennan 2, Bettinson, Sims, G: Sims 2
Nov 18	WIDNES	W 16-15	4,280	T: Bettinson, Murphy, Nestor, Sims, G: Sims 2
Nov 25	WORKINGTON TOWN	L 9-10	3,919	T: McInnes, G: Sims 2, Clare
Dec 3	Rochdale Hornets	W 17-4	2,713	T: Murphy, Sims, Whitehead, G: McInnes 2, Sims 2
Dec 17	Liverpool City	L 4-8	842	G: Sims 2
Dec 26	HUDDERSFIELD	L 5-13	5,332	T: Hughes, G: Sims
Dec 27	Wigan	L 11-28	8,545	T: Bettinson, G: McInnes 3, Sims
Dec 31	Bramley	W 10-2	810	T: Southward, Whitehead, G: McInnes 2
Jan 13	ROCHDALE HORNETS	D 4-4	4,539	G: McInnes 2
Jan 21	Oldham	L 4-17	3,856	G: McInnes, Sims
Jan 28	HULL	W 14-6	3,348	T: Southward, Whitehead, G: McInnes 2, Sims 2
Feb 3	ST HELENS (RLC-1)	D 5-5	14,109	T: Murphy, G: Sims
Feb 7	St Helens (RLC-1 Replay)	W 8-3	14,133	T: Bettinson, Murphy, G: Sims
Feb 10	HUNSLET	L 12-16	5,898	T: Bettinson, Sims, G: Sims 3
Feb 17	Barrow	L 9-15	3,723	T: Hughes, G: Sims 3
Feb 25	Wigan (RLC-2)	W 18-6	25,342	T: Bettinson, Ogden, G: Sims 4, McInnes 2
Mar 3	WHITEHAVEN	W 27-15	5,321	T: Murphy 3, Brennan, McInnes, Southward, Whitehead, G: Sims 3
Mar 10	Warrington	L 7-16	5,668	T: Murphy, G: Sims 2
Mar 18	Dewsbury (RLC-3)	L 7-9	13,557	T: Bettinson, G: McInnes, Sims
Mar 24	Blackpool Borough	W 23-18	1,800	T: Collier 2, Breen, Murphy, Southward, G: McInnes 2, Murphy, Sims
Mar 25	Swinton	W 7-3	7,800	T: Ogden, G: Sims 2
Mar 27	WIGAN	W 17-4	9,767	T: Brennan, Ogden, Whitehead, G: Sims 2, Burdell, McInnes
Apr 15	Wakefield Trinity (NRL-1)	L 8-48	8,381	T: Southward, Whitehead, G: Sims

Salford RL Match Results

1967-1968

	Opponent	Result	Attendance	Scorers
Aug 11	Wakefield Trinity (RRC)	W 29-6	4,309	T: Hughes 2, Murphy 2, Argent, Burdell, Southward, G: Murphy 3, McInnes
Aug 19	Wigan (LC-1)	W 18-14	10,592	T: Murphy 2, Brennan, Whitehead, G: Murphy 3
Aug 21	Barrow	L 20-23	4,692	T: Bettinson 2, Whitehead 2, G: Murphy 4
Aug 25	Castleford	L 14-21	6,156	T: Brennan, Southward, G: Murphy 4
Aug 28	SWINTON	W 17-8	9,894	T: Hesketh, Murphy, Southward, G: Murphy 3, McInnes
Sep 1	ST HELENS	L 3-15	7,587	T: Henighan
Sep 4	Workington Town (LC-2)	L 0-33	3,056	
Sep 8	Halifax	L 18-27	4,415	T: Bott, Henighan, Jackson, Sims, G: Murphy 2, Sims
Sep 15	CASTLEFORD	L 14-19	7,361	T: Collier 2, Breen, Ogden, G: Sims
Sep 20	ROCHDALE HORNETS	W 30-4	4,963	T: Whitehead 2, Bettinson, Breen, Brennan, McInnes, G: D Hill 6
Sep 25	Leigh	L 9-15	6,529	T: McInnes, G: D Hill 3
Sep 29	LIVERPOOL CITY	W 18-5	4,059	T: Hesketh 2, D Hill, Whitehead, G: D Hill 2, McInnes
Oct 3	LEIGH (FT-1)	L 3-5	4,000	T: Murphy
Oct 7	Whitehaven	W 10-0	787	T: D Hill, McInnes, G: D Hill 2
Oct 17	WHITEHAVEN	W 23-7	3,087	T: Hesketh 3, Brennan 2, G: D Hill 4
Oct 20	OLDHAM	W 12-6	10,117	T: Burdell, Watkins, G: Watkins 2, D Hill
Oct 28	Workington Town	L 8-13	1,546	T: Bettinson, D Hill, G: D Hill
Nov 3	FEATHERSTONE ROVERS	L 11-12	6,821	T: D Hill, G: D Hill 3, Watkins
Nov 13	Oldham	W 4-0	4,236	G: D Hill 2
Nov 17	HALIFAX	W 14-3	5,643	T: Murphy, Watkins, G: D Hill 4
Nov 24	St Helens	W 7-4	5,000	T: D Hill, G: D Hill 2
Dec 1	WIDNES	W 15-3	6,325	T: Watkins 2, Breen, G: Watkins 2, D Hill
Dec 22	Widnes	W 14-0	4,000	T: Bettinson, D Hill, G: D Hill 3, Watkins
Dec 26	Batley	W 9-7	2,000	T: Brennan, G: D Hill 3
Dec 29	WORKINGTON TOWN	W 14-5	7,049	T: Brennan, D Hill, G: Watkins 2, D Hill, McInnes

Salford RL Match Results

1967-1968 *continued*

Date	Opponent	Result	Attendance	Scorers
Jan 1	BLACKPOOL BOROUGH	W 17-0	5,684	T: Hesketh, D Hill, McInnes, G: D Hill 4
Jan 7	Featherstone Rovers	W 10-9	4,500	T: Brennan, Whitehead, G: D Hill, Watkins
Jan 19	BARROW	W 6-5	8,027	G: D Hill, McInnes, Watkins
Jan 27	Liverpool City	W 12-7	1,100	T: Crank, Whitehead, G: D Hill 2, McInnes
Feb 3	BLACKPOOL BOROUGH (RLC-1)	W 16-5	6,500	T: Kelly, Whitehead, G: D Hill 5
Feb 5	GREAT BRITAIN (F)*	A 0-12	4,500	
Feb 13	Warrington	L 8-10	5,336	G: D Hill 3, McInnes
Feb 16	LEIGH	W 11-2	10,932	T: Kelly, G: D Hill 3, Watkins
Feb 24	WAKEFIELD TRINITY (RLC-2)	L 4-8	14,079	G: D Hill, Watkins
Mar 1	WARRINGTON	L 6-14	7,199	G: D Hill 2, Watkins
Mar 9	Rochdale Hornets	W 31-0	3,609	T: D Hill 2, Bettinson, Brennan, Kelly, Smethurst, Watkins, G: D Hill 5
Mar 22	BATLEY	W 21-2	6,369	T: Watkins 2, Brennan, G: D Hill 6
Mar 29	WIGAN	W 15-13	11,834	T: Brennan, Watkins, Whitehead, G: D Hill 3
Apr 5	GREAT BRITAIN (F)*	L 5-20	6,000	T: Hesketh, G: D Hill
Apr 12	Blackpool Borough	W 18-4	3,338	T: Hesketh, Whitehead, G: D Hill 5, Watkins
Apr 13	Swinton	L 17-20	7,856	T: Bott, Brennan, Smethurst, G: D Hill 4
Apr 15	Wigan	L 14-25	10,797	T: Bott, Whitehead, G: D Hill 3, Watkins
Apr 19	Castleford (NRL-1)	L 15-47	5,500	T: Prosser, Watkins, Whitehead, G: D Hill 3
May 5	CAVAILLON (France) (F)	W 43-0	–	T: Whitehead 3, Brennan 2, Hesketh, Kelly, Redford, Watkins, G: Redford 5, D Hill 3
May 29	Hull Kingston Rovers (F)**	L 33-36	1,000	T: Murphy 2, Bettinson, Bott, Brennan, D Hill, Kelly, Prosser, Watkins, G: D Hill 2, Bettinson
Jun 1	Bradford Northern (F)***	L 22-46	11,500	T: D Hill, Mills, Prosser, Watkins, G: D Hill 5

Practice match for Great Britain for 1968 World Cup – first match abandoned 35 mins (snowstorm)
** At Jedburgh   *** At Abertillery

Salford RL Match Results

1968-1969

	Opponent	Result	Attendance	Scorers
Aug 14	Bradford Northern	W 11-5	9,229	T: Watkins, G: Watkins 2, Halliwell, D Hill
Aug 16	HULL	W 19-2	5,395	T: Bott, Halliwell, Murphy, G: D Hill 4, Watkins
Aug 21	Widnes	L 9-21	5,300	T: Whitehead, G: D Hill 2, Watkins
Aug 24	Wakefield Trinity	L 12-31	6,869	T: Halliwell, Watkins, G: D Hill 3
Aug 27	BRADFORD NORTHERN	W 18-12	6,950	T: Bettinson, Brennan, Jackson, Prosser, G: Murphy 2, Jackson
Sep 2	SWINTON	L 3-11	9,651	T: Prosser
Sep 6	WARRINGTON (LC-1)	W 14-3	8,500	T: Bott 2, Hesketh, D Hill, G: Halliwell
Sep 15	Doncaster	W 18-12	1,542	T: Southward 2, Hesketh, Prosser, G: D Hill 2, Brennan
Sep 20	WHITEHAVEN	W 18-7	3,762	T: Brennan, D Hill, Jackson, Whitehead, G: D Hill 3
Sep 22	Whitehaven (LC-2)	W 17-4	2,345	T: Hesketh 2, Watkins, G: D Hill 2, Halliwell, Watkins
Sep 28	Wigan	L 11-18	10,562	T: Prosser, G: D Hill 3, Watkins
Oct 1	Leeds (FT-1)	L 19-24	4,227	T: Southward 2, Smethurst, G: D Hill 3, Smethurst, Watkins
Oct 4	ST HELENS	D 10-10	8,441	T: Bettinson, Hardicre, G: D Hill 2
Oct 9	OLDHAM (LC-SF)	L 9-12	12,000	T: Whitehead, G: D Hill 3
Oct 12	Whitehaven	W 21-2	413	T: Burdell, D Hill, Jackson, G: D Hill 5, Brennan
Oct 18	ROCHDALE HORNETS	L 7-10	7,000	T: AN Other, G: D Hill 2
Oct 30	OLDHAM	W 4-2	5,500	G: Murphy 2
Nov 1	Warrington	L 8-12	4,868	G: Murphy 3, Watkins
Nov 8	WORKINGTON TOWN	L 10-18	4,500	T: Brennan, Murphy, G: McInnes, Murphy
Nov 16	St Helens	D 9-9	5,400	T: Jackson, G: D Hill 3
Nov 22	BARROW	D 14-14	5,000	T: Coulman, R Hill, G: D Hill 3, McInnes
Nov 29	Leigh	W 20-5	6,000	T: Jackson 2, Hesketh, R Hill, G: D Hill 4
Dec 6	DONCASTER	W 44-2	4,000	T: McInnes 3, Jackson 2, Halliwell, Hesketh, Watkins, G: R Hill 10
Dec 20	WAKEFIELD TRINITY	W 17-3	7,969	T: McInnes, Rabbitt, Whitehead, G: R Hill 4

Salford RL Match Results

1968-1969 *continued*

	Opponent	Result	Attendance	Scorers
Jan 1	BLACKPOOL BOROUGH	W 39-8	6,690	T: Bott, Burdell, Burgess, Dixon, McInnes, Ogden, Rabbitt, Watkins, Whitehead, G: R Hill 6
Jan 10	LEIGH	D 6-6	9,000	G: R Hill 2, Watkins
Jan 18	Oldham	L 12-22	3,758	T: Coulman, Rabbitt, G: R Hill 2, Watkins
Jan 25	BATLEY (RLC-1)	W 17-2	6,514	T: Brennan, Gwilliam, R Hill, G: R Hill 4
Jan 27	Hull	D 5-5	3,800	T: Ogden, G: R Hill
Jan 31	Huyton*	W 18-5	5,500	T: Watkins 2, Jackson, Whitehead, G: R Hill 3
Feb 23	WORKINGTON TOWN (RLC-2)	W 12-5	13,534	T: Burgess, R Hill, G: R Hill 3
Mar 2	WIDNES (RLC-3)	W 20-7	21,000	T: Burgess, Coulman, Dixon, Hesketh, G: R Hill 3, Watkins
Mar 4	WARRINGTON	W 33-10	12,000	T: Dixon 2, Ogden 2, Prosser, Smethurst, Whitehead, G: D Hill 6
Mar 15	Rochdale Hornets	W 23-8	3,349	T: Whitehead 2, Burgess, Hesketh, McInnes, G: R Hill 4
Mar 22	Warrington (RLC-SF)**	W 15-8	20,600	T: Burgess, Jackson, Whitehead, G: R Hill 3
Mar 28	Barrow	W 11-8	4,500	T: Burgess, G: R Hill 4
Apr 1	WIDNES	W 29-3	6,000	T: R Hill 2, Burgess, Dickens, Hesketh, Ogden, Watkins, G: R Hill 4
Apr 4	Blackpool Borough	W 49-7	5,000	T: Coulman 3, Burgess 2, R Hill 2, Jackson 2, Hesketh, Ogden, Rabbitt, Watkins, G: R Hill 5
Apr 5	Swinton	W 19-3	11,800	T: Brennan, Burgess, Hesketh, G: R Hill 5
Apr 7	WIGAN	W 37-5	15,300	T: Burdell 2, Burgess 2, Bott, Dixon, Hesketh, G: R Hill 7, Watkins
Apr 11	HUYTON	L 5-8	7,000	T: Burgess, G: R Hill
Apr 14	Workington Town	L 4-5	1,601	G: D Hill 2
Apr 27	YORK (NRL-1)	W 13-7	9,200	T: Burgess, Coulman, Jackson, G: Watkins 2
May 3	Wigan (NRL-2)	W 26-21	16,683	T: Burgess 3, Brennan, Smethurst, Whitehead, G: R Hill 4

Salford RL Match Results

1968-1969 *continued*

	Opponent	Result	Attendance	Scorers
May 10	Leeds (NRL-SF)	L 12-22	15,690	T: Dixon 2, G: R Hill 3
May 17	Castleford (RLC-Final)***	L 6-11	97,939	G: R Hill 3

*Away match played at Salford   ** At Wigan   *** At Wembley*

Rugby League Challenge Cup runners-up

1969-1970

	Opponent	Result	Attendance	Scorers
Aug 10	Huyton	W 60-5	3,090	T: Coulman 3, Hesketh 2, R Hill 2, Whitehead 2, Dickens, Jackson, Prosser, Smethurst, Watkins, G: R Hill 9
Aug 16	Wigan (LC-1)	L 9-25	13,631	T: Dickens, G: R Hill 2, Watkins
Aug 19	Oldham	W 20-11	4,890	T: Hesketh, R Hill, Prosser, Whitehead, G: R Hill 4
Aug 30	Rochdale Hornets	L 10-15	3,925	T: Coulman, Watkins, G: R Hill 2
Sep 1	SWINTON	W 8-5	10,592	T: Jackson, Watkins, G: Watkins
Sep 5	WARRINGTON	W 20-13	8,332	T: Hardicre, McInnes, Prosser, Watkins, G: R Hill 3, McInnes
Sep 10	WIGAN	L 4-14	11,614	G: R Hill, McInnes
Sep 12	Hull Kingston Rovers	L 5-12	5,187	T: Prosser, G: R Hill
Sep 19	WORKINGTON TOWN	L 6-22	8,023	G: R Hill 2, McInnes
Sep 26	HUYTON	W 32-3	5,364	T: Hesketh 2, Jackson 2, Brennan, Burgess, Dixon, Watkins, G: McInnes 4
Oct 3	ROCHDALE HORNETS	W 41-0	6,989	T: Burgess 2, Whitehead 2, Bott, Burdell, Hesketh, Ogden, Watkins, G: McInnes 6, Watkins
Oct 10	Warrington	W 14-10	9,450	T: Burgess, Watkins, G: Watkins 3, McInnes
Oct 15	LEIGH	W 15-5	11,608	T: Bott, Jackson, Whitehead, G: Watkins 3
Oct 21	CASTLEFORD (FT-1)	L 12-16	7,583	T: Hesketh, Richards, G: D Hill 3
Oct 29	ST HELENS	W 16-12	9,600	T: Hesketh 2, G: D Hill 5
Oct 31	Widnes	W 19-2	5,980	T: Burgess, Dixon, Richards, G: D Hill 5
Nov 7	BATLEY	W 28-9	5,668	T: Burgess 2, Charlton, D Hill, Richards, Watkins, G: D Hill 5

Salford RL Match Results

1969-1970 *continued*

	Opponent	Result	Attendance	Scorers
Nov 22	Whitehaven	W 13-7	2,953	T: Burgess 2, Hesketh, G: D Hill 2
Nov 28	WAKEFIELD TRINITY	W 17-12	6,109	T: Coulman, Hesketh, Richards, G: D Hill 4
Dec 13	HULL KINGSTON ROVERS	L 7-22	5,218	T: Richards, G: D Hill 2
Dec 21	Workington Town	W 6-4	1,338	G: R Hill 3
Dec 26	BARROW	W 14-7	8,099	T: Burgess, Watkins, G: R Hill 3, Watkins
Jan 1	BLACKPOOL BOROUGH	W 36-14	5,510	T: Watkins 3, Burgess 2, Coulman, Dixon, Prosser, Richards, Whitehead, G: R Hill 3
Jan 2	WHITEHAVEN	W 7-2	5,821	T: Richards, G: D Hill, McInnes
Jan 11	Wakefield Trinity	L 5-7	5,025	T: Jackson, G: Richards
Jan 16	CASTLEFORD	L 7-12	8,630	T: Charlton, G: Richards 2
Jan 27	St Helens	W 16-15	6,538	T: Bott, Dixon, Hesketh, Whitehead, G: Richards 2
Jan 30	WIDNES	W 19-7	7,256	T: Watkins 2, Coulman, Dixon, J Ward, G: Richards 2
Feb 8	Featherstone Rovers (RLC-1)	W 7-2	14,500	T: Burgess, G: Richards 2
Feb 22	Huddersfield (RLC-2)	D 0-0	10,353	
Feb 26	HUDDERSFIELD (RLC-2 Replay)*	W 11-5	13,637	T: Jackson, G: Richards 3, Watkins
Feb 27	OLDHAM	W 30-3	6,789	T: Richards 3, Henighan 2, Hesketh, Jackson, Whitehead, G: Richards 3
Mar 1	Leigh	D 6-6	12,434	G: Richards 2, Charlton
Mar 7	Castleford (RLC-3)	L 0-15	15,000	
Mar 13	Barrow	L 6-9	4,314	T: Coulman, Henighan
Mar 20	Castleford	L 5-20	5,946	T: Richards, G: Richards
Mar 27	Blackpool Borough	W 41-11	2,631	T: Dixon 2, Henighan 2, Burgess, Charlton, Richards, Smethurst, Whitehead, G: Richards 7
Mar 28	Swinton	L 5-12	6,750	T: Henighan, G: Richards
Mar 30	Wigan	L 11-24	12,929	T: Burgess, Charlton, Richards, G: Richards
Apr 12	Batley	W 23-0	1,845	T: Burgess, Coulman, Henighan, Smethurst, Watkins, G: Watkins 4
Apr 19	HULL (NRL-1)	W 11-4	7,911	T: Coulman, Hesketh, Jackson, G: Watkins
Apr 24	Hull Kingston Rovers (NRL-2)	L 16-27	5,118	T: Dixon 2, Coulman, Smethurst, G: Watkins 2

Salford RL Match Results

1969-1970 *continued*

	Opponent	Result	Attendance	Scorers
May 7	Swinton (F)	L 18-28	1,815	T: Bott, Smethurst, Snell, Whitehead, G: Watkins 3

* Home tie played at Swinton

Lancashire League Championship runners-up

1970-1971

	Opponent	Result	Attendance	Scorers
Aug 7	St Helens (F)*	L 12-29	4,000	T: Watkins, Whitehead, G: D Hill 3
Aug 14	Keighley (F)	W 43-17	1,379	T: Henighan 2, Richards 2, Bott, Charlton, Crank, Prosser, Watkins, G: Watkins 6, R Hill, Richards
Aug 21	Hull Kingston Rovers	L 11-12	5,000	T: Whitehead, G: Watkins 4
Aug 29	Oldham (LC-1)	W 35-12	4,060	T: Charlton 2, Hesketh 2, Coulman, Egan, Jackson, G: Watkins 7
Aug 31	SWINTON	W 30-4	10,000	T: Charlton 2, Richards 2, Henighan, Jackson, G: Watkins 6
Sep 4	Wigan	L 7-13	11,011	T: Bott, G: Watkins 2
Sep 9	CASTLEFORD	L 11-13	7,806	T: Jackson 2, J Ward, G: Egan
Sep 11	WIDNES	L 8-13	6,902	T: Charlton, Dixon, G: D Hill
Sep 13	WIGAN (LC-2)	D 12-12	11,600	T: Prosser, Whitehead, G: Watkins 3
Sep 16	Castleford	W 36-6	5,482	T: Hesketh 2, Prosser 2, Charlton, Richards, G: Watkins 9
Sep 19	Bradford Northern	W 25-9	5,108	T: Jackson 3, Henighan, Richards, G: Watkins 5
Sep 20	Wigan (LC-2 Replay)	L 6-32	20,021	G: Watkins 3
Sep 23	Leigh	L 14-20	9,698	T: Jackson, Watkins, G: Watkins 4
Sep 25	FEATHERSTONE ROVERS	W 45-7	6,880	T: Coulman 3, Richards 2, Brennan, Charlton, Jackson, Watkins, G: Watkins 9
Sep 30	LEIGH	L 7-19	9,187	T: Prosser, G: Watkins 2
Oct 4	Huddersfield	W 10-8	3,656	T: Jackson, Watkins, G: Watkins 2
Oct 9	HULL KINGSTON ROVERS	W 20-0	7,150	T: Charlton, Colloby, Smethurst, Whitehead, G: Watkins 4

Salford RL Match Results

1970-1971 *continued*

	Opponent	Result	Attendance	Scorers
Oct 14	Rochdale Hornets	L 9-20	2,816	T: Richards, G: Watkins 3
Oct 16	WAKEFIELD TRINITY	W 25-10	7,644	T: Jackson 2, Dixon, Orr, Richards, G: Watkins 5
Oct 20	WIDNES (FT-1)	L 2-7	4,135	G: Watkins
Nov 11	NEW ZEALAND (Tour)	L 7-8	2,226	T: Whitehead, G: MacCorquodale 2
Nov 14	Whitehaven	W 10-4	1,823	T: Hesketh, Jackson, G: Colloby, Gill
Nov 20	ST HELENS	L 0-4	7,042	
Nov 29	Warrington	W 50-0	4,148	T: Richards 4, Charlton 2, Jackson 2, Dixon, Hesketh, Prosser, Watkins, G: Watkins 7
Dec 4	WHITEHAVEN	W 33-20	5,516	T: Colloby 2, Dixon 2, Charlton, Watkins, Whitehead, G: Watkins 6
Dec 12	Hull	D 12-12	2,600	T: Jackson, Richards, G: Watkins 3
Dec 26	BARROW	W 21-11	6,062	T: Jackson 2, Hesketh, G: Watkins 6
Jan 10	Wakefield Trinity	L 7-14	10,606	T: Richards, G: Watkins 2
Jan 15	WARRINGTON	W 40-15	6,750	T: Charlton 2, Richards 2, Clarke, Colloby, Coulman, Prosser, Watkins, Whitehead, G: Watkins 5
Jan 24	WAKEFIELD TRINITY (RLC-1)	D 6-6	14,278	G: Watkins 3
Jan 27	Wakefield Trinity (RLC-1 Replay)	W 15-8	11,733	T: Richards 2, Watkins, G: Watkins 3
Jan 29	LEEDS	L 4-42	9,235	G: Watkins 2
Feb 6	St Helens	L 4-26	7,000	G: Watkins 2
Feb 12	HULL	W 24-5	5,809	T: Banner, Charlton, Colloby, Coulman, Dixon, Hesketh, G: Watkins 3
Feb 21	WARRINGTON (RLC-2)	W 20-9	13,424	T: Colloby 2, Charlton, Hesketh, G: Watkins 4
Feb 27	Leeds	L 13-24	8,000	T: Richards 2, Charlton, G: MacCorquodale 2
Mar 6	Castleford (RLC-3)	L 8-9	8,357	T: Coulman, Watkins, G: Watkins
Mar 14	Featherstone Rovers	W 43-24	3,802	T: Watkins 3, Coulman 2, Dixon 2, Charlton, Richards, G: Watkins 8
Mar 19	BRADFORD NORTHERN	W 23-2	5,899	T: Coulman, Devlin, Hesketh, Orr, Watkins, G: Watkins 4

Salford RL Match Results

1970-1971 *continued*

	Opponent	Result	Attendance	Scorers
Mar 26	HUDDERSFIELD	W 17-5	5,854	T: Coulman 2, Hesketh, G: Watkins 4
Mar 30	ROCHDALE HORNETS	W 18-9	5,592	T: Coulman, Dixon, Hardicre, Hesketh, G: Watkins 3
Apr 9	Barrow	W 20-16	4,900	T: Gill, Hesketh, Richards, Watkins, G: Watkins 4
Apr 10	Swinton	W 23-20	8,122	T: Hesketh 2, Dixon, Jackson, Richards, G: Jackson 2, Richards 2
Apr 12	WIGAN	W 16-7	8,819	T: Coulman, Watkins, G: Watkins 5
Apr 16	Widnes	L 5-17	4,100	T: Jackson, G: Watkins
Apr 25	HALIFAX (NRL-1)	W 33-2	7,462	T: Coulman 2, Dixon 2, Banner, Gill, Watkins, G: Watkins 5, Bott
May 1	Leeds (NRL-2)	L 22-37	7,439	T: Jackson, Prosser, Watkins, Whitehead, G: Watkins 5

* Gallie Cup

1971-1972

	Opponent	Result	Attendance	Scorers
Jul 27	Oldham (F)	W 35-8	2,000	T: Colloby 2, Jackson 2, Watkins 2, Charlton, Hesketh, Richards, G: Watkins 4
Jul 30	ST HELENS (F)*	W 28-3	5,048	T: Watkins 2, Coulman, Grice, Hurst, Richards, G: Watkins 5
Aug 8	WORKINGTON TOWN (LC-1)	W 46-5	5,591	T: Dixon 2, Watkins 2, Charlton, Gill, Hesketh, Richards, G: Watkins 11
Aug 15	Swinton (LC-2)	L 11-20	9,005	T: Colloby, Richards, Watkins, G: Watkins
Aug 20	WARRINGTON	W 8-6	7,584	G: Watkins 4
Aug 24	HUYTON	W 53-13	5,096	T: Charlton 3, Richards 3, Colloby 2, Banner, Grice, Kirkbride, G: Watkins 10
Aug 28	Halifax	W 45-2	2,178	T: Charlton 2, Dixon 2, Richards 2 Watkins 2, Colloby, Coulman, Prosser, G: Watkins 6

Salford RL Match Results

1971-1972 *continued*

	Opponent	Result	Attendance	Scorers
Aug 30	SWINTON	W 34-9	9,109	T: Banner, Charlton, Richards, J Ward, G: Watkins 11
Sep 5	Huyton	W 18-7	2,040	T: Charlton, Colloby, G: Watkins 6
Sep 7	HUDDERSFIELD	W 37-4	7,142	T: Colloby 3, Banner, Dixon. Hesketh, Kirkbride, G: Watkins 8
Sep 12	Warrington	W 15-13	9,787	T: Richards, G: Watkins 6
Sep 17	LEEDS	W 27-2	10,514	T: Banner, Charlton, Colloby, Richards, Watkins, G: Watkins 6
Oct 2	St Helens	L 12-23	8,151	T: Jackson, Watkins, G: Watkins 3
Oct 10	WAKEFIELD TRINITY	W 25-5	8,836	T: Dixon 2, Charlton, Colloby, Richards, G: Watkins 5
Oct 19	ROCHDALE HORNETS (FT-1)	L 15-17	3,661	T: Coulman, Richards, Watkins, G: Watkins 3
Oct 22	NEW ZEALAND (Tour)	W 31-30	7,127	T: Watkins 3, Coulman 2, Gill, Richards, G: Watkins 5
Oct 24	HULL	W 17-7	7,138	T: Charlton, Hesketh, Watkins, G: Watkins 4
Oct 30	Leeds	L 5-34	11,507	T: Gwilliam, G: Watkins
Nov 7	BATLEY	W 21-3	5,122	T: Richards 3, Banner, Coulman, Dixon, Watkins
Nov 14	Hull Kingston Rovers (JP-1)	L 14-17	6,415	T: Colloby, Richards, G: Watkins 3, Gill
Nov 21	Workington Town	L 5-9	1,020	T: Coulman, G: Watkins
Nov 26	WARRINGTON (TTC)	W 38-7	4,000	T: Richards 3, Watkins 2, Colloby, Coulman, Dixon, Hesketh, Whitehead, G: Watkins 4
Dec 5	Dewsbury	L 17-22	3,000	T: Davies, Hesketh, Watkins, G: Watkins 4
Dec 10	CASTLEFORD	W 25-9	6,600	T: Richards 2, Charlton, Gill, Whitehead, G: Watkins 5
Dec 17	Hull Kingston Rovers	W 22-8	3,004	T: Richards 2, Coulman, P Ward, G: Watkins 4, Gill
Dec 26	LEIGH	W 27-9	11,409	T: MacCorquodale, Watkins, Whitehead, G: Watkins 9
Jan 2	Leigh	W 10-9	9,515	G: Watkins 5
Jan 7	KEIGHLEY	W 65-3	5,340	T: Coulman 3, Charlton 2, Jackson 2, MacCorquodale 2, Davies, Richards, Watkins, Whitehead, G: Watkins 13

Salford RL Match Results

1971-1972 *continued*

	Opponent	Result	Attendance	Scorers
Jan 16	Wakefield Trinity	L 2-9	6,185	G: Watkins
Jan 21	HULL KINGSTON ROVERS	W 22-11	5,500	T: Dixon 2, Coulman, Richards, G: Watkins 3, G: MacCorquodale 2
Jan 30	WIGAN (RLC-1)	L 12-16	17,900	T: Gwilliam, Richards, G: Watkins 2, MacCorquodale
Feb 6	Batley	W 31-7	2,500	T: Richards 3, Clarke, Dixon, MacCorquodale, Prosser, G: Watkins 5
Feb 13	WIGAN	L 14-24	9,236	T: Watkins 2, Richards, P Ward, G: Watkins
Feb 27	HALIFAX	W 25-2	6,888	T: Charlton 2, Coulman, Dixon, Prosser, G: Watkins 5
Mar 5	Hull	L 14-22	3,500	T: Watkins 4, G: Watkins
Mar 10	WORKINGTON TOWN	W 28-0	5,087	T: Richards 3, Banner, Jackson, Watkins, G: Watkins 5
Mar 17	Castleford	L 12-19	3,358	T: Jackson, Watkins, G: Watkins 3
Mar 24	ST HELENS	L 0-7	8,300	
Mar 31	Swinton	W 2-0	9,200	G: Watkins
Apr 3	Wigan	W 13-10	8,029	T: Dixon, Gill, Richards, G: Watkins 2
Apr 7	DEWSBURY	W 20-9	5,221	T: P Ward 2, Whitehead 2, G: Watkins 4
Apr 9	Huddersfield	W 14-9	3,773	T: Charlton, Watkins, G: Watkins 4
Apr 16	Keighley	W 35-12	2,681	T: Watkins 3, Coulman 2, Whitehead 2, Charlton, Dixon, G: Watkins 4
Apr 23	DEWSBURY (NL-1)	W 23-7	6,575	T: Dixon, Hesketh, P Ward, G: Watkins 7
Apr 30	Wigan (NL-2)	W 21-9	11,416	T: Coulman, Dixon, Gill, G: Watkins 6
May 5	Leeds (NL-SF)	L 0-10	11,211	

* Gallie Cup

1972-1973

	Opponent	Result	Attendance	Scorers
Aug 4	DEWSBURY (F)	L 14-15	2,957	T: Colloby, Whitehead, G: Watkins 4
Aug 11	ST HELENS (F)	D 12-12	3,500	T: Dixon, P Ward, G: Watkins 3

Salford RL Match Results

1972-1973 *continued*

	Opponent	Result	Attendance	Scorers
Aug 19	LEEDS	L 10-15	4,879	G: Watkins 5
Aug 23	Featherstone Rovers	L 15-27	2,199	T: Colloby, Hesketh, Watkins, G: Watkins 3
Aug 26	Whitehaven	W 32-17	1,100	T: Charlton 3, Watkins 2, Banner, Hesketh, Richards, G: Watkins 4
Aug 28	SWINTON	L 8-13	6,369	T: Colloby, Hesketh, G: Watkins
Sep 1	OLDHAM (LC-1)	W 41-17	5,415	T: Charlton 2, Colloby 2, Clarke, Dixon, Watkins, G: Watkins 10
Sep 9	Leeds	L 10-19	7,125	T: Charlton, Hesketh, G: Watkins 2
Sep 15	ROCHDALE HORNETS (LC-2)	W 46-13	5,959	T: Colloby 3, Charlton 2, Dixon, Gill, Hesketh, G: Watkins 11
Sep 17	Leigh	W 27-16	4,782	T: Couman 2, Charlton, Colloby, Dixon, G: Watkins 6
Sep 24	Barrow (JP-1)	W 17-2	1,801	T: Colloby, Richards, Whitehead, G: Watkins 4
Sep 29	HUYTON	W 62-10	4,773	T: Richards 4, Charlton 2, Gill 2, Hesketh 2, Banner, Coulman, Dixon, Watkins, G: Watkins 10
Oct 3	Oldham (FT-1)	L 8-12	4,507	G: Watkins 4
Oct 6	Wigan (LC-SF)	W 14-2	6,027	T: Hesketh, Richards, G: Watkins 4
Oct 8	Blackpool Borough	W 37-10	2,045	T: Colloby 2, Richards 2, Charlton, Dixon, McKay, G: Watkins 5, Colloby 2, Charlton
Oct 13	BLACKPOOL BOROUGH	W 43-13	4,510	T: Hesketh 2, Charlton, Colloby, Eastham, Gill, Richards, J Ward, Watkins, G: Watkins 8
Oct 21	Swinton (LC-Final)*	W 25-11	6,865	T: Banner, Charlton, Eastham, Richards, Watkins, G: Watkins 5
Nov 5	Huyton	W 34-3	1,000	T: Richards 2, Colloby, Coulman, Eastham, Kirkbride, G: Watkins 8
Nov 10	ROCHDALE HORNETS	W 30-7	3,877	T: Richards 3, Eastham, Orr, Watkins, G: Watkins 6
Nov 17	Warrington	L 11-16	5,368	T: Colloby, G: Watkins 4

Salford RL Match Results

1972-1973 *continued*

	Opponent	Result	Attendance	Scorers
Nov 19	NEW ZEALAND (Tour)	W 50-4	3,572	T: Colloby 2, Gill 2, Charlton, Dixon, Kirkbride, Prescott, Richards, Watkins, G: Watkins 10
Nov 24	DEWSBURY (JP-2)	W 19-3	4,039	T: Charlton, Hesketh, Richards, G: Watkins 4, Gill
Nov 26	WORKINGTON TOWN	W 27-10	4,454	T: Colloby, Charlton, Gill, Orr, Richards, G: Watkins 6
Dec 1	BARROW	W 51-10	3,700	T: Watkins 3, Colloby 2, Devlin 2, Richards 2, Charlton, Kirkbride, G: Watkins 9
Dec 10	BRADFORD NORTHERN (JP-3)	W 39-2	6,271	T: Charlton, Devlin, Dixon, Gill, Prescott, Richards, Watkins, G: Watkins 9
Dec 13	Oldham	W 14-12	3,010	T: Charlton, Devlin, G: Watkins 4
Dec 15	LEIGH	W 18-2	5,647	T: Charlton. Gill, Hesketh, Watkins, G: Watkins 3
Dec 24	Bradford Northern	W 19-11	4,545	T: Richards 2, Dixon, G: Watkins 5
Dec 26	Workington Town	W 12-3	1,405	T: Banner, Charlton, G: Watkins 3
Dec 30	Hull Kingston Rovers (JP-SF)	W 15-13	2,946	T: Richards, G: Watkins 5, Dixon
Jan 3	BRADFORD NORTHERN	W 30-4	4,655	T: Charlton 3, Hesketh 2, Richards, G: Watkins 6
Jan 7	Rochdale Hornets	W 13-11	5,348	T: Charlton, Colloby, Gill, G: Watkins 2
Jan 12	FEATHERSTONE ROVERS	W 16-12	4,724	T: Gill, J Ward, G: Watkins 4, Gill
Jan 28	Featherstone Rovers (RLC-1)	L 11-18	9,300	T: Richards, G: Watkins 4
Feb 2	WHITEHAVEN	W 25-7	4,520	T: Davies, Gill, Hesketh, Richards, J Ward, G: Watkins 4, Gill
Feb 11	Barrow	W 28-10	1,000	T: Banner, Charlton, Colloby, Gill, Richards, Watkins, G: Watkins 5
Feb 23	ST HELENS	W 15-10	5,042	T: Colloby, Devlin, Richards, G: Watkins 3
Mar 7	Widnes	W 18-9	3,800	T: Davies, Dixon, Hesketh, McKay, G: Watkins 3
Mar 9	DEWSBURY	W 15-7	5,652	T: Richards 3, G: Watkins 3
Mar 16	St Helens	L 4-21	5,300	G: Watkins 2
Mar 24	Leeds (JP-Final)**	L 7-12	10,102	T: Dixon, G: Watkins 2

Salford RL Match Results

1972-1973 *continued*

	Opponent	Result	Attendance	Scorers
Mar 30	WARRINGTON	L 7-10	8,297	T: Richards, G: Gill, Watkins
Apr 6	WIDNES	W 17-7	4,924	T: Charlton 2, Richards, G: Watkins 4
Apr 13	OLDHAM	W 18-10	5,617	T: Banner, Charlton, Hesketh, Richards, G: Watkins 3
Apr 15	Dewsbury	L 7-14	4,000	T: Devlin, G: Watkins 2
Apr 17	Wigan	L 6-23	5,000	G: Watkins 3
Apr 20	Swinton	W 29-11	6,200	T: Charlton, Devlin, Hesketh, Ramshaw, Richards, G: Watkins 7
Apr 23	WIGAN	W 15-3	6,700	T: Watkins 2, Richards, G: Watkins 3
Apr 29	ROCHDALE HORNETS (NL-1)	L 10-14	9,348	T: Holland 2, G: Watkins 2
May 23	Swinton (F)	W 27-21	3,666	T: Prescott 2, Hesketh, Kirkbride, Richards, J Taylor, Watkins, G: Watkins 2, Prescott

* At Warrington   ** At Huddersfield

Lancashire Cup winners
Player's No.6 Trophy runners-up

1973-1974

	Opponent	Result	Attendance	Scorers
Aug 3	DEWSBURY (F)	W 25-6	3,139	T: Gill, Hesketh, McKay, Walker, Watkins, G: Watkins 5
Aug 10	St Helens (F)	W 18-15	4,000	T: Charlton, Fielding, Gill, Richards, G: Watkins 3
Aug 17	LEIGH	W 31-4	5,500	T: Richards 2, Davies, Gill, Watkins, G: Watkins 8
Aug 25	Bramley	W 14-7	1,500	T: Charlton, Richards, G: Watkins 4
Aug 31	WIDNES (LC-1)	W 12-11	5,399	T: Charlton, Watkins, G: Watkins 3
Sep 7	FEATHERSTONE ROVERS	W 34-4	5,977	T: Gill 2, Fielding, Hesketh, Richards, Walker, G: Watkins 8
Sep 14	ROCHDALE HORNETS (LC-2)	W 24-3	6,365	T: Banner, Fielding, McKay, Watkins, G: Watkins 6
Sep 16	DONCASTER (JP-1)	W 47-17	4,132	T: Hesketh 3, Fielding 2, Knighton 2, McKay, Prescott, Richards, Watkins, G: Watkins 7

Salford RL Match Results

1973-1974 *continued*

	Opponent	Result	Attendance	Scorers
Sep 23	Widnes	W 23-10	4,300	T: Banner, Charlton, Fielding, G: Watkins 7
Sep 25	Whitehaven (LC-SF)	W 23-9	5,000	T: Fielding 2, Charlton, Prescott, Watkins, G: Watkins 4
Sep 28	Hull Kingston Rovers	W 24-2	2,954	T: Charlton 2, Dixon, Holland, G: Watkins 6
Sep 30	AUSTRALIA (Tour)	L 12-15	11,064	T: Fielding, Holland, G: Watkins 3
Oct 5	CASTLEFORD	W 16-5	6,606	T: Fielding 2, Dixon, Watkins, G: Watkins 2
Oct 13	Wigan (LC-Final)*	L 9-19	8,012	T: Watkins, G: Watkins 3
Oct 19	WIGAN	W 8-4	5,799	T: Holland, Knighton, G: Watkins
Oct 23	WARRINGTON (FT-1)	W 26-4	4,389	T: Knighton 2, Banner, McKay, G: Watkins 7
Oct 28	Warrington	L 13-20	9,400	T: Hesketh, G: Watkins 4, Banner
Nov 6	WIDNES (CM-1)	W 32-9	3,709	T: Fielding 2, Charlton, Dixon, J Taylor, Watkins, G: Watkins 6, Holland
Nov 9	Whitehaven	W 15-3	1,500	T: Coulman, Fielding, J Taylor, G: Watkins 2, Holland
Nov 18	Workington Town (CM-2)	L 5-10	1,403	T: Watkins, G: Watkins
Nov 20	WIDNES (FT-2)	L 11-15	2,422	T: Fielding, G: Watkins 4
Dec 9	WHITEHAVEN	W 52-5	4,870	T: Fielding 3, Hesketh 3, Holland 2, Watkins 2, Charlton, Coulman, G: Watkins 8
Dec 16	LEEDS (JP-2)	L 4-17	5,848	G: Watkins 2
Dec 26	DEWSBURY	W 39-2	5,194	T: Fielding 3, Dixon 2, Banner, Charlton, Richards, Watkins, G: Watkins 6
Jan 1	OLDHAM	W 15-12	8,245	T: Fielding 3, G: Watkins 3
Jan 6	Castleford	W 16-11	3,515	T: Fielding, Watkins, G: Watkins 5
Jan 12	BRAMLEY	W 14-10	4,138	T: Charlton, Coulman, G: Watkins 4
Jan 13	WAKEFIELD TRINITY	W 22-7	7,127	T: Fielding 3, Richards, G: Watkins 5
Jan 27	ST HELENS	L 11-12	9,781	T: Charlton, Dixon, Richards, G: Watkins
Feb 3	OLDHAM (RLC-1)	W 26-12	11,792	T: Hesketh 2, Watkins 2, Coulman, Fielding, G: Watkins 4
Feb 10	WIDNES	W 19-7	7,430	T: Dixon, Hesketh, Richards, G: Watkins 5

Salford RL Match Results

1973-1974 *continued*

	Opponent	Result	Attendance	Scorers
Feb 23	Leeds (RLC-2)	L 6-10	12,296	G: Watkins 3
Mar 3	HULL KINGSTON ROVERS	W 23-22	5,688	T: Fielding 2, Davies, Hesketh, Richards, G: Watkins 4
Mar 10	ROCHDALE HORNETS	W 24-16	6,392	T: Fielding 2, Knighton 2, Devlin, Richards, G: Watkins 3
Mar 17	LEEDS	W 61-13	8,082	T: Charlton 2, Devlin 2, Dixon 2, Richards 2, Watkins 2, Fielding, Gill, Hesketh, G: Watkins 11
Mar 19	St Helens	D 19-19	7,000	T: Fielding 2, Richards, G: Watkins 5
Mar 24	Rochdale Hornets	W 8-3	4,091	G: Watkins 4
Mar 26	Dewsbury	L 10-14	2,700	T: Fielding, Watkins, G: Watkins 2
Mar 31	Wakefield Trinity	W 32-13	4,915	T: Fielding 3, Coulman, Dixon, Richards, G: Watkins 7
Apr 2	Leeds	L 5-7	5,605	T: Charlton, G: Watkins
Apr 7	Featherstone Rovers	L 16-27	5,000	T: Fielding 2, Dixon, Watkins, G: Prescott, Watkins
Apr 9	WARRINGTON	W 21-3	8,067	T: Charlton, Dixon, Fielding, Gill, Hesketh, G: Watkins 3
Apr 12	Leigh	W 24-21	3,500	T: Fielding 3, Gill, Richards, Watkins, G: Watkins 3
Apr 13	Oldham	L 2-4	3,000	G: Watkins
Apr 15	Wigan	W 21-12	9,642	T: Fielding, Gill, Richards, J Taylor, Watkins, G: Watkins 2, Walker
Apr 21	BRADFORD NORTHERN (CC-1)	D 16-16	10,236	T: Gill, Hesketh, Richards, Watkins, G: Watkins 2
Apr 25	Bradford Northern (CC-1 Replay)	L 8-17	8,140	T: Watkins 2, G: Watkins

* *At Warrington*

First Division Championship winners
Lancashire Cup runners-up

Salford RL Match Results

1974-1975

Date	Opponent	Result	Attendance	Scorers
Aug 13	SWINTON (RRC)	W 19-14	3,098	T: Coulman, Grimes, Redford, G: Knowles 5
Aug 25	Keighley	L 7-11	2,570	T: Fielding, G: Fielding 2
Aug 26	HALIFAX	W 37-0	3,971	T: Richards 4, Banner, Charlton, Coulman, Graham, P Ward, G: Knowles 5
Aug 30	BLACKPOOL BOROUGH (LC-1)	W 25-8	4,058	T: Knighton 2, Banner, Charlton, Richards, G: Richards 3, Knowles 2
Sep 6	Featherstone Rovers	L 11-12	5,538	T: Richards 2, Charlton, G: Fielding
Sep 8	HUYTON (LC-2)	W 17-15	3,076	T: Fielding 3, G: Fielding 4
Sep 15	York	W 24-14	3,361	T: Fielding 3, Corcoran, G: Fielding 6
Sep 20	DEWSBURY	W 29-13	5,221	T: Fielding 2, Hesketh 2, Gill, Richards, Turnbull, G: Fielding 4
Sep 27	CASTLEFORD (JP-1)	W 36-5	4,755	T: Hesketh 2, Banner, Charlton, Corcoran, Graham, Knighton, Richards, G: Fielding 6
Oct 2	KEIGHLEY	W 45-2	4,563	T: Fielding 3, Gill 3, Banner, Charlton, Graham, G: Fielding 9
Oct 6	Widnes	W 8-7	5,000	T: Graham, Richards, G: Fielding
Oct 11	WORKINGTON TOWN (LC-SF)	W 17-10	5,498	T: Devlin, Fielding, Richards, G: Fielding 4
Oct 19	Wigan	L 8-14	6,139	T: Charlton, Fielding, G: Fielding
Oct 25	YORK	W 42-15	5,262	T: Fielding 3, Charlton 2, Coulman 2, Knighton, Prescott, Richards, G: Fielding 6
Oct 29	HUDDERSFIELD (FT-1)	W 16-2	2,926	T: Knighton, Richards, G: Fielding 5
Nov 2	Widnes (LC-Final)*	L 2-6	7,403	G: Fielding
Nov 8	BRAMLEY (JP-2)	W 14-9	4,295	T: Fielding, Richards, G: Fielding 4
Nov 12	St Helens (FT-2)	W 11-7	4,500	T: Banner, G: Fielding 4
Nov 15	CASTLEFORD**	V 13-10	6,470	T: Dixon, Fielding, Richards, G: Fielding 2
Nov 23	Leeds	L 15-28	6,161	T: Charlton, Coulman, Devlin, G: Redford 3
Nov 29	WARRINGTON	W 11-7	6,294	T: Fielding, Prescott, Richards, G: Fielding

Salford RL Match Results

1974-1975 *continued*

	Opponent	Result	Attendance	Scorers
Dec 3	HULL KINGSTON ROVERS (FT-SF)	W 27-10	3,727	T: Fielding 4, Brophy, Devlin, Knighton, G: Fielding 3
Dec 7	Hull Kingston Rovers (JP-3)	L 17-25	3,927	T: Knighton, Prescott, Richards, G: Fielding 4
Dec 15	Bradford Northern	L 5-14	5,065	T: Charlton, G: Brophy
Dec 17	WARRINGTON (FT-Final)	D 0-0	4,473	
Dec 22	Bramley	W 15-8	2,380	T: Graham 2, Charlton, G: Fielding 3
Dec 26	WIDNES	W 10-9	6,599	T: Brophy, Coulman, G: Fielding 2
Dec 29	ST HELENS	L 0-14	8,575	
Jan 1	ROCHDALE HORNETS	W 18-0	5,416	T: Charlton, Coulman, Graham, Richards, G: Fielding 3
Jan 5	Featherstone Rovers	L 12-18	2,826	T: Prescott, Richards, G: Fielding 3
Jan 10	WAKEFIELD TRINITY	L 6-16	6,402	T: Knighton, Watkins
Jan 19	Warrington	L 2-7	7,117	G: Fiddler
Jan 24	CASTLEFORD	D 11-11	5,251	T: Knighton, Richards, Stead, G: Watkins
Jan 28	Warrington (FT-Final Replay)	W 10-5	5,778	T: Fielding, Richards, G: Watkins 2
Feb 2	St Helens	L 5-18	8,600	T: Richards, G: Watkins
Feb 9	Featherstone Rovers (RLC-1)	W 17-7	6,000	T: Coulman, Fielding, Stead, G: Watkins 4
Feb 23	LEEDS (RLC-2)	L 12-17	12,041	T: Fiddler, Prescott, G: Watkins 3
Mar 7	Castleford	W 15-12	2,730	T: Coulman, Graham, Hesketh, G: Fiddler 3
Mar 11	BRADFORD NORTHERN	L 7-9	4,625	T: Richards, G: Fiddler 2
Mar 21	BRAMLEY	W 28-8	4,000	T: Banner, Charlton, Fielding, Prescott, Richards, Stead, G: Fiddler 5
Mar 23	Wakefield Trinity	L 10-12	2,911	T: Fielding, Gill, G: Fiddler 2
Mar 28	Rochdale Hornets	L 9-18	2,510	T: Fiddler, G: Fiddler 3
Mar 31	WIGAN	L 20-30	5,715	T: Richards 3, Coulman, G: Fiddler 4
Apr 8	LEEDS	W 12-3	4,501	T: Gill, Watkins, G: Fiddler 3
Apr 13	Dewsbury	L 16-17	3,133	T: Butler 2, Charlton, Richards, G: Fiddler 2
Apr 20	Halifax	W 13-4	1,984	T: Fielding, G: Fiddler 5
Apr 27	Widnes (PT-1)	W 20-12	7,500	T: Butler 2, Fielding, Watkins, G: Fiddler 4

Salford RL Match Results

1974-1975 *continued*

	Opponent	Result	Attendance	Scorers
Apr 29	Wigan (PT-2)	L 17-35	6,316	T: Devlin, Fielding, Knighton, G: Fiddler 4
Apr 30	France (F)***	L 13-23	–	T: Banner, Fielding, Hesketh, G: Fiddler 2

Scoring values: Drop-goal decreased to 1 point from this season

* At Wigan   ** Declared void after Castleford protested pitch invasion in closing seconds – replay ordered   *** At Marseille

BBC2 Floodlit Trophy winners
Lancashire Cup runners-up

1975-1976

	Opponent	Result	Attendance	Scorers
Aug 5	SWINTON (RRC)	W 15-12	3,000	T: Banner, G: Watkins 6
Aug 8	ST HELENS (F)	W 17-15	3,000	T: Prescott, Richards, Sheffield, G: Watkins 4
Aug 15	DEWSBURY	W 39-2	3,922	T: Fielding 3, Knighton 2, Richards 2, Butler, Gill, G: Watkins 6
Aug 22	WARRINGTON	W 25-11	6,033	T: Fielding 2, Butler, Hesketh, Richards, G: Fielding 5
Aug 25	SWINTON	W 13-2	6,267	T: Butler 2, Richards, G: Fielding 2
Aug 31	HUYTON (LC-1)	W 44-17	3,812	T: Fielding 2, Richards 2, Gill, Graham, Hesketh, Nash, Prescott, Turnbull, G: Fielding 7
Sep 5	WIDNES	W 30-10	6,694	T: Nash 3, Butler, Richards, Watkins, G: Watkins 6
Sep 14	Leigh (LC-2)	W 23-6	4,922	T: Butler 2, Fiddler, Richards, G: Watkins 5, DG: Nash
Sep 23	St Helens (LC-SF)	W 21-8	9,000	T: Butler, Graham, Richards, Turnbull, G: Watkins 4, DG: Nash
Sep 26	MAYFIELD (JP-1)	W 57-3	3,500	T: Butler 2, Fielding 2, Graham 2, Richards 2, Fiddler, Hawksley, Watkins, G: Watkins 12
Sep 30	Wigan (FT-Preliminary)	D 14-14	3,774	T: Knighton, Watkins, G: Watkins 4
Oct 4	Widnes (LC-Final)*	L 7-16	7,566	T: Richards, G: Watkins 2
Oct 7	WIGAN (FT-Prelim Replay)	L 19-25	5,402	T: Butler, Coulman, Fielding, Gill, Hawksley, G: Nash 2

Salford RL Match Results

1975-1976 *continued*

Date	Opponent	Result	Attendance	Scorers
Oct 14	AUSTRALIA (Tour)	L 6-44	5,357	T: Fiddler, Mayor
Oct 17	CASTLEFORD	W 18-10	5,217	T: Hesketh 2, Knighton, Richards, G: Fiddler 3
Nov 2	Huddersfield	W 40-13	3,030	T: Richards 4, Coulman 2, Graham, Nash, Stead, G: Prescott 6, DG: Prescott
Nov 9	OLDHAM (JP-2)	W 46-3	6,483	T: Fielding 3, Turnbull 2, Coulman, Graham, Hesketh, Knighton, Richards, G: Watkins 8
Nov 16	Oldham	W 37-10	3,914	T: Butler 2, Hesketh 2, Fielding, Turnbull, Watkins, G: Watkins 8
Nov 23	WORKINGTON TOWN (JP-3)	W 16-8	5,020	T: Fielding, Watkins, G: Watkins 5
Nov 28	FEATHERSTONE ROVERS	W 13-7	5,444	T: Hesketh, Richards, G: Fiddler 2, Watkins, DG: Nash
Dec 7	Bradford Northern	W 12-11	5,518	T: Hesketh, Richards, G: Watkins 3
Dec 13	HULL (JP-SF)	L 14-22	4,070	T: Graham, Watkins, G: Watkins 4
Dec 22	WAKEFIELD TRINITY	L 9-16	4,702	T: Watkins, G: Watkins 3
Dec 26	Widnes	L 14-19	7,800	T: Fielding, Richards, G: Watkins 4
Dec 28	BRADFORD NORTHERN	W 20-10	6,358	T: Gill 2, Hesketh, Watkins, G: Watkins 4
Jan 1	OLDHAM	D 8-8	4,152	T: Fielding, Richards, G: Watkins
Jan 3	Leeds	L 14-28	6,145	T: Fielding, Richards, G: Watkins 3, Nash
Jan 11	Warrington	L 7-8	6,406	T: Graham 2, DG: Gill
Jan 16	KEIGHLEY	W 20-10	4,507	T: Richards 2, Coulman, Knighton, G: Watkins 4
Jan 25	Wakefield Trinity	W 13-4	3,698	T: Fielding 2, Hesketh, G: Watkins 2
Feb 3	WIGAN	W 36-20	5,226	T: Butler 2, Hesketh 2, Richards 2, Prescott, Watkins, G: Watkins 6
Feb 6	Castleford	W 19-16	2,851	T: Butler, Fielding, Richards, G: Watkins 5
Feb 14	Castleford (RLC-1)	W 25-3	4,872	T: Butler, Coulman, Fielding, Knighton, Richards, G: Watkins 5
Feb 20	LEEDS	W 7-5	6,676	G: Watkins 3, DG: Watkins
Feb 29	ST HELENS (RLC-2)	L 11-17	13,023	T: Fielding, G: Watkins 4
Mar 5	ST HELENS	W 10-9	6,051	T: Dixon, Richards, G: Watkins 2

Salford RL Match Results

1975-1976 *continued*

	Opponent	Result	Attendance	Scorers
Mar 10	Hull Kingston Rovers	L 10-15	3,387	T: Coulman, Nash, G: Fielding, Nash
Mar 14	Dewsbury	W 13-2	1,800	T: Graham 2, Fielding, G: Watkins 2
Mar 21	Featherstone Rovers	L 6-21	5,370	G: Watkins 3
Mar 30	St Helens	L 7-24	5,550	T: Richards, G: Watkins 2
Apr 2	HULL KINGSTON ROVERS	W 19-3	4,026	T: Hesketh 2, Nash, Richards, Watkins, G: Watkins 2
Apr 9	HUDDERSFIELD	W 24-9	4,369	T: Coulman, Grice, Prescott, Richards, G: Watkins 6
Apr 16	Swinton	W 30-22	6,083	T: Fielding 2, Watkins 2, Devlin, Richards, G: Watkins 6
Apr 19	Wigan	W 24-15	7,204	T: Butler 2, Fielding, Sheffield, G: Watkins 6
Apr 25	Keighley	W 18-10	3,043	T: Coulman, Dixon, Fielding, Richards, G: Watkins 3
Apr 30	HULL KINGSTON ROVERS (PT-1)	W 21-6	5,607	T: Coulman, Prescott, Richards, G: Watkins 6
May 11	WAKEFIELD TRINITY (PT-SF)	W 10-5	5,381	T: Nash, Richards, G: Watkins 2
May 16	Wakefield Trinity (PT SF)	W 14-5	7,048	T: Butler, Hesketh, Richards, G: Watkins 2, DG: Watkins
May 22	St Helens (PT-Final)**	L 2-15	18,082	DG: Watkins 2

* At Wigan   ** At Swinton

First Division Championship winners
Premiership Trophy runners-up
Lancashire Cup runners-up

1976-1977

	Opponent	Result	Attendance	Scorers
Aug 13	SWINTON (RRC)	W 36-8	2,500	T: Corcoran 2, Butler, Frodsham, Gill, Nash, Rawlinson, Turnbull, G: Knowles 6
Aug 17	DEWSBURY (F)	W 39-11	1,724	T: Fielding 2, Gill 2, Rawlinson 2, Devlin, Dixon, Sheffield, G: Fielding 6

Salford RL Match Results

1976-1977 *continued*

Date	Opponent	Result	Attendance	Scorers
Aug 22	HUYTON (LC-1)	W 46-14	3,151	T: Gill 3, Richards 3, Dixon, Fielding, Graham, Knighton, G: Fielding 8
Aug 29	Warrington (LC-2)	L 13-14	6,481	T: Coulman, Richards, Sheffield, G: Watkins 2
Sep 3	WARRINGTON	W 16-5	5,761	T: Butler, Knighton, Richards, G: Watkins 3, DG: Watkins
Sep 12	Featherstone Rovers	W 23-12	4,114	T: Gill 2, Fielding, G: Watkins 7
Sep 18	Widnes	L 12-15	4,942	T: Hesketh, Watkins, G: Watkins 3
Sep 24	HULL KINGSTON ROVERS	D 16-16	5,334	T: Hesketh, Mantle, G: Watkins 5
Sep 28	Leigh (FT-1)	L 18-22	2,724	T: Butler, Fielding, Knighton, Richards, G: Watkins 3
Oct 3	Wigan	L 15-32	4,501	T: Dixon, Fielding, Hesketh, G: Watkins 3
Oct 8	ROCHDALE HORNETS	W 33-6	5,185	T: Turnbull 2, Dixon, Gill, Graham, Hesketh, Mantle, G: Watkins 6
Oct 17	Wakefield Trinity	W 18-12	2,794	T: Hesketh 2, Butler, Turnbull, G: Watkins 3
Oct 24	ACE AMATEURS (Hull) (JP-1)	W 39-15	3,037	T: Butler 2, Gill 2, Warren 2, Dixon, Graham, Richards, G: Watkins 6
Oct 29	ST HELENS	L 15-18	6,824	T: Mantle, Richards, G: Watkins 4, DG: Watkins
Nov 6	Leeds (JP-2)	L 17-18	5,201	T: Butler, Gill, Richards, Turnbull, G: Watkins 2, DG: Nash
Nov 12	Castleford	W 14-9	4,160	T: Richards, Watkins, G: Watkins 4
Nov 28	Bradford Northern	L 16-25	5,717	T: Butler, Gill, G: Watkins 5
Dec 5	WAKEFIELD TRINITY	W 22-13	4,450	T: Coulman, Gill, Hesketh, Richards, G: Watkins 5
Dec 12	Warrington	L 10-44	3,869	T: Butler, Mantle, G: Watkins 2
Dec 19	LEIGH	L 12-13	4,551	T: Nash, Richards, G: Watkins 3
Dec 26	WIDNES	L 9-13	7,450	T: Gill, G: Watkins 3
Jan 2	OLDHAM	W 33-12	5,975	T: Fielding 2, Coulman, Gill, Nash, Richards, Watkins, G: Watkins 6
Jan 9	Hull Kingston Rovers	L 10-15	4,758	T: Richards, Turnbull, G: Watkins 2

Salford RL Match Results

1976-1977 *continued*

	Opponent	Result	Attendance	Scorers
Jan 14	WORKINGTON TOWN	W 17-5	4,305	T: Fielding 3, Hesketh, Turnbull, G: Watkins
Jan 23	Leigh	W 45-8	4,312	T: Richards 3, Watkins 2, Butler, Fielding, Graham, Hesketh, Mantle, Prescott, G: Watkins 6
Jan 30	BARROW	W 38-13	4,565	T: Fielding 3, Butler 2, Hesketh 2, Richards 2, Turnbull, G: Fielding 3, Gill
Feb 5	Leeds	W 28-13	4,335	T: Coulman, Dixon, Gill, Hesketh, Nash, Richards, G: Fielding 5
Feb 11	HUDDERSFIELD (RLC-1)	W 25-2	3,997	T: Fielding 2, Graham, Prescott, Turnbull, G: Watkins 4, Fielding
Feb 27	Workington Town (RLC-2)	L 4-13	7,400	G: Watkins 2
Mar 6	St Helens	L 9-29	6,315	T: Prescott, G: Watkins 3
Mar 11	FEATHERSTONE ROVERS	L 17-18	4,982	T: Butler, Fielding, Knighton, G: Watkins 4
Mar 24	Workington Town	W 12-6	1,702	T: Dixon, Knighton, G: McGreal 3
Mar 27	Rochdale Hornets	L 10-11	2,052	T: Fielding, Richards, G: Watkins 2
Apr 3	Oldham	W 37-8	1,508	T: Fielding 4, Coulman 2, Mantle, Prescott, Richards, G: Watkins 5
Apr 8	Barrow	W 15-12	2,955	T: Coulman, Gill, Graham, G: Watkins 3
Apr 11	WIGAN	W 14-10	6,285	T: Fielding, Richards, G: Watkins 4
Apr 15	CASTLEFORD	W 12-7	5,613	T: Coulman, Dixon, G: Watkins 3
Apr 22	BRADFORD NORTHERN	W 32-2	5,058	T: Coulman 3, Fielding 3, Gill, Watkins, G: Watkins 4
Apr 24	LEEDS*	A 2-5	4,209	G: Watkins
May 1	Castleford (PT-1)	L 17-25	5,391	T: Fielding, Hesketh, Mayor, G: Watkins 4

* Abandoned 38 mins (after tragic death of Leeds player Chris Sanderson)

Salford RL Match Results

1977-1978

Date	Opponent	Result	Attendance	Scorers
Aug 10	LEIGH (F)	W 23-15	2,500	T: Dixon 2, Knighton, Prescott, Watkins, G: Watkins 4
Aug 14	Swinton (RRC)	W 35-15	2,000	T: Fielding 2, Grice 2, Knighton, Turnbull, Prescott, G: Watkins 6, Oldham
Aug 21	Workington Town (LC-1)	L 12-17	2,537	T: Prescott, G: Watkins 4, DG: Watkins
Aug 30	NEW HUNSLET (FT-Preliminary)	W 39-5	1,962	T: Richards 3, Butler, Coulman, Nash, Prescott, Stead, Turnbull, G: Watkins 6
Sep 2	FEATHERSTONE ROVERS	W 7-3	5,011	T: Knighton, G: Watkins 2
Sep 11	Bradford Northern	L 14-35	5,893	T: Coulman, Dixon, G: Watkins 4
Sep 14	Warrington	W 17-14	3,778	T: Fielding, Gill, Prescott, G: Watkins 4
Sep 18	New Hunslet	W 17-14	2,750	T Prescott, G: Watkins 6, DG: Watkins 2
Sep 25	WARRINGTON	W 21-10	4,917	T: Hesketh, Nash, Richards, Turnbull, G: Watkins 4, DG: Watkins
Oct 2	Dewsbury	W 20-10	2,304	T: Fielding 2, Prescott, Turnbull, G: Watkins 4
Oct 4	Whitehaven (FT-1)	W 6-5	1,700	T: Nash, G: Watkins, DG: Watkins
Oct 7	NEW HUNSLET	W 30-12	4,579	T: Fielding 4, Richards 2, Hesketh, G: Watkins 4, DG: Watkins
Oct 21	ROCHDALE HORNETS (JP-1)	W 27-8	5,013	T: Fielding 2, Butler, Nash, Richards, G: Watkins 6
Oct 28	HULL KINGSTON ROVERS	W 23-9	4,786	T: Richards 2, Evans, Gill, Turnbull, G: Watkins 4
Nov 1	OLDHAM (FT-2)	W 29-10	2,410	T: Richards 3, Butler 2, Dixon, Fielding, G: Watkins 4
Nov 6	Warrington (JP-2)	L 10-19	6,042	T: Hesketh, Richards, G: Fielding, Richards
Nov 13	Wakefield Trinity	L 7-14	3,661	T: Prescott, G: Watkins 2
Nov 27	St Helens	L 12-13	7,286	T: Fielding, Richards, G: Watkins 3
Dec 4	CASTLEFORD	W 37-8	4,461	T: Richards 3, Gill 2, Fielding, Grice, Irving, Watkins, G: Watkins 5
Dec 6	St Helens (FT-SF)	L 4-7	3,500	G: Fielding 2
Dec 9	Hull Kingston Rovers	L 10-13	4,769	T: Evans, Nash, G: Fielding 2

Salford RL Match Results

1977-1978 *continued*

	Opponent	Result	Attendance	Scorers
Dec 18	WAKEFIELD TRINITY	W 21-9	4,286	T: Fielding 2, Gill, Irving, Richards, G: Fielding 3
Dec 26	Widnes	L 10-16	8,212	T: Nash, Williams, G: Gill, Nash
Jan 1	WORKINGTON TOWN	L 13-19	4,757	T: Fielding 2, Irving, G: Watkins 2
Jan 8	Bramley	W 21-13	1,750	T: Dixon 2, Corcoran, Evans, Fielding, G: Fielding 3
Jan 11	DEWSBURY	W 20-7	2,145	T: Fielding 2, H Henney, Prescott, G: Fielding 4
Jan 18	WIGAN	L 0-10	4,377	
Jan 22	Featherstone Rovers	L 8-40	3,058	T: Fielding 2, G: Watkins
Jan 27	BRAMLEY	L 13-14	2,543	T: Evans, Prescott, Richards, G: Watkins 2
Feb 2	LEEDS	W 21-3	3,317	T: Grice, H Henney, Irving, G: Watkins 6
Feb 24	BRAMLEY (RLC-1)	W 9-7	4,132	T: Butler, G: Watkins 3
Mar 3	HULL	W 27-18	3,845	T: Fielding 3, Prescott 2, Butler, Graham, G: Watkins 3
Mar 12	Huddersfield (RLC-2)	L 3-13	5,709	T: Graham
Mar 21	ST HELENS	L 11-24	4,159	T: Fielding, H Henney, Watkins, G: Watkins
Mar 24	Workington Town	L 7-9	3,633	T: Turnbull, G: Watkins 2
Mar 27	Wigan	W 17-10	6,320	T: Butler, Fielding, Richards, Turnbull, G: Watkins 2, DG: Nash
Mar 31	WIDNES	L 12-20	6,086	T: Butler, H Henney, G: Watkins 3
Apr 3	Castleford	W 22-14	3,728	T: Richards 2, Fielding, Knighton, Watkins, G: Watkins 3, DG: Watkins
Apr 5	BRADFORD NORTHERN	W 21-13	3,961	T: Fielding 2, Harris, Hesketh, G: Watkins 4, DG: Watkins
Apr 15	Leeds	L 7-34	6,271	T: Irving, G: Watkins 2
Apr 23	Hull	L 4-18	4,607	G: Watkins 2
Apr 30	St Helens (PT-1)	L 11-29	6,000	T: Fielding 2, Nash, G: Watkins

1978-1979

	Opponent	Result	Attendance	Scorers
Aug 6	Leigh (F)	L 10-16	2,500	T: Dixon, Hesketh, G: Watkins 2
Aug 8	SWINTON (RRC)	W 21-2	3,000	T: Butler, Irving, Nash, G: Watkins 6

Salford RL Match Results

1978-1979 *continued*

	Opponent	Result	Attendance	Scorers
Aug 13	Blackpool Borough (F)	W 31-0	250	T: Fielding 2, Nash 2, Richards 2, Butler, G: Rule 5
Aug 18	OLDHAM (LC-1)	W 30-15	4,197	T: Dixon, Fielding, Irving, Prescott, Richards, Turnbull, G: Watkins 6
Aug 27	Whitehaven (LC-2)	W 19-6	4,700	T: Butler, Fielding, Irving, Rule, Williams, G: Rule 2
Sep 1	FEATHERSTONE ROVERS	W 24-10	4,745	T: Dixon 2, Fielding, H Henney, G: Watkins 6
Sep 6	Huddersfield	W 25-10	2,000	T: Fielding 2, Ashcroft, Graham, Rule, G: Rule 5
Sep 9	Leeds	L 16-30	6,049	T: Dixon, Richards, Rule, Turnbull, G: Rule 2
Sep 13	WORKINGTON TOWN (LC-SF)	L 8-9	5,729	T: Fielding, G: Watkins 2, DG: Nash
Sep 15	WARRINGTON	L 7-23	5,432	T: Jones, G: Rule 2
Sep 22	ROCHDALE HORNETS (JP-1)	W 25-7	4,470	T: Fielding 2, Hesketh, Nash, Watkins, G: Watkins 5
Sep 29	BRADFORD NORTHERN	W 17-8	4,258	T: Coulman, Turnbull, Watkins, G: Watkins 4
Oct 13	HULL KINGSTON ROVERS	L 14-19	5,308	T: Butler, Rule, G: Rule 4
Oct 17	ST HELENS (FT-1)	L 15-17	4,632	T: Butler, Dixon, Stead, G: Watkins 3
Oct 22	Leigh	W 31-2	4,361	T: Rule 2, Butler, Richards, Stead, G: Rule 8
Oct 27	WORKINGTON TOWN	L 8-24	4,410	T: Richards, Rule, G: Rule
Nov 1	AUSTRALIA (Tour)	L 2-14	6,155	G: Watkins
Nov 7	Widnes	L 5-16	6,349	T: McGreal, G: Watkins
Nov 12	Wakefield Trinity	D 10-10	4,167	T: Fielding, McGreal, G: Watkins 2
Nov 17	BARROW	W 24-7	3,355	T: Fielding 2, Butler, Coulman, Prescott, Rule, G: Watkins 3
Nov 24	Castleford	L 10-34	3,429	T: Fielding, Richards, G: Rule 2
Dec 3	Hull Kingston Rovers (JP-2)	L 14-16	5,504	T: Fielding, Butler, Rule, G: Rule 2, DG: Ashcroft
Dec 10	ST HELENS	L 13-16	4,498	T: Dootson, Philbin, Richards, G: Rule 2
Dec 26	WIDNES	D 10-10	5,863	T: Prescott, G: Watkins 3, DG: Watkins
Jan 23	ROCHDALE HORNETS	L 4-13	2,884	G: Johns 2
Feb 2	LEIGH	L 15-22	3,007	T: Dixon, Stead, Stephenson, G: Rule 3
Feb 11	BRAMLEY (RLC-1)	D 6-6	3,639	T: Fielding, G: Watkins, DG: Watkins

Salford RL Match Results

1978-1979 *continued*

	Opponent	Result	Attendance	Scorers
Feb 27	Bramley (RLC-1 Replay)	D 2-2	1,750	G: Watkins
Mar 1	Bramley (RLC-1 2nd Replay)*	L 5-7	2,543	T: Prescott, G: Johns
Mar 9	LEEDS	L 0-3	2,743	
Mar 14	CASTLEFORD	W 16-5	2,668	T: Harris, Hey, O'Neill, G: Fielding 3, DG: Nash
Mar 20	Hull Kingston Rovers	L 7-19	4,831	T: McGreal, G: Whitfield 2
Mar 23	WAKEFIELD TRINITY	L 6-15	3,640	T: Fielding, Lang
Apr 1	Rochdale Hornets	W 8-5	1,968	T: Fielding, Wilson, G: Watkins
Apr 3	Bradford Northern	W 12-8	5,129	T: Driver, Williams, G: Whitfield 3
Apr 6	HUDDERSFIELD	W 38-3	3,168	T: Ashcroft, Dixon, Fielding, Nash, Prescott, Stephenson, Turnbull, Williams, G: Whitfield 7
Apr 16	WIGAN	W 23-15	5,552	T: Richards 3, Fielding, Turnbull, Williams, G: Fielding, Whitfield, DG: Stephenson
Apr 19	Workington Town	L 0-5	2,947	
Apr 22	Barrow	L 3-32	2,841	T: McGreal
Apr 29	Featherstone Rovers	L 8-20	2,060	T: Hesketh, Johns, G: Johns
May 2	Warrington	L 5-12	3,741	T: Nash, G: Fielding
May 12	Wigan	W 26-13	3,543	T: Fielding 4, Richards, Stephenson, G: Whitfield 4
May 13	St Helens	L 4-26	4,800	G: Whitfield 2

* At Swinton

1979-1980

	Opponent	Result	Attendance	Scorers
Aug 8	LEIGH (F)	W 20-6	2,500	T: Whitfield 2, Dixon, Fielding, G: Whitfield 4
Aug 12	Swinton (RRC)	W 38-15	2,500	T: Stephenson 3, Coulman, Driver, Harris, Turnbull, Williams, G: Rule 7
Aug 19	Workington Town (LC-1)	L 8-14	3,335	T: Coulman, Stephenson, G: Rule
Sep 2	Blackpool Borough	W 22-2	2,400	T: Fielding, O'Neill, Richards, Wilson, G: Rule 5
Sep 7	ST HELENS	W 25-21	4,430	T: Fielding 3, Gill, Harris, G: Rule 5
Sep 14	HUDDERSFIELD (JP-1)	W 47-5	3,597	T: Coulman 3, Fielding 2, Prescott 2, Rule 2, G: Rule 10
Sep 21	LEEDS	W 24-7	5,046	T: Fielding, McGreal, Prescott, Williams, G: Rule 6

Salford RL Match Results

1979-1980 *continued*

	Opponent	Result	Attendance	Scorers
Sep 30	BRAMLEY (JP-2)	W 23-9	4,500	T: Coulman, Prescott, Wilson, G: Rule 7
Oct 7	Warrington	W 30-7	6,931	T: Fielding 2, Richards 2, Coulman, G: Rule 7, DG: Ashcroft
Oct 9	WIGAN (FT-1)	W 24-6	4,717	T: Fielding 2, Richards, Wilson, G: Rule 6
Oct 14	WIDNES	D 16-16	11,982	T: Fielding, Richards, G: Rule 4, DG: Rule, Stephenson
Oct 21	Castleford (JP-3)	W 13-6	5,240	T: Ashcroft, Wilson, G: Rule 3, DG: Rule
Oct 26	HULL KINGSTON ROVERS	W 17-5	5,303	T: Fielding 2, McGreal, G: Rule 4
Nov 3	Widnes (JP-SF)*	L 3-19	6,567	T: Whitfield
Nov 9	WIGAN	W 29-13	4,178	T: Whitfield 2, Coulman, Fielding, O'Neill, G: Rule 7
Nov 23	HUNSLET	W 19-12	3,675	T: Rule, Turnbull, Whitfield, G: Rule 5
Nov 28	WORKINGTON TOWN	W 19-7	3,525	T: Fielding 2, Driver, Rule, G: Rule 3, DG: Rule
Nov 30	St Helens (FT-2)	L 10-15	6,000	T: Rule, G: Rule 2, DG: Rule 3
Dec 2	York	W 16-12	3,698	T: Dootson, Whitfield, Williams, G: Rule 3, DG: Rule
Dec 16	Hunslet	W 7-4	1,500	G: Rule 3, DG: Rule
Dec 23	BRADFORD NORTHERN	L 11-14	6,500	T: Fielding, G: Rule 4
Dec 26	Widnes	L 6-16	7,494	T: Stephenson, G: Rule, DG: Rule
Dec 29	Hull Kingston Rovers	L 10-23	4,842	T: Harris, Rule, G: Rule 2
Jan 12	St Helens	W 18-17	4,111	T: Coulman, Prescott, Whitfield, G: Rule 4, DG: Ashcroft
Jan 20	BLACKPOOL BOROUGH	L 7-11	3,337	T: Stephenson, G: Rule 2
Jan 26	Leeds	L 2-24	7,400	G: Rule
Feb 1	CASTLEFORD	W 22-12	2,985	T: Dixon, Fielding, Gourley, Prescott, G: Rule 5
Feb 10	Huyton (RLC-1)	W 25-0	1,500	T: Coulman, Dixon, Harris, Rule, Whitfield, G: Rule 5
Feb 17	Hull	L 2-16	9,796	G: Rule
Feb 24	Rochdale Hornets (RLC-2)	W 20-2	3,350	T: Fielding 2, Coulman, Gourley, G: Rule 4
Mar 8	WIDNES (RLC-3)	L 8-9	9,711	T: Stephenson, G: Rule, DG: Rule 2, Ashcroft
Mar 14	Castleford	W 20-8	3,069	T: H Henney, Prescott, Richards, Rule, G: Rule 4

Salford RL Match Results

1979-1980 *continued*

	Opponent	Result	Attendance	Scorers
Mar 16	WAKEFIELD TRINITY	W 27-5	3,883	T: Fielding 2, Nash, Richards, Stephenson, G: Rule 6
Mar 21	YORK	W 32-11	2,937	T: Fielding 2, Coulman, Gill, O'Neill, Prescott, Richards, Stephenson, G: Rule 2, Whitfield 2
Mar 23	Bradford Northern	L 0-15	6,132	
Mar 28	WARRINGTON	W 21-13	3,889	T: Coulman, Fielding, Richards, Stephenson, G: Whitfield 4, DG: Whitfield
Apr 4	Leigh	L 10-24	5,247	T: Fielding, McGreal, G: Whitfield 2
Apr 7	Wigan	L 15-18	4,667	T: Fielding, Prescott, Wilson, G: Whitfield 3
Apr 11	HULL	W 15-3	4,897	T: Dixon, Whitfield, Wilson, G: Whitfield 3
Apr 13	Wakefield Trinity	W 23-14	4,120	T: Stephenson 2, Fielding, Gourley, Williams, G: Whitfield 4
Apr 16	Workington Town	W 20-5	2,109	T: Fielding, Prescott, Richards, Stead, G: Whitfield 4
Apr 20	LEIGH	L 10-19	6,119	T: Coulman, Wilson, G: Whitfield 2
Apr 27	LEEDS (PT-1)	L 13-27	5,382	T: Stephenson 2, Prescott, G: Whitfield 2

* At Warrington

1980-1981

	Opponent	Result	Attendance	Scorers
Aug 8	SWINTON (RRC)	W 26-9	2,500	T: Richards 2, Wilson 2, Lang, Smith, G: Oldham 3, Smith
Aug 10	Dewsbury (F)	W 23-21	–	T: Nash 2, Driver, Richards, Williams, G: Smith 4
Aug 17	LEIGH (LC-1)	W 23-12	3,579	T: Fielding, O'Neill, Turnbull, Williams, Wilson, G: Whitfield 4
Aug 24	Oldham (LC-2)	L 13-15	3,445	T: Fielding, Richards, G: Whitfield 3, DG: Nash
Aug 31	Hull Kingston Rovers	L 20-28	7,911	T: Fielding 3, Prescott, G: Rule 3, Whitfield
Sep 5	HALIFAX	W 41-16	2,837	T: Wilson 3, Coulman, Fielding, Prescott, Richards, Stephenson, Turnbull, G: Whitfield 7

Salford RL Match Results

1980-1981 *continued*

	Opponent	Result	Attendance	Scorers
Sep 14	Castleford	L 8-37	3,060	T: Fielding, Wilson, G: Whitfield
Sep 19	ST HELENS	L 19-25	3,990	T: Coulman, Richards, Sheffield, G: Whitfield 5
Sep 26	WORKINGTON TOWN	W 36-8	2,735	T: Fielding 2, Ashcroft, Coulman, McGovern, Richards, Smith, Stephenson, G: Whitfield 6
Oct 5	Widnes	W 26-10	5,086	T: Stephenson 2, Latham, O'Neill, Richards, G: Johns 3, Nash, Whitfield, DG: Nash
Oct 12	HULL	L 16-34	6,306	T: Driver, Latham, Richards, Smith, G: Smith 2
Oct 19	Bradford Northern	L 5-27	5,494	T: Wilson, G: Smith
Oct 24	FEATHERSTONE ROVERS	W 13-9	2,499	T: Stephenson 2, Williams, G: Nash 2
Nov 9	Wakefield Trinity	L 18-42	3,439	T: Coulman, Latham, Nash, Stephenson, G: Stephenson 2, Fielding
Nov 14	WAKEFIELD TRINITY	L 17-32	2,523	T: Burns, O'Neill, Richards, G: Johns 4
Nov 19	OLDHAM	L 7-22	3,394	T: Williams, G: Whitfield 2
Nov 23	WIGAN (JP-1)	W 17-9	3,715	T: Coulman, O'Neill, Richards, G: Whitfield 4
Nov 30	Hull	L 10-15	10,191	T: Driver, Williams, G: Whitfield 2
Dec 7	CASTLEFORD (JP-2)	L 8-15	3,452	T: O'Neill, Richards, G: Whitfield
Dec 14	BRADFORD NORTHERN	W 18-9	3,044	T: O'Neill 2, Stephenson, G: Whitfield 4, DG: Stephenson
Dec 21	Workington Town	L 12-15	1,982	T: H Henney, Richards, G: Whitfield 3
Dec 26	WIDNES	W 16-8	3,444	T: Coulman 2, Cherrie, Whitfield, G: Whitfield 2
Dec 28	LEEDS	L 5-10	3,533	T: Coulman, G: Whitfield
Jan 1	Leigh	L 10-11	4,031	T: Fielding, Williams, Wilson, DG: Whitfield
Jan 4	St Helens	L 14-29	4,396	T: Francis, H Henney, G: Johns 3, Fielding
Jan 14	Leeds	L 9-26	3,734	T: Fielding, H Henney, G: Johns, DG: Nash
Jan 18	Warrington	L 10-17	4,702	T: Coulman, Richards, G: Johns, Whitfield
Jan 25	Halifax	L 19-23	4,359	T: Wilson 2, Williams, G: Rule 5

Salford RL Match Results

1980-1981 *continued*

	Opponent	Result	Attendance	Scorers
Feb 1	WARRINGTON	L 13-19	4,324	T: Stephenson, G: Whitfield 5
Feb 8	Barrow	L 15-18	4,391	T: R Henney, Richards, Williams, G: Whitfield 3
Feb 15	BRADFORD NORTHERN (RLC-1)	W 17-13	5,371	T: Cross, O'Neill, Richards, G: Rule 4
Feb 22	CASTLEFORD	W 17-15	2,660	T: O'Neill, Richards, G: Rule 5, DG: Nash
Mar 1	LEIGH (RLC-2)	W 12-3	8,759	T: O'Neill, Williams, G: Rule 3
Mar 15	Hull Kingston Rovers (RLC-3)	L 8-19	14,315	T: O'Neill, Yates, G: Rule
Mar 20	HULL KINGSTON ROVERS	W 20-15	3,473	T: Stephenson 2, G: Rule 7
Mar 29	Featherstone Rovers	L 8-24	2,240	T: Williams, G: Rule 2, DG: Whitfield
Apr 3	BARROW	W 20-9	2,560	T: Coulman, H Henney, Rule, Yates, G: Rule 4
Apr 17	LEIGH	W 13-12	4,544	T: Stephenson, Whitfield, Williams, G: Rule 2
Apr 24	Oldham	D 18-18	2,222	T: Coulman 2, Smith, G: Rule 4, DG: Nash

1981-1982

	Opponent	Result	Attendance	Scorers
Aug 7	DEWSBURY (F)	W 25-5	975	T: Francis, H Henney, Nash, Thomas, Yates, G: Whitfield 5
Aug 14	Oldham (LC-1)	W 17-7	2,915	T: Richards, Stephenson, G: Rule 5, DG: Nash
Aug 23	FULHAM (LC-2)	W 19-3	3,462	T: Fielding, Richards, Williams, G: Rule 4, DG: Nash, Whitfield
Aug 30	Cardiff City	W 26-21	9,247	T: Fielding, H Henney, Richards, Whitfield, G: Rule 7
Sep 2	Widnes (LC-SF)	L 2-33	5,849	G: Rule
Sep 4	DONCASTER	W 59-13	2,111	T: Francis 3, H Henney 2, Stephenson 2, Williams 2, Fielding, Rule, G: Rule 13
Sep 13	Huyton	W 26-3	455	T: Fielding 2, Richards 2, Williams, Yates, G: Rule 4
Sep 18	BRAMLEY	W 43-0	2,514	T: Rogers 3, Coulman, Fielding, Francis, McGreal, Stephenson, Williams, G: Rule 8
Sep 23	ROCHDALE HORNETS	W 7-2	2,448	T: Richards, G: Rule 2
Sep 27	Batley	L 11-15	1,187	T: Nash, G: Rule 4

Salford RL Match Results

1981-1982 *continued*

	Opponent	Result	Attendance	Scorers
Oct 2	WORKINGTON TOWN	W 17-16	2,765	T: Rogers, Stephenson, Williams, G: Rule 4
Oct 18	Whitehaven (JP-1)	W 19-11	3,351	T: Coulman, H Henney, Rule, G: Rule 4, DG: Nash 2
Oct 23	CARDIFF (CITY	L 14-17	3,883	T: Francis, Stephenson, G: Rule 4
Oct 25	Blackpool Borough	L 0-3	1,400	
Nov 1	Keighley (JP-2)	W 11-10	2,730	T: Nash, Yates, G: Rule 2, DG: Stephenson
Nov 8	Keighley	L 15-18	1,699	T: Fletcher, McGreal, O'Neill, G: Rule 3
Nov 15	SWINTON (JP-3)	L 0-6	6,728	
Nov 27	BLACKPOOL BOROUGH	W 30-10	1,970	T: McGreal 2, Nash, Rule, Stephenson, Yates, G: Rule 6
Dec 2	BATLEY	W 44-8	1,692	T: Coulman 2, H Henney, McGreal, O'Neill, Richards, Rule, Yates, G: Rule 10
Dec 6	Carlisle	L 18-21	3,107	T: Richards, Rule, Stephenson, Yates, G: Rule 3
Jan 3	OLDHAM	L 7-17	3,612	T: Richards, G: Rule 2
Jan 20	HUNSLET	W 12-3	1,690	T: Richards, Williams, G: Rule 3
Jan 24	Dewsbury	W 25-10	1,061	T: Stephenson 2, Byrne, Fielding, Williams, G: Rule 5
Jan 29	CARLISLE	L 7-19	2,584	T: Yates, G: Rule 2
Feb 7	Halifax	L 10-15	3,525	T: Yates 2, G: Rule 2
Feb 14	Hull (RLC-1)	L 15-29	13,697	T: Nash, Richards, Yates, G: Rule 3
Feb 19	DEWSBURY	W 25-7	1,717	T: Stockley 2, Heaney, H Henney, O'Neill, Richards, Williams, G: Rule 2
Feb 28	Bramley	W 25-11	800	T: Byrne, H Henney, Murray, Williams, Yates, G: Yates 3, Rule 2
Mar 5	HALIFAX	W 20-10	2,576	T: Byrne, H Henney, Stockley, Yates, G: Yates 4
Mar 7	Hunslet	D 10-10	860	T: Rogers, Yates, G: Yates 2
Mar 12	HUDDERSFIELD	W 15-9	1,802	T: Fielding 2, Stead, G: Yates 2, Stockley
Mar 14	Doncaster	W 20-8	389	T: Yates 2, Byrne, Williams, G: Yates 3, Nash
Mar 21	Workington Town	L 16-41	1,736	T: Yates 2, Byrne, Fielding, G: Yates 2
Apr 4	Rochdale Hornets	W 20-16	1,174	T: O'Neill 2, Coulman, Fielding, G: Rule 4
Apr 9	SWINTON	W 28-16	3,156	T: Richards 2, Byrne, Coulman, H Henney, Yates, G: Rule 5

Salford RL Match Results

1981-1982 *continued*

	Opponent	Result	Attendance	Scorers
Apr 12	Oldham	L 10-20	2,912	T: Rogers, Yates, G: Rule 2
Apr 18	Huddersfield	W 29-11	1,274	T: Fielding 2, Richards 2, Byrne, Smith, Williams, G: Rule 4
Apr 21	HUYTON	W 44-7	1,682	T: Richards 2, Smith 2, Coulman, Fielding, H Henney, O'Neill, Williams, Yates, G: Rule 6, Coulman
Apr 23	KEIGHLEY	W 20-9	2,257	T: Richards 2, Fielding, O'Neill, G: Rule 4
May 3	Swinton	L 3-45	2,863	T: Fielding

1982-1983

	Opponent	Result	Attendance	Scorers
Aug 15	Dewsbury (F)	L 7-23	700	T: Williams, G: O'Neill, Rule
Aug 22	Hunslet	W 35-18	2,000	T: Yates 3, Byrne, O'Neill, Richards, Smith, G: Rule 7
Aug 25	WHITEHAVEN	W 14-10	1,734	T: Coulman, Stockley, G: Rule 4
Aug 29	BRAMLEY	W 23-5	1,635	T: O'Neill 2, Stockley, Williams, G: Rule 5, DG: Coulman
Sep 5	Wigan (LC-1)	L 13-18	7,033	T: McGreal, Richards, Smith, G: Rule 2
Sep 12	Batley	W 23-9	1,010	T: Byrne 2, Yates 2, Stead, G: Yates 4
Sep 15	ROCHDALE HORNETS	W 26-11	1,611	T: Byrne, O'Neill, Smith, Williams, G: Smith 5, Yates 2
Sep 19	Huyton	W 22-12	390	T: Fielding 3, Stead, G: Smith 5
Sep 26	FULHAM	L 13-26	2,494	T: Aspey, Richards, Smith, G: Smith 2
Oct 3	Cardiff City	W 28-18	1,418	T: Richards 2, Byrne, Coulman, Driver, Major, G: Smith 5
Oct 6	HUDDERSFIELD	W 22-6	1,536	T: Byrne, H Henney, O'Neill, Yates, G: Smith 5
Oct 17	DEWSBURY	W 40-8	1,699	T: H Henney 2, McTigue 2, Byrne, Coulman, O'Neill, Stockley, G: Smith 8
Oct 24	Blackpool Borough	W 26-4	1,215	T: Driver 3, Coulman, Williams, Yates, G: Smith 4
Oct 31	YORK	W 20-16	2,035	T: O'Neill 2, Smith 2, G: Smith 3, Yates
Nov 7	Wakefield Trinity	L 5-18	2,995	T: O'Neill, G: Smith

Salford RL Match Results

1982-1983 *continued*

	Opponent	Result	Attendance	Scorers
Nov 12	HUYTON	W 47-3	1,428	T: Smith 3, O'Neill 2, Beckett, Coulman, Driver, Fletcher, Maggs, Stockley, G: Smith 7
Nov 21	Huddersfield	L 5-13	700	T: Driver, G: Yates
Dec 5	HUNSLET (JP-1)	W 23-11	1,471	T: Coulman, Fletcher, Nash, O'Neill, Stockley, G: Smith 4
Dec 12	HUDDERSFIELD (JP-2)	W 21-19	1,924	T: Stockley 2, Aspey, Byrne, McTigue, G: Fletcher 2, Smith
Dec 18	WIGAN (JP-3)	L 4-5	3,237	G: Smith 2
Dec 26	SWINTON	W 18-4	3,555	T: Smith 2, Williams 2, G: Smith 3
Jan 2	Whitehaven	L 7-8	2,254	T: Williams, G: Smith 2
Jan 9	DONCASTER	W 55-5	1,509	T: Fletcher 3, Byrne 2, O'Neill 2, Williams 2, Coulman, Maggs, Nash, Smith, G: Smith 6, Fletcher, Rule
Jan 16	York	W 26-5	1,694	T: Williams 2, Coulman, Driver, Fielding, Fletcher, G: Rule 4
Jan 23	CARDIFF CITY	W 12-8	2,020	T: Byrne, Fielding, G: Smith 3
Jan 30	BATLEY	W 39-8	1,410	T: Driver 3, Fletcher 2, Coulman, H Henney, Nash, O'Neill, G: Rule 6
Feb 6	Fulham	L 9-17	3,681	T: Byrne, G: Smith 3
Feb 13	LEIGH (RLC-1)	W 12-5	6,519	T: Driver, O'Neill, G: Smith 3
Feb 20	KEIGHLEY	W 20-11	2,112	T: Fielding 2, Smith 2, Coulman, Driver, G: Smith
Feb 27	FEATHERSTONE ROVERS (RLC-2)	L 11-17	4,169	T: Aspey, Byrne, Fielding, G: Smith
Mar 20	BLACKPOOL BOROUGH	W 26-7	1,672	T: Blackwood, Fielding, Fletcher, McTigue, Nicholls, Williams, G: Rule 2, Smith 2
Mar 27	Doncaster	W 20-9	477	T: Stockley 2, Fielding, Smith, G: Rule 4
Apr 1	Swinton	W 16-7	3,533	T: Byrne 2, Driver, Fletcher, G: Rule 2
Apr 4	HUNSLET	W 21-15	1,907	T: McTigue, O'Neill, Stockley, G: Rule 6
Apr 6	Rochdale Hornets	W 7-0	827	T: Fletcher, G: Rule 2
Apr 10	WAKEFIELD TRINITY	L 10-19	2,466	T: Fielding, Williams, G: Rule 2

Salford RL Match Results

1982-1983 *continued*

	Opponent	Result	Attendance	Scorers
Apr 17	Bramley	L 17-42	750	T: Byrne, Fielding, Fletcher, G: Rule 4
Apr 20	Keighley	L 5-18	576	T: Byrne, G: Beckett
Apr 24	Dewsbury	W 29-5	650	T: O'Neill 2, Byrne, Fletcher, McTigue, G: Rule 7

1983-1984

	Opponent	Result	Attendance	Scorers
Aug 14	DEWSBURY (F)	W 46-14	577	T: Bloor 2, O'Neill 2, Fletcher, McTigue, Ruddy, Smith, G: Smith 7
Aug 21	WIGAN	L 14-16	3,858	T: McTigue, Richards, G: Smith 3
Aug 28	Leeds	L 10-40	4,253	T: Driver, Glynn, G: Smith
Sep 4	FULHAM (LC-1)	W 16-15	1,986	T: Driver, Fletcher, Williams, G: Smith 2
Sep 7	LEIGH	L 6-38	3,723	T: Groves, G: Smith
Sep 11	WAKEFIELD TRINITY	W 27-26	1,900	T: Bloor, Byrne, H Henney, Williams, G: Smith 5, DG: Nash
Sep 14	BARROW (LC-2)	L 2-13	1,625	G: Smith
Sep 18	Widnes	L 4-28	4,231	T: Williams
Sep 25	CASTLEFORD	L 14-34	2,249	T: Williams 2, G: Twist 3
Oct 2	Bradford Northern	L 14-38	4,853	T: Driver, Shuttleworth, G: Twist 3
Oct 9	WARRINGTON	L 8-12	2,733	T: Shuttleworth, Williams
Oct 16	Wakefield Trinity	W 16-5	2,135	T: Byrne 2, Williams, G: Twist 2
Oct 30	Hull	L 6-58	8,589	T: Byrne, G: Twist
Nov 6	Doncaster (JP-1)	W 22-11	458	T: Shuttleworth 2, Williams, Wood, G: Smith 3
Nov 11	BRADFORD NORTHERN	L 12-14	2,730	T: Byrne, Maggs, G: Smith 2
Nov 20	Wigan (JP-2)	L 15-24	7,290	T: Byrne, Wood, G: Smith 2, Shuttleworth, DG: Shuttleworth
Nov 27	Whitehaven	W 13-10	1,383	T: Byrne 3, DG: Shuttleworth
Dec 4	LEEDS	L 10-24	2,748	T: Bentley, Byrne, G: Shuttleworth
Dec 11	Castleford	L 12-40	2,998	T: Byrne, Nash, G: Shuttleworth 2
Dec 20	ST HELENS	L 16-18	1,833	T: Wood 2, Byrne, G: Shuttleworth 2
Dec 26	Oldham	L 6-18	3,975	T: Bloor, G: Shuttleworth
Jan 2	FULHAM	L 4-6	1,847	T: Williams

Salford RL Match Results

1983-1984 *continued*

	Opponent	Result	Attendance	Scorers
Jan 8	Featherstone Rovers	L 18-30	2,269	T: McTigue 2, Smith, G: Smith 3
Jan 27	Warrington	L 8-14	2,474	T: O'Neill, G: Shuttleworth 2
Feb 5	St Helens	L 0-20	3,431	
Feb 12	LEEDS (RLC-1)	L 16-24	4,299	T: Bloor, Groves, Ruddy, G: Shuttleworth 2
Feb 19	FEATHERSTONE ROVERS	L 6-10	1,865	T: Bentley, G: Shuttleworth
Feb 26	WHITEHAVEN	W 26-16	1,472	T: Byrne 2, Bloor, Williams, G: Shuttleworth 5
Mar 4	Leigh	L 22-31	3,297	T: Byrne 2, Groves, G: Fletcher 5
Mar 11	HULL	L 6-42	2,692	T: Byrne, G: Fletcher
Mar 18	Hull Kingston Rovers	L 32-51	6,139	T: Glynn 2, E Bentley, Bloor, Byrne, G: Fletcher 6
Mar 23	WIDNES	L 12-22	1,825	T: Shuttleworth, Williams, G: Fletcher 2
Apr 1	XIII Catalan (F)*	L 7-8	2,502	T: Groves, G: Shuttleworth, DG: Bloor
Apr 8	Fulham	W 12-10	1,622	T: Prescott, Williams, G: Fletcher 2
Apr 10	HULL KINGSTON ROVERS	L 0-32	1,816	
Apr 15	Wigan	L 8-34	6,653	T: Glynn, Rogers
Apr 20	OLDHAM	L 10-50	2,700	T: McTigue, Maggs, G: Shuttleworth

Scoring values: Try increased to 4 points from this season

* At Perpignan

1984-1985

	Opponent	Result	Attendance	Scorers
Aug 17	FEATHERSTONE ROVERS (F)	L 20-28	1,390	T: Bentley, Glynn, Smith, J Taylor, G: Fletcher 2
Aug 26	Rochdale Hornets (F)	W 40-16	630	T: McTigue 2, Bentley, Bloor, Byrne, Gee, G: Fletcher 8
Sep 2	Whitehaven	L 8-18	1,634	T: Stacey, G: Fletcher 2
Sep 7	ROCHDALE HORNETS	W 36-1	1,790	T: Glynn 2, Bentley, Fletcher, Groves, Stacey, Williams, G: Fletcher 3, Glynn
Sep 16	WHITEHAVEN (LC-1)	W 19-14	1,700	T: Byrne, Stacey, G: Fletcher 5, DG: Glynn
Sep 23	Sheffield Eagles	W 13-6	1,159	T: Groves, Ritter, G: Fletcher 2, DG: Boyd
Sep 27	BLACKPOOL BOROUGH (LC-2)	W 15-6	1,917	T: Bentley, Fletcher, Muller, G: Fletcher, DG: Glynn

Salford RL Match Results

1984-1985 *continued*

Date	Opponent	Result	Attendance	Scorers
Sep 30	BRIDGEND	W 64-18	1,738	T: Byrne 3, Stacey 2, Williams 2, Bentley, Dickens, Fletcher, Meachin, Muller, G: Fletcher 8
Oct 7	Runcorn Highfield	D 16-16	980	T: Williams 2, Byrne, Stacey
Oct 10	WIGAN (LC-SF)	L 8-19	7,492	T: Muller, G: Twist 2
Oct 14	CARLISLE	L 12-19	1,655	T: Glynn, Prescott, G: Twist 2
Oct 19	Bramley	W 18-8	993	T: Jamieson, Muller, G: C Griffiths 5
Oct 28	WHITEHAVEN	W 22-12	1,897	T: Fletcher, C Griffiths, Groves, Prescott, G: C Griffiths 3
Nov 4	Bridgend	W 38-17	580	T: C Griffiths 2, Groves, Lamb, Major, Prescott, G: C Griffiths 7
Nov 9	FULHAM	W 28-12	1,504	T: C Griffiths 2, Bentley, Bloor, J Taylor, G: C Griffiths 4
Nov 18	Dewsbury (JP-1)	L 8-14	1,176	T: Bloor, G: C Griffiths 2
Nov 25	Rochdale Hornets	D 9-9	882	T: Fletcher, G: C Griffiths 2, DG: Glynn
Dec 9	HUDDERSFIELD BARRACUDAS	D 23-23	1,690	T: Byrne 2, Glynn, J Taylor, G: C Griffiths 3, DG: Fletcher
Dec 16	Fulham	W 19-13	650	T: Byrne, McTigue, Prescott, G: C Griffiths 3, DG: C Griffiths
Dec 23	SHEFFIELD EAGLES	W 50-16	1,740	T: Marsh 3, Byrne 2, C Griffiths 2, Fletcher, Ritter, G: C Griffiths 7
Dec 26	Swinton	L 5-18	3,977	G: C Griffiths 2, DG: C Griffiths
Dec 30	BLACKPOOL BOROUGH	W 16-13	2,015	T: Bloor, Dickens, C Griffiths, G: C Griffiths 2
Jan 6	York	L 9-10	1,573	T: Byrne, G: C Griffiths 2, DG: C Griffiths
Jan 29	FEATHERSTONE ROVERS (RLC-Preliminary)	W 14-6	1,652	T: Fletcher, McTigue, G: C Griffiths 3
Feb 3	YORK	W 51-0	1,824	T: Byrne 2, Glynn 2, Groves, Marsh, Muller, J Taylor, G: C Griffiths 9, DG: Bloor
Feb 20	SWINTON (RLC-1)	W 31-6	4,267	T: Byrne, Fletcher, Glynn, Marsh, Pendlebury, G: C Griffiths 5, DG: C Griffiths

Salford RL Match Results

1984-1985 *continued*

	Opponent	Result	Attendance	Scorers
Feb 24	Bramley (RLC-2)	L 10-24	2,700	T: Lamb, G: C Griffiths 3
Mar 10	Southend Invicta	W 56-12	114	T: Fletcher 3, C Griffiths 3, Bentley, Byrne, Major, Marsh, G: C Griffiths 8
Mar 16	SOUTHEND INVICTA	W 42-6	1,134	T: Bloor 3, C Griffiths 2, Byrne, Marsh, Muller, G: C Griffiths 5
Mar 24	WAKEFIELD TRINITY	W 50-10	1,871	T: Bloor 3, Groves 2, Dickens, Glynn, C Griffiths, Lamb, G: C Griffiths 7
Mar 31	BRAMLEY	W 48-14	1,588	T: Byrne 2, J Taylor 2, Bloor, Groves, Marsh, Muller, G: C Griffiths 8
Apr 5	Blackpool Borough	W 30-4	1,036	T: Byrne 2, Marsh 2, Glynn, G: Griffiths 5
Apr 8	SWINTON	L 5-9	4,972	G: C Griffiths 2, DG: C Griffiths
Apr 14	RUNCORN HIGHFIELD	W 54-7	1,603	T: Byrne 4, C Griffiths 2, Blease, Bloor, Foy, S Griffiths, Turnbull, G: C Griffiths 5
Apr 21	Wakefield Trinity	W 16-15	1,419	T: Bloor, Glynn, C Griffiths, G: C Griffiths 2
Apr 24	Carlisle	W 28-17	550	T: Byrne, Foy, Marsh, Pendlebury, Turnbull, G: C Griffiths 4
Apr 28	Huddersfield Barracudas	W 21-10	871	T: C Griffiths, Lamb, McTigue, G: C Griffiths 4, DG: C Griffiths

1985-1986

	Opponent	Result	Attendance	Scorers
Aug 4	Leigh (F)	L 12-16	1,705	T: Bloor, McTigue, G: Pendlebury 2
Aug 16	SHEFFIELD EAGLES (F)	W 37-7	485	T: Glynn 2, Jamieson, Lamb, McTigue, Marsh, G: C Griffiths 6, DG: Fletcher
Aug 18	MANSFIELD MARKSMAN (F)	W 42-0	685	T: Glynn 3, C Griffiths, Jamieson, Lamb, Pendlebury, G: C Griffiths 7
Sep 1	York	L 12-14	1,815	T: Fletcher, Groves, G: C Griffiths 2
Sep 4	WIGAN	W 12-8	4,404	T: Bloor, K O'Loughlin, G: C Griffiths 2
Sep 8	HALIFAX	W 22-6	3,266	T: Bloor, Fletcher, C Griffiths, Groves, G: C Griffiths 2, DG: Baker 2

Salford RL Match Results

1985-1986 *continued*

	Opponent	Result	Attendance	Scorers
Sep 15	SWINTON (LC-1)	W 18-14	3,482	T: Bloor, K O'Loughlin, Pendlebury, G: C Griffiths 2, DG: Baker, Bloor
Sep 22	Featherstone Rovers	W 16-12	1,897	T: Baker, Bloor, K O'Loughlin, G: C Griffiths 2
Sep 25	Wigan (LC-2)	L 20-22	11,188	T: Baker, Bloor, Marsh, G: C Griffiths 4
Sep 29	LEEDS	L 16-22	3,721	T: Baker 2, G: C Griffiths 4
Oct 6	Warrington	L 19-41	3,199	T: Major 2, Battese, G: C Griffiths 3, DG: Baker
Oct 13	OLDHAM	L 20-34	3,563	T: Baker, C Griffiths, Ruddy, G: C Griffiths 4
Oct 23	Widnes	L 12-27	3,629	T: Bloor, Gribbin, G: C Griffiths 2
Oct 27	Halifax	L 12-23	4,013	T: Battese, Glynn, G: Pendlebury 2
Nov 3	HULL KINGSTON ROVERS	W 27-24	2,359	T: Bloor 2, Gribbin 2, K O'Loughlin, G: Baker 3, DG: Baker
Nov 10	Wigan	L 8-20	12,588	T: Bloor, G: Baker 2
Nov 15	YORK	W 22-18	1,730	T: Baker, Major, Moylan, Pobjie, G: C Griffiths 3
Nov 24	ROCHDALE HORNETS (JP-1)	W 18-12	2,844	T: Baker, Bloor, Marsh, G: C Griffiths 3
Dec 1	Hull (JP-2)	L 10-30	5,659	T: Fletcher, G: C Griffiths 3
Dec 8	Oldham	L 10-32	4,859	T: Baker, Blease, G: Baker
Dec 15	CASTLEFORD	W 9-8	1,888	T: Baker, Fletcher, DG: Baker
Dec 26	SWINTON	W 21-17	3,374	T: Battese 2, Baker, Glynn, G: Baker 2, DG: Glynn
Jan 1	Dewsbury	L 10-12	1,006	T: Glynn, G: C Griffiths 3
Jan 15	BRADFORD NORTHERN	W 9-8	1,709	T: Glynn, Wiltshire, DG: Baker
Jan 19	FEATHERSTONE ROVERS	W 26-12	1,674	T: Herbert 2, Baker, Byrne, K O'Loughlin, G: Baker 3
Feb 2	WIDNES	W 22-6	2,289	T: Glynn 2, Fletcher, Wiltshire, G: Pendlebury 3
Feb 9	Doncaster (RLC-1)	L 12-18	842	T: Bloor, Marsh, G: Pendlebury 2
Feb 27	Leeds	L 12-34	4,701	T: Ford, Pendlebury, G: Pendlebury 2
Mar 5	HULL	W 15-12	1,281	T: K O'Loughlin, Wiltshire, G: Pendlebury 3, DG: Pendlebury
Mar 16	WARRINGTON	L 10-19	2,356	T: Byrne, Wiltshire, G: Pendlebury

Salford RL Match Results

1985-1986 *continued*

	Opponent	Result	Attendance	Scorers
Mar 19	St Helens	L 10-28	4,500	T: Bloor, K O'Loughlin, G: Pendlebury
Mar 23	Hull	L 16-34	4,985	T: Bloor, Byrne, Glynn, G: Pendlebury 2
Mar 28	DEWSBURY	W 36-8	1,404	T: Blease 2, Dickens 2, Byrne, McTigue, K O'Loughlin, G: Pendlebury 4
Mar 31	Swinton	W 24-0	2,631	T: Byrne, Fletcher, Herbert, Pendlebury, Wiltshire, G: Pendlebury 2
Apr 13	ST HELENS	L 28-30	2,790	T: Bloor 2, Fletcher 2, Pendlebury, G: Pendlebury 4
Apr 16	Hull Kingston Rovers	W 28-4	2,880	T: McTigue 2, K O'Loughlin, Pendlebury, Wiltshire, G: Pendlebury 4
Apr 20	Castleford	L 16-30	2,947	T: Byrne, Major, Wiltshire, G: Pendlebury 2
Apr 22	Bradford Northern	L 8-18	2,221	T: S Griffiths, G: Pendlebury 2

1986-1987

	Opponent	Result	Attendance	Scorers
Aug 24	LEIGH (F)	L 18-28	1,195	T: Fletcher, McTigue, Andy Mercer, G: Austin 3
Aug 31	Wigan	L 12-42	10,671	T: Fletcher, Moylan, G: Austin 2
Sep 3	ST HELENS	L 4-38	2,817	G: Austin 2
Sep 7	BRADFORD NORTHERN	L 12-22	2,396	T: Austin, Bentley, G: Austin 2
Sep 14	Warrington (LC-1)	L 20-28	3,617	T: Bloor 2, Fletcher, G: Fazackerley 4
Sep 21	Warrington	L 14-42	2,981	T: McTigue 2, Austin, G: Fazackerley
Sep 28	BARROW	L 12-24	1,328	T: McTigue, Ruddy, G: Fazackerley 2
Oct 5	Leeds	L 10-46	6,346	T: Groves, Wakefield, G: Fazackerley
Oct 12	HULL KINGSTON ROVERS	L 14-34	1,759	T: Foy, Morris, G: Fazackerley 3
Oct 17	St Helens	L 14-32	5,712	T: Ruddy, Selby, Wiltshire, G: Austin
Oct 26	Featherstone Rovers	L 6-16	1,600	T: Wiltshire, G: Pendlebury
Nov 2	WARRINGTON	L 10-25	2,546	T: Byrne, McTigue, G: O'Shea
Nov 9	WIGAN	L 0-34	5,391	

Salford RL Match Results

1986-1987 *continued*

	Opponent	Result	Attendance	Scorers
Nov 16	Castleford	W 21-20	3,225	T: Bloor, Glynn, K O'Loughlin, G: O'Shea 4, DG: Austin
Nov 23	WIDNES	W 22-16	1,414	T: O'Shea 2, Austin, Fletcher, G: O'Shea 3
Nov 30	HULL (JP-1)	L 12-27	2,100	T: Bloor 2, G: O'Shea 2
Dec 21	Halifax	L 8-18	3,410	T: Selby, G: O'Shea 2
Dec 26	Oldham	L 18-34	4,011	T: Blease, Byrne, Glynn, G: O'Shea 3
Jan 1	LEIGH	W 20-12	2,502	T: Austin, K O'Loughlin, Selby, G: O'Shea 3, Austin
Jan 4	Wakefield Trinity	W 16-10	1,600	T: O'Shea 2, Moran, G: O'Shea 2
Jan 25	HULL	W 29-18	1,858	T: Austin 2, Byrne, O'Shea, Wiltshire, G: O'Shea 4, DG: Glynn
Feb 1	LEEDS (RLC-1)	L 0-4	4,534	
Feb 8	Widnes	L 12-13	3,101	T: McTigue, Selby, G: Austin, O'Shea
Feb 15	FEATHERSTONE ROVERS	W 26-16	1,967	T: Byrne, Fletcher, K O'Loughlin, O'Shea, G: O'Shea 4, Austin
Feb 20	CASTLEFORD	W 36-10	2,024	T: O'Shea 2, Austin, Herbert, Marsh, Selby, G: O'Shea 6
Mar 1	WAKEFIELD TRINITY	W 36-12	1,530	T: K O'Loughlin 2, Byrne, Herbert, Major, Selby, Wakefield, G: O'Shea 4
Mar 8	LEEDS	L 12-14	2,152	T: Austin, Glynn, G: O'Shea 2
Mar 15	Barrow	W 26-20	2,030	T: Austin 2, Fletcher, McTigue, Major, G: O'Shea 3
Mar 22	HALIFAX	W 16-8	4,192	T: Bloor, Byrne, O'Shea, G: O'Shea 2
Mar 25	Hull	W 14-8	3,664	T: Austin 2, G: O'Shea 3
Apr 5	Hull Kingston Rovers	L 16-20	3,084	T: Austin, Herbert, K O'Loughlin, G: Austin 2
Apr 9	Leigh	W 14-10	5,441	T: Bloor, Byrne, G: Austin 3
Apr 17	OLDHAM	W 36-30	4,222	T: Byrne 3, Austin 2, K O'Loughlin, G: Austin 6
Apr 21	Bradford Northern	W 23-12	4,040	T: Austin 2, Fletcher, Marsh, G: Austin 3, DG: Bloor

Salford RL Match Results

1987-1988

	Opponent	Result	Attendance	Scorers
Aug 23	SPRINGFIELD BOROUGH (F)	L 10-24	673	T: Bentley, Disley, G: K Jones
Aug 30	BRADFORD NORTHERN	L 12-16	2,514	T: Herbert, G: K Jones 4
Sep 6	Hull	L 11-16	3,758	T: Jones, G: K Jones 3, DG: Glynn
Sep 13	FULHAM (LC-1)	W 58-4	1,640	T: Bloor 3, Blacker, Bullough, Gibson, Groves, K Jones, McTigue, Major, G: K Jones 9
Sep 20	HULL KINGSTON ROVERS	W 34-32	2,005	T: K Jones 2, Blacker, Blease, Gibson, Marsh, G: K Jones 5
Sep 23	Wigan (LC-2)	L 2-42	11,633	G: K Jones
Sep 27	Leeds	L 6-60	6,583	T: McTigue, G: K Jones
Oct 4	WIDNES	L 0-18	4,190	
Oct 18	Hunslet	W 14-12	1,418	T: Austin 2, O'Shea, G: K Jones
Oct 25	ST HELENS	L 8-18	4,549	T: M Worrall, G: K Jones 2
Nov 1	Halifax	L 20-29	5,231	T: Austin 2, K O'Loughlin, M Worrall, G: K Jones, M Worrall
Nov 8	HULL	W 20-6	2,395	T: Blease, Gibson, K O'Loughlin, G: K Jones 4
Nov 15	Swinton (JP-1)	W 18-12	3,459	T: Austin, Jack, McTigue, G: K Jones 2, M Worrall
Nov 22	DEWSBURY (JP-2)	W 14-5	2,129	T: Blease, Glynn, G: K Jones 3
Nov 29	WIGAN (JP-3)	L 12-16	7,986	T: Austin, Cairns, G: M Worrall 2
Dec 6	HUNSLET	W 21-14	2,000	T: Bloor, McTigue, Moran, G: K Jones 4, DG: Bloor
Dec 13	Castleford	L 0-14	3,382	
Dec 27	SWINTON	W 36-8	4,498	T: Blease, Bloor, Jack, K Jones, Shaw, M Worrall, G: K Jones 6
Jan 1	Leigh	L 0-18	3,818	
Jan 10	Hull Kingston Rovers	L 8-20	3,420	T: Herbert, Jack
Jan 17	WIGAN	L 6-14	6,459	T: Gibson, G: M Worrall
Jan 24	Widnes	L 2-22	4,698	G: M Worrall
Jan 31	SWINTON (RLC-1)	W 16-6	3,425	T: Austin, M Worrall, G: K Jones 4
Feb 14	SPRINGFIELD BOROUGH (RLC-2)	W 12-10	2,352	T: Gibson, K O'Loughlin, G: K Jones 2
Feb 19	CASTLEFORD	L 12-28	2,304	T: Austin, Gibson, G: K Jones 2
Feb 28	ST HELENS (RLC-3)	W 22-18	7,964	T: M Worrall 2, Gibson, K Jones, G: K Jones 3

Salford RL Match Results

1987-1988 *continued*

	Opponent	Result	Attendance	Scorers
Mar 6	LEEDS	W 14-10	3,548	T: Bloor, Gibson, G: O'Shea 3
Mar 12	Wigan (RLC-SF)*	L 4-34	20,783	T: Blease
Mar 16	St Helens	L 10-24	6,376	T: K Jones 2, G: K Jones
Mar 20	Bradford Northern	L 4-34	3,320	T: Shaw
Mar 23	LEIGH	W 28-21	3,421	T: Gibson 3, Bentley, P Williams, G: K Jones 4
Mar 27	WARRINGTON	L 14-34	4,118	T: Gormley, Herbert, G: K Jones 3
Apr 1	Swinton	W 10-6	3,841	T: Bloor, P Williams, G: K Jones
Apr 10	Warrington	W 20-19	3,412	T: Cairns, P Williams, M Worrall, G: K Jones 4
Apr 13	Wigan	L 22-52	10,125	T: Fox, K Jones, J O'Loughlin, Potts, G: K Jones 3
Apr 17	HALIFAX	W 36-16	6,716	T: P Williams 2, Bentley, Bloor, Gibson, M Worrall, G: K Jones 6

* At Bolton

1988-1989

	Opponent	Result	Attendance	Scorers
Aug 14	Oldham (F)	W 20-18	2,313	T: Bloor, J O'Loughlin, Walsh, P Williams, G: Gibson, K Jones
Aug 21	Chorley Borough (F)	W 22-16	–	T: P Williams 2, Herbert, Burgess, G: M Worrall 2, K Jones
Aug 28	HULL KINGSTON ROVERS	W 24-14	3,519	T: Bentley 2, Gibson, K Jones, P Williams, G: K Jones 2
Sep 4	Bradford Northern	L 18-42	4,403	T: P Williams 2, K Jones, G: K Jones 3
Sep 11	WARRINGTON	W 25-18	5,809	T: Bentley, Blease, Evans, Gibson, K Jones, G: K Jones 2, DG: Cairns
Sep 18	WHITEHAVEN (LC-1)	W 42-8	2,551	T: Bentley 2, Evans 2, Gibson, Herbert, K Jones, Moran, G: K Jones 5
Sep 25	Wakefield Trinity	W 36-18	4,276	T: Bentley 3, Gibson 2, M Worrall, G: K Jones 6
Sep 28	Oldham (LC-2)	W 18-2	5,497	T: Gibson, Gormley, K Jones, G: K Jones 3
Oct 2	WIDNES	W 15-12	6,684	T: Hadley 2, Moran, G: K Jones, DG: Cairns

Salford RL Match Results

1988-1989 *continued*

	Opponent	Result	Attendance	Scorers
Oct 5	WARRINGTON (LC-SF)	W 15-2	7,316	T: Bentley, Evans, G: Hadley 3, DG: Bentley
Oct 9	Castleford	L 12-38	6,208	T: Bentley, Evans, Gibson
Oct 16	OLDHAM	W 38-20	5,954	T: P Williams 2, Evans, Gibson, Gormley, Hadley, Horo, G: P Brown 5
Oct 23	Wigan (LC-Final)*	L 17-22	19,154	T: Bentley, Evans, Herbert, G: P Brown 2, DG: M Worrall
Nov 6	St Helens	L 14-30	8,420	T: Blease, Gibson, G: M Worrall 3
Nov 13	Halifax (JP-1)	L 4-22	6,661	T: Hadley
Nov 20	WIGAN	W 24-16	8,533	T: Gormley, Horo, K Jones, Shaw, G: P Brown 4
Nov 27	LEEDS	L 6-24	6,025	T: Bragger, G: P Brown
Dec 4	Featherstone Rovers	L 18-22	2,637	T: Blease 2, Bentley, M Worrall, G: P Brown
Dec 11	BRADFORD NORTHERN	W 33-18	4,130	T: Bragger 3, Bentley, Cairns, Kerry, G: Kerry 4, DG: M Worrall
Dec 18	FEATHERSTONE ROVERS	L 8-12	3,126	T: Bragger, P Williams
Dec 26	Oldham	L 22-23	6,406	T: Hadley 2, Bentley, Bragger, G: Kerry 3
Jan 8	WAKEFIELD TRINITY	W 18-8	3,692	T: Bentley, Bragger, Shaw, G: Kerry 3
Jan 15	Widnes	L 8-50	11,871	T: Hadley, P Williams
Jan 22	Leeds	L 16-18	10,135	T: Bragger 2, Gormley, G: Kerry 2
Jan 29	WIDNES (RLC-1)	L 14-18	7,094	T: Gibson, Kerry, G: Kerry 3
Feb 5	HULL	L 6-18	3,484	T: Cairns, G: Kerry
Feb 17	CASTLEFORD	L 18-20	4,460	T: Bragger 2, Hadley, G: P Brown 2, Kerry
Mar 5	Halifax	L 12-21	6,708	T: Horo, P Williams, G: P Brown 2
Mar 14	ST HELENS	W 22-4	5,003	T: Kerry 2, P Brown, Horo, G: Kerry 3
Mar 19	Hull Kingston Rovers	W 24-18	3,384	T: Kerry 2, Hadley, P Williams, G: Kerry 4
Mar 27	Warrington	L 6-18	4,408	T: Gibson, G: Kerry
Apr 2	HALIFAX	W 22-4	3,508	T: Bragger, Gibson, Kerry, McTigue, P Williams, G: Kerry
Apr 9	Wigan	L 18-28	14,247	T: Bragger 2, Kerry, G: Kerry 3
Apr 16	Hull	L 6-12	7,174	T: Gibson, G: Kerry

At St Helens

Lancashire Cup runners-up

Salford RL Match Results

1989-1990

	Opponent	Result	Attendance	Scorers
Aug 20	Swinton (F)*	W 42-20	–	T: Bragger 2, Bradshaw, Burgess, Hadley, Kerry, K Jones, G: K Jones 4, Kerry 3
Aug 27	OLDHAM (F)	W 42-28	2,100	T: Bragger 2, Gibson 2, Evans, Gibson, Kerry, Moran, G: Kerry 7
Sep 3	Widnes	L 18-46	8,591	T: Evans, Hadley, Sherratt, P Williams, G: Kerry
Sep 10	WIGAN	L 12-56	7,318	T: Bragger, Burgess, G: Kerry 2
Sep 17	ROCHDALE HORNETS (LC-1)	W 52-12	3,094	T: Bragger 4, Gibson 2, Kerry 2, Gormley, G: Kerry 8
Sep 24	Leeds	L 28-34	8,575	T: Blease, Evans, Hadley, Kerry, G: Kerry 6
Sep 27	WARRINGTON (LC-2)	L 4-27	4,994	G: Kerry 2
Oct 1	BRADFORD NORTHERN	L 12-36	4,059	T: Gibson, M Worrall, G: K Jones, Kerry
Oct 7	LEIGH	W 19-6	2,241	T: Evans, Kerry, G: Kerry 5, DG: Kerry
Oct 15	Hull	L 8-44	5,858	T: Evans, Hadley
Oct 31	WIDNES	L 16-28	5,453	T: Gibson, M Worrall, G: Kerry 4
Nov 4	St Helens	L 16-40	4,437	T: Bentley, Bragger, Cairns, G: Hadley, Kerry
Nov 12	LEEDS	L 18-38	4,624	T: S Brown, Hadley, P Williams, G: S Brown 3
Nov 19	Barrow	W 36-2	1,801	T: Kerry 2, Burgess, Gibson, Hadley, Rampling, G: Kerry 6
Nov 26	SHEFFIELD EAGLES	D 20-20	3,020	T: Fell, Gormley, Hadley, Kerry, G: Kerry 2
Dec 3	Hull (RT-1)	W 21-18	4,587	T: Kerry 2, Brooke-Cowden, G: Kerry 4, DG: Kerry
Dec 10	Halifax (RT-2)	L 6-20	6,005	T: Evans, G: Kerry
Dec 17	Warrington	L 15-18	3,910	T: Rampling, P Williams, G: Kerry 3, DG: Kerry
Dec 26	Leigh	L 10-18	4,123	T: Gibson, G: Kerry 2, DG: Kerry 2
Jan 7	FEATHERSTONE ROVERS	L 14-15	3,104	T: Cassidy, Evans, P Williams, G: Kerry
Jan 14	Wakefield Trinity	L 4-28	4,119	T: Hadley
Jan 21	ST HELENS	L 10-25	5,187	T: Gormley, G: Burgess 3
Jan 28	BISON SPORTS (Leeds) (RLC-1)	W 56-6	1,935	T: M Worrall 3, Cassidy 2, Burgess, Evans, Gormley, Lee, Mercer, O'Neill, G: Birkett 4, Burgess 2

Salford RL Match Results

1989-1990 *continued*

	Opponent	Result	Attendance	Scorers
Feb 2	BARROW	W 36-4	2,167	T: Evans 2, Burgess, Cassidy, Gibson, Kerry, M Worrall, G: Kerry 4
Feb 11	OLDHAM (RLC-2)	L 7-18	6,472	T: S Brown, G: Birkett, DG: Lee
Feb 18	Wigan	L 26-32	11,368	T: Gibson 2, Kerry 2, Evans, G: Kerry 3
Feb 25	CASTLEFORD	L 18-24	3,178	T: S Brown, Howard, Kerry, G: Kerry 3
Mar 4	Bradford Northern	L 12-18	3,459	T: Gibson 2, G: Kerry 2
Mar 11	Featherstone Rovers	W 33-20	3,318	T: Gibson 2, Kerry 2, Brooke-Cowden, M Worrall, G: Kerry 4, DG: O'Neill
Mar 18	HULL	L 5-21	2,829	T: Mercer, DG: Cairns
Mar 25	Sheffield Eagles	L 12-17	1,121	T: Kerry, M Worrall, G: Kerry 2
Apr 1	Castleford	L 0-65	4,756	
Apr 8	WAKEFIELD TRINITY	L 18-28	2,217	T: Fell 2, S Brown, G: Kerry 3
Apr 16	WARRINGTON	L 5-16	2,960	T: Clare, DG: S Brown

* Agecroft Cup

1990-1991

	Opponent	Result	Attendance	Scorers
Aug 12	SWINTON (F)*	W 34-14	1,420	T: Fell 2, Evans, Gibson, Kerry, Mercer, G: Kerry 5
Aug 19	Rochdale Hornets (LC-Preliminary)	W 41-12	2,049	T: Hadley 2, Evans, Fell, Gibson, Lee, P Williams, G: Kerry 6, DG: Lee
Aug 26	OLDHAM (LC-1)	W 27-24	4,236	T: Burgess 2, Birkett, Gibson, Hadley, G: Kerry 3, DG: S Brown
Sep 2	ST HELENS (LC-2)	W 21-7	5,574	T: Birkett, Evans, Gibson, Hadley, G: Kerry 2, DG: Lee
Sep 9	Barrow	W 31-0	1,368	T: Blease 2, Birkett, Bradshaw, Evans, Gibson, G: Kerry 3, DG: Lee
Sep 12	LEIGH (LC-SF)	W 16-7	6,939	T: Fell 2, G: Kerry 4
Sep 16	WORKINGTON TOWN	W 30-8	2,011	T: Evans 2, Bradshaw, Fell, Hadley, Kerry, G: Kerry 3
Sep 23	Batley	W 21-10	1,375	T: Bradshaw, Cassidy, Evans, Gilfillan, G: Kerry 2, DG: Kerry
Sep 29	Widnes (LC-Final)**	L 18-24	7,485	T: Blease, Fell, P Williams, G: Kerry 3

Salford RL Match Results

1990-1991 *continued*

	Opponent	Result	Attendance	Scorers
Oct 3	DONCASTER	W 21-4	2,237	T: Clare, Gilfillan, Hadley, G: Kerry 4, DG: Kerry
Oct 7	Ryedale-York	W 19-12	2,444	T: Gilfillan, Sherratt, G: Birkett 4, DG: Cassidy, Kerry, Lee
Oct 14	BARROW	W 76-10	2,360	T: Gilfillan 3, Fell 2, Gibson 2, O'Neill 2, Blease, Bradshaw, Burgess, Evans, Hadley, G: Kerry 10
Oct 21	Chorley	W 50-2	1,609	T: Burgess 3, Bradshaw 2, Hadley 2, Gibson, G: Kerry 9
Oct 30	TRAFFORD BOROUGH	W 38-12	2,376	T: Kerry 2, Blease, Burgess, Cassidy, G: Kerry 8, DG: Kerry, Lee
Nov 4	BRAMLEY	W 40-0	2,158	T: Hadley 2, Birkett, Evans, Fell, Gibson, Gilfillan, Tunks, G: Kerry 4
Nov 18	Runcorn Highfield	W 26-6	1,540	T: Evans, Fell, Gibson, Gilfillan, Hadley, G: Kerry 3
Nov 25	WHITEHAVEN	W 40-6	2,042	T: Fell 3, Gibson, Gilfillan, Kerry, Sherratt, G: Kerry 6
Dec 2	Oldham (RT-1)	L 6-26	4,932	T: Gibson, G: Kerry
Dec 16	Whitehaven	W 38-12	1,093	T: Blease, Cassidy, Evans, Gibson, Kerry, M Worrall, G: Kerry 7
Jan 1	SWINTON	W 13-0	4,647	T: Cassidy, Hadley, G: Kerry 2, DG: Cassidy
Jan 6	Dewsbury	W 50-2	1,053	T: Birkett, Bradshaw, Burgess, Evans, Gibson, Gilfillan, Hadley, Kerry, P Williams, G: Kerry 7
Jan 9	Leigh	W 20-4	2,218	T: Blease, Fell, P Williams, G: Kerry 4
Jan 20	RYEDALE-YORK	W 22-12	2,521	T: Blease, Hadley, Kerry, G: Kerry 5
Jan 22	RUNCORN HIGHFIELD	W 50-6	1,702	T: Blease 3, Kerry 2, Evans, Gilfillan, Hadley, Hansen, Lee, G: Kerry 5
Jan 27	CUTSYKE (RLC-Preliminary)	W 44-4	1,788	T: Birkett 2, Fell 2, Bradshaw, Evans, Kerry, Hadley, M Worrall, G: Kerry 4
Jan 30	Doncaster	W 14-12	1,602	T: Kerry, Gelling, G: Kerry 2, DG: Cassidy, Lee
Feb 15	BATLEY (RLC-1)	W 36-14	2,050	T: Fell 2, Blease, Hadley, O'Neill, M Worrall, G: Kerry 6
Feb 24	Sheffield Eagles (RLC-2)	W 19-16	1,990	T: Burgess, Fell, Hansen, Kerry, G: Kerry, DG: Lee

Salford RL Match Results

1990-1991 *continued*

	Opponent	Result	Attendance	Scorers
Feb 27	DEWSBURY	W 32-6	1,837	T: O'Neill 3, Kerry 2, G: Kerry 6
Mar 3	Keighley	W 22-21	1,020	T: Hadley 3, Birkett, G: Kerry 3
Mar 10	Oldham (RLC-3)	L 3-40	6,503	G: Kerry, DG: Kerry
Mar 13	CHORLEY	W 46-2	1,472	T: Kerry 2, Birkett, Cassidy, Gilfillan, Howard, J O'Loughlin, Stephenson, G: Kerry 7
Mar 17	Workington Town	L 0-7	2,743	
Mar 21	BATLEY	W 32-14	1,643	T: Fell, Gibson, Hadley, J O'Loughlin, P Williams, G: Kerry 6
Mar 24	Bramley	W 27-18	928	T: Gibson 2, Birkett, Kerry, G: Kerry 5, DG: Cassidy
Mar 29	LEIGH	W 18-11	3,122	T: Birkett, Cassidy, Hadley, G: Kerry 3
Apr 1	Swinton	D 10-10	4,102	T: Birkett, J O'Loughlin, G: Kerry
Apr 10	Trafford Borough	W 40-12	1,500	T: Fell 2, Hadley, 2, Bentley, Dean, M Worrall, G: Kerry 6
Apr 14	KEIGHLEY	W 30-0	2,274	T: Hadley 3, Blease, M Worrall, G: Kerry 5
Apr 21	CARLISLE (PT-1)	W 26-12	1,697	T: O'Neill 2, Gibson, Hadley, G: Kerry 5
May 5	WORKINGTON TOWN (PT-SF)	D 9-9	4,291	T: Hadley, G: Kerry 2, DG: Lee
May 7	Workington Town (PT-SF Replay)	W 26-6	5,500	T: Birkett 2, Evans, Hadley, Kerry, G: Kerry 2, DG: Kerry, Lee
May 12	Halifax (PT-Final)***	W 27-20	42,043	T: Kerry 2, Evans, Gilfillan, G: Kerry 4, DG: Cassidy, Kerry, Lee

*Agecroft Cup ** At Wigan *** At Old Trafford, Manchester

Second Division Championship winners

Second Division Premiership Trophy winners

Lancashire Cup runners-up

Salford RL Match Results

1991-1992

	Opponent	Result	Attendance	Scorers
Aug 18	Swinton (F)*	W 24-12	–	T: Birkett, Fell, Gibson, M Worrall, G: Kerry 4
Sep 1	Warrington	L 20-22	5,032	T: Birkett, Gibson, Kerry, G: Kerry 4
Sep 8	CASTLEFORD	L 10-18	4,022	T: Burgess, Hadley, G: Kerry
Sep 15	WARRINGTON (LC-1)	W 22-16	3,656	T: Hadley 2, Reid, Staziker, G: Kerry 3
Sep 22	Bradford Northern	L 24-48	3,310	T: Gibson 2, Fell, Reid, G: Birkett 4
Sep 26	Rochdale Hornets (LC-2)	L 18-25	1,829	T: Birkett, Evans, Gibson, G: Kerry 3
Sep 29	WIDNES	L 10-18	4,124	T: Sherratt, Staziker, G: Kerry
Oct 6	Hull	W 24-12	4,254	T: Birkett, Evans, Hadley, M Worrall, G: Kerry 4
Oct 13	HALIFAX	W 34-14	5,356	T: Evans 2, Hadley 2, Birkett, Bradshaw, G: Kerry 5
Oct 23	St Helens	L 16-25	6,955	T: Birkett, Sherratt, P Williams, G: Kerry 2
Oct 27	HULL	W 26-8	3,128	T: Blease, Evans, Fell, Gibson, G: Birkett 5
Nov 3	Featherstone Rovers	W 27-22	3,280	T: Blease, Evans, Fell, Gibson, Hadley, G: Birkett 3, DG: Lee
Nov 13	WIGAN	W 24-10	5,377	T: Reid 2, Evans, Hadley, G: Birkett 4
Nov 17	TRAFFORD BOROUGH (RT-1)	W 74-10	1,783	T: Gibson 4, Gilfillan 2, Hadley 2, M Worrall 2, Bradshaw, Cruickshank, Evans, Lee, G: Birkett 9
Nov 24	Wakefield Trinity (RT-2)	W 30-10	4,577	T: Evans, Gibson, Hadley, Reid, Reynolds, Staziker, G: Birkett 3
Nov 30	WIGAN (RT-3)	W 24-14	4,608	T: Evans 2, Birkett, Cruickshank, Hadley, G: Birkett 2
Dec 7	Leeds (RT-SF)**	L 15-22	7,275	T: Birkett 2, Gilfillan, G: Birkett, DG: Lee
Dec 15	Halifax	L 12-29	5,573	T: Cassidy, Evans, G: Birkett 2
Dec 22	Hull Kingston Rovers	L 7-28	3,460	T: Evans, G: Birkett, DG: S Brown
Dec 26	SWINTON	W 48-4	4,280	T: Bradshaw 3, Birkett 2, Cassidy, Evans, Gibson, G: Birkett 8

Salford RL Match Results

1991-1992 *continued*

	Opponent	Result	Attendance	Scorers
Jan 1	Leeds	L 10-36	12,519	T: Evans, Reynolds, G: Birkett
Jan 5	ST HELENS	L 6-15	3,680	T: Evans, G: Birkett
Jan 9	Chorley Borough (RLC-Preliminary)	W 64-13	932	T: Birkett 2, Bradshaw 2, Gibson 2, Gilfillan, Lee, Reid, Reynolds, P William, Young, G: Birkett 8
Jan 12	Castleford	L 12-26	4,598	T: Birkett, Bradshaw, G: Birkett 2
Jan 18	LEEDS	L 10-27	2,913	T: Birkett 2, G: Birkett
Feb 2	WIGAN (RLC-1)	L 6-22	11,173	T: P Williams, G: Birkett
Feb 9	Wakefield Trinity	L 10-27	3,647	T: Evans, Fell, G: Birkett
Feb 16	FEATHERSTONE ROVERS	W 26-4	3,232	T: Fell, Kerry, Lee, Reid, G: Kerry 5
Feb 28	BRADFORD NORTHERN	W 23-6	3,743	T: Blease, Burgess, Evans, Kerry, G: Kerry 3, DG: Lee
Mar 15	WAKEFIELD TRINITY	L 12-18	3,349	T: Hansen, G: Kerry 4
Mar 22	Wigan	L 7-28	13,231	T: M Worrall, G: Kerry, DG: Lee
Mar 29	WARRINGTON	L 10-14	3,130	T: Hansen, Reid, G: Birkett
Apr 5	Widnes	W 24-20	3,800	T: Evans, Fox, Hadley, Reid, G: Birkett 4
Apr 12	HULL KINGSTON ROVERS	W 22-10	2,880	T: Evans, Gibson, Hansen, Reid, G: Birkett 3
Apr 20	Swinton	W 26-18	3,487	T: Hadley 3, Gilfillan, G: Birkett 5

* Agecroft Cup   ** At Bradford

1992-1993

	Opponent	Result	Attendance	Scorers
Aug 23	SWINTON (F)*	W 36-8	1,506	T: Fell 3, Critchley, Cruickshank, Gibson, P Williams, G: S Brown 3, Gibson
Aug 30	HULL KINGSTON ROVERS	L 10-14	3,178	T: Cruickshank, G: Birkett 3
Sep 6	Castleford	W 24-20	4,500	T: Blease, Critchley, Ford, Gilfillan, G; Birkett 4
Sep 13	WHITEHAVEN (LC-1)	W 60-8	1,985	T: Ford 5, Coleman 2, Critchley 2, Blease, Reid, P Williams, G: Birkett 6
Sep 20	HALIFAX	W 27-22	5,515	T: Coleman 2, Birkett, Critchley, G: Birkett 5, DG: Lee

Salford RL Match Results

1992-1993 *continued*

	Opponent	Result	Attendance	Scorers
Sep 23	WORKINGTON TOWN (LC-2)	W 42-20	2,143	T: Ford 2, Birkett, S Brown, Burgess, Evans, Gibson, G: Birkett 7
Sep 27	St Helens	L 8-48	9,159	T: Coleman, G: Birkett 2
Oct 4	Bradford Northern	L 26-28	4,017	T: Lee 2, Critchley, Ford, P Williams, G: Birkett 3
Oct 7	St Helens (LC-SF)	L 5-18	9,289	G: S Brown 2, DG: S Brown
Oct 11	WAKEFIELD TRINITY	W 14-8	3,734	T: Critchley, Ford, G: S Brown 3
Oct 16	CASTLEFORD	W 21-18	2,945	T: Ford 2, Critchley, Young, G: S Brown 2, DG: Lee
Nov 1	Hull Kingston Rovers	W 16-10	3,978	T: Evans, Ford, Staziker, G: S Brown 2
Nov 8	FEATHERSTONE ROVERS (RT-1)	L 14-18	3,088	T: Ford, Lee, G: Birkett 3
Nov 15	ST HELENS	L 12-15	6,013	T: Burgess, Ford, G: Young 2
Nov 22	WIGAN	L 18-26	7,681	T: Blease, Bradshaw, Gilfillan, G: Blakeley 3
Nov 29	Hull	L 10-42	4,047	T: Evans, G: Blakeley 3
Jan 1	Leeds	L 14-38	14,828	T: Blakeley, Lee, G: Blakeley 3
Jan 6	WIDNES	L 12-48	3,586	T: Evans, Gibson, G: Blakeley 2
Jan 10	Wakefield Trinity	L 14-34	3,750	T: Blakeley, Evans, Ford, G: Blakeley
Jan 13	LEIGH	W 24-16	3,389	T: Bradshaw, Coleman, Evans, Ford, G: Blakeley 4
Jan 17	LEEDS	L 15-46	5,244	T: Evans 2, Blease, G: Blakeley, DG: Lee
Jan 24	Sheffield Eagles	L 16-30	2,278	T: T: Coleman, Critchley, Ford, G: Blakeley 2
Jan 31	WAKEFIELD TRINITY (RLC-1)	L 12-20	3,732	T: Birkett, Critchley, G: Birkett 2
Feb 7	Halifax	L 14-36	5,795	T: Burgess, Evans, Lee, G: Birkett
Feb 19	BRADFORD NORTHERN	W 38-4	2,842	T: Ford 2, Burgess, Critchley, Evans, Forber, Howard, Young, G: Blakeley 3
Mar 7	HULL	W 26-10	3,043	T: Critchley, Evans, Forber, Ford, Howard, G: Blakeley 3
Mar 14	Wigan	L 6-70	12,420	T: Blakeley, G: Blakeley
Mar 21	SHEFFIELD EAGLES	W 48-12	3,105	T: Blease 3, Critchley 2, Birkett, Burgess, Reid, Staziker, G: Blakeley 6

Salford RL Match Results

1992-1993 *continued*

	Opponent	Result	Attendance	Scorers
Mar 26	Widnes	L 22-38	4,139	T: Critchley, Laurie, Lee, Reid, G: Birkett 3
Apr 4	WARRINGTON	L 23-24	3,693	T: Critchley 3, Blease, Evans, G: Young, DG: Lee
Apr 12	Leigh	L 20-46	2,253	T: Blakeley, Evans, Forber, Young, G: Blakeley 2
Apr 18	Warrington	L 20-22	2,809	T: Blease, Coussons, Reid, G: Young 4

*Swinton Liberal Club Cup

1993-1994

	Opponent	Result	Attendance	Scorers
Aug 8	Barrow (F)	W 30-13	700	T: Naylor 2, Coussons, Critchley, Potts, Swift, G: Tyrer 3
Aug 22	Swinton (F)	W 48-6	1,300	T: Forber 2, O'Neill 2, Birkett, Critchley, Quigley, P Williams, Young, G: Blakeley 5, Birkett
Aug 29	SHEFFIELD EAGLES	L 20-32	3,119	T: Blakeley, Burgess, Forber, G: Blakeley 4
Sep 5	St Helens	L 14-22	7,587	T: Blease, Jack, G: Blakeley 3
Sep 12	WIDNES	W 33-19	4,293	T: Critchley 2, Blease, Ford, Jack, G: Blakeley 6, DG: Lee
Sep 19	Hull	L 12-28	3,982	T: Forber, Ford, G: Birkett 2
Sep 26	LEEDS	W 23-18	4,943	T: Critchley 2, Neil, G: Blakeley 5, DG: Blakeley
Oct 3	WIGAN	L 2-24	8,765	G: Blakeley
Oct 8	Halifax	L 12-20	5,096	T: Blakeley, Ford, G: Blakeley 2
Oct 24	CASTLEFORD	L 0-34	3,769	
Oct 31	Bradford Northern	L 24-44	5,609	T: Critchley 2, Burgess, Evans, G: Blakeley 4
Nov 5	WARRINGTON	L 6-20	2,746	T: Critchley, G: Blakeley
Nov 13	LEEDS (RT-2)	W 21-12	1,799	T: Lee 2, Critchley, Forber, G: Birkett 2, DG: S Brown
Nov 21	Hull Kingston Rovers	W 10-6	2,529	T: Jack, P Williams, G: Birkett
Nov 28	FEATHERSTONE ROVERS	W 34-24	3,526	T: Critchley 2, Jack 2, S Brown, Ford, Lee, G: Birkett 3
Dec 5	WAKEFIELD TRINITY	W 22-8	3,525	T: Critchley 2, Forber, Ford, Jack, G: S Brown
Dec 14	Batley (RT-3)	W 12-8	809	T: A Gregory, O'Connor, G: Blakeley 2

Above: 1990-91. Back: C Whiteley, S Gibson, I Sherratt, M Worrall, I Blease, T Conroy. Middle: D Fell, A Hadley, T Evans, A Bradshaw, P Williams, A Burgess, F Cassidy. Front: M Birkett, S Kerry, T Cassidy (assistant coach), JA Wilkinson (chairman), K Tamati (coach), S O'Neill (Alliance coach), M Lee, S Brown.

Above: 1990-91. Skipper Ian Blease (with trophy) leads the celebration at Old Trafford after his side had beaten Halifax to clinch the Second Division Premiership.

Above: 1994-95. Back: A Burgess, P O'Neill, S Gibson, S Hansen, S Naylor, I Blease, P Forber, P Williams. Middle: D Betts, T Howard, D Fell, S Blakeley, W Reid, G Stazicker, D Young, J Gilfillan, M Birkett. Front: T Evans, J Quigley, G Jack (team manager), JA Wilkinson (chairman), H Cartwright (coach), M Lee, J Critchley.

Above: 1996. Ecstatic Salford trio Paul Forber, Andy Burgess and Nathan McAvoy acknowledge the fans after overcoming Keighley in the Divisional Premiership decider at Old Trafford.

Above: 1997. The players (in kit) and coach are, back row: P Maitland, P Southern, D Rogers, I Blease, S Naylor, C Eccles, P Coussons, N McAvoy, J Cartwright. Middle: E Faimalo, P Edwards, F Sini, D Hulme, L Savelio. Front: I Watson (kneeling), C Randall, J Laurence, S Martin, A Gregory (head coach), S Blakeley, A Burgess, M Lee, A Platt, P Forber (kneeling).

Above left: Hooker Malcolm Alker made his first Salford appearance in 1997 and went on to play in 360 matches including eight seasons as captain.

Above right: Centre Stuart Littler's Salford debut was in 1998. His 329 matches incorporated a club record of 163 consecutive appearance.

Above left: Stand-off Steve Blakeley signed from Wigan in 1992, his final appearance being in 2003. A prolific scorer he stands third in the club's all-time list of leading goal and point scorers behind David Watkins and Gus Risman.

Above right: Paul Highton proved himself to be one of Salford's most consistent forwards during the summer era notching 269 appearances from 1998 to 2008.

Above: 2006. Back: K Fitzpatrick, K McGuinness, J Clough, S Littler, S Baldwin, S Rutgerson, R Clayton, A Moule, D Hodgson, A Dunemann. Middle: J Langi, G Haggerty, T Jonkers, P Highton, A Coley, A Brocklehurst, J Wilshere, S Myler, C Charles, S Finnigan, M Stringer. Front: A Hunte (assistant coach), S Naylor (assistant coach), J Lowes (assistant coach), L Robinson, K Harrison (head coach), M Alker, JA Wilkinson (chairman), I Sibbit, A Stewart, E McGuinness (fitness co-ordinator), C Holmes (physio).

Above: 2011. A historic moment as the Salford team pose for the camera following the final match to be played at The Willows, on 11th September. Back: S Wild, M Smith (slightly obscured), W Godwin, S Gleeson, C Nero (slightly obscured), L Jewitt, I Palea'aesina, J Broughton, D Williams, A Gibson, S Ratchford, D Holdsworth. Front: L Adamson, R Boyle, M Henry, R Cashmere, A Neal, L Patten.

Above: 2012. Salford's first official match at their new stadium was against Castleford on 4th February. Televised live, it took place in a snowstorm giving the playing area a surreal illuminated appearance.

Above: 2019. Back: R Lui, L Tomkins, G Griffin, J Turgut, G Dudson, G Burke, G Johnson. Middle: J Lussick, K Sio, B Nakubuwai, A Walker, T McCarthy, D Murray, A Lawton, J Jones, J Bibby. Front: E Chamberlain, N Evalds, K Welham, M Flanagan, I Watson (head coach), M Gleeson (assistant coach), L Mossop, J Sa'u, J Hastings, J Wood, D Olpherts.

Above: 2019. The Red Devils provided the biggest upset of 2019 through reaching the Super League Grand Final at Old Trafford. Jake Bibby is shown diving in at the corner for Salford's only try. Despite losing to St Helens it was a significant event as it was the club's first major final of the summer era.

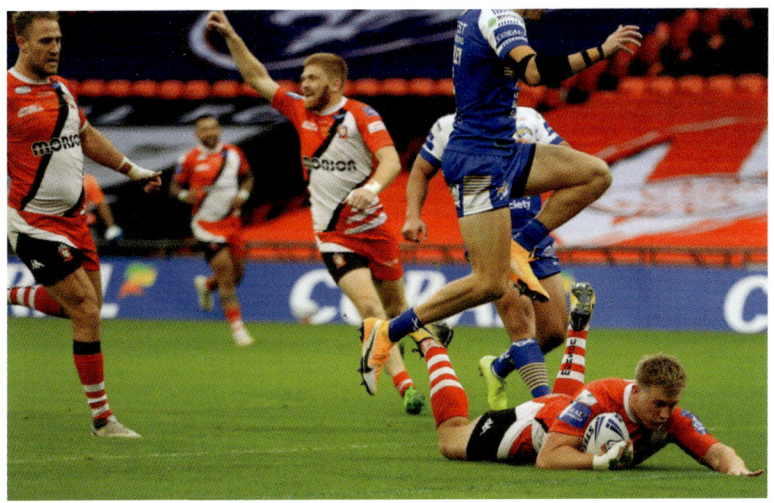

Above: 2020. James Greenwood registers Salford's third try as the club bridged a 51-year gap by returning to Wembley where they faced Leeds Rhinos. Losing by the narrowest of margins, 17-16, it was Salford's eighth appearance in a Rugby League Challenge Cup final and fourth at Wembley.

Above left: Australian half-back Jackson Hastings joined Salford in 2018 as a virtual unknown but quickly made headlines through his outstanding performances. He was the catalyst in the teams spectacular rise during 2019, his contribution recognised when he became Salford's first player to receive the prestigious Steve Prescott Man of Steel award as the sports leading player.

Above right: Brodie Croft is another Australian half-back who joined Salford for the 2022 season and, along with Ryan Brierley, Marc Sneyd and Andy Ackers, created what was rated by many as the best 'spine' in Super League. Croft's outstanding contribution, which helped the Red Devils reach the Super League play-off semi-final, earned him the ultimate accolade as Salford's second player to be named Man of Steel.

Above: 2022. Back: R Brierley, A Gerrard, S Akauola, D Addy, D Sarginson, K Watkins. Middle: J Johnson, J Wells, T Lafai, J Greenwood, S Wright, H Livett, J Ormondroyd, K Sio, J Burgess, K Vuniyayawa, G Burke, R Lannon, S Luckley, A Bourouh. Front (seated): M Escare, A Ackers, R Williams, D Cross, B Croft, E Taylor, M Sneyd, C Atkin, M Costello, J Stevens.

Above: 2023. All set for the 150th Anniversary season! Back: Andrew Dixon (Toulouse Olympique), R Lannon, D Addy, Oliver Partington (Wigan), M Costello, J Greenwood, D Sarginson, K Sio, T Lafai. Middle: S Wright, A Gerrard, T Dupree, Sam Stone (Leigh), K Vuniyayawa, J Ormondroyd, J Burgess, Adam Sidlow (Leigh), Ben Hellewell (Featherstone Rovers), Ellis Longstaff (Warrington, on loan). Front: R Brierley, D Cross, A Bourouh, B Croft, K Watkins, M Sneyd, A Ackers, R Williams, C Atkin. Results and players records for 2023 are not included in this book as the season was still in progress at the time of publication, therefore first names and previous teams are shown for new squad members. Note that Dixon, Hellewell (previously on loan) and Sidlow joined Salford for a second time.

Salford RL Match Results

1993-1994 *continued*

	Opponent	Result	Attendance	Scorers
Dec 19	HULL (RT-4)	W 26-6	3,207	T: A Gregory 2, Forber, Marsden, Tauro, G: S Brown 3
Dec 22	Sheffield Eagles	L 22-28	1,605	T: Forber 2, Jack, Webster, G: S Brown 2, Blakeley
Dec 26	Oldham	W 20-8	4,576	T: Ford, Marsden, P Williams, G: Blakeley 4
Jan 2	LEIGH	W 23-10	4,338	T: Burgess, Forber, Ford, P Williams, G: Blakeley 3, DG: A Gregory
Jan 8	WIGAN (RT-SF)	L 12-18	7,483	T: Ford, Marsden, G: Blakeley 2
Jan 12	ST HELENS	W 34-2	4,439	T: Critchley, Ford, O'Connor, O'Neill, Tauro, Young, G: S Brown 4, Blakeley
Jan 16	Widnes	L 22-30	4,589	T: Critchley 3, Jack, O'Neill, G: S Brown
Jan 23	HULL	L 11-22	3,459	T: Critchley, Ford, G: Young, DG: Lee
Jan 30	Castleford (RLC-4)	L 4-36	5,662	T: Blakeley
Feb 6	Leeds	L 16-22	8,315	T: Critchley, Marsden, G: Blakeley 4
Feb 20	Wigan	L 12-34	11,911	T: Jack, Young, G: Blakeley 2
Feb 27	HALIFAX	W 34-14	4,304	T: Critchley 2, Burgess, Forber, Ford, Young, G: Blakeley 5
Mar 18	BRADFORD NORTHERN	L 6-14	3,189	T: Lee, G: Blakeley
Mar 23	Castleford	L 14-22	3,639	T: Blakeley, Critchley, P Williams, G: Blakeley
Mar 27	Warrington	L 14-18	4,587	T: Blease, Critchley, Evans, G: Blakeley
Apr 1	OLDHAM	L 23-26	4,317	T: Ford, Lee, Naylor, O'Connor, G: Blakeley 3, DG: Lee
Apr 4	Leigh	W 19-18	2,833	T: Blakeley, S Brown, P Williams, G: Blakeley 3, DG: Lee
Apr 10	Wakefield Trinity	L 18-25	2,685	T: Critchley 2, Swift, G: Blakeley 3
Apr 17	HULL KINGSTON ROVERS	W 30-12	2,871	T: Tyrer 2, Blakeley, Jack, Swift, Tauro, G: Blakeley 3
Apr 24	Featherstone Rovers	L 24-46	2,958	T: Blakeley, Critchley, Evans, P Williams, G: Blakeley 3, A Gregory

Salford RL Match Results

1994-1995

	Opponent	Result	Attendance	Scorers
Aug 12	SWINTON (F)	W 44-16	1,524	T: Ford 3, Birkett, Critchley, Panapa, Swift, G: Blakeley 8
Aug 21	Wakefield Trinity	L 10-13	3,355	T: Blakeley, G: Blakeley 3
Aug 28	HULL	W 33-28	3,247	T: Blakeley 2, Forber, Ford, Young, G: Blakeley 6, DG: S Brown
Aug 31	Widnes	L 16-24	3,402	T: Blakeley, S Brown, Forber, G: Blakeley 2
Sep 4	St Helens	L 28-34	7,239	T: Birkett, Blakeley, Critchley, Ford, Mahon, G: Blakeley 4
Sep 11	FEATHERSTONE ROVERS	D 24-24	3,410	T: McAvoy 2, Coussons, Mahon, G: Mahon 2, Blakeley, S Brown
Sep 18	Leeds	L 20-26	11,598	T: Ford 2, McAvoy 2, Panapa
Sep 25	HALIFAX	L 12-24	4,681	T: Coussons, Randall, G: S Brown 2
Oct 2	DONCASTER	W 22-12	3,147	T: Ford 2, Critchley, Panapa, G: Mahon 2, S Brown
Oct 9	Castleford	L 6-34	4,036	T: Randall, G: Mahon
Oct 16	Wigan	L 22-52	12,740	T: Mahon 2, Ford, McAvoy, G: A Gregory 3
Nov 4	WAKEFIELD TRINITY	W 48-8	2,647	T: Blakeley, Forber, A Gregory, McAvoy, Mahon, Naylor, Randall, J Williams, G: Blakeley 8
Nov 13	Hull	L 16-29	4,042	T: McAvoy, Panapa, Randall, G: Blakeley 2
Nov 27	ST HELENS	W 39-12	5,558	T: Blakeley, Critchley, Ford, Lee, Mahon, J Williams, G: Blakeley 7, DG: Blakeley
Dec 4	LONDON BRONCOS (RT-2)	W 16-14	2,088	T: Forber, Ford, Panapa, G: Blakeley 2
Dec 11	Featherstone Rovers	W 20-12	2,707	T: J Williams 3, G: Blakeley 4
Dec 17	WARRINGTON (RT-3)	L 24-31	2,189	T: Critchley, McAvoy, Panapa, Randall, G: Blakeley 4
Dec 26	OLDHAM	L 12-16	4,984	T: Blakeley, G: Blakeley 4
Jan 1	Bradford Northern	L 18-24	5,056	T: Blease 2, Webster, G: Blakeley 3
Jan 8	SHEFFIELD EAGLES	W 24-20	2,427	T: Ford 2, Birkett, Naylor, J Williams, G: Blakeley 2

Salford RL Match Results

1994-1995 *continued*

Date	Opponent	Result	Attendance	Scorers
Jan 22	Workington Town	L 0-34	3,325	
Feb 5	Halifax	W 27-24	5,292	T: Naylor 2, Critchley, Panapa, Tyrer, G: A Gregory 3, DG: A Gregory
Feb 12	Hunslet (RLC-4)	D 32-32	1,112	T: Ford 2, Blakeley, Marsden, Quigley, Tyrer, G: Blakeley 4
Feb 15	HUNSLET (RLC-4 Replay)	W 52-10	1,931	T: Webster 2, Blakeley, Critchley, Ford, Lee, McAvoy, Panapa, Tyrer, G: Blakeley 7, Birkett
Feb 19	Doncaster	W 19-12	2,030	T: Blakeley, Critchley, McAvoy, Panapa, G: Blakeley, DG: Blakeley
Feb 26	FEATHERSTONE ROVERS (RLC-5)	L 10-30	4,064	T: Lee 2, G: Tyrer
Mar 1	LEEDS	L 8-26	3,271	T: Naylor, G: S Brown 2
Mar 12	CASTLEFORD	L 16-48	2,670	T: Ford, Marsden, Naylor, Webster
Mar 15	WARRINGTON	L 16-32	2,590	T: McAvoy 2, Panapa, G: Tyrer 2
Mar 19	WIGAN	L 8-42	7,091	T: Lee, G: Tyrer 2
Mar 26	Warrington	L 22-58	4,023	T: McAvoy 2, Eccles, Randall, G: Watson 3
Apr 2	Sheffield Eagles	L 16-29	1,983	T: Evans, Myler, Panapa, G: Myler 2
Apr 9	WORKINGTON TOWN	W 46-14	2,551	T: Panapa 3, Ford 2, Martin, Quigley, Randall, G: Blakeley 5, Myler 2
Apr 14	Oldham	L 16-28	3,965	T: Panapa, Quigley, G: Blakeley 4
Apr 17	BRADFORD NORTHERN	L 14-16	2,647	T: Martin 2, Naylor, G: Blakeley
Apr 23	WIDNES	W 35-18	3,094	T: Blakeley, Critchley, Martin, Naylor, Quigley, Randall, G: Blakeley 5, DG: Lee

Salford RL Match Results

1995-1996

Date	Opponent	Result	Attendance	Scorers
Aug 11	ST HELENS (F)	L 22-32	–	T: Neil Kenyon, Randall, Southern, trialist, G: Watson 3
Aug 23	Whitehaven	W 14-2	1,819	T: Eccles, Webster, G: Watson 2, A Gregory
Aug 27	WIDNES	W 45-4	2,886	T: McAvoy 2, Randall 2, Eccles, Martin, Webster, Young, G: Watson 5, Hampson, DG: Watson
Sep 3	Featherstone Rovers	W 38-16	2,407	T: Hampson 2, McAvoy 2, Eccles, Panapa, Rogers, G: Watson 4, DG: Hampson, Watson
Sep 10	BATLEY	W 52-24	2,455	T: Ford 2, Panapa 2, Eccles, Hampson, Lee, Martin, Webster, G: Watson 7, DG: Watson 2
Sep 17	Huddersfield	W 48-20	2,803	T: McAvoy 2, Panapa 2, Blakeley, Forber, Ford, Naylor, G: Blakeley 8
Sep 20	KEIGHLEY COUGARS	L 14-22	5,194	T: McAvoy, G: Blakeley 5
Sep 24	Rochdale Hornets	W 32-27	1,639	T: Edwards 2, Panapa, Rogers, Young, G: Blakeley 6
Oct 1	HULL	W 38-22	2,383	T: Ford 2, Blakeley, Edwards, Forber, Panapa, G: Blakeley 7
Nov 1	WAKEFIELD TRINITY	W 40-12	2,029	T: Blakeley 2, McAvoy 2, Edwards, Panapa, G: Blakeley 8
Nov 5	Dewsbury	W 23-8	1,640	T: Blakeley 2, Eccles, G: Blakeley 3, Hampson, DG: Hampson 3
Nov 12	Leeds (RT-2)	L 22-46	7,589	T: Blakeley, Forber, Hampson, Martin, G: Blakeley 3
Nov 14	WHITEHAVEN	W 58-18	1,670	T: Webster 3, Hampson 2, Eccles, Forber, McAvoy, Panapa, Sini, G: Blakeley 9
Nov 29	Batley	D 12-12	884	T: McAvoy, Panapa, G: Blakeley 2
Dec 3	HUDDERSFIELD	W 31-12	2,044	T: Sini 2, Lee, McAvoy, Young, G: Blakeley 5, DG: Hampson
Dec 10	Keighley Cougars	W 34-6	4,812	T: Lee, Naylor, Panapa, Webster, G: Blakeley 8, DG: Hampson 2
Dec 17	ROCHDALE HORNETS	W 42-4	1,933	T: Naylor 2, Eccles, McAvoy, Martin, Randall, Young, G: Blakeley 7

Salford RL Match Results

1995-1996 *continued*

	Opponent	Result	Attendance	Scorers
Jan 1	FEATHERSTONE ROVERS	W 24-6	2,326	T: Panapa 3, Naylor, G: Blakeley 4
Jan 4	Widnes	L 22-24	2,795	T: Edwards, McAvoy, Randall, Rogers, G: Blakeley 3
Jan 7	Hull	W 20-15	3,206	T: Edwards 2, Naylor, G: Blakeley 4
Jan 14	Wakefield Trinity	W 28-6	2,463	T: Blakeley, McAvoy, Naylor, Savelio, Young, G: Blakeley 4
Jan 21	DEWSBURY	W 46-18	3,182	T: McAvoy 2, Blakeley, Davys, Martin, Naylor, Rogers, Savelio, G: Blakeley 7

Centenary First Division Championship winners

Renamed Salford Reds from November 14

1996

	Opponent	Result	Attendance	Scorers
Jan 28	FEATHERSTONE ROVERS (RLC-4)	W 35-12	2,116	T: Edwards, Forber, Lee, McAvoy, Sevelio, G: Blakeley 7, DG: Hampson
Feb 11	WIGAN (RLC-5)	W 26-16	10,048	T: Naylor 2, Martin, Young, G: Blakeley 5
Feb 24	ST HELENS (RLC-6)	L 26-46	8,134	T: McAvoy 2, Burgess, Edwards, Panapa, Rogers, G: Blakeley
Mar 24	WIGAN (F)	D 34-34	1,535	T: Rogers 2, Coussons, Forber, Lee Hudson, Knowles, Mansson, G: Blakeley 2, Blease
Mar 31	Huddersfield Giants	W 26-21	4,043	T: Martin 2, Eccles, McAvoy, Young, G: Blakeley 3
Apr 5	WIDNES	W 46-14	4,219	T: McAvoy 2, Blakeley, Coussons, Edwards, Martin, Rogers, Webster, G: Blakeley 7
Apr 14	Whitehaven	W 38-14	1,025	T: Blakeley, Eccles, Forber, McAvoy, Mansson, Sini, G: Blakeley 7
Apr 21	Wakefield Trinity	W 32-26	3,010	T: Forber 2, Edwards, McAvoy, Martin, Rogers, G: Blakeley 4

Salford RL Match Results

1996 *continued*

Date	Opponent	Result	Attendance	Scorers
May 5	ROCHDALE HORNETS	W 36-16	2,645	T: Rogers 2, Eccles, Edward, Hampson, McAvoy, Savelio, G: Blakeley 4
May 12	Hull	L 28-30	3,354	T: Blakeley 2, Lee, McAvoy, G: Blakeley 6
May 19	FEATHERSTONE ROVERS	W 32-10	3,130	T: McAvoy 2, Burgess, Panapa, Savelio, Sini, G: Blakeley 4
May 24	DEWSBURY	W 54-0	2,611	T: Edwards 2, Sini 2, Blease, Coussons, Lee, McAvoy, Panapa, Rogers, G: Blakeley 7
Jun 2	Keighley Cougars	W 45-8	6,564	T: Sini 3, Blakeley, Coussons, Naylor, Panapa, Rogers, G: Blakeley 6, DG: Lee
Jun 9	Batley Bulldogs	W 56-18	1,262	T: Coussons 3, Blakeley 2, Blease, Lee, Rogers, Sini, G: Blakeley 10
Jun 16	HUDDERSFIELD GIANTS	W 26-20	4,107	T: Panapa 2, Martin, Naylor, Rogers, G: Blakeley 3
Jun 23	Widnes	W 32-20	2,823	T: McAvoy 2, Hampson, Lee, Panapa, Rogers, G: Blakeley 4
Jul 7	WHITEHAVEN	W 38-12	3,343	T: Hampson 2, Rogers 2, Blakeley, McAvoy, Martin, Naylor, G: Blakeley, Hampson, Watson
Jul 14	WAKEFIELD TRINITY	W 42-24	3,072	T: Rogers 3, Sini 2, McAvoy, Martin, Savelio, G: Blakeley 5
Jul 19	Rochdale Hornets	W 42-6	1,838	T: McAvoy 2, Blakeley, Davys, Edwards, Hampson, Martin, Randall, G: Blakeley 3, Hampson 2
Jul 28	HULL	W 23-14	4,059	T: Sini 2, Edwards, G: Blakeley 5, DG: Lee
Aug 4	Dewsbury	W 46-6	1,303	T: Edwards 2, Randall 2, Burgess, Martin, Naylor, Rogers, G: Blakeley 4, Sini 3
Aug 11	KEIGHLEY COUGARS	W 21-4	5,317	T: Sini 2, Forber, Rogers, G: Blakeley, Hampson, DG: Lee
Aug 18	BATLEY BULLDOGS	W 60-6	2,444	T: Naylor 2, Blease, Burgess, Davys, Eccles, Forber, Laurence, Savelio, Sini, G: Sini 6, Hampson 4
Aug 25	Featherstone Rovers	L 10-29	1,673	T: Coussons, Forber, G: Sini

Salford RL Match Results

1996 *continued*

	Opponent	Result	Attendance	Scorers
Sep 1	HULL KINGSTON ROVERS (PT-SF)	W 36-16	2,339	T: Lee 2, Blakeley, McAvoy, Panapa, Sini, G: Blakeley 5, Hampson
Sep 8	Keighley Cougars (PT-Final)*	W 19-6	35,013	T: Naylor 2, Blakeley, G: Blakeley 3, DG: Blakeley

* At Old Trafford, Manchester

First Division Championship winners

Divisional Premiership Trophy winners

1997

	Opponent	Result	Attendance	Scorers
Jan 19	Warrington Wolves (F)	W 37-30	6,453	T: Edwards 2, Eccles, E'Faimalo, Laurence, McAvoy, G: Watson 5, Laurence, DG: Watson
Feb 9	Castleford Tigers (RLC-4)	W 36-18	5,935	T: Rogers 3, Edwards, Hulme, Lee, Sini, G: Watson 3, Sini
Feb 23	PARIS ST GERMAIN (RLC-5)	W 8-4	5,275	T: Sini, G: Watson 2
Mar 8	Warrington Wolves (RLC-6)	W 29-10	6,218	T: McAvoy 2, Cartwright, Coussons, Forber, G: Blakeley 4, DG: Lee
Mar 16	CASTLEFORD TIGERS	W 4-0	5,726	T: Coussons
Mar 22	St Helens (RLC-SF)*	L 20-50	12,580	T: Blakeley, McAvoy, Rogers, G: Blakeley 4
Mar 28	OLDHAM BEARS	W 35-26	5,295	T: Blakeley, Forber, Naylor, Platt, Rogers, Watson, G: Blakeley 5, DG: Watson
Mar 31	PARIS ST GERMAIN	W 27-26	3,195	T: Rogers 2, Naylor, Sini, G: Blakeley 5, DG: Blakeley
Apr 6	Halifax Blue Sox	W 28-16	5,971	T: Broadbent, McAvoy, Martin, Naylor, G: Blakeley 5, DG: Watson 2
Apr 11	SHEFFIELD EAGLES	W 17-16	4,686	T: Blakeley, Edwards, G: Blakeley 4, DG: Watson
Apr 15	St Helens	L 12-19	10,213	T: Sini, Watson, G: Blakeley 2
Apr 18	London Broncos	L 12-48	4,495	T: Edwards, Naylor, G: Watson 2
Apr 25	WIGAN WARRIORS	W 14-4	6,626	T: Rogers, Watson, G: Blakeley 3

Salford RL Match Results

1997 *continued*

	Opponent	Result	Attendance	Scorers
May 11	LEEDS RHINOS	L 20-33	5,921	T: Forber, McAvoy, Sini, Watson, G: Blakeley 2
May 18	Castleford Tigers	L 10-12	3,265	T: Blakeley, Rogers, G: Blakeley
May 22	ST HELENS	W 39-26	5,549	T: Broadbent 3, Coussons, Lee, McAvoy, G: Blakeley 7, DG: Lee
May 26	Oldham Bears	L 10-19	4,254	T: Rogers, G: Blakeley 3
Jun 1	BRADFORD BULLS	L 24-40	8,241	T: E Faimalo, McAvoy, Martin, R Smith, Watson, G: Blakeley, Watson
Jun 8	Adelaide Rams (WCC)	L 8-50	11,009	T: Broadbent, G: Blakeley 2
Jun 21	North Queensland Cowboys (WCC)	L 8-44	15,560	T: McAvoy, G: Blakeley 2
Jun 27	WARRINGTON WOLVES	W 26-14	3,477	T: McAvoy 2, Coussons, Sini, G: Blakeley 5
Jul 2	Paris St Germain	W 24-16	500	T: McAvoy, Martin, Rogers, G: Blakeley 6
Jul 6	Leeds Rhinos	L 18-34	8,508	T: Blakeley, Martin, Watson, G: Blakeley 3
Jul 11	Bradford Bulls	L 14-34	14,095	T: Rogers, Sini, G: Blakeley 3
Jul 27	N QUEENSLAND COWBOYS (WCC)	L 14-24	7,448	T: Edwards, Rogers, G: Blakeley 3
Aug 3	ADELAIDE RAMS (WCC)	W 14-12	6,995	T: Rogers, G: Blakeley 4, DG: Lee 2
Aug 10	Warrington Wolves	L 8-23	5,546	T: Rogers, G: Blakeley 2
Aug 17	Wigan Warriors	W 21-14	6,518	T: Blakeley, Broadbent, Edwards, G: Blakeley 4, DG: Lee
Aug 22	LONDON BRONCOS	L 16-27	3,997	T: Blakeley, Broadbent, Lee, G: Blakeley 2
Aug 25	Sheffield Eagles	L 12-30	2,943	T: Randall, G: Blakeley 4
Aug 31	HALIFAX BLUE SOX	W 37-18	4,509	T: McAvoy 3, Forber, Naylor, Sini, G: Blakeley 6, DG: Lee
Sep 7	PARIS ST GERMAIN (PT-Preliminary)	W 48-6	2,045	T: Blakeley 2, Cartwright 2, Hulme 2, McAvoy, Naylor, Rogers, G: Blakeley 6
Sep 12	St Helens (PT-1)	L 12-26	4,367	T: Naylor, Rogers, G: Blakeley 2

*At Wigan

Salford RL Match Results

1998

	Opponent	Result	Attendance	Scorers
Jan 25	WARRINGTON WOLVES (F)	W 16-14	3,653	T: Blakeley, McAvoy, White, G: Blakeley 2
Feb 14	Ovenden (RLC-4)*	W 74-0	1,415	T: Rogers 3, White 3, McAvoy 2, Randall 2, Coussons, Crompton, Martin, Naylor, G: Blakeley 9
Mar 1	Widnes Vikings (RLC-5)	W 48-6	5,019	T: Martin 2, Randall 2, Blakeley, Bradbury, Naylor, Rogers, Savelio, G: Blakeley 6
Mar 15	HULL SHARKS (RLC-6)	W 41-10	6,210	T: McAvoy 2, White 2, Broadbent, Forber, Naylor, G: Blakeley 4, White 2, DG: Blakeley
Mar 28	Sheffield Eagles (RLC-SF)**	L 18-22	6,961	T: Edwards, Rogers, White, G: Blakeley 2, DG: Blakeley, Crompton
Apr 5	ST HELENS	L 14-18	7,337	T: Crompton, Eccles, Hulme, G: White
Apr 10	Warrington Wolves	W 37-4	5,567	T: Rogers 2, Bradbury, Broadbent, Forber, Hulme, Naylor, G: Crompton 4, DG: Crompton
Apr 19	HULL SHARKS	W 12-4	5,227	T: Blakeley, Rogers, G: Blakeley 2
Apr 24	Leeds Rhinos	L 12-31	10,288	T: Crompton, E Faimalo, G: Blakeley 2
May 10	HUDDERSFIELD GIANTS	W 40-6	4,195	T: Bradbury 2, McAvoy 2, Blakeley, Edwards, Hassan, Rogers, G: Blakeley 4
May 17	SHEFFIELD EAGLES	L 8-28	3,752	T: McAvoy, G: Blakeley 2
May 24	London Broncos	L 12-21	2,448	T: Crompton, Martin, G: Crompton 2
May 31	CASTLEFORD TIGERS	L 8-18	4,143	T: Martin, Rogers
Jun 7	Wigan Warriors	L 6-34	10,075	T: Alker, G: Russell
Jun 14	Halifax Blue Sox	L 6-34	5,218	T: McAvoy, G: Southern
Jun 21	BRADFORD BULLS	W 11-10	6,319	T: Bradbury, White, G: White, DG: Lee
Jun 28	St Helens	L 12-48	6,130	T: Alker, Randall, G: White 2
Jul 5	WARRINGTON WOLVES	L 14-25	4,538	T: Alker 2, Randall, G: White
Jul 10	Leeds Rhinos***	L 16-34	4,122	T: Alker, McAvoy, Martin, G: Svabic 2
Aug 2	Hull Sharks	L 0-32	4,593	
Aug 9	LEEDS RHINOS	L 6-40	4,043	T: Hassan, G: Svabic
Aug 16	Huddersfield Giants	W 16-12	2,932	T: Naylor 2, White, G: Svabic 2

Salford RL Match Results

1998 *continued*

	Opponent	Result	Attendance	Scorers
Aug 21	Sheffield Eagles	D 18-18	2,571	T: Littler, Randall, Rogers, G: Svabic 2, Southern
Aug 30	LONDON BRONCOS	W 23-20	3,681	T: P Highton, Naylor, Rogers, G: Blakeley 5, DG: White
Sep 6	Castleford Tigers	L 12-30	4,865	T: Hulme, Waring, G: Blakeley 2
Sep 13	WIGAN WARRIORS	L 2-34	4,895	G: Blakeley
Sep 20	HALIFAX BLUE SOX	L 16-34	3,487	T: White 2, Southern, G: Svabic 2
Sep 27	Bradford Bulls	L 18-40	11,102	T: Bradbury, Broadbent, White, G: Svabic 3

*At Halifax ** At Leeds *** 'On The Road' league fixture at Gateshead

1999

	Opponent	Result	Attendance	Scorers
Jan 22	BARROW BORDER RAIDERS (F)	W 36-12	1,211	T: Broadbent 2, Svabic 2, Alker, Crompton, G: Blakeley 6
Jan 24	Lancashire Lynx (F)	W 17-14	461	T: J Faimalo, Iain Marsh, Svabic, G: Svabic 2, DG: Waring
Feb 13	SHEFFIELD EAGLES (RLC-4)	W 16-6	2,359	T: Martin, H Smith, G: Blakeley 4
Feb 28	Huddersfield Giant (RLC-5)	W 22-14	4,992	T: Casey 2, Crompton, Martin, G: Blakeley 3
Mar 7	ST HELENS	L 12-30	6,378	T: Crompton, Hayes, G: Blakeley 2
Mar 13	Castleford Tigers (RLC-6)	L 10-30	5,236	T: Broadbent, G: Blakeley 3
Mar 21	Wakefield Trinity Wildcats	L 10-22	4,004	T: Carige, Casey, G: Casey
Apr 2	WARRINGTON WOLVES	L 22-26	6,249	T: Alker 2, Briggs, Hulme, G: Blakeley 3
Apr 6	Halifax Blue Sox	L 14-30	3,724	T: Casey, Crompton, P Highton, G: Casey
Apr 11	CASTLEFORD TIGERS	L 17-29	3,663	T: Baynes, J Faimalo, Littler, G: Blakeley 2, DG: Briggs
Apr 18	HUDDERSFIELD GIANTS	L 14-15	4,125	T: Carige, Blakeley, G: Blakeley 3
Apr 25	Gateshead Thunder	L 14-38	1,780	T: Hayes, Martin, Svabic, G: Blakeley
May 3	WIGAN WARRIORS	L 6-46	4,418	T: Briggs, G: Blakeley
May 9	Bradford Bulls	L 6-46	11,863	T: Thompson, G: Blakeley
May 12	LEEDS RHINOS	L 30-38	3,455	T: M Johnson 2, Blakeley, Makin, H Smith, G: Blakeley 5

Salford RL Match Results

1999 *continued*

	Opponent	Result	Attendance	Scorers
May 16	LONDON BRONCOS	W 31-14	3,052	T: Blakeley 3, M Johnson, Thompson, G: Blakeley 5, DG: Blakeley
May 22	Sheffield Eagles	D 26-26	3,100	T: Carige 2, Hulme, M Johnson, G: Blakeley 3, Casey 2
May 30	HULL SHARKS	W 38-18	3,699	T: Brown 3, Alker, Broadbent, J Faimalo, M Johnson, G: Blakeley 3, Casey 2
Jun 6	St Helens	L 0-48	7,402	
Jun 13	WAKEFIELD T WILDCATS	W 28-14	4,632	T: Crompton, P Highton, M Johnson, H Smith, Thompson, G: Southern 4
Jun 20	Warrington Wolves	L 14-28	4,869	T: Carige, Crompton, J Faimalo, G: Casey
Jun 23	Hull Sharks	L 12-18	3,100	T: Casey, P Highton, G: Casey 2
Jun 27	HALIFAX BLUE SOX	L 20-22	3,536	T: Briggs, Brown, H Smith, G: Casey 4
Jul 4	Castleford Tigers	L 10-38	5,786	T: P Highton, M Johnson, G: Casey
Jul 11	Huddersfield Giants	W 24-10	3,191	T: M Johnson 2, Baynes, Littler, G: Casey 2, Southern 2
Jul 18	GATESHEAD THUNDER	L 18-31	5,611	T: Carige, Broadbent, H Smith, G: Casey 3
Jul 25	Wigan Warriors	L 2-64	7,144	G: Casey
Aug 1	BRADFORD BULLS	L 20-58	6,680	T: Ayres, Blakeley, P Highton, Southern, G: Casey 2
Aug 7	London Broncos	L 14-28	2,153	T: Blakeley, J Faimalo, Littler, G: Casey
Aug 15	SHEFFIELD EAGLES	W 26-12	3,307	T: M Johnson 2, Broadbent, Thompson, G: Blakeley 4, Southern
Aug 18	Leeds Rhinos	L 16-50	10,117	T: Carige, M Johnson, Waring, G: Ayres 2
Aug 22	ST HELENS	L 10-23	5,149	T: Crompton, G: Blakeley 3
Aug 29	Wakefield Trinity Wildcats	L 10-36	2,736	T: J Faimalo, M Johnson, G: Southern
Sep 5	WARRINGTON WOLVES	W 42-26	3,627	T: Brown 2, Broadbent, Crompton, J Faimalo, M Johnson, H Smith, G: Blakeley 7
Sep 10	Halifax Blue Sox	L 20-32	5,764	T: Bradbury, M Johnson, Littler, Thompson, G: Thompson 2

Renamed Salford City Reds from July 18

Salford RL Match Results

2000

	Opponent	Result	Attendance	Scorers
Jan 28	WIGAN WARRIORS (F)	L 16-30	4,021	T: Alker, Holroyd, Offiah, G: Svabic 2
Feb 13	Barrow Border Raiders (RLC-4)	W 34-18	3,630	T: Pinkney 2, Alker, Littler, Offiah, Southern, G: Brown 5
Feb 27	London Broncos (RLC-5)	W 22-21	1,577	T: P Highton, Offiah, Pinkney, Webber, G: Southern 2, Brown
Mar 5	Huddersfield-Sheffield Giants	W 18-10	3,480	T: Svabic 2, Webber, G: Svabic 3
Mar 12	WARRINGTON WOLVES (RLC-6)	L 20-22	6,700	T: Brown, Offiah, James Smith, Tassell, G: Svabic 2
Mar 19	CASTLEFORD TIGERS	L 16-22	5,534	T: Offiah, Tassell, Webber, G: Svabic 2
Apr 2	WIGAN WARRIORS	L 0-32	6,663	
Apr 9	London Broncos	W 33-24	2,549	T: Brown 2, Crompton, Offiah, James Smith, G: Brown 6, DG: Crompton
Apr 16	BRADFORD BULLS	L 1-52	6,468	DG: Offiah
Apr 21	Hull FC	L 22-26	5,862	T: Webber 2, Crompton, Offiah, Tassell, G: Southern
Apr 24	WAKEFIELD TRINITY WILDCATS	L 14-22	4,224	T: Makin, Tassell, G: Southern 2, Duffy
May 2	Leeds Rhinos	L 16-42	10,008	T: Broadbent, J Faimalo, Offiah, G: Svabic 2
May 7	HALIFAX BLUE SOX	L 20-38	3,703	T: Alker 2, Pinkney, G: Blakeley 4
May 14	WARRINGTON WOLVES	W 31-12	4,005	T: Nicol 2, Littler, Pinkney, James Smith, G: Blakeley 5, DG: Duffy
May 21	St Helens	L 22-46	7,862	T: Alker, Broadbent, James Smith, Webber, G: Blakeley 3
May 26	Castleford Tigers	L 4-30	6,303	T: Brown
Jun 4	HUDDERSFIELD-SHEFFIELD GIANTS	W 18-8	3,149	T: Broadbent, Southern, Wainwright, G: Blakeley 3
Jun 11	Wigan Warriors	L 20-52	7,748	T: Blakeley, Brown, Pinkney, James Smith, G: Blakeley 2
Jun 18	LONDON BRONCOS	W 42-26	3,011	T: Holroyd 2, Webber 2, Broadbent, Pinkney, Wainwright, G: Blakeley 7
Jun 25	Bradford Bulls	L 16-96	11,596	T: Napolitano, Nicol, Pinkney, G: Blakeley 2

Salford RL Match Results

2000 *continued*

	Opponent	Result	Attendance	Scorers
Jul 2	Wakefield Trinity Wildcats	L 10-36	3,345	T: Littler, Offiah, G: Blakeley
Jul 9	HULL FC	W 30-22	3,494	T: Pinkney 2, James Smith, Tassell, Webber, G: Blakeley 5
Jul 16	LEEDS RHINOS	L 26-34	5,057	T: Alker 2, Baynes, Offiah, G: Blakeley 5
Jul 23	HALIFAX BLUE SOX	W 27-26	3,320	T: Alker, Nicol, Offiah, Pinkney, G: Blakeley 5, DG: Offiah
Jul 30	ST HELENS	L 4-58	5,409	T: Webber
Aug 6	Warrington Wolves	L 18-32	5,609	T: M Johnson, Pinkney, Webber, G: Blakeley 3
Aug 13	London Broncos	W 16-10	2,040	T: Broadbent, Offiah, G: Blakeley 4
Aug 20	WIGAN WARRIORS	L 18-30	4,704	T: Broadbent 2, Nicol, G: Roper 3
Aug 27	St Helens	L 28-50	6,694	T: Offiah 2, Alker, Broadbent, Southern, G: Blakeley 4
Sep 3	HULL FC	W 33-24	3,526	T: Offiah 2, Alker, Pinkney, Roper, Tassell, G: Blakeley 3, Holroyd, DG: Holroyd
Sep 10	Halifax Blue Sox	W 29-12	4,646	T: Holroyd, James Smith, Tassell, G: Blakeley 7, Holroyd, DG: Holroyd
Sep 17	Warrington Wolves	L 10-38	6,969	T: Offiah, Tassell, G: Holroyd

2001

	Opponent	Result	Attendance	Scorers
Dec 26	Warrington Wolves (F)	W 36-20	3,600	T: Baynes, Broadbent, Holroyd, Littler, Maloney, Pinkney, G: Holroyd 6
Jan 24	Wigan Warriors (F)	L 16-42	5,186	T: Blakeley 2, Pinkney, G: Holroyd 2
Feb 11	Leigh Centurions (RLC-4)	L 12-16	6,408	T: Jowitt 2, G: Blakeley 2
Feb 21	WIGAN WARRIORS (F)	L 6-40	1,372	T: Offiah, G: Blakeley
Mar 4	Hull FC	L 34-46	6,628	T: Maloney 2, P Highton, Offiah, Pinkney, Tassell, G: Goulding 5
Mar 16	BRADFORD BULLS	L 6-40	4,355	T: Jowitt, G: Goulding
Mar 25	Warrington Wolves	W 39-14	6,147	T: Maloney 2, Pinkney 2, Alker, Broadbent, Offiah, G: Goulding 5, DG: Holroyd

Salford RL Match Results

2001 *continued*

	Opponent	Result	Attendance	Scorers
Apr 8	HUDDERSFIELD GIANTS	W 28-14	3,793	T: Alker, Hancock, Maloney, Tassell, G: Goulding 6
Apr 13	Castleford Tigers	W 24-22	6,816	T: Maloney 2, Jowitt, Pinkney, G: Goulding 4
Apr 16	LONDON BRONCOS	L 12-14	3,967	T: Coley, Pinkney, G: Goulding 2
Apr 22	LEEDS RHINOS	L 14-19	5,069	T: Hancock, Littler, G: Goulding 2, Holroyd
Apr 30	Wakefield Trinity Wildcats	L 22-32	2,940	T: Maloney 2, Coley, Pinkney, G: Holroyd 3
May 6	Halifax Blue Sox	L 18-30	4,180	T: Maloney 2, Blakeley, Wainwright, G: Holroyd
May 13	WIGAN WARRIORS	W 31-30	5,691	T: Pinkney 3, Hancock, Offiah, G: Holroyd 5, DG: Holroyd
May 18	St Helens	L 16-66	7,837	T: Alker 2, Brown, G: Maloney 2
May 27	Bradford Bulls	L 10-42	10,907	T: Arnold, Littler, G: Blakeley
Jun 3	HULL FC	L 24-36	4,143	T: Alker 2, Hancock, Maloney, G: Blakeley 3, Goulding
Jun 10	WARRINGTON WOLVES	W 26-18	4,963	T: Pinkney 2, P Highton, Maloney, G: Blakeley 5
Jun 17	Huddersfield Giants	W 32-24	2,721	T: Littler 2, Alker, Blakeley, Coley, G: Blakeley 5, Maloney
Jun 23	CASTLEFORD TIGERS	L 18-26	3,530	T: Coley, Offiah, Tassell, G: Blakeley 3
Jul 1	London Broncos	W 37-14	2,941	T: Offiah 2, Blakeley, Hammond, Tassell, Wainwright, G: Blakeley 6, DG: Goulding
Jul 6	Leeds Rhinos	L 6-56	10,119	T: Littler, G: Blakeley
Jul 15	HALIFAX BLUE SOX	L 34-50	3,597	T: Arnold 3, Hancock, Pinkney, Tassell, G: Goulding 3, Blakeley 2
Jul 20	Wigan Warriors	L 4-70	8,085	T: Pinkney
Jul 29	ST HELENS	L 18-56	5,234	T: Arnold, Broadbent, Wainwright, G: Holroyd 3
Aug 5	WAKEFIELD TRINITY WILDCATS	W 26-16	3,509	T: Hancock, Littler, Nicol, Offiah, G: Holroyd 3, Blakeley, DG: Alker, Goulding
Aug 12	Huddersfield Giants	L 14-35	2,815	T: Maloney 2, Littler, G: Holroyd

Salford RL Match Results

2001 continued

	Opponent	Result	Attendance	Scorers
Aug 19	Wakefield Trinity Wildcats	L 20-23	2,376	T: Littler, Maloney, Nicol, G: Holroyd 4
Aug 26	HALIFAX BLUE SOX	L 30-41	3,649	T: Offiah 2, Blakeley, Holroyd, Maloney, Pinkney, G: Holroyd 3
Sep 2	LONDON BRONCOS	L 12-50	2,618	T: Driscoll, Maloney, G: Holroyd 2
Sep 9	Hull FC	L 8-40	6,262	T: Littler, G: Holroyd 2
Sep 16	WAKEFIELD TRINITY WILDCATS	L 24-32	4,264	T: Baynes, Hancock, Littler, Maloney, G: Holroyd 4

2002

	Opponent	Result	Attendance	Scorers
Dec 26	Halifax Blue Sox (F)*	L 8-28	1,741	T: Wainwright, G: L Marsh 2
Jan 13	HALIFAX BLUE SOX (F)*	L 6-36	1,231	T: Littler, G: Goulding
Jan 25	Warrington Wolves (F)	W 34-26	2,654	T: Baxter, Broadbent, Gibson, Gorski, Littler, Pinkney, G: Goulding 5
Feb 10	Castleford Tigers (RLC-4)	L 6-19	5,394	G: Goulding 3
Mar 3	HULL FC	L 10-24	4,693	T: Pinkney, G: Goulding 3
Mar 8	St Helens	L 2-34	10,160	G: Goulding
Mar 23	Wakefield Trinity Wildcats	L 18-32	2,475	T: Pinkney 2, Nicol, G: Holroyd 3
Mar 29	WARRINGTON WOLVES	W 31-18	5,478	T: Arnold, Gibson, Pinkney, Shaw, Treacy, G: Goulding 5, DG: Goulding
Apr 1	Halifax Blue Sox	W 15-12	3,808	T: Maloney, Wainwright, G: Goulding 3, DG: Goulding
Apr 7	CASTLEFORD TIGERS	L 16-74	4,101	T: Goulding 2, Arnold, G: Goulding 2
Apr 19	WIDNES VIKINGS	L 20-24	4,372	T: Littler, Treacy, Wainwright, G: Goulding 4
Apr 29	Bradford Bulls	L 18-44	9,652	T: Blakeley, Nicol, Platt, G: Pinkney 3
May 5	LEEDS RHINOS	L 16-48	4,460	T: Baynes, Blakeley, Treacy, G: Goulding 2
May 10	Wigan Warriors	L 0-32	8,765	
May 19	LONDON BRONCOS	L 18-42	2,211	T: Maloney 2, Nicol, G: Maloney 2, Goulding
May 26	Hull FC	L 8-28	6,262	T: Hunte, G: Holroyd 2
Jun 1	ST HELENS	L 24-28	4,102	T: Alker, Gibson, Holroyd, Southern, G: Holroyd 4
Jun 9	Castleford Tigers	L 2-24	5,025	G: Holroyd

Salford RL Match Results

2002 *continued*

	Opponent	Result	Attendance	Scorers
Jun 23	BRADFORD BULLS	L 10-48	4,806	T: Maloney, Pinkney, G: Goulding
Jun 30	Widnes Vikings	W 26-16	5,641	T: Holroyd 2, Arnold, Hunte, G: Goulding 5
Jul 7	WAKEFIELD TRINITY WILDCATS	W 42-18	3,845	T: Arnold, P Highton, Hunte, Littler, Southern, Treacy, Watson, G: Holroyd 7
Jul 14	HALIFAX BLUE SOX	L 14-28	3,573	T: Hunte, Wainwright, G: Holroyd 3
Jul 21	Warrington Wolves	L 9-18	5,751	T: Baynes, G: Blakeley 2, DG: Watson
Jul 26	Leeds Rhinos	L 38-39	8,200	T: Arnold 2, Alker, Holroyd, Hunte, Treacy, G: Holroyd 7
Aug 4	WIGAN WARRIORS	L 24-46	4,247	T: Blakeley, Coley, Hunte, Maloney, G: Holroyd 4
Aug 11	London Broncos	L 19-26	2,892	T: Reardon, Wainwright, G: Holroyd 3, Blakeley 2, DG: Holroyd
Aug 17	WAKEFIELD TRINITY WILDCATS	D 22-22	3,217	T: Arnold 2, Blakeley, Watson, G: Holroyd 3
Aug 25	Hull FC	L 16-60	5,303	T: Blakeley, Hunte, Treacy, G: Blakeley, Holroyd
Sep 1	Widnes Vikings	L 14-15	6,956	T: D Highton, Maloney, G: Blakeley 3
Sep 8	HALIFAX BLUE SOX	L 26-34	4,135	T: Reardon 2, Alker, Gibson, Maloney, G: Holroyd 2, Blakeley
Sep 13	Warrington Wolves	W 22-2	5,864	T: Hunte 2, Ebrill, Nicol, G: Blakeley 2, Treacy
Sep 22	CASTLEFORD TIGERS	L 10-20	5,541	T: D Highton, G: Blakeley 3

* Colin Dixon Memorial Trophy

2003

	Opponent	Result	Attendance	Scorers
Dec 29	Halifax (F)*	L 12-28	1,713	T: Alker, Coley, G: Blakeley 2
Jan 19	SWINTON LIONS (NLC)	W 58-6	3,334	T: Flowers 2, Hunte 2, Baldwin, Beverley, Blakeley, Clinch, Coley, Littler, L Marsh, G: Clinch 3, Blakeley 2, L Marsh 2
Jan 26	TOULOUSE SPACERS (RLC-3)	W 26-10	1,590	T: Flowers 2, Beverley, Hunte, Littler, G: Clinch 2, L Marsh

Salford RL Match Results

2003 *continued*

	Opponent	Result	Attendance	Scorers
Feb 9	Barrow Raiders (RLC-4)	W 22-6	1,392	T: Alker, Baldwin, Bowker, Littler, G: Clinch 3
Feb 16	Leigh Centurions (NLC)	D 20-20	4,445	T: Littler 2, Baynes, Hunte, G: L Marsh 2
Feb 23	ROCHDALE HORNETS (NLC)	W 58-16	2,346	T: Alker 2, Beverley 2, Flowers 2, Kirk 2, Clinch, Coley, D Highton, G: L Marsh 5, Clinch 2
Feb 28	Hull Kingston Rovers (RLC-5)	W 12-2	2,533	T: Hunte, Littler, G: Clinch 2
Mar 9	Oldham (NLC)	W 62-4	2,839	T: Charles 3, Alker 2, Littler 2, Beverley, Flowers, D Highton, Kirk, G: Clinch 5, Blakeley 4
Mar 16	ST HELENS (RLC-6)	L 6-54	5,717	T: Hunte, G: Charles
Mar 19	Gateshead Thunder (NLC)	W 90-8	172	T: Alker 2, Arnold 2, Beverley 2, Blakeley 2, Hunte 2, Lowe 2, Charles, D Highton, Kirk, L Marsh, G: Blakeley 13
Mar 23	GATESHEAD THUNDER (NLC)	W 100-12	1,653	T: Fitzpatrick 3, Beverley 2, Flowers 2, Hunte 2, Littler 2, Alker, Bowker, Clough, P Highton, Kirk, Lowe, L Marsh, G: Blakeley 14
Mar 30	LEIGH CENTURIONS (NLC)	W 22-10	3,099	T: Beverley 2, Hunte, Kirk, Platt, G: Blakeley
Apr 2	Swinton Lions (NLC)	W 72-0	954	T: Alker 4, Beverley 3, Kirk 2, Fitzpatrick, Flowers, D Highton, Platt, G: Blakeley 10
Apr 6	Rochdale Hornets (NLC)	W 44-16	1,067	T: Clinch 2, Hunte 2, Blakeley, Charles, D Highton, Kirk, G: Blakeley 6
Apr 13	OLDHAM (NLC)	W 54-12	2,162	T: Beverley 2, Arnold, Baldwin, Coley, Haggerty, D Highton, Hunte, Kirk, L Marsh, G: L Marsh 7
Apr 18	Whitehaven	D 22-22	2,136	T: Platt 2, Littler, Lowe, G: L Marsh 2, Charles
Apr 21	BATLEY BULLDOGS	W 54-12	2,074	T: Beverley 3, Charles 3, Kirk 2, Hunte, Littler, G: Charles 7
May 4	Featherstone Rovers	L 16-18	1,616	T: Alker, Arnold, Beverley, G: Blakeley, Charles

Salford RL Match Results

2003 *continued*

Date	Opponent	Result	Attendance	Scorers
May 10	OLDHAM	W 44-12	1,657	T: Hunte 3, Alker 2, Baldwin, Lowe, L Marsh, G: Charles 5, Blakeley
May 18	Barrow Raiders (NLC-1)	W 40-20	936	T: Beverley 2, Baldwin, Charles, Littler, Lowe, Kirk, G: Charles 6
May 25	Doncaster Dragons	W 34-24	1,069	T: Kirk 2, Baldwin, Clinch, Coley, Littler, G: Charles 3, Blakeley 2
Jun 1	DEWSBURY RAMS	W 76-4	1,698	T: Hunte 5, Beverley 3, Alker 2, Coley 2, Berne, Flowers, G: Charles 10
Jun 8	BATLEY BULLDOGS (NLC-SF)	W 68-6	1,379	T: Charles 3, Littler 2, Alker, Baldwin, Berne, Beverley, Bowker, P Highton, Hunte, G: Charles 7, Beverley 3
Jun 15	Rochdale Hornets	W 32-16	1,571	T: Beverley 2, Arnold, D Highton, Littler, G: Blakeley 3, Charles 3
Jun 22	Leigh Centurions	W 32-12	4,000	T: Arnold, Beverley, Clinch, Flowers, Hunte, G: Charles 4, Beverley 2
Jun 29	WHITEHAVEN	D 26-26	2,056	T: Kirk 2, Arnold, Beverley, Littler, G: Charles 2, Blakeley
Jul 6	Leigh Centurions (NLC-Final)**	W 36-19	6,486	T: Arnold, Coley, Haggerty, Hunte, Kirk, Littler, G: Blakeley 5, Charles
Jul 13	HULL KINGSTON ROVERS	W 24-12	2,063	T: Littler 2, Alker, Beverley, Hunte, G: Charles 2
Jul 20	Batley Bulldogs	W 54-16	835	T: Kirk 2, Arnold, Baldwin, Baynes, Beverley, Charles, Flowers, P Highton, G: Blakeley 7, Charles 2
Jul 27	FEATHERSTONE ROVERS	W 36-20	2,025	T: Alker, Baynes, Coley, Flowers, Kirk, Littler, G: Charles 5, Clinch
Aug 3	Oldham	W 32-22	1,765	T: Alker, Beverley, Bowker, Coley, Hunte, Littler, G: Charles 4
Aug 10	DONCASTER DRAGONS	W 72-0	1,620	T: Flowers 2, D Highton 2, Kirk 2, Beverley, Clinch, Coley, Haggerty, P Highton, Littler, Lowe, G: Blakeley 10

Salford RL Match Results

2003 *continued*

Date	Opponent	Result	Attendance	Scorers
Aug 17	Dewsbury Rams	W 58-18	972	T: Clinch 2, Baldwin, Baynes, Beverley, Blakeley, Coley, Flowers, D Highton, P Highton, G: Charles 5, Blakeley 3, Hunte
Aug 24	ROCHDALE HORNETS	W 58-18	2,204	T: Clinch 3, Davies 2, Littler 2, Baldwin, Beverley, Hunte, G: Charles 6, Blakeley 3
Aug 31	LEIGH CENTURIONS	W 46-24	4,121	T: Littler 2, Alker, Baldwin, Beverley, P Highton, Hunte, Kirk, G: Blakeley 6, Hunte
Sep 7	Hull Kingston Rovers	L 16-18	2,060	T: Baldwin, Beverley, Davies, G: Clinch 2
Sep 21	LEIGH CENTURIONS (NL-Qualifying SF)	W 26-18	3,660	T: Arnold, Baldwin, Littler, Moana, G: Charles 5
Oct 5	Leigh Centurions (NL-Final)***	W 31-14	9,186	T: Hunte 2, Beverley, Littler, G: Charles 6, Blakeley, DG: Blakeley

*Colin Dixon Memorial Trophy   ** At Rochdale   *** At Widnes*

National League One Grand Final winners

National League One Minor Premiers

National League Cup winners

2004

Date	Opponent	Result	Attendance	Scorers
Jan 25	BATLEY (F)	W 36-22	957	T: Littler 2, Alker, Coley, A Johnson, Naylor, Stewart, G: Caine 4
Feb 1	Warrington (F)	L 22-32	3,336	T: Beverley, Caine, Charles, G: Caine 3, Charles 2
Feb 6	St Helens (F)	L 10-20	4,664	T: Caine, Stewart, G: Charles
Feb 22	WIDNES VIKINGS	W 24-12	5,049	T: Clinch, Coley, Little, G: Caine 5, Charles
Feb 29	London Broncos (RLC-4)	L 8-24	2,454	T: Alker, Stewart
Mar 7	Wigan Warriors	L 10-20	11,172	T: Littler, Stewart, G: Charles

Salford RL Match Results

2004 *continued*

	Opponent	Result	Attendance	Scorers
Mar 20	WAKEFIELD TRINITY WILDCATS	L 20-27	2,825	T: Kirk 2, Fitzpatrick, A Johnson, G: Charles 2
Mar 28	London Broncos	L 30-35	2,198	T: Beverley 2, Baldwin, Haggerty, Moana, Stewart, G: Fitzpatrick 2, Caine
Apr 2	Bradford Bulls	L 18-25	11,976	T: Beverley 3, G: Charles 3
Apr 9	Huddersfield Giants	L 16-24	4,062	T: Beverley, Stewart, G: Charles 4
Apr 12	LEEDS RHINOS	L 0-44	5,462	
Apr 16	St Helens	L 4-40	7,649	T: Littler
Apr 24	WARRINGTON WOLVES	L 18-37	3,624	T: Beverley, Fitzpatrick, A Johnson, G: Charles 3
May 2	Hull FC	L 6-82	9,869	T: Littler, G: Charles
May 8	LONDON BRONCOS	W 30-12	2,529	T: Beverley, Caine, Charles, Littler, Stewart, G: Charles 5
May 23	Castleford Tigers	W 36-32	6,961	T: Baynes, Caine, Haggerty, P Highton, A Johnson, Stewart, G: Caine 6
May 28	Leeds Rhinos	L 6-34	14,239	T: Baynes, G: Charles
Jun 6	HUDDERSFIELD GIANTS	L 18-25	3,271	T: Haggerty, A Johnson, McGuinness, G: Charles 3
Jun 13	BRADFORD BULLS	L 28-35	5,006	T: Alker, Beverley, Caine, Coley, G: Charles 6
Jun 20	Wakefield Trinity Wildcats	L 20-21	3,426	T: Beverley, Coley, Littler, G: Charles 4
Jun 27	CASTLEFORD TIGERS	W 30-14	3,313	T: Alker 2, Charles, Coley, Shipway, G: Charles 5
Jul 11	WIGAN WARRIORS	L 16-32	6,037	T: A Johnson, Kirk, Stewart, G: Charles 2
Jul 18	Widnes Vikings	W 15-14	5,573	T: Caine, Kirk, G: Charles 3, DG: Clinch
Jul 25	HULL FC	L 20-44	3,515	T: Baynes, Charles, Coley, G: Charles 3, Caine
Aug 1	Warrington Wolves	L 20-46	8,641	T: A Johnson, Littler, McAvoy, McGuinness, G: Charles 2
Aug 8	ST HELENS	W 30-20	4,897	T: Alker 2, Baynes, Caine, Littler, G: Charles 5
Aug 14	WIDNES VIKINGS	W 14-13	3,067	T: Caine, A Johnson, Kirk, G: Charles
Aug 22	Wakefield Trinity Wildcats	L 18-46	3,641	T: Coley 2, Caine, G: Charles 3
Aug 29	WARRINGTON WOLVES	L 6-32	4,019	T: Littler, G: Charles
Sep 5	Castleford Tigers	W 24-22	5,809	T: Fitzpatrick 2, Alker, Coley, G: Charles 4

Salford RL Match Results

2004 *continued*

Date	Opponent	Result	Attendance	Scorers
Sep 12	HULL FC	L 8-12	3,307	T: Alker, G: Charles 2
Sep 19	Huddersfield Giants	L 22-28	3,083	T: Littler 2, Caine, Rutgerson, G: Charles 3

2005

Date	Opponent	Result	Attendance	Scorers
Jan 2	SWINTON LIONS (F)	W 34-16	1,946	T: Coley, Dickens, Fitzpatrick, Haggerty, Littler, Mark Stevens, G: Dickens 3, Charles, Fitzpatrick
Jan 25	WIGAN WARRIORS (F)	W 20-16	2,182	T: Fitzpatrick, Hodgson, Robinson, Stewart, G: Charles 2
Jan 30	Warrington Wolves (F)	L 24-26	4,323	T: Fitzpatrick 3, Haggerty, G: Robinson 3, Fitzpatrick
Feb 11	Wigan Warriors	L 4-15	13,687	T: Alker
Feb 18	LONDON BRONCOS	W 20-16	3,315	T: Fitzpatrick 2, Sibbit, Stewart, G: Charles 2
Feb 26	Leigh Centurions	W 32-6	4,180	T: Fitzpatrick, Haggerty, Hodgson, McGuinness, Shipway, Sibbit, G: Charles 3, Robinson
Mar 5	HULL FC	L 12-22	3,568	T: Haggerty, Hodgson, Stewart
Mar 11	St Helens	L 12-46	9,971	T: Alker, Baldwin, G: Charles, Dickens
Mar 18	LEEDS RHINOS	L 12-30	5,118	T: Baldwin, Hodgson, G: Dickens, Robinson
Mar 25	WARRINGTON WOLVES	W 42-10	6,004	T: Littler 3, Hodgson, McAvoy, Robinson, Sibbit, G: Charles 4, Dickens 2, Robinson
Mar 28	Huddersfield Giants	L 12-26	4,760	T: Beverley, McGuinness, G: Charles 2
Apr 3	Rochdale Hornets (RLC-4)	W 30-24	1,971	T: Sibbit 2, Alker, Baldwin, Dickens, Robinson, G: Charles 3
Apr 8	WAKEFIELD TRINITY WILDCATS	W 16-14	3,378	T: Robinson 2, Hodgson, G: Charles 2
Apr 17	Widnes Vikings	W 22-6	5,878	T: Littler 2, Robinson 2, G: Charles 3
Apr 22	LEIGH CENTURIONS	W 42-6	5,021	T: Littler 3, Robinson 2, Coley, Haggerty, Sibbit, G: Robinson 3, Charles 2
May 1	Hull FC	L 6-20	8,929	T: Beverley, G: Charles

Salford RL Match Results

2005 *continued*

	Opponent	Result	Attendance	Scorers
May 8	LONDON BRONCOS (RLC-5)	L 12-26	2,339	T: Bamford, McGuinness, G: Charles 2
May 13	BRADFORD BULLS	L 0-58	4,102	
May 22	London Broncos	L 18-34	2,997	T: Haggerty, McAvoy, Rutgerson, G: Charles 3
May 30	WIGAN WARRIORS	L 20-34	5,526	T: Coley 2, Alker, Stewart, G: Charles 2
Jun 5	Wakefield Trinity Wildcats	L 24-36	3,536	T: Hartley, Hodgson, Robinson, Rutgerson, G: Charles 4
Jun 10	ST HELENS	L 22-33	4,704	T: Hartley 2, Charles, Littler, G: Charles 3
Jun 19	Warrington Wolves	L 14-48	10,925	T: Beverley, Hartley, Shipway, G: Charles
Jul 2	HUDDERSFIELD GIANTS	W 24-16	2,682	T: Beverley, Charles, Robinson, G: Charles 6
Jul 8	WIDNES VIKINGS	W 34-16	4,507	T: Hodgson 2, Haggerty, Littler, Robinson, Sibbit, G: Charles 5
Jul 15	Leeds Rhinos	L 14-54	13,904	T: Littler 2, Hartley, G: Charles
Jul 22	BRADFORD BULLS	L 18-24	3,684	T: Coley, Fitzpatrick, Langi, G: Charles 3
Aug 5	Wigan Warriors	L 12-40	10,156	T: Brocklehurst, Littler, G: Charles 2
Aug 14	Bradford Bulls	L 12-58	10,113	T: Alker, A Smith, G: Charles 2
Aug 19	WAKEFIELD TRINITY WILDCATS	W 37-0	3,005	T: Stewart 3, Coley, Fitzpatrick, Robinson, G: Charles 5, Robinson, DG: Robinson
Sep 4	Warrington Wolves	L 22-32	9,619	T: Fitzpatrick, Littler, Sibbit, Stewart, G: Charles 3
Sep 9	LONDON BRONCOS	W 26-18	2,683	T: Fitzpatrick, Haggerty, Langi, Littler, Stewart, G: Charles 3
Sep 16	Leigh Centurions	W 20-14	3,519	T: Hodgson 2, Littler, Stewart, G: Charles 2

2006

	Opponent	Result	Attendance	Scorers
Feb 1	Warrington Wolves (F)	L 6-26	3,187	T: P Highton, G: Charles
Feb 5	SWINTON LIONS (F)	W 38-8	1,768	T: Hodgson 2, Sibbit 2, Clough, James Lowes, Stewart, G: Charles 4, Fitzpatrick

Salford RL Match Results

2006 *continued*

	Opponent	Result	Attendance	Scorers
Feb 12	Warrington Wolves	W 24-6	10,835	T: Wilshere 2, Hodgson, Langi, G: Hodgson 4
Feb 17	CATALANS DRAGONS	W 16-0	4,660	T: Littler 2, Brocklehurst, G: Hodgson 2
Feb 24	Bradford Bulls	L 4-34	10,062	T: Hodgson
Mar 3	WIGAN WARRIORS	W 28-10	5,494	T: Coley, Dunemann, Finnigan, Hodgson, Wilshere, G: Hodgson 4
Mar 11	WAKEFIELD TRINITY WILDCATS	W 48-10	4,060	T: Finnigan 3, P Highton 2, Brocklehurst, Fitzpatrick, Robinson, G: Hodgson 8
Mar 17	Leeds Rhinos	L 12-20	15,242	T: Finnigan, Hodgson, Langi
Mar 25	Catalans Dragons	W 28-22	6,547	T: Fitzpatrick 2, Moule 2, Coley, Finnigan, G: Hodgson 2
Apr 2	DEWSBURY RAMS (RLC-4)	W 32-4	1,899	T: Hodgson 2, Coley, Finnigan, McGuinness, Stringer, G: Wilshere 4
Apr 7	HUDDERSFIELD GIANTS	W 36-18	4,084	T: Fitzpatrick 3, Hodgson, Robinson, Sibbit, G: Wilshere 6
Apr 14	Warrington Wolves	W 22-6	10,744	T: Fitzpatrick, Hodgson, Littler, Robinson, G: Wilshere 3
Apr 17	LEEDS RHINOS	L 18-24	7,609	T: Finnigan 2, Wilshere, G: Wilshere 3
Apr 21	ST HELENS	L 10-12	7,234	T: Finnigan, Hodgson, G: Wilshere
Apr 30	Castleford Tigers	L 26-28	6,069	T: Finnigan, Hodgson, Langi, Moule, Wilshere, G: Wilshere 3
May 5	WAKEFIELD TRINITY WILDCATS	W 26-12	4,086	T: Wilshere 2, Clayton, Moule, G: Wilshere 5
May 14	Huddersfield Giants	L 18-32	5,289	T: Moule, S Myler, Robinson, G: S Myler 2, Wilshere
May 19	WIGAN WARRIORS (RLC-5)	W 16-4	5,888	T: Littler, Moule, Rutgerson, G: S Myler, Wilshere
May 29	HARLEQUINS	L 28-29	3,295	T: Littler 3, Haggerty, Sibbit, G: S Myler 4
Jun 4	Huddersfield Giants (RLC-6)	L 14-44	4,200	T: Hodgson 2, Moule, G: Hodgson

Salford RL Match Results

2006 *continued*

	Opponent	Result	Attendance	Scorers
Jun 11	Wakefield Trinity Wildcats	W 36-18	3,871	T: Fitzpatrick 2, Brocklehurst, P Highton, Robinson, Sibbit, G: Hodgson 5, S Myler
Jun 16	LEEDS RHINOS	L 18-19	4,517	T: Coley, Hodgson, G: Hodgson 5
Jun 24	St Helens	L 6-28	8,307	T: Haggerty, G: S Myler
Jun 30	BRADFORD BULLS	W 17-16	4,203	T: Langi 2, Robinson, G: Hodgson, S Myler, DG: Dunemann
Jul 8	HULL FC	L 20-24	4,076	T: Hodgson, Moule, Wilshere, G: S Myler 4
Jul 14	Wigan Warriors	L 12-20	13,613	T: Clayton, Moule, G: S Myler 2
Jul 22	Catalans Dragons	L 6-26	5,070	T: Coley, G: Hodgson
Aug 4	HARLEQUINS	W 34-0	3,046	T: Coley, Haggerty, McGuinness, Moule, Robinson, Rutgerson, G: Hodgson 5
Aug 11	WARRINGTON WOLVES	W 35-34	5,016	T: Coley 2, Finnigan, Haggerty, Moule, Robinson, G: Hodgson 5, DG: Dunemann
Aug 20	Hull FC	L 10-11	10,117	T: Finnigan, Wilshere, G: Hodgson
Sep 3	Huddersfield Giants	L 18-24	5,027	T: Coley, Fitzpatrick, Hodgson, Wilshere, G: Charles
Sep 8	CASTLEFORD TIGERS	W 26-16	6,106	T: Alker, Coley, Hodgson, Robinson, Daley Williams, G: Charles 2, Hodgson
Sep 16	Harlequins	L 18-40	3,053	T: Charles, Hodgson, Robinson, G: Charles 3
Sep 23	Bradford Bulls (SL-Elimination)	L 6-52	8,611	T: Hodgson, G: Charles

2007

	Opponent	Result	Attendance	Scorers
Jan 28	WARRINGTON WOLVES (F)	L 12-24	2,900	T: Adamson, Halliwell, Hodgson
Jan 31	WIGAN WARRIORS (F)	L 15-20	2,902	T: Hodgson 2, Gower, G: Robinson, DG: Hodgson
Feb 4	Swinton Lions (F)	L 34-40	931	T: Ambler, Ballard, Adi Dootson, Halliwell, Ratchford, Viane, G: Adi Dootson 4, Halliwell
Feb 11	LEEDS RHINOS	L 26-30	8,070	T: Moule 2, Wilshere 2, Haggerty, G: Robinson 3

Salford RL Match Results

2007 *continued*

	Opponent	Result	Attendance	Scorers
Feb 17	Harlequins	D 18-18	3,515	T: Coley, Korkidas, Robinson, Wilshere, G: Hodgson
Feb 25	Wakefield Trinity Wildcats	L 24-36	6,385	T: Adamson, Finningan, Haggerty, Daley Williams, G: Wilshere 4
Mar 3	CATALANS DRAGONS	W 10-0	4,085	T: Alker, Dorn, G: Wilshere
Mar 11	Bradford Bulls	L 18-56	10,640	T: Coley, Dorn, Daley Williams, G: Wilshere 3
Mar 16	WIGAN WARRIORS	L 6-25	6,025	T: McGuinness, G: Wilshere
Mar 25	Huddersfield Giants	W 18-16	5,275	T: Robinson 2, Turner, G: Wilshere 3
Mar 30	GATESHEAD THUNDER (RLC-4)*	W 64-4	1,283	T: Robinson 4, Hodgson 2, Brocklehurst, Coley, Finningan, Halliwell, P Highton, G: Wilshere 10
Apr 6	WARRINGTON WOLVES	L 32-34	6,177	T: Dorn, Hodgson, Littler, Robinson, Daley Williams, Wilshere, G: Wilshere 4
Apr 9	St Helens	L 4-48	9,409	T: Coley
Apr 13	HULL FC	L 18-35	4,077	T: Dorn, Moule, Wilshere, G: Wilshere 3
Apr 22	Hull Kingston Rovers	W 28-24	6,299	T: Dorn, Hodgson, Moule, Robinson, Wilshere, G: Wilshere 4
Apr 27	WIGAN WARRIORS	L 24-50	6,603	T: Coley 2, Finnigan, Moule, G: Wilshere 4
May 6	Warrington Wolves**	L 18-50	26,447	T: Brocklehurst, Dorn, McGuinness, G: Wilshere 3
May 11	HUDDERSFIELD GIANTS (RLC-5)	L 10-36	2,694	T: Dorn, Littler, G: Wilshere
May 19	Catalans Dragons	L 6-66	8,820	T: Dorn, G: Wilshere
May 25	HUDDERSFIELD GIANTS	W 14-12	3,379	T: Hodgson, McGuinness, Viane, G: Wilshere
Jun 1	St Helens	L 26-27	7,801	T: Wilshere 2, Coley, Hodgson, Ratchford, G: Wilshere 2, Hodgson
Jun 15	HARLEQUINS	W 5-2	4,067	G: Wilshere 2, DG: Robinson
Jul 6	WAKEFIELD TRINITY WILDCATS	L 18-35	4,178	T: Finnigan, Hodgson, Robinson, G: Wilshere 3
Jul 15	Warrington Wolves	L 6-42	9,634	T: Dorn, G: Wilshere
Jul 21	BRADFORD BULLS	W 14-10	3,438	T: Robinson, Viane, G: Wilshere 3

Salford RL Match Results

2007 *continued*

	Opponent	Result	Attendance	Scorers
July 29	Hull FC	L 26-48	13,338	T: Moule 2, Dorn, Finnigan, Wilshere, G: Wilshere 3
Aug 3	HULL KINGSTON ROVERS	L 24-30	7,165	T: Barnett, Finningan, Hodgson, Moule, G: Wilshere 4
Aug 10	Leeds Rhinos	L 14-52	15,637	T: Coley, Dorn, Littler, G: Wilshere
Aug 17	ST HELENS	L 20-32	5,031	T: Wilshere 2, Littler, G: Wilshere 4
Aug 31	Wigan Warriors	L 16-40	13,611	T: Fitzpatrick, P Highton, McGuinness, G: Wilshere 2
Sep 8	Harlequins	L 16-22	2,347	T: Barnett, Dorn, Wilshere, G: Hodgson, Wilshere
Sep 14	WARRINGTON WOLVES	L 26-34	5,152	T: Barnett 2, McGuinness 2, Turner, G: Wilshere 3

* Away tie switched to Salford ** Millennium Magic weekend at Cardiff

2008

	Opponent	Result	Attendance	Scorers
Jan 27	WARRINGTON WOLVES (F)	L 18-22	2,008	T: Leuluai, Littler, Sidlow, G: Wilshere 3
Feb 3	Rochdale Hornets (NLC)	W 54-12	1,478	T: Fitzpatrick 2, Alker, Borgese, Jiminez, R Myler, Sibbit, Stapleton, White, Wilshere, G: Turner 4, Wilshere 3
Feb 8	OLDHAM (NLC)	W 40-12	4,224	T: Littler 3, Gardner, Jiminez, Turner, White, G: Ballard 6
Feb 17	Swinton Lions (NLC)	W 48-8	1,664	T: Turner 3, Fitzpatrick 2, Gardner, Leuluai, Ratchford, White, G: Ratchford 3, Wilshere 3
Feb 22	Oldham (NLC)	L 14-18	1,350	T: Ballard, Brocklehurst, Turner, G: Ballard
Feb 29	SWINTON LIONS (NLC)	W 70-6	6,042	T: Gardner 3, White 2, Alker, Ballard, Fitzpatrick, Jewitt, R Myler, Sibbit, Turner, Wilshere, G: Ballard 9
Mar 7	WARRINGTON WIZARDS (RLC-3)	W 66-10	1,348	T: Ballard 2, Gardner 2, Borgese, Brocklehurst, Fitzpatrick, R Myler, Nash, Walton, White, Wilshere, G: Ballard 9

Salford RL Match Results

2008 *continued*

Date	Opponent	Result	Attendance	Scorers
Mar 14	ROCHDALE HORNETS (NLC)	W 68-0	3,758	T: Ballard 2, R Myler 2, Ratchford 2, Fitzpatrick, Gardner, Littler, Stapleton, White, Wilshere, G: Ballard 10
Mar 20	Leigh Centurions	W 24-8	3,708	T: Ballard, Stapleton, White, Wilshere, G: Ballard 4
Mar 24	FEATHERSTONE ROVERS	W 42-12	5,139	T: Gardner 2, Ballard, Littler, Ratchford, Sibbit, Turner, White, G: Ballard 5
Mar 30	Batley Bulldogs	W 48-22	1,207	T: White 2, Wilshere 2, Bannister, Brocklehurst, Gardner, Littler, Turner, G: Ballard 6
Apr 4	BRAMLEY BUFFALOES (NLC-Qual)	W 62-6	1,780	T: Paul 2, Turner 2, Adamson, Gardner, P Highton, Littler, R Myler, Sibbit, White, G: Ballard 9
Apr 11	WIDNES VIKINGS	D 16-16	6,143	T: Ballard, Brocklehurst, Littler, G: Ballard 2
Apr 20	WAKEFIELD TRINITY WILDCATS (RLC-4)	L 8-38	2,159	T: Alker, G: Ballard 2
Apr 24	WHITEHAVEN	W 36-10	3,252	T: R Myler 3, Alker, Gardner, Ratchford, G: Turner 4, Ratchford 2
May 2	Sheffield Eagles	D 24-24	1,058	T: Alker, Gardner, Stapleton, Turner, White, G: Ratchford, Turner
May 15	CELTIC CRUSADERS	W 24-22	3,438	T: White 2, Leuluai, Littler, Wilshere, G: Wilshere 2
May 22	Featherstone Rovers (NLC-1)	W 30-12	1,314	T: Fitzpatrick 2, R Myler 2, Wilshere, G: Wilshere 5
May 29	Whitehaven	L 22-26	2,189	T: Paul, Sidlow, Stapleton, White, G: Wilshere 3
Jun 6	SHEFFIELD EAGLES	W 34-10	3,526	T: Leuluai, R Myler, Ratchford, Stapleton, White, Wilshere, G: Wilshere 5
Jun 14	Celtic Crusaders (NLC-SF)	W 36-20	1,760	T: R Myler 2, White 2, Wilshere 2, G: Wilshere 6
Jun 19	Widnes Vikings	L 18-20	8,189	T: Paul, Walton, White, G: Wilshere 3
Jun 27	HALIFAX	W 30-24	4,373	T: Fitzpatrick, Gardner, Littler, Paul, Ratchford, G: Wilshere 5

Salford RL Match Results

2008 *continued*

Date	Opponent	Result	Attendance	Scorers
Jul 6	Doncaster (NLC-Final)*	W 60-0	6,328	T: White 3, R Myler 2, Fitzpatrick, Paul, Sidlow, Sibbit, Stapleton, G: Wilshere 10
Jul 13	Dewsbury Rams	W 70-22	1,320	T: Turner 3, R Myler 2, Ratchford 2, Wilshere 2, Alker, Bannister, Littler, White, G: Wilshere 9
Jul 20	Featherstone Rovers	D 30-30	1,756	T: Ballard 2, Alker, Bannister, Gardner, Ratchford, G: Wilshere 3
Jul 25	LEIGH CENTURIONS	W 46-12	4,554	T: Alker, Gardner, R Myler, Ratchford, Sidlow, Turner, White, Wilshere, G: Wilshere 7
Jul 31	Halifax	W 36-18	2,571	T: Gardner, Littler, Ratchford, Turner, Wilshere, G: Wilshere 8
Aug 8	DEWSBURY RAMS	W 58-6	3,046	T: Gardner 2, White 2, Adamson, Leuluai, Littler, R Myler, Ratchford, Sibbit, G: Wilshere 6, Bannister 2, Turner
Aug 17	BATLEY BULLDOGS	W 46-0	2,761	T: Alker, Adamson, Ambler, Littler, R Myler, Ratchford, Sibbit, Turner, G: Turner 4, Bannister 3
Aug 23	Celtic Crusaders	L 10-20	1,447	T: Gardner, Ratchford, G: Bannister
Sep 11	CELTIC CRUSADERS (NL-Qualifying SF)	L 18-44	2,607	T: R Myler 2, Bannister, G: Bannister 2, Wilshere
Sep 18	WHITEHAVEN (NL-Final Eliminator)	W 62-18	1,871	T: Bannister 2, Turner 2, Adamson, Gardner, P Highton, R Myler, Sibbit, White, Wilshere, G: Wilshere 9
Sep 28	Celtic Crusaders (NL-Final) (AET)**	W 36-18	7,104	T: White 2, Fitzpatrick, Gardner, R Myler, Sibbit, G: Wilshere 6

* At Blackpool ** At Warrington

National League One Grand Final winners

National League One Minor Premiers

National League Cup winners

Salford RL Match Results

2009

	Opponent	Result	Attendance	Scorers
Dec 28	Leigh Centurions (F)	W 26-6	4,775	T: Fitzpatrick, Brad Hargreaves, Ratchford, Jeremy Smith, White, G: Ratchford 2, Lewis Palfrey
Jan 17	Leeds Rhinos (F)*	L 10-12	5,700	T: Talau, Parker, G: Wilshere
Jan 27	Widnes Vikings (F)	W 40-12	1,938	T: Paul 2, Fitzpatrick, Littler, R Myler, Talau, Turner, G: Paul 3, Turner 2, Wilshere
Feb 6	Hull Kingston Rovers (F)	L 16-18	3,570	T: Littler, Jeremy Smith, Wilshere, G: Wilshere 2
Feb 14	CELTIC CRUSADERS	W 28-16	4,026	T: Henry, R Myler, Sibbit, Stapleton, H: Wilshere 6
Feb 22	Wakefield Trinity Wildcats	L 10-29	6,578	T: R Myler, Talau, G: Wilshere
Feb 28	Castleford Tigers	L 16-52	7,052	T: Fitzpatrick, Henry, Talau, G: Wilshere 2
Mar 6	HARLEQUINS	L 18-48	3,367	T: Parker, Paul, Wilshere, G: Wilshere 3
Mar 13	St Helens	L 12-38	9,723	T: Fitzpatrick, Thornley, G: Ratchford 2
Mar 20	WIGAN WARRIORS	L 12-38	7,016	T: R Myler 2, G: Ratchford, Turner
Mar 29	Hull Kingston Rovers	L 12-28	8,104	T: Adamson, White, G: Wilshere 2
Apr 5	Hull FC (RLC-4)	W 22-18	8,945	T: Littler, R Myler, Wilshere, G: Wilshere 5
Apr 10	WARRINGTON WOLVES	W 18-16	6,150	T: R Myler 2, Adamson, G: Wilshere 3
Apr 13	Leeds Rhinos	W 30-20	14,381	T: Henry, R Myler, Paul, Turner, Wilshere, G: Wilshere 5
Apr 18	Catalans Dragons	L 6-38	8,327	T: Ratchford, G: Wilshere
Apr 25	HULL FC	L 14-18	4,165	T: Goulding 2, R Myler, G: Wilshere
May 2	Harlequins**	L 16-24	29,627	T: Ratchford 2, R Myler, G: Wilshere 2
May 10	Batley Bulldogs (RLC-5)	W 66-4	1,298	T: Henry 4, Adamson, Alker, McGilvray, R Myler, Paul, Ratchford, Wilshere, G: Wilshere 11
May 17	Huddersfield Giants	W 24-4	6,903	T: Goulding, Henry, R Myler, Wilshere, G: Wilshere 4
May 22	BRADFORD BULLS	W 18-10	4,383	T: Adamson, Henry, Littler, G: Wilshere 3
May 29	Wigan Warriors (RLC-6)	L 6-28	9,466	T: Adamson, G: Wilshere

Salford RL Match Results

2009 *continued*

	Opponent	Result	Attendance	Scorers
Jun 5	Wigan Warriors	L 18-34	11,550	T: Alker, Henry, Swain, G: Wilshere 3
Jun 19	Hull FC	L 12-14	11,218	T: Goulding, Jeremy Smith, G: Wilshere 2
Jun 26	HUDDERSFIELD GIANTS	L 10-34	3,721	T: Turner, Wilshere, G: Wilshere
Jul 3	ST HELENS	W 20-10	4,808	T: Ratchford 2, Goulding, Henry, G: Wilshere 2
Jul 11	Celtic Crusaders	L 12-25	3,009	T: Adamson, Littler, G: Wilshere 2
Jul 17	CASTLEFORD TIGERS	L 12-18	3,487	T: McGilvray, Ratchford, G: Wilshere 2
Jul 26	Warrington Wolves	L 20-62	8,906	T: Henry, Littler, R Myler, Jeremy Smith, G: Wilshere 2
July 31	WAKEFIELD TRINITY WILDCATS	L 24-30	3,151	T: Leuluai 2, McGilvray 2, G: Wilshere 4
Aug 7	CATALANS DRAGONS	L 16-18	2,475	T: Stapleton, Wilshere, G; Ratchford 4
Aug 15	Harlequins	W 26-22	2,612	T: Wilshere 2, McGilvray, Nash, Swain, G: Wilshere 3
Aug 21	HULL KINGSTON ROVERS	L 10-14	4,224	T: Ratchford, Sidlow, G: Wilshere
Sep 6	Bradford Bulls	L 18-44	8,167	T: Wilshere 2, Henry, G: Ratchford 3
Sep 11	LEEDS RHINOS	L 24-30	6,101	T: Adamson, Littler, Ratchford, Wilshere, G: Wilshere 4

* At Jacksonville, USA ** Murrayfield Magic weekend at Edinburgh

2010

	Opponent	Result	Attendance	Scorers
Jan 17	SWINTON LIONS (F)	W 50-12	1,800	T: Cashmere, Fitzpatrick, Ratchford, Sibbit, Jeremy Smith, M Smith, Swain, Talau, Tyrer, G: Ratchford 5, Tyrer 2
Jan 24	Widnes Vikings (F)	W 36-0	1,774	T: Fitzpatrick 2, Tyrer 2, L Adamson, Broughton, Gibson, Sidlow, G: Ratchford 2
Feb 7	Hull Kingston Rovers	L 12-30	9,123	T: Broughton, M Smith, G: Ratchford 2
Feb 12	CRUSADERS	L 16-36	3,421	T: Fitzpatrick, Holdsworth, M Smith, G: Ratchford 2
Feb 19	Leeds Rhinos	L 10-22	12,700	T: Gibson, Talau, G: Ratchford

Salford RL Match Results

2010 *continued*

	Opponent	Result	Attendance	Scorers
Feb 26	BRADFORD BULLS	L 0-7	3,806	
Mar 5	CATALANS DRAGONS	L 12-24	3,022	T: Gibson, Talau, G: Ratchford 2
Mar 14	Harlequins	W 26-22	2,395	T: Tyrer 3, Broughton, Fitzpatrick, G: Holdsworth 3
Mar 21	Wakefield Trinity Wildcats	L 6-36	4,883	T: Littler, G: Ratchford
Mar 27	HULL FC	W 27-20	3,535	T: Broughton 2, Fitzpatrick 2, Sidlow, G: Holdsworth 3, DG: Holdsworth
Apr 2	Warrington Wolves	L 2-32	11,467	G: Holdsworth
Apr 5	HUDDERSFIELD GIANTS	W 30-18	4,014	T: Gibson, Holdsworth, Sidlow, Tyrer, G: Holdworth 7
Apr 11	WIGAN WARRIORS	L 4-18	6,618	T: Gibson
Apr 18	Catalans Dragons (RLC-4)	L 8-30	5,238	T: Broughton 2
Apr 25	Castleford Tigers	L 12-30	5,025	T: Gibson, Henry, G: Holdsworth 2
May 1	Warrington Wolves*	L 16-68	26,642	T: Ratchford 2, M Smith, G: Holdsworth 2
May 15	ST HELENS	W 42-34	5,685	T: M Smith 3, Gibson 2, Boyle, Broughton, Holdsworth, G: Holdsworth 5
May 22	Catalans Dragons	W 22-14	5,115	T: Fitzpatrick, Leuluai, Littler, G: Holdsworth 5
Jun 4	WARRINGTON WOLVES	L 10-27	6,093	T: Broughton, Henry, G: Tyrer
Jun 11	Hull FC	L 12-34	11,397	T: Fitzpatrick, Sidlow, G: M Smith 2
Jun 20	CASTLEFORD TIGERS	L 22-28	3,130	T: Broughton, Fitzpatrick, Littler, Sibbit, G: Holdsworth 3
Jun 25	St Helens	L 34-58	7,728	T: Sidlow 2, Boyle, Gibson, Henry, Holdsworth, G: Holdsworth 5
Jul 2	HARLEQUINS	W 17-14	2,672	T: M Smith, Swain, G: Holdsworth 4, DG: M Smith
Jul 9	Wigan Warriors	L 10-60	12,221	T: Broughton, Holdsworth, G: Holdsworth
Jul 18	Bradford Bulls	W 30-26	6,382	T: Broughton 2, Fitzpatrick, Littler, Tyrer, G: Holdsworth 5
Jul 25	LEEDS RHINOS	L 22-31	4,651	T: Gibson 2, Broughton, Cashmere, G: Tyrer 3
Aug 1	Crusaders	L 16-60	2,412	T: Cashmere, Fitzpatrick, Ratchford, G: M Smith 2

Salford RL Match Results

2010 *continued*

	Opponent	Result	Attendance	Scorers
Aug 15	HULL KINGSTON ROVERS	L 18-44	4,111	T: Cashmere, Parker, M Smith, G: Tyrer 3
Aug 22	Huddersfield Giants	L 4-52	6,697	T: Broughton
Sep 5	WAKEFIELD TRINITY WILDCATS	W 16-12	3,401	T: Cashmere, Littler, Tyrer, G: Tyrer 2

* Murrayfield Magic weekend at Edinburgh

2011

	Opponent	Result	Attendance	Scorers
Dec 27	Leigh Centurions (F)	L 12-13	2,200	T: Clay, Godwin, G: Ratchford 2
Jan 16	WIGAN WARRIORS (F)	L 24-30	2,425	T: Broughton, Nero, Parker, Ratchford, G: Holdsworth 2, M Smith 2
Jan 21	SWINTON LIONS (F)	W 42-16	985	T: M Smith 2, Goldwin, Jack Holmes, Neal, Ratchford, Sidlow, G: Ratchford 6, M Smith
Jan 30	Hull Kingston Rovers (F)	L 6-40	4,023	T: Ratchford, G: Holdsworth
Feb 13	Crusaders*	L 12-42	29,323	T: Holdsworth, Patten, G: Holdsworth 2
Feb 18	ST HELENS	L 22-56	5,929	T: Broughton, Gibson, Patten, Ratchford, G: Holdsworth 3
Feb 27	Wakefield Trinity Wildcats	W 32-6	6,823	T: Henry 2, Parker, Ratchford, Sidlow, Wild, G: Holdsworth 4
Mar 4	WIGAN WARRIORS	L 16-32	6,266	T: Gibson, Nero, Parker, G: Ratchford, Sneyd
Mar 11	Leeds Rhinos	L 12-46	13,068	T: Ratchford, Sidlow, G: Holdsworth 2
Mar 18	HULL KINGSTON ROVERS	W 34-18	4,408	T: Boyle, Broughton, S Gleeson, Ratchford, M Smith, Sneyd, G: Holdsworth 4, Ratchford
Mar 26	Catalans Dragons	W 22-10	7,156	T: Broughton 4, G: Holdsworth 3
Apr 2	CRUSADERS	L 10-16	3,416	T: Broughton, Cashmere, G: Holdsworth
Apr 10	Castleford Tigers	L 20-52	6,741	T: Anderson, Broughton, Holdsworth, Sidlow, G: Holdsworth 2
Apr 16	BRADFORD BULLS	W 56-16	2,809	T: Gibson 3, Henry 2, Adamson, Broughton, Holdsworth, Ratchford, M Smith, G: Holdsworth 8

Salford RL Match Results

2011 *continued*

	Opponent	Result	Attendance	Scorers
Apr 22	WARRINGTON WOLVES	L 0-60	7,496	
Apr 26	Huddersfield Giants	L 22-52	6,042	T: Henry, Holdsworth, Ratchford, Sidlow, G: Holdsworth 3
Apr 30	Harlequins	W 34-16	1,957	T: Clay 2, Anderson, Godwin, Nero, Palea'aesina, Patten, G: Holdsworth 3
May 8	Hunslet Hawks (RLC-4)	W 68-2	649	T: Adamson 2, Broughton 2, Clay 2, Palea'aesina 2, Jewitt, Neal, Nero, Ratchford, G: Holdsworth 6, Ratchford 3, M Smith
May 13	HULL FC	L 16-32	3,983	T: Clay, Gibson, Ratchford, G: Holdsworth 2
May 20	HULL KINGSTON ROVERS (RLC-5)	L 0-25	2,087	
May 29	Bradford Bulls	L 14-28	12,487	T: Henry 3, G: Holdsworth
Jun 3	WAKEFIELD TRINITY WILDCATS	W 34-12	3,213	T: Ratchford 3, Adamson, Broughton, Holdsworth, Jewitt, G: Holdsworth 3
Jun 12	Warrington Wolves	W 18-16	10,339	T: S Gleeson, Henry, Patten, G: Holdsworth 3
Jun 17	CASTLEFORD TIGERS	L 8-15	3,587	T: Broughton, Holdsworth
Jun 24	Crusaders	W 22-18	2,576	T: Adamson, Godwin, Ratchford, Sidlow, G: Holdsworth 3
Jul 1	HARLEQUINS	W 26-18	3,065	T: Gibson 2, Anderson, Broughton, Henry, G: Holdsworth 3
Jul 8	Hull FC	L 16-52	11,699	T: Anderson, Broughton, Nero, G: Holdsworth 2
Jul 17	Hull Kingston Rovers	L 8-21	7,834	T: Anderson, G: Holdsworth 2
Jul 29	LEEDS RHINOS	L 22-30	4,024	T: Anderson, Broughton, Jewitt, Patten, G: Holdsworth 3
Aug 14	Wigan Warriors	L 18-52	13,607	T: Danny Williams 2, S Gleeson, G: Holdsworth 3
Aug 19	HUDDERSFIELD GIANTS	W 24-18	3,458	T: Danny Williams 3, Holdsworth, G: Holdsworth 4
Sep 2	St Helens	L 6-31	7,377	T: Danny Williams, G: Holdsworth
Sep 11	CATALANS DRAGONS	L 18-44	10,146	T: Danny Williams 2, Adamson, G: Holdsworth 3

* Millennium Magic weekend at Cardiff

Final season at The Willows

Salford RL Match Results

2012

Date	Opponent	Result	Attendance	Scorers
Jan 7	LEIGH CENTURIONS (F)	L 12-36	2,818	T: Danny Williams 2, G: Holdsworth 2
Jan 15	HALIFAX (F)*	W 46-16	1,234	T: M Smith 2, Anderson, Gibson, Holdsworth, Howarth, Owen, Patten, G: Holdsworth 5, M Smith 2
Jan 24	WIGAN WARRIORS (F)	L 10-16	2,732	T: Danny Williams, Palea'aesina, G: Holdsworth
Feb 4	CASTLEFORD TIGERS	L 10-24	5,242	T: Ashurst, M Smith, G: Holdsworth
Feb 10	St Helens	L 10-38	15,547	T: Broughton, Gibson, G: Holdsworth
Feb 19	Widnes Vikings	W 38-18	5,053	T: Holdsworth 2, Patten 2, Broughton, Owen, Palea'aesina, G: Holdsworth 5
Feb 24	HULL FC	W 24-22	5,186	T: Gibson 2, Ashurst, S Gleeson, G: Holdsworth 4
Mar 2	LONDON BRONCOS	W 44-12	5,250	T: S Gleeson 2, Nero 2, Adamson, Moon, Palea'aesina, M Smith, G: Holdsworth 6
Mar 10	Catalans Dragons	L 18-40	8,158	T: Howarth, Owen, Veivers, G: Holdsworth 3
Mar 16	LEEDS RHINOS	L 16-56	6,891	T: Anderson, Owen, Patten, G: Holdsworth 2
Mar 25	Bradford Bulls	W 38-18	11,219	T: Moon 2, Ashurst, Gibson, Owen, Patten, Veivers, G: Holdsworth 5
Mar 30	WIGAN WARRIORS	L 20-40	6,774	T: Holdsworth, James, Patten, Danny Williams, G: Holdsworth 2
Apr 6	Huddersfield Giants	L 10-36	6,988	T: Broughton, Moon, G: Holdsworth
Apr 9	HULL KINGSTON ROVERS	L 10-18	5,000	T: Gibson, Patten, G: Holdsworth
Apr 15	Whitehaven (RLC-4)	W 58-18	751	T: Moon 2, Sneyd 2, Adamson, Ashurst, S Gleeson, Nero, M Smith, Veivers, G: Sneyd 9
Apr 21	Wakefield Trinity Wildcats	L 22-26	6,748	T: Gibson 2, Holdsworth, Nero, G: Holdsworth 3
Apr 29	LEEDS RHINOS (RLC-5)	L 10-16	2,947	T: Broughton, Jewitt, G: Holdsworth
May 6	Warrington Wolves	L 20-24	10,437	T: Gibson 2, Holdsworth, Danny Williams, G: Holdsworth 2

Salford RL Match Results

2012 *continued*

	Opponent	Result	Attendance	Scorers
May 18	BRADFORD BULLS	D 20-20	6,121	T: Danny Williams 2, Broughton, Sidlow, G: Holdsworth 2
May 27	Huddersfield Giants**	W 38-34	32,953	T: Broughton 2, Moon 2, Sidlow 2, S Gleeson, G: Holdsworth 5
Jun 1	CATALANS DRAGONS	W 34-30	4,220	T: Broughton 2, S Gleeson, Holdsworth, Moon, Patten, G: Holdsworth 3, M Smith 2
Jun 10	Castleford Tigers	L 30-34	5,877	T: Anderson, Broughton, S Gleeson, Moon, Wild, G; Sneyd 5
Jun 22	ST HELENS	L 10-32	5,447	T: Anderson, Danny Williams, G: Holdsworth
Jun 29	WARRINGTON WOLVES	W 48-24	6,179	T: Anderson 2, Broughton 2, Danny Williams 2, Patten 2, M Smith, G: Holdsworth 6
Jul 8	Hull Kingston Rovers	W 24-22	7,213	T: Danny Williams 2, Broughton, Gledhill, Moon, G: Holdsworth 2
Jul 20	WIDNES VIKINGS	L 8-46	5,196	T: Gibson, Danny Williams
Jul 29	Hull FC	L 26-34	10,766	T: Gibson 2, S Gleeson 2, Broughton, G: Holdsworth 3
Aug 4	London Broncos	L 28-40	1,517	T: Gibson 2, Anderson, Ashurst, Broughton, S Gleeson, G: Holdsworth 2
Aug 10	HUDDERSFIELD GIANTS	L 20-30	3,615	T: Anderson, Broughton, S Gleeson, Danny Williams, G: Holdsworth 2
Aug 20	Wigan Warriors	L 6-38	13,703	T: James, G: Holdsworth
Aug 31	Leeds Rhinos	L 12-46	15,081	T: Patten 2, G: Holdsworth 2
Sep 8	WAKEFIELD TRINITY WILDCATS***	L 34-42	2,380	T: Gibson 2, Anderson, Ashurst, S Gleeson, Danny Williams, G: Holdsworth 4, Adamson

* Colin Dixon Memorial Trophy ** Magic Weekend at Etihad Stadium, Manchester
*** Home match played at Leigh

Home matches played at Salford City Stadium, Barton, from this season

Salford RL Match Results

2013

	Opponent	Result	Attendance	Scorers
Jan 6	SWINTON LIONS (F)	W 52-12	1,811	T: Broughton 3, Ashurst, Boyle, Fages, Gibson, Godwin, Wild, G: Sneyd 8
Jan 17	WIGAN WARRIORS (F)	L 16-34	3,000	T: Fages, Nero, Owen, G: Sneyd 2
Feb 1	WIGAN WARRIORS	L 0-42	5,383	
Feb 9	Catalans Dragons	L 6-40	6,872	T: Evalds, G: Murphy
Feb 15	Leeds Rhinos	L 14-42	12,558	T: Gibson 2, Evalds, G: Sneyd
Feb 24	HULL KINGSTON ROVERS	W 38-34	1,989	T: Gibson 2, Dixon, Godwin, Murphy, Sneyd, Danny Williams, G: Sneyd 5
Mar 1	LONDON BRONCOS	L 4-38	2,333	T: Godwin
Mar 10	Wakefield Trinity Wildcats	D 23-23	6,986	T: Broughton, Fages, Jewitt, Murphy, G: Sneyd 3, DG: Sneyd
Mar 15	WARRINGTON WOLVES	L 4-46	3,932	T: Owen
Mar 22	St Helens	L 10-14	5,348	T: Foran, Sneyd, G: Sneyd
Mar 29	HUDDERSFIELD GIANTS	W 21-20	2,788	T: Broughton, Gaskell, Gibson, James, G: Sneyd 2, DG: Sneyd
Apr 1	Bradford Bulls	L 24-36	7,503	T: Dixon, Gaskell, Murphy, Nero, G: Sneyd 4
Apr 7	Widnes Vikings	L 24-58	5,562	T: Broughton, Fages, James, Jewitt, G: Sneyd 4
Apr 13	HULL FC	L 18-24	2,698	T: Broughton, Owen, Danny Williams, G: Sneyd 3
Apr 21	Gloucestershire All Golds (RLC-4)	W 82-6	867	T: Ford 3, Gibson 2, Hope 2, Broughton, Emmitt, Evalds, Mauro, Tyson, Sneyd, A Walne, J Walne, G: Sneyd 11
Apr 27	CASTLEFORD TIGERS	W 34-30	2,306	T: Ashurst, Dixon, Fages, McGoldrick, Mauro, Danny Williams, G: Sneyd 5
May 3	Wigan Warriors	L 6-46	12,489	T: A Walne, G: Sneyd
May 12	Warrington Wolves (RLC-5)	L 6-52	5,451	T: Broughton, G: Gaskell
May 17	BRADFORD BULLS	L 7-28	5,106	T: McGoldrick, G: Sneyd, DG: McGoldrick
May 26	Widnes Vikings*	W 28-22	31,249	T: James 2, Fages, Gaskell, M Gleeson, G: Sneyd 4
Jun 2	Warrington Wolves	L 10-68	9,560	T: Broughton, Gaskell, G: Sneyd
Jun 10	WAKEFIELD TRINITY WILDCATS	L 10-46	2,327	T: Broughton, Danny Williams, G: Gaskell
Jun 21	ST HELENS	L 10-52	3,248	T: Broughton, M Gleeson, G: Sneyd

Salford RL Match Results

2013 *continued*

	Opponent	Result	Attendance	Scorers
Jun 29	London Broncos	W 44-30	2,079	T: Gaskell 3, Broughton 2, Fages, Gibson, Godwin, G: Sneyd 6
Jul 7	Hull Kingston Rovers	L 18-28	6,974	T: Ashurst, Godwin, Wild, G: Sneyd 3
Jul 19	CATALANS DRAGONS	W 16-12	2,200	T: Dixon, Wild, Danny Williams, G: Sneyd 2
Aug 4	Huddersfield Giants	L 4-46	5,345	T: Evalds
Aug 9	LEEDS RHINOS	L 16-42	3,235	T: Fages, Gaskell, Gibson, G: Gaskell, Sneyd
Aug 16	Hull FC	L 13-18	11,180	T: McGoldrick, Danny Williams, G: Sneyd 2, DG: Sneyd
Sep 1	Castleford Tigers	L 30-44	6,870	T: Broughton 3, Danny Williams 2, G: Sneyd 5
Sep 6	WIDNES VIKINGS	L 4-24	3,775	T: Sneyd

* Magic Weekend at Etihad Stadium, Manchester

2014

	Opponent	Result	Attendance	Scorers
Jan 24	Leigh Centurions (F)	W 26-16	1,887	T: Dixon, G Johnson, Mullaney, Puletua, Danny Williams, G: Mullaney 3
Feb 5	Warrington Wolves (F)	L 8-14	3,022	T: G Johnson, Meli
Feb 16	WAKEFIELD TRINITY WILDCATS	W 18-14	7,102	T: Dixon, Hansen, Hock, G: Mullaney 3
Feb 22	London Broncos	W 44-18	1,246	T: Fages 2, Hansen 2, Meli, Mullaney, T Smith, Danny Williams, G: Mullaney 5, T Smith
Feb 27	ST HELENS	L 0-38	6,353	
Mar 6	Widnes Vikings	L 18-32	5,291	T: Fages, G Johnson, Lee, G: Mullaney 3
Mar 14	WARRINGTON WOLVES	L 12-28	6,260	T: Manfredi 2, G Johnson
Mar 23	CASTLEFORD TIGERS	W 23-16	5,823	T: Dixon 2, M Gleeson, G Johnson, G: Mullaney 3, DG: Chase
Mar 28	Hull FC	L 8-30	9,821	T: G Johnson, Sa'u
Apr 3	Hull FC (RLC-4) (AET)	W 37-36	5,435	T: Meli 3, Chase, Fages, Sa'u, G: Mullaney 6, DG: Chase

Salford RL Match Results

2014 *continued*

Date	Opponent	Result	Attendance	Scorers
Apr 11	Bradford Bulls	W 38-24	6,144	T: Ashurst, Chase, Meli, Mullaney, Puletua, Sa'u, T Smith, G: Mullaney 5
Apr 18	HUDDERSFIELD GIANTS	L 22-42	5,068	T: Meli 3, Ashurst, Morley, G: Mullaney
Apr 21	Leeds Rhinos	L 4-32	14,013	T: Tomkins
Apr 27	WIDNES VIKINGS (RLC-5)	L 20-30	2,630	T: Hock 2, Tasi, Sa'u, G: Lee 2
May 3	Catalans Dragons	L 24-37	7,862	T: Eden, Hock, Meli, Danny Williams, G: T Smith 4
May 10	HULL KINGSTON ROVERS	D 16-16	2,903	T: Meli 2, M Gleeson, G: Mullaney 2
May 17	Widnes*	L 24-30	36,339	T: Ashurst, Chase, Meli, Sa'u, Danny Williams, G: Mullaney 2
May 22	WIGAN WARRIORS	L 4-25	3,706	T: Meli
May 30	St Helens	L 12-32	10,391	T: Evalds, Hock, G: T Smith 2
Jun 15	BRADFORD BULLS	W 46-18	3,407	T: Chase 2, Sa'u 2, Dixon, Evalds, Meli, Tomkins, G: Chase 7
Jun 22	Warrington Wolves	L 20-36	10,120	T: Evalds 2, Morley, Sa'u, G: Chase 2
Jun 28	Castleford Tigers	L 10-14	5,937	T: Hock, Sa'u, G: Chase
Jul 5	Huddersfield Giants	W 36-10	5,689	T: Ashurst, Caton-Brown, Chase, Fages, G Johnson, Locke, G: Locke 6
Jul 12	HULL FC	W 35-22	3,421	T: Caton-Brown 2, Chase, D Griffin, J Griffin, G Johnson, G: J Griffin 4, Chase, DG: Chase
Jul 20	Hull Kingston Rovers	W 38-18	8,213	T: J Griffin 2, Caton-Brown, Evalds, Fages, G Johnson, Sa'u, G: J Griffin 5
Jul 25	LEEDS RHINOS	L 18-22	5,012	T: Fages, Sa'u, J Walne, G: J Griffin 3
Jul 31	Wigan Warriors	L 4-45	12,962	T: J Griffin
Aug 15	CATALANS DRAGONS	W 34-22	3,100	T: Locke 2, Evalds, Fages, Puletua, Sa'u, G: Locke 3, Chase 2
Aug 31	Wakefield Trinity Wildcats	L 6-42	4,016	T: Hansen, G: Locke
Sep 7	LONDON BRONCOS	W 58-26	3,268	T: J Griffin 3, G Johnson 3, Lee, Tomkins, J Walne, Walton, G: J Griffin 9
Sep 12	WIDNES VIKINGS	W 36-6	3,268	T: Sa'u 2, Chase, J Griffin, Hansen, Puletua, G: J Griffin 6

Salford RL Match Results

2014 *continued*

* Magic Weekend at Etihad Stadium, Manchester

Note the latter two identical attendances are as reported

Renamed Salford Red Devils from this season

Salford City Stadium renamed A J Bell Stadium (from Sep 13, 2013)

2015

Date	Opponent	Result	Attendance	Scorers
Jan 11	Dewsbury Rams (F)	L 12-28	1,313	T: Brad England, Forster, G: Hood 2
Jan 18	SWINTON LIONS (F)	W 66-4	1,552	T: Chase 4, Hock 2, Locke 2, Evalds, Fages, Jon Ford, Puletua, G: J Griffin 9
Jan 24	Hunslet Hawks (F)	W 46-0	512	T: Caton-Brown 2, Chase 2, Evalds, Fages, J Johnson, Taylor, G: Chase 7
Feb 7	Warrington Wolves	L 8-22	11,864	T: Jones-Bishop 2
Feb 12	ST HELENS	L 6-52	4,975	T: Jones-Bishop, G: Dobson
Feb 28	HULL FC	W 32-28	3,606	T: Evalds 2, J Griffin 2, Fages, Sa'u, G: J Griffin 4
Mar 7	Catalans Dragons	D 40-40	8,864	T: Paterson 2, Chase, Fages, J Griffin, Lee, Sa'u, G: J Griffin 6
Mar 15	WAKEFIELD TRINITY WILDCATS	W 24-18	2,712	T: Chase, Hauraki, G Johnson, Sa'u, G: J Griffin 4
Mar 20	Castleford Tigers	L 16-30	6,901	T: Hauraki, Jones-Bishop, Lee, G: J Griffin 2
Mar 26	WIDNES VIKINGS	W 36-8	3,476	T: J Griffin, Hauraki, G Johnson, Jones-Bishop, Paterson, Tasi, Taylor, G: J Griffin 4
Apr 3	Huddersfield Giants	W 18-12	6,003	T: Forster, J Griffin, Jones-Bishop, G: J Griffin 3
Apr 6	WIGAN WARRIORS	W 24-18	6,561	T: Evalds 2, Dobson, Jones-Bishop, G: J Griffin 4
Apr 12	LEEDS RHINOS	L 18-28	4,489	T: Evalds 2, Tasi, G: Dobson 3
Apr 18	Leigh Centurions (RLC-5)	L 18-22	6,358	T: Evalds 2, Fages, G: Paterson 2, Dobson
Apr 26	CASTLEFORD TIGERS	L 20-22	3,397	T: Locke 2, Fages, Taylor, G: G Johnson, Locke

Salford RL Match Results

2015 *continued*

Date	Opponent	Result	Attendance	Scorers
May 1	Hull FC	L 20-24	9,385	T: Gildart, Greenwood, Locke, G: Fages 4
May 8	HUDDERSFIELD GIANTS	L 0-19	1,972	
May 22	WARRINGTON WOLVES	L 18-34	6,159	T: Evalds, Paterson, Sa'u, G: Paterson 3
May 30	Widnes Vikings*	L 16-38	40,871	T: G Johnson, Jones-Bishop, Paterson, G: J Griffin 2
Jun 5	St Helens	L 12-32	11,664	T: Chase, Evalds, G: Paterson 2
Jun 14	Wakefield Trinity Wildcats	W 24-16	3,240	T: Hansen 2, Fages, Taylor, G: J Griffin 4
Jun 19	Wigan Warriors	L 12-19	13,710	T: G Griffin, Paterson, G: J Griffin 2
Jun 30	Hull Kingston Rovers	L 28-34	6,717	T: Jones-Bishop 2, Caton-Brown, Taylor, J Walne, G: J Griffin 4
Jul 5	CATALANS DRAGONS	W 18-14	5,078	T: Dobson 2, Evalds, G: J Griffin 3
Jul 12	HULL KINGSTON ROVERS	W 31-18	4,415	T: Jones-Bishop 2, Evalds, Fages, J Griffin, Hauraki, G: Dobson 3, DG: Dobson
Jul 17	Leeds Rhinos	L 6-70	14,190	T: Evalds, G: Paterson
Jul 26	Widnes Vikings	L 20-21	5,477	T: Evalds, Paterson, Taylor, G: J Griffin 4
Aug 9	WAKEFIELD TRINITY WILDCATS (S8)	W 34-26	3,100	T: J Griffin 2, Paterson 2, Chase, G Griffin, G: J Griffin 4, Paterson
Aug 16	LEIGH CENTURIONS (S8)	W 46-18	4,547	T: Chase 2, Evans, G Johnson, Jones-Bishop, Sa'u, Taylor, Thornley, G: Dobson 7
Aug 23	Bradford Bulls (S8)	L 10-41	6,593	T: Chase, Thornley, G: Dobson
Sep 5	Halifax (S8)	W 50-28	2,186	T: Evalds 3, G Johnson 3, Jones-Bishop 3, G: J Griffin 4, Dobson 3
Sep 13	SHEFFIELD EAGLES (S8)	W 53-34	3,000	T: J Griffin 2, Evalds, G Griffin, Hansen, Hauraki, Hood, Tasi, Thornley, G: Dobson 7, J Griffin, DG: Dobson
Sep 20	Widnes Vikings (S8)	W 24-10	5,285	T: J Griffin, Paterson, Sa'u, Taylor, G: Dobson 4
Sep 27	Hull Kingston Rovers (S8)	L 22-46	7,543	T: Hansen, G Johnson, Lannon, Tasi, G: Jones-Bishop 3

Magic Weekend at Newcastle

Salford RL Match Results

2016

	Opponent	Result	Attendance	Scorers
Jan 10	Rochdale Hornets (F)	W 44-16	1,325	T: J Carney, Evalds, Forster, J Griffin, Krasniqi, Lui, Sarsfield, Sa'u, G: Dobson 3, J Griffin 3
Jan 24	WIGAN WARRIORS (F)	W 32-16	2,000	T: Dobson, Flanagan, J Griffin, G Johnson, Lannon, Lui, G: Dobson 4
Feb 5	Hull FC	L 20-42	12,265	T: Sa'u 2, Evalds, J Griffin, G: Dobson, J Griffin
Feb 11	ST HELENS	W 44-10	4,386	T: Evalds 2, Lui 2, Dobson, G Johnson, Kopczak, A Walne, G: Dobson 4, J Griffin 2
Feb 21	WIDNES VIKINGS	W 28-20	5,098	T: Flanagan 2, J Carney, J Griffin, G Johnson, G: Dobson 3, O'Brien
Feb 25	Wigan Warriors	L 16-20	10,897	T: J Griffin, Murdoch-Masila, Sa'u, G: J Griffin, O'Brien
Mar 3	WARRINGTON WOLVES	L 30-31	4,381	T: Sa'u 2, J Griffin, G Johnson, Jones, G: O'Brien 4, Dobson
Mar 13	Castleford Tigers	W 32-16	8,151	T: J Carney 2, J Griffin 2, G Johnson, G: O'Brien 6
Mar 20	Hull Kingston Rovers	L 30-44	6,593	T: G Griffin 2, Kopczak 2, G Johnson, G: O'Brien 5
Mar 25	CATALANS DRAGONS	L 12-26	3,485	T: G Johnson 2, J Griffin
Mar 28	Huddersfield Giants	W 26-24	4,885	T: J Carney, Evalds, J Griffin, Kopczak, O'Brien, G: Dobson 3
Apr 2	Wakefield Trinity Wildcats	L 18-32	4,048	T: J Carney, O'Brien, Sarsfield, G: O'Brien 2, Dobson
Apr 9	LEEDS RHINOS	W 14-10	4,912	T: Lui, Tomkins, G: Dobson 2, O'Brien
Apr 17	Hunslet Hawks (RLC-5)	W 50-14	834	T: J Griffin 3, Bibby 2, Lui 2, Lannon, Wood, G: O'Brien 4, Dobson 3
Apr 23	Catalans Dragons	L 32-42	9,686	T: Sa'u 3, Evalds 2, J Carney, G: Dobson 2, O'Brien 2
Apr 30	HULL KINGSTON ROVERS	W 44-26	3,048	T: Sa'u 3, Lui 2, Evalds, G Griffin, Jones, G: O'Brien 4, Dobson 2
May 7	Castleford Tigers (RLC-6)	L 18-32	3,317	T: Sa'u 2, Lui, G: O'Brien 3
May 13	St Helens	L 20-34	9,299	T: Evalds 3, J Carney, G: Dobson, O'Brien

Salford RL Match Results

2016 *continued*

	Opponent	Result	Attendance	Scorers
May 21	Widnes Vikings*	W 18-12	39,331	T: Vidot 2, J Carney, G: O'Brien 2, Dobson
May 27	WAKEFIELD TRINITY WILDCATS	W 38-8	3,022	T: Lannon 2, Evalds, Flanagan, G Griffin, Lui, Sa'u, G: O'Brien 4, Dobson
Jun 3	WIGAN WARRIORS	L 20-23	4,096	T: Dobson 2, Jones, Vidot, G: Dobson, Lui
Jun 10	Leeds Rhinos	L 0-8	14,462	
Jun 17	HUDDERSFIELD GIANTS	L 30-31	1,958	T: Jones 2, Vidot 2, Kopczak, G: O'Brien 5
Jul 1	CASTLEFORD TIGERS	W 22-18	2,275	T: Caton-Brown, Dobson, O'Brien, G: O'Brien 5
Jul 7	Warrington Wolves	L 14-40	9,024	T: J Griffin, Lui, Sa'u, G: O'Brien
Jul 15	Widnes Vikings	W 32-24	4,636	T: Caton-Brown 3, J Carney, Jones, G: O'Brien 5, Dobson
Jul 22	HULL FC	L 20-28	3,225	T: Caton-Brown, Dobson, Evalds, Lui, G: O'Brien 2
Aug 7	HUDDERSFIELD GIANTS (S8)	W 34-12	2,184	T: Caton-Brown 3, G Griffin, Hauraki, Murdoch-Massila, G: O'Brien 5
Aug 13	Leigh Centurions (S8)	L 26-32	4,547	T: Caton-Brown 2, Evalds, Lui, Murdoch-Masila, G: O'Brien 3
Aug 19	HULL KINGSTON ROVERS (S8)	L 12-29	2,074	T: Caton-Brown, O'Brien, G: O'Brien 2
Sep 2	Leeds Rhinos (S8)	L 8-30	13,996	T: G Griffiths, G: O'Brien 2
Sep 11	FEATHERSTONE ROVERS (S8)	W 70-16	1,759	T: Hauraki 2, Jones 2, Murdoch-Masila 2, Sa'u 2, Dobson, Evalds, Krasniqi, Tomkins, Vidot, G: O'Brien 9
Sep 17	LONDON BRONCOS (S8)	L 16-19	2,521	T: J Griffin 2, G Griffin, G: O'Brien 2
Sep 25	Batley Bulldogs (S8)	W 42-14	1,520	T: Hauraki 2, O'Brien 2, J Griffin, G Johnson, Lui, Sa'u, G: O'Brien 5
Oct 1	Hull Kingston Rovers (S8) (AET)**	W 19-18	6,562	T: Evalds 2, G Johnson, Murdoch-Masila, G: O'Brien, DG: O'Brien

* Magic Weekend at Newcastle ** 'Million Pound Game' to retain Super League place

Salford RL Match Results

2017

	Opponent	Result	Attendance	Scorers
Jan 15	Rochdale Hornets (F)	W 44-18	834	T: G Johnson 3, Bibby, Jones, O'Brien, Sa'u, Welham, G: Dobson 3, O'Brien 2, Wood
Jan 22	Halifax (F)*	W 13-6	970	T: Brining, Kopczak, G: Dobson 2, DG: Lui
Jan 29	HULL FC (F)	W 18-6	1,461	T: G Griffin, Sa'u, Welham, G: O'Brien 2, Dobson
Feb 11	WIGAN WARRIORS	L 16-26	6,527	T: Brining, Dobson, Sa'u, G: O'Brien 2
Feb 16	Huddersfield Giants	W 30-20	6,017	T: O'Brien 2, Jones, Sa'u, G: O'Brien 7
Feb 24	Leeds Rhinos	L 14-20	14,575	T: O'Brien, Tomkins, Welham, G: O'Brien
Mar 4	WARRINGTON WOLVES	W 24-14	5,492	T: Sa'u 2, Brining, G Griffin, G: O'Brien 4
Mar 12	Wakefield Trinity	L 22-24	4,964	T: G Griffin, G Johnson, Murdoch-Masila, Welham, G: O'Brien 3
Mar 19	CASTLEFORD TIGERS	W 13-12	5,221	T: Murdoch-Masila 2, G: O'Brien 2, DG: O'Brien
Mar 24	Widnes Vikings	W 46-10	5,565	T: J Carney, Dobson, G Griffin, G Johnson, Lui, Murdoch-Masila, O'Brien, Tasi, Welham, G: Dobson 3 O'Brien 2
Mar 30	ST HELENS	W 22-14	3,686	T: Dobson 2, Kopczak, G: Dobson 4, O'Brien
Apr 7	Hull FC	W 54-18	11,016	T: G Johnson 2, Kopczak 2, J Carney, Dobson, G Griffin, Lui, Murdoch-Masila, Sa'u, G: O'Brien 4, Dobson 3
Apr 14	LEIGH CENTURIONS	W 12-6	5,834	T: O'Brien, Welham, G: Dobson, O'Brien
Apr 17	Catalans Dragons	L 6-38	10,804	T: J Carney, G: O'Brien
Apr 23	TORONTO WOLFPACK (RLC-5)	W 29-22	1,318	T: G Johnson 2, Dobson, O'Brien, Welham, G: Dobson 3, O'Brien, DG: O'Brien
Apr 30	WIDNES VIKINGS	W 30-10	3,127	T: Murdoch-Masila 2, Bibby, Evalds, G Johnson, G: Dobson 5
May 5	Wigan Warriors	W 31-16	11,861	T: Evalds 2, G Johnson, Murdoch-Masila, Welham, G: Dobson 4, O'Brien, DG: O'Brien

Salford RL Match Results

2017 *continued*

	Opponent	Result	Attendance	Scorers
May 12	HULL KINGSTON ROVERS (RLC-6)	W 24-14	3,100	T: Brining, Kopczak, Lannon, Murdoch-Masila, G: Dobson 4
May 21	Leigh Centurions**	W 36-22	30,046	T: Johnson 2, Murdoch-Masila 2, Evalds, Welham, G: Dobson 5, O'Brien
May 26	CATALANS DRAGONS	W 50-12	4,957	T: Brining, Evalds, Flanagan, Jones, Krasniqi, Lannon, Lui, O'Brien, Welham, G: Dobson 7
May 29	Warrington Wolves	W 38-12	10,684	T: Evalds 3, Sa'u 2, Bibby, Brining, G: O'Brien 5
Jun 4	WAKEFIELD TRINITY	L 24-34	3,277	T: Bibby 2, Kopczak, Tasi, G: Dobson 4
Jun 9	HULL FC	L 10-34	2,678	T: Evalds, Hauraki, G: Dobson
Jun 15	WAKEFIELD TRINITY (RLC-7)	W 30-6	2,808	T: Evalds, G Johnson, Kopczak, Lannon, Murdoch-Masila, G: Dobson 5
Jun 23	St Helens	L 24-25	10,001	T: Evalds 2, G Johnson, Lui, G: T Carney 4
Jul 2	HUDDERSFIELD GIANTS	W 36-20	3,718	T: Sa'u 2, G Johnson, Lui, Murdoch-Masila, O'Brien, Welham, G: Dobson 4
Jul 9	LEEDS RHINOS	L 24-50	5,056	T: Murdoch-Masila 2, Dobson, Wood, G: Dobson 4
Jul 14	Castleford Tigers	L 14-38	7,094	T: Bibby, O'Brien, Welham, G: Dobson
Jul 21	Leigh Centurions	L 0-25	7,002	
Jul 30	Wigan Warriors (RLC-SF)***	L 14-27	10,796	T: G Johnson, McCarthy, G: Dobson 3
Aug 4	Hull FC (S8)	L 18-32	10,239	T: Vatuvei 2, Evalds, Lui, G: Lui
Aug 11	CASTLEFORD TIGERS (S8)	L 4-23	2,811	T: Vatuvei
Aug 18	Wigan Warriors (S8)	L 6-42	11,229	T: Evalds, G: O'Brien
Sep 1	WAKEFIELD TRINITY (S8)	L 18-43	2,489	T: G Johnson, Kopczak, McCarthy, G: T Carney 3
Sep 9	HUDDERSFIELD GIANTS (S8)	W 52-14	1,405	T: Welham 2, Vatuvei 2, Bibby, Evalds, Jones, McCarthy, Murdoch-Masila, G: O'Brien 8
Sep 15	Leeds Rhinos (S8)	L 2-44	13,094	G: O'Brien
Sep 21	ST HELENS (S8)	L 4-30	2,840	T: Evalds

*Colin Dixon Memorial Trophy ** Magic Weekend at Newcastle *** At Warrington*

Salford RL Match Results

2018

Date	Opponent	Result	Attendance	Scorers
Jan 14	SWINTON LIONS (F)	W 50-12	2,036	T: Olpherts 2, Bennion, Evalds, G Johnson, Lui, McCarthy, O'Brien, Welham, G: O'Brien 7
Jan 20	Warrington Wolves (F)	L 6-18	3,208	T: Lui, G: O'Brien
Feb 2	WIGAN WARRIORS	L 12-40	5,506	T: Evalds, Welham, G: O'Brien 2
Feb 9	Wakefield Trinity	L 12-14	4,262	T: Evalds, Lui, Welham
Feb 23	HULL KINGSTON ROVERS	W 36-12	2,948	T: Evalds 2, Bibby, Lui, O'Brien, Sa'u, G: O'Brien 6
Mar 4	St Helens	L 2-34	10,008	G: O'Brien
Mar 11	Castleford Tigers	L 8-22	7,480	T: Bibby, Sa'u
Mar 16	HULL FC	W 24-8	2,902	T: G Johnson, Littlejohn, Lui, Nakubuwai, G: Lui 4
Mar 22	Widnes Vikings	L 16-24	4,007	T: Hauraki, Kopczak, G: Lui 4
Mar 30	CATALANS DRAGONS	W 32-16	2,328	T: Bibby, Evalds, G Johnson, Jones, Welham, G: Lui 6
Apr 2	Leeds Rhinos	L 0-20	10,718	
Apr 7	WARRINGTON WOLVES	L 6-22	3,428	T: Lui, G: Lui
Apr 15	Huddersfield Giants	W 30-12	4,385	T: Bibby 2, Flanagan, Hauraki, Nakubuwai, G: Lui 5
Apr 20	WAKEFIELD TRINITY	W 38-4	2,686	T: Bibby 2, G Griffin, G Johnson, Lannon, McCarthy, Sa'u, G: Lui 2, McCarthy 2, Littlejohn
Apr 26	ST HELENS	L 10-60	3,105	T: McCarthy, Welham, G: Shorrocks
May 4	Wigan Warriors	L 0-30	10,733	
May 11	Leigh Crusaders (RLC-6)	L 10-22	4,024	T: Evalds, G Griffin, G: Shorrocks
May 20	Catalans Dragons*	L 12-26	25,438	T: G Griffin, Hauraki, G: Lui 2
May 25	HUDDERSFIELD GIANTS	L 16-24	2,343	T: Sa'u 2, Evalds, G: Lui 2
Jun 8	Hull FC	L 14-45	10,606	T: G Griffin, G Johnson, Olpherts, G: Lui
Jun 14	WIDNES VIKINGS	W 26-12	2,248	T: Welham 2, Bibby, Burke, Lui, G: Lui 3
Jun 29	Warrington Wolves	L 14-30	9,171	T: Littlejohn 2, Bibby, G: Lui
Jul 8	Hull Kingston Rovers	L 22-52	7,698	T: Sa'u 2, Bibby, G Johnson, G: Chamberlain 3
Jul 13	CASTLEFORD TIGERS	L 6-24	2,681	T: Bibby, G: Chamberlain
Jul 21	Catalans Dragons	L 10-44	8,672	T: Olpherts, Wood, G: Chamberlain

Salford RL Match Results

2018 *continued*

	Opponent	Result	Attendance	Scorers
Jul 27	LEEDS RHINOS	W 38-22	2,387	T: Evalds 2, Chamberlain, Hastings, Jones, Lannon, Lui, G: Chamberlain 5
Aug 10	Hull Kingston Rovers (S8)	W 28-10	7,081	T: Evalds, Lui, J Lussick, Wood, G: Hastings 4, Chamberlain 2
Aug 18	WIDNES VIKINGS (S8)	W 32-6	2,317	T: Sa'u 2, Evalds, Flanagan, Lui, G: Chamberlain 6
Sep 2	Halifax (S8)	W 62-4	2,555	T: Olpherts 3, Hastings 2, Sa'u 2, Chamberlain, Nakubuwai, Tasi, Welham, Wood, G: Chamberlain 7
Sep 8	TORONTO WOLFPACK (S8)	W 28-16	2,509	T: Chamberlain, Hastings, Lannon, Lui, G: Chamberlain 6
Sep 14	Leeds Rhinos (S8)	L 16-18	11,202	T: Burke, Evalds, Olpherts, G: Chamberlain 2
Sep 22	London Broncos (S8)	L 8-11	809	T: G Johnson 2
Sep 27	TOULOUSE OLYMPIQUE (S8)	W 44-10	2,130	T: Evalds, Hastings, G Johnson, J Lussick, McCarthy, Olpherts, Welham, G: Hastings 7, Burgess

* *Magic Weekend at Newcastle*

2019

	Opponent	Result	Attendance	Scorers
Jan 11	SWINTON LIONS (F)	W 52-6	1,798	T: G Johnson 2, J Lussick 2, Sio 2, Chamberlain, Evalds, Hastings, Lui, Olpherts, G: Chamberlain 3, J Lussick
Jan 20	WIGAN WARRIORS (F)	L 18-28	2,190	T: Bibby, J Lussick, Olpherts, Sio, G: Chamberlain
Feb 1	Huddersfield Giants	W 34-14	5,387	T: Evalds 3, Sio 2, Olpherts, Sa'u, G: J Lussick 2, Sio
Feb 10	LONDON BRONCOS	W 24-0	3,246	T: Evalds, Hastings, Jones, Sio, G: Hastings 4
Feb 17	LEEDS RHINOS	L 14-46	4,385	T: Jones, J Lussick, G: Sio 3
Feb 23	Hull Kingston Rovers	W 24-22	7,565	T: Jones, Lui, J Lussick, Olpherts, Sio, G: Sio 2
Feb 28	ST HELENS	L 4-26	4,064	T: Olpherts
Mar 9	Catalans Dragons	W 46-0	8,021	T: Bibby 2, G Griffin 2, Evalds, Hastings, J Lussick, Sio, G: Sio 7
Mar 17	Castleford Tigers	L 20-24	7,750	T: Bibby 2, J Lussick, Turgut, G: J Lussick 2

Salford RL Match Results

2019 *continued*

	Opponent	Result	Attendance	Scorers
Mar 24	WIGAN WARRIORS	L 22-30	4,470	T: Evalds, Jones, Olpherts, Walker, G: Chamberlain 3
Mar 31	Wakefield Trinity	L 22-33	4,356	T: Evalds, Hastings, Olpherts, Welham, G: Chamberlain 3
Apr 7	HULL FC	L 16-23	3,609	T: Evalds, Hastings, Jones, G: Chamberlain 2
Apr 12	ROCHDALE HORNETS (RLC-5)	W 76-6	1,101	T: Evalds 4, Bibby 2, Burke, Chamberlain, Dudson, G Griffin, Inu, Lui, Tomkins, G: Chamberlain 6, Inu 6
Apr 19	Warrington Wolves	W 36-12	11,867	T: Bibby, Lui, J Lussick, Murray, Welham, G: Inu 8
Apr 22	WIGAN WARRIORS	L 26-30	4,017	T: Evalds, G Griffin, J Lussick, Walker, G: Inu 5
Apr 27	London Broncos	W 30-10	1,133	T: Evalds, Hastings, J Lussick, Mossop, Murray, G: Inu 5
May 3	LEEDS RHINOS	W 28-16	3,368	T: Walker 2, Lui, J Lussick, Mossop, G: Inu 4
May 11	HULL KINGSTON ROVERS (RLC-6)	L 18-32	1,842	T: Evalds, Inu, J Lussick, G: Inu 3
May 17	St Helens	L 30-32	9,446	T: Evalds 2, Dudson, Lui, Olpherts, G: Inu 5
May 26	Hull Kingston Rovers*	L 20-22	26,812	T: Sio 2, J Lussick, Pauli, G: Inu 2
Jun 7	Hull FC	L 32-35	9,914	T: Bibby 2, Pauli 2, Evalds, Lui, G: Inu 4
Jun 16	WAKEFIELD TRINITY	W 44-20	2,950	T: Evalds 3, Bibby 2, Lui, J Lussick, Welham, G: Inu 6
Jun 21	CASTLEFORD TIGERS	W 26-16	2,829	T: Evalds, Hastings, Mossop, Olpherts, G: Inu 5
Jun 28	Wigan Warriors	L 12-28	12,066	T: Olpherts, Welham, G: Inu 2
Jul 4	HUDDERSFIELD GIANTS	L 18-36	2,368	T: McCarthy 2, Sio, Welham, G: Inu
Jul 12	Warrington Wolves	W 22-12	9,509	T: Inu 2, Lannon, Welham, G: Inu 3
Jul 21	CATALANS DRAGONS	W 40-14	2,785	T: Welham 2, Evalds, Flanagan, J Johnson, Lolohea, Olpherts, G: Inu 3, Lolohea 3
Aug 4	London Broncos	W 58-28	1,445	T: Evalds 3, Inu 2, Flanagan, Hastings, Jones, Lolohea, Welham, G: Lolohea 8, Inu

Salford RL Match Results

2019 *continued*

	Opponent	Result	Attendance	Scorers
Aug 11	HUDDERSFIELD GIANTS	W 32-12	3,032	T: Flanagan, Inu, Lolohea, Tomkins, G: Inu 8
Aug 17	Hull FC	W 44-22	11,217	T: Inu 2, Mossop 2, Sio 2, Bibby, Hastings, G: Inu 6
Aug 29	WARRINGTON WOLVES	W 22-6	4,879	T: Sio 3, Inu, G: Inu 3
Sep 6	Leeds Rhinos	W 20-12	12,436	T: Bibby, Evalds, J Lussick, G: Inu 4
Sep 13	HULL KINGSTON ROVERS (AET)**	W 17-16	5,393	T: Bibby, Lolohea, J Lussick, G: Inu 2, DG: Inu
Sep 20	Wigan Warriors (SL-Qualifying play-off)	L 12-18	9,247	T: G Griffin, Hastings, G: Inu 2
Sep 26	CASTLEFORD TIGERS (SL-Elimination S-F)	W 22-0	4,800	T: Bibby, Hastings, McCarthy, G: Inu 5
Oct 4	Wigan Warriors (SL-Final Eliminator)	W 28-4	9,858	T: Dudson, J Lussick, Mossop, G: Inu 8
Oct 12	St Helens (SL-Grand Final)***	L 6-23	64,102	T: Bibby, G: Inu

* Magic Weekend at Liverpool   ** Extra time introduced this season for League matches
*** At Old Trafford, Manchester

Super League Grand Final runners-up

2020

	Opponent	Result	Attendance	Scorers
Jan 5	SWINTON LIONS (F)	W 52-4	1,747	T: Evalds 2, Welham 2, Atkin, Dudson, J Johnson, Lannon, Sio, Williams, G: Inu 3, Chamberlain 2, Atkin
Jan 11	LEIGH CENTURIONS (F)	W 40-14	1,611	T: Williams 2, Chamberlain, Greenwood, J Johnson, J Lussick, Sio, G: Inu 3, Lolohea 3
Jan 23	Warrington Wolves (F)	L 10-26	4,046	T: Sarginson 2, G: Lolohea
Jan 31	St Helens	L 8-48	12,006	T: Sio, G: Lolohea 2
Feb 8	TORONTO WOLFPACK*	W 24-16	4,593	T: Brown, Evalds, Lolohea, Sarginson, Williams, G: Lolohea 2
Feb 14	HUDDERSFIELD GIANTS	L 10-12	3,350	T: Sarginson, Sio, G: Lolohea
Feb 22	LEEDS RHINOS	L 8-22	4,757	T: Evalds, Lolohea
Mar 1	WAKEFIELD TRINITY	L 12-22	3,801	T: Sio 2, Lolohea
Mar 7	Catalans Dragons	L 14-30	7,940	T: Sio 2, Evalds, G: Lolohea

Salford RL Match Results

2020 *continued*

	Opponent	Result	Attendance	Scorers
Mar 13	WIGAN WARRIORS	W 18-14	4,796	T: Evalds 2, Brown, G: Lolohea 3
Aug 9	HULL FC**	W 54-18	BCD	T: Lolohea 2, Sio 2, Williams 2, Atkin, Evalds, Welham, Yates, G: Lolohea 7
Aug 29	Leeds Rhinos***	L 12-50	BCD	T: Evalds 2, G: Lolohea 2
Sep 3	CASTLEFORD TIGERS**	L 30-37	BCD	T: Brown, Evalds, J Lussick, Williams, Yates, G: Inu 5
Sep 18	Catalans Dragons (RLC-7) (AET)****	W 22-18	BCD	T: Sarginson 2, Greenwood, Inu, G: Inu 3
Sep 24	Hull FC***	W 28-22	BCD	T: Inu 2, Ackers, J Lussick, Williams, G: Inu 4
Sep 29	WARRINGTON WOLVES	W 20-18	BCD	T: Gilmore, Kear, Williams, G: Inu 4
Oct 3	Warrington Wolves (RLC-SF)****	W 24-22	BCD	T: Greenwood, Inu, J Lussick, Watkins, G: Inu 4
Oct 10	Huddersfield Giants**	W 24-16	BCD	T: Inu 3, Atkin, G: Inu 4
Oct 13	Hull Kingston Rovers***	L 22-24	BCD	T: Ashall-Bott, Chamberlain, Jones, Yates, G: Chamberlain 3
Oct 17	Leeds Rhinos (RLC-Final)*****	L 16-17	BCD	T: Greenwood, Pauli, Williams, G: Inu 2
Oct 23	Wigan Warriors****	L 12-58	BCD	T: Lolohea, Watkins, G: Inu 2
Oct 26	ST HELENS**	W 12-10	BCD	T: Inu, Pauli, G: Inu 2
Nov 2	CATALANS DRAGONS	W 42-24	BCD	T: Inu 3, Lolohea 2, Watkins, Williams, G: Inu 7
Nov 6	Wakefield Trinity**	W 28-20	BCD	T: Chamberlain, Evalds, Inu, Lolohea, McCarthy, G: Inu 4

* Result expunged from league table after Toronto withdrew ** At Leeds *** At Warrington **** At St Helens ***** At Wembley

Due to Covid-19 fixtures suspended mid-March to August – no spectators allowed upon resumption

Salford unable to raise team v Warrington (at St Helens) on Oct 30 – awarded to Warrington 24-0

Rugby League Challenge Cup runners-up

Salford RL Match Results

2021

Date	Opponent	Result	Attendance	Scorers
Mar 14	WIGAN WARRIORS (F)	W 20-6	BCD	T: Escare, Inu, Sio, Watkins, G: Inu 2
Mar 26	St Helens*	L 6-29	BCD	T: Sio, G: Inu
Apr 3	HULL FC**	L 4-35	BCD	T: Sio
Apr 10	WIDNES VIKINGS (RLC-3)	W 68-4	BCD	T: Costello 2, Escare 2, Ackers, Atkin, Ikahihifo, Lolohea, Ormondroyd, Patton, Watkins, Williams, G: Inu 10
Apr 17	Catalans Dragons	L 6-42	BCD	T: Livett, G: Escare
Apr 23	LEIGH CENTURIONS	W 34-8	BCD	T: Brown 2, Atkin, Greenwood, Livett, Sio, G: Inu 5
Apr 30	CASTLEFORD TIGERS	L 18-28	BCD	T: Ackers, Brown, Lolohea, G: Livett 2, Brown
May 8	Castleford Tigers (RLC-4)*	L 18-19	BCD	T: Livett 2, Mossop, G: Livett 3
May 17	St Helens	L 0-18	4,000	
May 22	WIGAN WARRIORS	L 16-17	2,033	T: Livett, Wells, G: Livett 4
May 27	WARRINGTON WOLVES	L 18-62	2,306	T: Livett, D Lussick, Sio, G: Livett 3
Jun 11	Hull Kingston Rovers	L 4-40	4,000	T: Sio
Jun 16	Huddersfield Giants	W 9-8	2,352	T: Ackers, G: Patton 2, DG: Atkin
Jun 27	LEEDS RHINOS	L 12-38	2,219	T: Atkin, Escare, G: Atkin, Patton
Jul 11	Castleford Tigers	W 70-18	3,900	T: Escare 2, Williams 2, Atkin, Costello, Davies, Norman, Ormondroyd, Patton, Roberts, Sio, G: Inu 11
Jul 16	WAKEFIELD TRINITY	W 24-14	1,323	T: Inu 2, Escare, Sio, G: Inu 4
Jul 23	Leeds Rhinos	L 16-38	10,515	T: Inu, Lolohea, Sio, G: Inu 2
Aug 6	Wigan Warriors	L 6-16	9,431	T: Burgess, G: Livett
Aug 13	HUDDERSFIELD GIANTS	W 18-12	3,066	T: Lolohea, Ormondroyd, Williams, G: Inu 3
Aug 22	Leigh Centurions	L 22-32	3,304	T: Sio 2, Livett, Williams, G: Inu 3
Aug 26	CATALANS DRAGONS	L 14-42	2,742	T: Escare, Livett, Sarginson, G: Inu
Aug 30	HULL FC	W 42-14	3,297	T: Sio 4, Atkin, Burgess, Livett, G: Inu 7
Sep 4	Castleford Tigers***	L 18-29	35,104	T: Burgess, Hingano, Sio, G: Inu 3

Salford RL Match Results

2021 *continued*

	Opponent	Result	Attendance	Scorers
Sep 11	Warrington Wolves	L 19-20	7,351	T: Sio 2, Lolohea, G: Escare 2, Inu, DG: Lolohea
Sep 17	ST HELENS	W 26-14	5,130	T: Sio 2, Atkin, Costello, Robson, G: Atkin 2, Inu

*At Leeds ** At St Helens *** Magic Weekend at Newcastle

Covid-19 restrictions eased – spectators allowed from May 17

2022

	Opponent	Result	Attendance	Scorers
Jan 15	SWINTON LIONS (F)	W 48-12	1,688	T: Ackers 2, Brierley, Costello, Croft, Cross, Sio, Williams, Wright, G: Atkin 3, Sneyd 3
Jan 21	HALIFAX PANTHERS (F)*	W 32-10	1,280	T: Brierley 2, Bourouh, Costello, Vuniyayawa, Williams, G: Sneyd 4
Feb 4	Warrington Wolves (F)	L 14-30	1,798	T: Joseph Brady, Lannon, Jacob Lee, G: Stevens
Feb 11	Castleford Tigers	W 26-16	10,050	T: Cross, Sio, Vuniyayawa, G: Sneyd 7
Feb 20	TOULOUSE OLYMPIQUE	W 38-12	4,003	T: Sio 4, Brierley, Lafai, Sneyd, G: Sneyd 5
Feb 26	Hull FC	L 16-48	10,081	T: Lafai 2, Sio, G: Sneyd 2
Mar 6	Huddersfield Giants	L 2-34	5,702	G: Sneyd
Mar 11	HULL KINGSTON ROVERS	L 16-26	3,950	T: Burgess, Sio, Wright, G: Sneyd 2
Mar 16	LEEDS RHINOS	W 26-12	5,756	T: Atkin, Brierley, Sio, Taylor, G: Sneyd 5
Mar 25	Wigan Warriors (RLC-6)	L 0-29	6,005	
Apr 3	Wakefield Trinity	L 24-30	4,371	T: Sio 2, Williams 2, Cross, G: Sneyd 2
Apr 14	Warrington Wolves	L 18-32	8,486	T: Ackers, Brierley, Sio, G: Sneyd 3
Apr 18	CATALANS DRAGONS	L 10-36	3,221	T: Cross, Sio, G: Sneyd
Apr 24	Wigan Warriors	L 24-30	10,783	T: Costello, Gerrard, Sio, Vuniyayawa, G: Brierley 4
Apr 29	St Helens	L 10-14	10,988	T: Costello, Escare, G: Atkin
May 15	LEEDS RHINOS	W 23-8	4,473	T: Ackers, Brierley, Burgess, Sio, G: Sneyd 3, DG: Sneyd
May 20	CASTLEFORD TIGERS	W 30-14	5,355	T: Burgess 3, Cross, Lafai, G: Sneyd 5

Salford RL Match Results

2022 *continued*

	Opponent	Result	Attendance	Scorers
Jun 5	Hull Kingston Rovers	L 16-43	7,023	T: Burgess, Cross, Watkins, G: Sneyd 2
Jun 10	WIGAN WARRIORS	L 12-30	5,944	T: Cross, Watkins, G: Sneyd 2
Jun 26	WAKEFIELD TRINITY	W 74-10	4,047	T: Burgess 3, Brierley 2, Cross 2, Sio 2, Alauola, Croft, Lafai, Watkins, G: Sneyd 11
Jul 3	Warrington Wolves	W 32-24	8,559	T: Ormondroyd 2, Atkin, Brierley, Cross, Williams, G: Sneyd 4
Jul 10	Huddersfield Giants**	L 18-30	25,333	T: Croft, Cross, Luckley, G: Sneyd 3
Jul 17	CATALANS DRAGONS	W 32-6	2,607	T: Sio 3, Croft, Ormondroyd, G: Sneyd 6
Jul 23	Toulouse Olympique	W 24-11	3,706	T: Burgess 2, Sio 2, G: Sneyd 4
Jul 31	ST HELENS	W 44-12	6,041	T: Burgess 2, Watkins 2, Akauola, Burke, Croft, Sarginson, G: Sneyd 6
Aug 7	Leeds Rhinos	L 14-34	14,668	T: Burgess, Croft, Sio, G: Sneyd
Aug 13	HUDDERSFIELD GIANTS	W 33-16	4,400	T: Brierley, Burgess, Lafai, Livett, Sio, Watkins, G: Sneyd 4, DG: Sneyd
Aug 20	Catalans Dragons	W 46-14	7,133	T: Watkins 2, Atkin, Brierley, Croft, Cross, Sio, Sneyd, G: Sneyd 5, Brierley 2
Aug 25	HULL FC	W 28-18	3,968	T: Brierley, Cross, Sio, Watkins, Williams, G: Sneyd 4
Aug 29	Castleford Tigers	W 50-10	7,322	T: Sneyd 2, Croft, Cross, Ormondroyd, Sio, Watkins, Wright, G: Sneyd 9
Sep 3	WARRINGTON WOLVES	L 14-32	5,123	T: Greenwood, Myles-Dalton, G: Livett 3
Sep 10	Huddersfield Giants (SL-Eliminator)	W 28-0	6,374	T: Ackers, Brierley, Burgess, Watkins, G: Sneyd 6
Sep 17	St Helens (Super League-SF)	L 12-19	12,357	T: Brierley, Watkins, G: Sneyd 2

* Colin Dixon Memorial Trophy   ** Magic Weekend at Newcastle

Salford NU/RL Records (1896-2022)

Appearances (200-plus)

Maurice Richards	498	Alf Middleton	285
Bert Day	488	Billy Brown	276
Mike Coulman	463	Ken Gill	275
Chris Hesketh	452	Steve Nash	275
Willie Thomas	442	Harold Osbaldestin	271
Billy Williams	435	Paul Highton	269
Gus Risman	427	Jack Williams	269
Colin Dixon	418	Walter Clegg	267
Barney Hudson	411	Harry Council	262
Jack Feetham	409	Reg Meek	260
David Watkins	407	Dave Preston	256
Dai John	405	John Cheshire	255
Dai Davies	370	Mark Lee	254
Malcolm Alker	360	Ian Blease	252
Billy Watkins	360	Bob Brown	251
Tommy Harrison	359	Emlyn Jenkins	246
Fergie Southward	350	Alan Grice	245
Teddy Haines	342	Jack Davies	241
Jack Muir	338	Hugh Duffy	240
Jackie Brennan	329	Graham Jones	239
Stuart Littler	329	Paul Charlton	234
Dai Moses	328	Bryn Hartley	231
Les Bettinson	319	George Heath	227
Keith Fielding	319	Stuart Whitehead	223
Sammy Miller	319	Stewart Williams	223
Jimmy Lomas	312	Pat Tunney	222
Evan Thomas	306	Syd Williams	222
Syd Boyd	299	David Major	221
Joe Bradbury	299	Jack Brown	218
Paddy Dalton	291	Jimmy Burgess	218
Eric Prescott	291	Dan Smith	218
Jack Rhapps	286	Bernard Mesley	215
		Silas Warwick	209

Most tries

Maurice Richards	297	Graham Jones	119
Barney Hudson	282	Stuart Littler	113
Keith Fielding	253	Niall Evalds	111
Jimmy Lomas	208	Jack Feetham	109
David Watkins	147	Paul Charlton	99
Gus Risman	144	Jimmy Cook	98
Bob Brown	136	Willie Thomas	92
Mike Coulman	135	Colin Dixon	91
Alan Edwards	128	Fergie Southward	90
Chris Hesketh	128	Bryn Hartley	89

Salford NU/RL Records (1896-2022)

Most goals

David Watkins	1241
Gus Risman	796
Steve Blakeley	789
Jack Davies	470
Jimmy Lomas	470
Steve Rule	395
Steve Kerry	318
John Wilshere	269
Chris Charles	231
Krisnan Inu	196
Daniel Holdsworth	191
Doug Hill	170
Bernard Mesley	170
Syd Lowdon	161
Fergie Southward	158
Clive Griffiths	157
Ken Richards	152
Gareth O'Brien	146
John Cheshire	141
Keith Fielding	133

Note: Includes all goals

Most 1-point drop goals

Mark Lee	35
Steve Nash	17
David Watkins	16
Steve Kerry	12
Steve Rule	11

Most points

David Watkins	2907
Gus Risman	2024
Steve Blakeley	1877
Jimmy Lomas	1564
Jack Davies	1087
Keith Fielding	1025
Barney Hudson	962
Maurice Richards	956
Steve Rule	848
Steve Kerry	812
John Wilshere	742
Bernard Mesley	601
Fergie Southward	586
Chris Charles	526
Krisnan Inu	487
Daniel Holdworth	453
Stuart Littler	452
Syd Lowdon	445
Niall Evalds	444
Alan Edwards	442

Most tries in a season
46 by Keith Fielding, 1973-74

Most tries in a match
6 by Frank Miles v Lees (Oldham), 5 March 1898; Ernie Bone v Goole, 29th March 1902; Jack Hilton v Leigh, 7 October 1939

Most goals in a season
221 by David Watkins, 1972-73

Most goals in a match
14 by Steve Blakeley v Gateshead Thunder, 23 March 2003

Most points in a season
493 by David Watkins, 1972-73

Most points in a match
39 by Jimmy Lomas v Liverpool City, 2 February 1907

Most consecutive appearances
163 (including 16 as a sub) by Stuart Littler, July 2004-September 2009

Most consecutive starts
140 by David Watkins, April 1971-April 1974

Most appearances in a season
50 by Bert Day, 1938-39

Salford NU/RL Records (1896-2022)

Club honours board
(*chronological sequence*)
1913-14 Rugby League Championship
1931-32 Lancashire Cup
1932-33 Lancashire League Championship
Rugby League Championship
1933-34 Lancashire League Championship
1934-35 Lancashire Cup
Lancashire League Championship
1935-36 Lancashire Cup
1936-37 Lancashire Cup
Lancashire League Championship
Rugby League Championship
1937-38 Rugby League Challenge Cup
1938-39 Lancashire League Championship
Rugby League Championship
1972-73 Lancashire Cup
1973-74 Rugby League Championship
1974-75 BBC2 Floodlit Trophy
1975-76 Rugby League Championship
1990-91 Division Two Championship
Division Two Premiership
1995-96 Centenary Division One (2nd tier) Championship
1996 Division One (2nd tier) Championship
Divisional Premiership
2003 Arriva Trains National League Cup
National League One Minor Premiers
National League One Grand Final
2008 Northern Rail National League Cup
National League One Minor Premiers
National League One Grand Final

Most consecutive wins
19, March-September 1933

Most consecutive matches unbeaten
20 (19 wins, 1 draw), March-September 1933

Biggest win
100-12 v Gateshead Thunder, 23 March 2003

Highest home attendances
26,470 v Warrington, 13 February 1937
26,327 v Warrington, 17 March 1951
26,000 v St Helens, 25 February 1950
25,000 v Wigan, 12 March 1910
25,000 v Wigan, 22 April 1935
25,000 v Wigan, 29 March 1937
24,442 v Halifax, 24 February 1934
24,000 v Castleford, 7 March 1936
23,500 v Swinton, 26 March 1932
23,000 v Leeds, 21 February 1931
23,000 v Hunslet, 18 February 1939

SALFORD FOOTBALL CLUB

Official Programme
(Issued by Authority of the Directors.)

No. 12   February 5th, 1916.   Price 1d.

The Dewsbury Match.

Commenting on the prospects of this match in our issue of January 22nd, we said "Given a decent day the game ought to be a sparkler." Well it was an excellent day and the game was in every way in keeping with the weather, and everyone present must have been delighted. Both teams played good, clean and honest football—not a semblance of foul play, all the players are entitled to thanks for their work. We were glad to annex the points but Mr. Wallwork's one slip nearly caused us to have to divide them, and his sigh of relief when the ball travelled wide could be heard a long way off.

It was a pity that owing to the late arrival of Dewsbury the game was limited to two 30's but the visitors are rather to be condoled with than blamed, as their train was due Manchester 2-10 and to make sure of a punctual start they ordered five taxis to meet them. But Football Committees propose and Railway Companies dispose—the train was forty minutes late.

The Wigan Match.

Once again has Central Park been fatal to us. We quite hoped to succeed last Saturday and in the early part of the game looked like doing so, but ultimately we had to give way and the final was 9. 3. against us. We used to look upon Central Park as a happy hunting ground—now we look upon it as, more or less, a cemetery.

Jack Bevon's Case.

We have received an acknowledgment from the County Committee of our protest against this player's suspension for an alleged offence in the Leigh match, and an expression of regret that nothing can be done as the Committee will not meet again before the suspension expires.

This is most unsatisfactory—the more that Bevon was suspended without an opportunity of defending himself. Bevon was ordered off on January 8th, and suspended three days later. No one expected the case would come up so early, indeed we did not know there was a meeting on Jan. 11th.

Benevolent Funds.

We are glad to say that the Williams' Family Fund is doing fairly well but we would like it to do "weller". Barrow have kindly promised to help by making a collection on their ground when we visit them on March 4th. We are very grateful to Barrow. We mentioned on January 8th that we intended to do something for the family of George Thom. We have arranged for the players of both sides to make a collection at half-time, the amount taken will be equally divided between the Thom fund and the Comforts Fund, which latter is much depleted. We are giving £5 from our Benevolent Fund to the Thom Fund and hope, later on, to play a benefit match or give half the gross gate of one of our ordinary fixtures.

Our Engagements.

To-day we meet Broughton Rangers whom we have already played twice this season. Let us hope for a good game and a good win.

Next Saturday Huddersfield will appear at the Willows. Their performances are so well known to every Rugby follower that we need not enlarge upon them. May the day be more propitious than the last one when Huddersfield were here.

Salford continued to produce a four-page programme throughout World War One. During such uncertain times it was impossible to name the 13 players that would take part, Salford listing 21 for this match against Broughton Rangers.

4

The Great War (World War One)
1915-16 – 1918-19

Britain's declaration of war against Germany on 4th August 1914 signalled its entry into what subsequently became known as The Great War, referred to today as World War One. With expectations that the conflict would soon be over, the Northern Union's 1914-15 season went ahead. However, the war gained momentum and the Northern Union called a halt to competitive fixtures from 1915-16.

Although many players answered the call to arms, clubs continued to play a full programme of friendly fixtures, albeit fielding teams invariably supplemented with retired players, juniors and guests. Very often the make-up of a team was not finalised until just before kick-off, with players involved in the war effort, understandably, being unable to guarantee their availability.

Some newspapers – the *Yorkshire Post* in particular – created interest by producing unofficial 'League' tables based on the match results, although all games were non-competitive. Following the Armistice on 11th November 1918, competitive fixtures recommenced in January 1919. In total, Salford played 102 wartime friendly matches, from 4th September 1915 until 1st January 1919.

At a time when the football and rugby results were, rightly, secondary to the war effort, obtaining full match details in newspapers that were already reduced in size due to paper shortages proved a challenge.

The Great War – 1915-16 – 1918-19

The players known to have taken part in those 102 friendly matches are listed in the following players' records section. There are seven instances – all during 1917-18 – when Salford, in common with other clubs, agreed to take to the field with 12 players, shedding one of the forwards. In total there are 47 appearances unaccounted for, 44 of which emanate from five matches during 1918-19 when the conflict was virtually over.

The score details are included in the season-by-season results indicated by 'F' after the opponents' name.

Salford – World War One Players

Name	Pos	WW1 Debut	WW1 Last	App	Tries	G	Pts
Ainsworth, Arthur	W	25/03/1916	28/12/1918	38	7	0	21
Anderson, Tom (Swinton)	HB	25/12/1918	25/12/1918	1	0	0	0
Antrobus, Edward	HB	23/09/1916	30/09/1916	2	0	0	0
Bailey, - (Leigh)	F	12/01/1918	12/01/1918	1	0	0	0
Baker, -	HB	21/10/1916	21/10/1916	1	0	0	0
Banks, H	HB	02/10/1915	29/01/1916	16	1	0	3
Barber, Jack	HB	13/10/1917	27/04/1918	3	0	0	0
Barnes, Jimmy (Broughton R)	C	01/04/1916	01/04/1916	1	0	0	0
Bevan, David William	W	18/09/1915	18/03/1916	2	1	0	3
Bevon, Jack	F	04/09/1915	16/03/1918	24	0	0	0
Blackledge, John (Swinton)	C	24/04/1916	24/04/1916	1	0	0	0
Bloor, -	F	11/09/1915	11/09/1915	1	0	0	0
Boardman, Horace (Swinton)	C	15/04/1916	15/04/1916	1	2	0	6
Brady, Billy	HB	25/12/1917	29/12/1917	2	0	0	0
Braithwaite, W	F	09/09/1916	09/09/1916	1	0	0	0
Brockbank, Chris (Swinton)	W	23/03/1918	25/12/1918	4	1	0	3
Brown, W 'Billy'	F	09/02/1918	09/02/1918	1	0	0	0
Brown, R (York)	FB	02/10/1915	09/10/2015	2	0	0	0
Burgess, A	C	17/02/1917	17/02/1917	1	0	0	0
Burgess, Jimmy (Runcorn)	F	09/10/1915	01/01/1919	67	16	6	60
Burke, J	F	29/09/1917	14/12/1918	21	0	0	0
Burrows, Robert	W	01/03/1917	01/01/1919	12	2	0	6
Campbell, - (Army/Heaton Park)	W	01/12/1917	28/12/1918	12	2	0	6
Clegg, Walter	T	04/09/1915	28/12/1918	82	14	1	44
Clifford, Reg	W	04/09/1915	12/01/1918	44	15	0	45
Coates, Tom (senior)	F	02/10/1915	01/01/1919	54	2	0	6
Collins, -	C	01/04/1918	01/04/1918	1	0	0	0
Cooper, Frank (Broughton R)	F	14/04/1917	27/04/1918	14	0	0	0
Costigan, Steve	W	28/10/1916	07/04/1917	11	1	0	3
Cotton, R	F	29/09/1917	29/09/1917	1	0	0	0
Currie, George	F	11/09/1915	07/04/1917	47	0	0	0
Dagnall, -	F	09/09/1916	09/09/1916	1	0	0	0
Dawson, Jimmy (Swinton)	C	09/02/1918	09/02/1918	1	0	0	0
Deacon, -	HB	16/02/1918	16/02/1918	1	0	0	0
Dixon, H	F	09/09/1916	01/04/1918	27	1	0	3
Empson, GW	C	30/09/1916	25/11/1916	3	0	0	0
Evans, Sam	HB	03/11/1917	03/11/1917	1	0	0	0
Evans, L (Hull Kingston Rovers)	C	24/04/1916	24/04/1916	1	0	0	0
Gagon, Frank	W	08/01/1916	29/01/1916	3	1	0	3
Gatley, -	W	20/01/1917	20/01/1917	1	0	0	0
Goldsmith, Harry	F	04/09/1915	07/04/1917	27	7	0	21
Gotheridge, Tom (Leigh)	F	12/01/1918	12/01/1918	1	0	0	0
Greatorex, H	W	04/09/1915	19/02/1916	15	3	0	9
Hall, - (Swinton)	W	29/12/1917	19/01/1918	2	0	0	0
Hampson, John	HB	05/02/1916	07/10/1916	8	0	1	2

Salford – World War One Players

Name	Pos	WW1 Debut	WW1 Last	App	Tries	G	Pts
Harold, John	F	09/03/1918	09/03/1918	1	0	0	0
Harrison, Edwin	FB	11/09/1915	25/09/1915	2	0	0	0
Harrison, G	W	01/04/1918	01/04/1918	1	0	0	0
Harrison, Harold	F	23/09/1916	21/04/1917	13	1	0	3
Hesketh, George (Wigan)	HB	02/03/1918	02/03/1918	1	0	0	0
Higson, -	F	26/12/1916	26/12/1916	1	0	0	0
Higson, - (Wigan)	W	02/03/1918	02/03/1918	1	0	0	0
Hill, Robert (Broughton R)	T	15/09/1917	28/12/1918	19	0	0	0
Hindshaw, Alec	F	23/09/1916	23/09/1916	1	0	0	0
Hobson, R	F	18/12/1915	29/04/1916	8	0	0	0
Holden, - (Swinton)	F	23/03/1918	23/03/1918	1	0	0	0
Hutson, W	W	03/11/1917	26/12/1917	3	0	0	0
John, WD 'Dai'	HB	04/09/1915	01/01/1917	49	8	49	122
Jones, - (St Helens)	C	13/01/1917	13/01/1917	1	0	0	0
Jones, William	F	28/10/1916	12/05/1917	14	0	0	0
Knott, James	F	07/12/1918	07/12/1918	1	0	0	0
Lambert, -	F	22/09/1917	22/09/1917	1	0	0	0
Landers, Fred	F	24/02/1917	27/04/1918	34	1	0	3
Launce, Harry	FB	04/09/1915	01/01/1919	87	0	11	22
Lewis, - (Barrow)	W	16/02/1918	16/02/1918	1	0	0	0
Livesey, Albert	F	23/11/1918	28/12/1918	4	1	0	3
Lomas, Jimmy (York)	C	06/04/1917	28/04/1917	3	2	1	8
Loveluck, Arthur	C	04/09/1915	25/03/1916	23	3	0	9
Martindale, J (Barrow)	F	16/09/1916	28/12/1918	22	0	0	0
May, Edgar	HB	12/02/1916	29/03/1918	46	2	0	6
Melling, - (Leigh)	F	02/03/1918	02/03/1918	1	0	0	0
Mesley, Bernard	W	07/10/1916	07/10/1916	1	1	0	3
Morton, Sam	W	01/01/1918	01/01/1918	1	0	0	0
Oldham, W	HB	26/12/1917	28/12/1918	16	0	0	0
Parr, - (Leigh)	FB	12/01/1918	12/01/1918	1	0	0	0
Pennaluna, - (Barrow)	FB	16/02/1918	16/02/1918	1	0	0	0
Ratcliffe, Joe	W	11/03/1916	14/12/1918	4	1	0	3
Rees, Charlie	F	04/09/1915	26/12/1916	24	4	0	12
Reeves, C	W	22/09/1917	30/03/1918	4	0	0	0
Ritchie, Bob	F	04/09/1915	01/04/1916	22	1	3	9
Roberts, T	F	15/09/1917	16/02/1918	7	0	0	0
Robinson, W	W	21/10/1916	28/04/1917	5	3	0	9
Scott, - (Broughton Rangers)	F	23/03/1918	23/03/1918	1	0	0	0
Shaw, -	C	12/01/1918	12/01/1918	1	0	0	0
Shirley, J	W	13/10/1917	20/10/1917	2	0	0	0
Spencer, LF	C	13/01/1917	06/10/1917	12	1	1	5
Stansfield, - (Huddersfield)	F	25/03/1916	25/03/1916	1	0	0	0
Sykes, Edward	F	11/09/1915	07/12/1918	64	4	0	12
Taylor, -	F	26/12/1916	26/12/1916	1	0	0	0
Taylor, A (Broughton Rangers)	F	26/12/1917	23/02/1918	2	0	0	0

Salford – World War One Players

Name	Pos	WW1 Debut	WW1 Last	App	Tries	G	Pts
Thomas, C (Army/Heaton Park)	C	01/12/1971	01/12/1917	1	0	0	0
Thomas, Evan J	F	18/09/1915	08/01/1916	4	0	0	0
Thomas, R 'Bob'	F	25/09/1915	12/01/1918	11	0	0	0
Thomas, Willie	C	04/09/1915	01/01/1919	57	7	6	33
Thompson, AJ 'Jack'	F	18/09/1915	17/02/1917	3	0	0	0
Tranter, Jim (Warrington)	C	08/04/1916	12/05/1917	4	0	0	0
Traynor, H (Barrow)	F	16/09/1916	28/12/1918	2	0	0	0
Walker, -	C	24/02/1917	24/02/1917	1	0	0	0
Wanklyn, Bullig	HB	18/11/1916	28/12/1918	43	2	0	6
Whitchurch, J	FB	13/10/1917	03/11/1917	4	0	0	0
Whitney, Harold 'George'	F	16/09/1916	01/01/1919	19	2	0	6
Whitworth, J	W	29/09/1917	27/10/1917	2	0	0	0
Wilkinson, William	F	04/09/1915	04/09/1915	1	0	0	0
Williams, -	C	17/02/1917	17/02/1917	1	0	0	0
Winstanley, Jack (Swinton)	W	09/02/1918	09/02/1918	1	0	0	0
Winter, -	F	26/12/1917	26/12/1917	1	0	0	0
Wood, Sam	W	28/04/1917	28/04/1917	1	1	0	3
Woods, Ernie	F	04/09/1915	28/12/1918	44	4	0	12
Yorke, - (RU player)	W	09/02/1918	09/02/1918	1	0	0	0
AN Other	F	24/03/1917	24/03/1917	1	0	0	0

Salford Royal Hospital Senior Rugby Challenge Cup.
Presented by Messrs GROVES-WHITNALL, Ltd., 1924.

The Salford Royal Hospital Cup was provided by local brewers Groves and Whitnall at a cost of 100 guineas (£105).

5

The Salford Royal Hospital Cup 1924-25 – 1947-48

The Salford Royal Hospital Cup was instigated by Broughton Rangers, local brewers Groves and Whitnall providing a gold cup for annual competition. The proceeds were donated to the original Salford Royal Hospital in Chapel Street, which exists today as an apartment block. The tournament began in 1924-25 and continued until 1947-48, when it was discontinued after fund raising for the hospital was no longer thought necessary following the launch of the National Health Service in July 1948.

Initially, Broughton Rangers, Salford, Swinton and Leigh competed for the trophy in a four-team knock-out contest. From 1929-30 until 1937-38 it operated as a three-team competition as Leigh did not participate, reverting to four again for 1947-48 after Leigh returned.

From 1930-31 to 1937-38 it was decided to only hold the final, the previous season's winners standing down. Altogether the competition took place 13 times, Salford winning six, Swinton five, and Broughton Rangers two. Salford played in 14 matches, winning ten and losing four. The score details are included in the season-by-season results indicated by 'SHC' in brackets after the opponents name. The complete players' records for all 14 matches are included here.

Salford Royal Hospital Cup Players

Name	First	Last	App	Tries	G	Pts
Aspinall, George	1947-48	1947-48	2	1	0	3
Beaver, William	1924-25	1924-25	2	0	0	0
Boon, Wilf	1926-27	1926-27	1	0	0	0
Bowen, Trevor	1935-36	1935-36	1	0	0	0
Boyd, Syd	1924-25	1930-31	9	2	0	6
Bradbury, Joe	1930-31	1937-38	3	0	0	0
Brogden, Stan	1947-48	1947-48	1	0	0	0
Brown, Jack	1947-48	1947-48	2	1	0	3
Brown, Bob	1933-34	1937-38	2	2	0	6
Burgess, Jimmy	1924-25	1926-27	3	0	1	2
Butterworth, Frank	1924-25	1926-27	5	0	0	0
Casewell, Aubrey	1933-34	1933-34	1	0	0	0
Chapman, Herbert	1947-48	1947-48	2	0	0	0
Coates, Jack	1927-28	1927-28	1	0	0	0
Curran, George	1947-48	1947-48	2	0	0	0
Dalton, Patrick 'Paddy'	1933-34	1937-38	3	1	0	3
Davies, DM 'Dai'	1947-48	1947-48	2	1	0	3
Davies, William	1926-27	1926-27	1	0	0	0
Day, Eric	1947-48	1947-48	2	1	0	3
Day, HC 'Bert'	1933-34	1937-38	3	0	0	0
Dobing, George	1929-30	1929-30	2	0	0	0
Doran, Billy	1930-31	1930-31	1	1	0	3
Edwards, Alan	1937-38	1937-38	1	0	0	0
Evans, Cliff	1935-36	1935-36	1	0	0	0
Feetham, Jack	1930-31	1937-38	3	0	0	0
Flanagan, John	1947-48	1947-48	2	1	0	3
Fox, Thomas	1926-27	1926-27	1	0	0	0
Gallagher, J	1924-25	1924-25	2	0	0	0
Gardner, Joe	1935-36	1935-36	1	0	0	0
Garland, Sam	1926-27	1926-27	3	0	0	0
Gear, Albert	1937-38	1947-48	2	0	0	0
Gore, Jack	1924-25	1927-28	6	1	0	3
Haines, EC 'Teddy'	1924-25	1930-31	7	3	0	9
Hall, Clifford	1927-28	1927-28	1	0	0	0
Halton, Jack	1924-25	1924-25	2	0	0	0
Harris, George	1935-36	1935-36	1	0	0	0
Harrison, Tommy	1947-48	1947-48	2	1	0	3
Hudson, Bernard 'Barney'	1929-30	1937-38	4	6	1	20
Hurst, Alex 'Sandy'	1924-25	1924-25	2	0	0	0
Jenkins, Emlyn	1930-31	1933-34	2	0	0	0
Jones, Reg	1947-48	1947-48	2	3	0	9
Kenny, Russ	1947-48	1947-48	2	1	0	3
Lindley, Jimmy	1927-28	1927-28	1	0	0	0
Mann, Fred	1926-27	1926-27	2	0	0	0
Manning, Dick	1927-28	1929-30	2	1	0	3

Salford Royal Hospital Cup Players

Name	First	Last	App	Tries	G	Pts
Mannion, Tom	1926-27	1927-28	4	0	1	2
Marsden, W 'Bill'	1929-30	1929-30	1	0	0	0
Matthews, Eddie	1929-30	1929-30	2	1	0	3
Meek, Reg	1926-27	1930-31	5	0	2	4
Middleton, Alf	1929-30	1933-34	3	0	0	0
Miller, Sammy	1929-30	1937-38	5	1	0	3
Moses, Dai	1947-48	1947-48	2	0	0	0
Muir, Jack	1924-25	1930-31	8	0	0	0
Osbaldestin, Harold	1933-34	1937-38	3	0	1	2
Peacock, Charlie	1924-25	1926-27	4	1	0	3
Pearson, Leslie	1933-34	1935-36	2	0	0	0
Price, Billy	1926-27	1927-28	4	0	0	0
Risman, AJ 'Gus'	1929-30	1937-38	5	3	7	23
Schofield, Dave	1935-36	1935-36	1	0	2	4
Shaw, Fred	1929-30	1929-30	2	0	0	0
Smith, JH	1927-28	1927-28	1	0	0	0
Southward, Ferguson 'Fergie'	1924-25	1929-30	7	5	2	19
Spruce, Joe	1935-36	1935-36	1	0	0	0
Summerville, Wilf	1926-27	1926-27	1	0	0	0
Thomas, Harold	1937-38	1937-38	1	1	1	5
Watkins, Billy	1933-34	1933-34	1	0	0	0
Watson, Robert	1926-27	1926-27	1	0	0	0
Whitehead, JF	1927-28	1929-30	2	0	0	0
Williams, John	1924-25	1924-25	2	0	0	0
Williams, Llewellyn	1926-27	1929-30	5	0	3	6
Williams, Syd	1947-48	1947-48	2	2	8	22
Williams, WA 'Billy'	1930-31	1937-38	4	1	0	3

Action from the opening match of Salford's 1934 French tour versus Paris XIII, as depicted on the front page of the French weekly *Le Miroir Des Sports*.

6

France Tour 1934
(Birth of 'The Red Devils')

As 1933-34 drew to a close, reports circulated that the French had requested that Salford visit them for a promotional tour in their bid to establish rugby league in France. The French had sent a touring side to England during March 1934 and viewed Salford as 'the premier side in the game' after playing against them on that tour. Initially, they wanted Salford to visit during August or September 1934, but with a new season just starting, it was delayed until late October. Salford was the first club side* invited to France and they won all six matches in spectacular fashion.

The opening game, on 21st October 1934 in Paris, was just one day after Salford's Lancashire Cup Final win over Wigan, following an overnight sea journey from Folkestone to Dunkirk. It was also the first time that Salford had played on a Sunday. The programme for that first match described the visitors as 'Les Diables Rouges de Salford' and the legend of the Salford Red Devils was born.

Salford played their six matches over a 15-day period, the scores for which appear in the match results section for 1934-35. Unfortunately, the players' records section shown here are missing seven appearances. Whilst it has been possible to confirm the full line-up for the first three matches, three are unknown for the meeting with Albi and two each versus Perpignan and Villeneuve.

* *During May 1934 a 'Yorkshire Select' consisting of 16 Leeds and two York players undertook a five-match tour of France.*

France Tourists 1984

Name	App	Tries	Goals	Points
Bradbury, Joe	2	0	0	0
Brown, Bob	5	8	0	24
Casewell, Aubrey	3	1	0	3
Dalton, Patrick 'Paddy'	2	2	0	6
Day, HC 'Bert'	6	1	0	3
Evans, Cliff	3	5	0	15
Feetham, Jack	6	5	0	15
Harris, George	3	0	1	2
Hudson, Bernard 'Barney'	6	10	0	30
Jenkins, Emlyn	6	4	8	28
Middleton, Alf	5	5	0	15
Miller, Sammy	1	1	0	3
Osbaldestin, Harold	6	7	0	21
Pearson, Leslie	1	0	2	4
Risman, AJ 'Gus'	4	2	25	56
Watkins, Billy	6	3	1	11
Williams, WA 'Billy'	6	3	0	9

7

Festival of Sports 1951-52 – 1952-53

At the conclusion of 1951-52 and 1952-53 Salford participated in a four-team knock-out competition as part of a Festival of Sports Fortnight organised by Blackpool Corporation.

Both contests were held at the Oval in Stanley Park, Blackpool, during June. In the 1951-52 semi-final Salford defeated Barrow 19-12 and then overcame Doncaster – conquerors of Dewsbury by 26-7 in the final. Twelve months later, Barrow gained revenge, beating Salford 25-10 in a semi-final rematch.

The score details are included in the season-by-season results indicated by 'FoS' in brackets after the opponents name. The complete players' records for all three matches are included here.

Festival of Sports 1951-52 – 1952-53

Name	First	Last	App	Tries	Goals	Points
Alder, Frank	1951-52	1951-52	2	1	0	3
Baines, Albert	1952-53	1952-53	1	1	0	3
Birkin, Frank	1951-52	1951-52	2	1	0	3
Caudwell, Peter	1951-52	1951-52	2	0	0	0
Danby, Tom	1951-52	1951-52	2	1	0	3
Davies, Eifion, 'Jack'	1951-52	1952-53	3	2	10	26
Finnan, Bill	1951-52	1952-53	3	1	0	3
Grainger, Jim	1951-52	1952-53	3	0	0	0
Harrison, Tommy	1951-52	1952-53	3	0	1	2
Hartley, Bryn	1951-52	1952-53	3	4	0	12
Hindle, Ray	1952-53	1952-53	1	0	0	0
Hughes, Bill	1951-52	1951-52	1	0	0	0
McKinney, Tom	1951-52	1952-53	3	0	0	0
Marston, Peter	1952-53	1952-53	1	0	0	0
Moses, Dai	1951-52	1952-53	3	0	0	0
Robson, Bob	1951-52	1951-52	2	0	0	0
Rogers, Jack	1952-53	1952-53	1	0	0	0
Smith, Fred	1952-53	1952-53	1	0	0	0
Whalley, Joe	1952-53	1952-53	1	0	0	0
Williams, Syd	1951-52	1951-52	1	0	0	0

8

The Red Rose Cup
1954-55 – 1980-81

Following the demise of the Salford Royal Hospital Cup in 1948, a new annual charity fixture between Salford and Swinton was launched in 1954.

It was arranged primarily as a pre-season game with all proceeds donated to junior rugby league and local charities. The trophy used was a half-size replica of the Rugby League Challenge Cup, presented to Salford by brewers Groves and Whitnall in 1938 to honour the clubs Wembley success that year. The breweries Red Rose Ales brand had recently been introduced and was advertised in Salford's match programme at the time.

The Red Rose Cup was competed for 19 times between 1954-55 and 1980-81, two of the matches (1966-67 and 1967-68) being contested instead by Salford and Wakefield Trinity. Salford claimed ten victories (including the two matches with Trinity) and Swinton nine. The score details are included in the season-by-season results indicated by 'RRC' in brackets after the opponents name. The complete players' records for all 19 matches are included here.

The Red Rose Cup 1954-55 – 1980-81

Name	First	Last	App	Sub	Total	Tries	G	Pts
Alder, Frank	1954-55	1958-59	3	0	3	0	0	0
Argent, Joe	1966-67	1967-68	2	0	2	1	0	3
Ashcroft, Kevin	1979-80	1980-81	2	0	2	0	0	0
Ayles, Eric	1956-57	1957-58	2	0	2	0	0	0
Bailey, Gary	1977-78	1977-78	0	1	1	0	0	0
Baines, Albert	1956-57	1960-61	3	0	3	1	0	3
Banks, Billy	1959-60	1959-60	1	0	1	0	0	0
Banner, Peter	1974-75	1975-76	2	0	2	1	0	3
Bettinson, Les	1957-58	1966-67	8	0	8	1	0	3
Birkin, Frank	1954-55	1954-55	1	0	1	0	0	0
Boardman, Frank	1954-55	1960-61	3	0	3	0	0	0
Bott, Charlie	1967-68	1967-68	1	0	1	0	0	0
Bradbourne, Terry	1955-56	1955-56	1	0	1	0	1	2
Breen, Aiden	1966-67	1966-67	1	0	1	0	0	0
Brennan, Jackie	1961-62	1955-56	5	1	6	0	0	0
Brunt, Ken	1961-62	1961-62	1	0	1	0	0	0
Burdell, Bob	1967-68	1967-68	1	0	1	1	0	3
Burgess, -	1956-57	1956-57	1	0	1	0	0	0
Butler, John	1975-76	1978-79	4	0	4	2	0	6
Cheshire, John	1956-57	1962-63	5	0	5	0	4	8
Clare, Mick	1966-67	1966-67	1	0	1	0	0	0
Clark, Mick	1963-64	1963-64	1	0	1	0	0	0
Collier, Frank	1967-68	1967-68	1	0	1	0	0	0
Corcoran, John	1974-75	1977-78	1	2	3	2	0	6
Coulman, Mike	1974-75	1979-80	3	1	4	2	0	6
Council, Harry	1955-56	1961-62	5	0	5	0	0	0
Critch, Jon	1980-81	1980-81	1	0	1	0	0	0
Critchley, Ernie	1966-67	1966-67	1	0	1	0	0	0
Devlin, Ellis	1975-76	1976-77	1	1	2	0	0	0
Dixon, Colin	1977-78	1977-78	1	0	1	0	0	0
Dodd, Frank	1955-56	1955-56	1	0	1	0	0	0
Donoghue, Peter	1960-61	1960-61	1	0	1	0	0	0
Dorning, Alan	1962-63	1963-64	2	0	2	0	0	0
Driver, David	1979-80	1980-81	2	0	2	1	0	3
Duffy, Hugh	1955-56	1961-62	7	0	7	0	0	0
Dunn, Terry	1960-61	1963-64	4	0	4	2	0	6
Evans, Dave	1966-67	1967-68	2	0	2	1	0	3
Evans, Dick	1977-78	1977-78	1	0	1	0	0	0
Fairhurst, Jim	1955-56	1955-56	1	0	1	0	0	0
Farrington, John	1954-55	1956-57	2	0	2	0	0	0
Fieldhouse, Derek	1957-58	1957-58	1	0	1	0	0	0
Fielding, Keith	1977-78	1979-80	2	0	2	2	0	6
Frodsham, Peter	1976-77	1977-78	0	2	2	1	0	3
Gill, Ken	1976-77	1979-80	2	0	2	1	0	3
Gourley, Tony	1979-80	1979-80	1	0	1	0	0	0

The Red Rose Cup 1954-55 – 1980-81

Name	First	Last	App	Sub	Total	Tries	G	Pts
Graham, Gordon	1978-79	1978-79	1	0	1	0	0	0
Grainger, Jim	1954-55	1954-55	1	0	1	0	0	0
Greenslade, Alan	1959-60	1959-60	1	0	1	0	0	0
Gregory, Arthur	1956-57	1961-62	5	0	5	0	0	0
Gregory, Harold	1958-59	1958-59	1	0	1	0	0	0
Grice, Alan	1974-75	1979-80	4	1	5	2	0	6
Grimes, Paul	1974-75	1974-75	1	0	1	1	0	3
Halsall, Albert	1963-64	1963-64	1	0	1	1	0	3
Hancock, John	1956-57	1963-64	5	0	5	0	2	4
Harris, David	1979-80	1979-80	1	0	1	1	0	3
Harrison, Tommy	1954-55	1954-55	1	0	1	0	0	0
Hartley, Bryn	1954-55	1961-62	5	0	5	1	0	3
Harwood, George	1961-62	1961-62	1	0	1	0	0	0
Hemmings, John	1956-57	1956-57	1	0	1	0	0	0
Henighan, Mick	1966-67	1966-67	1	0	1	0	0	0
Henney, Harold	1978-79	1978-79	1	0	1	0	0	0
Hesketh, Chris	1967-68	1978-79	4	0	4	0	0	0
Hey, Steve	1978-79	1978-79	1	0	1	0	0	0
Hindley, Jim	1963-64	1963-64	1	0	1	0	0	0
Houghton, Joe	1954-55	1954-55	1	0	1	0	0	0
Hughes, Arthur	1966-67	1967-68	2	0	2	2	0	6
Hutson, Bill	1963-64	1963-64	1	0	1	0	0	0
Irving, Bob	1978-79	1978-79	1	0	1	1	0	3
Johns, Graeme	1979-80	1979-80	0	1	1	0	0	0
Jones, Eric	1960-61	1960-61	1	0	1	0	0	0
Jones, Graham	1955-56	1961-62	7	0	7	3	0	9
Keavney, Brian	1955-56	1958-59	3	0	3	0	1	2
Kettle, Bob	1979-80	1979-80	0	1	1	0	0	0
Kilgannon, Derek	1958-59	1962-63	2	0	2	0	0	0
Knighton, John	1974-75	1977-78	4	0	4	1	0	3
Knowles, Graham	1974-75	1976-77	3	0	3	0	11	22
Lambert, Roy	1955-56	1955-56	1	0	1	1	0	3
Lang, David	1980-81	1980-81	1	0	1	1	0	3
Latham, Keith	1979-80	1980-81	2	0	2	0	0	0
Leonard, Ken	1962-63	1962-63	1	0	1	0	0	0
Lowdon, Syd	1958-59	1958-59	1	0	1	1	2	7
Lowe, Johnny	1954-55	1954-55	1	0	1	1	0	3
McAlone, Eddie	1962-63	1963-64	2	0	2	0	0	0
McArthur, Walter 'Wally'	1957-58	1957-58	1	0	1	0	3	6
McGreal, Chris	1975-76	1975-76	1	0	1	0	0	0
McGuinness, Jack	1959-60	1959-60	1	0	1	0	0	0
McInnes, Alan	1967-68	1967-68	1	0	1	0	1	2
McKay, Graham	1974-75	1975-76	1	1	2	0	0	0
Major, David	1980-81	1980-81	0	1	1	0	0	0
Marston, Peter	1954-55	1955-56	2	0	2	1	0	3

The Red Rose Cup 1954-55 – 1980-81

Name	First	Last	App	Sub	Total	Tries	G	Pts
Mayor, Graham	1975-76	1975-76	0	1	1	0	0	0
Moses, Dai	1956-57	1956-57	1	0	1	0	0	0
Murphy, Paul	1962-63	1967-68	2	0	2	2	3	12
Nash, Steve	1976-77	1980-81	3	0	3	2	0	6
Nestor, Vince	1967-68	1967-68	1	0	1	0	0	0
Ogden, Terry	1966-67	1966-67	1	0	1	0	0	0
Ogle, Denis	1978-79	1978-79	0	1	1	0	0	0
Oldham, Alan	1977-78	1980-81	0	4	4	0	4	8
O'Neill, Paul	1978-79	1980-81	2	1	3	0	0	0
Openshaw, Arthur	1957-58	1957-58	1	0	1	0	0	0
Parr, Jim	1956-57	1956-57	1	0	1	0	0	0
Parsons, George	1959-60	1959-60	1	0	1	0	0	0
Pearce, Ray	1963-64	1963-64	1	0	1	0	1	2
Preece, Bob	1959-60	1959-60	1	0	1	0	1	2
Prescott, Eric	1976-77	1979-80	4	0	4	1	0	3
Rabbitt, Trevor	1966-67	1966-67	1	0	1	0	0	0
Rawlinson, John	1975-76	1976-77	2	0	2	1	0	3
Redford, Tony	1974-75	1974-75	1	0	1	1	0	3
Rees, Graham	1961-62	1962-63	2	0	2	1	0	3
Richards, Ken	1962-63	1962-63	1	0	1	0	3	6
Richards, Maurice	1975-76	1980-81	3	0	3	2	0	6
Rogers, Jack	1954-55	1955-56	2	0	2	0	1	2
Roughley, George	1954-55	1954-55	1	0	1	0	0	0
Rule, Steve	1978-79	1979-80	1	1	2	0	7	14
Sheffield, Bill	1975-76	1978-79	3	1	4	0	0	0
Simcox, Dennis	1962-63	1962-63	1	0	1	0	0	0
Sims, Geoff	1966-67	1967-68	1	1	2	0	2	4
Smart, Geoff	1963-64	1963-64	1	0	1	0	0	0
Smith, Derek	1959-60	1959-60	1	0	1	0	0	0
Smith, Fred	1954-55	1957-58	2	0	2	0	0	0
Smith, Ron	1980-81	1980-81	1	0	1	1	1	5
Southward, Joe	1966-67	1967-68	2	0	2	2	1	8
Starkey, -	1966-67	1966-67	0	1	1	0	0	0
Stead, Frank	1974-75	1980-81	3	0	3	0	0	0
Stephenson, David	1979-80	1979-80	1	0	1	3	0	9
Stoddart, Ray	1957-58	1957-58	1	0	1	0	0	0
Storey, Tony	1958-59	1958-59	1	0	1	0	0	0
Stott, Roy	1958-59	1959-60	2	0	2	0	0	0
Taylor, John	1974-75	1974-75	1	0	1	0	0	0
Taylor, Mark	1966-67	1966-67	1	0	1	1	0	3
Todd, William	1955-56	1955-56	1	0	1	0	0	0
Turnbull, Sam	1975-76	1980-81	6	0	6	3	0	9
Walker, Peter	1974-75	1975-76	2	0	2	0	0	0
Walker, Ron	1956-57	1956-57	1	0	1	0	0	0
Ward, Phil	1974-75	1974-75	1	0	1	0	0	0

The Red Rose Cup 1954-55 – 1980-81

Name	First	Last	App	Sub	Total	Tries	G	Pts
Warren, Wayne	1977-78	1977-78	1	0	1	0	0	0
Watkins, David	1975-76	1978-79	3	0	3	0	18	36
Whitehead, Stuart	1967-68	1967-68	1	0	1	0	0	0
Williams, Stewart	1977-78	1980-81	2	2	4	1	0	3
Wilson, Frank	1980-81	1980-81	1	0	1	2	0	6
Wilson, Terry	1963-64	1963-64	1	0	1	0	0	0
AN Other	1974-75	1974-75	1	0	1	0	0	0
AN Other	1980-81	1980-81	1	0	1	0	0	0
AN Other	1980-81	1980-81	0	1	1	0	0	0

Jimmy Lomas was the Salford captain for over eight years.

9

Salford Chairmen, Coaches and Captains

Club Officials 1873-2022

Season	Chairman	Coach	Captain
1873-74	none	none	RG MacKay
1874-75	none	none	RG MacKay
1875-76	none	none	RG MacKay
1876-77	none	none	RG MacKay
1877-78	none	none	RG MacKay
1878-79	none	none	RG MacKay
1879-80	none	none	RG MacKay
1880-81	none	none	Tom Hardy
1881-82	none	none	Hugh Williamson
1882-83	none	none	Hugh Williamson
1883-84	James Jackson	none	Hugh Williamson
1884-85	Daniel Wellwood	none	WH 'Bill' Buckley
1885-86	Daniel Wellwood	none	Connie Varley
1886-87	Daniel Wellwood	none	Connie Varley
1887-88	Daniel Wellwood	none	Sam Williams
1888-89	Daniel Wellwood	none	Harry Eagles
1889-90	Daniel Wellwood	none	Sam Williams
1890-91	Daniel Wellwood	none	Harry Eagles
1891-92	Lees Knowles (P)	none	Tom Craven
1892-93	Lees Knowles (P)	none	Frank Miles
1893-94	Lees Knowles (P)	none	Tom Kent
1894-95	Lees Knowles (P)	none	Alf Barrett
1895-96	Lees Knowles (P)	none	W 'Billy' Manwaring
1896-97	Lees Knowles (P)	none	W 'Billy' Manwaring
1897-98	William Barron-Smith	none	Frank Miles
1898-99	James Higson	none	Tom Williams
1899-00	James Higson	Jack Roberts (T)	Tom Williams
1900-01	James Higson	Jack Roberts (T)	Tom Williams
1901-02	Edwin Mather	George Cook (T)	Tom Williams
1902-03	Edwin Mather	George Cook (T)	Tom Williams/ Jimmy Lomas
1903-04	Edwin Mather	George Cook (T)	Jimmy Lomas
1904-05	Edwin Mather	George Cook (T)	Jimmy Lomas
1905-06	E Mather/F Hampson	Joe White (T)	Jimmy Lomas
1906-07	Fred Hampson	Joe White (T)	Jimmy Lomas
1907-08	Fred Hampson	Joe White (T)	Jimmy Lomas
1908-09	Fred Hampson	Joe White (T)	Jimmy Lomas
1909-10	Fred Hampson	George Bracegirdle (T)	Jimmy Lomas
1910-11	Fred Hampson	George Bracegirdle (T)	Jimmy Lomas/ WS 'Willie' Thomas
1911-12	Fred Hampson	Joe White (T)	WS 'Willie' Thomas
1912-13	Geoffrey C Swire (OR)	Joe White (T)	WS 'Willie' Thomas
1913-14	Geoffrey C Swire (OR)	Joe White (T)	WS 'Willie' Thomas
1914-15	SM Williams	Joe White (T)	WS 'Willie' Thomas
1915-16	SM Williams	none	WS 'Willie' Thomas

Club Officials 1873-2022

Season	Chairman	Coach	Captain
1916-17	SM Williams/ Arthur Holt	none	WS 'Willie' Thomas
1917-18	Arthur Holt	none	WS 'Willie' Thomas
1918-19	Arthur Holt	none	WS 'Willie' Thomas
1919-20	Thomas A Rich	George Bracegirdle (T)	WS 'Willie' Thomas
1920-21	Thomas A Rich	George Bracegirdle (T)	WS 'Willie' Thomas
1921-22	Thomas A Rich	George Bracegirdle (T)	WS 'Willie' Thomas/ R 'Bob' Keegan/ TH 'Harry' Smith
1922-23	Thomas A Rich	George Bracegirdle (T)	TH 'Harry' Smith
1923-24	Thomas A Rich	Joe White (T)	Alex 'Sandy' Hurst
1924-25	Joseph Priestley	Jimmy Lomas	Ferguson 'Fergie' Southward
1925-26	Joseph Priestley	Joe White (T)	Jack Gore
1926-27	Joseph Priestley	William Taylor (T)	Jack Gore
1927-28	Charles B Riley	William Taylor (T)	Jack Gore
1928-29	Charles B Riley	Lance B Todd (TM)	Ferguson 'Fergie' Southward
1929-30	Charles B Riley	Lance B Todd (TM)	Alf Middleton
1930-31	Charles B Riley	Lance B Todd (TM)	Alf Middleton
1931-32	Charles B Riley	Lance B Todd (TM)	Alf Middleton/ WA 'Billy' Williams
1932-33	Charles B Riley	Lance B Todd (TM)	WA 'Billy' Williams
1933-34	Charles B Riley	Lance B Todd (TM)	WA 'Billy' Williams
1934-35	Charles B Riley	Lance B Todd (TM)	WA 'Billy' Williams
1935-36	Charles B Riley	Lance B Todd (TM)	AJ 'Gus' Risman
1936-37	Charles B Riley	Lance B Todd (TM)	WA 'Billy' Williams
1937-38	Charles B Riley	Lance B Todd (TM)	AJ 'Gus' Risman
1938-39	Charles B Riley	Lance B Todd (TM)	WA 'Billy' Williams
1939-40	Charles B Riley	Lance B Todd (TM)	AJ 'Gus' Risman
1940-41	James B Goldstraw	Lance B Todd (TM)	Sammy Miller
1941-42	none	none	none
1942-43	none	none	none
1943-44	none	none	none
1944-45	none	none	none
1945-46	James B Goldstraw	Jimmy Dawson (TM)/ Cyril Braund (TM)	AJ 'Gus' Risman/ Alan Edwards/
1946-47	James B Goldstraw	Cyril Braund (TM)	DM 'Dai' Davies
1947-48	James B Goldstraw	Cyril Braund (TM)	DM 'Dai' Davies
1948-49	James B Goldstraw	Cyril Braund (TM)/ Jimmy Douglas (TM)	DM 'Dai' Davies
1949-50	James B Goldstraw	Jimmy Douglas (TM)	Eifion 'Jack' Davies
1950-51	James B Goldstraw	Jimmy Douglas (TM)	Tommy Harrison
1951-52	James B Goldstraw	Jimmy Douglas (TM)	Tommy Harrison
1952-53	James B Goldstraw	Jimmy Douglas (TM)	Tom Danby/ Frank Birkin

Club Officials 1873-2022

Season	Chairman	Coach	Captain
1953-54	James B Goldstraw	Jimmy Douglas (TM)	Frank Birkin/ George Roughley
1954-55	James B Goldstraw/ James W Hammond	Jimmy Douglas (TM)	George Roughley
1955-56	Thomas H Mellor	Jimmy Douglas(TM)/ AJ 'Gus' Risman (TM)	Brian Keavney
1956-57	Thomas H Mellor	AJ 'Gus' Risman (TM)	Brian Keavney/ Eric Ayles
1957-58	Thomas H Mellor/ George S Cadman	AJ 'Gus' Risman (TM)	Eric Ayles/ Syd Lowdon
1958-59	George S Cadman	AJ 'Gus' Risman (TM)	Syd Lowdon
1959-60	William S 'Willie' Thomas	AJ 'Gus' Risman (TM)	Billy Banks
1960-61	William S 'Willie' Thomas	George Parsons	Les Bettinson
1961-62	WS 'Willie' Thomas/ James W Hammond	George Parsons	Terry Dunn
1962-63	James W Hammond	George Parsons	Terry Dunn/ Mick Clark
1963-64	James W Hammond/ G Brian Snape	Ted Cahill	Mick Clark/ Les Bettinson
1964-65	G Brian Snape	Griff Jenkins	Les Bettinson/ Brian Sparks
1965-66	G Brian Snape	Griff Jenkins	Brian Sparks/ Arthur Hughes
1966-67	G Brian Snape	Griff Jenkins	Arthur Hughes
1967-68	G Brian Snape	Griff Jenkins	Jackie Brennan
1968-69	G Brian Snape	Griff Jenkins	David Watkins
1969-70	G Brian Snape	Griff Jenkins	David Watkins
1970-71	G Brian Snape	Cliff Evans	David Watkins
1971-72	G Brian Snape	Cliff Evans	David Watkins
1972-73	G Brian Snape	Cliff Evans	David Watkins
1973-74	G Brian Snape	Cliff Evans/ Les Bettinson	David Watkins
1974-75	G Brian Snape	Les Bettinson	Chris Hesketh
1975-76	G Brian Snape	Les Bettinson	Chris Hesketh
1976-77	G Brian Snape	Led Bettinson/ Colin Dixon	Chris Hesketh
1977-78	G Brian Snape	Colin Dixon/ Stan McCormick	Chris Hesketh
1978-79	H Keith Snape	Alex Murphy	Steve Nash
1979-80	H Keith Snape	Alex Murphy	Keith Fielding
1980-81	H Keith Snape	Alex Murphy/ Kevin Ashcroft	Frank Wilson/ Steve Nash
1981-82	HK Snape/JA Wilkinson	Kevin Ashcroft	Steve Nash
1982-83	John A Wilkinson	Mal Aspey	Steve Nash
1983-84	John A Wilkinson	Mal Aspey/ Mike Coulman	Steve Nash/ Peter Glynn

Club Officials 1873-2022

Season	Chairman	Coach	Captain
1984-85	John A Wilkinson	Kevin Ashcroft (TM)	Denis Boyd/ Paul Groves
1985-86	John A Wilkinson	Kevin Ashcroft (TM)	Paul Groves/ John Pendlebury
1986-87	John A Wilkinson	Kevin Ashcroft (TM)	John Pendlebury/ Mark Wakefield
1987-88	John A Wilkinson	Kevin Ashcroft (TM)	Darren Bloor
1988-89	John A Wilkinson	Kevin Ashcroft (TM)	Darren Bloor/ Peter Williams
1989-90	John A Wilkinson	Kevin Ashcroft (TM)/ Kevin Tamati	David Cairns Mick Worrall
1990-91	John A Wilkinson	Kevin Tamati	Ian Blease
1991-92	John A Wilkinson	Kevin Tamati	Ian Blease
1992-93	John A Wilkinson	Kevin Tamati	Ian Blease
1993-94	John A Wilkinson	Garry Jack (TM)	David Young
1994-95	John A Wilkinson	Garry Jack (TM)/ Andy Gregory	David Young
1995-96	John A Wilkinson	Andy Gregory	David Young
1996	John A Wilkinson	Andy Gregory	David Young/ Steve Blakeley
1997	John A Wilkinson	Andy Gregory	Steve Blakeley/ Andy Platt
1998	John A Wilkinson	Andy Gregory	Andy Platt
1999	John A Wilkinson	Andy Gregory/ John Harvey (HC)	David Hulme
2000	John A Wilkinson	John Harvey (HC)	Darren Brown
2001	John A Wilkinson	John Harvey (HC)/ Steve McCormack (HC)	Darren Brown/ Bobbie Goulding
2002	John A Wilkinson	Steve McCormack (HC)/ Karl Harrison (HC)	Bobbie Goulding/ Darren Treacy
2003	John A Wilkinson	Karl Harrison (HC)	Malcolm Alker
2004	John A Wilkinson	Karl Harrison (HC)	Malcolm Alker
2005	John A Wilkinson	Karl Harrison (HC)	Malcolm Alker
2006	John A Wilkinson	Karl Harrison (HC)	Malcolm Alker
2007	John A Wilkinson	Karl Harrison (HC)/ Shaun McRae (HC)	Malcolm Alker
2008	John A Wilkinson	Shaun McRae (HC)	Malcolm Alker
2009	John A Wilkinson	Shaun McRae (HC)	Rob Parker/ Malcolm Alker
2010	John A Wilkinson	Shaun McRae (HC)	Malcolm Alker
2011	John A Wilkinson	Shaun McRae (HC)/ Matt Parrish (HC)	Daniel Holdsworth
2012	John A Wilkinson	Phil Veivers (HC)	Stephen Wild
2013	John A Wilkinson/ Marwan Koukash	Phil Veivers (HC)/ Brian Noble (HC)	Stephen Wild/ Martin Gleeson

Club Officials 1873-2022

Season	Chairman	Coach	Captain
2014	Marwan Koukash	Brian Noble (HC)/ Iestyn Harris (HC)	Adrian Morley
2015	Marwan Koukash	Iestyn Harris (HC)/ Ian Watson (HC)	Harrison Hansen
2016	Marwan Koukash	Ian Watson (HC)	Tommy Lee/ Michael Dobson
2017	Marwan Koukash	Ian Watson (HC)	Michael Dobson
2018	Andrew Rosler	Ian Watson (HC)	Mark Flanagan, Lee Mossop (joint)
2019	Paul King	Ian Watson (HC)	Lee Mossop
2020	Paul King	Ian Watson (HC)	Lee Mossop
2021	Paul King	Richard Marshall (HC)	Lee Mossop/ Kevin Brown
2022	Paul King	Paul Rowley (HC)	Elijah Taylor

P-president
T-trainer
OR – official receiver
TM-team manager
HC-head coach

10
Statistical Notes

Statistical Notes – Player Records

'Name' column

Wherever possible the player's first name is shown as that by which he was commonly known, for example Robert may be 'Bob', Richard could be 'Dick' or 'Richie' and perhaps, most famously, A. J. Risman was always referred to as 'Gus'. In some instances it has not been possible to trace a first name, particularly for the years prior to the 1950s when the press generally referred to players by their surname only.

Refer also to 'Statistical Notes – Miscellaneous' under 'Assumed names', 'Illegal registrations', and 'Wartime appearances'.

'Pos' (position) column

The following abbreviations are used:
FB – full-back, T – three-quarter, W – wing, C – centre, HB – half-back, SO – stand-off, SH – scrum-half, F – forward, H – hooker.

The position given for each player is based on whichever he occupied the most for Salford. However, there are exceptions. Those regularly utilised at both centre and wing are identified as a three-quarter ('T'). Similarly, half-backs adept at either stand-off or scrum-half are identified as a half-back ('HB'). All forwards, with the exception of hooker ('H') are identified as forwards ('F').

Refer also to 'Statistical Notes – Miscellaneous' under 'Evolvement of positions'.

'Brn' (where born) column

The country of each player's birth is identified by the following abbreviations:
A – Australia, AL – Albania, C – Congo, E – England, F – France, FJ – Fiji, IR – Ireland, NL – Netherlands, NZ – New Zealand, PN – Papua New Guinea, S – Scotland, SA – South Africa, SM – Samoa, W – Wales. Where the entry is left blank, the player is assumed to have been born in England.

Refer also to 'Statistical Notes – Miscellaneous' under 'Countries of birth' and 'Earliest overseas signings'.

Statistical Notes – Player Records

'Previous team' column

Whenever possible each player's previous team in given which, in the majority of cases, will be the club they transferred from. There are, however, some instances where the club name is followed in brackets by 'trialist' (appeared on trial but not subsequently signed), 'loan' (loaned by the named club) or 'guest' (appeared as a guest from the named club during World War Two). In some cases it has not been possible to identify the club for former amateur rugby league players, only the area they were signed from, hence some are referred to as 'local ARL' others by, for example, 'Wigan district ARL'.

The following abbreviations are used:
AFC – Association Football Club, ARL – Amateur Rugby League, NU – Northern Union club, RU – Rugby Union club

'Representative' column

Representative honours achieved by players whilst attached to Salford. (Note that in many cases additional honours have been gained whilst with other clubs.) These include appearances in full international, county, and regional representative sides. Not included are appearances for England Knights, England Under-24s, England Under-21s, and combinations that played under the name of British Empire XIII, English Rugby League XIII, Lancashire League, Northern Rugby League XIII, Rugby League XIII, United Kingdom XIII, and Welsh XIII.

The following abbreviations have been used:

International teams: CN – Combined Nations, E – England, EX – Exiles, F – France, FJ – Fiji, GB – Great Britain, IR – Ireland, ON – Other Nationalities, PN – Papua New Guinea, S – Scotland, SA – South Africa, SM – Samoa, T – Tonga, TR – Touring Team, US – United States, W – Wales, WS – Western Samoa.
County teams: C – Cumberland/Cumbria, CH – Cheshire, DN – Durham & Northumberland, GM – Glamorgan & Monmouthshire, L – Lancashire, MM – Monmouthshire, OC – Other Nationalities (county level), WM – Westmorland, Y – Yorkshire.

Statistical Notes – Player Records

Regional teams: MS – Midlands & South (of England), N – North (of England), WW – Wales & West of England.

Each of these abbreviations is followed by the number of appearances. Substitute appearances are shown separately and preceded by a plus ('+') sign. Note the latter excludes substitutes that did not play. In the case of selection for a touring team ('TR') the number that follows indicates the number of tours undertaken.

Refer also to 'Statistical Notes – Miscellaneous' under 'Welsh internationals', 'Grandparent rule', 'Great Britain', and 'County qualification'.

Statistical Notes – Match Results

'Opponent' column

Where the opposing team is shown in capital letters it indicates a 'home' match. Almost all matches that are listed up to and including 1895-96 (Salford's rugby union era) are friendly games (termed 'ordinary' fixtures at the time). Exceptions are matches played in the Lancashire Club Championship (indicated in brackets by 'LCC'), a competition Salford competed in from 1892-93 until 1895-96.

From 1896-97 onwards (under Northern Union/Rugby League) all matches listed are League games unless specified otherwise in brackets. The League competitions Salford competed in are as follows:

1896-97 to 1900-01: Lancashire Senior Competition
1901-02: Northern Rugby League Championship
1902-03 to 1904-05: First Division Championship
1905-06 to 1914-15: Northern Rugby League Championship
1918-19: Lancashire League Championship
1919-20 to 1938-39: Northern Rugby League Championship
1945-46 to 1961-62: Northern Rugby League Championship
1962-63 to 1963-64: Second Division Championship
1964-65 to 1972-73: Northern Rugby League Championship
1973-74 to 1980-81: First Division Championship
1981-82 to 1982-83: Second Division Championship
1983-84: First Division Championship
1984-85: Second Division Championship
1985-86 to 1989-90: First Division Championship
1990-91: Second Division Championship
1991-92 to 1994-95: First Division Championship
1995-96: Centenary First Division Championship (2nd tier)
1996: First Division Championship (2nd tier)
1997 to 2002: Super League
2003: National League One (2nd tier)
2004 to 2007: Super League
2008: National League One (2nd tier)
2009 to 2020: Super League (CHECK)

Note: The Northern Rugby League Championship incorporated fixtures in

Statistical Notes – Match Results

the Lancashire League Championship for the following seasons: 1907-08 to 1914-15, 1918-19 to 1938-39, 1945-46 to 1961-62, 1964-65 to 1969-70.

Matches from 1896-97 onwards that are not in the above League competitions are indicated in brackets by the following abbreviations:

CC – Club Championship
CM – Captain Morgan Trophy
F – Friendly (including benefit and charity matches)
FT – BBC2 Floodlit Trophy
FoS – Festival of Sports
JP – Players No. 6 Trophy (1971-72 to 1976-77), John Player Trophy (1977-78 to 1982-83), John Player Special Trophy (1983-84 to 1988-89)
LC – Lancashire Challenge Cup
NL – National League One play-off
NLC – National League Cup
NRL – Northern Rugby League Championship play-off
NUC – Northern Union Challenge Cup
PT – Premiership Trophy (Second Division Premiership Trophy 1990-91, Divisional Premiership Trophy 1996)
RLC – Rugby League Challenge Cup
RRC – Red Rose Cup,
RT – Regal Trophy,
S8 – Super 8s (The Qualifiers 2015, 2016, 2018, Super League Super 8s 2017)
SELL – South East Lancashire League
SHC – Salford Royal Hospital Cup
SL – Super League play-off
TTC – Players No.6 Top Tries Contest
WCC – World Club Championship
WD – Western Division Championship
WEL – (Lancashire) War Emergency League
WSL – (Wartime) Summer League

Note 1: Matches indicated as 'Tour' in brackets cover home fixtures against overseas touring teams, except in 1934-35 when it indicates the matches played by Salford during its six-match tour of France.
Note 2: 'AET' indicates extra-time was played.

Statistical Notes – Match Results

'Result' column

The following abbreviations are used: W – won, L – lost, D – drawn, A – abandoned, V – void, NRA – no result available (applies to Cavendish fixtures only as explained in the introduction to that section), g – goals, t – tries.

Note: In the seasons up to and including 1890-91, each teams score is shown in terms of number of goals (g) and number of unconverted tries (t). At that time if a try was converted into a goal it was reflected in the score as a goal and the try was not shown. From 1891-92, a point system was introduced, continuing to the present day, albeit with revised values.

'Attendance' column

The following abbreviation appears for matches played during 2020 and 2021: BCD – behind closed doors.

This relates to matches played after the Covid-19 pandemic struck when spectators were not admitted for health reasons. When spectators were again admitted during 2021 the numbers were initially limited for 'social distance' reasons.

'Scorers' column

The following abbreviations are used: T – try, C – conversion, G – goal, DG – drop-goal, PG – penalty goal, GM – goal from mark.

Note 1: Scorers names are listed alphabetical within the number of tries or goals scored. The scorers' initials are included where players from the same period share surnames.

Note 2: 'G' (goal) is used from 1897-98 when all goals, however scored, became valued at 2 points. From 1974-75 drop-goals ('DG') are shown separately due to their reduced value of 1 point.

Note 3: A goal attempt from a mark ('GM') was abolished by the Rugby Football League in 1922. A mark resulted after a player caught the ball directly from an opponent's kick. The player would 'mark' the ground with his heel, typically shouting 'mark' at the same time thus earning his team a free kick including an option to kick for goal.

Statistical Notes – Miscellaneous

Assumed names

The following players are known to have appeared under assumed names:
Jimmy Burgess played under the name of J. Fishwick throughout 1917-18.
Howard Burt played under the name of Howard Jones during his 1945-46 debut season.
Jim Holcroft had played under the name of George Taylor for his previous club Warrington.
Bob Ritchie was actually Robert Armstrong and had played under that name in rugby union for Tynedale and Northumberland.
Harold 'George' Whitney, who played under that name throughout his career at Salford, was actually George Arthur Thompson.

Illegal registrations

The following players signed for Salford when already registered with another club:
Radley Thomas came from West Hartlepool RU and played on 15th January 1898 at home to Runcorn. It was then discovered he had already signed for Castleford. Salford – who were probably unaware of the situation – were deducted two points for fielding an ineligible player. Thomas did not actually play for Castleford during 1897-98 and it was subsequently agreed to transfer him to Salford prior to 1898-99.
Jack Elliott was suspended for one week during February 1906 after having signed professional forms for both Salford and the local Egerton club. No blame was attached to Salford. He eventually played four matches for Salford during April 1906.

Wartime appearances

Several players that assisted Salford during World War One are worthy of comment:
Billy Brown came out of retirement at the age of 41 to play one match in February 1918 having played his last game for Salford in December 1908.
Jimmy Burgess joined his local club Runcorn in 1912 but played as a guest for Salford throughout World War One due to working in Salford as a dock labourer. Following the demise of Runcorn, he signed for Salford in February 1919, making a further 218 appearances until his last in 1928.

Statistical Notes – Miscellaneous

Harry Goldsmith was born in Napier, New Zealand, and arrived at Salford in 1912 asking for a trial after playing for the Olympic rugby union club in San Francisco, United States.

Jimmy Lomas first signed for Salford in 1901, transferring to Oldham in January 1911. In 1914 he joined York, playing three wartime matches for Salford as a guest during April 1917. He subsequently returned to Salford as a coach in 1922, coming out of retirement to play in eight matches during 1923, the last at the age of 44.

Evolvement of positions

Throughout the late-1800s, as rugby developed, playing positions were not clearly defined, other than being designated as a full-back, three-quarter, half-back or forward. Only the three-quarters had any semblance of structure in that the idea of having two (usually faster) outside men as wingers was developed and references to right wing, right centre, left centre and left wing began to appear in the press in the mid-1890s. In the early 1900s half-back roles became more distinctive with terms like 'scrum-half' or 'scrum-worker' and 'stand-off' or 'outside-half' being reported.

It was also in the early 1900s that the specialised role of the hooker began to emerge. The pre-World War One period also saw the emergence of the 'roving' or 'loose' forward, a quicker breed of forward that would break away from the 'pack' and link with the backs. The final piece of evolution, in the early 1920s, was the creation of the front row (prop) forward, whereby the stronger forwards would pack down first alongside the hooker, replacing the previous method of grouping around the hooker in order of arrival at the scrummage.

From the mid-1920s it became possible to determine from match reports which positions players occupied. Previously it was not always clear whether three-quarters filled the right or left flank or which half-back played at scrum-half. Similarly the forwards were not listed in a way that indicated their positions. For these reasons it is not always possible to identify which player was at hooker, scrum-half or stand-off prior to the 1920s.

Statistical Notes – Miscellaneous

Countries of birth

There are several players who require further explanation:

Aubrey Casewell (signed from local amateur RL) was born in Welshpool, Wales.

Ephraim Curzon (signed from Kirkcaldy RU, Scotland) was born in Crumpsall, Manchester. He had worked in Edinburgh for the three years prior to joining Salford.

Eric Day (signed from local amateur RL) was born in Salford. There has been confusion over his nationality as he had previously lived in Canada and reportedly played Canadian 'Gridiron' Football prior to joining Salford. He later transferred to Bradford Northern before returning to Canada in 1952.

Eifion 'Jack' Davies (signed from Harlequins RU, London) was born in Penclawdd, Wales.

Albert Gear (signed from Torquay Athletic RU) was born in Newport, Wales.

Harry Goldsmith (signed from Olympic RU, United States) was born in Napier, New Zealand.

John Hancock (signed from Newport RU and born in Newport, Wales) had represented England RU through parentage.

Tom Harris (signed from Llwynypia RU) was born in Chard, Somerset.

Tom McKinney (signed from Jed-Forest RU, Scotland) was born in Ballymena, Ireland.

Pat Tunney (signed from Tudhoe RU, Durham) was born in County Mayo, Ireland.

The players' record section covering Salford's Rugby Football Union period does not include the countries of birth. However, those known to have been born outside of England are:

James Jackson (signed from Leigh) was born in Chepstow, Wales. In 1886 he became the first Salford player to represent Lancashire.

Arthur Paul (signed from Swinton) was born in Belfast, Ireland. He had previously been a member of the inaugural British rugby touring team in 1888.

Thomas Ryan (signed from Leeds Parish Church) was born in County Down, Ireland.

Angus Stuart (signed from Manchester Athletic) was born in Scotland. He

Statistical Notes – Miscellaneous

subsequently joined Dewsbury and was included in the 1888 British rugby touring team.

Earliest overseas signings

In the 'Introduction' to this publication, reference was made to five overseas players that appeared for Salford prior to the dramatic increase in Australasian-based recruits that began in the 1980s. To recap, they were *Joe Lavery* (signed 1910), *Harry Goldsmith* (1912), *Noel Sligar* and *J. H. Smith* (both 1928), and *Wally McArthur* (1957). There are, however, several others who, for varying reasons, did not make it into Salford's first team but are, nonetheless, worthy of mention:

B. F. Fischer was a 21-year-old Australian forward from Port Macquarie, New South Wales, who was signed during February 1913, making his 'A' team debut the following month. It did not work out and, according to the official Northern Union register, he was 'transferred' in September 1913.

R. E. 'Reggie' Walker was from Durban, South Africa, and signed by Salford during October 1920 at the age of 31. He was a famous athlete having won the 100 metres at the 1908 Olympic Games in London. During the early 1920s he was based in Britain, competing in various events as a professional sprinter. There is, however, no evidence of him appearing in Salford's first or 'A' team.

Carl J. Burger was a rugby union forward from South African who was listed as a Salford player ahead of the 1929-30 season. There is, however, no evidence that he subsequently appeared for Salford's first or 'A' team. He originally came to England in 1924, joining Wigan from South Africa's Simmer and Jack club before transferring to Barrow in 1926.

Frank Fisher was an Australian stand-off that, according to a 1987 Australian publication, Salford attempted to sign from Barambah, Queensland, in 1936 after impressing for Wide Bay against that year's Great Britain touring side. Reportedly born in 1905 he would have been over 30 years old at the time. It is claimed he was sent a contract but refused permission to travel by the Queensland state authorities due to restrictive laws then controlling the movement of Australian Aboriginals. However, there are no contemporary British newspaper reports to support that story. Had Fisher signed, he would have preceded Wally McArthur as the first Aboriginal player to join a British club.

Harry Shiells was a 20-year-old Australian wingman who Salford tried to

Statistical Notes – Miscellaneous

sign ahead of the 1959-60 season. Employed by a Salford company at that time, he was unable to obtain clearance from the Sydney rugby league authorities.

Welsh internationals

No Wales full international matches took place between 1953 and 1968 depriving many fine Welsh born players the opportunity to represent their country. During this period a Welsh XIII was twice selected against France (1959 and 1963) but these matches do not count as full internationals and it is worth pointing out, to avoid confusion, that they have mistakenly been accepted in some publications as the full Wales national side. Their reduced status denied Salford's *John Cheshire*, *Graham Jones* and *George Parsons* a Welsh cap, as well as long serving *Dai Moses* who appeared in the 1959 match after joining Swinton.

Grandparent rule

Since the mid-1970s many players have represented countries other than where they were born (as indicated under the 'Brn' column). This is due to the so-called 'grandparent rule' that qualifies players to represent the country of their parents or grandparents birth. The first Salford beneficiary was *Peter Banner* in 1975 who qualified for Wales due to his Newport-born grandfather. After rugby union became fully professional in 1995 this trend accelerated due to the dearth of Welsh players defecting to Rugby League.

Also in 1995, Ireland and Scotland debuted in Rugby League's international arena and, since that time, all three of those home nations have mostly consisted of players born in England, Australia or New Zealand, qualifying via the grandparent rule. Similarly, this ruling has provided the Pacific island nations, such as the Cook Islands, Fiji, Samoa, and Tonga, with New Zealand and Australian-born players, whose family originated in those countries.

Great Britain

The Great Britain name was introduced for the 1947 test series against New Zealand. Previously Britain's test side had played as the Northern Union (1908-1922) and England (1924-1946). Official records have retrospectively

Statistical Notes – Miscellaneous

included these latter matches under the banner of Great Britain, and this is reflected in this publication for players' representative honours.

However, an anomaly was that, during 1933-34, England played two matches against Australia and one against France, none of which had test status. Previously they had been credited in players records as England appearances despite the fact that several Welshmen played in the England team. In 2022, the Rugby League Record Keepers' Club (relaunched in 2020 and, like its predecessor, granted official status) in conjunction with International Rugby League (IRL) took the logical step of reclassifying these as Great Britain matches. The effect of this is to add two Great Britain appearances each for *Paddy Dalton* and *Emlyn Jenkins* and one each for *Barney Hudson* and *Gus Risman*, subtracting the same number from their previous 'England' appearance total.

County qualification

Players have often represented counties that were not the county of their birth. This is due to the vagaries of the qualification rules. On occasions it restricted selection to players born within the county whilst, at other times, it was based on the county of their club rather than their birthplace.

As a result of this, a total of 16 Salford players born outside of Lancashire have represented that county. Two played during the club's rugby union era; *James Jackson* (born Chepstow, Monmouthshire) and *Tom Kent* (Nottingham). The remaining 14 have been chosen during the Northern Union/Rugby League period. Nine were born in Wales, namely *Arthur Buckler*, *Herbert Buckler*, *Ben Griffiths*, *Joe Hoskins*, *Dai Rees*, *Jack Rhapps*, *Dan Smith*, *Jack Williams* and *Tom Williams*. The non-Welsh five are *Mike Coulman* (born Stone, Staffordshire), *Keith Fielding* (Birmingham), *Jimmy Lomas* (Maryport, Cumberland), *Pat Tunney* (County Mayo, Ireland), and *Herbert 'Harry' Woodhead* (Goole, Yorkshire).

Chris Hesketh captained Salford, Great Britain and Lancashire during his 12-year career at The Willows.